Program Authors

Peter Afflerbach

Camille Blachowicz

Candy Dawson Boyd

Wendy Cheyney

Connie Juel

Edward Kame'enui

Donald Leu

Jeanne Paratore

P. David Pearson

Sam Sebesta

Deborah Simmons

Sharon Vaughn

Susan Watts-Taffe

Karen Kring Wixson

Editorial Offices: Glenview, Illinois • Parsippany, New Jersey • New York, New York
Sales Offices: Needham, Massachusetts • Duluth, Georgia • Glenview, Illinois
Coppell, Texas • Sacramento, California • Mesa, Arizona

About the Cover Artist

As a kid growing up in Cincinnati, Ohio, Dan Cosgrove always liked to draw. After majoring in Graphic Design in college, he worked for the National Park Service in Colorado and then for a design firm in Cincinnati. Now he works in Chicago, Illinois, drawing and designing in his studio overlooking the Chicago River, where he specializes in both digital and traditional illustration for a variety of national clients. His work has appeared in numerous ads and posters and on packaging.

ISBN: 0-328-10839-1

1 2 3 4 5 6 7 8 9 10 V063 14 13 12 11 10 09 08 07 06 05

Dear Reader,

A new school year is beginning. Are you ready? You are about to take a trip along a famous street—*Scott Foresman Reading Street.* During this trip you will meet exciting people, such as Thomas Edison, a girl who finds a stray dog, a boy who learns to survive alone in the wilderness, and the great opera singer Marian Anderson. You will visit places from the past, such as the great ancient civilizations of Egypt and Greece.

As you read selections about the rain forests, Cesar Chavez, paleontologists studying dinosaur fossils, and a crow who became a family's pet, you will gain exciting new information that will help you in science and social studies.

While you're enjoying these exciting pieces of literature, you will find that something else is going on— you are becoming a better reader, gaining new skills and polishing old ones.

Have a great trip— and send us a postcard!

Sincerely,
The Authors

Loyalty and Respect

What draws us to people and things around us and makes us care?

Space and Time

Read It ONLINE
sfsuccessnet.com

Why might things far away and long ago be important to us now?

6

Challenges and Obstacles

Read It
ONLINE
sfsuccessnet.com

How are the results of our efforts sometimes greater than we expect?

Explorers, Pioneers, and Discoverers

How have those who've gone first influenced those who've gone after?

Resources

What are resources and why are they important to us?

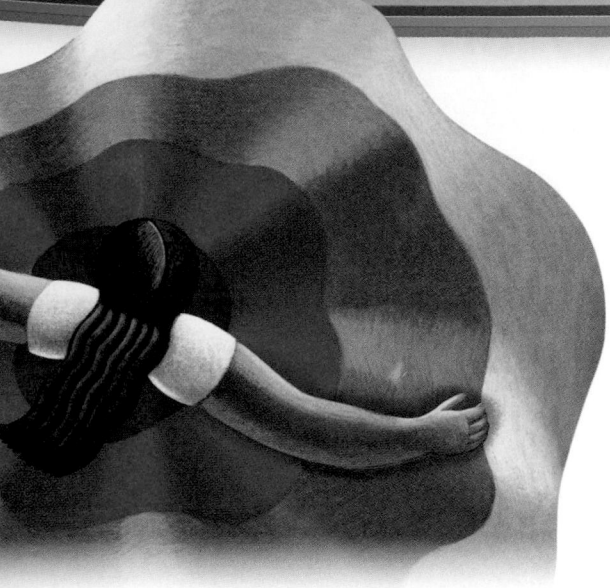

Exploring Cultures

In what ways does one culture affect another?

Read It
ONLINE
sfsuccessnet.com

Loyalty and Respect

What draws us to people and things around us and makes us care?

Old Yeller

A dog protects his family.

Classic Fiction

Mother Fletcher's Gift

A family receives a valuable gift.

Realistic Fiction

Viva New Jersey

A recent immigrant makes a new friend.

Realistic Fiction

Saving the Rain Forests

Rain forests need to survive and thrive.

Expository Nonfiction

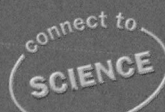

When Crowbar Came

A family learns from a pet bird.

Autobiography

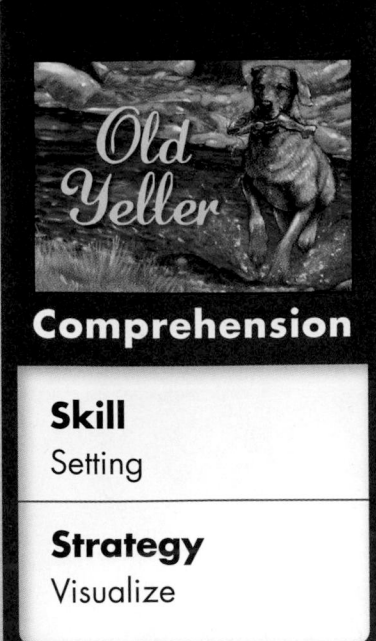

Comprehension

Skill
Setting

Strategy
Visualize

 # Setting

- The setting is the time and place in which a story occurs. Sometimes the author tells you the setting, but sometimes you have to figure it out from clues in the story.

- The setting can determine what kinds of events happen in a story.

- The setting can also influence the behavior of characters in a story.

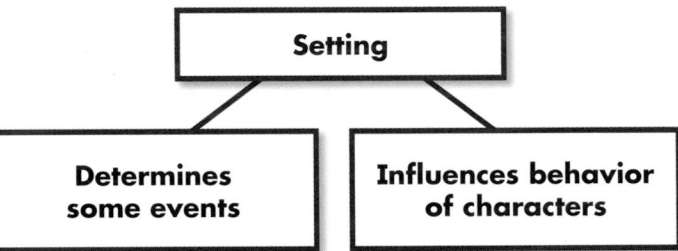

Strategy: Visualize

Good readers visualize, or create mental pictures of what they read. They picture themselves in the text, becoming part of it with all their senses. Words and phrases in the text will help you form pictures in your mind. Visualizing is a good way to picture the setting of a story. You can also "see" how the setting affects plot events and characters.

 **Write**

1. Read "High Plains Childhood." Make a graphic organizer like the one above in order to identify how the setting influences a character's behavior and helps determine an event in the story.

2. Write about how the setting influenced or affected the character you chose.

High Plains Childhood

My parents moved us to the treacherous high plains of West Texas in 1853, when I was seven and my sister Jenny was twelve. We lived in the middle of a gigantic, rolling prairie and were stunned by how dry and hot it was and by how many wild animals were around. We encountered many challenging circumstances.

One time we were caught in a violent sandstorm. It was around noon, and Jenny and I were walking back to our cabin. Suddenly the wind picked up, the sky blackened, and blowing grains of sand struck our faces and arms. It stung terribly. I screamed, and Jenny pulled me to the ground. The storm pounded us for about ten minutes, and all we could do was lie there. When it ended, the sand covered our bodies and filled our clothing.

Then, just three days later, I was stopped in my tracks by a rattlesnake. I stood there like a statue, eyes unblinking, as the snake stared menacingly at me. After a few horrifying moments it slithered off, and I ran like the wind back home. I then sat down and wept the fear out of my body.

Skill The author states the place and time in this first sentence. What is the setting?

Strategy What images come to mind when you read the author's description of the high plains of Texas?

Skill Could this event have occurred in other settings? Why or why not?

Strategy How do you picture the way the narrator looked at this point? How did he feel?

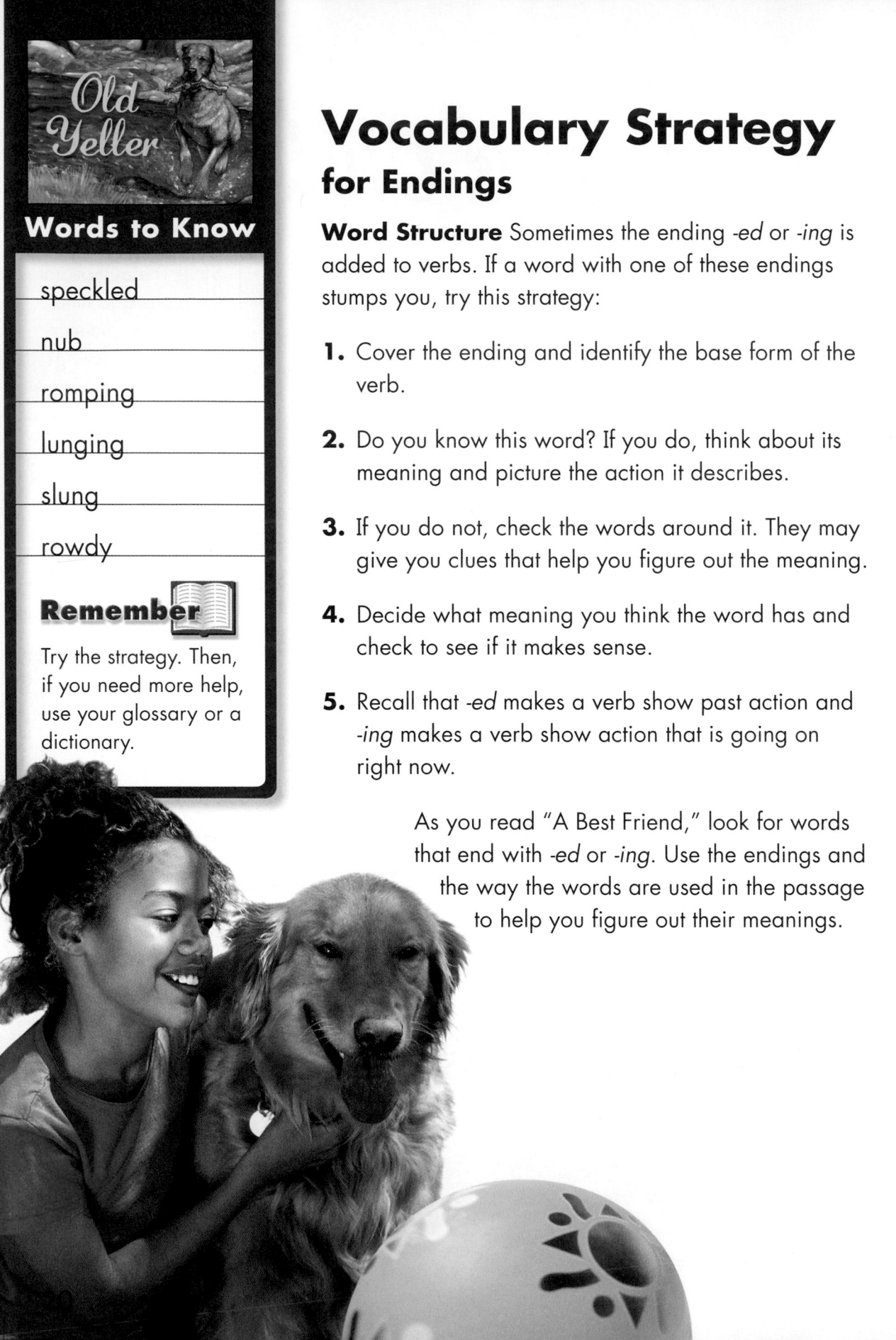

Old Yeller

Words to Know

speckled
nub
romping
lunging
slung
rowdy

Remember

Try the strategy. Then, if you need more help, use your glossary or a dictionary.

Vocabulary Strategy
for Endings

Word Structure Sometimes the ending *-ed* or *-ing* is added to verbs. If a word with one of these endings stumps you, try this strategy:

1. Cover the ending and identify the base form of the verb.

2. Do you know this word? If you do, think about its meaning and picture the action it describes.

3. If you do not, check the words around it. They may give you clues that help you figure out the meaning.

4. Decide what meaning you think the word has and check to see if it makes sense.

5. Recall that *-ed* makes a verb show past action and *-ing* makes a verb show action that is going on right now.

As you read "A Best Friend," look for words that end with *-ed* or *-ing*. Use the endings and the way the words are used in the passage to help you figure out their meanings.

A Best Friend

The bond between people and dogs runs deep and strong. Owners just fall in love with their dogs. These four-legged friends return the feeling many times over. The size, shape, and breed of the dog do not seem to matter. It might be a speckled, sleek Dalmatian. It might be a stubby-legged, wiry-haired Scottie with a nub of a tail. All dogs adore their people.

Romping with the kids on the lawn, the family dog shows joy with its whole body. Lunging for a Frisbee™ in the park, it leaps higher and farther than muscles should allow. Happiness seems to give the dog extra lift. Even a quiet old dog sitting by its master's feet seems to want nothing more.

Worn out after a shared run or walk, owner and dog lie down together for a nap. A child sleeps with a trusting arm slung over the dog's back. This picture says a lot about the connection we feel with these family members with fur. Whether the time together has been rowdy or calm, the dog is content. It seems to say with every inch of its being, nothing makes me happier than spending time with you!

Write

Does a dog own you? Or would you love to get a dog? Write a description of how you and the dog might play. Use as many words from the Words to Know list as you can.

Old Yeller

by Fred Gipson
illustrated by Lori Lohstoeter

Genre

Historical fiction is fiction that takes place in the past. What clues tell you that *Old Yeller* takes place in the past?

How might a dog show loyalty to a family?

The year is 1867 on the frontier of Texas. Fourteen-year-old Travis takes charge of the family homestead while his father is away. Left behind with Travis, his mother, and five-year-old brother named Arliss, is a stray yellow dog. The family calls him Old Yeller.

That little Arliss! If he wasn't a mess! From the time he'd grown up big enough to get out of the cabin, he'd made a practice of trying to catch and keep every living thing that ran, flew, jumped, or crawled.

Every night before Mama let him go to bed, she'd made Arliss empty his pockets of whatever he'd captured during the day. Generally, it would be a tangled-up mess of grasshoppers and worms and praying bugs and little rusty tree lizards. One time he brought in a horned toad that got so mad he swelled out round and flat as a Mexican *tortilla* and bled at the eyes. Sometimes it was stuff like a young bird that had fallen out of its nest before it could fly, or a green-speckled spring frog, or a striped water snake. And once he turned out of his pocket a wadded-up baby copperhead that nearly threw Mama into spasms. We never did figure out why the snake hadn't bitten him, but Mama took no more chances on snakes. She switched Arliss hard for catching that snake. Then she made me spend better than a week taking him out and teaching him to throw rocks and kill snakes.

That was all right with Little Arliss. If Mama wanted him to kill his snakes first, he'd kill them. But that still didn't keep him from sticking them in his pockets along with everything else he'd captured that day. The snakes might be stinking by the time Mama called on him to empty his pocket, but they'd be dead.

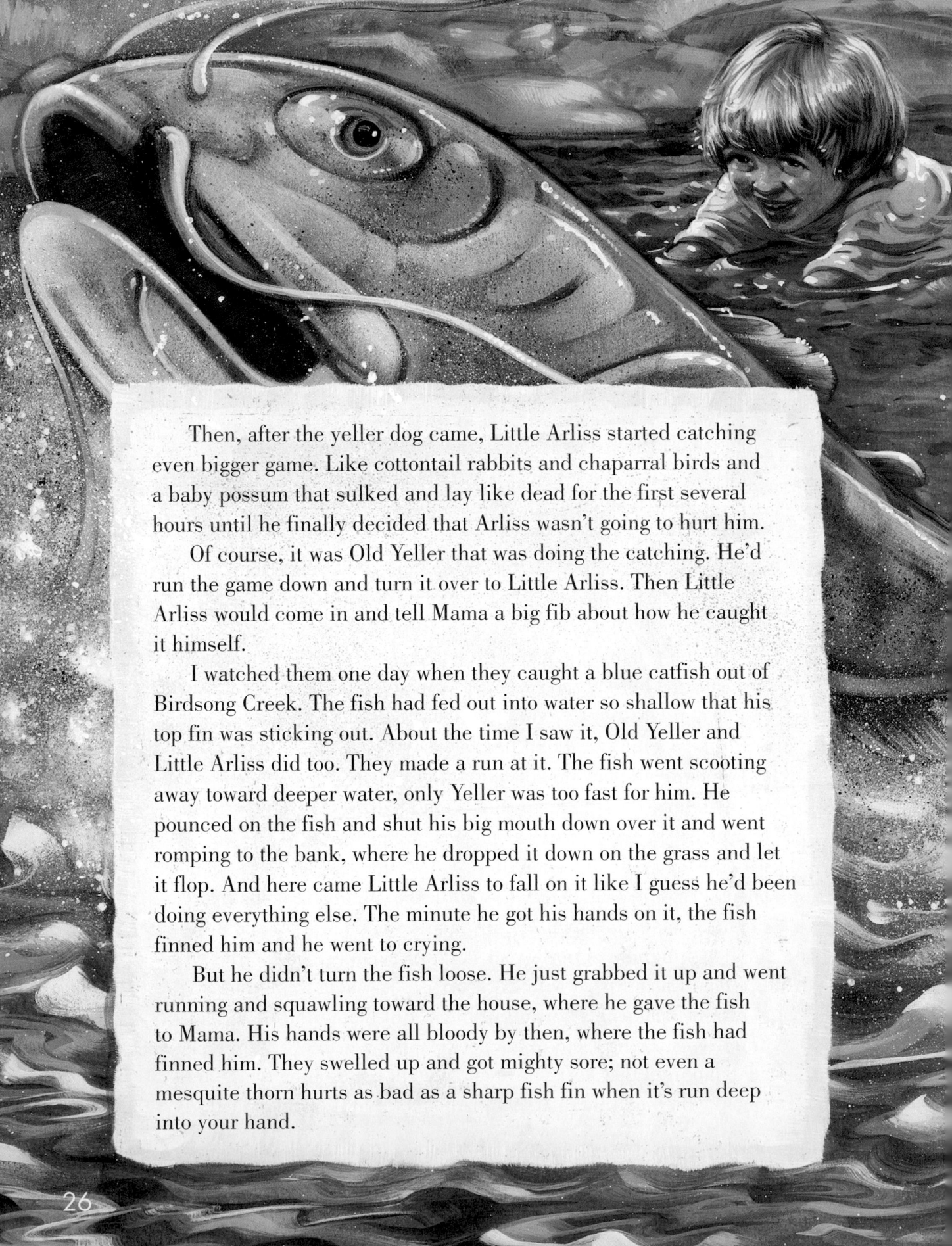

Then, after the yeller dog came, Little Arliss started catching even bigger game. Like cottontail rabbits and chaparral birds and a baby possum that sulked and lay like dead for the first several hours until he finally decided that Arliss wasn't going to hurt him.

Of course, it was Old Yeller that was doing the catching. He'd run the game down and turn it over to Little Arliss. Then Little Arliss would come in and tell Mama a big fib about how he caught it himself.

I watched them one day when they caught a blue catfish out of Birdsong Creek. The fish had fed out into water so shallow that his top fin was sticking out. About the time I saw it, Old Yeller and Little Arliss did too. They made a run at it. The fish went scooting away toward deeper water, only Yeller was too fast for him. He pounced on the fish and shut his big mouth down over it and went romping to the bank, where he dropped it down on the grass and let it flop. And here came Little Arliss to fall on it like I guess he'd been doing everything else. The minute he got his hands on it, the fish finned him and he went to crying.

But he didn't turn the fish loose. He just grabbed it up and went running and squawling toward the house, where he gave the fish to Mama. His hands were all bloody by then, where the fish had finned him. They swelled up and got mighty sore; not even a mesquite thorn hurts as bad as a sharp fish fin when it's run deep into your hand.

But as soon as Mama had wrapped his hands in a poultice of mashed-up prickly-pear root to draw out the poison, Little Arliss forgot all about his hurt. And that night when we ate the fish for supper, he told the biggest windy I ever heard about how he'd dived 'way down into a deep hole under the rocks and dragged that fish out and nearly got drowned before he could swim to the bank with it.

But when I tried to tell Mama what really happened, she wouldn't let me. "Now, this is Arliss's story," she said. "You let him tell it the way he wants to."

I told Mama then, I said: "Mama, that old yeller dog is going to make the biggest liar in Texas out of Little Arliss."

But Mama just laughed at me, like she always laughed at Little Arliss's big windies after she'd gotten off where he couldn't hear her. She said for me to let Little Arliss alone. She said that if he ever told a bigger whopper than the ones I used to tell, she had yet to hear it.

Well, I hushed then. If Mama wanted Little Arliss to grow up to be the biggest liar in Texas, I guessed it wasn't any of my business.

All of which, I figure, is what led up to Little Arliss's catching the bear. I think mama had let him tell so many big yarns about his catching live game that he'd begun to believe them himself.

When it happened, I was down the creek a ways, splitting rails to fix up the yard fence where the bulls had torn it down. I'd been down there since dinner, working in a stand of tall slim post oaks. I'd chop down a tree, trim off the branches as far up as I wanted, then cut away the rest of the top. After that I'd start splitting the log.

I'd split the log by driving steel wedges into the wood. I'd start at the big end and hammer in a wedge with the back side of my axe. This would start a little split running lengthways of the log. Then I'd take a second wedge and drive it into this split. This would split the log further along and, at the same time, loosen the first wedge. I'd then knock the first wedge loose and move it up in front of the second one.

Driving one wedge ahead of the other like that, I could finally split a log in two halves. Then I'd go to work on the halves, splitting them apart. That way, from each log, I'd come out with four rails.

Swinging that chopping axe was sure hard work. The sweat poured off me. My back muscles ached. The axe got so heavy I could hardly swing it. My breath got harder and harder to breathe.

An hour before sundown, I was worn down to a nub. It seemed like I couldn't hit another lick. Papa could have lasted till past sundown, but I didn't see how I could. I shouldered my axe and started toward the cabin, trying to think up some excuse to tell Mama to keep her from knowing I was played clear out.

That's when I heard Little Arliss scream.

Well, Little Arliss was a screamer by nature. He'd scream when he was happy and scream when he was mad and a lot of times he'd scream just to hear himself make a noise. Generally, we paid no more mind to his screaming than we did to the boggle of a wild turkey.

But this time was different. The second I heard his screaming, I felt my heart flop clear over. This time I knew Little Arliss was in real trouble.

I tore out up the trail leading toward the cabin. A minute before, I'd been so tired out with my rail splitting that I couldn't have struck a trot. But now I raced through the tall trees in that creek bottom, covering ground like a scared wolf.

Little Arliss's second scream, when it came, was louder and shriller and more frantic-sounding than the first. Mixed with it was a whimpering crying sound that I knew didn't come from him. It was a sound I'd heard before and seemed like I ought to know what it was, but right then I couldn't place it.

Then, from way off to one side came a sound that I would have recognized anywhere. It was the coughing roar of a charging bear. I'd just heard it once in my life. That was the time Mama had shot and wounded a hog-killing bear and Papa had had to finish it off with a knife to keep it from getting her.

My heart went to pushing up into my throat, nearly choking off my wind. I strained for every lick of speed I could get out of my running legs. I didn't know what sort of fix Little Arliss had got himself into, but I knew that it had to do with a mad bear, which was enough.

The way the late sun slanted through the trees had the trail all cross-banded with streaks of bright light and dark shade. I ran through these bright and dark patches so fast that the changing light nearly blinded me. Then suddenly, I raced out into the open where I could see ahead. And what I saw sent a chill clear through to the marrow of my bones.

There was Little Arliss, down in that spring hole again. He was lying half in and half out of the water, holding onto the hind leg of a little black bear cub no bigger than a small coon. The bear cub was out on the bank, whimpering and crying and clawing the rocks with all three of his other feet, trying to pull away. But Little Arliss was holding on for all he was worth, scared now and screaming his head off. Too scared to let go.

How the bear cub ever came to prowl close enough for Little Arliss to grab him, I don't know. And why he didn't turn on him and bite loose, I couldn't figure out, either. Unless he was like Little Arliss, too scared to think.

But all of that didn't matter now. What mattered was the bear cub's mama. She'd heard the cries of her baby and was coming to save him. She was coming so fast that she had the brush popping and breaking as she crashed through and over it. I could see her black heavy figure piling off down the slant on the far side of Birdsong Creek. She was roaring mad and ready to kill.

And worst of all, I could see that I'd never get there in time!

Mama couldn't either. She'd heard Arliss, too, and here she came from the cabin, running down the slant toward the spring, screaming at Arliss, telling him to turn the bear cub loose. But Little Arliss wouldn't do it. All he'd do was hang with that hind leg and let out one shrill shriek after another as fast as he could suck in a breath.

30

Now the she bear was charging across the shallows in the creek. She was knocking sheets of water high in the bright sun, charging with her fur up and her long teeth bared, filling the canyon with that awful coughing roar. And no matter how fast Mama ran or how fast I ran, the she bear was going to get there first!

I think I nearly went blind then, picturing what was going to happen to Little Arliss. I know that I opened my mouth to scream and not any sound came out.

Then, just as the bear went lunging up the creek bank toward Little Arliss and her cub, a flash of yellow came streaking out of the brush.

It was that big yeller dog. He was roaring like a mad bull. He wasn't one-third as big and heavy as the she bear, but when he piled into her from one side, he rolled her clear off her feet. They went down in a wild, roaring tangle of twisting bodies and scrambling feet and slashing fangs.

As I raced past them, I saw the bear lunge up to stand on her hind feet like a man while she clawed at the body of the yeller dog hanging to her throat. I didn't wait to see more. Without ever checking my stride, I ran in and jerked Little Arliss loose from the cub. I grabbed him by the wrist and yanked him up out of that water and slung him toward Mama like he was a half-empty sack of corn. I screamed at Mama. "Grab him, Mama! Grab him and run!" Then I swung my chopping axe high and wheeled, aiming to cave in the she bear's head with the first lick.

But I never did strike. I didn't need to. Old Yeller hadn't let the bear get close enough. He couldn't handle her; she was too big and strong for that. She'd stand there on her hind feet, hunched over, and take a roaring swing at him with one of those big front claws. She'd slap him head over heels. She'd knock him so far that it didn't look like he could possibly get back there before she charged again, but he always did. He'd hit the ground rolling, yelling his head off with the pain of the blow; but somehow he'd always roll to his feet. And here he'd come again, ready to tie into her for another round.

I stood there with my axe raised, watching them for a long moment. Then from up toward the house, I heard Mama calling: "Come away from there, Travis. Hurry, son! Run!"

That spooked me. Up till then, I'd been ready to tie into that bear myself. Now, suddenly, I was scared out of my wits again. I ran toward the cabin.

But like it was, Old Yeller nearly beat me there. I didn't see it, of course, but Mama said that the minute Old Yeller saw we were all in the clear and out of danger, he threw the fight to that she bear and lit out for the house. The bear chased him for a little piece, but at the rate Old Yeller was leaving her behind, Mama said it looked like the bear was backing up.

But if the big yeller dog was scared or hurt in any way when he came dashing into the house, he didn't show it. He sure didn't show it like we all did. Little Arliss had hushed his screaming, but he was trembling all over and climbing to Mama like he'd never let her go. And Mama was sitting in the middle of the floor, holding him up close and crying like she'd never stop. And me, I was close to crying, myself.

Old Yeller, though, all he did was come bounding in to jump on us and lick us in the face and bark so loud that there, inside the cabin, the noise nearly made us deaf.

The way he acted, you might have thought that bear fight hadn't been anything more than a rowdy romp that we'd all taken part in for the fun of it.

35

Reader Response

Open for Discussion Think about all the action in this story. Where, in all of the excitement, can you find examples of devotion and loyalty? Describe these examples.

1. Reread the incident with Little Arliss and the bear cub, paying special attention to the verbs the author uses to describe the action. Make a list of five of these verbs and explain their effect on the reader.

2. How does the setting of *Old Yeller* contribute to the story? Could this have taken place in a setting such as the desert? the city?

3. Look back at page 28 to reread the passage that describes Travis splitting rails. When you visualize this scene, how do you picture Travis? Describe the details you picture in your mind.

4. Work with a partner to find the sentences that use words from your Words to Know list. Write the sentences on a piece of paper. Discuss words the author might have used instead. Which words work best and why?

Look Back and Write Look back at page 25. What does the information on this page tell you about the setting of Old Yeller? Write a paragraph using your own words to describe the setting.

Read more books by Fred Gipson.

Fred Gipson once described the home where he grew up as "a little 'dry-land' farm in the heart of the Hill Country of Texas." He said that as a boy he liked to hunt, fish, and follow his hounds in search of fox, raccoon, and wildcat. "That's how and where I learned about boys and dogs and the great outdoors and the wild animals I was later to write about," he said.

Mr. Gipson believed he was born with "the urge" to write. He wrote fiction and nonfiction for adults and young people, but the setting was always the cattle ranching country he loved. His stories are filled with adventure. They show boys who are growing up, learning about nature, and discovering that dogs make good companions.

The Newbery Medal is a well-known children's book award. *Old Yeller,* Fred Gipson's most famous book, is a Newbery Honor book. When it was made into a movie, Mr. Gipson was invited to Los Angeles to work on the screenplay.

Fred Gipson died at his ranch in 1973. By a proclamation of the governor, he was buried in the State Cemetery in Austin, Texas. The headstone says, "His books are his monument."

Little Arliss

Curly and the Wild Boar

Expository Nonfiction

Genre

- Expository nonfiction provides facts and explanations.

- The author of expository nonfiction might include well-supported opinions on the subject, but the majority of the writing should be factual.

Text Features

- A story is included to capture the reader's interest and support an opinion.

- Information from the past and present supports the author's favorable view of dogs and their qualities.

Link to Social Studies

Research some different breeds of dog. Choose a breed and learn about ways it originally helped humans. Report to the class on what you learn.

A DOG'S LIFE

by Iain Zaczek

In the 14th century, a French historian named Froissart told the story of a prince who had to find a husband for his younger sister. The girl in question had three suitors, each of whom was brave, noble and chivalrous. Indeed, these knights had so many fine qualities that the prince found it impossible to choose among them. So in the end, he decided to leave the final choice up to fate. Remembering his sister's fondness for her pet greyhound, he had the dog brought before the suitors, and declared that the princess would marry whichever man the animal preferred. It was a short contest. As soon as the greyhound was let off its leash, it ran over to the tallest of the three, started

Greyhound

Bulldog

to sniff his leg, and then began licking his hand with great affection. With this, the matter was decided. The princess accepted her brother's decision and the wedding took place within a week.

What the prince didn't realize, of course, was that his sister had been meeting the lucky suitor in secret for some time, and that the young man had already befriended the dog. All of which goes to show that you should never underestimate the usefulness of keeping a dog. Ever since the beginning of time, dogs and humans have lived together and helped each other. Dogs can do many things better than people; they can run faster, their hearing is more acute, and their sense of smell is much stronger. Because of this, they have often been used for hunting, to provide food for their owners, or else as alert guard dogs. Some have helped detectives track down criminals, while others are sent out to rescue mountaineers trapped in snowdrifts. Shepherds always have dogs, to keep their sheep under control, and guide dogs are equally invaluable to the blind.

Search-and-rescue worker talks on walkie-talkie with German shepherd on duty.

Setting How does knowing the setting help you understand the historian's story?

Poodle

There are many different breeds of dog, because some are better than others at carrying out certain types of tasks. Today, most dogs are kept as household pets, so their original purpose has often been forgotten. Poodles, for example, were originally bred as water dogs, helping huntsmen to fetch their prey from lakes and rivers. Their hair was clipped short, so that they could move more easily through the water, but was left longer at the joints to prevent rheumatism. The name comes from *puddeln,* a German word for "splashing about." Similarly, dachshunds were deliberately bred with short legs and long bodies, so that they could wriggle down holes and chase badgers *(dachs-hund* means "badger dog"). Dalmatians were used as carriage dogs, running alongside their owners' horse-drawn coach to protect them against highwaymen. Fortunately, all these practices have long since been abandoned, and the animals can lead a much more pleasant life as pets.

Dachshund

Dalmatian

Why are dogs so keen to help us? Apart from the fact that we give them food, they are used to living in packs and are adaptable enough to think of humans as part of this extended family. So when your pet tries to convince you that he would rather sleep in your bedroom than in the kitchen or the yard, he is following a perfectly natural instinct. He is trying to remain as close as possible to you, the honorary leader of his pack.

Reading Across Texts

From what you read about Old Yeller, which of the dogs mentioned in "A Dog's Life" seems most like him?

Writing Across Texts Write a comparison of Old Yeller with the dog you chose.

 **Visualize** | How can visualizing help you understand the dogs' names?

Skill
Character

Strategy
Summarize

Character

- Characters are the people or animals who take part in the events of a story.

- You can understand the characters by examining their words and actions. You can also understand characters by the way other people speak about them and act toward them.

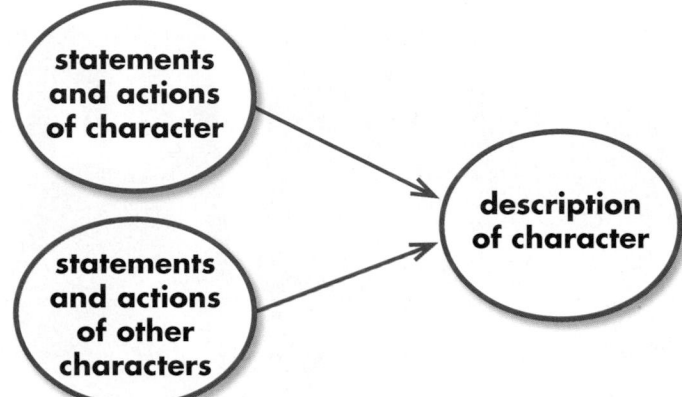

statements and actions of character

statements and actions of other characters

description of character

Strategy: Summarize

Good readers summarize in order to check their understanding of what they read. To summarize, you state the most important ideas about something. You can summarize what a character is like by stating important ideas you have learned about the character's personality.

Write

1. Read "Linda and Val." Choose one character and make a graphic organizer like the one above to tell what the character is like.

2. Use your graphic organizer to write a summary of the personality of the character you chose.

LINDA AND VAL

"Today we'll weigh objects. For homework, you'll make a graph of the weights," Mr. Daniels said. "Linda, you work with Val."

Linda's eyes widened in disbelief. "*Val?*" Linda said. Val had joined the class just last week. She had cerebral palsy.

Linda looked at Val, who was attempting to stand up. Her arms and legs shook. Linda rolled her eyes. Val slowly wobbled over and said, "Hi, Linda." Linda did not reply.

Once Val sat down, Linda asked, "Have you ever weighed an object?"

"Sure, even shaky old me," Val joked. The humorous reply surprised Linda, and she relaxed a little.

Val tried to place a weight on the scale, but her hand stayed closed. Then her clenched fist began to shake. "Could you pry that open for me?" Val asked. Linda slowly peeled Val's fingers back until the weight dropped. "Nice job," Val said, smiling. "You didn't even need a crowbar."

Linda smiled. "Do you want me to put the next weight on?" she asked.

"Sure, this time I might never let go!" Val quipped. Both girls laughed and continued working. At the end of the class, Val asked, "Do you want to come over to my home after school? We could work on the graph together."

Linda didn't even hesitate. "Sure."

Skill Remember you can learn about a character by the way he or she acts. What does Linda's facial expression tell you about her?

Strategy Here is a good point to start summarizing. What things have you learned about Linda so far?

Skill Linda has begun to change her actions and words toward Val. What does this tell you about Val's character?

Strategy How would you summarize Val's character?

43

Words to Know

apparently

flimsy

incident

fixtures

subscribe

survive

Remember

Try the strategy. Then, if you need more help, use your glossary or a dictionary.

Vocabulary Strategy
for Greek and Latin Roots

Word Structure Sometimes when you are reading, you come across a word you don't know. Does it have a word part that other words have? Many words are built from Greek or Latin roots. For example, in *vivid* is *viv* from the Latin word *vivere,* meaning "to live." *Scribe* is in the Latin word *scribere,* meaning "to write." A scribe is a person who writes.

1. Check the unknown word for any Greek or Latin word parts whose meanings you know.

2. Use the meaning of the word part to help you figure out the meaning of the unknown word.

3. Reread the sentence. Does this meaning make sense?

As you read "Saving the Past," study vocabulary words to see if you find a root whose meaning you can learn.

Saving the Past

Have you ever known people who are trying to save an old building from being torn down? You may have said, "So what? What's the big deal?" As far as you can see, it apparently is worthless. The roof is caving in, and the paint has faded and peeled. It looks tired and ugly and flimsy. Why not tear it down, you ask? Something cool like an arcade or movie rental store could go there.

The building may be a historic landmark. You probably have several in your area. These are buildings that are rich in history. They have importance to the people of the community. Perhaps some historic incident took place there, like the birth of a President or the creation of an important invention. Maybe the building shows the details and style of a time we want to remember.

Its roof, trim, and antique fixtures capture the charm of an era that is past.

Most people subscribe to the idea that we should save these buildings. They need to be preserved and treasured. While they survive, we can take pride in remembering part of who we were and are.

What building or location in your community is a part of history? Write about this place, and tell why it should be saved. Use as many words from the Words to Know list as you can.

Genre

Realistic fiction is fiction about imaginary people and events that could be possible. Look for realistic actions and events as you read.

Mother Fletcher's Gift

by Walter Dean Myers
illustrated by William Low

How can one person make a difference in the life of another?

It was rumored that Mother Fletcher was well over ninety years old. She had become a legend on 145th Street. If anybody wanted to know what the neighborhood looked like in the twenties, where Jack Johnson had lived, perhaps, or where James Baldwin's father had preached, Mother Fletcher could tell you. Patrolman William Michael O'Brien had heard about her shortly after his assignment to the precinct, but it wasn't until nearly three months later that he actually met the old woman.

He was on foot patrol and had stopped to pass a few words with one of the local shopkeepers when a young black girl came running up to him and told him that Mother Fletcher was sick and needed an ambulance. O'Brien knew that in this neighborhood it was nearly impossible to get a doctor who would make house calls. But he had also been told that sometimes the people used ambulances just to go downtown.

He followed the girl into one of the buildings and into a first-floor apartment. The place was small but spotless. The floor was covered with a linoleum rug that was worn through in several spots. The porcelain in the kitchen sink was discolored but the brass fixtures were shining brightly.

"She's in here," the girl said, and went into the adjoining room.

49

Mother Fletcher sat upright in the white-sheeted bed, her pale green housecoat pinned at the neck. O'Brien had never seen as black a person in his entire life. Her skin was a dull ebony that seemed almost purple in the light of the lamp by her bed.

Her gray hair, still streaked with wisps of black and thinner on the sides than on the top, framed her face and, catching the light, made her look like a black version of a painted medieval saint. She was a small person, in the delicate way that a child is small, but with the quiet grace of her years. But what stood out most on the old woman were her eyes.

They were, if it was possible, even darker than her skin. Black shiny eyes that darted brightly about, checking the room for anything that might have been out of place.

"Didn't my great-great-grandchild there tell you I was sick?" Mother Fletcher shot a glance in the direction of the girl. "I gave her a dime to tell you."

"I mean," O'Brien said, "what *exactly* is the matter?"

"How do I know? I'm not a doctor." Mother Fletcher pulled the housecoat tighter around her thin shoulders.

"What's your name, please?"

"Mother Fletcher."

"What's your first name?"

"I'm Mother Fletcher, that's all. Now, are you going to get me an ambulance or do I have to send that child out for another officer?"

"We can't just call an ambulance any time someone says to call one," O'Brien said.

"Boy, I am not someone," the old woman said. "I am Mother Fletcher and you can call for an ambulance. You know how to use that radio you got."

"What is your age?" O'Brien flipped out his radio and called the emergency network.

"Full-grown," came the flat reply.

O'Brien stepped into the next room and told the operator what he had. The ambulance arrived some fifteen minutes later. Two slim attendants carried the old woman out. O'Brien wrote up the incident in his book and promptly put it out of his mind.

A week later he was called into one of the precinct offices, where a lieutenant and two patrolmen were waiting for him.

"O'Brien." Lt. Stanton rolled a cigar from one side of his mouth to the other. "What's this I hear about you taking graft?"

"I don't know what you're talking about," O'Brien answered.

"Well, this package just came in from someone on your beat and it's addressed to your shield number." The lieutenant was enjoying this. "Looks like graft to me, O'Brien. Open it up."

O'Brien looked at the childish scrawl on the top of the box. *To Officer 4566.* There was no return address. He flipped open the flimsy box and took out the contents. It was a knitted green cardigan. Instead of a brand name on the label it simply repeated his badge number, 4566. O'Brien tried it on and was surprised to discover that it fit even his long arms.

"I wonder who it's from?"

"Mother Fletcher," the lieutenant said. "You do anything for her?"

"Mother Fletcher? Oh, yes, the old black lady. I called an ambulance for her. No big thing."

"She probably started making that sweater for you on the way to the hospital," Lt. Stanton said. "We had another guy here about two years ago that straightened out a hassle she had with her landlord. She made him a sweater too. Then she decided that the landlord was right after all and she made *him* a sweater. I guess it makes her feel good. You can put a couple of bucks in the precinct fund to make up for the sweater. And don't forget to go around and thank Mother Fletcher. It's good for community P.R."

O'Brien got around to thanking the old woman a few days later, telling her how his wife had been jealous of such a fine sweater. Three weeks later another package arrived at the station house. It was a sweater for his wife. When he went over to thank Mother Fletcher for the second sweater he was careful not to mention that he had a six-year-old daughter.

Over the next months O'Brien learned more about Mother Fletcher from people on his beat. Some stories were a bit far-fetched, but they were all told in a way that said that people loved the old woman. She did her own shopping, always carrying the same blue cloth shopping bag, and always walking on the sunny side of the street "to keep the bones warm." Once O'Brien met her on the corner of 147th Street and asked how she was feeling.

"I'm feeling just fine. I'm not cutting the rug," she said, "but I'm not lying on it, either."

O'Brien talked to her now and again when he saw her on the street, and started writing down everything she said, trying to piece together enough information to determine her true age. In truth, Mother Fletcher was the only one in his precinct that he thought of during his off-duty hours. The struggle and hassles of Harlem were not what he wanted to bring home with him. It didn't take O'Brien long to subscribe to the precinct motto—Eight and Straight. Eight hours on the job and straight out of the neighborhood.

To O'Brien, "out of the neighborhood" meant home to a ranch-style house in suburban Staten Island. He looked forward to the day when his wife, Kathy, could quit her job with the utility company and stay home with their daughter, Meaghan. He had told Kathy about Mother Fletcher and they had gone over his notes in the evenings trying to figure her age. Beyond this O'Brien was careful to keep his job apart from his family. At least he was until just before Christmas.

"Hi, honey," Bill called out as he ducked in from the light snow.

"Dinner's almost ready," Kathy answered as she came from the kitchen. "Did you ask Mother Fletcher if she remembered when Woodrow Wilson was elected President?"

"Yep."

"Well, what did she say?" Kathy wiped her hands on her apron.

"She said she remembered it."

"Did she remember how old she was then?"

"Nope, unless you can figure how old ''bout half grown' is," Bill said. He tousled his daughter's hair and sat on the couch.

"What else did she say?" Kathy folded one leg under herself and sat on it.

"Not much. I think she knows that I'm trying to figure out her age, and she's playing with me." Bill glanced toward the kitchen and sniffed the air. "Is that roast beef?"

"Chicken," Kathy answered. "So that's all she said today?"

"No, she complained about how loud the teenagers play their radios and, oh, yes, she invited us to Christmas dinner."

"Who invited us to dinner?" Meaghan looked up from her book.

"A lady Daddy knows in Harlem, sweetheart."

"Can we take presents over?"

"We won't be going over," Bill said.

"Why, Daddy?"

"We have other plans. We're going to . . . what are we doing for Christmas, Kathy?"

"Nothing."

"Then we can go!" Meaghan said.

"Kathy, will you deal with your daughter?" Bill smiled as he reached for the paper. "She's too much for me."

"No, I won't." Kathy got up. "I'm going to start serving dinner. And Meaghan has a right to ask a question."

"Hey, let's not make an issue of this," Bill said.

"She just asked for a simple explanation, Bill." Kathy was annoyed.

"The lady is a little different, that's all." Bill spoke to his daughter. "The place she lives in isn't very nice, and Daddy would rather not spend his Christmas in that kind of a neighborhood."

"Is she a poor lady?"

"Yes, she's a poor lady."

"Then we can take her a present because poor people like presents."

"We'll send her a present if you want, Meaghan." Bill rose from the couch and went into the living room, snapping on the television before sitting down. Kathy followed him in.

"I don't like the idea of being made out to be a bad guy, Kathy," Bill said without looking away from the six o'clock news. "One word from you could have helped that little situation in there."

"Why didn't you just give her the same answer you gave Mother Fletcher? What did you tell her?"

"There are times, Kathy, when you don't give direct answers to questions. It's a way of dealing with people. You don't reject them, and you don't get yourself involved in a whole scene. Like this one, I might add."

"Would you mind giving *me* a direct answer? What did you tell her?"

"I told her yes, we'd come. But they know we don't come into that neighborhood when we're off duty," Bill answered. "And they're not that anxious to have us come, either."

"You said yes? That you'd come?" Kathy pulled her glasses from the top of her head and put them on. "That's your way of not answering a question directly?"

"I'll send her a present."

"That's awfully sweet of you, Mr. O'Brien." Kathy went back to the kitchen.

Bill turned up the television and watched as some senator complained about the military budget. If his wife had chosen this occasion to have one of her special "I simply don't understand" periods he wasn't going to fight her.

He also heard snatches of the conversation drifting from the kitchen. Meaghan was talking about getting a kitten and was trying to decide between a calico and a tabby. At any rate she seemed to have forgotten Mother Fletcher. He only hoped that Kathy would too.

And apparently she had. For that was the last O'Brien heard about visiting the old woman. That is, it was the last thing until just after eleven on Christmas morning. He was sitting in his favorite armchair, feeling especially regal in the smoking jacket that Kathy had given him, watching a college football game, when Kathy and Meaghan came into the room with their coats on.

"Going for a walk?" Bill asked, hoping he wouldn't be expected to leave his comfortable spot.

"We're going to Mother Fletcher's for dinner," Meaghan said brightly.

"You're not going to Mother Fletcher's, Kathy. And that's that!"

"Well, then I suggest you arrest me, Mr. O'Brien." The sunlight through the window caught the flare in Kathy's eyes. "Because that will be the only way you're going to prevent our going."

"I brought her a scarf." Meaghan held a small square package.

"What is this all about?" Bill felt his face getting red. "You don't even know this woman. Why do you have to drag Meaghan all the way to Harlem?"

"I'm not dragging her anywhere. I'm giving her the present of a visit to an old lady that even you like. Now, from what you say, all I have to do is go over to the neighborhood and ask anyone where she lives because they all know, right? Or would you like to drop us off?"

The silence of the long drive was broken only by an occasional observation from Meaghan. O'Brien took his wife slowly, carefully, through the worst streets he could find until he finally pulled up in front of Mother Fletcher's place.

"Well, well, well!" Mother Fletcher was wearing an ankle-length green dress with a white lace collar. She wore a red and gold pin shaped like a tree. "I thought I was going to be having Christmas dinner by myself this year." Bill shot a glance in Kathy's direction as they entered the small apartment. The smell of the ham in the oven filled the room.

"Mother Fletcher, this is my wife, Kathy, and this is Meaghan."

"Well, ain't she the prettiest little thing. Look just like her mama too. Sit on down in here while I see if I can't get something together for dinner. Did I wish you a Merry Christmas yet? Merry Christmas, children."

"Merry Christmas, and here's a present." Meaghan gave Mother Fletcher the package.

"Thank you, child," Mother Fletcher said.

"Daddy didn't want to come," Meaghan said, pulling off her coat.

"I just didn't want to put you out," Bill said quickly.

"Child, I don't blame you one bit," Mother Fletcher said. "You working here all week and then coming back on a holiday. But it's good for you to see we have holidays here too. You see the people in the street all wishing each other a Merry Christmas and dressed up in their churchgoing clothes. You see them in this frame and you get a different picture of them. Don't you think so, Officer?"

"Yeah, I guess you're right," Bill answered.

"You can take your coat off," Mother Fletcher said. "I'll put it in a safe place."

"Those plates are so lovely!" Kathy went to the kitchen table where three plates were set out. "Are they antiques?"

"Everything in this house is an antique, including me," Mother Fletcher said as she took another plate from the cabinet.

"It's a lovely setting and there sure are a lot of pots on the stove for you not to be expecting anyone."

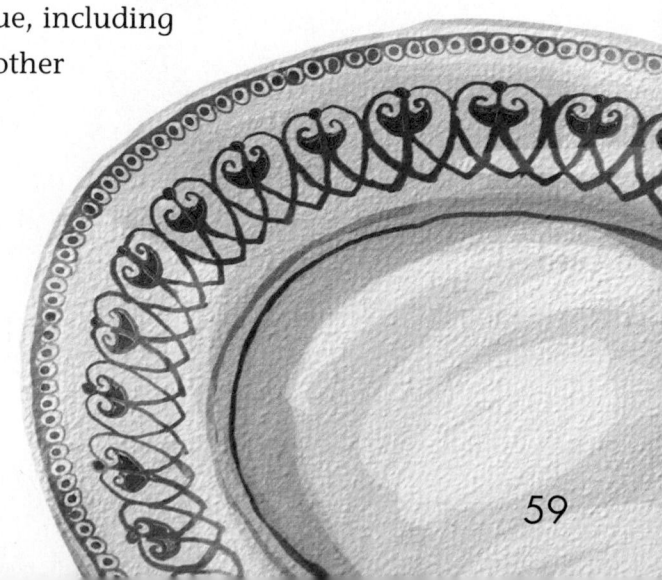

"Well, honey, let me tell you something. You don't survive, and that's what I been doing all these years, you don't survive sitting around expecting folks to act right." She opened the oven door, poked a fork in the ham and watched the clear juices run down its side, and then closed it. "'Cause the more you expect the more you get your heart broke up. But you got to be ready when they do act right because that's what makes the surviving worth surviving. That make any sense to you, honey?"

"It makes quite a bit of sense."

"That child of yours eat sweet potatoes?"

"Yes, she loves them," Kathy said. "Can I help you with anything?"

"You can help me with anything you have a mind to," Mother Fletcher said. "'Bout time you asked me too, old as I am."

"You're not as old as Santa Claus," volunteered Meaghan.

"Santa Claus?" Mother Fletcher put down the dish towel and turned her head to one side. "Child, I knew Santa Claus when he wasn't nothing but a little fellow. Let's see now. He wasn't any bigger than you when I knew him. Me and him used to play catch down near the school yard."

And Mother Fletcher went off into telling stories to Meaghan about how long she had known Santa Claus and how she used to have to lend him her handkerchief because his nose was always running.

And the Christmas dinner wasn't the best that the O'Briens would ever have but it was far from being the worst. But then, that's not what this story is about. This story is about how a policeman's young family brought a few hours of happiness to an old woman. Or perhaps it's about how an old woman taught a young family something about sharing. Or maybe, just maybe, it is about how a six-year-old girl found the only person in the world who played catch with Santa Claus when he was a little boy, even though she was a lot older than he was.

Reader Response

Open for Discussion In the last paragraph, the narrator says that this story might be about three different things. Do you think it is about any of these, or do you think it is about something else?

1. Mother Fletcher is a fictional character, but the author describes her in a way that makes her seem real. Find details from the story that help bring Mother Fletcher to life for the reader.

2. The author reveals Officer O'Brien's character through the things he does. Find at least three examples that help show Officer O'Brien's character. What are they?

3. On pages 55–56 Officer O'Brien and his wife Kathy have a disagreement. Summarize the events in this passage.

4. The author refers to Officer O'Brien's first meeting with Mother Fletcher as an *incident*. Make a list of at least three other incidents that occur in the story.

Look Back and Write At first, Officer O'Brien didn't want to go to Mother Fletcher's for Christmas dinner. Look back at the last page of the selection. Write a paragraph from Officer O'Brien's point of view explaining how he felt after having dinner at Mother Fletcher's with his family.

Walter Dean Myers

Read more books by Walter Dean Myers.

Walter Dean Myers lost his mother at age three. His father, too poor to care for him, gave up his son to foster parents. Fortunately, the Deans were good, loving people. "From them I received the love that was ultimately to strengthen me, even when I had forgotten its source."

A speech impediment made school difficult for Mr. Myers. "I arrived in school ready to conquer the world, but no one could understand a thing I was saying. That was very frustrating for me, and I responded by being angry." Mr. Myers began to write poems and short stories. "Writing was about the only thing I was praised for in school," he says. In high school, his speech difficulties led to social isolation and at sixteen he dropped out to join the army. When he returned, he took jobs that didn't require him to speak. "I loaded trucks. I worked for the post office."

At night, though, Mr. Myers wrote, mainly for magazines. One day he came across a contest for black writers of children's books and decided to enter. That decision changed his life. He won the contest and the book he submitted *Where Does the Day Go?* was soon published. From then on he never stopped, and the prizes kept coming. About half of the books he publishes win awards.

Amistad:
A Long Road to Freedom

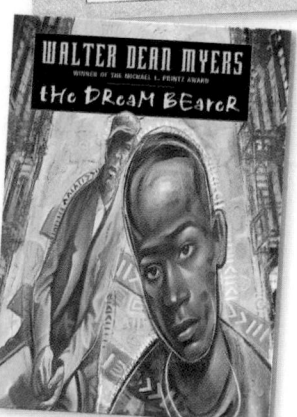

The Dream Bearer

Expository Nonfiction

Genre

- **Expository nonfiction informs us about real people and places of the past or present.**

- **Short pieces of nonfiction are usually in the form of essays or articles.**

- **If you want to explore further the topics you learn about, you would seek other articles or books of expository nonfiction.**

Text Features

- **The author organizes the facts in a logical order to aid your discovery of the Harlem Renaissance.**

- **Facts, such as who was a part of the Harlem Renaissance, where it took place, and why it came about, are detailed in the writing.**

Link to Social Studies

Research some writers, poets, singers, actors, composers, and painters of the Harlem Renaissance. Choose one person and present what you discover.

THE HARLEM RENAISSANCE

from *Cobblestone* magazine

IN THE 1920S AND EARLY 1930S, Harlem was the largest black urban community in the country. Many African Americans had moved there from the South in the two decades since 1900. Harlem was a community of families, homes, and businesses. It also was the spiritual center of the Harlem Renaissance, a 1920s artistic movement made up of black writers, poets, dancers, singers, actors, composers, and painters. A renaissance is a rebirth or rediscovery and is often a time when much artistic activity takes place. Black artists in the 1920s were interested not only in rediscovering their African roots and culture but also in understanding their place in American society.

The times—the Roaring Twenties— played a big role in giving these artists the opportunity to voice their black experiences. World War I had just ended, times were better economically for most people, including the black middle class, and people everywhere were eager to shed old ideas and accept new ones. Caught up in the

ZORA NEALE HURSTON

excitement of the times, black artists were eager to be heard, and many people listened.

The artists of the Harlem Renaissance were not a formal, organized group. They did not attend scheduled weekly meetings with set agendas or share a common political or philosophical belief. It was this growing black city, Harlem, and their common cultural experience that brought them together. Most of these artists lived in Harlem at one time or another and saw each other on the streets, in the library, and at parties, clubs, formal dinners, and readings. Many were friends. The Harlem artists also had strong relationships with their patrons, mostly whites who lived downtown. With their connections to publishing houses, art dealers, and the wealthy class, these patrons helped get African American art published, performed, and exhibited.

LANGSTON HUGHES

In the 1930s, when the economy collapsed and times got bad, the Harlem Renaissance lost its momentum. Money was no longer available to support the artists, and Harlem lost its focus as the center of the movement. But the creativity it inspired did not die. The spirit of the renaissance and the enormous body of art it produced have continued into the present to enrich those who enjoy it and to inspire new artists, both black and white.

Reading Across Texts
Mother Fletcher says she lived in Harlem during its renaissance. Do you think her life would have been easier or more difficult back then?

Writing Across Texts
Write a paragraph explaining your answer.

 **Summarize** What information is most important to remember?

Comprehension

Skill
Compare
and Contrast

Strategy
Summarize

Compare and Contrast

- Comparing is telling how things are alike. Contrasting is telling how things are different.

- Similes and metaphors make comparisons of very different things. Similes use the clue words *like, as,* or *than.* For example: *She is as sly as a fox.* Metaphors do not use clue words. For example: *He's the engine that drives this team.*

- You can use summarizing skills to clearly state how two people or things are alike and different. For example, *James is quiet and enjoys reading, while Kevin is outgoing and likes sports.*

Character A
Trait
Trait

Trait
Trait

Character B
Trait
Trait

Strategy: Summarize

Good readers understand text better when they summarize, or briefly state, the most important ideas in a selection. When summarizing a comparison piece, focus on the main ideas rather than the details.

1. Read "This New Town." Make a graphic organizer like the one above to compare and contrast Marville and Abbey Creek.

2. Use the graphic organizer above to write a summary of the two towns' similarities and differences.

This New Town

It's been a year since we moved to Abbey Creek. I am still getting acquainted with my new town.

In Marville, we could play outside even after dusk. All summer long we'd play games in the street. There weren't many cars to be concerned about. Because there is so much traffic in Abbey Creek, we play in the yards instead of the street. The yards in Marville were really spacious. The yards here are like postage stamps.

In some ways, though, Abbey Creek is superior to Marville. The houses here are more interesting. Each one is unique. In Marville, the houses all looked similar. There are more places to visit here. There are convenience stores and comic book shops. Abbey Creek is like a carnival; Marville was like a golf course.

Despite the differences, the two towns have things in common. Both of them have outstanding schools. Each town's park districts offer a lot of classes and sports.

Abbey Creek has a terrific public library, just like Marville. And like Marville, it has a lot of kids, although I'm not familiar with all of them yet.

Strategy Which of the following sentences best summarizes what this paragraph is all about?

(a) It was easier to play in Marville than in Abbey Creek.

(b) Marville has bigger yards than Abbey Creek.

(c) Marville had far fewer cars than Abbey Creek.

Skill What does comparing the yards to postage stamps tell you about the yards?

Skill Compare the houses in the two towns. How are they different?

Strategy Summarizing here helps you remember the likenesses and differences.

Words to Know

mongrel

menacing

groping

pleas

persisted

destination

corridors

Remember

Try the strategy. Then, if you need more help, use your glossary or a dictionary.

Vocabulary Strategy
for Unfamiliar Words

Context Clues Sometimes you can use context clues—the words and sentences around an unfamiliar word—to help you figure out the meaning of the word.

1. Read the words and sentences around the unknown word. The author may give you a definition of the word, examples, or a relationship that can help you predict the word's meaning.

2. If not, say what the sentence means in your own words.

3. Predict a meaning for the unknown word.

4. Try your predicted meaning in the sentence. Does it make sense?

As you read "The Traveler," use the context to help you figure out the meanings of the vocabulary words.

The Traveler

The dog I found standing in the yard was a hungry-looking mongrel. He was put together like a puzzle of many different breeds. Every rib stuck out. He might have been lost or maybe abandoned. I knew he had belonged to someone, for he was not one bit menacing. He wagged his tail politely and lowered his head to be petted. This dog had manners, and someone had taught them to him.

The feel of his ribs made me wince. I made for the kitchen. While I was groping in the cupboard for some bread, I thought I saw a movement. Sure enough, he had started trotting down the road. I tore back to the yard like a sprinter, hollering after him. He was deaf to my pleas that he return. Instead, he persisted in moving off at a brisk pace. It was as if he had a destination set in his mind. How far did he have to go, and how would he survive?

In the years since then, I have often wondered with a twinge of regret whether that dog made it home. I cannot forget his faithful path through the dusty corridors of that lost summer.

Write

Write about an animal you have wanted to rescue. Use words from the Words to Know list.

VIVA NEW JERSEY

by Gloria Gonzalez
illustrated by Melodye Rosales

70

How do we find new friends?

As far as dogs go, it wasn't much of a prize—a hairy mongrel with clumps of bubble gum wadded on its belly. Pieces of multicolored hard candies were matted in its fur. The leash around its neck was fashioned from a cloth belt, the kind usually seen attached to old bathrobes. The dog's paws were clogged with mud from yesterday's rain, and you could see where the animal had gnawed at the irritated skin around the swollen pads.

The dog was tied to an anemic tree high about the cliffs overlooking the Hudson River and the majestic New York City skyline.

Lucinda traveled the route each day on her way to the high school, along the New Jersey side of the river. The short walk saddened her, despite its panoramic vista of bridges and skyscrapers, for the river reminded her of the perilous journey six months earlier, when she and her family had escaped from Cuba in a makeshift boat with seven others.

They had spent two freezing nights adrift in the ocean, uncertain of their destination, till a U.S. Coast Guard cutter towed them to the shores of Key West.

From there they wound their way north, staying temporarily with friends in Miami and finally settling in West New York, New Jersey, the most densely populated town in the United States. Barely a square mile, high above the Palisades, the town boasted a population of 47,000. Most of the community was housed in mammoth apartment buildings that seemed to reach into the clouds. The few private homes had cement lawns and paved driveways where there should have been backyards.

Lucinda longed for the spacious front porch where she'd sat at night with her friends while her grandmother bustled about the house, humming her Spanish songs. Lucinda would ride her bike to school and sometimes not see a soul for miles, just wild flowers amid a forest of greenery.

Now it was cement and cars and trucks and motorcycles and clanging fire engines that seemed to be in constant motion, shattering the air with their menacing roar.

Lucinda longed painfully for her grandmother. The old woman had refused to leave her house in Cuba, despite the family's pleas, so she had remained behind, promising to see them again one day.

The teenager, tall and slight of build with long dark hair that reached down her spine, was uncomfortable among her new classmates, most of whom she towered over. Even though the majority of them spoke Spanish and came from Cuba, Argentina, and Costa Rica, they were not like any of her friends back home. These "American" girls wore heavy makeup to school, dressed in jeans and high heels, and talked about rock singers and TV stars that she knew nothing of. They all seemed to be busy, rushing through the school corridors, huddling in laughing groups, mingling freely with boys, and chatting openly with teachers as if they were personal friends.

It was all too confusing.

Things weren't much better at home. Her parents had found jobs almost immediately and were often away from the tiny, cramped apartment. Her brother quickly made friends and was picked for the school baseball team, traveling to nearby towns to compete.

All Lucinda had were her memories—and now this dog, whom she untied from the tree. The animal was frightened and growled at her when she approached, but she spoke softly and offered a soothing hand, which he tried to attack. Lucinda persisted, and the dog, perhaps grateful to be freed from the mud puddles, allowed her to lead him away.

She didn't know what she was going to do with him now that she had him. Pets were not allowed in her building, and her family could be evicted. She couldn't worry about that now. Her main concern was to get him out of the cold.

Even though it was April and supposedly spring, the weather had yet to top fifty degrees. At night she slept under two blankets, wearing warm socks over her cold feet. Another night outdoors, and the dog could freeze to death.

Lucinda reached her building and comforted the dog, "I'm not going to hurt you." She took off her jacket and wrapped it quickly around the animal, hoping to disguise it as a bundle under her arm. "Don't make any noise," she begged.

She waited till a woman with a baby stroller exited the building and quickly dashed inside, unseen. She opted not to take the elevator, fearful of running into someone, and instead lugged the dog and her schoolbag up the eight flights of stairs.

Lucinda quickly unlocked the apartment door and plopped the dog on her bed. The animal instantly shook its hair free and ran in circles atop her blanket.

"Don't get too comfortable," Lucinda cautioned. "You can't stay."

She dashed to the kitchen and returned moments later with bowl of water and a plate of leftover chicken and yellow rice.

The dog bolted from the bed and began attacking the food before she even placed it on the floor. The girl sat on the edge of the bed and watched contently as he devoured the meal.

"How long has it been since you've eaten?"

The dog swallowed the food hungrily, not bothering to chew, and quickly lapped up the water.

It was then, with the dog's head lowered to the bowl, that Lucinda spotted the small piece of paper wedged beneath the belt around its neck. She slid it out carefully and saw the word that someone had scrawled with a pencil.

"Chauncey. Is that your name?"

The dog leaped to her side and nuzzled its nose against her arm.

"It's a crazy name, but I think I like it." She smiled. Outside the
window, eight stories below, two fire engines pierced the afternoon
with wailing sirens. Lucinda didn't seem to notice as she stroked the
animal gently.

Working quickly, before her parents were due to arrive, she filled
the bathtub with water and soap detergent and scrubbed the animal
clean. The dog didn't enjoy it—he kept trying to jump out—so Lucinda
began humming a Spanish song her grandmother used to sing to her
when she was little. It didn't work. Chauncey still fought to get free.

Once the animal was bathed, Lucinda attacked the clumps of hair
with a scissors and picked out the sticky globs of candy.

"Look at that—you're white!" Lucinda discovered. While using her
brother's hair blower, she ran a quick comb through the fur, which now

was silvery and tan with faint traces of black. "You're beautiful." The girl beamed.

The dog seemed to agree. It picked up its head proudly and flicked its long ears with pride.

Lucinda hugged him close. "I'll find you a good home. I promise," she told the animal.

Knowing that her parents would arrive any moment, Lucinda gathered up the dog, covering him with her coat, and carried him down nine flights to the basement. She crept quietly past the superintendent's apartment and deposited the animal in a tiny room behind the bank of washing machines.

The room, the size of a small closet, contained all the electrical levers that supplied power to the apartments and the elevator.

Chauncey looked about, confused. He jumped up as if he knew he was about to be abandoned again. His white hairy paw came dangerously close to hitting the protruding, red master switch near the door.

Lucinda knelt to the animal. "I'll be back. Promise."

She closed the door behind her, hoping the dog wouldn't bark, and hurried away. An outline of a plan was taking shape in her mind.

Ashley.

The girl sat in front of her in English and always went out of her way to say hi. She didn't seem to hang out with the other kids, and whenever they passed in the corridor, she was alone. But what really made her even more appealing was that she lived in a real house. Just a block away. Lucinda had seen her once going in. Maybe Ashley would take Chauncey.

Lucinda's parents arrived from work, and she quickly helped her mother prepare the scrumptious fried bananas. Her father had stopped at a restaurant on his way home and brought a *cantina* of food—white rice, black beans, avocado salad, and meat stew. Each food was placed in its own metal container and clipped together like a small pyramid. The local restaurant would have delivered the food to the house each day, if the family desired, but Lucinda's father always liked to stop by and check the menu. The restaurant also made fried bananas, but Lucinda's mother didn't think they were as tasty as her own.

One of the nice surprises of moving to New Jersey was discovering that the Latin restaurants supplied *cantina* service.

"How was school today?" her mother asked.

"Okay," Lucinda replied.

The dinner conversation drifted, as it always did, to Mama's problems at work with the supervisor and Papa's frustration with his job. Every day he had to ride two buses and a subway to get to work, which he saw as wasted hours.

"You get an education, go to college," Lucinda's father sermonized for the thousandth time, "and you can work anywhere you like— even in your own house, if you want. Like a doctor! And if it is far away, you hire someone like me, with no education, to drive you."

Lucinda had grown up hearing the lecture. Perhaps she would have been a good student anyway, for she certainly took to it with enthusiasm. She had discovered books at a young age. School only heightened her love of reading, for its library supplied her with an endless source of material. She excelled in her studies and won top honors in English class. She was so proficient at learning the English language that she served as a tutor to kids in lower grades.

Despite her father's wishes, Lucinda had no intention of becoming a doctor or lawyer. She wasn't sure what she would do—the future seemed far too distant to address it—but she knew somehow it would involve music and dance and magnificent costumes and glittering shoes and plumes in her hair.

They were talking about her brother's upcoming basketball game when suddenly all the lights in the apartment went out.

"*Qué pasó!*" her father exclaimed.

Agitated voices could be heard from the outside hallway. A neighbor banged on the door, shouting. "Call the fire department! Someone's trapped in the elevator!"

Groups of tenants mingled outside their apartments, some carrying candles and flashlights. The building has been pitched into darkness.

"We'll get you out!" someone shouted to the woman caught between floors.

Lucinda cried: "Chauncey!"

He must've hit the master switch. She could hear the distant wail of the fire engines and knew it was only a matter of minutes before they checked the room where the dog was hidden.

"I'll be right back!" Lucinda yelled to her mother as she raced out the door. Groping onto the banister, she felt her way down the flights of steps as people with candles hurried to escape.

The rescuers reached the basement before she did. Two firemen were huddled in the doorway checking the power supply. Lucinda looked frantically for the dog, but he was gone.

She raced out into the nippy night, through the throng of people crowded on the sidewalk, and searched for the dog. She was afraid to look in the street, expecting to see his lifeless body, the victim of a car.

Lucinda looked up at the sound of her name. Her mother was calling to her from the window.

"Come home! What are you doing?"

The girl shouted, "In a minute!" The crowd swelled about her as she quickly darted away.

Lucinda didn't plan it, but she found herself in front of Ashley's house minutes later. She was on the sidewalk, with the rest of her neighbors, gazing up the block at the commotion in front of Lucinda's building.

"``" Lucinda stammered.

Ashley took a moment to place the face and then returned the smile. "Hi."

Lucinda looked about nervously, wondering if any of the adults belonged to Ashley's family. She didn't have a moment to waste.

"What happens," she blurted out, "when a dog runs away? Do the police catch it?"

The blond, chubby teenager, with light green eyes and glasses with pink frames, shrugged. "Probably. If they do, they only take it to the pound."

"What's that?" It sounded bad, whatever it was.

"A shelter. Where they keep animals. If nobody claims 'em, they kill 'em."

Lucinda started to cry. She couldn't help it. It came upon her suddenly. Greatly embarrassed, she turned quickly and hurried away.

"Wait up!" The blonde hurried after her. "Hey!"

Lucinda stopped, too ashamed to meet her eyes.

"Did you lose your dog?" Ashley's voice sounded concerned.

Lucinda nodded.

"Well, let's go find him," Ashley prodded.

They searched the surrounding neighborhood and checked underneath all the cars parked in the area in case he was hiding. They searched basements and rooftops. When all else failed, they walked to the park along the river, where Lucinda pointed out the tree where she had found him.

The girls decided to sit on a nearby bench in case Chauncey reappeared, though they realized there was little hope.

Lucinda knew her mother would be frantically worried.

"She probably has the police looking for me," she told Ashley.

"You've only been gone an hour."

"It's the first time I've left the house, except to go to school, since we moved here," she revealed.

It was a beautiful night, despite the cold tingling breeze that swept up from the river. The New York skyline was ablaze with golden windows silhouetted against dark, boxlike steel structures. You could make out the red traffic lights along the narrow streets. A long, thin barge sailed down the river like a rubbery snake.

Lucinda learned that Ashley's mother was a lawyer, often away from home for long periods, and her father operated a small business in New York's Chinatown, which kept him busy seven days a week. An only child, she spent her time studying and writing letters.

"Who do you write to?" Lucinda asked.

"My grandmother, mostly. She lives
in Nevada. I spend the summers with her."

Lucinda told her how lucky she was to be able to see her
grandmother. She felt dangerously close to tears again and quickly
changed the subject. "I never see you with any friends in school. Why?"

Ashley shrugged. "Guess I'm not the friendly type. Most of the girls
are only interested in boys and dates. I intend to be a famous writer one
day, so there's lot of books I have to read. Just so I know what's been done."

It made sense.

"What are you going to be?"

Lucinda admitted she had no ambition. No particular desire. But maybe, if she had her choice, if she could be anything she wanted, it would probably be a dancer.

"My grandmother used to take me to her friend's house who used to be a famous ballerina in Cuba. She'd let me try on her costumes, and she'd play the records and teach me the steps. It hurt my feet something awful. Hers used to bleed when she first started, but she said it got easier after the first year."

Ashley told her, "You have the body for it. I bet you'd make a wonderful dancer."

When it became apparent that Chauncey would never return, the girls walked home together.

Despite all that had happened, Lucinda found herself sad to have the evening end. For the first time since leaving her homeland, she felt somewhat at peace with herself. She now had someone to talk to. Someone who understood. Someone who carried her own pain.

"Wanna have lunch tomorrow?" Ashley asked her. "I usually run home and eat in front of the television. I'm a great cook. My first book is going to be filled with exotic recipes of all the countries I plan to visit. And if you want," she gushed excitedly, "after school we can go to the library. You can get out a book on how to be a ballerina."

Lucinda agreed immediately, "That would be wonderful!"

The girls parted on the sidewalk, and Lucinda raced home where her irate father and weeping mother confronted her angrily.

"Where have you been! I was only going to wait five more minutes and then I was calling the police! Where were you?"

Before she could stammer a reply, the lights went out.

"Not again!" her mother shrieked.

Lucinda's heart throbbed with excitement.

Chauncey was back!

She ran out of the apartment, unmindful of the darkness, with her mother's screams in the air: "Come back here!"

This time Lucinda made it to the basement before the firemen, and she led her pal safely out the building. She reached Ashley's doorstep just as the first fire engine turned the corner.

Reader Response

Open for Discussion Suppose you found a stray dog. How do you think you might react to the dog, and what would you do, if anything, to help it?

1. The author leaves the story a bit open-ended. What effect does this kind of ending have on you as a reader?

2. In what ways are Ashley and Lucinda different from one another? In what ways are they similar? Make a list of these likenesses and differences.

3. Summarize what happens in the time between the power outage in the building where Lucinda's family lives and the point when Lucinda arrives at Ashley's house.

4. Write a journal entry Lucinda might have written that night after she got home from Ashley's house. Use words from the Words to Know list as well as other words in the story.

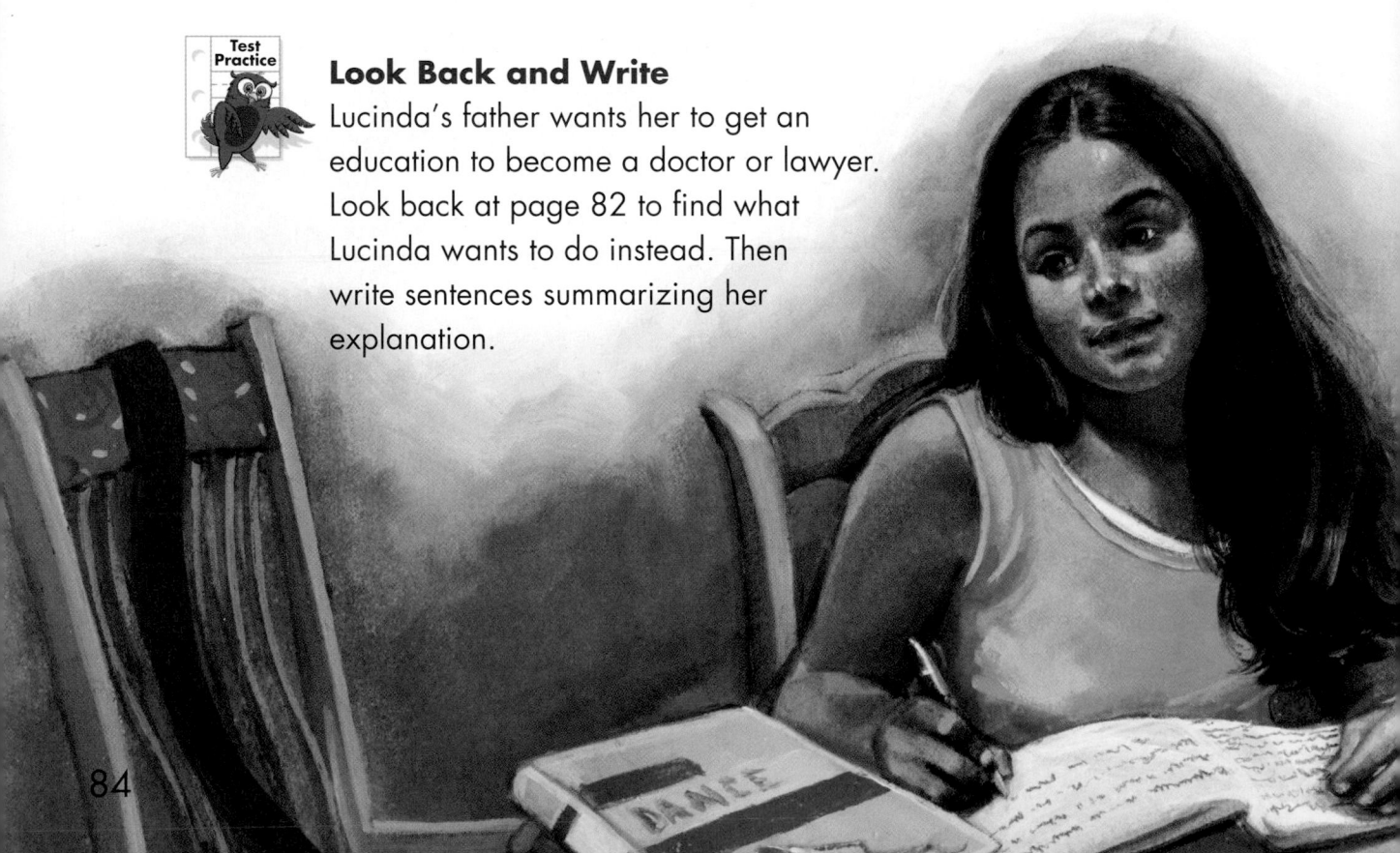

Look Back and Write
Lucinda's father wants her to get an education to become a doctor or lawyer. Look back at page 82 to find what Lucinda wants to do instead. Then write sentences summarizing her explanation.

GLORIA GONZALEZ

Read more books about young people and dogs.

A Girl's Best Friend
by Harriet May Savitz

Gloria Gonzalez lived for many years in West New York, New Jersey, where her story "Viva New Jersey" takes place. However, she grew up in New York City, across the Hudson River from West New York. While growing up, she spoke Spanish at home because her father came from the Canary Islands of Spain.

Ms. Gonzalez began her career as an investigative reporter for various New Jersey newspapers. Although she has written novels for young people and for adults, she is, perhaps, best known as a playwright. Her play *Curtains* was named one of the Best Short Plays of 1976. After her play *Gaucho* appeared on television, she rewrote it as a novel for young adults.

In addition to "Viva New Jersey," Ms. Gonzalez has written the short story "The Boy with Yellow Eyes" about two boys who capture a Nazi spy.

Wanted . . . Mud Blossom
by Betsy Byars

E-Mail

Genre

- Electronic mail, also known as e-mail, is a message sent over the Internet from one user to another.
- E-mail lets you communicate with people all over the world.

Text Features

- The "To" box shows to whom a message is going.
- The message itself looks like the body of a letter.

Link to Social Studies

Find out about some of Cuba's recent past and present history. Why do many people leave that country? Share what you find out with your class.

Visiting Another Country

Elizabeth got scared when her parents told her they were going to Israel for the summer. "I'll be just like Lucinda in 'Viva New Jersey.' I won't have any friends and I won't know what to do," she thought. Elizabeth wanted to know more about Israel. With her parents' permission, Elizabeth surfed the Internet and found a great Web site about travel for kids. At the site, she found a link for contacting people there and sent an e-mail.

Compare & Contrast What is a good way to compare two countries?

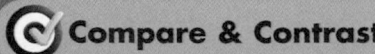

Take It to the NET™
ONLINE
more activities sfsuccessnet.com

86

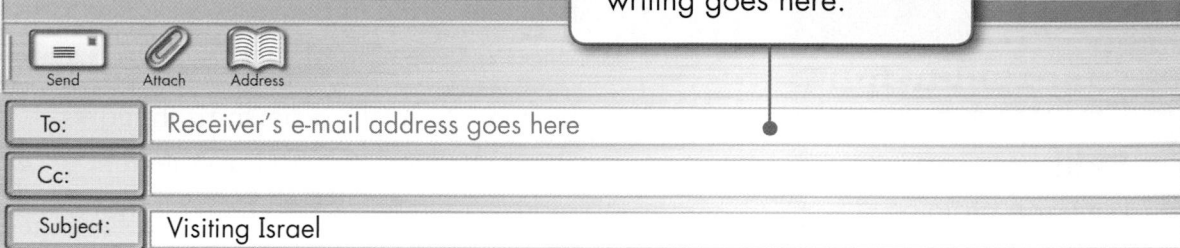

The e-mail address of the person to whom you are writing goes here.

Send Attach Address

To: Receiver's e-mail address goes here

Cc:

Subject: Visiting Israel

Dear Sir or Madam:

My parents just told me that we're visiting Israel for the summer. They were both very young when they moved from Israel to the United States. Can you help me find information on what a kid can do there? Thank you very much.

Elizabeth

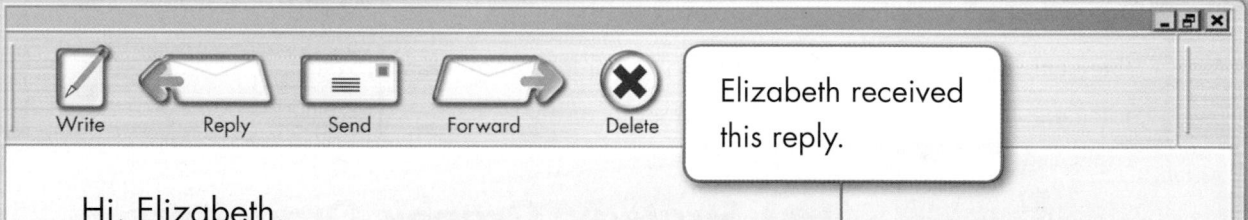

Write Reply Send Forward Delete

Elizabeth received this reply.

Hi, Elizabeth,

The first reaction some people have when they think of Israel is that it may not be very exciting for kids. Israel has religious importance for many of the people who visit, but there are also many other things for kids to see and do. Click on the links at our Web site to find breathtaking sights, activities, and books to read. And have a great trip!

Web site Editor

Reading Across Texts

Lucinda and Elizabeth each are having experiences with new countries. How are the two experiences different?

Writing Across Texts Write at least two paragraphs explaining how moving to another country is different from visiting another country.

87

Comprehension

Skill
Fact and Opinion

Strategy
Graphic Organizers

Fact and Opinion

- A statement that can be proved true or false is called a statement of fact.

- A statement that tells a person's thoughts, feelings, or ideas is called a statement of opinion. Statements of opinion cannot be proved true or false.

- Statements of opinion may be either *valid* or *faulty*. Valid statements of opinion are supported by facts or are stated by experts. Faulty statements of opinion are not supported by facts—they are supported only by personal opinions or by the opinions of people who are not experts.

Statement of Opinion	Support	Valid or Faulty
Statement	Facts from reference book	Valid
Statement	Opinion or incorrect fact	Faulty

Strategy: Graphic Organizers

Using graphic organizers can help you comprehend what you read. During reading, you can complete a graphic organizer to help monitor your comprehension and to think about the statements of fact and opinion in the text you are reading.

1. Read "Give the Oceans a Break!" Make a graphic organizer like the one above in order to identify valid and faulty statements of opinion in the article.

2. Look at the statements you labeled as faulty statements of opinion. Write a sentence or two for each one telling why the statement is faulty.

GIVE THE OCEANS A BREAK!

Why do humans harm the ocean when it is so important to them?

The ocean provides humans with many important things, such as fish. Overall, humans really like fish. Each year millions of tons of ocean fish are caught and eaten by humans.

The ocean is also a source of energy. Millions of barrels of oil are pumped from the ocean each day. Ocean energy is important because if we didn't have it, we would not have electricity.

The most important thing humans get from the ocean is minerals. My friend Tom, who lives near the ocean, says, "The ocean gives us sand, gravel, and sometimes even gold and silver."

But humans have really harmed the oceans. Many areas of the oceans have been heavily polluted by raw sewage, garbage, and toxic chemicals. In other areas, the fertilizers and pesticides that humans use enter the ocean and make it harder for sea animals to survive.

Overfishing has also hurt sea life. The populations of many sea creatures, such as whales and crustaceans, have declined over the years because of humans fishing. I think all ocean fishing should be illegal.

I think it's time we took better care of our oceans.

Strategy This statement should go on your chart as a statement of opinion. Think about its support.

Skill How can you tell that this statement of opinion is faulty?

(a) It is supported by only one fact.

(b) It was stated by an energy expert.

(c) It is based on incorrect information.

Skill As you read, watch to see if this statement of opinion is supported.

Strategy To keep track of the different things that pollute the ocean, make and fill in a web.

89

Words to Know

basin

tropics

equator

evaporates

recycled

industrial

exported

erosion

charities

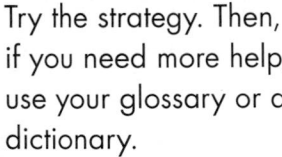

Try the strategy. Then, if you need more help, use your glossary or a dictionary.

Vocabulary Strategy
for Endings

Word Structure The endings *-ed* and *-s* may be added to verbs. The ending *-s* is also added to nouns. You may be able to use the endings to help you figure out the meanings of words.

1. Cover the ending and read the base word. Keep in mind that the spelling of a word sometimes changes when endings are added.

2. Reread the sentence and determine what part of speech the word is. (The ending -s may signal a plural noun or a present tense, singular verb.)

3. Do you know the meaning of the verb or noun? If not, look for clues in the sentence.

4. Decide what meaning you think the word has and then see if that meaning makes sense in the sentence.

As you read "The Amazing Amazon," look for words that end with *-ed* or *-s*. Use the endings and the way the words are used to help you figure out their meanings.

The Amazing Amazon

The basin of the Amazon River in South America is the area covered by the Amazon River and the rivers that flow into it. It is an area of Brazil that holds amazing wealth. Its riches lie in its vast forests. This area is part of the tropics, the land near the equator. The forests of the Amazon Basin are thought to hold millions of species of plants and animals. Many organisms can live there because of the warmth and heavy rainfall.

It rains every day in the tropical forest. Then the hot sun evaporates water from the soil and trees and other plants. This water vapor goes into the air, becomes clouds, and falls again as rain. Water is thus recycled and kept in the region. It is believed that many valuable medicines and other products can be made from the plants and animals that live there.

However, people who live in the region want to live well. They want Brazil to become an industrial nation.

Many square miles of forest are being cut down every year to make way for industry. Some wood is exported, but much is burned. The tropical soil is thin, and soon erosion carries it away. Then the bare land is poor. The people often use the help of charities to help them find ways to exist without destroying their forests.

Write

Choose a picture from the next selection and write a description of it. Use words from the Words to Know list.

91

Why are tropical rain forests valuable and important?

Genre

Expository nonfiction gives information about real people, places, and events. Note the features in this selection that show that what you're reading about is real.

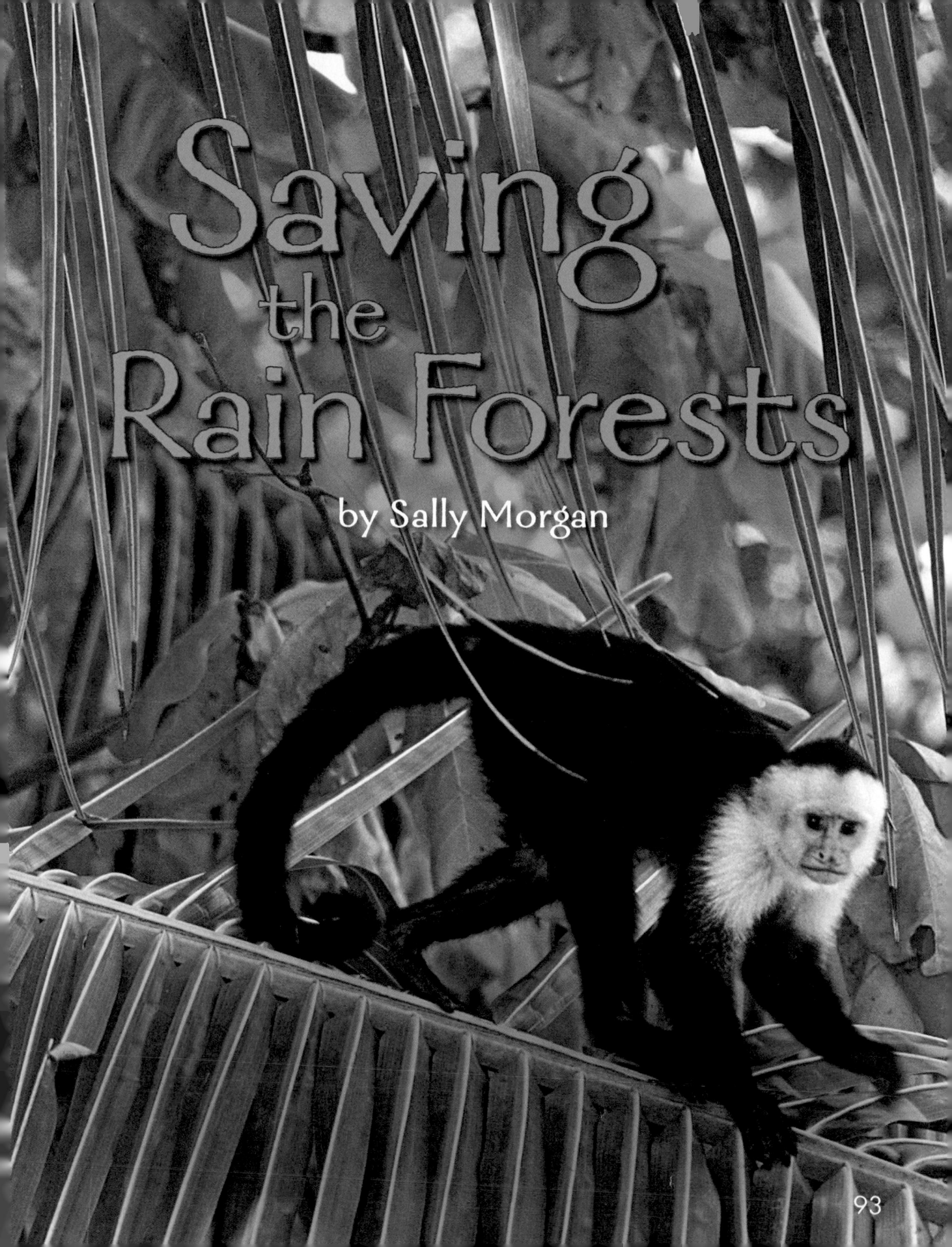

Saving
the
Rain Forests

by Sally Morgan

What Is a Rain Forest?

A rain forest is a special kind of forest that grows in warm, wet places. The trees are tall and grow close together. There are three main types of rain forest.

TROPICAL FORESTS

Tropical rain forests grow near the equator (an imaginary line around the middle of Earth). The climate is hot and rain falls nearly every day. The rain forest trees are evergreen trees—they have leaves year-round.

The largest area of rain forest is the Amazon rain forest, in the huge Amazon River basin in South America. There are also tropical rain forests in Central Africa, Southeast Asia, and Australia.

Lush vegetation in a tropical rain forest

CLOUD FORESTS

Rain forests that cover mountains in tropical regions are called cloud forests because they are up in the clouds. The air is cooler higher up a mountain, and there is more moisture in the air. Trees in cloud forests are shorter than those in tropical forests, and they are deciduous—they drop their leaves once a year.

TEMPERATE FORESTS

Temperate rain forests grow farther from the equator, where the climate is cooler. Here there are distinct seasons, when some parts of the year are cool and others warm. Many of the trees are conifer trees, which have needlelike leaves that drop gradually all through the year. The trees are covered in mosses and lichens. There are temperate rain forests in Australia, New Zealand, North America, and parts of South America.

Tropical and cloud rain forests
Temperate rain forests

ECO THOUGHT

In the tropics, more than one billion people depend on the water that falls on rain forests. They need it for drinking, cooking, and watering crops.

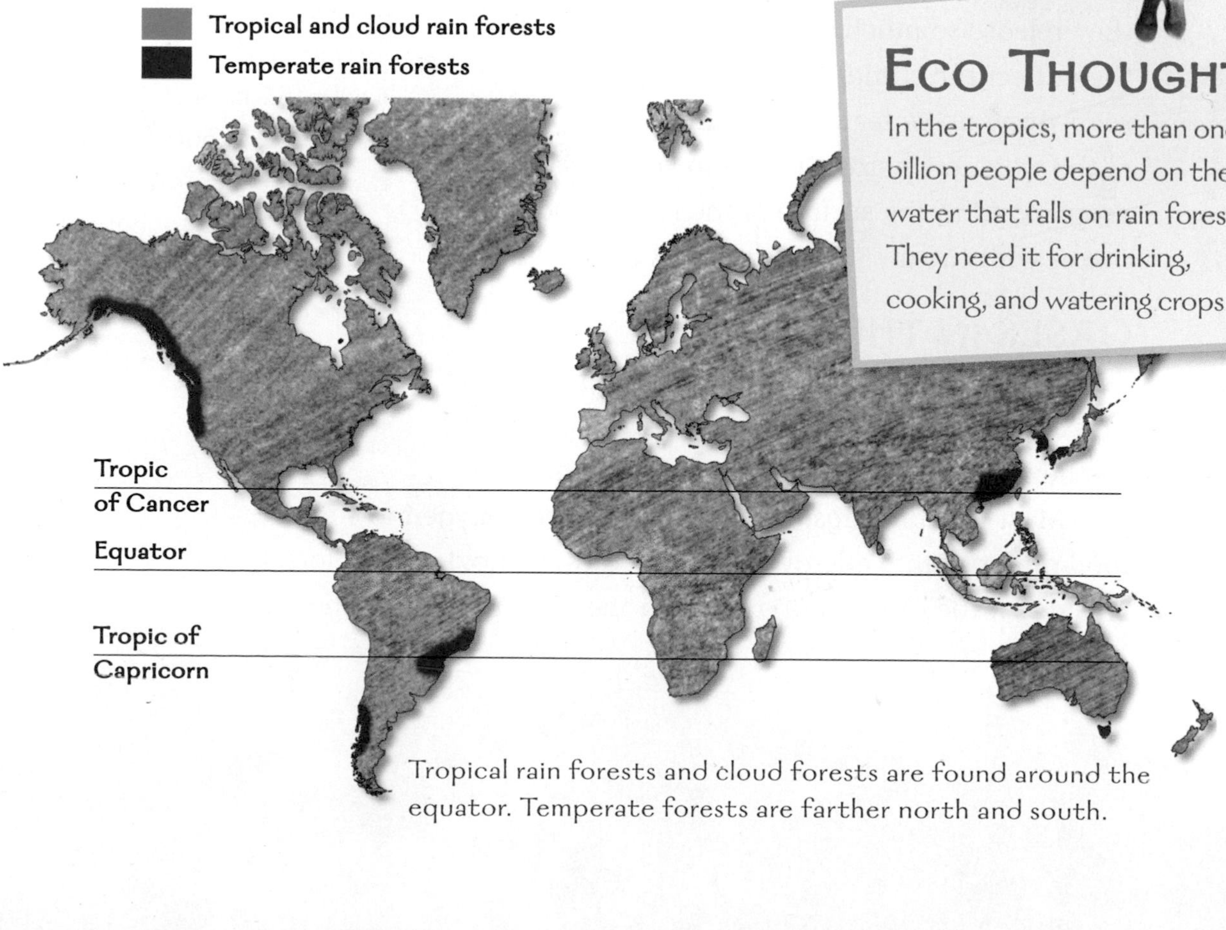

Tropic of Cancer

Equator

Tropic of Capricorn

Tropical rain forests and cloud forests are found around the equator. Temperate forests are farther north and south.

95

This rare bird, called an iiwi, resides in the rain forests of Hawaii.

Rain Forests at Risk

In the last few years, huge fires in the rain forests of Brazil and Indonesia have hit the news. On television, we have seen dramatic pictures of the fires and the damage they have caused. Forest fires are common, so why should they worry us?

MILLIONS OF PLANTS AND ANIMALS

We should worry because forests are important. Scientists think that about ten million different species (types) of plants and animals live on Earth. The rain forests are home to nearly two-thirds of these. Some animals live among the leaves, others on tree trunks, and some on the forest floor. Because of this, scientists say rain forests have a high biodiversity (variety of living things).

WATER AND CLIMATE

We should also save rain forests because they release so much water into the air that they affect the climate of the tropics. Plant roots draw up water from the ground. A lot of the water evaporates (turns to vapor, or tiny droplets) from the surface of the leaves and mixes with the air. This helps form rain clouds.

ECO THOUGHT

In a patch of rain forest 4 miles (6.7 kilometers) square, there can be 1,500 species of flowering plants, 400 species of birds, 150 species of butterflies, 100 species of reptiles, and 60 species of amphibians.

GASES IN THE AIR

Leaves use the energy of sunlight to join water and carbon dioxide gas from the air to make food. As they do this, they give off the gas oxygen.

Most living things, including trees, need oxygen to convert food material into energy for their bodies. Removing rain forests cuts down the amount of oxygen in the air, threatening the lives of many plants and animals.

How a Tree Takes Up and Loses Water

Water vapor from leaves

Flow of water

As fallen leaves rot, nutrients return to the soil.

Water travels up from the roots through the stem to the leaves.

Disappearing Forests

As the world's population gets larger, more food and building materials are needed. Half the world's rain forests have been destroyed to provide timber or farmland. It will take centuries for them to grow back.

LAND FOR FARMING

In Central and South America, land that was once forest is now pasture for cattle. In many countries, the best farmland outside the forest is all owned by rich people. Poorer farmers need somewhere to live, so they clear forestland for farms. They grow crops and use wood as fuel. In many parts of the world, wood is the only fuel available for cooking and for heating water.

An Indonesian farmer clearing brush after cutting trees in this rain forest area.

TROPICAL WOODS

Tropical wood is used a lot in building. In Southeast Asia and Africa, logging for timber is the main reason for clearing the forests. Timber companies build roads into the forests so they can bring in machinery to cut down the trees and pull out the logs. The logs are sent by road, or floated down rivers, to ports. From the ports, they are exported all over the world and used to make tables and other furniture.

BIG BUSINESS

Huge areas of rain forests are burned to clear land. On much of this land, cash crops (crops grown for sale) such as coffee, bananas, and rubber are grown instead of fruit and vegetables for local people.

Mining, industrial development, and the building of large dams all damage the rain forests too. Even tourism is threatening some of the more popular rain forests.

These young rubber trees in West Africa will be planted in land that was once rain forest.

Washed Away

In parts of the tropics (regions of the world near the equator), there are heavy downpours of rain almost every day. About 6 inches (15 centimeters) of rain can fall in just a few hours. New York might get that much rain in a month.

A HUGE SPONGE

The rain forest is like a huge sponge. The plants soak up most of the rainwater. This evaporates from the leaves, creating mist and low clouds.

The water in the clouds falls back onto the forest as rain. The water is recycled over and over again. Some of the water drains into streams and rivers. The rain forests release this water slowly, so the rivers never run dry.

SOIL EROSION

If the trees are cleared away, there are no roots to hold the soil. Rain washes it away. This is called soil erosion. Soil washes into streams and rivers and chokes them with mud. Aquatic (water) plants and animals that need clear and clean water die.

Cascade in Hana Rain Forest

LESS RAIN

With fewer trees, rainwater drains away quickly. At first, farmers have more water for their crops. But then, less water evaporates, so less falls as rain. The climate of the rain forest changes. Instead of reliable rainfall, there may be droughts.

Erosion in Papua New Guinea's Star Mountains caused by mining and heavy tropical rainfall

A Normal Tropical Rain Forest

Water drains from the forest soil into rivers.

Tropical Rain Forest with Soil Erosion

Without the trees, rain washes away the soil. Mud clogs up the rivers.

Rich Resources

Rain forests are rich in materials used in industry. These are called resources. Wood, such as teak and mahogany, is used in building and to make furniture. The rocks beneath the forests may contain oil and metals, such as gold, silver, and zinc.

LOGGING

Many rain forests produce hardwood, which is tough and long lasting. It is ideal for building and making furniture such as tables. Unfortunately, the best trees are scattered through the forest. In reaching them, loggers damage other trees and the soil, making it hard for young trees to grow.

VALUABLE TIMBER

Most hardwood is sold and transported to other countries. There, it is usually sold again for hundreds of times more than the local people were paid for it. Often, this valuable wood is wasted when it is used to make throw-away objects such as packing crates and chopsticks.

Huge numbers of logs are floated away from a tropical rain forest on a river in Borneo.

This mine in Guinea-Bissau, Africa, is an important source of money, but it has damaged the rain forest.

ECO THOUGHT

After logging, as many as three out of four of the trees left behind in the forest may have been badly damaged. It takes hundreds of years for the trees to regrow fully.

MINING

Huge areas of forest are cleared so that mining companies can reach the rock that contains oil and valuable metals. Sometimes they remove whole hillsides.

Digging quarries produces a lot of waste material, and this is usually dumped on nearby land. Water running off this waste and from the quarries may be polluted and can harm the aquatic life of streams and rivers.

In Colombia, South America, local people extract gold from a hillside in the rain forest.

New Finds

Scientists believe that they have only found about one-tenth of the animals and plants in the world's rain forests. New species (kinds) are being discovered every day. Many forest plants could be the source of new medicines or foods.

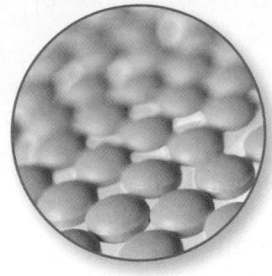

NEW MEDICINES

About a quarter of all modern drugs came originally from rain forests. The forest people discovered most of these long ago. They use plants to treat headaches, fevers, cuts, snakebites, toothaches, and skin infections.

Scientists have tested only a hundredth of the rain forest plants to see if they can be used in medicine. It is important to test more, because they may help to cure many diseases.

EXOTIC FOODS

Crops such as rice, coffee, bananas, and peanuts all came first from rain forests. There may be around 75,000 types of edible plants in the world, but we eat only a few hundred of them. Our diets could be far more varied and healthy if we used more rain forest plants.

MAKING DISCOVERIES

Scientists are discovering useful rain forest plants all the time. There are fruits containing more vitamin C than oranges, and substances 300 times sweeter than sugar. One tree produces a kind of oil that can be used in diesel engines. Some plants contain insecticides (substances that kill insect pests).

No one is sure how many useful plants there may be. But if the forests disappear, we will never know.

A scientist studies a weed growing in a rain forest in Hawaii.

What Can We Do?

The future of the rain forests is important to everyone. People and governments need to work together to make sure this precious resource is used well.

THE EARTH SUMMIT

In 1992, there was a meeting in Brazil called the Earth Summit. Politicians and experts from 150 countries discussed biodiversity, the importance of rain forests, and global warming. They drew up a biodiversity action plan—they agreed to list the plants and animals found in their countries, to set up more nature reserves and national parks, and to manage forests in a sustainable way.

RAIN FOREST CHARITIES

Some charities raise money to work with rain forest peoples. Others set up nature reserves to protect wildlife. We can help to protect the rain forests by supporting these charities.

The challenge for the future is finding ways for people to live in rain forests, find sufficient food in them, earn a living from them, and look after them, all at the same time.

In Uganda, Africa, children help grow new trees to plant in the rain forest.

Reader Response

Open for Discussion This article has a purpose: to make you aware of a problem. What is the problem? What is the evidence? What can you do about the problem?

1. How do photos and diagrams help convey the author's message? Chose three examples that could be used effectively in a speech about rain forests.

2. The author states that "many rain forests produce hardwood, which is tough and long lasting." Is this a statement of fact or a statement of opinion? How do you know?

3. Make a three-column chart. Title the chart *Forests* and label the three columns *Tropical, Cloud,* and *Forest.* Write at least two pieces of information about each type of forest in the appropriate column.

4. Write a magazine advertisement designed to get people to help the rain forests survive and thrive. Use words from the Words to Know list and from the selection.

Look Back and Write The Earth Summit meeting's action plan included three ideas to help solve the rain forest problem. Look on page 105; then write the three ideas in your own words.

Test Practice

Read more books by Sally Morgan.

The Ozone Hole

Acid Rain

Sally Morgan was once the head of a biology department at a high school. Today she is a writer and has more than fifty books on science to her credit. Like *Saving the Rain Forests,* many of her books are about ecology and the environment.

For younger readers, she has written a series of books about shapes. The books demonstrate how spirals, for example, are found in the objects we see around us every day. For older readers, she has written on a wide variety of subjects ranging from plants and animals to energy and power. She has also published books on water, sound, and light, but her special interests are conservation, genetic engineering, and health.

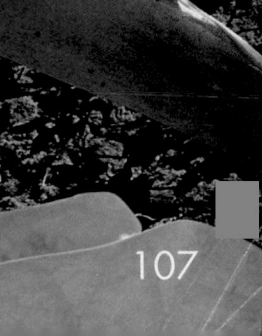

Expository Nonfiction

Genre

- Expository nonfiction can prove or support an author's opinion while also explaining facts.

- Expository nonfiction can give surprising information that may startle and raise the awareness of the reader.

Text Features

- The unusual title of this piece gains the reader's attention.

- Three introductory paragraphs are the author's way of linking together the captions of the photographs.

- Most of the information is carried in the captions.

Link to Science

Research water pollution sites in your area using information from the Internet as well as local newspapers, journals, city water department workers, and environmentalists. Share your findings with the class.

Not a Drop to Drink

from *Kids Discover* magazine

Water covers about two-thirds of Earth's surface. Ninety-seven percent of Earth's water is found in oceans, as saltwater. Two percent is stored in glaciers, ice caps, and on snowy mountain ranges. That leaves one percent of Earth's water available to us for our daily needs. Much of that is in hard-to-reach places, but some is found in lakes, rivers, and streams.

As Earth's population grows, the overall quality of our water has declined due to pollution, overuse, and problems tied to global warming.

Lakes are a resource that no one can take for granted.

If all the world's water could be put in a bathtub, the usable part would barely fill a teaspoon.

The Fermi-1 nuclear power plant on Lake Erie was closed in 1972 due to reactor problems. This power plant, Fermi-2, has had problems with leaks in recent years. Nuclear power plants such as this one are often responsible for polluted water conditions.

NO SWIMMING ALLOWED
WATER POLLUTED
NO LIFE GUARD ON DUTY
CITY OF ROCKY RIVER
CUYAHOGA COUNTY-BOARD OF HEALTH

LAKE POLLUTION COMES FROM MANY SOURCES, including nuclear power plants, chemicals, sewage, farm fertilizers, and acid rain. The 1972 Clean Water Act helped save many threatened U.S. lakes. For example, Lake Erie was so polluted that in 1970 *Life* magazine pronounced it dead. Today some fish populations have rebounded, and people can swim in parts of the lake that are away from urban centers. But Erie remains polluted.

 **Fact & Opinion** Are statements of opinion supported by facts and logic?

SOME OF THE WORLD'S LAKES ARE BEING STARVED

for water. Asia's Aral Sea has lost more than 60 percent of its water since 1960. Two rivers that were major sources of freshwater to the sea have been rerouted. At least 24 of its native fish species have disappeared.

WATER MAY SPARK CONFLICT in the Middle East in the 21st century. Both Israel and Syria rely heavily on the freshwater Sea of Galilee. Its water level has dropped sharply in recent years because of drought and increased dependence as other sources of water dry up. Meanwhile, Turkey has angered both Iraq and Syria by damming the Tigris and Euphrates Rivers, choking off millions of gallons of freshwater that people in those countries would normally get downstream.

LAKES, RIVERS, AND BEACHES are now America's favorite vacation spots. Sadly, many lakes are being loved to death. Motorboats and jet skis leave behind oil in the water, which is deadly to plants and animals. Also, the sheer number of vacationers drives away wildlife.

PROBLEMS OFTEN ARISE when people introduce non-native plants or animals to a lake. For instance, the water hyacinth, which comes from South America, has spread worldwide because of its beautiful flower. Unfortunately, this fast-growing water weed takes oxygen and sunlight away from fish and plankton. This causes water to stagnate, creating a breeding ground for disease-carrying mosquitoes. Water hyacinths have strangled huge sections of Lake Victoria in East Africa, the source of the Nile.

FLOODING ON LAKES has long been a hazard. Strong rainy seasons near China's Dongting Lake frequently cause thousands to be evacuated. Global warming is adding a new twist to this problem. It is causing the world's glaciers to melt much more rapidly, filling up some glacial lakes in high mountain areas. In some cases, the additional water might cause them to burst. A wall of water could suddenly plunge down narrow valleys and destroy everything in its path. In mountainous countries such as Peru and India, thousands of people can live in such valleys.

Reading Across Texts

The authors of *Saving the Rain Forests* and "Not a Drop to Drink" have positions they want to promote. What environmental message does each author try to persuade us to heed?

Writing Across Texts

Tell which message you felt was more compelling and why.

Ⓒ Graphic Organizers Could charts and graphs get across this information better?

Comprehension

Skill
Fact and Opinion

Strategy
Answer Questions

Fact and Opinion

- Statements of fact can be proved true or false. They can be proved by reading, observing, or asking an expert.

- Statements of opinion are judgments or beliefs. They cannot be proved true or false, but they can be supported by facts and logic.

- Sometimes statements express both a fact and an opinion.

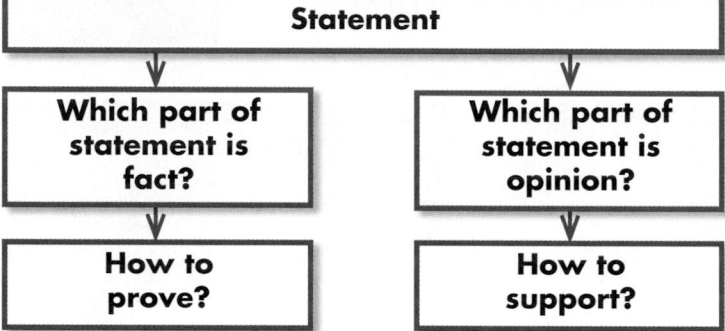

Strategy: Answer Questions

Good readers give complete, accurate, and focused answers to questions. Sometimes you must use your background knowledge to answer a question. For example, to answer whether a statement is a fact or an opinion, think of ways you know to prove a statement, such as using references. Be able to explain your answer.

1. Read "All About Birds." Make a graphic organizer like the one above to identify three sentences that contain both facts and opinions.

2. For each of the three, write how the part with the statement of fact could be proved or disproved and the opinion supported.

All About Birds

Did you know that birds are the only animals with feathers? There are about 8,700 different kinds of these fascinating creatures in the world.

All birds lay eggs, usually in nests. A nest may be a hole in a tree, a scrape in the sand, or a woven structure made of mud, sticks, or feathers.

Bird eggs take between 11 and 80 days to hatch. Some birds imprint. Soon after hatching, they follow the first moving object they see. This object is usually their mother. Imprinting helps make sure the young bird will be fed and protected. It is also nature's excellent way of making sure the bird will "learn" to be a bird.

Some birds, such as chickens, are able to look for food right away. Other young birds, such as songbirds, are fed by their parents until they can fly. Birds do not need to learn how to fly, but they do need to practice to become expert fliers.

Birds use audio signals, like chirping, for many reasons. They may make sounds to scare off other birds, to alert other birds to danger, or to attract mates. Some birds even have the amusing ability to imitate human speech.

Skill A descriptive word clue tells you that part of this last sentence is an opinion. What is it that could not be proved true or false?

Strategy Where could you check to see if this statement of fact were true? Use your knowledge of reference books.

Skill There is a statement in this third paragraph that contains both a fact and an opinion. Which sentence is it?

Strategy What are three facts from this article that describe bird behavior? Use your knowledge of facts and how to prove them to answer that question.

113

When Crowbar Came

Words to Know

dubiously

frustration

tolerated

secretive

detect

materialize

aggressive

migration

imprinted

Remember

Try the strategy. Then, if you need more help, use your glossary or a dictionary.

Vocabulary Strategy
for Suffixes

Word Structure Sometimes when you are reading, you come across a word you don't know. Check to see if the word has a suffix at the end. Suffixes add meaning. For example, *-ly* means "a characteristic of"; *-ion* means "the action of"; and *-ize* means "to make or cause to be." The meaning of the suffix combines with the meaning of the base word.

1. Cover the suffix and identify the base form of the word.

2. Decide its meaning if you don't know the word.

3. Look at the suffix, and decide what extra meaning it adds.

4. Combine the meanings from steps 2 and 3.

5. Use this meaning in the sentence. Does it make sense?

As you read "Wild Thing!" look for words that end with suffixes. Analyze the base words and the suffixes to figure out meaning.

WILD THING!

What puts the *wild* in wildlife? The birds and squirrels that visit our feeders have grown used to people to some extent. They look upon us dubiously when we emerge from the house. Get too close and they scatter. It is clear they think we cannot be trusted. Yet their frustration when we fail to fill the feeders is obvious too. They let us know in many ways that we are only tolerated, not accepted.

Further from us, in deep woods, live animals so secretive that they never show themselves to people if they can help it. If they detect a human, they behave as if a warning bell sounds in their brains. They hide quickly and silently. They do not materialize again until they feel danger has passed.

There are animals that display other degrees and signs of wildness. Some wild creatures become aggressive when threatened. They will attack if they feel it is "my life or yours." They also may be locked into a cycle of migration. Some wild animals travel thousands of miles to reach feeding and breeding grounds. A few may become imprinted on humans when first born. Otherwise, wild animals would never choose to spend time with people.

Write

Write about a time when you observed a wild animal. Use as many words from the Words to Know list as you can.

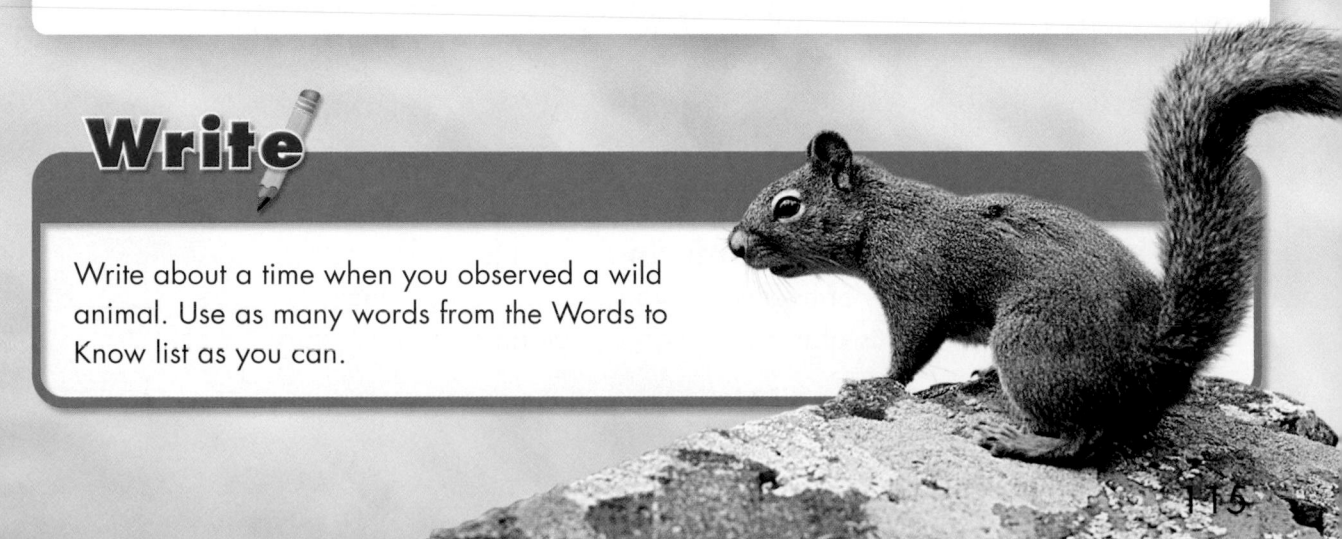

When
Crowbar
Came

from *The Tarantula in My Purse*

by Jean Craighead George
illustrated by Greg Newbold

Are crows intelligent animals?

Jean Craighead George lived in rural New York State. Her three children were Craig, Twig, and Luke. The George family often took in wild animals in need of aid. Some of the animals the family helped were a robin named Pete and four crows named Bituminous, Light Foot, New York, and last of all, Crowbar.

SEVERAL YEARS AFTER Light Foot, Bituminous, and then New York came and went, Crowbar came into our lives.

Craig found him on the ground in a spruce grove. A violent windstorm had knocked bird and nest out of a tree. Craig looked around for his parents, saw none, and tucked the almost-naked nestling into his shirt and carried him home.

"His name's Crowbar," he said as he put him on the kitchen table. The little crow was somewhat younger than New York had been when we brought him home, and so we knew this bird was going to be more deeply imprinted on us. He would indeed be a member of the family.

The scrappy little crow looked at us, rolled to his back, and clawed the air as if to tear us to pieces. He screamed like an attacking warrior.

I went to the refrigerator, took out a cold cheeseburger, and stuffed a bite in his mouth pressing it with my finger to make sure he swallowed. He did, and instantly changed his tune. He blinked his pale-blue eyes and got to his feet. Taking a wide stance to keep from falling over, he fluttered his stubby wings. In bird talk this means, "I am a helpless baby bird—feed me." We fed him until he couldn't open his beak.

At the end of the day we had a pet crow. Crows are smart. They know a good thing when they see it.

But it was not just the food. He was young and craved our attention. He cuddled against Luke, begged until Craig petted his head and chin, and dropped spoons and forks off the kitchen table until someone talked to him. He was ours, and he let us know what that meant.

He did concede one thing to his heredity, however: He slept in the apple tree outside the kitchen window. This greatly pleased me. Although a red fox named Fulva; two mink, Vison and Mustelid;

and three skunks had trained themselves to use a litter box while in the house, Crowbar, New York, and our other crows had no inclination to do so. Fortunately they spent most of their time outside, and when they did come in, they treated the house like their nest and kept it clean.

By autumn Crowbar was Crowbar George to Twig, Craig, and Luke. He would wake them at dawn by rapping on their windows with his beak. The three would come downstairs and set the table, including a place for Crowbar. They would scramble the eggs, serve them up, and open the window. Crowbar would fly to his plate and gulp his food like the young gluttonous crow that he was.

Then he would fly out the window to the apple tree and wait until Twig, Craig, and now Luke came out the door and down the front steps on their way to school. He would drop to the ground and walk beside them all the way down the hill to the school bus stop. Like New York he would sit on the rail fence. When the bus came, he would fly back to the kitchen window, and I would know my children were safely on their way to school. Other mothers had to go down to the bus stop and wait. I sent a crow.

Meanwhile I was reading every scientific paper about crows that I could get my hands on. I read that crows are hard to study because they're so smart. They easily elude and outwit the observer. They hide. They sneak through tree limbs. They count. A farmer learned that if he went crow hunting in the woods, he would not see a crow. They knew about guns. To foil them, the farmer took a friend into the woods with him. The farmer hid and the friend walked out across the fields and away. The crows did not make an appearance until the farmer left.

CROWS, I ALSO READ, have a language. They communicate with each other. Three caws are an identification—"I'm so-and-so crow." Five desperately given caws mean there is an enemy around—a hawk, an owl, a man with a gun. Many caws given with passion and fury say "Come—mob the owl." The crow fact that amazed me most, however, was that they can detect poisoned food and warn each other not to eat it.

They can recognize death in any form it takes. In an experiment by Dr. Kalmbach, two farmers who shot some crows in their cornfield found they could never again get close enough to the crows to shoot. Their wives could, however. When they came to the fields, the crows went right on eating within ten feet of them. The farmers decided that the crows recognized them because they wore pants. They put on skirts and aprons and went out to shoot the crows. They still could not get within gunshot range. Putting their heads together once more, they figured the crows must see the guns and know they meant death. They disguised the guns in brooms and went out to the cornfields to kill the crows. Before they got within range the crows were gone.

It must be, wrote Dr. Kalmbach, that when a man picks up a gun, he takes on an aggressive attitude that the crows read. They flee.

Appended to one report on crows was this: "Crows can learn to talk as do parrots or myna birds."

With that we began Crowbar's English lessons.

"Hello, hello, hello," we said slowly and distinctly many times over.

"Hello, hello, hello." This went on for days and weeks.

He did not speak. He looked at us intently, his throat feathers rising and falling. Then he would wipe his beak, a reaction to frustration.

"I give up," I said to Twig, and had no more than gotten the words out of my mouth than John Priori, who delivered the milk, came in the back door.

"Oh, good," he said. "You're in the kitchen. I thought I heard you up in the apple tree saying 'hello.'"

"It's Crowbar," we shouted. "Crowbar is talking." Twig and I ran outside to listen.

"Hello," said the clever bird. "Hello, hello, hello,"

"Crowbar," Twig said slowly and thoughtfully, "is really the smartest person on the block."

Crowbar did not rest on his laurels. He soon figured out how to make use of that word.

The neighbors on our wooded hillside come outside in summer to picnic and cook on their grills. Most have moved to the suburbs from New York City and know little about the country, much less its wild membership. Crowbar discovered that if he alit on a food-laden table and said, "Hello," he terrified these people. A large black bird might be tolerated, but one that spoke English was too much. They ran into their houses and closed their doors. Crowbar then helped himself to the hamburgers, strawberry shortcake, cheese, and nuts. When he was stuffed, he flew back to his apple tree.

Twig and I were walking under his tree one day as he was returning from one of these picnics. He alit, cocked his eye, and said, "Hiya, Babe."

Because Crowbar was completely free, our new neighbors had no idea he was a pet. Soon the police began to get complaints about a bird that took the clothespins out of their laundry and dumped clean shirts and towels on the ground.

The officers would arrive and, finding only an ordinary crow sitting on a fence or flying off through the trees, they would peg the complainers as cranks and depart. The complaints persisted, however, and one policeman, a hunter and wise to the ways of crows, brought a BB gun to the scene.

As the officer rounded the house, gun in hand, Crowbar gave five frantic caws. Birds stopped singing; crows disappeared. The policeman stood in a silent world where nothing moved but a breeze-touched shirt that Crowbar had not yet released to the ground.

"That bird won't be back," he said to the complainer. "Crows see a gun and they're off—for good."

He left, smiling at his own cleverness. When the patrol car was out of sight, Crowbar dropped down to the wash line and dropped the breeze-touched shirt to the ground.

So much for knowing it all.

Crowbar Goes to the Bank

THE SANDBOX WAS CROWBAR'S FAVORITE SPOT. When Twig and Craig played in the sandbox with Luke, they dumped into the sand a bucket of glittering spoons, bottle caps, toy soldiers, coffee cans and lids. At the sight of the sparkle, Crowbar would materialize from the trees and join them. He walked around forts and castles, picking up bright treasures and carrying them to the apple tree.

One day as I was working at my desk, Twig came to the door of the sunporch, her hands on her hips.

"I'm not going to play with that crow anymore," she said. "He takes all my toys."

I smiled. Here was my Twig. She was seeing the human in Crowbar. But she did have a point, after all. It must be maddening when you are counting on shaping a castle turret with a spoon and a crow steals it.

"Why don't you slide down the slide?" I suggested. "Crows can't slide down slides. Their feet have pads that hold them fast to perches."

She went back to her brothers, and the next time I looked up the three were sliding down the slide.

Then down from the roof sailed Crowbar. He swept his black wings upward, then down, and alit on the top of the slide. We all stared. Would he slide? He stepped on the steeply slanted metal board—and was stuck. Twig waved to me; I waved back to her. We had outwitted a crow, which we both knew was a very hard thing to do.

No sooner had we gone on with our businesses than Crowbar flew to the sandbox. He picked up a coffee-can lid, carried it to the top of the slide, stepped on it, and—*zoom*—we had a sliding crow.

CROWBAR WAS INDEED A CHARACTER. In the morning when the children were in school, he would sit beside my foot when I was working at my typewriter and brood over it. He would lift his feathers and lean against my ankle as if it were some cherished object. Sometimes he would go into a trance and fall over.

Unaware that I was being used, I would pick him up and pet him. He would make soft noises, then hop to my desk and fly off with a paper clip. I would laugh, knowing I had been had—but I never learned. He repeated this game many times, and I always fell for it.

When school reopened after spring vacation, Crowbar began to disappear every day at noon. He would walk to the open door, fly to the ash tree, and sneak uphill into the woods.

For hours I would neither see nor hear him. I assumed he was resting quietly in some leafy tree, which birds do for longer periods than most people realize.

One day a little neighbor girl, Sally, came to my door.

"Mrs. George," she said, "I think Crowbar has enough money to buy a sports car."

"What do you mean?" I asked.

"He comes down to the middle school every day for lunch," she said. "We feed him sandwiches and throw him our milk money. He picks up the money and flies off with it. He must be very rich."

"The middle school," I said, and remembered the crow's-eye view of the ecosystem. Of course: While soaring above the trees, he had spotted the kids and their food and shiny money. I wondered what else Crowbar knew about our town. He probably knew about the baseball games and picnics, the people getting on and off the trains, and the town dumpsters. But apparently most fascinating to him were the kids at the middle school eating sandwiches and flipping shiny coins into the air, and so it was to them he went at noon.

"We can't find where he hides his money," Sally went on. "Could you help us?"

"I'll try," I answered dubiously, "but crows are clever. He may be investing it in Wall Street."

She didn't laugh, so I answered more seriously. "I'll meet you on the playground tomorrow at noon, and we'll see what he's up to."

Crowbar was walking among the children when I arrived. Sally saw me and came running. Crowbar, who undoubtedly knew I was there, ignored me. A boy waved a coin and spun it in the air. When it sparkled to the ground, Crowbar hopped upon it and took it in his beak.

When he had a beakful of money, he skimmed low over the grass and laboriously climbed into a sugar maple tree that edged the playground. He looked as if he had stolen the crown jewels.

"See?" Sally said. "He hides the money, but we don't know where. He won't hide it while we're watching."

"He sure won't," I said, "Crows are very secretive. Other birds' nests are easy to find by following the parents when they are carrying food home to the young. But not crows.

"They won't go near their nests while you're watching. Those bright coins are kind of like Crowbar's nest. He doesn't want you to find them."

"Seems so," said Sally. "He waits till the bell rings and we have to go inside; then he flies away and we can't see where he goes."

The bell rang, Sally dashed off, and I sat down to see if I could outwait my friend. I could not. After half an hour I gave up and went home.

About a week later I came out of the bank, which is next to the middle school, and saw Crowbar flying low over the recreation field, laboriously carrying his load of quarters and dimes.

I stepped back into the doorway. He flew over the fence and the parked cars, then swept up to the rainspout of the bank. He looked around and then deposited his money in the bank's rainspout.

There is something uncanny about crows.

NEW YORK GAVE ME MY FIRST EXPERIENCE with this otherworldly attribute.

One afternoon the director of the Bronx Zoo and his wife, who were friends of my aunt and uncle, came to visit. Mrs. Tee Van was a very accomplished nature artist, and I was flattered that she would come calling. The day before, I had returned from a speaking engagement and had brought home to Twig the hotel shampoo, soap, and shoe-shine rag. She had put the shoe-shine rag in the dollhouse that stood on the porch.

We adults sat down in the living room to get acquainted. The children and New York played on the porch in view of us. At one point in the conversation Mrs. Tee Van looked out the window and saw New York walking on the porch railing. She smiled when she saw him.

"I had a pet crow when I was young," she said, and walked to the window. "I adored him. He was so clever." She paused. "Your crow's legs are so shiny. How do you manage that?"

Hardly had she spoken than New York flew to the dollhouse, picked up the shoe-shine cloth, and walked with it in his beak slowly along the porch railing.

Dr. Tee Van and I chuckled, but Mrs. Tee Van did not. She turned to me, visibly upset by what seemed to be a crow answering her question.

"We must go," she said. "That's just too uncanny."

"A funny coincidence," I said, forcing myself to laugh.

"No," she answered. "Crows are eerie. We have a lot to learn."

A Crow Kidnapping

CROWBAR STAYED. Two and a half years had passed since he had joined the family. After Pete left, he strutted down to the bus stop on school days, kept me company, and flew to the middle school at noon to call on his moneyed friends.

One morning as the sun was coming up, I heard crows yelling from my trees and yard. I ran to the window. Thirty or forty of the big black birds, who were on migration, were gathered on limbs, lawn, and picnic table. They were directing their caws at Crowbar.

"You're a crow. You're a crow. Come with us," I was certain they were saying. Crows do not like to see their kind become pet crows.

I tried to pick out Crowbar from the mob, but could not. They all looked alike. This was embarrassing, since Crowbar would fly right to my shoulder when I got off the train. He could find me in a mass of humans, but I could not find him in a crowd of crows.

The kids awoke, and we hung out the windows watching the drama below.

"He's going to go away with them," said Luke when the chorus rose to a frantic pitch.

"Get the hamburger," Twig said, and she and Craig dashed downstairs. Before they returned, the sun had flooded the hillside with light and the crows had taken off. Sitting alone was Crowbar. We ran outside and fed him until he could eat no more.

"Crows do know a good thing when they see it," said Luke, glad the family crow had stayed.

The next morning the birds returned. Crows are very sensible migrants. None of this flying fifteen thousand miles from the Arctic to the tip of South America and then back again, as some birds do, or for that matter even from New York to Florida. Crows migrate only as far as their favorite winter roosting sites, which can be no more than twenty miles away.

The telephone rang the third morning of the crow visitation.

"What are all the crows doing here?" asked Art Buckley, who lived at the bottom of the hill. "I've never, in all the twenty years I've lived here, seen so many crows." Then he added, "They wake me up at five. What can we do about it?"

"Wait," I said. "They'll go away."

I was not sure about that. I had never had a massive gang of crows come to abduct a pet. What would happen if they all came to recognize a good thing when they saw it and stayed on too?

On the fifth day we heard a new note in the communal voice of the crows. It was an unmistakable jubilation. Excitement infused their cacophony. Craig sped down to the refrigerator for food.

He got back in time to see the crows take off. They beat their black taffeta wings and flew up over our trees and down the valley— and there was no more Crowbar.

Despite our tears, it was a beautiful ending to a wild-pet story.

Reader Response

Open for Discussion Have you ever heard of setting a place at the breakfast table for a crow, or a crow with a bank account? What else did this amazing real-life Crowbar do that would make good conversation?

1. After reading this selection, how well do you know Crowbar? Look how precisely and respectfully Jean Craighead George has written about his movements. Find favorite examples that demonstrate how well you know Crowbar.

2. On page 125, there are both statements of fact and statements of opinion. Name one of each and explain how you know the statement is one of either opinion or fact.

3. What did the title "When Crowbar Came" tell you about the selection before you even began to read?

4. The author uses the word *secretive* to describe the way Crowbar behaves at times. Make a list of other words she uses to describe Crowbar's actions.

Look Back and Write How did Crowbar use the English language to get food? Look back at page 123 to help remember. Describe Crowbar's strategy in writing.

132

Meet the Author

Jean Craighead George

Read more books by Jean Craighead George.

Visitors to Jean Craighead George's Web site are greeted with this message: "I write for children. Children are still in love with the wonders of nature, and I am too. So I tell them stories about a boy and a falcon, a girl and an elegant wolf pack, about owls, weasels, foxes, prairie dogs, the alpine tundra, the tropical rain forest. And when the telling is done, I hope they will want to protect all the beautiful creatures and places."

Ms. George was born into a family of naturalists. As a child, she learned to climb trees and make fishing hooks from twigs. Her first pet was a turkey vulture.

After graduating from college, Ms. George worked as a reporter and member of the White House Press Corps. Then she married, had children, and began bringing home wild animals, 173 in all. When her children Twig, Craig, and Luke were old enough to carry backpacks, she took them camping. They learned about nature, and she wrote books about what she observed.

Ms. George began writing when she was in the third grade. To date, she has written over one hundred books. Her advice to young writers is "read, write, and talk to people, hear their knowledge, hear their problems. Be a good listener. The rest will come."

The Summer of the Falcon

Everglades

Narrative Nonfiction

Genre

- **Narrative nonfiction tells true stories.**

- **These factual stories may be long, or they may be short, interesting anecdotes.**

Text Features

- **In this selection, the author uses short, numbered sections to tell about various animals.**

- **The title gives a clue about the subject. Previewing the rest of the article by looking at the pictures and captions can further help the reader locate key information.**

Link to Science

Use reference materials to research an animal that interests you. Research that animal's behavior to find facts about its personality. Create a chart to display the information you find.

They've Got Personality

from *National Geographic WORLD*
by Aline Alexander Newman

"Personality is what makes a person (or an animal) unique as an individual," says Samuel D. Gosling, a psychologist at the University of Texas at Austin. Animal personality has become a hot new topic with scientists who study animals.

WORLD asked wildlife experts to share their four favorite stories about the personalities of memorable animals. Here are the tales of a few characters they've come across.

1 A bossy gray parrot rules the roost.

Who's the Boss?

Patricia Simonet's African gray parrot Max gets his kicks by giving orders. One time when Max was home alone in Incline Village, Nevada, a visitor knocked at the door. "Come on in," the parrot shouted. And the man did!

Whenever Simonet's other pet bird begins squawking, Max yells at him, "Pierre, be quiet!" Peace is restored.

Even the cat obeys Max. "Oh, Valentine!" Max calls in a singsong voice that practically beckons. The cat comes running to Max's cage. Max tosses a corn kernel onto the floor. Then the game begins. As the playful feline "soccer" player kicks and chases the kernel all around the room, "coach" Max sits on his perch watching, completely entertained.

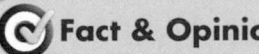 **Fact & Opinion** | What statements of opinion are mixed among the facts?

Do Not Disturb!

Ursula, a giant Pacific octopus who lived at the Seattle Aquarium in Washington State, had excellent aim. The trouble was her choice of targets. Every night this crabby sea creature blasted water out through the breathing tube on the side of her head, completely drenching the researcher whose job it was to check Ursula's tank. "This woman actually felt picked on," says biologist Roland Anderson. "Ursula never soaked anyone else, only this researcher." The cold shower was obviously intentional, since an octopus can spray in any direction it wants to. And Ursula turned an angry red every time she did it.

What prompted these nightly temper tantrums? Nobody knows for sure. But Anderson suspects that the researcher's flashlight beam may once have irritated the sleeping giant. From then on, Ursula carried a grudge.

2 An armed octopus gets revenge

Friends "R" Us

Jenny, an abandoned circus elephant, lumbered into the barn at her home at The Elephant Sanctuary in Hohenwald, Tennessee. Then she stopped and stared. A new arrival, Shirley, stood in a stall. Jenny rumbled hello. But Shirley, who had spent many years in a zoo with no elephant companions, didn't reply.

Jenny trumpeted louder. She paced. She even tried to climb over the barrier that separated the two elephants. Still nothing. Jenny poked and prodded the newcomer with her trunk. Finally Shirley lifted her head.

3 Elephants: friends forever!

"Her eyes got huge and she started to trumpet," says Carol Buckley, cofounder of the sanctuary. "Both elephants began screaming and bellowing excitedly."

Jenny and Shirley had been barnmates 25 years earlier. After more than two decades apart, they recognized each other! Now they share everything. They're never apart and often stand touching. The mutual devotion of the animals amazes Buckley, who says she's never seen such togetherness. It's true that elephants never forget—especially their friends!

Smile, Please

Nibble. Nibble. The gray seal yanked and chewed on the scuba diver's swim fins. Feeling the tug, underwater photographer Brian Skerry spun around. But quick as a flash, the seal flipped backward and disappeared.

Many of these underwater acrobats glide around between the rocks in the Gulf of Maine off the coast of Acadia National Park. But they almost always stay out of sight.

This young seal was much braver than most. Moments after their first encounter, the animal returned. "His flippers came together and he kind of posed," says Skerry. "It was almost as if he were saying 'OK, I've had my fun. Now you can take my picture.'"

4 A seal poses politely.

Reading Across Texts

Crowbar and the animals in this article all had definite personalities. What word would you use to describe each animal?

Writing Across Texts Make a list of the animals and their main personality traits.

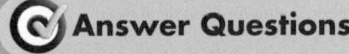 **Answer Questions** | Where is information that answers questions about these anecdotes?

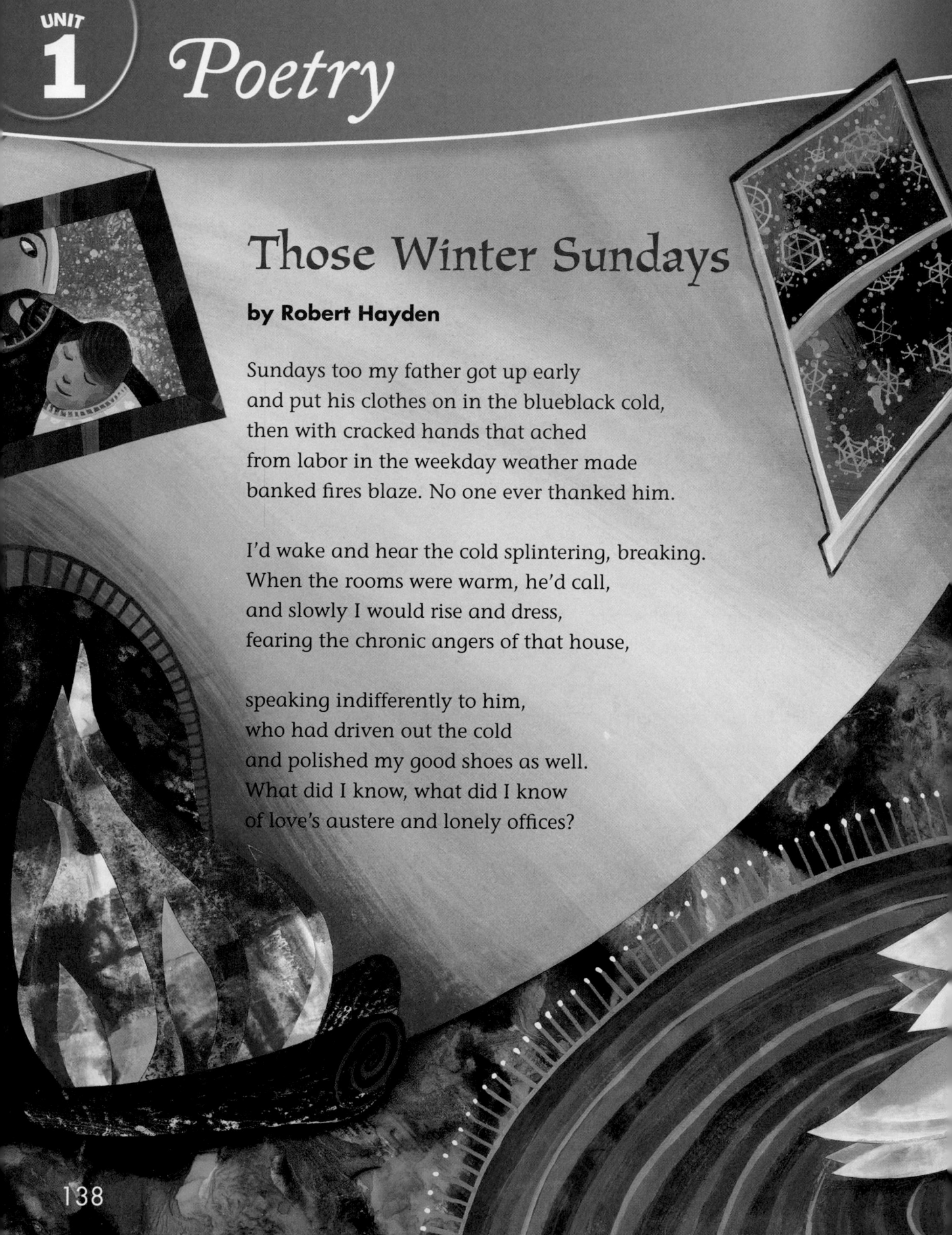

Those Winter Sundays

by Robert Hayden

Sundays too my father got up early
and put his clothes on in the blueblack cold,
then with cracked hands that ached
from labor in the weekday weather made
banked fires blaze. No one ever thanked him.

I'd wake and hear the cold splintering, breaking.
When the rooms were warm, he'd call,
and slowly I would rise and dress,
fearing the chronic angers of that house,

speaking indifferently to him,
who had driven out the cold
and polished my good shoes as well.
What did I know, what did I know
of love's austere and lonely offices?

Grandma

by Ralph Fletcher

On the first warm morning
she's kneeling in the dirt,
smiling and humming
like she does making bread.

Grandma's planting tulip bulbs
that are almost the same color
as her own worn knuckles.
Watch how her hands work

the dark mounds of soil
in that dirty confusion
of bulb and knuckle,
knuckle and bulb.

Song to Mothers

by Pat Mora

Your laugh is a green song,
canción verde,
that branches
through our house,
its yellow blooms smelling
like warm honey.
Your laugh peels apples
and stirs their cinnamon bubblings,
then opens a book and pulls me
onto your lap.
At night, your laugh kisses
us soft as a petal, smooths my pillow
and covers me, a soft leafy blanket,
green and yellow.
I snuggle into your laugh,
your canción verde
and dream of growing
into my own green song.

Louisa Jones Sings a Praise to Caesar

by Emanuel di Pasquale

Caesar is my king.
He is my guard dog
and barks at anything—
at visitors and strangers,
always trying to protect
Mom and me from danger.
For his reward
He gets the weirdest
breakfast, ice cream.
He loves me,
and when I play with him
or bring him fresh water,
he flaps his ears
and wags his tail
and even tries to sing.

141

Save the Rain Forest

You learned many facts about why the rain forest is important and how parts of it are being destroyed. Make a poster to inform people about why it's important to respect this ecosystem. List some things people can do to help preserve it.

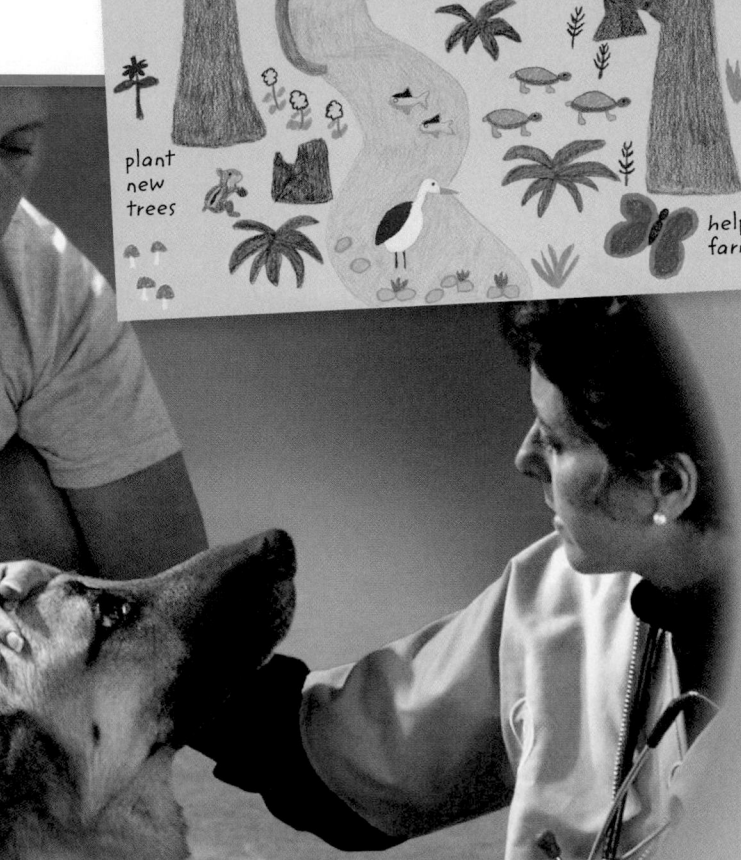

Save the Rain Forest for Our Future

cut down fewer trees

plant new trees

important medicines

new sources of food

help local farmers

What draws us to people and things around us and makes us care?

Adopt a Loyal Friend

connect to
WRITING

Chart the special ways in which the pets in Unit 1—Old Yeller, Crowbar, and Chauncey—enrich their owners' lives. Add some pets you know of, including your own. Then write a composition or poem around the idea of praising or valuing pets.

Pet	Owner	How the Pet Makes Life Better

R-E-S-P-E-C-T

connect to
DRAMA

Choose two characters from different selections in this unit. With a partner, dramatize the characters. Have a conversation in which the two characters each discuss a person or animal from one of the selections that they care about or greatly respect.

Read It ONLINE
sfsuccessnet.com

Space and Time

Why might things far away and long ago be important to us now?

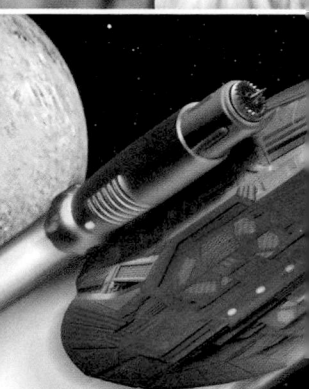

Comprehension

Skill
Main Idea
and Details

Strategy
Monitor and Fix Up

Skill

Main Idea
and Details

- To find the topic of a paragraph or section, ask yourself, "What is this all about?"

- To find the main idea, ask yourself, "What is the most important idea about the topic?"

- To help find the main idea, look for supporting details that explain or tell about the main idea.

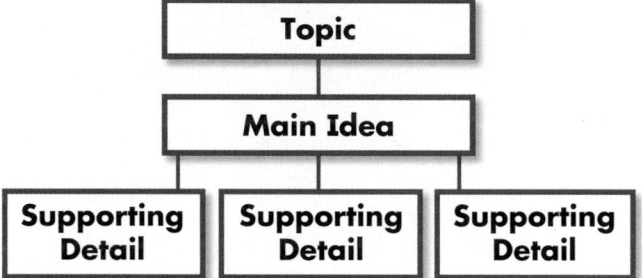

Topic

Main Idea

| Supporting Detail | Supporting Detail | Supporting Detail |

Strategy

Strategy: Monitor and Fix Up

Good readers check themselves to make sure they understand what they are reading. If you want to make sure you understand main ideas, you can look at text features such as headings. You can also scan a paragraph or section to look for key words. This is helpful when you are trying to identify the topic of a paragraph or section.

Write

1. Read "The Telescope." Make and complete a graphic organizer like the one above for the section headed "Optical Telescopes." Make another for the section headed "Radio Telescopes."

2. Use your graphic organizers to write a short summary of the kinds of telescopes that astronomers use to scan the skies.

The Telescope

For thousands of years humans studied the sky using only their eyes. Today, however, astronomers have a much more powerful tool to use: the telescope. There are two kinds of telescopes: optical and radio.

Optical Telescopes

Optical telescopes work by collecting light. The larger the aperture, or opening, of the telescope, the more powerful it is. The largest optical telescope in the world is in Russia. It has an opening 236 inches wide. Most of the world's large, powerful optical telescopes are in buildings called observatories. These are usually high on mountains, away from cities and lights. Some, such as the Hubble Space Telescope, are in space.

Radio Telescopes

Radio telescopes collect long energy waves from faraway objects in space through a "dish," a curved object that looks like a bowl. The world's largest radio telescope, in Germany, is almost 300 feet wide! The most powerful radio telescope, though, is in New Mexico. Scientists use it to study the solar system and other galaxies.

Without telescopes, we would know very little about the amazing objects in the sky.

Strategy Text features such as headings can help you find topics. What is the topic of the next paragraph?

Skill One of these is the big idea—the main idea—of the section headed "Optical Telescopes." Which is it?

(a) Optical telescopes work by collecting light.

(b) The largest optical telescope is in Russia.

(c) Most large optical telescopes are in observatories.

Strategy How can you determine the topic of the next paragraph? What is it?

Skill What is the main idea of the section headed "Radio Telescopes"?

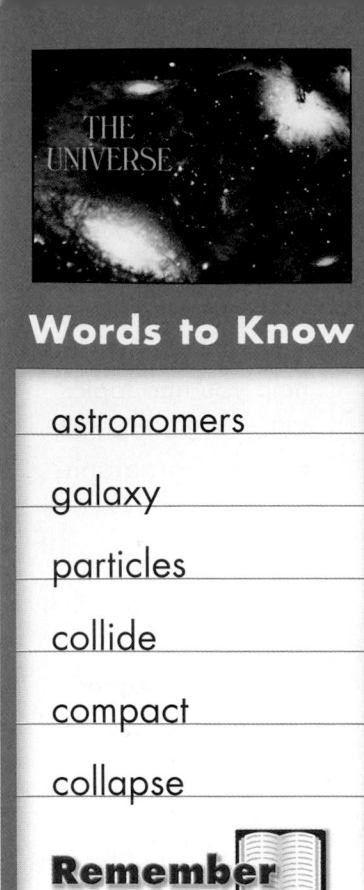
Words to Know

astronomers

galaxy

particles

collide

compact

collapse

Remember

Try the strategy. Then, if you need more help, use your glossary or a dictionary.

Vocabulary Strategy
for Greek and Latin Roots

Word Structure When you find a word you cannot read, see if you can find a familiar root in it. Greek and Latin roots, or basic original parts of words, are used in many English words. For example, the Latin word *sol* means "sun." The Greek root *astr-* means "star." It is used to build the words *astronaut*, *astrology*, and *astronomer*.

1. If the word has a prefix or suffix, cover it.

2. Do you recognize the root? Does the root make a base word that you know?

3. If so, see if the meaning of this base word is similar to a meaning that would make sense for the unknown word.

4. Add on the meaning(s) of the prefix and/or suffix and predict the meaning for the unknown word.

5. See if your meaning makes sense in the sentence.

As you read "The Birth and Death of Stars," look for Greek and Latin roots to help you figure out the meanings of unknown words.

The Birth and Death of Stars

For thousands of years, astronomers have gazed up into space and wondered. We are beginning to understand our galaxy, the huge cluster of stars in our corner of the universe. How do we think our sun and the planets of our solar system came to be?

One idea says that they formed from an enormous spinning cloud of gas and dust. The spinning pulled most of the matter in the cloud toward the center. However, smaller whirlpools also formed in the cloud. Some matter also collected in the whirlpools. The dust particles grew closer together and began to collide with each other. As they were pressed together, the balls of matter became more compact. The matter in the center formed the sun. The matter in the whirlpools formed the planets.

The sun, at the heart of our solar system, is a star. All stars have a life cycle of many billions of years. Some stars end as a cold piece of matter—a sort of space junk. Others may explode and then collapse into a black hole. We will not get to see how our sun dies. That ending is billions of years away.

Write

Use what you know about astronomy to write a story set in outer space. Include words from the Words to Know list in your story.

THE UNIVERSE

by Seymour Simon

Genre

Expository nonfiction explains the nature of an object, an idea, or a theme. Look for information about the nature of the universe as you read.

How do we know whether
a star is old or new?

From Earth we can look into space and study the universe with telescopes and other instruments. The moon is Earth's nearest neighbor in space, only about a quarter of a million miles away. That's very close in space, almost next door. Still, it's very far away compared to the distance between places on Earth's surface. You'd have to travel around the Earth ten times in order to match the distance from the Earth to the moon. The sun, the closest star to us, is over four hundred times farther away from us than the moon is—about ninety-three million miles.

The nearest star after our sun is much farther away than that. But measuring the distance between stars and planets in miles is like measuring the distance around the world in inches. We measure the distance to the stars in light-years: the distance that light travels in one year, which is close to six *trillion* miles. A spaceship speeding at ten miles per second would still take more than seventy thousand years to get to Alpha Centauri, the nearest star after the sun—a distance of 4.3 light-years, or twenty-five trillion miles.

For many years, our solar system was the only one we had ever seen. But in recent years, scientists using new instruments began to observe what looked like other solar systems in the making. These are two images (right) of gas-and-dust disks forming around young stars. The disks range in size from about two to eight times the diameter of our solar system. The glow in the center of each disk is a newly formed star, about one million years old.

The disks do not mean, for certain, that planets will form. But the building blocks for planets are there. Now that they know so many young stars have planetary disks, scientists feel more optimistic about the possibility of locating other solar systems.

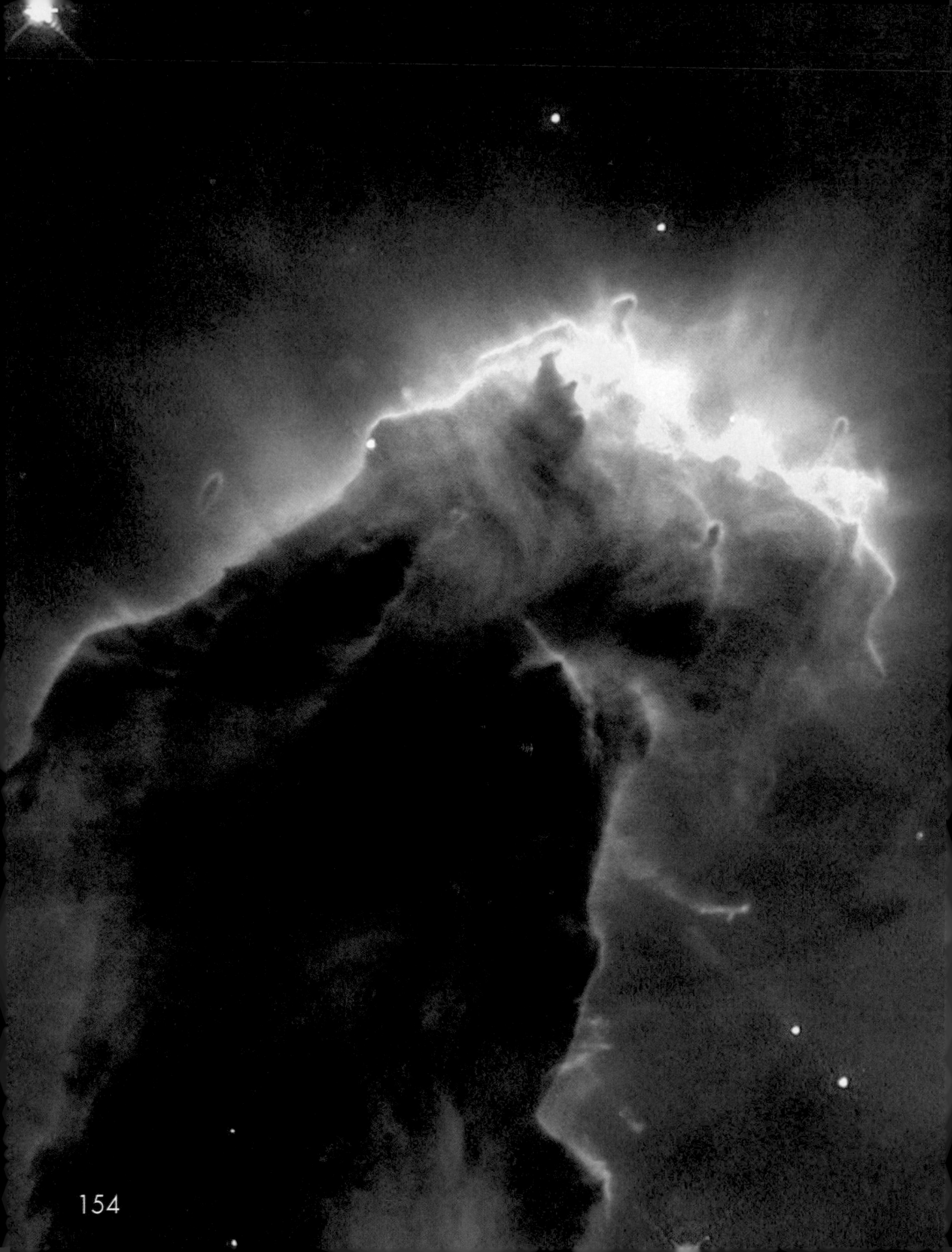

Finding individual planets is more challenging than finding planetary disks, because a single planet is much smaller and more compact than a whole solar system in the making. Still, we have discovered more planets around distant stars than in our own solar system.

All stars are born within nebulas, which are eerie, dark clouds of hydrogen gas and dust. Stars are not born singly but in groups or clusters. Usually each star grows at a different speed, and most clusters finally drift apart. Some of the young stars are ten thousand times brighter than our sun is now.

This photo of the Eagle Nebula—also called M-16—was taken by the Hubble Space Telescope in 1995. The Eagle Nebula is in a nearby star-forming region of the Milky Way galaxy. It is about seven thousand light-years away from Earth. The new stars are the bright lights inside the finger-like bulges at the top of the nebula. Each "fingertip" is tens of billions of miles across—larger than our entire solar system.

When stars get older, they cool off, swell up one hundred times larger, and turn red. These aging stars are called red giants. The red giants become very active, blowing off violent gusts of hot gas from their surfaces into space. When a red giant has shed its outer layers, the hot core within the star makes the surrounding cloud of gases glow. This cloud is called a planetary nebula because early astronomers thought its shape and color looked like a planet.

Planetary nebulas come in a variety of shapes: from narrow jets of exploding gases to peanut-shaped clouds to bright globes surrounding stars.

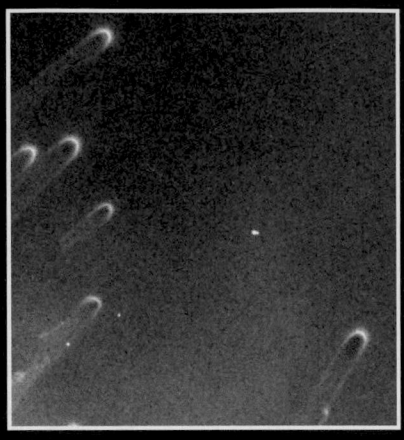

What look like spaceships from a science fiction movie are really the result of a dying star's final outbursts. These mysterious "space pods" (right) are gigantic tadpole-shaped clumps of gas, each several billion miles across, twice the size of our solar system. The comet-like tails fan out around the central star like the spokes on a wheel.

No one knows what will happen to the pods. Perhaps they will expand and disappear within a few hundred thousand years. Or perhaps the dust particles inside each gas ball will collide and stick together. Planets the size of Earth, but frigid and icy like the planet Pluto, might form over time. Thousands of these icy worlds might escape the dead star and roam the dark space between the stars forever.

Our sun is just one of about two hundred billion stars in the Milky Way galaxy, a vast spiral of stars about one hundred thousand light-years across. Viewed from the side, it looks like a lens, with a thick bright center of stars and flattened edges. All the stars we see in the night sky are in our galaxy. Other galaxies are much too distant for us to see their individual stars.

Our solar system is about thirty thousand light-years away from the center of the Milky Way. The central galaxy is much more crowded than our lonely part of space. In one star cluster near the center of the Milky Way, there are one hundred thousand stars in one cubic light-year. But in our remote corner of the galaxy, there are no stars within four light-years of our solar system.

This is a radio photo of a star called Sagittarius A*, near the center of the Milky Way. Hidden someplace within this photo, there might be an enormous black hole marking the true center of our galaxy.

Scientists class galaxies by their shape. There are four main types of galaxies: spirals, ellipticals, barred spirals, and irregular-shaped galaxies. Spirals are disk-shaped, with older stars in the center and newer stars in the arms. Ellipticals are the most common and are shaped like balls or eggs. They contain mostly old stars. Barred spirals are spirals whose central stars form a bar. Irregulars are the rarest and do not fit any known pattern.

Many galaxies in space are so distant that their light fades out before it reaches the Earth, and they can only be seen with radio telescopes. This radio image of a large elliptical galaxy called Fornax A is in the center of a distant cluster of galaxies. The central bright white region shines with the light of more than ten billion stars. Fornax A is so huge that it is swallowing nearby galaxies. The small spiral galaxy just above Fornax A may soon be captured.

Scientists think that there are at least one hundred billion galaxies in the universe, and each galaxy contains about one hundred billion stars. There are more stars in the universe than there are grains of sand on all the beaches in the world.

With a high-powered telescope, scientists discovered fifteen hundred galaxies in different stages of their lives. From Earth, some of these galaxies are as faint as a flashlight on the moon would be.

Looking at distant galaxies in the universe with a telescope is like using a time machine to peer into the past. Light from the dimmest galaxies has taken ten billion years to reach us.

Among the strangest objects in the universe are black holes. A black hole is a region of space where matter is squeezed together so tightly and the pull of its gravity is so powerful that nothing can escape from it, not even light. It is impossible to see a black hole, but we can see vast amounts of matter being sucked into the hole, never to return. Black holes seem to come in two sizes: small and super-large. The small ones are formed when stars collapse and are only a few miles in diameter. Most we cannot detect.

Scientists think that the super-large black holes are probably at the center of most galaxies. This drawing shows a spiral of dust and gases eight hundred light-years wide being sucked into a giant black hole in the center of a nearby galaxy. The black hole contains more than one billion times the amount of matter in our sun, all packed tightly together.

These discoveries have led to new mysteries: Does every galaxy have a black hole at its center? If there's a black hole in a galaxy, does that mean that all the stars in the galaxy will eventually disappear inside it? What starts a black hole, and does it ever end?

Quasars are as mysterious as black holes. Before stars vanish into a black hole, they give off energy in a burst of light and radio waves. This outpouring of energy is called a quasar. About the size of our solar system, quasars contain the mass of more than a million suns. Yet they pour out one hundred to one thousand times as much light as an entire galaxy of one hundred billion stars.

Does life exist on Earth-like planets in distant solar systems? Will the universe expand forever or finally stop and then collapse into a gigantic black hole? Searching for answers about the universe is like exploring a dark, mysterious ocean without being able to leave the shore. But with the Hubble Space Telescope and other new methods of gathering information, we are just at the beginning of a golden age of discovery. No one knows what fantastic places we will see.

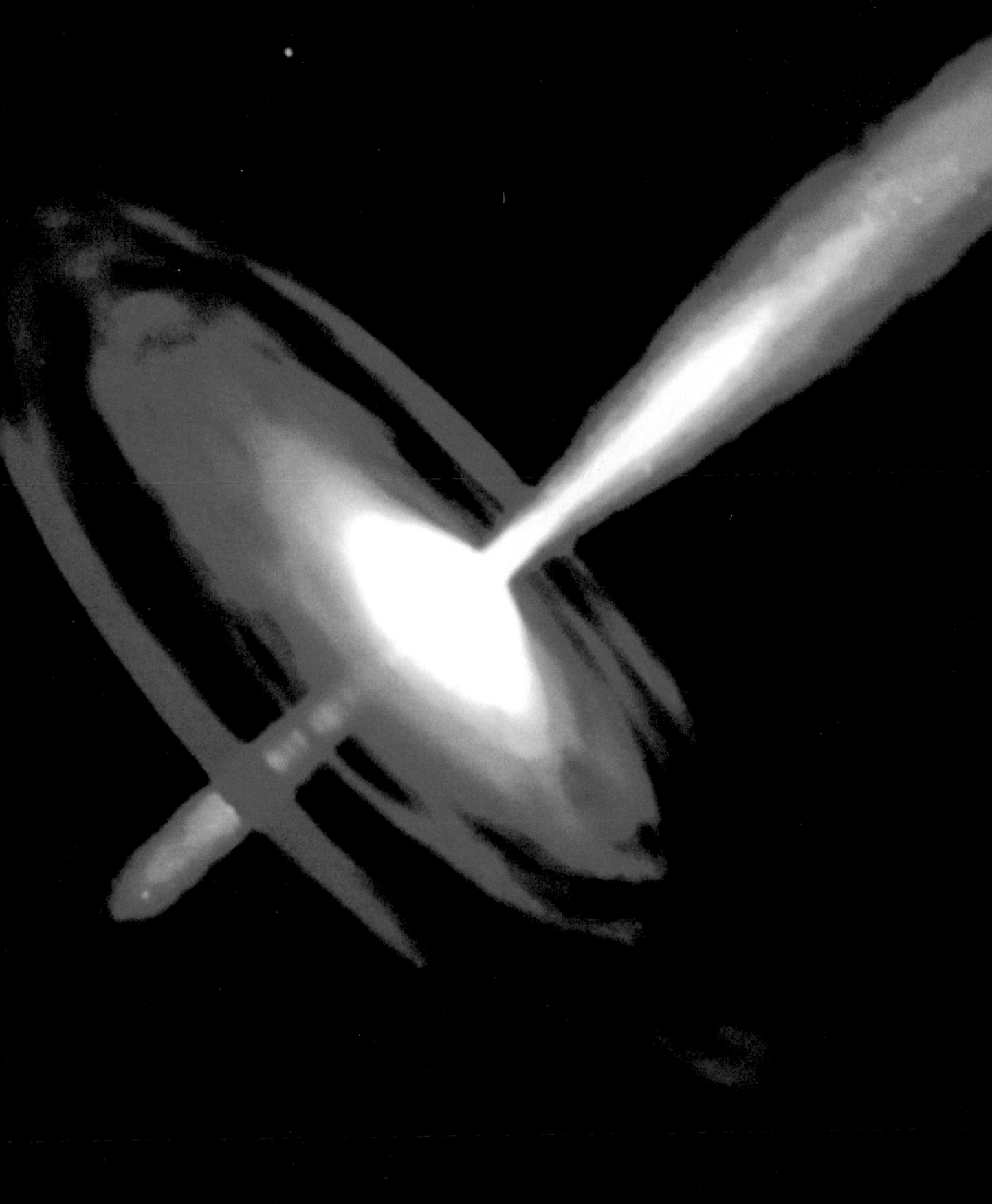

Reader Response

Open for Discussion   Seymour Simon writes about "our lonely part of space." What is the evidence that we are in a lonely part? Will a "golden age of discovery" make our place in the universe less lonely?

1. Vast sizes and distances are almost impossible to comprehend, but Seymour Simon comes to the rescue. Find sentences he wrote to help readers comprehend the vastness of the universe.

2. The main idea of the information in the first paragraph of page 159 is that there are different types of galaxies. What details from the paragraph support that statement?

3. How do the pictures on pages 156–157 help you better understand what you've read?

4. A new movie about the universe is due to be released soon. Write copy to go on a poster to advertise it. Use words from the Words to Know list and from the selection.

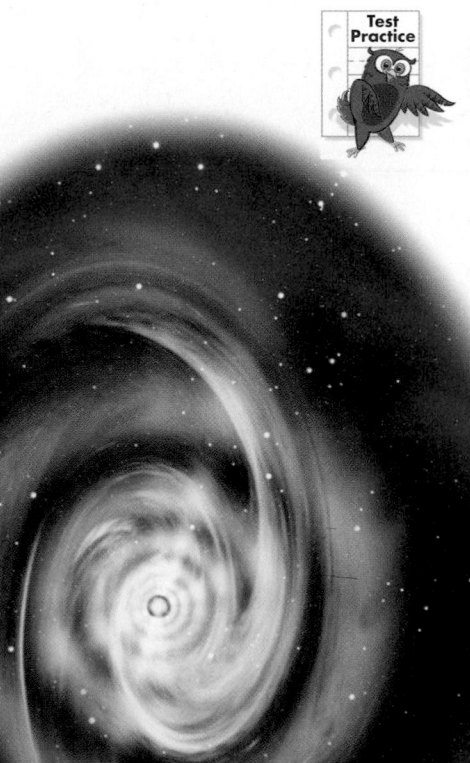

Look Back and Write   What is the relationship between a quasar and a black hole? Look back at page 160 to help you write an answer. Then write why that relationship may be of special interest to astronomers.

Seymour Simon

Read more books by Seymour Simon.

Seymour Simon is a widely recognized writer of science books for young people today. He is praised for his clear, interesting writing, but also for his attention to the latest research. You can count on a book by Seymour Simon to be accurate and reliable.

Mr. Simon grew up in the Bronx in New York. "When I was in junior high school I was very interested in space (and I still am)," he says. He was a member of the Junior Astronomy Club and even made his own telescope.

Mr. Simon was a New York City science teacher for 23 years. But in 1979, he retired from teaching so that he could write full time. He has now published over 200 books! Many of his books are on space, but he has also written books on animals, the weather, the human body, and icebergs.

Though he no longer teaches in the classroom, Mr. Simon's books teach thousands of readers about the world of science. "I haven't really given up teaching," he says, "and I suppose I never will, not as long as I keep writing."

The On-Line Spaceman and Other Cases (Einstein Anderson, Science Detective series)

Destination: Space

Expository Nonfiction

Genre

- **Informational articles are expository nonfiction. They explain topics and ideas.**

- **Using facts and information in a way that is understandable to the reader, the author explains a specific topic.**

Text Features

- **In this article, the author uses an informal, conversational tone with questions and words such as *you* and *we*, to make what he is saying interesting to the reader.**

- **Notice how the author uses people's everyday experiences to explain scientific phenomena. Look for examples of this as you read.**

Link to Science

The sun is a yellow dwarf star. Research the different types of stars at the library or on the World Wide Web.

So Long, Sol!

by Seth Shostak

What happens when a good sun goes bad?

Astronomers know the disturbing answer. They'll tell you that the bright, yellow star that warms our planet is doomed. It's sure to run low on fuel. When that happens, our good sun will start behaving very badly.

How will this affect us? You may be surprised to learn that as it ages, the sun doesn't just slowly cool off. In fact, as it gets older, it actually *heats up*. This isn't the global warming that everyone talks about. It's not an effect caused by auto exhaust or hair spray, a problem we have to worry about for the next century. This is the natural, long-term behavior of the sun.

The sun's temperature isn't rising very fast. The increase is about 0.0000000004 of a degree per day, far too little to notice even over an entire lifetime. But in a few hundred million years, this slow warming will start to change our atmosphere. Everyone knows about oxygen in the air—which we breathe—and carbon dioxide (CO₂), which plants breathe. Both gases are found in the ocean as well as the air. But as the sun heats up the ocean, more of the carbon dioxide that bubbles through it will combine chemically with rocks to make compounds called carbonates. Ultimately, that will remove a lot of the CO_2 from the atmosphere, locking it up as underwater stone.

When that happens, it will be bad news for plants. They will slowly suffocate. Of course, not all plants will die right away. Some, like corn, can survive even with reduced amounts of CO_2, but many cannot. Our forests will gradually disappear, and so will the majority of the plants that you find stacked up in your supermarket's produce section.

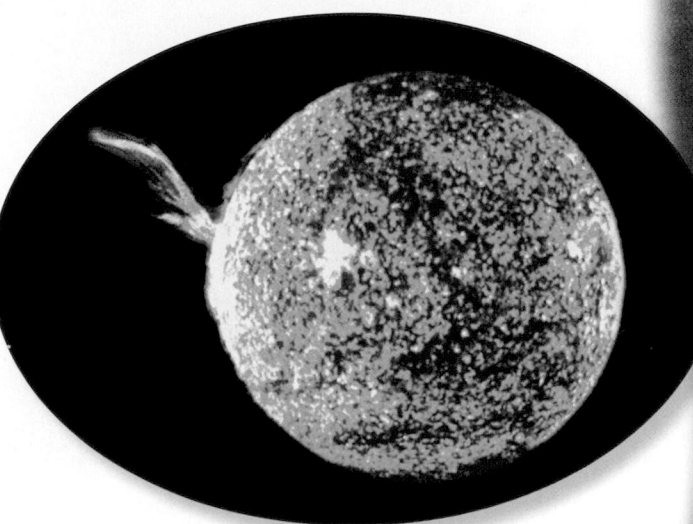

Solar flares, like the one you see here, occur when built-up energy on the sun is suddenly released.

Most of Earth's animals, including us, will perish unless we can stop this catastrophe. Fortunately, a few hundred million years from now we may be clever enough to do so. For example, we could construct giant factories to burn the carbonate rocks, releasing the CO_2 back into the atmosphere. Alternatively, we might be able to build huge, orbiting shields that would reduce the sunlight hitting Earth. Venetian blinds in space! These are just some of the ways that human intelligence might avoid natural calamity.

But there's worse in store. When the sun gets even older, it will start to go nuts. Thanks to hard work by astronomers, we know exactly what's going to happen. This is because stars are actually fairly simple. They're not like living things, whose deaths are uncertain. A tree, for example, could perish from old age, but it's more likely that something else will wipe it out much sooner. Lightning might toast it, or bugs might eat it. Dutch elm disease could rot it, or a lumber company might chop it down.

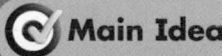 **Main Idea** | What main points does the author make?

The surface of the sun exhibiting solar flares.

Stars, on the other hand, die predictable, old-age deaths. In about five billion years, the sun will begin to swell up like an over-inflated balloon. Its outer surface will cool off a few thousand degrees, and its tint will turn from yellow-white to red. But despite the lower temperature, the sun's enormous size will guarantee that it puts out a thousand times as much energy as it does now.

As you can imagine, as the sun swells to red giant size, nasty things happen to the worlds that orbit it. It becomes big enough to swallow the planet Mercury. "No loss," you might say. After all, who cares about Mercury? But not long thereafter, the growing sun will devour Venus and will appear in our skies as a huge, red ball. By this point, the temperature on Earth will be several thousand degrees. Oceans will boil away, the atmosphere will start to evaporate, and the ground will be hot and soft,

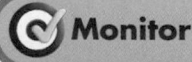 **Monitor**   Visualizing will help you understand the process.

like volcanic lava. Air conditioning won't help you very much, and no one will be keeping their cool under such circumstances.

So what should humans do to avoid expiring when our sun does? We might abandon Earth and retreat to the outer realms of the solar system. Our descendants could stall for time by taking up residence on the moons of Saturn, Uranus, or Neptune. But eventually the dying sun will puff off its outer gas layers and collapse to a white-hot little ball, only a few thousand kilometers across. Its engines will be dead, starved of fuel. After that, it's only a matter of time (a *long* time) before Old *Sol* will cool off to become an economy-size charcoal briquette.

That will be the end of our solar system. To survive, future generations— if there are any—will undoubtedly move to another sun. It's a long trip to the stars, but when you gotta go, you gotta go.

This could happen over and over, so hopping from star to star may be our long-term fate. But there's a limit to how long this can go on. When the universe is about ten times as old as it is now—100 billion years in the future—*all* the stars will be dead or dying, and there won't be enough raw material left to make new ones.

Then what? Is that it? If thinking beings are still around (a big "if") in this far-off future, will they be huddled around some dim and dying star, awaiting the end? Or will they figure out how to hang on for hundreds of billions of years more by scooping up the small amounts of still-fresh gas between these dull embers, to make their own, artificial suns?

That might be possible. Unlike the dinosaurs, we're smart enough to avoid catastrophe. If intelligent beings hope to survive for not just a few million years, but for a few hundred billion, we'll need to do more than just observe the universe—we'll need to rebuild it.

Reading Across Texts

Do the authors of *The Universe* and "So Long, Sol!" seem more optimistic or pessimistic about the future of our solar system?

Writing Across Texts Write about whether you are optimistic or pessimistic about our solar system and why you feel this way.

Dinosaur Ghosts

Comprehension

Skill
Main Idea
and Details

Strategy
Prior Knowledge

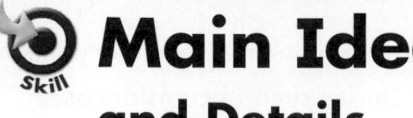

Main Idea
and Details

- The topic of a piece of writing can usually be stated in a few words.

- In a piece of writing, the main idea is the most important idea about the topic. Sometimes the main idea is given in a sentence. If it is not, you must figure it out on your own.

- Supporting details are smaller pieces of information that tell more about the main idea.

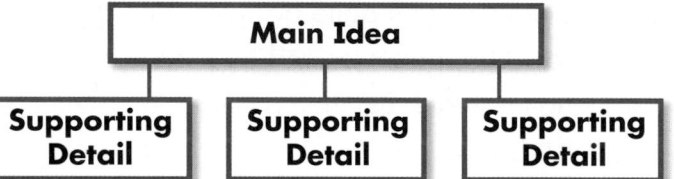

 **Strategy: Prior Knowledge**

Your prior knowledge is everything that you already know about a topic. Good readers connect their prior knowledge to what they are reading because that helps them understand better and remember more. First, read the title and headings to determine the topic. Ask yourself what you already know about it. As you read, connect details with what you know. This can help you find the main idea.

1. Read "Fossils." Make a graphic organizer like the one above for the section titled "What are fossils?" Make another for "How fossils form."

2. Use the main ideas from your graphic organizers to help you determine the main idea of the entire article. Write the main idea in your own words.

FOSSILS

Strategy Read the title and headings. List some things you already know about fossils.

Picture Earth long ago—giant ferns, huge dragonflies, and dinosaurs. How do we know that such plants and animals once lived? We learn about early forms of life by studying fossils.

What are fossils? A fossil is a trace of an animal or plant that once lived. It may be a body part, such as the shell of an ancient crab. Or it could be an impression made in rock, such as the footprint of a dinosaur.

Skill What is the main idea of this section?

(a) A fossil may be a body part.

(b) A fossil is a trace of a plant or an animal that once lived.

(c) Crab shells and dinosaur footprints are fossils.

How fossils form Most fossils come from the hard parts of animals, such as bones or shells, that are buried in the ground. Often these hard parts slowly change into a rocky substance. For example, the bones of an animal may slowly change into minerals. The animal bones no longer exist, but exact copies are left behind. In other cases, a shell may break up but leave an impression in the rock. When sand and soil fill in the impression and become hard, a copy of the shell is formed.

Strategy Have you ever seen a clay mold or a cake pan used? If so, that prior knowledge may help you understand how this type of fossil formed.

Sometimes the entire body of an animal or plant will be preserved, such as an insect in the sap of a tree or a wooly mammoth in ice. However, these fossils are rare.

Skill Add another leg for a third supporting detail to your graphic organizer for this section. Two supporting details are given in the first paragraph and another in this one.

Words to Know

- specimens
- volcanic
- sluggish
- poisonous
- fragile
- treacherous
- prey

Remember

Try the strategy. Then, if you need more help, use your glossary or a dictionary.

Vocabulary Strategy
for Suffixes

Word Structure Sometimes when you are reading, you come across a word you don't know. Check to see if the word has a suffix, or a word part added at the end of the word. Suffixes add meaning. For example, *-ic* means "related to" or "derived from"; *-ous* means "full of." These suffixes change a noun or a verb into an adjective.

1. Cover the suffix and see if you recognize the base word.

2. If you know this word, think about its meaning.

3. Look at the suffix. Think about its meaning or how it changes the part of speech of the base word.

4. Decide what meaning makes sense for the word in this sentence.

As you read "Fossils, Anyone?" look for words that have suffixes. Analyze the base words and the suffixes to figure out the meanings.

FOSSILS, ANYONE?

Last Saturday, we got to visit a museum that has dinosaurs. The dinosaurs are not alive, of course. The specimens on display are models. They have been created from fossils, or remains found in stone.

I read how some of these fossils had been found in volcanic rock. Maybe the dinosaurs were feeding when they suddenly began to feel sluggish and sleepy. The smoke coming from a volcano was poisonous and knocked them out. Then their bodies were trapped in the lava that flowed from the volcano. Over millions of years, their bones were replaced by stone. Then at last, they were discovered. Scientists chipped away the rock carefully to avoid hurting the fragile fossils. At the museum, other scientists used the bones to make strong models. These were put together to make the dinosaur shapes once more.

The dinosaurs look real and are posed to look as though they are on the attack. Their teeth and claws seem treacherous. Even the smaller dinosaurs seem like monsters. I would not like to be the prey trying to escape those teeth!

Write

Write a description of what you imagine you would find in the rock formed by a volcano. Use as many words from the Words to Know list as you can.

Dinosaur Ghosts

The Mystery of Coelophysis

by J. Lynett Gillette

pictures by Douglas Henderson

Genre

Expository nonfiction explains the nature of something. Look for explanations about the demise of *Coelophysis* as you read.

What kinds of clues do scientists use to figure out what happened to the *Coelophysis?*

The red and green hills of Ghost Ranch

There is a saying that the place called Ghost Ranch in New Mexico got its name because each night after dark, its fossils come out of the ground to play.

No one has really seen this happen, of course. But if there *were* such a thing as a dinosaur ghost, the red and green hills of this beautiful ranch would be filled with them. Hundreds of *Coelophysis* (SEEL-oh-FIE-sis) dinosaurs perished together here, in a tangle of necks, tails, arms, and legs. And for years scientists have been haunted by the question: Why did so many little dinosaurs die at Ghost Ranch?

To begin to answer that question, we must go back in time to the summer of 1947, when a scientist made a spectacular find.

A Big Find of Small Dinosaurs

Edwin "Ned" Colbert listened carefully to his field assistant's excited report. Bones—lots of very small ones—lay on a hillside in a nearby canyon!

Ned Colbert was a paleontologist (a scientist who studies prehistoric life) from the American Museum of Natural History in New York City. His plan was to spend that summer of 1947 collecting fossils in Arizona. On his way to Arizona,

Edwin Colbert, *center*, and the American Museum of Natural History's field crew at Ghost Ranch

Colbert had stopped to take a look around Ghost Ranch north of Albuquerque, New Mexico. He knew fossils had been collected there years earlier by several other paleontologists.

Some of the earlier fossils had been found by a professor named Charles Camp. Most of the bones Camp discovered were from animals that had lived during the Triassic period of the earth's history, which lasted from 245 to 208 million years ago. Every fossil discovery was faithfully recorded in Camp's field diary. (In this same diary, Camp had mentioned his fantasy of the fossils coming out to dance at night.)

None of Camp's fossils had ever been found in the canyons of Ghost Ranch. But Ned Colbert had an open mind about the canyons. Whenever people asked him his secret for finding fossils, he answered, "Fossils are where you find them, and you find them in the darndest places." He decided to investigate his assistant's report.

Colbert and his two helpers followed a trail of bone uphill. When the trail ended, the men dug into the hill—and dinosaur skeletons began appearing. The team had found *Coelophysis*, a meat-eating dinosaur about the size of a dog.

Colbert wasn't the first to find this little dinosaur. Back in

Charles Camp's field crew from the University of California at Berkeley, 1933

the 1880s, paleontologist Edward D. Cope hired a fossil collector to find bones for him in northern New Mexico. Traveling with a sure-footed burro, this fossil hunter discovered bits of backbones, a hipbone, a shoulder bone, and the end of a leg bone of a small reptile.

Cope said the fragile bones were those of a new small dinosaur. He named it *Coelophysis*, "hollow form," to suggest its hollow bones. The discovery didn't receive much publicity. Cope turned to other projects, and few people thought about this little dinosaur for nearly seventy years.

The Colbert team digs to uncover more and more bones.

But in the summer of 1947 Colbert's team began finding dozens and dozens of *Coelophysis* skeletons, buried in 225 million-year-old rocks from near the end of the Triassic period. There were so many skeletons that Colbert had to send a telegram back to the American Museum to ask for more help with the excavation.

This was a great find. Most dinosaurs are known from just a few specimens. Up until that time, the most familiar small dinosaurs were two chicken-sized *Compsognathus* skeletons. In a few days *The New York Times* announced the discovery of *Coelophysis* on its front page. A photographer from *Life* magazine visited the site. *Coelophysis* became the best-known small dinosaur ever discovered.

But why were all these dinosaurs buried in one place? Colbert wasn't sure. With Ghost Ranch's permission, he cut blocks of rock with the bones still inside to take to New York for study.

Because the dinosaurs were packed so tightly together, the blocks were made extra large to avoid cutting through a skeleton. Each block weighed a ton or more. Blocks of bone were shared with other museums and universities around the United States for examination, and new paleontologists joined the study of *Coelophysis*.

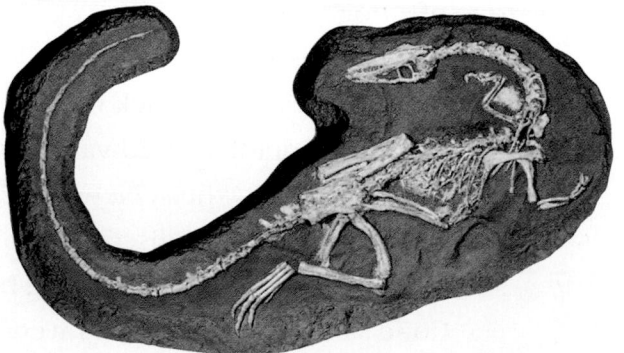

A nearly complete *Coelophysis* skeleton, showing curving and twisting of the neck after death. In the belly are bones of a young *Coelophysis*.

Bone Studies

Over the next fifty years a more complete picture of *Coelophysis* emerged. Paleontologists saw that the living animal had been a carnivore, or meat eater. Its teeth were sharp along the edges, much like a steak knife—perfect for slicing. Short front legs with sharp claws helped to hold the dinosaur's prey, but the long, flexible neck and strong jaws did most of the work.

They were lively, graceful animals, built for speed. The long, slender leg bones allowed *Coelophysis* to run upright, much like an African secretary bird does today. And just like a bird, *Coelophysis* had fragile, thin bones. If a technician working on *Coelophysis* sneezed, small bone fragments would fly into the air. Inside the whole length

of each thin leg and arm bone was a very wide space called the marrow cavity, where red blood cells were made. Active animals need plenty of red blood cells to carry oxygen.

Scientists think *Coelophysis* may have lived in large family groups, possibly in herds. We know that the young stayed with the adults for several years because all ages except embryos in eggs and newborn hatchlings have been found at Ghost Ranch. They probably ate other reptiles—such as young phytosaurs, which resembled alligators—plus fish, crayfish, clams, and in some cases even their own kind. Two skeletons of *Coelophysis* have their last meal still in the belly: small bones of a young *Coelophysis*. Some reptiles today still have this habit of cannibalism.

Unlike many other Triassic reptiles, *Coelophysis* dinosaurs had no armor to shield them from predators. Instead, speed and agility gave an advantage to *Coelophysis* when facing a hungry armored phytosaur. Large eyes also may have helped *Coelophysis* find prey, even in the dim light of early morning and evening when more sluggish reptiles might be napping.

What Happened Here?

After studying the *Coelophysis* bones to learn what these dinosaurs were like when they were alive, the scientists turned their attention to the positions of the bones in the ground. The arrangement of the bones might give some clues to the mystery of what happened to all these dinosaurs. Why and how did they die?

Many nearly complete skeletons were found with almost all their bones still joined together. These skeletons

Clusters of skeletons with separated bones.

lay flat on their sides with their heads, tails, hands, and feet all at about the same level. When these dinosaurs died, strong muscles in their necks tightened and pulled the neck and head back in a curve toward the tail.

In a different arrangement, some skeletons had missing bones and also were separated. Necks were no longer joined to bodies, tails were not attached to hips, ribs did not touch backbones. These bones had no unusual breaks or tooth marks, so we know the skeletons weren't scattered by predators.

All the skeletons—the nearly complete ones, stretched out on their sides, and the separated ones—lay close together. Some were even piled on top of one another. Other animals were discovered with the *Coelophysis* skeletons: a few fish, phytosaurs, small members of the crocodile family, and a very small lizard. The place where all these animals were buried is about thirty feet long and at least thirty feet wide. Around the bones are red rocks made of mud once carried by an ancient river.

Looking closely at the skeletons, paleontologists could see that none of the bones of any of the dinosaurs or the other animals seemed to be cracked from drying a long time in the sun. After considering this fact and all the other clues from the bones, the scientists have suggested a number of possible scenes that might explain the *Coelophysis* burial

179

ground at Ghost Ranch. We can test these scientific suggestions, or hypotheses, by comparing them with the evidence found in the bones and the rocks around them.

Stuck in the Mud?

A *Coelophysis* steps to the river's edge, coming to feed on several fish that are splashing in a pool of water. The dinosaur's feet sink deep in the dark, sticky earth. Other dinosaurs gather, also attracted by the splashing fish, but they too are caught in the treacherous ground. No matter how hard they struggle, they are all trapped, young and old alike.

The La Brea tar pits in California were once the site of scenes like this one. Thousands of animals were trapped there in sticky pools of black tar during the Ice Ages. Did a similar thing happen at Ghost Ranch? Probably not. If the dinosaurs *had* been trapped in mud, as they struggled their heavier legs would be buried more deeply than their arms and heads, and their bodies would be upright. (This is what scientists believe happened to a

Triassic dinosaur from Europe called *Plateosaurus* that died after being trapped in mud.) Since so many *Coelophysis* were found lying on their sides, most likely they didn't die this way.

Volcanic Violence?

The little dinosaurs are surprised by an erupting volcano as they gather at a river's edge to eat. They cannot breathe in the hot, swiftly moving clouds of ash and sulfurous gases. In great panic they fall down as they scramble to escape. Soon they are buried by mud slides flowing down the river valley and by ash falling from the sky.

Many of the Earth's great catastrophes have been caused by erupting volcanoes. When Mount St. Helens in Washington State blew its top in 1980, animals that couldn't run or burrow into the earth were killed by the heat, ash, and poisonous gases.

Does the scene at Ghost Ranch fit this picture? It doesn't seem likely to the geologists who have begun to study the rocks in which the *Coelophysis* skeletons are buried. If there were even traces of volcanic ash, under the microscope the rocks would have a few tiny smashed bubbles of the mineral silica. This silica would be present in the fiery blobs of ash shot into the sky. But no collapsed silica bubbles have been found yet in the rocks.

Asteroids from Outer Space?

The sun isn't as bright as usual, because high gray dust clouds shield the earth. The animals that the *Coelophysis* dinosaurs usually eat are becoming hard to find. The dinosaurs have become very thin; their scales are dull. Their tails—normally carried high—are drooping. Weak and exhausted, the dinosaurs fall, one by one, and do not get up.

Scientists Walter and Luis Alvarez of the University of California have suggested a reason why dinosaurs became extinct around 65 million years ago. The Alvarezes said that maybe a huge asteroid falling out of orbit from outer space struck the Earth. The collision would have sent great clouds of dust into the air that blocked sunlight and cooled the earth. A cooler earth couldn't support the same kinds of plants and animals. Many species that needed warm temperatures would die.

Not all paleontologists accept this reason for the extinction of dinosaurs, but it is an attractive one. A small amount of a rare element—iridium—has been found in many 65 million-year-old rocks. Asteroids often have more iridium than earth rocks, so an asteroid may indeed have brought this element to earth. Could an earlier asteroid, 225 million years ago, have caused climatic changes that killed *Coelophysis*?

The facts don't fit this picture at Ghost Ranch. The dinosaurs aren't scattered over a large area, as they would be if they collapsed, one by one, from hunger. And so far no one has found unusual amounts of iridium in the rocks. Asteroid extinctions don't seem to agree with what we have learned about *Coelophysis*.

Poisoned Water?

A group of *Coelophysis* gathers at a spring-fed pool of water along the river's edge. Balancing on their small front legs, they crouch down and drink, unaware that the water is poisoned. In a short time, one by one, they fall to the ground and die. Others come the next day, and the same thing happens again.

Do we find any poisons in the bones or the rocks around the dinosaur "graveyard" at Ghost Ranch? If the dinosaurs were killed this way, some poisons might remain, even after millions of years.

Geologists have tested the rocks and they did find a poison, arsenic, in both the rocks and the bones! But there are two problems with this theory.

First, we can't know exactly *when* the arsenic got into the bones and rocks. Just because arsenic is in the bones now doesn't mean that it was there when the dinosaurs died. The arsenic might have seeped in, carried by underground water, many years later.

And there's another idea to consider. Phytosaurs and fish were found with the dinosaurs. Could they have survived in a poisoned waterhole? Poison that would kill dinosaurs would probably make the water unfit for other animals too—especially ones that had to live *in* the water. For this reason arsenic doesn't seem to fit what we know either.

A Fearsome Flood?

A group of *Coelophysis* dinosaurs sleep in their resting area away from the riverbank under tall evergreen trees. It has been raining for days. This night the rising water spills over the top of the river channel and rushes down a wide valley. *Coelophysis* groups from many areas wake and begin to run, but the water is too fast. They are caught up and drowned by the churning flood. A few dinosaurs who run up the valley, instead of down, are saved.

Soon the rain clouds pass, and the river returns to its old channel. Down the valley rest the bodies of hundreds of dinosaurs, with a few phytosaurs, fish, and other reptiles. They are wrapped together, necks over tails, one on top of the other.

The rains aren't finished yet. Another tropical storm begins, and the river floods again. New mud and water flow into the old riverbed and cover the dinosaurs before other predators arrive.

The tangled positions and good condition of the skeletons (no cracks from the sun, no tooth marks from predators) might well have been caused by a flood. After the dinosaurs drowned, they could have been thrown together by a rush of floodwater and mud and buried quickly.

But if this is true, how do we explain those dinosaur skeletons that were found on their sides with the necks curved toward the tails? This position happens only if a dead animal, such as a cow lying in a field, is undisturbed long enough for its muscles and ligaments to shrink. Why were these dinosaurs arranged differently from the rest? Even the suggestion of a flood doesn't fit all the clues.

Water Worries?

The sun has burned in a cloudless sky for days and days. Ponds, streams, and lakes are drying up. Plants are dying. Plant eaters are starving. Crayfish are burrowing deep into mud to wait for wetter days. Fish are trapped by the hundreds in ever smaller puddles. *Coelophysis* gather to scoop up the helpless fish, but even more than meat, the dinosaurs need water.

As more fish are trapped, more *Coelophysis* of all ages come to eat. But the feeding activity doesn't last. The dinosaurs are weak with hunger and thirst, and there isn't enough food or drink to satisfy everyone. Hundreds die as they crowd around the last of the puddles.

When paleontologists began looking at the rocks around the bones of these dinosaurs, they sometimes found mud cracks, suggesting that some of the animals died on sun-baked mud. The skeletons with the curved necks were arranged like any animal who dries out in the hot sun after death.

Most of the fish bones were underneath the dinosaurs, as if they had attracted the little hunters to the site. And the scientists found many places where crayfish had burrowed into the mud.

But the drought picture does not tell the whole story. We already know that the dinosaurs' bones were not cracked by drying a long time in the sun. What if they spent only a short time—just a few days—in the sun? The real picture may be a combination of two suggestions—a drought *and* a flood.

185

Too Little Water—Then Too Much

Many of the little dinosaurs die at the end of a dry season when the earth is baked and the water holes are dry. One day the *Coelophysis* that are still alive discover a few sickly fish swimming slowly back and forth in a puddle at the bottom of the riverbed. Other fish bodies have already sunk into the mud. When a sudden rainstorm breaks the drought, a surge of water and thick mud flows swiftly over the riverbanks and down the valley. *Coelophysis* and other predators are trapped in the flood and drown.

When the waters dry up, they leave behind both the dinosaurs that had died a few days earlier in the drought and the newly drowned dinosaurs. Some are dropped in tangles; some lie alone, stretched out on the mud. The ones that lie in puddles begin to separate. Those outside the puddles begin to dry and shrink. Soon fresh rains bring more mud. The dinosaurs are buried completely in a few days, and they stay that way for millions of years. They are not uncovered until erosion in a canyon removes their blanket of rock in 1947.

This is our best idea for what happened to *Coelophysis* on those fateful days over two hundred million years ago. We can't say for sure that it is the right answer—but it's the explanation that fits most of the clues Ned Colbert and other scientists have discovered so far.

Could more information turn up that might point us toward a whole new scene? Of course, since the site is still being studied. Scientists are always ready to change their ideas to fit what they learn. New discoveries about the fossils and rocks at Ghost Ranch can still be made by anyone with the patience to study them—and the luck to find them "in the darndest places."

Reader Response

Open for Discussion Paleontologists help raise the curtain of time and look at the drama of the past. Do that now in your mind. Observe the drama of the little dinosaurs at a crucial time 245 million years ago. Don't look too close, but describe the scene from a safe distance.

1. Why do we seek answers to what happened millions of years ago? What are our motives? To find out, imagine asking a panel of experts including Edwin Colbert, author J. Lynett Gillette, and an eager reader. Report what they might say.

2. How do the headings in this article help you to determine the main ideas in each passage that follows?

3. You probably already know about some types of dinosaurs. How did that knowledge help you to better understand what you read in *Dinosaur Ghosts?*

4. Write a brief account for the Ghost Ranch newspaper telling about Ned Colbert's findings of the *Coelophysis* skeletons. Use some words from Words to Know list.

Look Back and Write Look back at page 179 to find the question posed by the author. Write it and then, in your own words, write the answer that paleontologists consider most likely to be true. Add a diagram if it will help.

Read more books by J. Lynett Gillette and Douglas Henderson.

J. Lynett Gillette studied journalism in college. When she got out, she says, "I wanted to write but felt I didn't have enough in-depth knowledge of any particular subject." So she began her lifelong study of anthropology, geology, and paleontology. Today she is the curator for a small museum of paleontology at Ghost Ranch, New Mexico.

"Now, after twenty-five years, I am returning to writing, this time with a deep appreciation for and love of the process of discovery in the sciences," she says. "I write for young people, hoping that some of their wonderful energy and creativity can be put to use in the future—solving all the puzzles that remain."

Douglas Henderson specializes in drawing dinosaurs. He works with paleontologists to be sure his illustrations reflect what they know. Though his work is based on science, it is also an art, he says. It requires imagination and experience. "All the time I had spent observing and drawing outside, studying landscapes of mountains, rivers, and forests, had taught me something about the natural world and the way it surely would have appeared long ago."

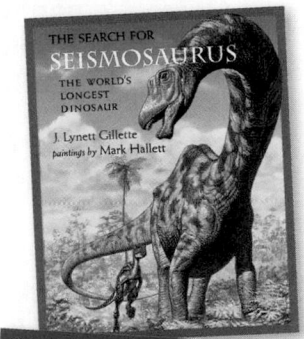

The Search for Seismosaurus: The World's Longest Dinosaur
by J. Lynett Gillette

Asteroid Impact
illustrated by Douglas Henderson

Narrative Nonfiction

Genre

- Narrative nonfiction tells a true story; it tells about an event that really happened.

- The author may or may not tell the events in strict sequence.

Text Features

- Narrative nonfiction may include pictures, maps, and illustrations that give additional information.

- Notice how the author includes valuable information in the captions. This helps to give the reader a better understanding of the visual information presented.

Link to Science

The students in the article found dinosaur ribs, eggshells, part of a skull, and even a backbone. If you were on a dig, what would you hope to unearth?

Dino Hunting

by Kristin Baird Rattini

photographs by O. Louis Mazzatenta

from *National Geographic WORLD*

This fossilized oyster shell dates back 150 million years, when an ocean covered part of Montana.

City kids head for the hills and discover more than old bones.

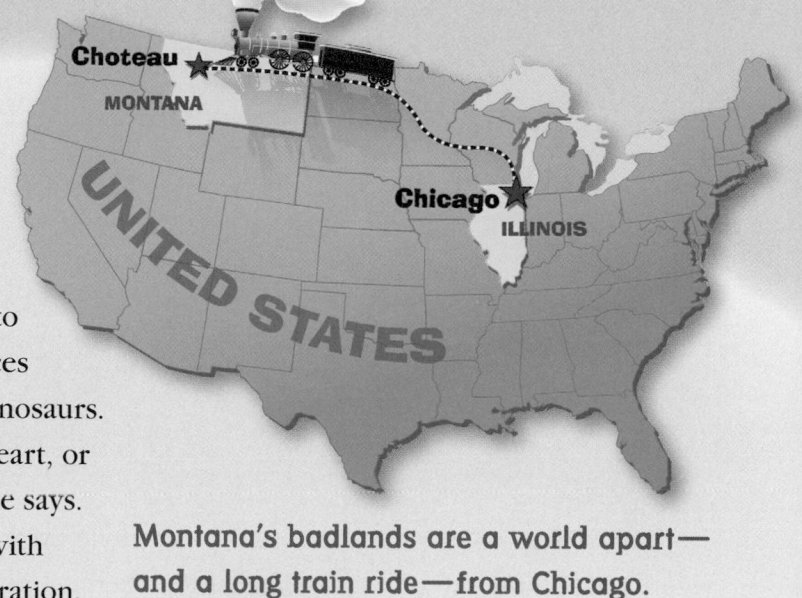

Sweat rolls down his back and rocks dig into his knees as José Rivera, 12, crawls along a hillside near Choteau, Montana. Eyes glued to the ground, he searches for tiny traces of the giants buried beneath him: dinosaurs.

"You need the right spirit and heart, or you're not going to find anything," he says.

As Junior Paleontologists (JPs) with an organization called Project Exploration, José and 13 other kids from Chicago, Illinois, found much more than dinosaur bones. Their week of dino hunting introduced them to a world far from their urban life. It also showed them that anything is within reach if they just keep on digging.

Montana's badlands are a world apart— and a long train ride—from Chicago.

José Rivera, 12, discovers a piece of fossilized eggshell.

✓ **Prior Knowledge** | Recall what you know about dinosaurs or digs.

191

The exhausting 500-foot climb up Indian Head Mountain was a first for many JPs, most of whom had never been out of Chicago.

Before their dig, led by co-founder Gabrielle Lyon, the JPs trained for about two weeks in the lab of paleontologist Paul Sereno, another co-founder and a National Geographic Explorer-in-Residence. But by the end of the program, the JPs had learned not just to dig with their hands, but to dig with their minds as well.

In Montana the JPs tracked dinosaurs that had thundered across the land 80 million years ago. Crumbling away dirt with picks and paintbrushes, they unearthed ribs, eggshells, even part of a skull. "We revealed a part of history," says Joseph Griffey, 15.

Notes:

If you want to go on your own dinosaur hunt, science museums around the country offer week-long or daily digs. Call a museum near you. Or to explore more about dinosaurs from home, Project Exploration recommends checking your local library or online for:
- *Dinosaurs*, by Eugene S. Gaffney
- *The Ultimate Dinosaur Book*, by David Lambert
- *The Illustrated Encyclopedia of Dinosaurs*, by David Norman

Paleontologist Paul Sereno

"It takes patience," says Timothy Hill, 15, as he uses dental tools to excavate what may be the jawbone of a hadrosaur.

But there's more to paleontology than meets the eye—and tongue! To distinguish between bone and rock, the JPs *licked* their finds. "Bone is porous (has holes), so when you put it to your tongue, it sticks," says Marco Mendez, 15 (left).

The thrill of the hunt kept the JPs dedicated until they made their biggest find: The last day, they discovered part of a backbone. They also discovered a lot about themselves. Says Susan Silva, 15: "There are many discoveries out there just waiting for us to find them."

Reading Across Texts

Where did the scientists in *Dinosaur Ghosts* and "Dino Hunting" do their work? How were their goals alike and different?

Writing Across Texts Make a chart that shows who the scientists in these selections were, where they worked, what their goals were, and what they found.

 **Main Idea** What main ideas will help you remember this article?

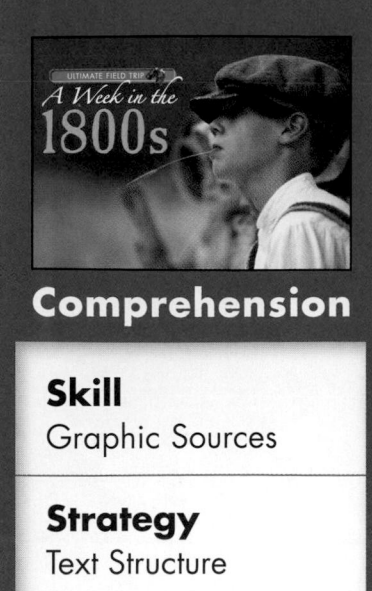

Comprehension

Skill
Graphic Sources

Strategy
Text Structure

Graphic Sources

- Graphic sources, such as charts, diagrams, and time lines, show information visually.

- While reading, compare the information in a graphic source with information you read in the text.

- Create your own graphic source with information in the text to help you understand and remember information. For example, you can make a time line to understand sequence of events.

| first event | second event | third event | fourth event |

Strategy: Text Structure

Good readers use the structure of an article to help them understand what they read. Before reading, preview a selection. Look at the title, headings, and graphic sources. Try to figure out what the article or story will be about. Headings help you see an outline of the article. Think about how the graphic sources might help you understand the material.

1. Read "An Early History of New Brunswick." Study the time line. Make a time line like the one above for the section titled "Political Changes."

2. Use the time lines to summarize the three groups that settled in New Brunswick beginning in the 1600s and the changes in its government beginning in the 1700s.

An Early History of New Brunswick

1600					1650					1700					1750					1800

1770s–1780s Loyalists settle

1604
French begin colony

1713
British take control

1755
French settlers forced out

Settlement Long ago Native Americans lived in the area now called New Brunswick, Canada. Then in 1604 the French began settling the land. They farmed, fished, and traded furs.

In 1713 the British took control. They forced the French settlers out in 1755. Many of these settlers, however, eventually returned. Even today, some people in New Brunswick speak French.

During the American Revolution, people loyal to England—called Loyalists—left what would become the United States and moved north to this area. The city of St. Johns was founded in 1785, and small farming settlements were started in the river valleys.

Political Changes In 1784 the area was named New Brunswick, and it became a British province. In 1848 the British allowed New Brunswick to rule itself. It became part of Canada in 1867.

Life in Early New Brunswick Forests covered much of this rolling, hilly land. In the 1800s many people began making their living by cutting timber or building ships. The soil was generally poor, and farming was difficult. The climate, too, was hard for early settlers. Though New Brunswick summers are mild, winters are long, cold, and snowy.

Strategy Based on this graphic source, what do you think this section will be about?
(a) the land in New Brunswick
(b) important events in New Brunswick
(c) large cities and towns in New Brunswick

Skill Use the time line to answer this question: What European people settled in New Brunswick first?

Skill Look for information in this section that you could use to make your own graphic source—a second time line.

Strategy What will the final section be about? How can you tell?

195

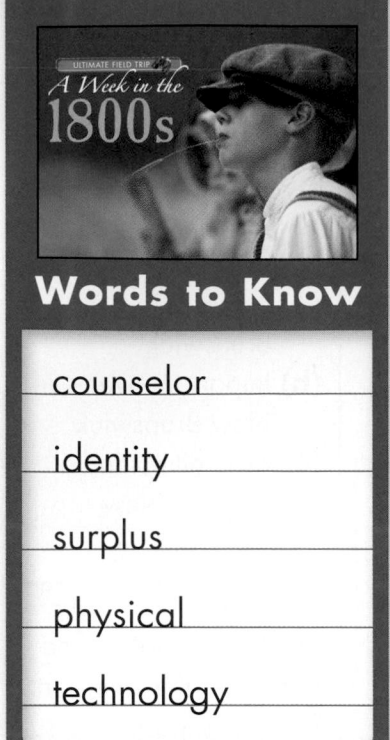

A Week in the 1800s

Words to Know

- counselor
- identity
- surplus
- physical
- technology

Vocabulary Strategy
for Unfamiliar Words

Dictionary/Glossary Sometimes when you are reading, you find a word you do not know. If the sentences around it do not give good clues to its meaning, you may need to look up the word in a dictionary or in the glossary of your book.

1. Check the back of your book to see if there is a glossary. If there is not, look in a dictionary.

2. Find the entry for the word. Words in both dictionaries and glossaries are listed in alphabetical order.

3. Read the pronunciation of the word, if one is given. You may recognize the word when you say it.

4. Read all of the meanings listed for the word.

5. Choose the meaning that makes sense in your sentence.

As you read "One-Room School," use your book's glossary or a dictionary to determine the meanings of unfamiliar words that the text does not define.

One-Room School

What would it have been like to attend school a century ago? Most likely, your school would have looked like a small wooden shanty with only one room. It would have had one teacher—usually a young single woman—who taught every grade. She was teacher, principal, nurse, counselor, and janitor all rolled into one.

There would have been no programs to help you discover your identity or plan your future. Classes in sports, art, and music simply did not exist. There were no career days. You came to school to learn to read and write and do arithmetic problems in chalk on your slate board. If you were lucky, you sat at a desk. Any surplus students sat on benches.

Today, you probably complain about spending so much time in school. Then, you would not have spent as much time in school because you were needed at home. You would have to help with the hard physical labor of planting, field work, and harvest. There had been no explosion of technology, so farm work was powered by horses and mules and men.

Look through the pictures in *A Week in the 1800s.* Choose one to write about. Use as many words from the Words to Know list as you can.

A Week in the 1800s

by Susan E. Goodman • photos by Michael J. Doolittle

How was life different in the 1800s?

Chapter One

A Leap Back in Time

Imagine traveling back in time to the 1800s. Suddenly, you're in a world without airplanes—or even automobiles. In a hurry to get somewhere? Your best bet, a coach with a team of fresh horses, will zip you along at the breakneck speed of nine miles an hour.

Hungry, but late for school? Forget about popping some instant oatmeal into the microwave. In the 1800s, almost all the foods you eat are made from scratch. If you have toast in the morning, it's because someone in your home has baked the bread and churned the butter that goes with it.

Your nineteenth-century evenings are lit by candles and oil lamps. In a time without telephones, you can talk to friends only when you actually see them. Long-distance communication is by letter—if you know how to write and can afford the postage.

Your music comes from singing and perhaps a friend's fiddle, not radios, tapes, or CDs.

You play checkers on a rainy day, not video games, and outdoor fun may include a new sport called baseball.

A group of modern kids stepped back into the 1800s at Kings Landing Historical Settlement in New Brunswick, Canada. For one week, these nine- to fourteen-year-olds wore the clothes of nineteenth-century young people—and tried their lives on for size as well.

Chapter Two

Starting the Journey

Garrett Hockenberry sat down with Rebecca, a counselor at Kings Landing.

"Garrett, this week you are going to be a cousin visiting the Heustis household," said Rebecca, introducing him to his nineteenth-century identity. "Your name will be Garrett Heustis."

"That's cool," said Garrett.

"It is," agreed Rebecca, "but since you're going to be living in the nineteenth century this week, *cool* is one word you shouldn't use. Not *cool* or *okay* or *wow*, because they didn't use those expressions back then. If you can't resist mentioning some twentieth-century things, try and think of a nineteenth-century way to say them. If you want to talk about your car, for example, you could change the word and say 'wagon.'"

"So . . . my father fixes and sells 'wagons'?" said Garrett, getting into the nineteenth-century spirit of things.

"You've got it!" said Rebecca.

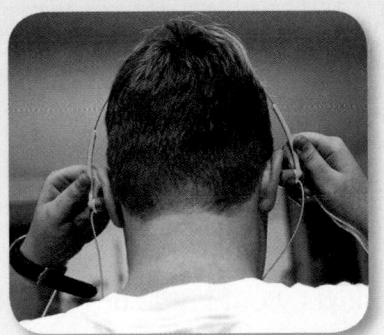

Meanwhile, Norma, the teacher at Kings Landing, was preparing another time traveler. "Did you pack anything modern in your suitcase?" she asked. "Magazines, cameras, earrings, or nail polish?"

"No," said Allison, "but I do have some money."

"Money! Young girls from the nineteenth century weren't allowed to carry money," replied Norma. "Give it to your mom to hold for you, and you'll be ready to go back in time."

In just moments, Garrett, Allison, and the rest of the group would start their journey. Kings Landing is a special kind of museum, a village of nineteenth-century farms, homes, shops, and mills that bring history to life. All the people who work there dress and act as if they were living in the 1800s. And that's what the kids were going to do as well.

But first they needed to look the part. Those shorts, sneakers, and T-shirts had to go. Next stop—the costume room.

Once their bonnets were tied and suspenders buttoned, the kids learned about the manners that went along with their nineteenth-century clothing.

"You all look so different; do you feel any different? Well, I do," said Norma, who had also changed her clothes. "This old-fashioned dress makes me feel more prim and proper. And people did behave differently in the nineteenth century, especially children."

Girls would never do anything so unladylike as run, Norma explained. They would skip instead. And they would never, goodness gracious, sit so their skirts would hike up. Both boys and girls were taught respect for their elders, which included never interrupting or talking back to any adult.

"I'm glad I didn't live back then," Catherine said (but not until later, when she wasn't interrupting anyone).

"When you greet people, say 'good day' or 'hello,'" said Darlene, continuing the lesson. "Girls, you can curtsy if you want to. Boys, you can take off your hats. But

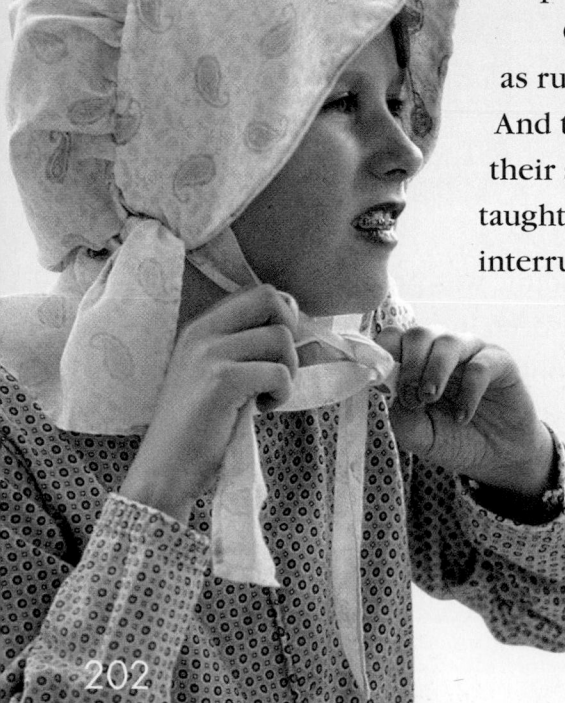

don't use the word *hi*, because it simply didn't exist yet. Does anyone know any other words that weren't used then?"

"Cool," shouted Garrett.

"That's right," answered Darlene. "*Cool* described the temperature outside. *Awesome* described mountains, and you didn't say *wicked* unless you were talking about someone very mean. Things that you liked were 'splendid' or 'very interesting.'

"At first, you'll make mistakes; it's hard to get used to acting as if you lived in a different time period," Darlene said. "But soon it will begin to feel natural. Then you can really have fun imagining yourself as a person in the eighteen hundreds!"

Chapter Three
Some Family History

The kids explored the village of Kings Landing together, but they each had their own home base. Kings Landing is filled with nineteenth-century houses that once belonged to real families. Some of these houses show what life was like in the 1820s and '30s, while others represent how people lived in the 1840s and the rest of the century. In the Morehouse house, for example, it is 1820, and Mrs. Morehouse cooks over a large open fireplace and gets her water from a well in the yard. By 1840, the Ingrahams have running water inside their home, and in 1860, the Joslins cook dinner on a wood-burning stove.

At night, the kids slept in a more modern house just outside the village. But they spent many daytime hours in the village's homes, visiting their "aunts" and "uncles" (played by museum interpreters). Talking to these "relatives," helping with chores, and sitting down to family dinners was the week's best history lesson.

"Sometimes, when I'm gardening or dusting and no one else is around, I can pretend I'm really from the eighteen hundreds," said Lorena.

"But it would be so different," said Amanda, thinking of life for her Hagerman family. "They didn't have electricity for refrigerators or lights. They didn't even have batteries—so when it was dark, it was really dark."

Looking at a bedroom with a bed, a dresser, and not much else, Brandon M. realized that people back then didn't have as many things

"This is a real pain in the neck," said Brandon M., wearing a yoke to carry two buckets of water.

"Can you imagine a grown-up scrunching into this bathtub?" asked Krista.

as we do today. "This room is okay," he said, "but my room at home has an alarm clock and books and a CD player and a real closet with a lot of clothes in it."

Comfort is another thing we have a lot more of too, especially where beds are concerned. Some houses in Kings Landing had beautiful canopy beds with feather mattresses. But others had beds with straw mattresses that felt lumpy and hard.

When the kids sat down to eat at noon, corn and carrots were only a small part of their meal. One time, for example, the menu included ham, potatoes, green beans, corn, biscuits, and pie for dessert (which was served at the same time as everything else). As Uncle Joslin explained to Allison, they called this meal "dinner," and it was the biggest one of the day. People needed food to fuel all the hard physical work that followed.

"I really like the food," said Stephanie.

"I do too," said Garrett. "And I like the fact that a lot of it comes from their own gardens."

"But I can't imagine having to make it all instead of buying some from the store," said Allison. "Even the milk is homemade!"

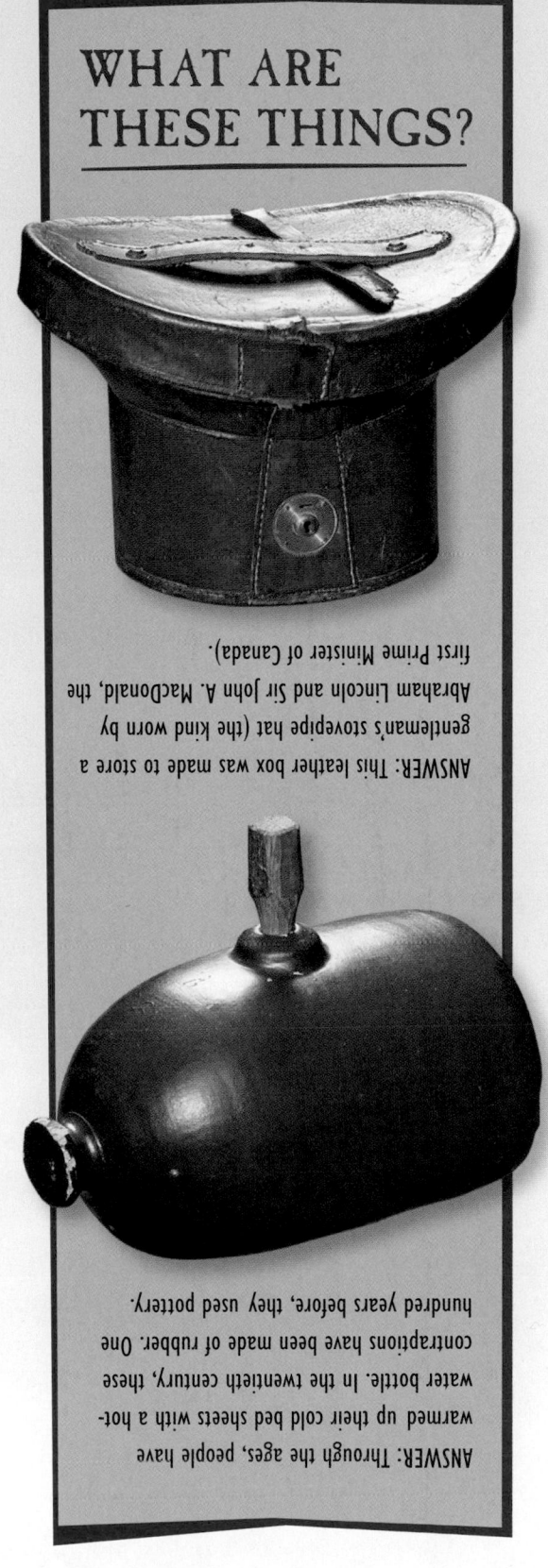

WHAT ARE THESE THINGS?

ANSWER: This leather box was made to store a gentleman's stovepipe hat (the kind worn by Abraham Lincoln and Sir John A. MacDonald, the first Prime Minister of Canada).

ANSWER: Through the ages, people have warmed up their cold bed sheets with a hot-water bottle. In the twentieth century, these contraptions have been made of rubber. One hundred years before, they used pottery.

Chapter Four

Women's Work

After their stay at Kings Landing, the girls had a new understanding of the expression "A woman's work is never done." In the nineteenth century, most women did not work outside their homes, but taking care of a house and children was work enough. Without electricity or modern appliances, women did all their chores by hand. Imagine first weaving the cloth, then sewing the clothes for an entire family. Imagine preparing three meals a day, when cooking included making every loaf of bread and hunk of cheese. Then there was the cleaning, the washing, the mending. . . .

The girls had known before that nineteenth-century women didn't have as many choices and rights. But they didn't like being in that position

Catherine pulls carrots for dinner.

Stephanie has her first cup of tea brewed from loose tea leaves.

themselves. "Why can't we go to work at the blacksmith shop or drive the oxen?" asked Erika.

"Well, you're not interested in such things," explained Wendy, trying to tell Erika about the person she would have been in the 1800s.

Erika wasn't buying it. "Oh yes I am interested," she said. "The nineteenth century wasn't fair."

ANSWER: This iron was heated up by dropping hot wood coals down its spout.

ANSWER: This ice-cream scoop has a knob on top that turns the inside blades and releases the ice cream.

Making samplers, girls practiced different sewing stitches and learned their letters and numbers at the same time.

Suffer little children to come unto me and forbid them not

aged 8

207

Laundry

"Girls, we're doing the Hagermans' laundry," announced a counselor named Sharlene. "Luckily they live in 1870 and are very modern. They have a washing machine."

The Hagermans' washing machine hardly fit in with the girls' idea of modern. They had to do the wash, rinse, and spin cycles themselves. The girls wet the clothes; then sudsed them up with soap made of beef fat and lye. Then they rocked the top of the machine back and forth to clean and rinse the clothes.

"This seems like a lot of work," said Amanda.

"Yes, but they washed less laundry than we do," Sharlene explained. "Most people could only afford one outfit besides their Sunday best. Luckily they also had different standards of hygiene."

"One outfit each week wouldn't be so bad," said Julie. "At least you wouldn't have to think about what to put on in the morning."

Baking

Baking in the 1800s meant no electric mixers or microwaves, not even a cake mix. In fact, in the early part of the century, cooks only had whole wheat flour to stir into their cookies and pies.

"We are lucky. It's 1870 in our house," said Aunt Perley while teaching the girls how to make crumb cake. "So we have baking powder and the lovely white flour that makes such a difference in baking."

As Sam and Stephanie measured and stirred, Aunt Perley explained that most women in the 1800s made their own bread, biscuits, and desserts. Then she showed the girls a nineteenth-century oven thermometer: She put her hand inside the oven. Since she was able to keep it there until she counted to ten, the oven was hot enough to bake, but not hot enough to burn.

"It *is* hot in here," said Sam as she put their cake in the oven.

"That's why ladies always have pink cheeks," said Aunt Perley.

WHAT ARE THESE THINGS?

ANSWER: These ice skates were used by screwing them into your shoes.

Chapter Five

Men's Work

In the nineteenth century, a boy often couldn't choose the work he'd do as a grown-up. He usually took on the job his father had, whether it was farming or printing or boot making. When a boy became an apprentice to another tradesman, however, he would often live and work with his new master. It was like attending blacksmithing or barrel-making school, but with only one teacher. Over the years, the apprentice worked for the tradesman, learning more and more, until he knew enough to become a master craftsman himself.

The boys at Kings Landing didn't like the idea of not being able to choose their own future. But they did like the different kinds of work that men did in the 1800s.

Farming

When the farmer discovered Brandon T. had never worked in his garden at home, he was surprised. "What do you do when you're not in school?" Harry asked.

"Play video games," answered Brandon.

"When I was your age," replied Harry, "I was milking cows morning and night."

In the nineteenth century, farming was more a way of life than a business. Farmers grew enough crops to feed their family and animals. They raised sheep to have wool for clothes and kept cows for milk, cheese, and butter. Any surplus—extra apples or cheese, for example—would be traded or sold to buy supplies at the general store.

It was harvesttime when the boys were at Kings Landing. After they dug up potatoes and picked cucumbers, they used a sickle to harvest corn-stalks. Harry explained that they fed these corn stalks and turnips to the cows.

"I hate turnips," replied Max. "That's what I would do if I grew 'em."

Farmers used every part of the corn plant. Corn was ground into cornmeal; the stalks were fed to cattle; and the leftover cobs were turned into pipes and dolls, even nineteenth-century toilet paper!

Blacksmith

"Come right in, boys," said the blacksmith. "I could use a few apprentices."

No surprise, a blacksmith usually had one of the busiest shops in any country town. The blacksmith made the tools men used on the farm and women used in the kitchen. He made shoes for the oxen; he even made the hinges for their barn doors.

A blacksmith's apprentice started learning the trade by making something much easier: a nail. Eventually an apprentice could make one nail every seven seconds, but the boys only had a chance to try once. They carefully heated a rod of iron in the forge and pounded the end on an anvil. Heat, pound, heat, pound, until the nail was done.

"Ouch! I didn't think it would still be hot!" said Alex, inspecting the red dot on his finger.

"Oh yes," said the blacksmith, "even when it's black, iron's temperature can still be eight hundred degrees."

"I'd be a blacksmith," said Brandon M., at the end of his turn. "I think it's fun."

"The only problem," the blacksmith answered, "is that blacksmiths often went deaf because of that constant loud sound of metal hitting metal."

"Are you deaf?" asked Garrett.

"What did you say?" the blacksmith jokingly replied.

WHAT IS THIS THING?

ANSWER: You might have guessed this was a lamp, but this courting lamp had a special use. When a young man came to visit a young woman, her father would fill a small lamp with oil. The boy could stay as long as the lamp kept burning.

Chapter Six

Back to the Future

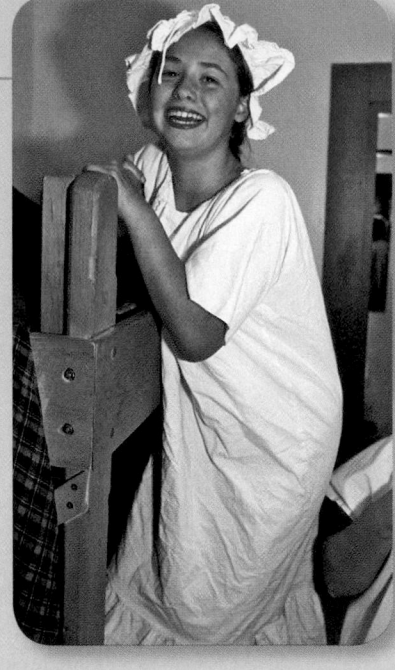

On their last night at Kings Landing, the kids started getting a little homesick for the twentieth century.

"I can't wait to go home and kill some aliens on my computer," said Garrett.

"Once I get my normal clothes on again, I'm not going to take them off," said Sam. "I think I'm gonna sleep in them my first night home."

As the girls changed into their nineteenth-century sleepwear, they all agreed that the nightcaps should stay in the 1800s where they belonged. But many were glad they could take their nightgowns home with them. And they wished they could take other parts of the nineteenth century home as well.

"I liked milking the cow," said Robin.

"I liked the fact that kids could go around the town all by themselves," said Krista. "Everybody knew everybody, so you didn't have to worry."

"I liked being able to walk to school instead of taking a long bus ride," said Amanda. "That way you could meet up with other kids and talk."

"I liked the quiet," said Allison. "No car horns or sirens, no jackhammers."

Many girls liked their nineteenth-century nightgowns, but when Brandon T. found out the kids could take their nightclothes home, he said, "I don't think I'll ever wear mine again."

But the kids also found their visit to the past gave them a fresh look at their lives in the present. Suddenly they valued parts of the twentieth century they had taken for granted because they had never known life without them. First and foremost phones, electricity, cars, the technology that affects every part of modern life.

"I'm sort of a TV fanatic and I've really missed it," said Garrett. "That and my remote-control car."

"After walking on rocks in these shoes all week, I really miss good roads," said Amanda.

"One thing I like a lot less here is the bugs," said Hilary.

"Wait a minute," said Catherine. "We have the same bugs now too."

"Yeah," Hilary answered, "but they didn't have anything to kill them with back then."

"The thing that surprised and bothered me most was that you weren't supposed to run," said Sarah.

WHAT IS THIS THING?

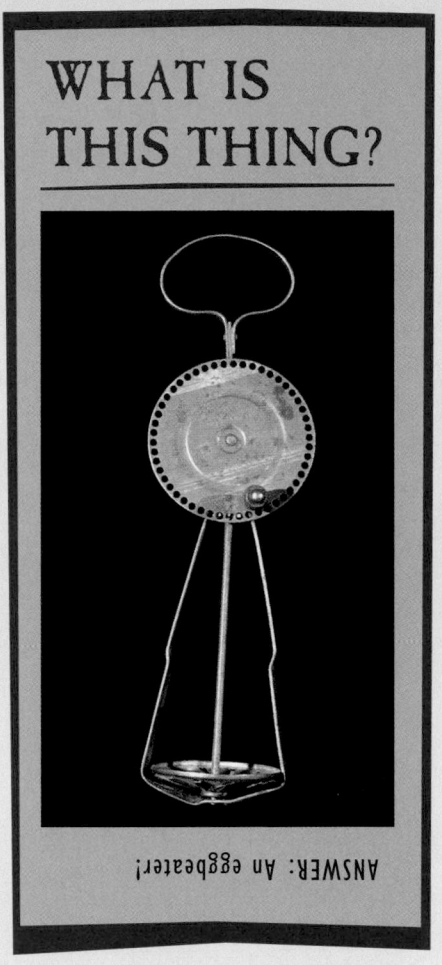

ANSWER: An eggbeater!

"That's right," agreed Allison, who started thinking about all the rules the nineteenth century had for girls. "At home, I'm used to acting normal instead of being so very, very, very polite."

"I can't imagine living in a time when women couldn't vote," said Catherine. "It would make me so mad."

Back to the twentieth century

"I don't like the fact that Kings Landing has a river the boys would be able to swim in back then—but not me," said Erika. "And I don't like that the guys got to do a lot of things we couldn't do."

"I'd like to be a blacksmith," said Hilary, "but I like sewing, too."

"That's right," said Amy, "I'd like to stay being a girl, but I'd like to do boy things."

213

Living in History

There are a number of places in both Canada and the United States where people can participate in living history. This map shows just a few the places where visitors can step into the past and experience a little taste of life as it used to be.

London, Ontario, Canada

Fanshawe Pioneer Village features demonstrations of trades of the past such as weavers, printmakers, blacksmiths, and farmers.

Pella, Iowa

In the **Pella Historical Village** tradespeople wearing Dutch costumes demonstrate wooden shoe-making and other traditional Dutch crafts.

Pittsfield, Massachusetts

In **Hancock Shaker Village** guests can try on traditional Shaker clothing. In the schoolhouse, they can learn how to write with a quill pen or how to spell with historic letter boards.

Williamsburg, Virginia

Colonial Williamsburg features living history of Colonial America in the late 1700s. In addition to townspeople, slaves, and free blacks, costumed interpreters here also portray famous historical Americans like Thomas Jefferson and Martha Washington.

Reader Response

Open for Discussion   Suppose you were on the field trip to this historical settlement. For a week you became a nineteenth century person. What impressed you? What didn't impress you? If next week offers another field trip to the time and place of your choice, where will you go?

1. In this report, direct quotes are often used instead of general statements about the role-players' likes and dislikes. Find samples of those quotes. How well do those direct quotes contribute to this report?

2. Look again at the sidebars on pages 205, 207, and 209. How do the descriptions of these items help you to better understand what life was like for those who lived in the nineteenth century?

3. How does the separation of information into different chapters help you to remember what you've read?

4. Make a list of words and their meanings from the selection that were used in the 1800s but are not much used today.

Look Back and Write
Erika didn't think the nineteenth century was fair. What was she referring to? Look back at pages 206–207 to find out. Write her reason and whether you agree or disagree with her—and why.

Susan E. Goodman

Read more books by Susan E. Goodman.

Ultimate Field Trip 1: Adventures in the Amazon Rain Forest

Ultimate Field Trip 5: Blasting Off to Space Academy

Do you think being a writer would be boring? Well, it hasn't been for Susan Goodman. For her, it has been an adventure!

Ms. Goodman's writing adventures include spending the night in an *underwater* hotel and swimming with dolphins. She has met many interesting people along the way. "I visited a guy who makes models of dinosaurs for museums and a zookeeper in charge of elephants. I met a guy who can tell when someone was murdered by studying the bugs on the dead body. It's great to talk to experts; their enthusiasm is catching."

Pretty cool life, don't you think?

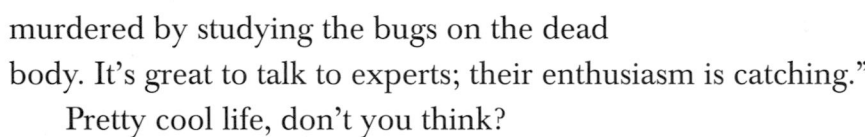

A Week in the 1800s is part of a series called *Ultimate Field Trips.* These are not your ordinary field trips. Ms. Goodman has gone with young people to Space Camp, to the Amazon Rain Forest, and to the ocean to study marine life.

A Week in the 1800s was fun to write. "I read a lot of Laura Ingalls Wilder as a kid and always wondered what it would be like to travel back in time," she says. Ms. Goodman learned a lot about history during her time at Kings Landing.

Web Site

Genre

- Web pages are found on Internet Web sites.

Text Features

- Every Web site has a home page. The home page is like the table of contents in a book. You move around a home page to find more information by clicking on links.

- Links are either buttons or words that are printed in a different color or underlined. When you click on these links, your computer will open a different window that contains the information indicated by the link.

Link to Social Studies

Find out what life was like for immigrant children in the 1890s and early 1900s. You might try looking up the El-lis Island website. Compare your life with those of immi-grant children.

Colonial Times

After reading about life in the 1800s, you might want to learn about how people lived in yet another time period. You may choose to learn about colonial times, when America was a new country.

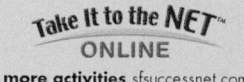
Take It to the NET™
ONLINE
more activities sfsuccessnet.com

217

A Web page like the one here can take you to other Web pages and Web sites as you follow its links.

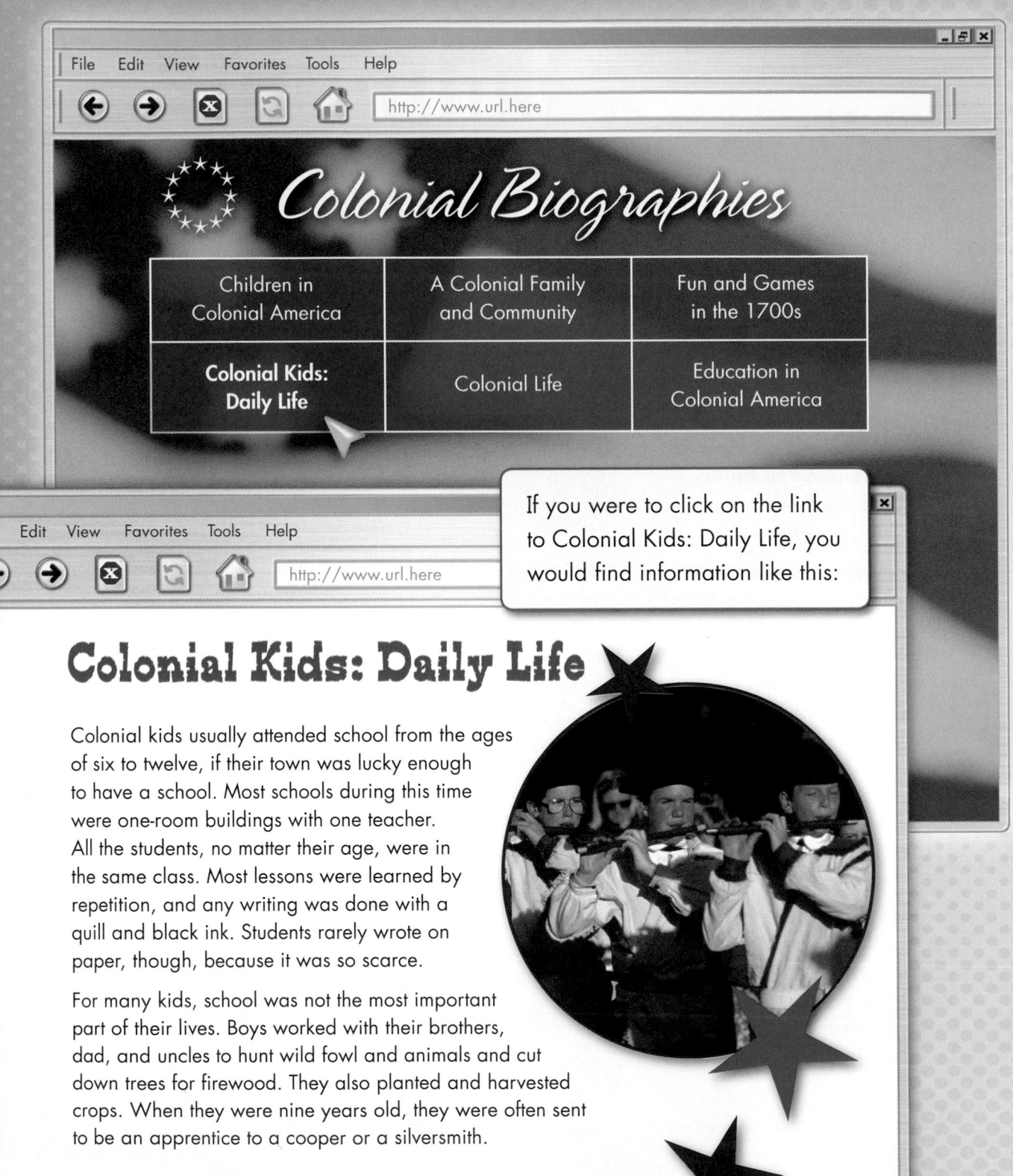

Colonial Biographies

Children in Colonial America	A Colonial Family and Community	Fun and Games in the 1700s
Colonial Kids: Daily Life	Colonial Life	Education in Colonial America

If you were to click on the link to Colonial Kids: Daily Life, you would find information like this:

Colonial Kids: Daily Life

Colonial kids usually attended school from the ages of six to twelve, if their town was lucky enough to have a school. Most schools during this time were one-room buildings with one teacher. All the students, no matter their age, were in the same class. Most lessons were learned by repetition, and any writing was done with a quill and black ink. Students rarely wrote on paper, though, because it was so scarce.

For many kids, school was not the most important part of their lives. Boys worked with their brothers, dad, and uncles to hunt wild fowl and animals and cut down trees for firewood. They also planted and harvested crops. When they were nine years old, they were often sent to be an apprentice to a cooper or a silversmith.

A master silversmith working on a small, etched cup

A cooper is someone who works with wood and repairs chairs or anything else manufactured from wood. A silversmith makes things out of silver, such as cups, plates, and eating utensils. Boys usually worked as apprentices for about seven years.

Girls were taught to be eager workers by their parents because laziness was considered a sin. They got up very early to do chores like making candles, sweeping, feeding and getting eggs from chickens, milking cows, watering livestock, picking berries, and gathering vegetables and herbs.

They helped prepare breakfast, a midday meal, and dinner. People in colonial times didn't really take many baths, but many washed in a pail with hot water about once a day. Most colonial families were very big. In addition to the children and parents, aunts, uncles, and grandparents all lived together. They were self-reliant, which means that they could meet their needs without assistance from anyone else.

Reading Across Texts

Compare being a young person in the 1800s with being one in colonial times.

Writing Across Texts Tell in which time you would rather have lived—the 1800s or colonial times—and why.

 **Text Structure** | How would the structure help you summarize "Colonial Kids"?

Comprehension

Skill
Compare
and Contrast

Strategy
Generate Questions

Skill

Compare and Contrast

- When you compare, you tell how two or more things are alike. When you contrast, you tell how two or more things are different.

- Sometimes authors use similes and metaphors to make comparisons. Similes use the clue words *like*, *as*, or *than*. Metaphors do not use clue words. Words such as *unlike*, *but*, and *however* can show contrasts.

- Ask questions while reading to compare and contrast such as, "How are these two characters alike and different?" or "What does this situation remind me of?"

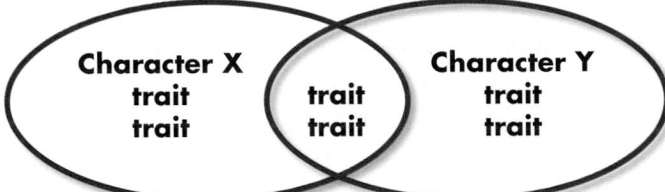

Character X
trait
trait

trait
trait

Character Y
trait
trait

Strategy

Strategy: Generate Questions

Asking questions helps you better comprehend the important ideas and information in the text. Ask questions before, during, and after you read. This can help you compare and contrast characters, ideas, or situations.

Write

1. Read "My Siblings." Make a graphic organizer like the one above to compare and contrast Anna and Charlie.

2. List the questions you asked while reading "My Siblings."

My Siblings

My older sibling is Anna, and my younger sibling is Charlie. We all come from the same family, but Anna and Charlie are like night and day.

Anna is 13, and I've never seen a better worker. She is as efficient and orderly as a perfectly programmed robot, and can multitask like you wouldn't believe. Anna can clean her room while doing her homework and talking on the phone. Everything she does turns out great. Sometimes I think that Anna is a powerful computer that has somehow acquired a human body.

Then there's Charlie, a very different species. It's clear to everyone in the family that he's from another planet. Charlie is the most imaginative creature I know. Despite being only 6 years old, he can build fabulous structures out of blocks, invent weird and wonderful games, and make up odd words and names. His mind is like a swarm of bees—constantly moving and swirling. He is a walking tornado, always leaving gigantic, complex messes in his wake. Kind? Yes—but as unique as they come.

What about me, you ask? Well, I'm nothing like either of them.

Skill Based on the simile *like night and day,* do you think Anna and Charlie are similar? Why or why not?

Strategy What question could you ask yourself to make sure you understand what Anna is like?
(a) "How would I describe Anna to someone else?"
(b) "Does Anna talk on the phone?"
(c) "How old is Anna?"

Strategy What questions might you be asking about the simile and the metaphor?

Skill Here is one point of contrast: how Anna and Charlie affect the family home. How are they different?

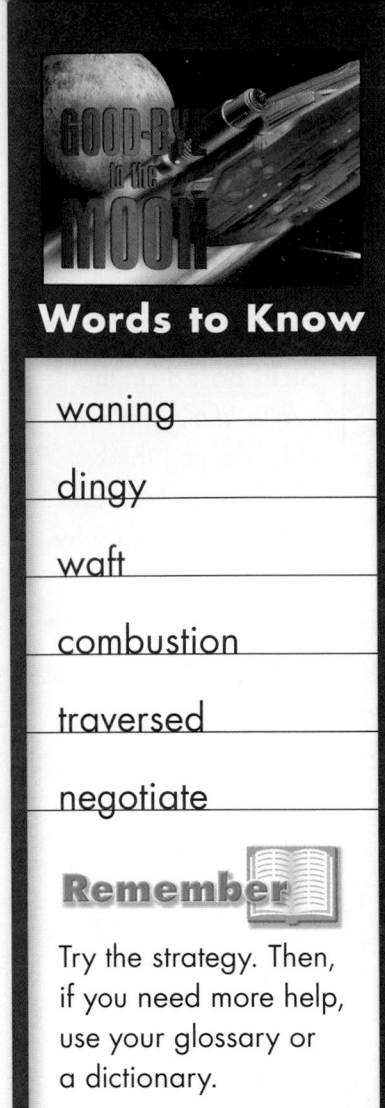

Words to Know

waning

dingy

waft

combustion

traversed

negotiate

Remember

Try the strategy. Then, if you need more help, use your glossary or a dictionary.

Vocabulary Strategy
for Unfamiliar Words

Context Clues Sometimes when you are reading, you come across a word you do not know. See if you can use context, or the words around the word, to figure out the meaning of the new word.

1. Reread the sentence in which the unknown word appears. Look for a synonym, example, or other clue to the word's meaning.

2. If you need more help, read the sentences around the sentence with the unknown word.

3. Ask yourself, "What is this about?" The subject matter, facts, or explanations may suggest the word's meaning.

4. Add up the clues you have found and predict the word's meaning. See if your meaning makes sense in the sentence.

As you read "Lunar Love Affair," look for context clues to help you find out the meanings of unknown words.

Lunar Love Affair

The love affair of humans for all things lunar reaches far back into history. For many thousands of years, humans have watched the moon in the night sky. They saw it gradually waxing, or growing round, and then waning, or growing ever smaller until only a sliver remained. It excited wonder and curiosity. No matter how dingy or ugly or hard life on Earth might be, the moon always glowed with a soft, pure light in the darkness. The perfume of blossoms might waft on the breeze to faces turned up to gaze at the mysterious moon.

Then, not so long ago, people invented internal combustion engines. By burning fuel in an enclosed space, they harnessed great power to drive vehicles, then airplanes, then jets. Before long, humans looked at the moon with a new question. Why not go there ourselves?

By 1969, astronauts had traversed outer space to go to the moon! Cameras showed us men in spacesuits taking great leaps across the rocky surface of the moon. It seemed the beginning of a new age. However, it seems that people have more plans than money for space travel. NASA, the U.S. agency responsible for space exploration, has to negotiate carefully for funding. Rather than return to the moon, humans have explored farther into space.

Imagine you are traveling to the moon. Write a journal entry about your trip. Use as many words from the Words to Know list as you can.

GOOD-BYE to the MOON

by Monica Hughes

illustrated by Mick Coulas

How might living on the Moon differ from living on Earth?

I sat in the darkened room of the space station and looked out at Earth. It was strangely familiar to me. The photograph of the blue globe with its whip-cream swirls of cloud hung in the Control Center of Lunar Lab 21. There was a small copy of the same famous picture in our own living unit. To my mother and father, it had meant home.

What was this Earth to me? It was a shining silver disk, waxing from crescent to full, and waning back again to crescent, that traversed the skies of our long lunar nights. It was the song my mother sang to me, the first child born on Moon:

Earth-shine, Earth-bright,
Grant the wish I wish tonight.

But that was long, long ago. Mother had been dead for five years, and I, Kepler Masterman, son of Moon Governor, was

actually going to Earth myself. Already I was over the first hurdle, the wearisome three-day journey on the old beat-up Moon ferry to the space station.

It was great to stretch my legs again and enjoy the low-grav of the station's slow spin after the weight of the moon-rocket's acceleration. I looked down at Earth, so close I felt I could reach out and touch. What was down there? . . . The Sphinx . . . the Taj Mahal . . . Skyscrapers. All the fantastic things I'd read about. I looked at my watch. Fifteen minutes to wait.

Restlessly I left the viewing room and glided down the long passageway to the hub of the space station. In the VIP lounge I could see Father, surrounded by reporters. Time for one last goodbye to Moon.

Down the passage to the right here. The view room was empty, and I slid into a couch in the center front row. The room was dark, and the window was set in an angle that fooled the eye. It was as if nothing separated me from the black infinity of space and from Moon. It was so small now, my Moon, no bigger than the silver identidisk on the chain around my neck.

My eyes picked out the familiar features. The terminator, that razor-edge between night and day, arced down through the Ocean of Storms. The oblique sunlight etched clearly in black shadow the huge circle of Copernicus, and, to its left, right on the edge of the terminator, I could see Kepler, the crater in which Lunar Lab was built. Home! Down there, a new Moon-day was just starting. The viewing ports of the Labs and the living units would automatically darken as the brilliant rays of the sun stabbed down white-hard against the rocks of the crater. The heat-exchange units would slowly adjust from two weeks of warming up the buildings to cooling them, as for the next fifteen days the sun would shine down on Lunar Lab 21.

Down there at home the kids would be getting ready for the party. There'd always been a party at sunrise, ever since I could remember, and I was the oldest kid on Moon. The adults used to tease us sometimes . . . "Imagine having a party every *day!*" But it was only twelve or thirteen times a year, and there was something special about the sunlight creeping so slowly across the surface of Moon, striking the peaks of the Apennines, sending shadows chasing across the Sinus

...esium, each Earth-day a little closer, until finally the two long weeks of night were over, and we were bathed in sunlight again. The astronomers hated daytime, except for the solar experts. They couldn't see the stars and had to stay in their rooms catching up on their paperwork. But everyone else loved it, especially the kids.

I sighed and thought of Ann. Wonder who'd be taking her to the party? We'd stood at the air lock to say goodbye. Ann had been crying, and her eyes were red. But she was as beautiful as ever. There had been an awful lump in my throat as I blurted out the words.

"I'll be seeing you, Ann."

"Oh, Kepler, take care of yourself."

"Sure. You, too, Ann. I'll write, I promise."

It was a terrible farewell. I'd worked out ahead of time exactly what I was going to say. It was terrific. It'd have bowled her over. But standing there by the air lock, I'd forgotten it all.

I squirmed at the memory and hoped that Ann wouldn't remember and laugh. Well, at least I could write. I knew I couldn't expect letters from Ann. Letter rates to Earth were crippling—so was the cost of everything that had to make the 240,000-mile haul. But I could write to

Ann. That was one advantage of having the Lunar Governor as Father. I could slip my letters into the diplomatic bag, and they would go rocketing to Moon with no questions asked. But six months away from home . . . I was going to miss her. *That* was the disadvantage of having a Governor for Father.

The door swung open behind me, letting in a shaft of light and a babble of excited voices. There was a waft of exotic perfume. Real French perfume! The ferry from Earth must have arrived. These would be passengers on Moon Safari. This was a trip only for the very, very wealthy. In fact, the tourist complex on the Sea of Serenity helped pay for some of the research expenses that the Moon administration was unable to wring from the reluctant cashbox of Earth.

I slipped out of the suddenly crowded room and down the passage to the central concourse. Father was standing there. There were last minute goodbyes.

"Good luck, George."

"We're counting on you, Governor!"

"See you in six months, at the latest."

I walked beside him, trying to copy his casual stroll. I wasn't about to look like some country Rube, even if it was my first Earth trip. But my first sight of the Earth-ferry threw me, and my jaw

dropped. It was magnificent, three times as big as our beat-up old Moon-ferries with their huge cargo holds and dingy cramped passenger quarters. Yet we had had to endure the lunar trip for three long days, and this was only going to take about three hours.

"Is everything on Earth this fancy?" I whispered to Father, as I snuggled down into the deep plush of my contour seat, and buckled my harness around me.

"Pretty much so—in the parts of the world you'll be seeing, anyway. It's a far cry from home, isn't it?"

Was it ever! I tried to imagine our living unit with a deep blue pile carpet and walls of cream

stippled with gold, instead of the standard issue green vinyl floor and plastic-coated steel walls. When I was a kid, I was always roaming into the wrong unit. They were all identical, and there just wasn't the money to ferry up from Earth the sort of things that would have made them look homey. . . .

. . . The ferry shivered delicately and then moved slowly out of its holding dock. I could feel my body pressing gently against the padded couch as the ferry surrendered itself to Earth-grav. It was amazingly quiet and comfortable. I'd hardly slept on the trip down from Moon, and now, in spite of myself, I found my eyes shutting.

It seemed only a few minutes before Father's voice woke me. "You're a pretty blasé traveler, Kepler! But you mustn't miss this sight. We're just turning into Earth orbit. Look!"

I craned my neck eagerly and looked through the port. I recognized the narrow spindle of Central America, and then the steely shimmer of the Atlantic lay beneath us. It went on and on.

"The planet's all water!" I gasped.

"Seven-tenths of it is," Father agreed.

"But . . . but. Oh, wow!" It was feeble, but what words could I have for it? A world that was seven-tenths *water!* Why, on Moon, water was harder to get than oxygen, much harder. Breathing was free. You could breathe as deeply and as often as you wished. Now that the hydroponic gardens were going, we didn't have to pay for our oxygen any more. But water was something else.

Every ounce of it was worth its weight in Moon minerals. Dirt was removed by electrostatic filters in the labs and living units. Washing was a luxury and drinking a special delight.

There was no free water on the Moon. Every ounce we used was extracted in the refinement of the ores we sent down to Earth. And the mining companies charged us for it—every drop! I had grown up thinking water was the most precious stuff in the Universe. Now with my own eyes I could see that Earth was covered with the stuff—slopping over with it.

We orbited across North Africa and Arabia. From my port I could see the island-spangled blueness of the Indian Ocean. Then the Pacific. I felt suddenly tired and a little sick. What sort of a place was this Earth and what were its people like? Half a world made of water, and yet they had charged us for every single cup. I shut my eyes and turned away from the port.

"You feeling groggy?" Father's voice was sympathetic. "They're starting their braking orbit, and I guess you'll really notice the weight difference. Don't worry. It'll get worse before it gets better. But it will get better. Just hang on!"

To the Earth passengers from the space station, I suppose the discomforts were minimal. Their apparent weight increased to double and momentarily three times their normal weight. I had not realized until this moment what my birthright of one-sixth Earth weight was going to mean when I tried to return "home." It was like a barrier separating me from all these other people. Already I weighed six times my normal weight. As the braking continued, it increased to twelve times, to. . . . The weight on my chest . . . I couldn't breathe. I felt as if my brain was going to burst.

When I came back to my senses, the enormous pressure had lifted. I felt heavy and very tired. I lifted my head and looked blurrily around. We had landed! There was a bustle of unstrapping harnesses, collecting belongings. I struggled with my own safety straps, and Father leaned over to help me. The expression on his face told me I didn't look good.

"Lie still, Kepler. You've had a nosebleed. I'll get a stewardess to help."

"I'm okay, Father." My tongue felt thick, and the words were blurry. The stewardess hurried over. She bent down to wash my face.

"I can do it," I muttered thickly, trying to take the cloth away from her.

"You just lie still, sonny. I'm just going to get you an ice pack. You really took the 'Gs' badly. You'll have two beautiful shiners in the morning."

Sonny! How old did she think I was, anyway? Two black eyes . . . oh, brother! That was really starting out on the right foot. Look out, Earth. Here comes Kepler Masterman—on a banana skin!

She glided back with the ice pack. How could she move so lightly on the heavy planet, I wondered. She looked no heavier than a grain of moondust.

She spoke to my father. "Governor, the Press and TV are waiting for you. Are you ready to leave the ferry yet?"

"Oh, sure. I'll come right away." He swung himself up from his couch and stretched. He was a big man, my father, and muscular. I wondered if I'd ever catch up. I was at the weedy stage, and in spite of secret body-building in my own room, I wasn't making much headway.

"Strange feeling going up to 170 pounds again. Don't think I like it much. Kepler, lie still and take your time. I'm sure this young lady will look after you."

I watched his broad back down the aisle and through the hatch, and then I took off the ice pack and swung my legs down to the floor. My head throbbed a bit, but it wasn't too bad. Standing was tougher, and walking was a nightmare of

wading through glue. I gritted my teeth and practiced, one foot and then the other, up and down the aisle, holding on to the seat backs for support.

Six months on this planet. How was I ever going to make out? I saw the stewardess watching me from the galley door. I wished she'd go away, but when she saw I'd seen her, she came down the aisle toward me.

"I could get you a wheelchair," she volunteered. "This low-grav syndrome can be a problem. It's happened before, you know, though I guess you're the first person who's never experienced Earth-weight in his life."

"I'm going to be fine, thanks. It just takes a little practice, that's all."

"Of course. Perhaps you'd like to clean up before you leave?" I took her hint and plodded back down the aisle to the washroom. Good grief, I was a disaster area! I took off my jacket—how crudely cut it looked in comparison with the Earth

234

fashions I'd seen on the ferry, and what rough material. Then I washed the rest of the blood off my face and combed my hair, what there was of it. It looked like a convict cut by Earth standards, but it would grow. There were red smudges under my eyes, but the shiners the stewardess had promised hadn't shown up yet.

I put on my jacket and plodded down to the exit hatch. I hesitated, my hand on the ramp rail, looking at the crowd of exotically dressed reporters, cameramen, and casual bystanders milling around my father. It really was a new world down there at the end of the ramp.

"Good luck," the stewardess said softly. She wasn't a bad sort, really, only a bit old to understand. I managed a smile, swallowed, and walked down the ramp to join my father. I was drowned in a storm of voices. How loudly these Earth people talked, as if they were constantly trying to shout each other down.

"Governor, would you say the differences between Earth and Moon people are irreconcilable?"

"I certainly would not. On the contrary, I am convinced that with a clearer understanding of our problem, the differences between us will be settled amicably."

"What do you intend to do if the U.N. vote goes against you?"

"I'm not even considering that possibility at the moment."

"Governor, how long do you intend to spend on Earth this trip?"

"I anticipate that it may take as long as six months to settle our differences, though of course we could strike lucky. . . . "

"One last question, Governor. Now you are back on Earth again, will you tell our listeners—which is really home to you, Earth or Moon?"

"That's a difficult question to answer. All my cultural ties are with Earth. But, like all immigrants who flocked to the New World and shaped it into a nation, I guess I must say that it is in this Newer World, Moon, that my present and future lie. My son was born there. My wife was buried there. My work is there. Yes, gentlemen, it is good to be back on Earth. But Moon is home!"

He saw me standing jammed among the reporters and casually gave me his arm. We walked together across the sun-splashed concrete of the landing pad. The sun was gently warm on my body and our shadows ran out ahead of us, soft, muzzy-edged. I looked up. The sky was a delicate blue with fluffy cumulus clouds, just like the ones in my old video tapes. They sailed gracefully across the sky, unbelievably beautiful. A sudden white shape plunged and screeched. I jumped and clutched Father's arm.

"What was that? . . . a bird?"

"Yes, Kepler. A seagull."

I walked along, breathing real air, not the canned stuff. It was strange being outdoors without a space-suit, scary but exciting. It looked as if Earth was going to be fun. If only my legs didn't ache so. . . .

"Is it far to the magnetrain, Father?"

"Hang on, son. It's right ahead."

Once aboard with my feet up, I didn't feel so much of a country cousin. The magnetrain had been developed on Moon, where the absence of any atmosphere had precluded the use of conventional jet, hovercraft, or internal combustion engines. Up there, we had perfected the magnetic lift system of propulsion, and our trains networked the lunar surface with silent pollution-free speeds of 500 miles an hour.

The idea had been enthusiastically adopted by an ecology-conscious Earth, and one of the items on my father's agenda was to negotiate an acknowledgment in terms of royalties of the Lunar discovery.

I lay back and thought of the pyramids and the Taj Mahal, the temples of Angkor Wat, and the mysterious jungle buildings of the Incas. Would six months be time enough to see it all?

236

Reader Response

Open for Discussion Kepler has one foot on Earth and one foot on the Moon. How will he cope during the next six months? Give him some advice.

1. The story is fiction (make-believe) plus science (natural world and technology). Cite examples to show how the author combines those two elements (fiction and science).

2. Kepler mentions many similarities and differences between life on the Moon and life on Earth. Name at least two similarities he mentions and two differences. Then describe which difference you would have the most trouble adjusting to.

3. Did the story tell you everything you wanted to know about Kepler's journey? What questions might you ask the author about the story if you could?

4. Find the words the author has made up to convey a sense of life on the Moon. Tell how they're used. One example is *identidisk*.

Look Back and Write What does "The reluctant cashbox of Earth" (page 228) tell you about relations between Earth and the Moon in the futuristic story? Write the answer and why it might be important.

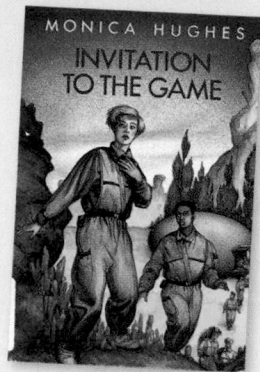

Invitation to the Game

Born in Liverpool, England, Monica Hughes immigrated to Canada, where she lived most of her life. She started out writing short stories, articles, and novels for adults but received only rejection slips from publishers. Then she read some novels written especially for young people and knew, she said, "I had found my voice."

She went on to become an award-winning author. On her death at the age of seventy-seven, Monica Hughes was considered the leading science fiction writer for young adults in Canada. During her lifetime, she wrote more than thirty books and credited some of her success with persisting in writing even after the rejections.

A Handful of Seeds

Ms. Hughes discovered that "ideas are everywhere." She learned to recognize ideas and write them down quickly. Because she was interested in "the tension between scientific progress and the health of the environment," she put newspaper clippings about scientific facts and human-interest stories into her file of ideas. She also used the library for research so that her science fiction books would have believable settings.

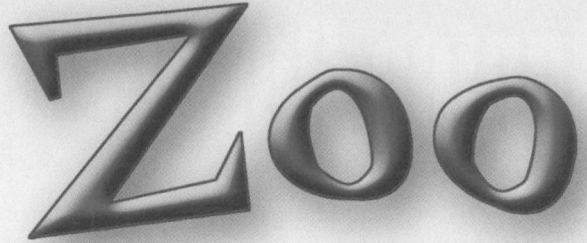

Zoo

by Edward D. Hoch

The children were always good during the month of August, especially when it began to get near the twenty-third. It was on this day that the great spaceship carrying Professor Hugo's Interplanetary Zoo settled down for its annual six-hour visit to the Chicago area.

Before daybreak the crowds would form, long lines of children and adults both, each one clutching his or her dollar and waiting with wonderment to see what race of strange creatures the Professor had brought this year.

In the past they had sometimes been treated to three-legged creatures from Venus, or tall, thin men from Mars, or even snake-like horrors from somewhere more distant. This year, as the great round ship settled slowly to Earth in the huge tri-city parking area just outside of Chicago, they watched with awe as the sides slowly slid up to reveal the familiar barred cages. In them were some wild breed of nightmare—small, horse-like animals that moved with quick, jerking motions and constantly chattered in a high-pitched tongue. The citizens of Earth clustered around as Professor Hugo's crew quickly collected the

240

PROFESSOR HUGO

⟲ Ask Questions | How will you find answers to questions you have?

241

waiting dollars, and soon the good Professor himself made an appearance, wearing his many-colored rainbow cape and top hat.

"Peoples of Earth," he called into his microphone. The crowd's noise died down and he continued. "Peoples of Earth, this year you see a real treat for your single dollar—the little-known horse-spider people of Kaan—brought to you across a million miles of space at great expense. Gather around, see them, study them, listen to them, tell your friends about them. But hurry! My ship can remain here only six hours!"

And the crowds slowly filed by, at once horrified and fascinated by these strange creatures that looked like horses but ran up the walls of their cages like spiders. "This is certainly worth a dollar," one man remarked, hurrying away. "I'm going home to get the wife."

All day long it went like that, until ten thousand people had filed by the barred cages set into the side of the spaceship. Then, as the six-hour limit ran out, Professor Hugo once more took the microphone in hand. "We must go now, but we will return next year on this date. And if you enjoyed our zoo this year, telephone your friends in other cities about it. We will land in New York tomorrow, and next week on to London, Paris, Rome, Hong Kong, and Tokyo. Then on to other worlds!"

He waved farewell to them, and as the ship rose from the ground, the Earth peoples agreed that this had been the very best Zoo yet. . . .

Some two months and three planets later, the ship of Professor Hugo settled at last onto the familiar jagged rocks of Kaan, and the odd horse-spider creatures filed quickly out of their cages. Professor Hugo was there to say a few parting words, and then they scurried away in a hundred different directions, seeking their homes among the rocks.

In one house, the she-creature was happy to see the return of her mate and offspring. She babbled a greeting in the strange tongue and hurried to embrace them. "It was a long time you were gone. Was it good?"

And the he-creature nodded. "The little one enjoyed it especially. We visited eight worlds and saw many things."

The little one ran up the wall of the cave. "On the place called Earth it was the best. The creatures there wear garments over their skins, and they walk on two legs."

"But isn't it dangerous?" asked the she-creature.

"No," her mate answered. "There are bars to protect us from them. We remain right in the ship. Next time you must come with us. It is well worth the nineteen commocs it costs."

And the little one nodded. "It was the very best Zoo ever. . . ."

Reading Across Texts

In "Goodbye to the Moon" and "Zoo," a father in each story travels with his child. Tell how the trip was different for the characters in each story.

Writing Across Texts Which parent and child do you think enjoyed themselves more? Write a paragraph telling why.

Compare & Contrast What surprise is caused by comparing the zoo visitors?

Comprehension

Skill
Graphic Sources

Strategy
Summarizing

 # Graphic Sources

- Graphic sources, or graphic aids, such as maps, charts, diagrams, pictures, and schedules, are used to show information visually.

- While reading, think about how the information in the graphic relates to what you read in the text. Sometimes the author will mention the graphic and explain how it connects to the text. At other times, you will need to make this connection on your own.

- Graphic sources are often used to summarize complex information.

Strategy: Summarizing

Summarizing helps you to determine which information in an article is most important. One kind of summary states the important ideas and does not include minor details. Another kind of summary can be in the form of a chart, graph, time line, or some other graphic aid, because the key information is put into the graphic with as few words as possible.

Rainfall in Egypt

Location	Rainfall as Inches per Year
Alexandria	7
Northern Sinai	5
Cairo	1
Aswan	1/10

1. Read "The Land of Egypt." Make a two-column chart similar to the one above for the section titled "Climate."

2. Use your own graphic organizer and the one above to help you write a summary of "The Land of Egypt."

The Land of Egypt

The Nile The Nile River is the most important body of water in Egypt. Aside from being the main source of fresh water, this mighty river divides Egypt into two sections, the Western and Eastern Deserts. A third area, the Sinai, is also a desert.

Mountains Egypt is not a completely flat country. There are mountains along the coast of the Red Sea. The highest of these rises 7,175 feet. The Sinai holds Egypt's highest mountain, Mount Catherine, which has an elevation of 8,668 feet.

Climate Egypt is a very sunny place. It averages 12 hours of sunshine per day in the summer, and about 10 hours in the winter. Winters are usually cool with temperatures around 65°F. In summer the highs range from 91°F in Cairo to 106°F in Aswan. Long winter cold spells and summer heat waves are not uncommon.

Precipitation On average, Egypt receives very little rain. Most of the rain comes during the winter months. However, the amount varies from place to place. The farther south you go in Egypt, the less it rains.

Strategy What is the most important information you read in this paragraph? You can summarize this first paragraph in one sentence.

Skill The map below can help you better understand the information in this paragraph.

Strategy Summarize the most important information in this paragraph.

Skill How did the "Rainfall in Egypt" graphic aid on page 244 help you understand the information presented in the article?

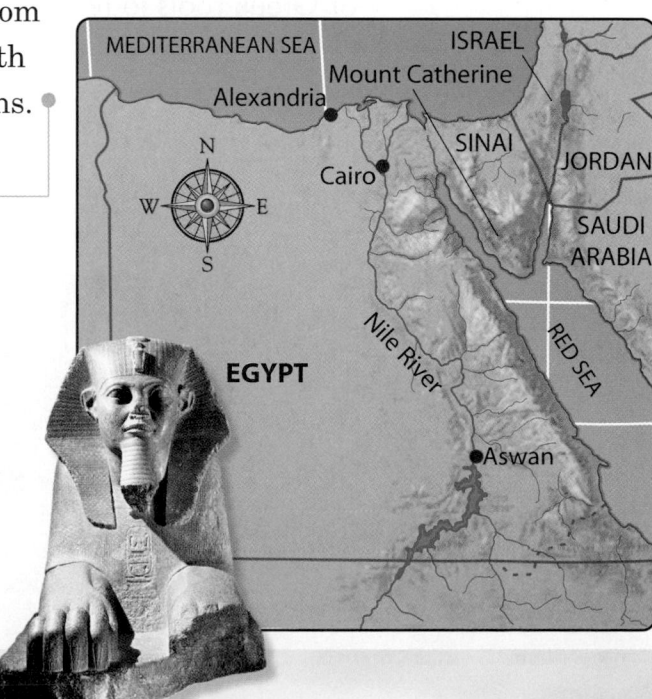

MEDITERRANEAN SEA
ISRAEL
Mount Catherine
Alexandria
SINAI
JORDAN
Cairo
SAUDI ARABIA
N
W E
S
EGYPT
Nile River
RED SEA
Aswan

Words to Know

reigned

decrees

artifacts

abundant

immortal

eternity

receded

Remember

Try the strategy. Then, if you need more help, use your glossary or a dictionary.

Vocabulary Strategy
for Latin and Greek Roots

Word Structure Many words in English are derived from Latin and Greek roots. If you recognize and know the meaning of a root, you can figure out an unfamiliar word's meaning. For example, *-mort-* is a Latin root meaning "death." (A mortal wound is a deadly one.) And *-reg-* or *-rex-* means "king." (*Tyrannosaurus rex* was king of the dinosaurs.)

1. Look at an unfamiliar word. Examine the word to see if it contains a Latin or Greek root you know.

2. Ask yourself how the meaning of the Latin or Greek root influences the meaning of the word.

3. Review the context in which the word is used. Does this meaning make sense?

4. If not, read on for other clues.

As you read "The Pharaohs of Egypt," look for Latin or Greek roots to help you find out the meanings of unfamiliar words.

The Pharaohs of Egypt

It has been more than 2,300 years since the last of the pharaohs reigned in Egypt, but we are still fascinated by these powerful rulers. They were believed to be gods. A pharaoh's power was absolute. The decrees of the ruler must be obeyed. His every wish would be carried out.

Artifacts from the tombs of the pharaohs tell us that they had fabulous wealth. Pharaohs were buried along with objects of solid gold inlaid with beautiful jewels. A royal tomb had many rooms in which abundant containers, furniture, and personal belongings were placed. Egyptians believed that the person who died would keep his earthly body in the next life, so he would need these belongings. In other words, Egyptians believed that a person could be immortal. He or she could enjoy food and clothing for all eternity.

We can only imagine what life was like for Egyptians so long ago. We know that a few were rich and many were poor. However, those favored few lived in splendor.

That ancient age has receded like the waters of the Nile River. Each year, the Nile's waters would rise and flood its banks. When the floods ended and the water went down, rich soil was left behind. Like the Nile's waters, the kings of Egypt have left a rich history.

Write

Look at the pictures in this selection and choose one to write about. Use as many words from the Words to Know list as you can.

Genre

Expository nonfiction explains the nature of something. Look for explanations about the nature of ancient Egyptian culture as you read.

EGYPT

by Ann Heinrichs

**Why is ancient Egypt
so important to us today?**

Detail showing Tutankhamen and Queen from decorated throne of Tutankhamen

Land of the Pharaohs

People were farming along the Nile as early as 7000 B.C. Eventually, they settled into two kingdoms—Upper Egypt in the south, and Lower Egypt in the northern Delta. In about 3100 B.C., Menes, a king of Upper Egypt, united the two kingdoms. Menes was honored as Egypt's first pharaoh, or king. (The word *pharaoh* comes from the words *per 'aa*, meaning "big house.")

Pharaohs liked to keep their power in the family. Ancient Egypt was governed by one dynasty, or ruling family, after another. Thirty-one dynasties of pharaohs reigned in Egypt between 3100 B.C. and 332 B.C.

Levels of Society

The pharaoh and his family were at the top rung of Egyptian society. They lived in great luxury. Alabaster lamps, golden beds and chairs, and exotic woods inlaid with ivory decorated their homes. Servants took care of their every need. Musicians and dancers amused guests at their lavish banquets. Other members of the upper class were priests, nobles, doctors, and high-ranking army officers.

Ancient Egyptian society greatly valued scribes. This painted limestone sculpture is on display at the Louvre Museum in Paris.

Artisans, merchants, and engineers made up the middle class. Scribes, or professional writers, held a special place of honor. Every family hoped to have a son who would become a scribe. The scribes wrote letters and government documents and recorded the pharaoh's decrees.

The common people were farmers, laborers, and soldiers. Farming took only part of the year so many farmers spent several months working on the pharaoh's construction projects.

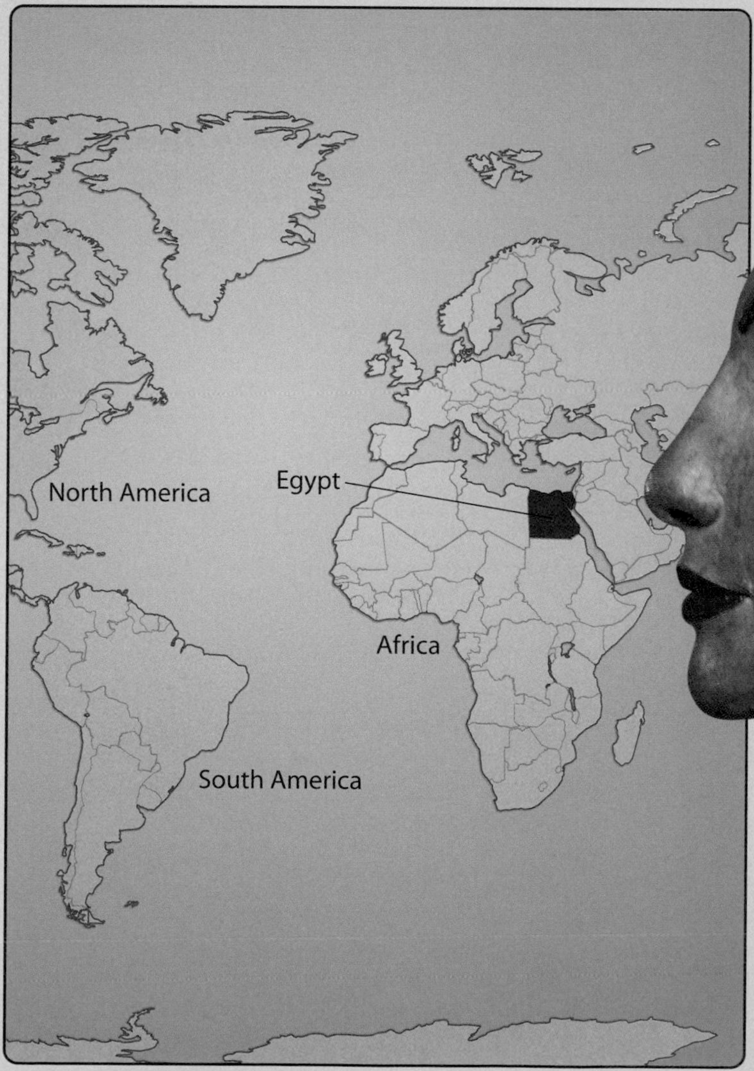

North America

Egypt

Africa

South America

Nefertiti, queen of Egypt during 1300s B.C., was noted for her beauty.

251

Love and Marriage

In ancient Egypt, love was an important part of marriage. Egyptians wrote beautiful love poems and songs. Druggists mixed love potions to help people charm their beloved. Pharaohs could keep several wives, but one wife was customary for everyone else.

Women in ancient Egypt had more rights than women in many cultures have today. They could own property, buy and sell goods, and inherit wealth. Wives could even sue for divorce if they had a good reason.

Statuette of Akhenaten and Nefertiti

Homes, Adornments, and Games

Most people lived in simple houses made of mud bricks. Very few of these houses remain today. Centuries of rain and wind have swept the soft materials away. In these simple homes, people sat and slept on woven mats on the floor. Candles and oil lamps provided light at night. Wealthy people had beautiful homes with dozens of rooms. Some were built around courtyards with gardens and pools.

Women kept their makeup in tiny bowls and jars. Cosmetics were made from minerals and plants. Gypsum was mixed with soot to make a sparkly eye shadow. A black substance called kohl was used as an eyeliner. Other substances made red coloring for lips and blush for cheeks.

Fresco painting of Nefertari playing *senet*

Women also painted their fingernails and wore hair ornaments. Upper-class women wore earrings, bracelets, armbands, and necklaces of gold and precious stones.

Both men and women wore lightweight linen skirts or robes. Lower-class people went barefoot, while the upper classes wore leather sandals. Shoulder-length head coverings protected workers from the heat of the sun. Upper-class men and women wore wigs. On festive evenings, women sometimes wore a cone of perfumed animal fat on their heads. As the night wore on, the fat melted, drenching them with sweet-smelling oil.

Ancient paintings and artifacts show how much the Egyptians loved games. Children played leapfrog and tug-of-war. Girls played catch with a ball, sometimes while riding piggyback. Wooden toys included monkeys on horseback and animals on wheels. Grown-ups played a game called *senet* by moving pieces on a checkered board. They played "snake" on a round board shaped like a coiled snake.

Ancient Cuisine

Egyptians ate using the first three fingers of the right hand. A typical meal might include vegetables such as broad beans, lentils, peas, cucumbers, or cabbage. People also enjoyed onions, garlic, turnips, and lettuce. Their fruit trees yielded figs, dates, and pomegranates. Other favorite fruits were melons and grapes.

Hunters went into the desert for wild game such as antelope and gazelle. In marshy areas, they shot ducks and geese with bows and arrows. Quail, pigeon, and beef were grilled or roasted. Fish from the Nile were salted or hung out to dry. Food was sweetened with honey collected from beehives.

Bread was a basic, everyday food. Pharaohs and nobles had their own bakeries. In most homes, women ground wheat and barley into flour and baked the loaves in clay pots or beehive-shaped clay ovens.

A wall relief which depicts men bearing poultry and joints of meats

The Cycle of Floods

Ancient Egyptians divided the year into three seasons of four months each. The new year began with the flooding of the Nile in July. This was the season of *akhet*. In November, as the waters receded, *peret*—the plowing and planting season—began. The dry season, *shemu*, lasted from March to July. Then crops were harvested and stored before the rains came again.

The floodwaters left a deposit of silt that fertilized the fields and produced abundant crops. Mud along the riverbank was made into pots, jars, tiles, and other ceramics. People measured the rise and fall of the Nile's water level with a *nilometer*—a series of marks on riverside rocks or cliffs.

Farmers produced more than enough food for Egypt's people. The pharaohs' storehouses brimmed over with food they collected as taxes. Ancient Egypt has been called the "granary [grainhouse] to the world." Grain and other crops were traded with neighboring peoples in Africa and Asia.

A hunting relief from the temple of Ramses II

Animal Life

Ancient Egypt swarmed with animals that no longer live there. Hippopotamuses bobbed in the Nile and lounged along the shore. Lions wandered in from the desert for water. Baboons and wildcats screeched in the thickets, and herds of gazelles trotted by. Golden jackals scoured the valleys for animal and human remains. Great flocks of rose-colored flamingos swooped in to nest along the Nile, and red-breasted geese flew in to winter in the marshes.

As the climate grew hotter and dryer, human settlements spread, and these animals went away. We know they once lived there because Egyptians left paintings of them. Ancient animals that still live in Egypt

Ancient Egyptian lion frescoe

255

include cobras, crocodiles, vultures, falcons, quails, and cows. Many animals were drawn in hieroglyphic symbols, and some were honored as gods.

Hieroglyphs

Egyptians were writing with picture symbols called hieroglyphs as early as 3000 B.C. Some hieroglyphs represented an object. For example, wavy lines stood for water, and a bird was—a bird. But a picture could also stand for an idea. Walking feet meant movement or the passage of time.

Some hieroglyphic symbols were homophones— words that sound alike but have different meanings. For example, the pharaoh Narmer's name was written

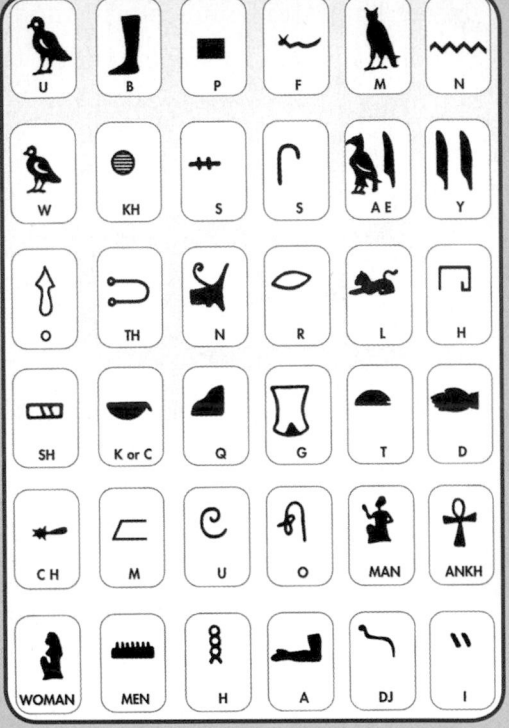

Chart of hieroglyphic symbols

as *n'r* (fish) plus *mr* (chisel). (Vowel sounds were often left out.) Some symbols stood for sounds. Others showed whether a word was singular or plural or a noun or a verb. By 300 B.C., the Egyptian alphabet consisted of more than 700 hieroglyphic symbols.

A loop with a royal name inside it was called a cartouche. You can make your cartouche using the symbols shown in the hieroglyphic chart.

Life Everlasting

The age of 110 was believed to be the perfect life span, but it was more an ideal than a reality. Most people in those days did not live past their thirties.

Hieroglyphs cover this obelisk at Luxor Temple.

256

But every Egyptian, from pharaoh to laborer, believed in life after death. Given the proper burial rites, they could be immortal.

The Egyptians believed that the jackal-headed god Anubis escorted each soul into the afterlife. Osiris, god of the underworld, made a final judgment by the "weighing of the heart." A feather was put on one side of a scale, and the person's heart on the other side. If the heart was as light as the feather, the soul could enter eternity.

Egyptians also believed that the dead would enjoy all their earthly comforts in the afterlife. Burial chambers were filled with favorite possessions, clothes, furniture, games, and food. Even pet cats were preserved and buried with their masters.

Mummies

After death, the body was made into a mummy to keep it from decaying. This ensured a successful journey into the afterlife. Mummification could take as long as seventy days.

First, the body was packed in a salt called natron, which dried the tissues and kept them from breaking down. Then the internal organs were removed. Some were preserved in jars and buried with the body. Other organs were treated with herbs and replaced in the body. The brain, believed to be worthless, was thrown away. Embalming fluids and pastes were then applied to preserve the skin and the body's interior.

Finally, the body was wrapped round and round with white linen strips. Mummies of some pharaohs were encased in jewel-encrusted gold and placed in a sarcophagus, or stone coffin,

A mummified body

257

in the burial chamber. Scrolls of the *Book of the Dead* were buried with the body. They contained special prayers and instructions for getting through the mysterious world of the dead.

Pyramids

To make sure they would have eternal life, pharaohs built fabulous tombs for themselves. The earliest pharaohs built tombs called *mastabas*—low, flat-topped, mud-brick structures with slanting sides.

Djoser, a pharaoh of the Third Dynasty, wanted a more glorious tomb, so his architect, Imhotep, built the first pyramid. It is called a step pyramid because its sides are like stair steps. Djoser's step pyramid still stands at Saqqara, near Memphis.

Fourth Dynasty pharaohs built the most famous pyramids—the three pyramids of Giza, just west of Cairo. Khufu built the largest one, called the Great Pyramid, around 2600 B.C.

> **GREAT PYRAMID FACTS**
>
> **Height:** 481 feet (147m)—taller than a forty-story building
>
> **Length of One Side:** 755 feet (230 m), or one-seventh of a mile
>
> **Area Covered:** 13 acres (5 ha), or about seven city blocks
>
> **Number of Limestone Blocks:** About 2.5 million
>
> **Average Weight of a Block:** 2.5 tons
>
> **Weight of Heaviest Blocks:** 15 tons
>
> **Contents:** Stolen by grave robbers, probably in ancient times

Two of the three pyramids of Giza. The capped pyramid of Khafre stands behind the Great Pyramid, also known as the Pyramid of Khufu.

A side view of the Great Sphinx in Giza, Egypt. The pyramid of Khafre looms in the background.

Khufu's pyramid was made of limestone blocks covered with sheer granite slabs that glistened in the sun. People could slide right down the sides. In later centuries, the granite was removed to make buildings in Cairo.

Khufu's son Khafre and the pharaoh Menkaure built the two other Giza pyramids. Nearby stands the Great Sphinx, a massive stone lion with the head of a man.

How Did They Build the Pyramids?

The ancient Egyptians left only a few clues about how they built the pyramids. From rock quarries at Aswan, stone blocks were floated down the Nile on rafts for 500 miles (800 km). Then the blocks were probably put on runners, like sleds, and hauled up wooden or stone ramps.

The Greek historian Herodotus says that 100,000 men worked on the Great Pyramid in three-month shifts. Then another 100,000 went to work. This went on for more than twenty years. How were the blocks lifted into place? According to Herodotus, they were lifted with a kind of crane that rested on lower-level stones.

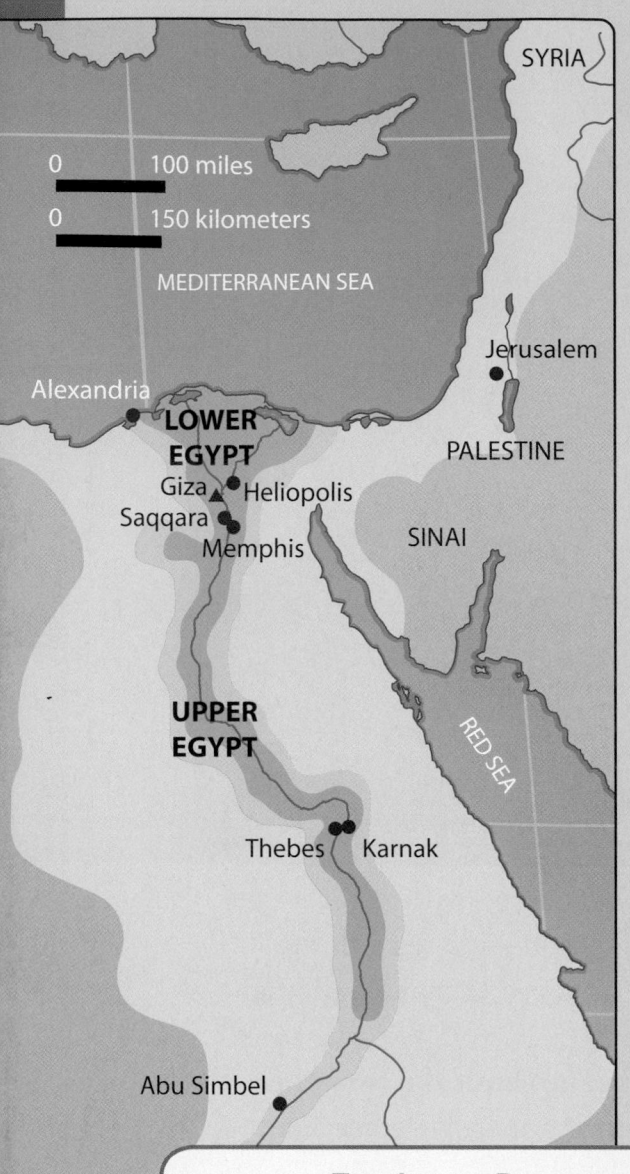

TIME LINE OF DYNASTIES

3110 B.C.	Founding of united Egypt by King Menes
C. 2686 B.C.–2160 B.C.	Old Kingdom
C. 2040 B.C.–1786 B.C.	Middle Kingdom
1570 B.C.–330 B.C.	New Kingdom

Ancient Egypt

- ▨ Old Kingdom
- ▨ Middle Kingdom
- ▨ New Kingdom

Kingdoms Unite and Divide

The history of ancient Egypt may be divided into three major periods—the Old Kingdom, the Middle Kingdom, and the New Kingdom. Memphis was Egypt's capital during the Old Kingdom period, beginning around 2686 B.C. Memphis lies about 15 miles (24 km) south of what is now Cairo. Even in this early period, Egyptians were making paper from papyrus fibers and writing in hieroglyphs.

In time, the pharaohs' power weakened, and Egypt once again broke into separate districts. Mentuhotep II pulled the kingdom together again around 2040 B.C. He built his capital at Thebes, on the Nile's east bank in Upper Egypt. His reign marks the beginning of the Middle Kingdom period. During this time, construction began on the temple of Amon at Karnak.

Asian people called the Hyksos rose to power in the 1600s B.C. They began ruling from their capital at Avaris in the Delta and later spread to Thebes. Egyptians learned much about the art of war from these foreign rulers. The Hyksos introduced horse-drawn chariots, bronze and iron swords, and other military gear.

The New Kingdom: Conquests and Construction

Ahmose, a Theban prince, drove the Hyksos out in the 1500s B.C. This began the New Kingdom period, with Thebes as the capital. With their new military skills, Egyptians now became a major world power. Under Thutmose III, they took over Nubia, Palestine, Syria, and northern Iraq. New lands meant new sources of wealth. Slaves, exotic woods, ivory, and precious metals and stones poured into the pharaohs' warehouses.

To show off their power, New Kingdom pharaohs built huge temples, monuments, and statues of themselves. Ramses II ("Ramses the Great") was the greatest builder of all. He built the temples of Abu Simbel and enlarged the temple at Karnak. Scholars also believe he was the pharaoh mentioned in the Bible's Book of Exodus story, in which Moses led the Hebrews out of slavery in Egypt.

For their tombs, New Kingdom rulers built huge necropolises, or cities of the dead. These tomb sites were on the west bank of the Nile, across from Thebes. Today they are named the Valley of the Kings, the Valley of the Queens, and the Tombs of the Nobles.

In 1995, archaeologist Kent Weeks discovered what may be the largest tomb in the Valley of the Kings. It holds most of Ramses II's fifty-two sons. So far, about sixty tombs have been found in the Valley of the Kings—only a fraction of those waiting to be discovered.

THE BOY KING

We know about Tutankhamen, or "King Tut," from his lavish tomb in the Valley of the Kings. Tutankhamen, the "boy king," reigned in the 1300s B.C. He died when he was about eighteen years old. More than 5,000 objects were found in his tomb, including furniture, games, weapons, and a golden chariot.

Reader Response

Open for Discussion   Picture yourself plopped down into the very heart of ancient Egypt. Based on what you've read here, describe what you observe and listen to on this visit.

1. Nonfiction can be *concise:* that is, it can give much information in not very much space. Explain, through examples, how Ann Heinrichs has made this article concise.

2. Do the graphic sources, such as the photos of Egyptian artifacts and the chart of hieroglyphic symbols, help you to better understand the text? Explain your answer.

3. In a few sentences, summarize the most influential parts of ancient Egypt's culture and how that culture has affected our own.

4. Create a hieroglyph or pictograph for some of the picturable words on the Words to Know list or from your life.

Look Back and Write   How long did Egypt exist under the thirty-one dynasties? Why is the length of time important? Look back at page 250 for help. Then write your response.

Meet the Author

Ann Heinrichs

Read more books by Ann Heinrichs.

While growing up in Arkansas, Ann Heinrichs read Doctor Dolittle books and became fascinated by faraway places. She now has traveled through the United States, Europe, Asia, and Africa. Her experiences in Egypt provided the background for this selection. She visited pyramids and tombs, and she rode a camel in the desert. She says, "Trips are fun, but the real work—tracking down all the factual information for a book—begins at the library. I head straight for the reference department. My favorite resources include United Nations publications, world almanacs, and the library's computer databases.

"To me, writing nonfiction is a bigger challenge than writing fiction. With nonfiction, you can't just dream something up; everything has to be researched. I study government reports, analyze statistics tables, then try to give the information a human face. And I'm always looking for what kids in the other countries are up to, so I can report back to kids here."

An author of more than one hundred books about countries throughout the world, Ms. Heinrichs also has two degrees in piano performance. She is also an award-winning martial artist who practices t'ai chi, nan chuan, and kung fu sword.

Pakistan: Enchantment of the World

Afghanistan

Expository Nonfiction

Genre

- Expository nonfiction gives factual information.

- Expository nonfiction can be presented in different ways or formats.

Text Features

- The question–answer format is a clear, logical way to organize information about the Rosetta Stone.

- The photograph gives you a helpful idea of the Rosetta Stone and its scripts.

Link to Social Studies

Locate Rosetta, Egypt, on a map. Find the Nile River and its delta. Is it surprising to you or is it logical that the French soldiers found the stone here? Why do you think this?

The Rosetta Stone

FROM THE BRITISH MUSEUM WEB SITE

What is the Rosetta Stone?

The Rosetta Stone is a stone with writing on it in two languages (Egyptian and Greek), using three scripts (hieroglyphic, demotic, and Greek).

Why is it in three different scripts?

The Rosetta Stone is written in three scripts because when it was written, there were three scripts being used in Egypt.

- The first was hieroglyphic, which was the script used for important or religious documents.

- The second was demotic, which was the common script of Egypt.

- The third was Greek, which was the language of the rulers of Egypt at that time.

The Rosetta Stone was written in all three scripts so that the priests, government officials, and rulers of Egypt could read what it said.

When was the Rosetta Stone made?

The Rosetta Stone was carved in 196 B.C.

When was the Rosetta Stone found?

The Rosetta Stone was found in 1799.

Who found the Rosetta Stone?

The Rosetta Stone was found by French soldiers who were rebuilding a fort in Egypt.

Where was the Rosetta Stone found?

The Rosetta Stone was found in a small village called Rosetta (Rashid) in the Delta of the Nile River.

Why is it called the Rosetta Stone?

It is called the Rosetta Stone because it was discovered in a town called Rosetta (Rashid).

What does the Rosetta Stone say?

The Rosetta Stone is a text written by a group of priests in Egypt to honor the Egyptian pharaoh. It lists all of the things that the pharaoh has done that are good for the priests and the people of Egypt.

Who deciphered hieroglyphs?

Many people worked on deciphering hieroglyphs over several hundred years. However, the structure of the script was very difficult to work out.

After many years of studying the Rosetta Stone and other examples of ancient Egyptian writing, Jean-François Champollion deciphered hieroglyphs in 1822.

How did Champollion decipher hieroglyphs?

Champollion could read both Greek and Coptic (the extinct language of Egypt that developed from ancient Egyptian).

He was able to figure out what the seven demotic signs in Coptic were. By looking at how these signs were used in Coptic he was able to work out what they stood for. Then he began tracing these demotic signs back to hieroglyphic signs.

By working out what some hieroglyphs stood for, he could make educated guesses about what the other hieroglyphs stood for.

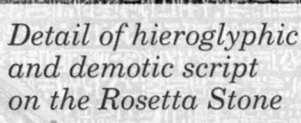

Detail of hieroglyphic and demotic script on the Rosetta Stone

Reading Across Texts

The Rosetta Stone honors an Egyptian pharaoh. What other ways of honoring pharaohs were stated in *Egypt?*

Writing Across Texts Make a list of ways in which pharaohs were honored in ancient Egyptian society.

 **Summarize** How can the question–answer format help you summarize?

Fossils

by Lilian Moore

Older than
books,
than scrolls,

older
than the first
tales told

or the
first words
spoken

are the stories

in the forests that
turned to
stone

in ice walls
that trapped the
mammoth

in the long
bones of
dinosaurs—

the fossil
stories that begin
Once upon a time

266

Tradition

by Eloise Greenfield

Pineapples! pumpkins! chickens! we
carry them on our heads you see
we can glide along forever
and not drop a thing, no never
never even use our hands
never put a finger to it
you know how we learned to do it?
knowledge came from other lands
Africans of long ago
passed it down to us and so
now we pass it on to you
for what is old is also new
pineapples, pumpkins, chickens, we
carry more than the things you see
we also carry history

Arrival

**by Florence Parry Heide
and Judith Heide Gilliland**

A very fast runner named Fay
ran faster and faster each day.
She was very athletic
and so energetic
she arrived at tomorrow today.

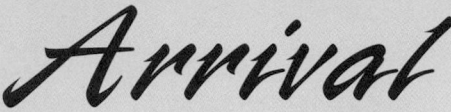

THE TIME MACHINE

by Florence Parry Heide and Judith Heide Gilliland

There was an inventor named Breen
who invented a Time Machine.
By mistake one time
he pressed rewind
and woke in his crib with a scream.

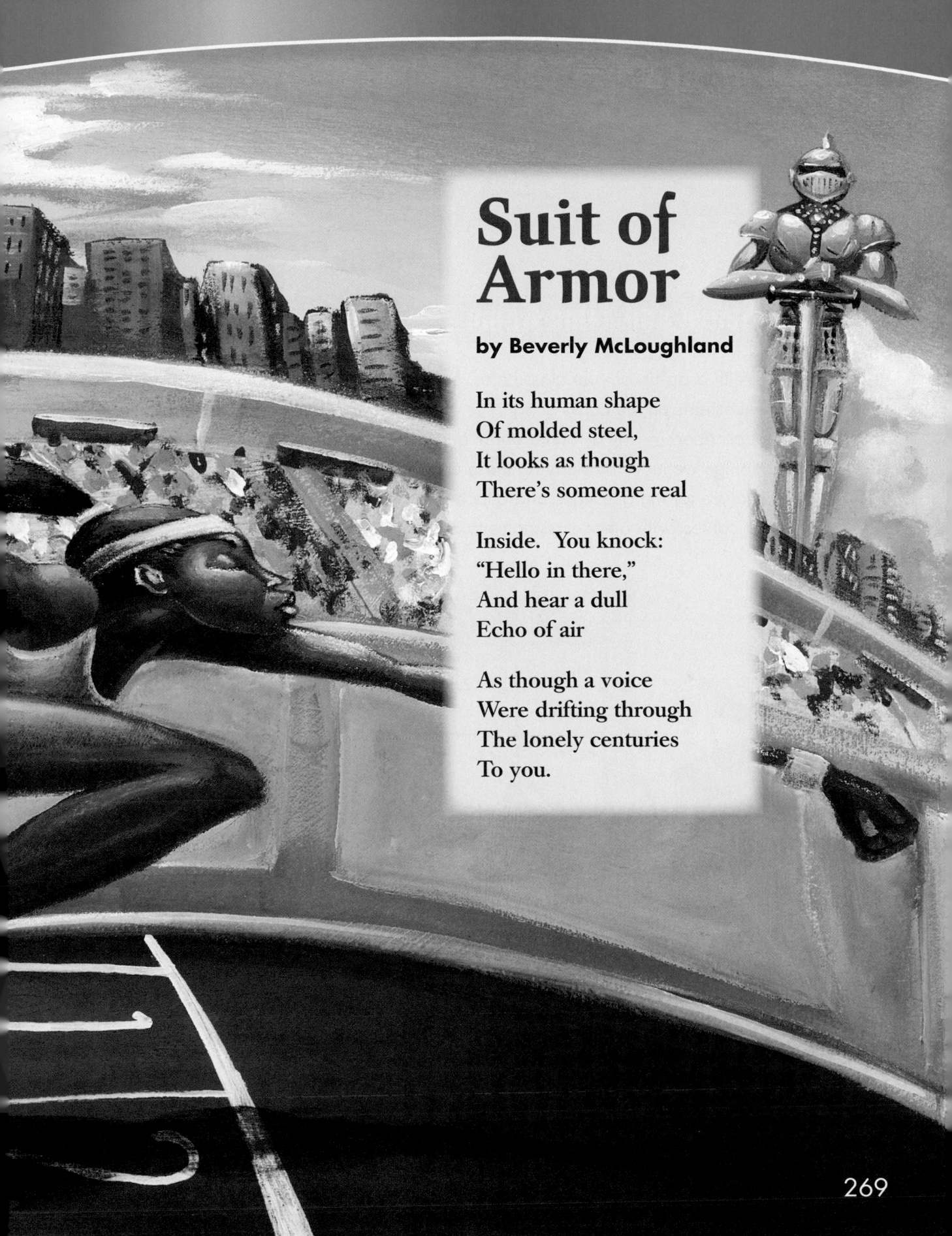

Suit of Armor

by Beverly McLoughland

In its human shape
Of molded steel,
It looks as though
There's someone real

Inside. You knock:
"Hello in there,"
And hear a dull
Echo of air

As though a voice
Were drifting through
The lonely centuries
To you.

Space and Time Game

connect to
SCIENCE

With a group of your classmates, construct a game by writing questions on file cards or squares of paper about the times and places described in Unit 2. Some of the questions should focus on important things we learn by studying these times and places. Assign point values for the questions and attach the cards to a board. Then have a contest with other classmates to answer the questions.

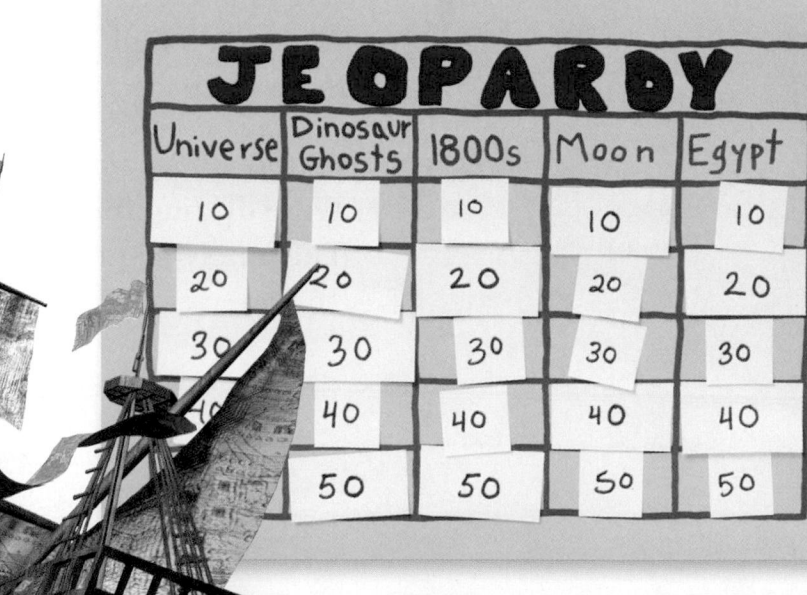

Why might things from far away and long ago be important to us now?

Time Machine

Build a model time machine or draw a picture of one. On the machine, write labels showing the time or place you read about in the unit. Then think about the place and time that you would most like to visit. Choose one and write a paragraph about what you would observe on your visit and a paragraph explaining why this visit would be an important choice.

If I Could Time Travel

Where	
When	
Why	
What to See	

Future Finds

What secrets of the natural world, ancient times, or outer space would you like to uncover some day? Write about your interest in one of these areas. Based on what you learned in Unit 2, also explain how certain findings from past explorations would help you to reach this goal.

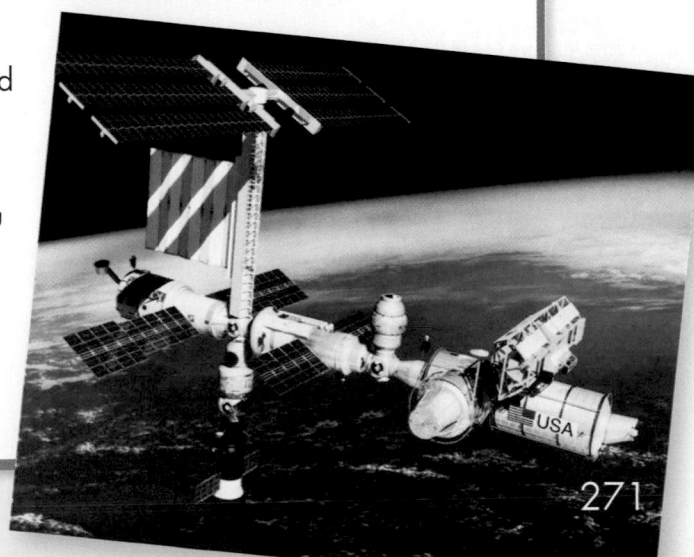

UNIT 3

Read It ONLINE
sfsuccessnet.com

Challenges and Obstacles

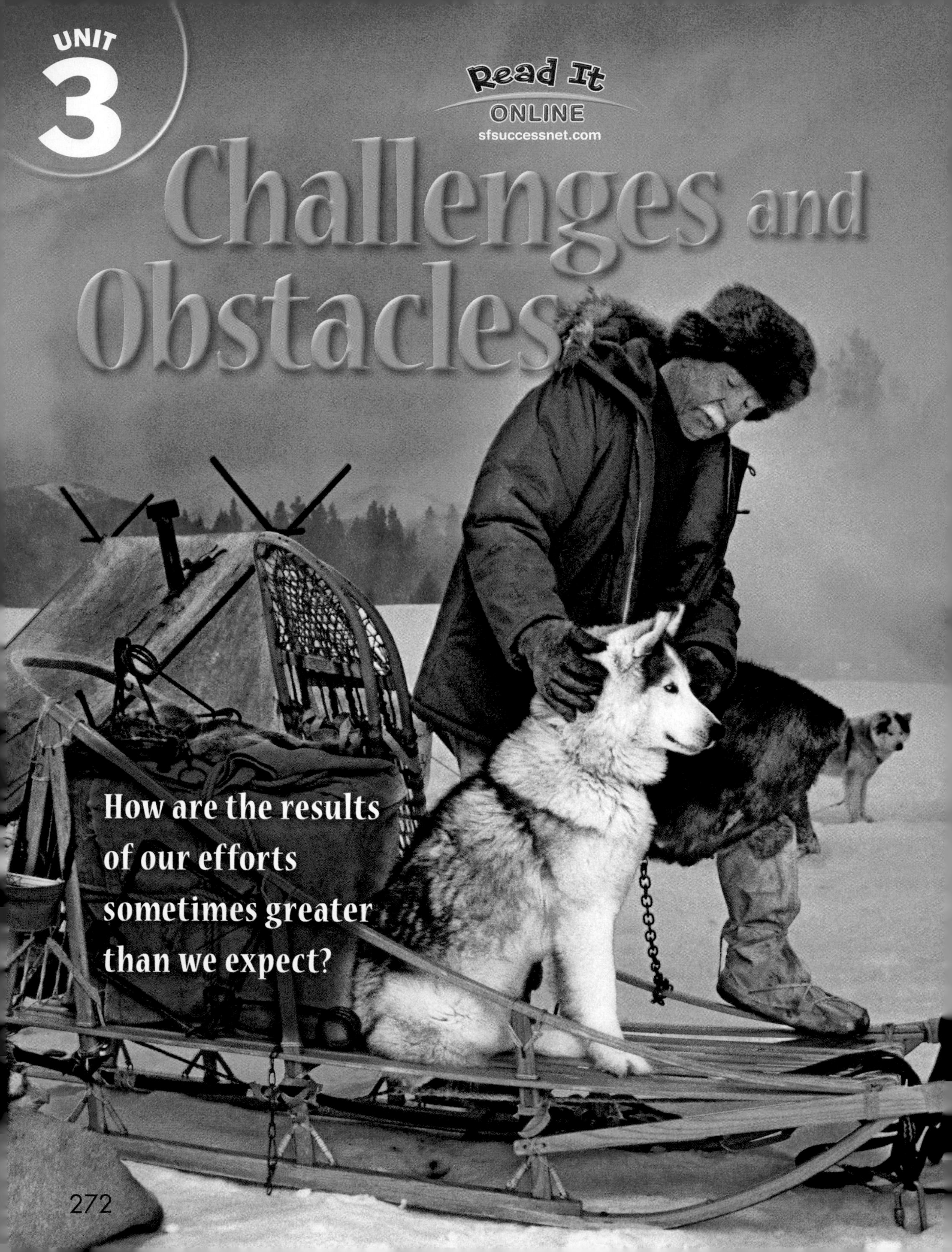

How are the results of our efforts sometimes greater than we expect?

connect to SOCIAL STUDIES

Hatchet
A boy learns to survive in the wild.

Realistic Fiction

connect to SOCIAL STUDIES

When Marian Sang
A woman finds her voice.

Biography

connect to SOCIAL STUDIES

Learning to Swim
A girl overcomes doubts about her strength.

Autobiography

connect to SOCIAL STUDIES

Juan Verdades: The Man Who Couldn't Tell a Lie
An employee is put to the test.

Folk Tale

connect to SOCIAL STUDIES

Elizabeth Blackwell: Medical Pioneer
An early American woman becomes a doctor.

Drama

Comprehension

Skill
Sequence

Strategy
Visualize

Sequence

- Sequence is the order of events in a story. Clue words such as *next, then,* and *yesterday* help to indicate the sequence in which events occur.

- Some events in a story happen simultaneously, or at the same time. Clue words such as *meanwhile* and *during* signal simultaneous events.

End

fourth event
third event
second event
first event

Beginning

Strategy: Visualize

Good readers visualize. That means they create pictures in their mind of what they read. They can become more involved in the story too — hearing the sounds, smelling the smells, touching and feeling objects. Visualizing helps you understand a story. It also is a good way to understand and keep track of the sequence of events.

1. Read "Incident at the Street Fair." Make a graphic organizer like the one above to keep track of the sequence of events in the story.

2. Select one of the main events on your sequence graphic organizer. Write a detailed description of the event as you visualize it.

Incident at the Street Fair

One Saturday Caleb, his sister Mandy, and their father rode the train downtown to the Garfield Street Festival. The street fair was packed with people!

First they treated themselves to some barbecue chicken and corn at a food booth. A live salsa band was entertaining the crowd from the main stage. While his father surveyed his festival map, Caleb gazed up at the glistening skyline, tilting his head w-a-a-a-y back.

"Dad, look at that awesome skyscraper," Caleb said, but there was no reply. Caleb anxiously glanced all around, but he didn't see a single familiar face.

Wide-eyed, Caleb wandered around, looking for his family in all directions. At one point he was sure he saw his father—the shirt was the same. But when Caleb pulled on the shirt and the person turned around, all Caleb saw was an old man eating a sloppy sandwich with barbecue sauce all over his face. Caleb was getting nervous.

The crowd swelled larger, and people bumped and jostled him. A rock band was now playing ear-blasting music. Then suddenly there was Mandy, and a moment later his father's face. It held a strange mixture of anger and relief.

Strategy Visualize the first event that has taken place in the story. What do you see in your mind?

Skill Which of the following events took place at the same time Caleb was looking at the skyline?
(a) He began to walk around.
(b) His father looked at a map.
(c) He ate chicken and corn.

Strategy Visualize Caleb's face at this point in the story. What event made him feel and look this way?

Skill What event marks the end of the story?

275

registered

stiffened

smoldered

hatchet

painstaking

ignite

quill

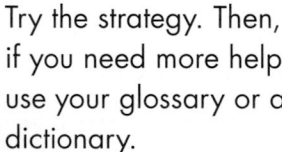

Remember

Try the strategy. Then, if you need more help, use your glossary or a dictionary.

Vocabulary Strategy
for Endings

Word Structure An ending is a letter or letters added to the end of a base word. For example, the endings *-ed* and *-ing* can be added to verbs to change their tense. You may be able to use endings to help you figure out the meanings of words.

1. Cover the ending and read the base word.

2. Think about the meaning of the base word. If you do not know its meaning, reread the sentence for clues that can help you.

3. See how the ending affects the meaning of the verb: *-ed* makes a verb show past action; *-ing* makes a verb show ongoing or current action. Sometimes the *-ed* or *-ing* form of a verb is used as an adjective, to describe.

4. Choose a meaning that seems correct and see if it makes sense in the sentence.

As you read "Wilderness Camp," use the endings *-ing* and *-ed* to help you figure out the meanings of verbs you do not know.

Wilderness Camp

I woke early to unfamiliar sounds. Slowly it registered in my mind that I was not at home but in a tent in the north woods of Michigan. My whole body had stiffened from sleeping with only a sleeping bag between me and the remarkably hard ground. Why had I signed on for Wilderness Camp? I wasn't sure I could take a month of roughing it.

Soon everyone was up and concentrating on breakfast. First we would have to build a fire. We had sat up late last night until the campfire was only ash and embers that smoldered. Our counselor Daniel had doused it well with water from the river. An unattended campfire could start a forest fire, and we didn't want that.

I took a hatchet and began to cut a dead branch into firewood. Daniel built the fire, using painstaking care. He started with wadded-up newspaper and small dead twigs. We would lean the larger pieces of wood around this and then ignite the paper. As we worked, I showed Daniel the curious hollow stick I had found yesterday. He told me it was a quill from a porcupine.

Write

Write a paragraph describing either how you would start a fire without matches or how you would survive in the woods. Use as many words from the Words to Know list as you can.

Hatchet

by Gary Paulsen

*Can a boy survive all alone
in the wilderness?*

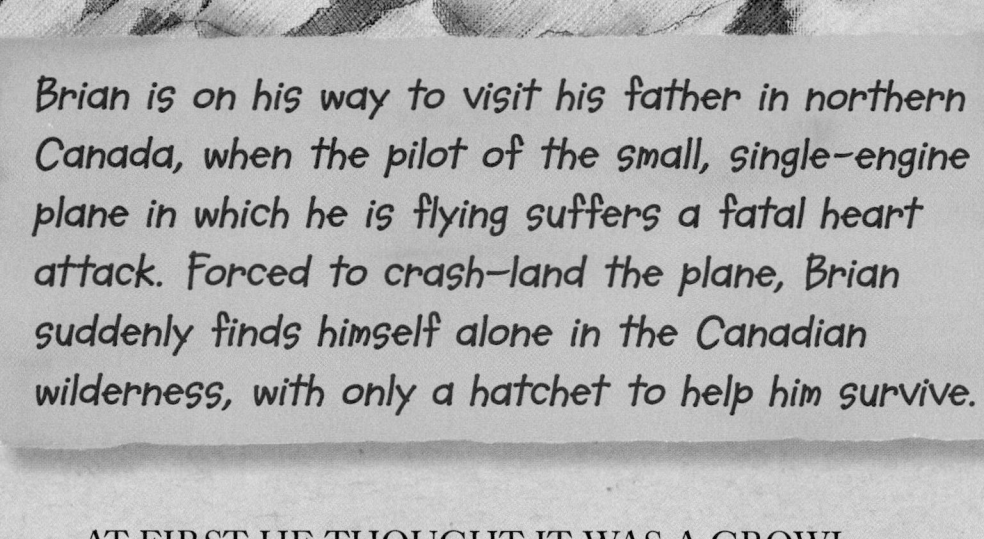

Brian is on his way to visit his father in northern Canada, when the pilot of the small, single-engine plane in which he is flying suffers a fatal heart attack. Forced to crash-land the plane, Brian suddenly finds himself alone in the Canadian wilderness, with only a hatchet to help him survive.

AT FIRST HE THOUGHT IT WAS A GROWL. In the still darkness of the shelter in the middle of the night his eyes came open and he was awake and he thought there was a growl. But it was the wind, a medium wind in the pines had made some sound that brought him up, brought him awake. He sat up and was hit with the smell.

It terrified him. The smell was one of rot, some musty rot that made him think only of graves with cobwebs and dust and old death. His nostrils widened and he opened his eyes wider, but he could see nothing. It was too dark, too hard dark with clouds covering even the small light from the stars, and he could not see. But the smell was alive, alive and full and in the shelter. He thought of the bear, thought of Bigfoot and every monster he had ever seen in every fright movie he had ever watched, and his heart hammered in his throat. Then he heard the slithering. A brushing sound, a slithering brushing sound near his feet—and he kicked out as hard as he could, kicked out and threw the hatchet at the sound, a noise coming from his throat. But the hatchet missed, sailed into the wall where it hit the rocks with a shower of sparks, and his leg was instantly torn with pain, as if a hundred needles had been driven into it. "Unnnngh!"

Now he screamed, with the pain and fear, and skittered on his backside up into the corner of the shelter, breathing through his mouth, straining to see, to hear.

The slithering moved again, he thought toward him at first, and terror took him, stopping his breath. He felt he could see a low dark form, a bulk in the darkness, a shadow that lived, but now it moved away, slithering and scraping it moved away, and he saw or thought he saw it go out of the door opening.

He lay on his side for a moment, then pulled a rasping breath in and held it, listening for the attacker to return. When it was apparent that the shadow wasn't coming back he felt the calf of his leg, where the pain was centered and spreading to fill the whole leg.

His fingers gingerly touched a group of needles that had been driven through his pants and into the fleshy part of his calf. They were stiff and very sharp on the ends that stuck out, and he knew then what the attacker had been. A porcupine had stumbled into his shelter and when he had kicked it, the thing had slapped him with its tail of quills.

He touched each quill carefully. The pain made it seem as if dozens of them had been slammed into his leg, but there were only eight, pinning the cloth against his skin. He leaned back against the wall for a minute. He couldn't leave them in, they had to come out, but just touching them made the pain more intense.

So fast, he thought.

So fast things change.

When he'd gone to sleep he had satisfaction and in just a moment it was all different. He grasped one of the quills, held his breath, and jerked. It sent pain signals to his brain in tight waves, but he grabbed another, pulled it, then another quill. When he had pulled four of them he stopped for a moment. The pain had gone from being a pointed injury pain to spreading in a hot smear up his leg, and it made him catch his breath.

Some of the quills were driven in deeper than others, and they tore when they came out. He breathed deeply twice, let half of the breath out, and went back to work. Jerk, pause, jerk—and three more times before he lay back in the darkness, done. The pain filled his leg now, and with it came new waves of self-pity. Sitting alone in the dark, his leg aching, some mosquitos finding him again, he started crying. It was all too much, just too much, and he couldn't take it. Not the way it was.

I can't take it this way, alone with no fire and in the dark, and next time it might be something worse, maybe a bear, and it wouldn't be just quills in the leg, it would be worse. *I can't do this,* he thought, again and again. *I can't.* Brian pulled himself up until he was sitting upright back in the corner of the cave. He put his head down on his arms across his knees, with stiffness taking his left leg, and cried until he was cried out.

He did not know how long it took, but later he looked back on this time of crying in the corner of the dark cave and thought of it as when he learned the most important rule of survival, which was that feeling sorry for yourself didn't work. It wasn't just that it was wrong to do, or that it was considered incorrect. It was more than that—it didn't work. When he sat alone in the darkness and cried and was done, was all done with it, nothing had changed. His leg still hurt, it was still dark, he was still alone, and the self-pity had accomplished nothing.

At last he slept again, but already his patterns were changing and the sleep was light, a resting doze more than a deep sleep, with small sounds awakening him twice in the rest of the night. In the last doze period before daylight, before he awakened finally with the morning light and the clouds of new mosquitos, he dreamed. This time it was not of his mother, but of his father at first and then of his friend Terry.

In the initial segment of the dream his father was standing at the side of a living room looking at him, and it was clear from his expression that he was trying to tell Brian something. His lips moved but there was no sound, not a whisper. He waved his hands at Brian, made gestures in front of his face as if he were scratching something, and he worked to make a word with his mouth but at first Brian could not see it. Then the lips made an *mmmmm* shape but no sound came. *Mmmmm-maaaa.* Brian could not hear it, could not understand it and he wanted to so badly; it was so important to understand his father, to know what he was saying. He was trying to help, trying so hard, and when Brian couldn't understand he looked cross, the way he did when Brian asked questions more than once, and he faded. Brian's father faded into a fog place Brian could not see, and the dream was almost over, or seemed to be, when Terry came.

He was not gesturing to Brian but was sitting in the park at a bench looking at a barbecue pit and for a time nothing happened. Then he got up and poured some charcoal from a bag into the cooker, then some starter fluid, and he took a flick type of lighter and lit the fluid. When it was burning and the charcoal was at last getting hot he turned, noticing Brian for the first time in the dream. He turned and smiled and pointed to the fire as if to say, *see, a fire.*

But it meant nothing to Brian, except that he wished he had a fire. He saw a grocery sack on the table next to Terry. Brian thought it must contain hot dogs and chips and mustard, and he could think only of the food. But Terry shook his head and pointed again to the fire, and twice more he pointed to the fire, made Brian see the flames, and Brian felt his frustration and anger rise and he thought *all right, all right, I see the fire but so what? I don't have a fire.*

I know about fire;
I know I need a fire.
I know that.

His eyes opened and there was light in the cave, a gray dim light of morning. He wiped his mouth and tried to move his leg, which had stiffened like wood. There was thirst, and hunger, and he ate some raspberries from the jacket. They had spoiled a bit, seemed softer and mushier, but still had a rich sweetness. He crushed the berries against the roof of his mouth with his tongue and drank the sweet juice as it ran down his throat. A flash of metal caught his eye, and he saw his hatchet in the sand where he had thrown it at the porcupine in the dark.

He scootched up, wincing a bit when he bent his stiff leg, and crawled to where the hatchet lay. He picked it up and examined it and saw a chip in the top of the head.

The nick wasn't large, but the hatchet was important to him, was his only tool, and he should not have thrown it. He should keep it in his hand and make a tool of some kind to help push an animal away. *Make a staff,* he thought, *or a lance, and save the hatchet.* Something came then, a thought as he held the hatchet, something about the dream and his father and Terry, but he couldn't pin it down.

"Ahhh . . ." He scrambled out and stood in the morning sun and stretched his back muscles and his sore leg. The hatchet was still in his hand, and as he stretched and raised it over his head it caught the first rays of the morning sun. The first faint light hit the silver of the hatchet and, flashed a brilliant gold in the light. Like fire. *That is it,* he thought. *What they were trying to tell me.*

Fire. The hatchet was the key to it all. When he threw the hatchet at the porcupine in the cave and missed and hit the stone wall, it had showered sparks, a golden shower of sparks in the dark, as golden with fire as the sun was now.

The hatchet was the answer. That's what his father and Terry had been trying to tell him. Somehow he could get fire from the hatchet. The sparks would make fire.

Brian went back into the shelter and studied the wall. It was some form of chalky granite, or a sandstone, but imbedded in it were large pieces of a darker stone, a harder and darker stone. It only took him a moment to find where the hatchet had struck. The steel had nicked into the edge of one of the darker stone pieces. Brian turned the head backward so he would strike with the flat rear of the hatchet and hit the black rock gently. Too gently, and nothing happened. He struck harder, a glancing blow, and two or three weak sparks skipped off the rock and died immediately.

He swung harder, held the hatchet so it would hit a longer, sliding blow, and the black rock exploded in fire. Sparks flew so heavily that several of them skittered and jumped on the sand beneath the rock, and he smiled and struck again and again.

There could be fire here, he thought.

sandstone

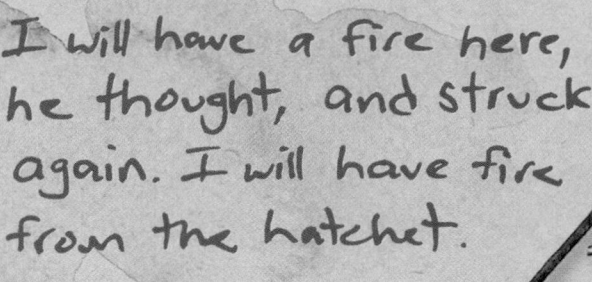

I will have a fire here,
he thought, and struck
again. I will have fire
from the hatchet.

Brian found it was
a long way from sparks to fire.

Clearly there had to be something for the sparks to ignite,
some kind of tinder or kindling—but what? He brought some
dried grass in, tapped sparks into it and watched them die.
He tried small twigs, breaking them into little pieces, but that
was worse than the grass. Then he tried a combination of the
two, grass and twigs.

Nothing. He had no trouble getting sparks, but the tiny bits
of hot stone or metal—he couldn't tell which they were—just
sputtered and died.

He settled back on his haunches in exasperation, looking
at the pitiful clump of grass and twigs.

He needed something finer, something soft and fine and
fluffy to catch the bits of fire.

Shredded paper would be nice, but he had no paper.

"So close," he said aloud, "so close. . . ."

He put the hatchet back in his belt and went out of the
shelter, limping on his sore leg. There had to be something,
had to be. Man had made fire. There had been fire for thousands,
millions of years. There had to be a way. He dug in his pockets
and found the twenty-dollar bill in his wallet. Paper. Worthless
paper out here. But if he could get a fire going. . . .

He ripped the twenty into tiny pieces, made a pile of pieces, and hit sparks into them. Nothing happened. They just wouldn't take the sparks. But there had to be a way—some way to do it.

Not twenty feet to his right, leaning out over the water were birches, and he stood looking at them for a full half-minute before they registered on his mind. They were a beautiful white with bark like clean, slightly speckled paper.

Paper.

He moved to the trees. Where the bark was peeling from the trunks it lifted in tiny tendrils, almost fluffs. Brian plucked some of them loose, rolled them in his fingers. They seemed flammable, dry, and nearly powdery. He pulled and twisted bits off the trees, packing them in one hand while he picked them with the other, picking and gathering until he had a wad close to the size of a baseball.

Then he went back into the shelter and arranged the ball of birchbark peelings at the base of the black rock. As an afterthought he threw in the remains of the twenty-dollar bill. He struck and a stream of sparks fell into the bark and quickly died. But this time one spark fell on one small hair of dry bark—almost a thread of bark—and seemed to glow a bit brighter before it died.

The material had to be finer. There had to be a soft and incredibly fine nest for the sparks.

I must make a home for the sparks, he thought. A perfect home or they won't stay or they won't make a fire.

He started ripping the bark, using his fingernails at first, and when that didn't work he used the sharp edge of the hatchet, cutting the bark in thin slivers, hairs so fine they were almost not there. It was painstaking work, slow work, and he stayed with it for over two hours. Twice he stopped for a handful of berries and once to go to the lake for a drink. Then back to work, the sun on his back, until at last he had a ball of fluff as big as a grapefruit—dry birchbark fluff.

He positioned his spark nest—as he thought of it—at the base of the rock, used his thumb to make a small depression in the middle, and slammed the back of the hatchet down across the black rock. A cloud of sparks rained down, most of them missing the nest, but some, perhaps thirty or so, hit in the depression and, of those, six or seven found fuel and grew, smoldered and caused the bark to take on the red glow.

Then they went out.

Close—he was close. He repositioned the nest, made a new and smaller dent with his thumb, and struck again.

More sparks, a slight glow, then nothing.

It's me, he thought. *I'm doing something wrong. I do not know this—a cave dweller would have had a fire by now, a Cro-Magnon man would have a fire by now—but I don't know this. I don't know how to make a fire.*

Maybe not enough sparks. He settled the nest in place once more and hit the rock with a series of blows, as fast as he could. The sparks poured like a golden waterfall. At first they seemed to take, there were several, many sparks that found life and took briefly, but they all died.

Starved.

He leaned back. They are like me. They are starving. It wasn't quantity, there were plenty of sparks, but they needed more.

I would kill, he thought suddenly, *for a book of matches. Just one book. Just one match. I would kill.*

What makes fire? He thought back to school. To all those science classes. Had he ever learned what made a fire? Did a teacher ever stand up there and say, "This is what makes a fire…"

He shook his head, tried to focus his thoughts. What did it take? *You have to have fuel,* he thought—and he had that. The bark was fuel. Oxygen—there had to be air.

He needed to add air. He had to fan on it, blow on it.

He made the nest ready again, held the hatchet backward, tensed, and struck four quick blows. Sparks came down and he leaned forward as fast as he could and blew.

Too hard. There was a bright, almost intense glow, then it was gone. He had blown it out.

Another set of strikes, more sparks. He leaned and blew, but gently this time, holding back and aiming the stream of air from his mouth to hit the brightest spot. Five or six sparks had fallen in a tight mass of bark hair, and Brian centered his efforts there.

The sparks grew with his gentle breath. The red glow moved from the sparks themselves into the bark, moved and grew and became worms, glowing red worms that crawled up the bark hairs and caught other threads of bark and grew until there was a pocket of red as big as a quarter, a glowing red coal of heat.

And when he ran out of breath and paused to inhale, the red ball suddenly burst into flame.

"Fire!" He yelled. "I've got fire! I've got it, I've got it, I've got it….."

But the flames were thick and oily and burning fast, consuming the ball of bark as fast as if it were gasoline. He had to feed the flames, keep them going. Working as fast as he could he carefully placed the dried grass and wood pieces he had tried at first on top of the bark and was gratified to see them take.

But they would go fast. He needed more, and more. He could not let the flames go out.

He ran from the shelter to the pines and started breaking off the low, dead, small limbs. These he threw in the shelter, went back for more, threw those in, and squatted to break and feed the hungry flames. When the small wood was going well he went out and found larger wood and did not relax until that was going. Then he leaned back against the wood brace of his door opening and smiled.

I have a friend, he thought—*I have a friend now. A hungry friend, but a good one. I have a friend named fire.*

" Hello, fire... "

The curve of the rock back made an almost perfect drawing flue that carried the smoke up through the cracks of the roof but held the heat. If he kept the fire small it would be perfect and would keep anything like the porcupine from coming through the door again.

A friend and a guard, he thought.

So much from a little spark. A friend and a guard from a tiny spark.

Reader Response

Open for Discussion Starting with a growl and ending with finding a friend in fire, could you act or direct this story without a script? Describe the action, bit by bit, for the entire sequence.

1. Read a page aloud, slowly and deliberately. Notice this: the pace of your reading matches the pace of Brian's movements. How does this matching pace help the story come alive?

2. Describe the sequence of events that occurred between Brian making sparks by throwing his hatchet against a rock and when he actually made a fire.

3. Look back at pages 281–282. Reread the passage that describes Brian examining his leg after the porcupine attack. Describe what you picture in your mind as you read this passage.

4. Write a journal entry that Brian might have made when his ordeal was over. Use words from the Words to Know list and the story.

Look Back and Write On page 283, Brian believes he has learned the most important rule of survival. Write that rule and why it is important.

292

Meet the Author

Gary Paulsen

Read more books about survival in the wilderness.

G ary Paulsen is one of the most important writers of books for young people in America today. *Hatchet* is a Newbery Honor Book (an important book award), as are two of his other novels.

He recalls how his life changed the day he met a librarian who encouraged him to read. To earn money, he was selling newspapers and went into a library to warm up. He says, "The librarian asked me if I would like a library card. I was a real cocky kid, and I said, 'Sure, why not.' So she gave me a card, and the most astonishing thing happened. This silly little card with my name on it gave me an identity I had not had. I felt I had become somebody."

Through his life, he has tried a number of jobs, from construction worker and ranch hand to sailor. He has run the Iditarod, the Alaskan dog sled race, twice. All of these adventures provided material for his writing. He is currently planning new adventures sailing on the high seas. Of his ten tips for survival, the first is "Stop. Don't panic. Breathe deeply and make yourself think slowly."

Brian's Winter
by Gary Paulsen

My Side of the Mountain
by Jean Craighead George

Expository Nonfiction

Genre

- Expository nonfiction provides information about people, places, events, and activities.

- Photos help the reader understand the information.

- Sometimes such articles seem to persuade—the reader wants to participate in what is described.

Text Features

- The author quotes the founders and campers to give further details about the camp and its purpose.

- The photographs help the reader visualize what takes place at the camp.

Link to Science

Choose and research one of the survival skills taught at Deep Wilds (making a shelter, foraging, and tracking). Using things in nature from your area, how could you survive alone and without supplies?

Call of the Deep Wilds

by Helen Strahinich

A summer camp teaches life skills to young people.

Jeannie McGartland used to be afraid of lots of things. She was frightened of the dark. She would get spooked by bees, hornets, and spiders, and she was so afraid of fire that she wouldn't even light a match.

Then one day, when Jeannie was ten years old, she enrolled in Deep Wilds, an unusual school in Brattleboro, Vermont. At overnight camps and day programs operated by Deep Wilds, kids learn how to survive, and even thrive, in the wilderness with little more than the clothes on their backs.

At Deep Wilds, Jeannie learned many useful skills, including how to make a fire using only two sticks. If Jeannie were to get lost in the woods now, she would know just how to use branches and leaves to make a shelter sturdy enough to withstand a fierce storm. And if she were to run out of food, no problem: Jeannie has learned to tell the difference between the plants that will nourish her and those that are poisonous. She can even distinguish beavers, bobcats, and coyotes from the appearance of their tracks.

Thanks to Deep Wilds, Jeannie, who lives in southern New Hampshire, has learned other valuable lessons as well: "I really learned about myself. I learned how to be aware of myself in my surroundings and of other people around me. I'm not as self-absorbed as I used to be."

Jeannie's words are music to the ears of her teachers, Mark Morey and Steve Young. When Morey and Young founded Deep Wilds in 1994, their goal was to help kids understand the natural world and find their place in it. The two met during a wilderness survival course in upstate New York. Until then, Steve had been confused about what he wanted to do with his life. But he and Mark discovered they

A group of campers prepare a raft before putting it into the water.

Sequence   Do you understand how and why Jeannie changed?

shared the same passions for nature and for teaching.

"Mark wanted to make a difference in the world, and so did I," Steve recalls.

Since then, Deep Wilds has blossomed into a full array of overnight and day camps. For kids ages seven to eleven, Deep Wilds offers

primitive cooking—using a stick and a rock to start a fire

the River Otter Day Camp. For girls ages nine to twelve and boys ten and twelve, there's overnight Raccoon Camp. And for teenagers ages thirteen to seventeen, Deep Wilds hosts its Coyote Camp.

Whatever their ages, Deep Wilds campers acquire all the skills necessary to survive in the wilderness. They learn how to forage for Indian cucumbers, wild groundnuts, onions, and nutritious greens, as well as blueberries, raspberries, and blackberries. They also learn to bake berry pies in "wilderness ovens," as Mark calls them, which campers make from mud, clay, stones, and straw. As well, they fashion their own spoons and bowls using hot charcoals and knives. Deep Wilds staffers also teach campers how to make "wilderness sleeping bags" from branches and leaves.

"This is real-time living off the land," says Mark. "We don't mess around. We don't need backpacks, sleeping bags, or tents. This is what our ancestors did to stay alive. *All* our ancestors."

But Deep Wilds is also about having fun. Campers learn to make slings with rope harvested from milkweed fibers. They make the bows and arrows they use from hickory branches and animal feathers. And at the end of the day, they get to break into smaller groups and play all-night tag games, using their wilderness tracking and stalking skills.

Visualize   To read this better, imagine yourself in the wilderness.

When Deep Wilds campers are ready, they get to do a "solo," which entails spending a whole night alone in the woods (under staff supervision, of course). Thirteen-year-old Liam Purvis, who lives in upstate New York, did his first solo last summer. He says it taught him how to be "a more self-reliant individual."

"When you're out there in the middle of everything, you find out who you are inside the baggy pants and the tee shirt."

As for Jeannie McGartland, she is now fourteen and a half and plans on becoming a counselor-in-training (CIT) this summer. "I used to be a fearful person," says Jeannie. "Now I'm learning how to help others conquer their fears."

a camper writing a letter in the wild

"When you're out there in the middle of everything, you find out who you are inside the baggy pants and the tee shirt." —Liam Purvis

Reading Across Texts

How would Brian, from *Hatchet,* have been better prepared by attending Deep Wilds?

Writing Across Texts Write about how Brian would have benefited from Deep Wilds.

Comprehension

Skill
Generalize

Strategy
Generate Questions

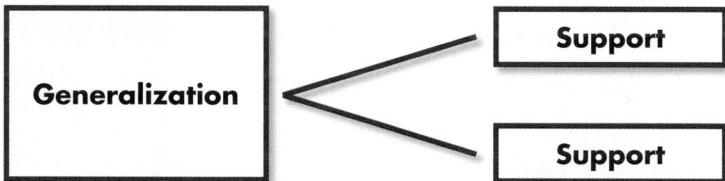

Generalize

- Sometimes authors write broad statements that apply to many examples. These statements are called generalizations. Often, clue words such as *most*, *all*, *sometimes*, *always*, and *never* help to identify generalizations.

- Generalizations supported by facts and logic are called valid generalizations. Faulty generalizations are not supported by facts.

- Generalizations should always be supported with facts from the text or your knowledge of the world.

```
┌─────────────────┐              ┌──────────────┐
│                 │──────────────│   Support    │
│ Generalization  │<             └──────────────┘
│                 │──────────────┌──────────────┐
└─────────────────┘              │   Support    │
                                 └──────────────┘
```

Strategy: Generate Questions

Active readers ask questions while they read. This can help them understand the text, make predictions, and determine the author's purpose. Asking questions is also useful when deciding whether or not an author's generalizations are valid or faulty. To evaluate generalizations, ask questions like, "Is this statement accurate?" or "Do the facts in the article or story support this generalization?"

1. Read "Ashley Helps Out" Make a graphic organizer like the one above to make a generalization about Ashley.

2. Write a paragraph making a generalization about Ashley and supporting it.

298

Ashley Helps Out

"I'll get it, Mom," said Ashley. She walked quickly to the buzzer and pressed it, granting her friend Karina entrance to the apartment. Ashley loved living in the apartment with her mother, but who wouldn't? Apartments are always better to live in than houses because you don't have to trim the hedges, and they are always luxurious inside.

"Mom, Karina and I are going to the shelter now, okay?"

"Okay, baby," said a groggy voice from the back bedroom. Ashley's mother usually worked nights and had to sleep during the day.

At the homeless shelter, the girls volunteered to help serve dinner to the people temporarily living there. Although the food wasn't particularly tasty (it never is at homeless shelters), Ashley dispensed the food with a smile and an encouraging word. Several hours later, the girls finished up and returned to the apartment.

"Mom, we're home," Ashley called as she entered.

"Hello, sweetie," said her mom, just waking up.

"Karina, how about we fix my mom a little dinner— or is it breakfast—while she gets ready for work?" said Ashley. Together, they made some tuna fish sandwiches and a Greek salad. When Ashley's mother moseyed out of the bedroom, she saw a lovingly prepared dinner on the table.

"Aw, sweetie, you're too much!" said her mom.

Strategy Asking questions before you read can help you predict what a story might be about. What questions come to mind from the title alone?

Skill Which of the following could you ask yourself to help determine if the author's generalization about apartments is valid or faulty?
(a) Are *all* apartments luxurious?
(b) Why doesn't Ashley live in a house?
(c) Does the apartment have hedges?

Strategy Write down some questions you have about Ashley's mother. See if they will be answered as you read.

Skill Is the generalization about homeless shelter food valid or faulty? Why do you think so?

Words to Know

opera

formal

recital

prejudice

privileged

application

momentous

dramatic

enraged

Remember

Try the strategy. Then, if you need more help, use your glossary or a dictionary.

Vocabulary Strategy
for Suffixes

Word Structure A suffix is a word part added to the end of a base word that changes its meaning, the way it is used in a sentence, and sometimes how it is spelled. The suffix *-ic* adds the meaning "pertaining to or associated with," as in *romantic*. The suffix *-ous* adds the meaning "full of," as in *joyous*. The suffix *-ation* makes a noun out of a verb, usually adding the meaning "the state of being," as in *starvation*. Knowing the meaning of a suffix may help you figure out the meaning of a word.

1. Look at the unknown word. See if you recognize a base word in it.

2. Check to see if the suffix *-ic*, *-ation*, or *-ous* has been added to the base word.

3. Ask yourself how the added suffix changes the meaning of the base word.

4. See if your meaning makes sense in the sentence.

As you read "From a Different Planet?" look for words that end with suffixes. Analyze the base words and the suffixes to figure out the meanings of words you do not know.

From a Different Planet?

The world of opera is much like another planet to most people. Not only do they have a difficult time trying to understand it, most also try to avoid it. Admittedly, this mixture of drama and music is much too formal for the taste of many Americans. Opera is quite different from other forms of recital and concert that most people are more familiar with. However, the roots of our prejudice against this art form are fed by other oddities.

To begin with, opera is usually sung in a language other than English. Many Americans do not learn to speak a second language. As a privileged people, we have come to expect the world to speak English for us. (Imagine if we had to complete a job application in French or Italian!)

Another fault we find with opera is actually one of its great strengths. It forces us to look at momentous occasions in someone's life. It takes a dramatic moment and multiplies its feelings times ten. Love brings the greatest joy. Loss brings awful sadness and even death. Jealousy drives an enraged lover to murder. The pageant of life is acted out before us with great feeling and color. If we can learn to live in this intense world for a few hours, we come away richer in spirit.

Write

Select one of the illustrations from this selection to write about. Use as many words from the Words to Know list as you can.

When Marian Sang

by Pam Muñoz Ryan

illustrations by Brian Selznick

Genre

A **biography** is the story of a real person's life, written by another person. As you read, note dates and other clues that indicate this story is about a real person.

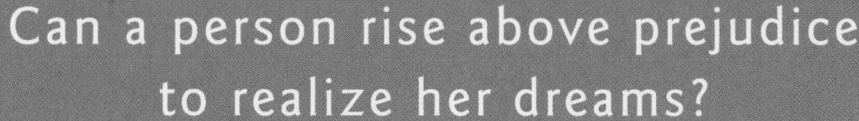

Can a person rise above prejudice
to realize her dreams?

No one was surprised

that Marian loved to sing. After all, she listened to Father singing in the morning as he dressed. Mother often hummed while she worked in the kitchen. Sometimes Marian and her little sisters, Ethel May and Alyse, sang songs all afternoon.

> *Let us break bread together*
> > *on our knees*
> *Let us break bread together*
> > *on our knees*
> *When I fall on my knees*
> > *with my face to the rising sun*
> *O Lord, have mercy on me.*

However, *her* voice was distinct—strong and velvety and able to climb more than twenty-four notes.

Everyone wanted to hear Marian sing.

Alexander Robinson, the choir director at the Union Baptist Church in South Philadelphia, wanted to hear Marian sing even though she was not quite eight years old and sometimes sang *too* loud. He asked her to perform a duet with her friend Viola Johnson. As Viola sang the high part and Marian sang the low, their harmony blended like a silk braid.

> *Dear to the heart of the Shepherd*
> *Dear are the sheep of His fold*
> *Dear is the love that He gives them*
> *Dearer than silver or gold.*

Church folks started whispering and followed with out-and-out talking about Marian's remarkable gift.

Neighboring churches heard the news and invited Marian to perform. One advertisement said: "COME AND HEAR THE BABY CONTRALTO, TEN YEARS OLD." And people came.

When Marian sang, it was often with her eyes closed, as if finding the music within. Audiences heard not only words, but feelings too: spirited worship, tender affection, and nothing short of joy.

She was chosen for the celebrated People's Chorus, a hundred voices from all the black church choirs in Philadelphia. She was one of the youngest members and had to stand on a chair so those in the back could see the pride of South Philadelphia.

Her father was proud too, but protective. He didn't want anyone taking advantage of his child. Father's love made Marian feel important. When he died after an injury at the Reading Terminal where he sold ice, tragedy filled Marian's heart and sometimes her songs.

> *Were you there when they laid Him*
> *in the tomb?*
> *Were you there when they laid Him*
> *in the tomb?*
> *Oh . . . oh . . . sometimes it causes me*
> *to tremble, tremble, tremble*
> *Were you there when they laid Him*
> *in the tomb?*

Mother was happy for Marian's success but reminded her that no matter what she studied she should take a little extra time and do it well.

Marian didn't need extra encouragement when it came to singing. She practiced her part of each song and often learned all the other parts too. For her, music was serious business, and more than anything, she hoped to someday go to music school. Church members promised tuition for "our Marian" if she was accepted.

Since Father's death, Marian worked at odd jobs and sang in concert programs in order to help support her family. It wasn't until 1915, when Marian was eighteen, that she finally went to a music school and patiently waited in

line for an application. But the girl behind the counter helped everyone except Marian. Was she invisible?

Finally, the girl said, "We don't take colored!" Her voice sounded like a steel door clanking shut.

Marian knew about prejudice. She had seen the trolley drive past her family as they stood at the corner. She knew that her people were always the last to be helped in a store. But she could not understand how anyone who was surrounded by the spirit and beauty of music could be so narrow-minded.

She felt sick in her stomach and in her heart. Didn't they know that her skin was different but her feelings were the same? Couldn't she be a professional singer if she was Negro?

With unwavering faith, Mother told her that there would be another way to accomplish what would have been done at that school. Marian believed her mother. She took voice lessons in her own neighborhood, continued with the choirs, and sometimes performed at Negro churches and colleges.

When Marian saw a Metropolitan Opera performance of the tragic opera *Madame Butterfly,* thoughts of a formal music education again came to mind. How wonderful it would be to sing on a grand stage, act out a dramatic role, and wear beautiful costumes. The passionate music inspired her and she was determined to study. But opera was simply the sun and the moon—a dream that seemed too far away to reach.

> *He's got the wind and the rain*
> *in His hands*
> *He's got the sun and the moon*
> *right in His hands*
> *He's got the wind and the rain*
> *in His hands*
> *He's got the whole world in His hands.*

As a young woman in her twenties, Marian was invited to many states to sing. Sometimes she traveled with her accompanist by train where they were seated in the dirty and crowded Jim Crow car reserved for Negroes. When she arrived at her destination, she often sang the same program twice, to separate audiences—one white and one black—or to segregated groups, whites in the best seats and blacks in the balcony. Many times, she was welcomed enthusiastically by her audiences, and then could not get a hotel room because she was Negro.

No matter what humiliations she endured, Marian sang her heart with dignity. Her voice left audiences weeping or in hushed awe as they strained to hold on to the memory of every opulent note.

> *When Israel was in Egypt's Land*
> *Let my people go*
> *Oppressed so hard they could not stand*
> *Let my people go*
> *Go down Moses*
> *Way down in Egypt's Land*
> *Tell ol' Pharaoh*
> *To let my people go.*

Marian still wanted to advance her singing with master teachers. With the help of friends, she was granted an audition with the fierce yet famous Giuseppe Boghetti.

When she arrived at his studio, Mr. Boghetti announced that he didn't have time or room for new students. Too afraid even to look at him, Marian took a deep breath. Slowly, with great emotion, she sang,

> *"Deep river, my home is over Jordan*
> *Deep river, Lord, I want to cross over*
> *   into campground*
> *Don't you want to go to that gospel feast*
> *That promised land where all is peace?*
> *O, deep river, Lord, I want to cross over*
> *   into campground."*

Marian finally lifted her eyes.

"I will make room for you right away." Mr. Boghetti said firmly, "and I will need only two years with you. After that, you will be able to go anywhere and sing for anybody."

Again, Marian's devoted church community raised the money for her lessons.

Marian worked hard with Mr. Boghetti, and sometimes, for practice, she sang scenes from Italian operas with him. Her recitals now included German songs too, but other languages troubled her. She didn't want simply to sing beautiful words like *Dunkel, wie dunkel in Wald und in Feld!* She wanted to know that the words meant *Dark, how dark in the woods and the fields!*

Other Negro singers had gone overseas to develop their voices and learn foreign languages. Why not her? After all, Europe was different. There, she would be able to sing to mixed audiences and travel without the restrictions put on her people in America.

Marian needed to grow and Mother agreed.

A bundle of trepidation and excitement, Marian boarded the *Ile de France* in October 1927. She had never been so far from her family. She knew her sisters would take good care of Mother, but still she already felt twinges of homesickness.

> *Sometimes I feel like a motherless child*
> *Sometimes I feel like a motherless child*
> *Sometimes I feel like a motherless child*
> *A long ways from home. A long ways from home.*
>
> *Sometimes I feel like I'm almost gone*
> *Sometimes I feel like I'm almost gone*
> *Sometimes I feel like I'm almost gone*
> *A long ways from home. A long ways from home.*

Marian studied and was eventually invited to perform in concert halls in Norway, Sweden, Finland, and Denmark. The enthusiasm for her singing was so overwhelming that one newspaper in Sweden called it "Marian Fever."

Audiences applauded in London, cheered in Paris, and pounded on the stage for encores in Russia. In Austria, the world-famous

conductor, Arturo Toscanini, announced that what he had heard, one was privileged to hear only once in a hundred years.

Marian felt as if she had finally achieved some success. She even asked Mother if there was anything she wanted that would make her happy because now Marian could afford to buy it for her. Mother said that all she wanted was for God to hold Marian in the highest of His hands.

It seemed like she was already there.

Mr. Boghetti had been right. She *could* go anywhere and sing for anyone . . .

. . . until she came home to the United States.

In 1939, Howard University in Washington, D.C., booked a concert with Marian Anderson and began looking for an auditorium big enough to hold the audience she attracted. They decided that the 4,000-seat Constitution Hall would be perfect. But the manager of the hall said it wasn't available *and* no other dates were offered because of their *white performers only* policy.

Marian's agent, Sol Hurok, wrote to the hall manager, pointing out that Marian Anderson was one of the greatest living singers of our time. But it did no good.

Enraged fans wrote letters to the newspaper. In protest, Eleanor Roosevelt, the first lady of the United States, resigned from the organization that sponsored Constitution Hall.

Howard University then tried to reserve a large high school auditorium from an all-white school. Again, they were denied.

Now teachers were angry and marched in support of Marian in front of the Board of Education. Washington, D.C., was a boiling pot about to spill over.

Wasn't there someplace in her own country's capital where Marian Anderson's voice could be heard?

Committees formed and held meetings. Finally, with President Roosevelt's approval, the Department of the Interior of the United States government invited Marian to sing on the steps of the Lincoln Memorial on Easter Sunday. Her country was offering her a momentous invitation, but she had concerns. Would people protest? Was it dangerous? Would anyone come?

Examining her heart, Marian realized that although she was a singer first and foremost, she also had become a symbol to her people and she wanted to make it easier for those who would follow her.

She said yes.

Standing in the shadow of the statue of Lincoln, waiting to be called out, she read the engraved words:

. . . THIS NATION UNDER GOD SHALL HAVE A NEW BIRTH OF FREEDOM. . . .

Marian looked out on a river of 75,000 people. Her heart beat wildly. Would she be able to utter one note?

She took a deep breath and felt the power of her audience's goodwill surge toward her. Marian's sisters were there, and

Mother too. Marian stood straight and tall. Then she closed her eyes and sang,

"My country 'tis of thee
Sweet land of liberty . . .
Let freedom ring!"

A roaring cheer followed every song. At the end of the program, the people pleaded for more.

When she began her thought-provoking encore,

"Oh, nobody knows the trouble I see
Nobody knows my sorrow. . . ."

. . . silence settled on the multitudes.

For almost sixteen years after the Lincoln Memorial performance, Marian sang for kings and queens, presidents and prime ministers, famous composers and conductors. She received medals, awards, and honorary degrees for her magnificent voice. But there was still one place Marian had not sung. When she was finally invited, a dream came true.

Marian wondered how people would react. No Negro singer had ever done such a thing. She would be the first. But she didn't need to worry. After she signed the contract, someone said, "Welcome home."

On opening night excitement charged the air. As Marian waited in the wings, the orchestra began. Her stomach fluttered. She walked onto the grand stage. Trembling, she straightened her costume and waited for the pounding music she knew to be her cue.

Tonight was her debut with the Metropolitan Opera. At long last, she had reached the sun and the moon.

The curtain parted . . .

. . . and Marian sang.

In order to address the era in which this story took place, the author has, with the greatest respect, stayed true to the references to African Americans as colored or Negro. Marian Anderson referred to herself and others of her race in this manner in the entirety of her autobiography.

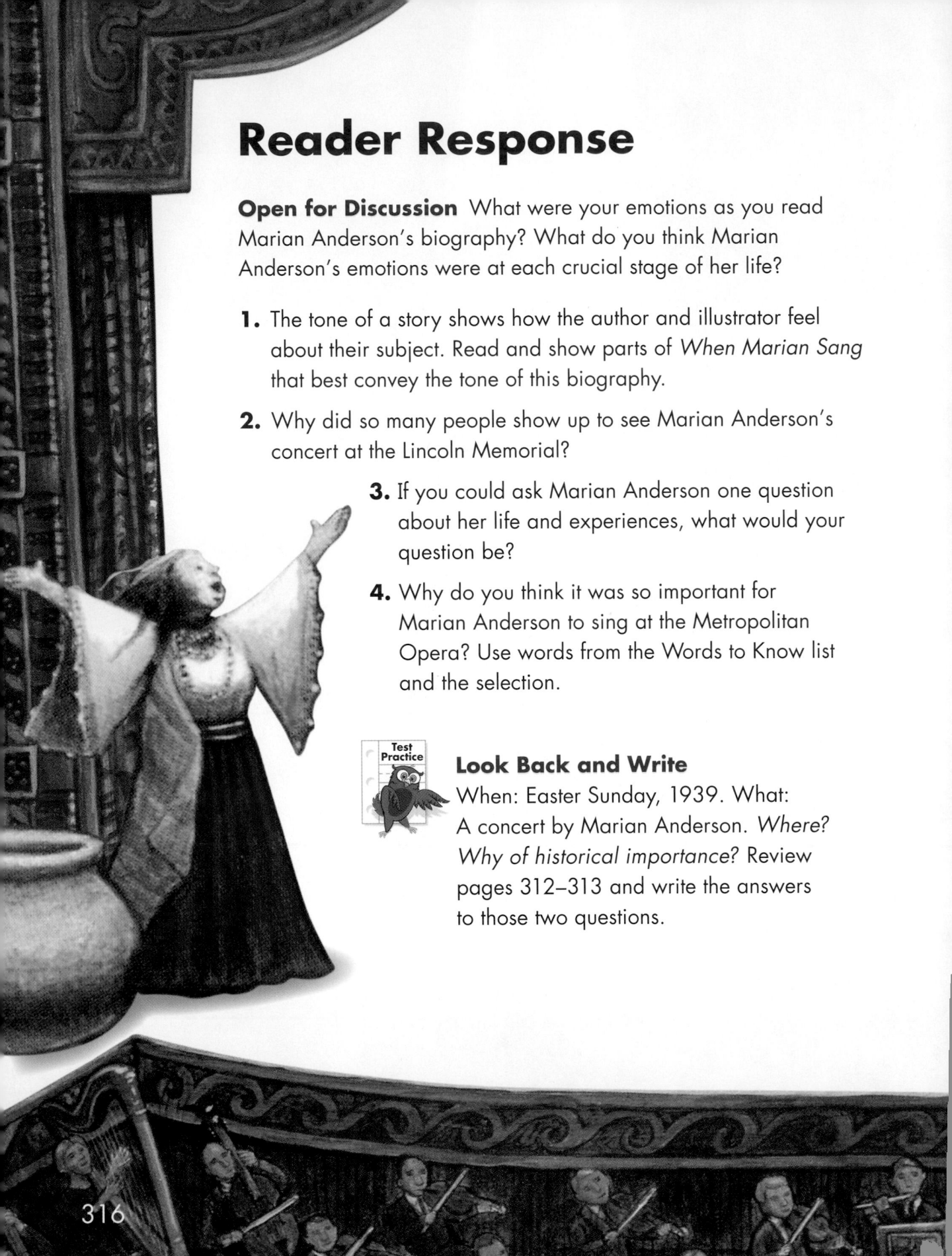

Reader Response

Open for Discussion What were your emotions as you read Marian Anderson's biography? What do you think Marian Anderson's emotions were at each crucial stage of her life?

1. The tone of a story shows how the author and illustrator feel about their subject. Read and show parts of *When Marian Sang* that best convey the tone of this biography.

2. Why did so many people show up to see Marian Anderson's concert at the Lincoln Memorial?

3. If you could ask Marian Anderson one question about her life and experiences, what would your question be?

4. Why do you think it was so important for Marian Anderson to sing at the Metropolitan Opera? Use words from the Words to Know list and the selection.

Test Practice

Look Back and Write
When: Easter Sunday, 1939. What: A concert by Marian Anderson. *Where? Why of historical importance?* Review pages 312–313 and write the answers to those two questions.

Meet the Author and the Illustrator
Pam Muñoz Ryan *and* Brian Selznick

Read these books about other famous singers and musicians.

Ella Fitzgerald
by Bud Kliment

Duke Ellington
by Ron Frankl

Pam Muñoz Ryan and **Brian Selznick** have worked together on several books. While working on *When Marian Sang*, Ms. Ryan got increasingly interested the more she researched. "Like many people I knew a little about Marian Anderson—specifically her Lincoln Memorial concert. . . . I began researching and became fascinated by the depth of her talent. Marian Anderson was someone of whom all Americans could be proud. I wanted more people to know about her inspiring story."

To prepare for illustrating the book, Mr. Selznick did a lot of research. "I studied many photographs and saw her singing, and listened again and again to recordings of her voice. I noticed that in many of the images of her singing, her eyes were closed, like she was feeling the music. I decided I would draw her with her eyes closed so the viewer could see her feeling the music."

Expository Nonfiction

Genre
- Expository nonfiction offers facts that explain about something or someone.

- Though expository nonfiction contains facts, it can convey vivid description.

Text Features
- Information about the Lincoln Memorial is arranged in a logical order.

- Photographs help the reader become more aware of the significance of this historic site and events that have occurred there.

Link to Social Studies

Research to discover other memorials or sites in Washington, D.C. Learn the history of the site you chose. Report what you learn to the class.

The Lincoln Memorial

by Sheri Buckner

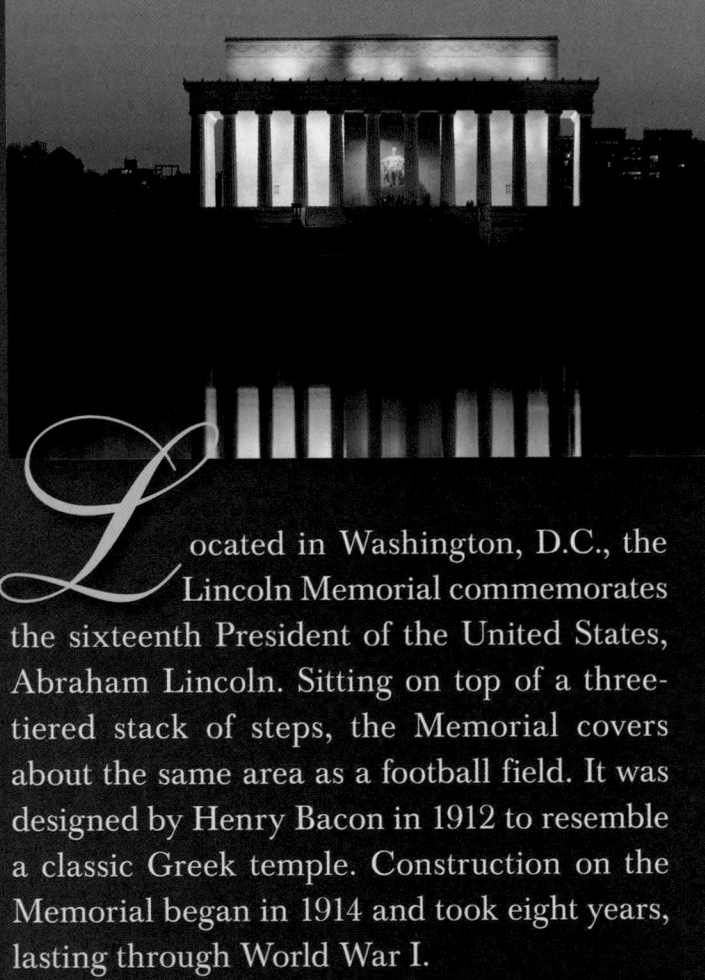

Located in Washington, D.C., the Lincoln Memorial commemorates the sixteenth President of the United States, Abraham Lincoln. Sitting on top of a three-tiered stack of steps, the Memorial covers about the same area as a football field. It was designed by Henry Bacon in 1912 to resemble a classic Greek temple. Construction on the Memorial began in 1914 and took eight years, lasting through World War I.

The outside of the building features thirty-six columns, one for each state in the Union at the time of Lincoln's death in 1865. There are three rooms inside. The central room features a statue by Daniel Chester French of the seated Lincoln.

At 19 feet high, this sculpture is almost as imposing as the Memorial itself. If the statue could stand, it would reach a towering height of 28 feet. The sculptor had a little help with the statue too. Casts, or molds, of Lincoln's hands and face were taken five years before his death. Daniel Chester French used these casts to help him recreate Lincoln's features.

In the south room of the Memorial, Lincoln's Gettysburg Address is etched, or cut, into a stone tablet. Lincoln's Second Inaugural Address is etched on a tablet in the north room. Above the Gettysburg Address is a mural showing the freeing of a slave; above the inaugural address is a mural on the theme of unity between the North and South.

Ask Questions What questions are you asking yourself as you read?

August 28, 1963

I have a dream...

Generalize Is the generalization about the Lincoln Memorial supported?

Marian Anderson's 1939 concert at the Memorial.

From all walks of life, people have come to be inspired by Abraham Lincoln's determination to save the Union and end the Civil War, as well as his great concern for those people who had been denied their freedom through slavery. The Memorial honors these accomplishments. But it has also become a place where people have come together to draw attention to other similar causes and issues.

Since its dedication on May 30, 1922, the Memorial has played host to a number of important historical events. In 1939, singer Marian Anderson gave a concert on the Memorial steps. She was not allowed to sing in any concert halls in Washington, D.C., because of the color of her skin. The free concert, on Easter Sunday, drew over 70,000 people. It was the largest concert crowd in the history of the city. It was also the first major gathering for the cause of civil rights at the feet of Lincoln. But it would not be the last.

Twenty-four years later, on August 28, 1963, Dr. Martin Luther King, Jr., delivered an address to more than 200,000 civil rights supporters at the Memorial. His "I Have a Dream" speech expressed the hopes of the civil rights movement, and moved a nation of citizens. But the Lincoln Memorial is not just a symbol of civil rights. Antiwar protesters came to the Memorial in the late 1960s and early 1970s to raise their voices against the war in Vietnam. In the years since, others have used the Memorial as a backdrop for rallies and protests.

The Lincoln Memorial, besides being a beautiful monument to an important President, has also come to symbolize for many people the ideals of American civil rights.

Reading Across Texts

What was important about Marian Anderson's performances at the Lincoln Memorial and at the Metropolitan Opera?

Writing Across Texts Which performance do you think was more important? Tell why you think as you do.

Comprehension

Skill
Sequence

Strategy
Predict

Sequence

Skill

- In both fiction and nonfiction, sequence is the order of events.

- The time of day and clue words such as *before* and *after* can help you determine the order in which things happen.

Strategy: Predict

Strategy

To predict means to tell what you think might happen in a story or article based on what has already happened. As you read, use the sequence of events in the text to try to predict what will happen next. Then check to see if your prediction was correct. Sometimes you will need to revise a prediction when you learn new information in the text.

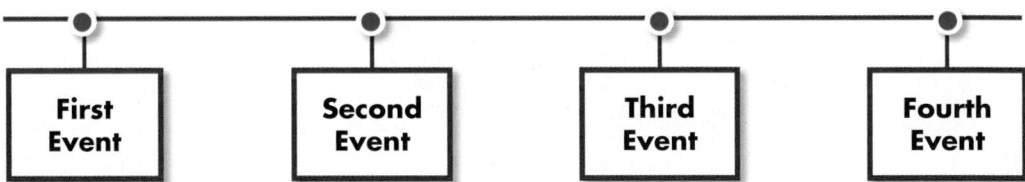

| First Event | Second Event | Third Event | Fourth Event |

1. Read "Slow Down." As you read, make a graphic organizer like the one above to show the sequence of events. Also write down what you predict will happen next. Try to make at least two predictions.

2. After you read, compare your time line with your predictions. Write about why you can't always predict the direction in which an author will take a story.

Slow Down

Thunder boomed. Glen and Felix huddled under an overhanging rock, but Dave, standing, said, "Let's keep going."

"No way," Felix snapped. There was too much thunder and lightning to evacuate their shelter. Dave scowled and sat down.

Once the storm passed, the three young men resumed their hike. They ambled through a small woods, then out onto a spacious meadow, where a herd of elk was grazing. Hours later the three approached a river. It was wide and fast. Glen and Felix walked along the bank to find a safe place to cross—someplace where the water was shallow and the current not too strong. Dave stayed right where he was.

"C'mon already!" Dave yelled. "We can make it across here." Felix and Glen didn't reply; it was crazy to even consider crossing there. A minute later Felix glanced back and saw Dave striding into the river. Felix rushed down the bank, but the current was already hurtling Dave downstream.

"The rope!" Felix yelled to Glen, who quickly pulled it out of his pack. Glen heaved one end of the rope to Dave and dragged him back to shore.

"I could've made it," Dave said, standing on shore soaking wet. Felix and Glen just rolled their eyes.

Skill Look for a phrase at the beginning of this paragraph that is a clue to sequence. Other clue words and phrases follow.

Strategy Think of how Dave acted during the storm. What do you predict he will do next?

Strategy Was your first prediction correct? What do you predict will happen next? Why do you think so?

Skill What do you think the last important event in the story should be on your time line?

323

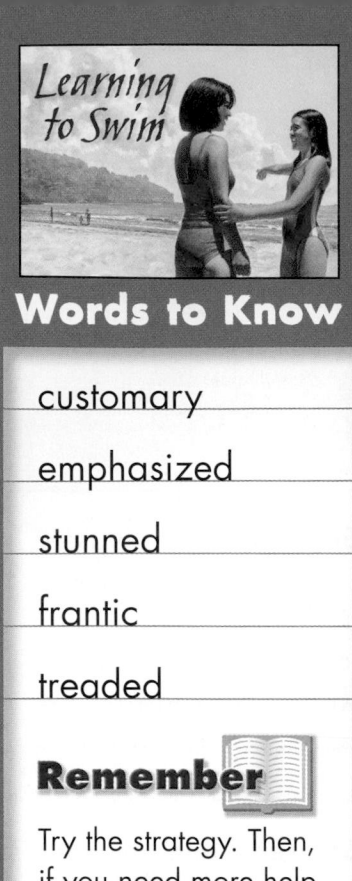

Learning to Swim

Words to Know

customary

emphasized

stunned

frantic

treaded

Remember

Try the strategy. Then, if you need more help, use your glossary or a dictionary.

Vocabulary Strategy
for Synonyms

Context Clues When you find a word you do not know, look at words near the unknown word. Often the author will provide clues to help you figure out the meaning of the word. One kind of clue that might help you determine a word's meaning is a synonym. A synonym is a word that has the same or almost the same meaning as another word.

1. Reread the sentence in which the unknown word appears.

2. Look for another word or words that give a clue to the unknown word's meaning.

3. Are two things being compared? Look for words that point to similarity, such as *like, also,* or *similarly.*

4. Identify the synonym and think about its meaning.

5. See if this meaning can be substituted for the unknown word. Does the sentence make sense?

As you read "Water Safety at the Beach," look for synonyms to help you figure out the meaning of unknown words.

Water Safety
at the Beach

A day at the beach sounds relaxing and fun. Who doesn't enjoy building sand castles, napping, and splashing in the blue-green water? However, if you choose to swim in the ocean, find out about what may be waiting in the waters.

It is customary for a beach to post a sign with any important information about swimming here. On the usual list, safety rules are emphasized. It may also focus on when and where the water becomes deep and whether there are rip tides, dangerous currents that flow swiftly outward from the shore.

People are stunned to learn that a rip tide can pull a good swimmer far out to sea in minutes. Many fight the current, trying to swim against it back to the beach. They become frantic as they see they are losing ground. Despite their frenzied work, they move farther out to sea. Too late, the swimmer may realize he or she should have treaded water to save strength. The best strategy is to swim at an angle to the current. Passing beyond it, the swimmer can then swim back toward shore.

Write

Write what you know about keeping safe in another dangerous situation. Use words from the Words to Know list in your writing.

Learning to Swim

by Kyoko Mori
illustrated by Kazuhiko Sano

Why is it a good idea to
stay calm during
a crisis?

327

I was determined to swim at least twenty-five meters in the front crawl. As we did every summer, my mother, younger brother, and I were going to stay with my grandparents, who lived in a small farming village near Himeji, in Japan. From their house, it was a short walk through some rice paddies to the river where my mother had taught me how to swim when I was six. First, she showed me how to float with my face in the water, stretching my arms out in front of me and lying very still so my whole body was like a long plastic raft full of air. If you thought about it that way, my mother said, floating was as easy as just standing around or lying down to sleep. Once I got comfortable with floating, she taught me to kick my legs and paddle my arms so I could move forward, dog-paddling with my face out of the water.

Now I was too old to dog-paddle like a little kid. My mother had tried to teach me the front crawl the previous summer. I knew what I was supposed to do—flutter kick and push the water from front to back with my arms, while keeping my face in the water and turning sideways to breathe—but somehow there seemed to be too much I had to remember all at once. I forgot to turn my head and found myself dog-paddling again after only a few strokes. This summer, I thought, I would work harder and learn to swim as smoothly and gracefully as my mother. Then I would go back to school in September and surprise my classmates and my teachers. At our monthly swimming test, I would swim the whole length of our pool and prove myself one of the better swimmers in our class.

At our school, where we had monthly tests to determine how far each of us could swim without stopping, everyone could tell who the best and the worst swimmers were by looking at our white cloth swimming caps. For every five or ten meters we could swim, our mothers sewed a red or black line on the front of the cap. At the last test we had, in late May, I had made it all the way across the width of the pool in an awkward combination of dog paddle and front crawl, earning the three red lines on my cap for fifteen meters. That meant I was an average swimmer, not bad, not great. At the next test, in September, I would have to try the length of the pool, heading toward the deep end. If I made it all the way across, I would earn five red lines for twenty-five meters. There were several kids in our class who had done that, but only one of them had turned around after touching the wall and swum farther, heading back toward the shallow end. He stopped halfway across, where the water was up to our chests. If he had gone all the way back, he would have earned five black lines, meaning "fifty meters and more." That was the highest mark.

All the kids who could swim the length of the pool were boys. They were the same boys I competed with every winter during our weekly race from the cemetery on the hill to our schoolyard. They were always in the first pack of runners to come back—as I was. I could beat most of them in the last dash across the schoolyard because I was a good sprinter, but in the pool they easily swam past me and went farther. I was determined to change that. There was no reason that I should spend my summers dog-paddling in the shallow end of the pool while these boys glided toward the deep end, their legs cutting through the water like scissors.

My brother and I got out of school during the first week of July and were at my grandparents' house by July 7—the festival of the stars. On that night if the sky was clear, the Weaver Lady and the Cowherd Boy would be allowed to cross the river of Heaven—the Milky Way—for their once-a-year meeting. The Weaver Lady and the Cowherd Boy were two stars who had been ordered to live on opposite shores of the river of Heaven as punishment for neglecting their work when they were together.

On the night of the seventh, it was customary to write wishes on pieces of colored paper and tie them to pieces of bamboo. On the night of their happy meeting, the Weaver Lady and the Cowherd Boy would be in a generous mood and grant the wishes. I wished, among other things, that I would be able to swim the length of the pool in September. Of course I knew, as my mother reminded me, that no wish would come true unless I worked hard.

Every afternoon my mother and I walked down to the river in our matching navy blue swimsuits. We swam near the bend of the river where the current slowed. The water came up to my chest, and I could see schools of minnows swimming past my knees and darting in and out among the rocks on the bottom. First I practiced the front crawl, and then a new stroke my mother was teaching me: the breaststroke.

"A good thing about this stroke," she said, "is that you come up for air looking straight ahead, so you can see where you are going."

We both laughed. Practicing the front crawl in the river—where there were no black lines at the bottom—I had been weaving wildly from right and left, adding extra distance.

As we sat together on the riverbank, my mother drew diagrams in the sand, showing me what my arms and legs should be doing. Then we lay down on the warm sand so I could practice the motions.

"Pretend that you are a frog," she said. "Bend your knees and then kick back. Flick your ankles. Good."

We got into the water, where I tried to make the motions I had practiced on the sand, and my mother swam underwater next to me to see what I was doing. It was always harder to coordinate my legs and arms in the water, but slowly, all the details that seemed so confusing at first came together, so I didn't have to think about them separately. My mother was a good teacher. Patient and humorous, she talked me out of my frustrations even when

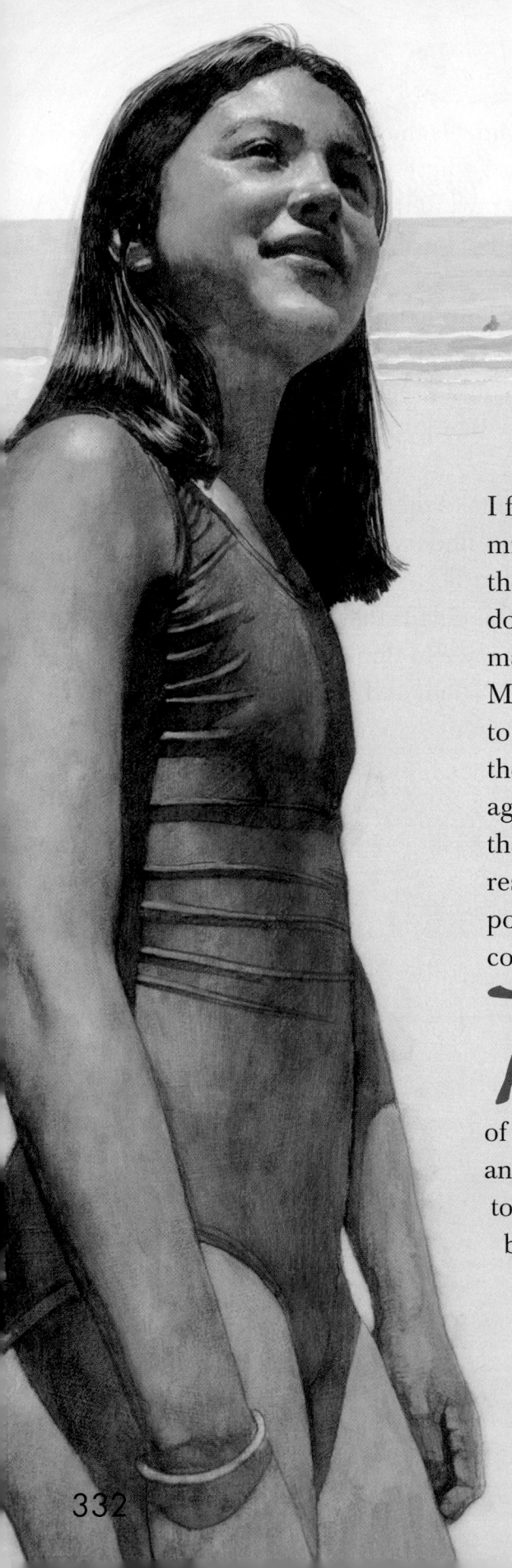

I felt sure I would never get better. By mid-August, in both the front crawl and the breaststroke, I could swim easily downstream—all the way to the rock that marked the end of the swimming area. My mother thought that the distance had to be at least fifty meters. When I reached the rock, I would turn around and swim against the current. It was harder going that way. I had to stop several times and rest, panting a little. But swimming in a pool where the water was still, I was sure I could easily go on for twenty-five meters.

That summer, during the third week of August, two of my uncles, their wives, and my mother decided to take a trip to the Sea of Japan for the weekend, bringing my brother, our cousins, and me. All of us kids were excited about going to the seacoast. It was on the less populated side of our country, which faced China, Korea, Russia, and other faraway northern places.

I had never been to that sea, though the river we swam in ended there. When my mother warned me not to swim past the rock that marked off the swimming area—because the current got strong—she said, "We don't want you carried past Ikaba, all the way to the Sea of Japan." Ikaba, a village to the north, got its name, which meant "fifty waves," because the river was so turbulent and wavy there. I imagined the water tumbling down rocky mountains from Ikaba to the faraway sea.

The next morning after breakfast, we dressed in our swimsuits and walked to the beach, which was just down the road from the inn. On a narrow strip of white sand, a few families were clustered around bright red, blue, and pink beach towels. Some people were already in the water. Even a long way out, the water came only to their waists or chests. Big waves were hitting the rocks on a piece of land that jutted out to the sea to our left.

While my uncles and aunts and their kids spread out their beach towels on the sand, my mother and I walked to the water's edge, leaving my brother behind with my cousins. I had never swum in the sea before, but I had seen pictures in my geography book of people floating on the Dead Sea. The writing underneath said that the salt in the water made it easier for people to float.

The sea was cold as my mother and I walked in—much colder than the pool or the river—but it was a hot sunny morning. I knew I would get used to it soon. We went in and splashed around for a while; then I started practicing my front crawl.

I couldn't tell if it really was easier to float. A big wave came and hit my face sideways just as I was turning my head to breathe. I stood up coughing. The water didn't taste like the salt water that I gargled with when I had a cold. Instead, it had a strong bitter taste that stung my nostrils and my throat. My eyes burned.

"Try floating on your back," my mother suggested, flopping back and closing her eyes. "It's easy."

She was right. In the pool, I could float on my stomach, but never on my back. But in the sea, my legs and head didn't start sinking while my chest and stomach stayed afloat. All of me was floating; I could almost take a nap.

Once we got tired of floating, my mother and I started jumping the waves. Side by side holding hands, we treaded water, each paddling with one arm instead of two, waiting for the next big wave to come surging our way. If we stopped moving at just the right time, we could crest over the top and glide down to the other side, falling slowly down the gentle slope till another wave came and lifted us up. All around us, other grownups and kids were doing the same thing. There were so many waves coming and going. Sometimes we couldn't see people who were only a few feet away until a wave lifted us up and dropped us almost on top of them. Laughing, we would apologize before another wave swept us away.

I don't know how long we were riding the waves before I noticed that my mother and I hadn't seen anyone for a long time. I thought of another thing too. When we first started, my feet had brushed against the sand bottom almost every time we came down. In the lull between the waves, I'd be standing in the water only up to my chest. That hadn't happened for a while. My feet hadn't touched bottom for at least twenty waves now. I stretched my body as straight as I could, trying to touch bottom with my toes. Nothing. Just as I opened my mouth to point that out to my mother, a big wave came, my head went under, and my hand was swept loose from hers. When I came up again, I was turned around, facing the shore for the first time. I couldn't believe what I saw. The people on the beach looked so small that I couldn't tell our family from anyone else's.

Before I really understood what this meant, another wave rose, my head went under again, and I came up coughing and spitting. My mother, to my relief, was right beside me, treading water.

"Mom," I tried to warn her, but the look on her face told me that she already knew. Her eyes were wide open and there was a big frown between her eyebrows.

"Turn around and swim," she said. "It's not as far as you think."

"I can't," I gasped before a wave pounded me, filling my mouth with a burning, bitter taste.

My mother was beside me again, treading water. She couldn't reach out and hold my hand now, I realized suddenly, because even she needed both of her arms to stay afloat. The water was moving underneath, pulling us sideways. The beach look farther and farther away. It was all I could do to keep my head from going under.

My mother started flinging her hand upward, trying to wave it from side to side. She was calling for help. That meant we were drowning.

Before the next wave hit us, I kicked my legs as hard as I could and lunged toward my mother, making up the short distance between us. The wave hit. We came up, both of us coughing and spitting, my arms clutched tightly around her neck.

"Listen," my mother said, in a choked-up voice. "You have to let go."

"But I'll drown," I wailed.

She stopped moving her arms for just a moment—long enough to put them around me and draw me closer. I could feel my shoulders, wet and slippery, pressed against her collarbone. "Let go," she said in voice that sounded surprisingly calm. "Now, or we'll both drown."

By the time the next wave went over my head I was swimming alone, flailing my arms and legs to come up for air, and my mother was beside me. If it weren't for me, I thought, she could easily swim back to the shore. She was a strong swimmer. We were drowning because of me.

"Stay calm," she said, "and float."

We treaded water for a while, and between the waves my mother looked around, no doubt trying to measure the distance we had to swim.

"Look over there," she said, turning away from the shore and pointing toward the piece of land jutting into the sea. "We can't swim back to the beach, but we can make it to those rocks."

The waves had been pushing us sideways, toward the rocks, as well as farther from the shore. From where we were now, the tip of that land was about as far away as I could swim in the river without stopping if the current was with me. That piece of land was our last chance. If I couldn't make it there, I would surely drown. Heading toward the rocks meant turning away from the beach completely, swimming farther out to sea. If I drifted too far to the side and missed the tip of the land, there wouldn't be anywhere else. Every time I came up for air, I'd better be looking at those rocks, making sure they were still in my sight. The only stroke that would allow me to do that was the breaststroke.

I took a big breath and started kicking my legs with my knees bent, flicking my ankles the way my mother had taught me in the river. The arms, I told myself, should draw nice big arcs, not a bunch of little frantic circles that would make me tired. My mother swam right beside me in her easy graceful breaststroke—she was between

me and the rest of the sea, guiding me toward the rocks, showing me how I should swim.

The waves we had been fighting were suddenly helping us. In just a few minutes, my mother and I stood on the rocky ground of that slip of land, looking back toward the shore. My legs felt wobbly, and I was breathing hard. The two of us looked at each other, too stunned to say anything. For a while we just stood trying to catch our breath, listening to the waves as they continued to crash at our feet. Then we started walking. The rocks formed a steep cliff above us, but at the bottom, there was enough room for us to walk side by side. Cautiously we picked our way back to the beach, trying not to cut our feet or slip back into the sea. On the way we noticed a group of people gathered on the sand, watching us. When we got there, they came rushing toward us. They were my uncles and several other men we had never seen.

"I waved for help," my mother said to them.

"We thought you were just waving for fun," one of my uncles said. "We didn't know anything was wrong until we saw you walking on those rocks."

One of the strangers, an old man in a shirt and trousers, shook his head. "You got caught in a rip tide," he said. "A fisherman drowned there a few years ago."

Several people were talking all at once, saying how lucky we were, but I wasn't listening very carefully. My brother was running toward us. Behind him, the beach was more crowded than when we had first started swimming. For the first time, I noticed an ice cream stand not too far away.

"Mom," I said. "My throat hurts from the seawater. I would love some ice cream."

When my mother told people the story of our near drowning, that was the detail she always emphasized—how I had calmly asked for ice cream as soon as we were back on the beach. Every time we remembered this incident, she said to me, "You are a brave girl. You let go of me when you had to."

The way she talked about it, our experience in the Sea of Japan was a great adventure that proved my courage: If I could swim well enough not to drown in a place where a fisherman had died in a rip tide, then I never again had to worry about drowning. I did not question her logic—though years later I realized that my mother had said just the right things to prevent me from becoming afraid.

If she had told stories of a near disaster, a close call—instead of the story about my courage—I might never have been able to swim again. Instead I believed that I had conquered that sea for good. All I had to do was be more careful and watch out for the rip tide. My mother and I swam at the same beach again the same afternoon and the two following days; we returned to my grandparents' house and continued our swimming lessons. I was getting so good, she said, that the following year she would teach me to butterfly.

Back at school in September, I swam the length of the pool in the breaststroke without stopping. When I got to the end, I touched the edge of the pool and turned around. The other side of the pool didn't look nearly as far away as the shore had from the sea the day I had almost drowned. The water wasn't moving or trying to pull me under. It was nothing. I started swimming back, past the first five meters where the pool was deep, then past the ten-meter mark, past the halfway mark, where the only other student from my class had stopped. I took a deep breath, changed to the front crawl, and swam all the way to the end. My hand hit the wall; I stood up. My mother would be pleased, I thought, to sew five black lines on my cap.

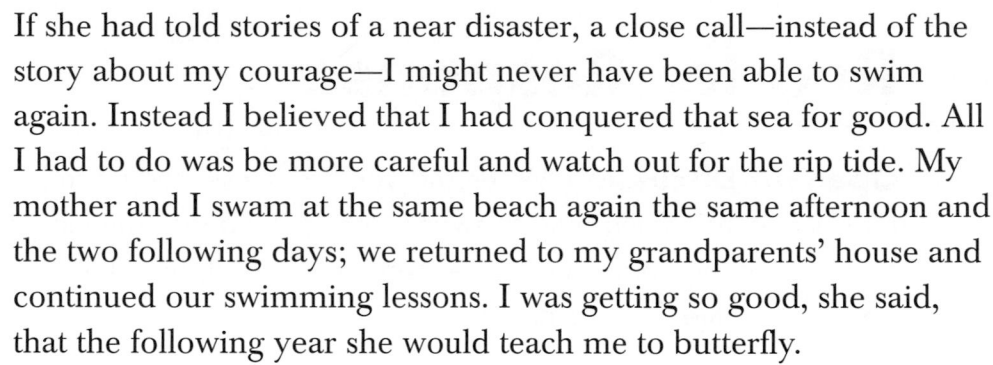

Reader Response

Open for Discussion When did you first sense danger in Kyoko Mori's account of learning to swim? Does this danger remind you of things you've read, seen, or experienced—and, hopefully, of happy outcomes? Make comparisons.

1. No screaming, no choking, no thrashing about: Kyoko Mori's autobiographical account is told so calmly that you may have to think twice before you realize what's happening. Find a sample section to read aloud to demonstrate this calm style.

2. At the beginning of her story, Kyoko Mori tells about how she first learned to swim. What swimming basics did she learn first, second, and last in that passage?

3. How good a swimmer do you predict that Mori became based on what you read in the story?

4. The words *stunned* and *frantic* were chosen by the author to convey danger of the situation she and her mother faced. Find other words and phrases that add to the mood of that time in the water.

Look Back and Write Look back at page 338 to recall how Kyoko's mother helped her not to be afraid after the near-drowning. In your own words, write what strategy the mother used and its effect.

340

Read more autobiographies.

Kyoko Mori learned that writing was enjoyable from two people in her family, her mother and her grandfather. "My mother sat down every Saturday to write a letter to her parents telling them about the flowers she was growing in the garden, the various recipes she had tried out, the funny things my brother and I had said. Her father—my grandfather—had been a schoolteacher though he was retired by the time I was born. Every summer when we visited, I saw him sitting down at the table in the morning to write in his journal."

Ms. Mori was born in Kobe, Japan. Sadly, her mother died when she was twelve. Later, she moved to the United States to attend college. In graduate school, she studied creative writing.

She says, "Much of what I write is based on the things I know. For instance I write about growing up in Japan, being a runner or a gardener, certain feelings I had as a teenager about wanting to be honest and wanting to be liked." Her stories come from what might have happened in her life but not what actually did happen. She says, "I think that the best thing about being a writer is that we get to make up things and tell the truth at the same time."

The Invisible Thread
by Yoshiko Uchida

Surprising Myself
by Jean Fritz

Search Engines

Genre

- Use a tool called a **search engine** to find Web sites on the Internet.

- Brainstorm a list of important words, called **keywords,** that you want to search for.

Text Features

- The search engine window is where you type in a keyword.

- You then click on the "Search" button. The search results are displayed in a list below the search window.

- Each item on the list is a link to a Web site that contains your keyword. Think about which may give the best information.

Link to Science

Kyoko discovers that it is easier to float in the ocean than in the river. Find out why it is easier to float in salt water.

Staying Safe in the Water

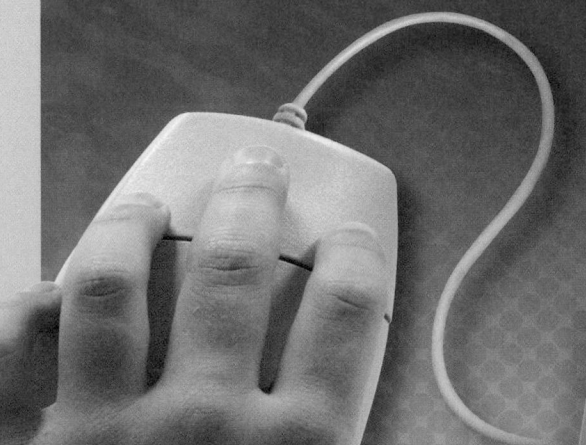

Just about everyone likes to be nearby or in water, whether at a pool, river, lake, or an ocean. Water can pose a challenge, though. If you wanted to know more about safety in the water, you could type in the keywords *water safety* into a search engine and click SEARCH.

342

Take It to the NET™
ONLINE
more activities sfsuccessnet.com

The search engine you choose might come up with a long list of Web sites about water safety. You might find results such as those below. You must decide which link will give you the information you want. You decide to click on the second link, *Water Safety*.

← → ☒ ↻ 🏠 | http://www.url.here

👤 **Search Engine** | water safety | **Search**

Beach Safety. Play It Safe at the Beach tips, safety advice, printable worksheets and more about **beach safety.**

● **Water Safety.** ▷ Playing at the beach, at a water park, by a lake, or in a pool can be a real treat on a hot day. But water can also mean danger.

Keeping Kids Safe at the Beach. Articles. From sun to swimming, we've got the goods on **beach safety.**

A computer screen such as this one appears. Look at the links. You then click on *Beaches* to learn more about ocean safety.

Water Safety

Check out more stuff below!

- Swimming Pools
- Lakes and Ponds
- ● **Beaches** ▷
- Water Parks

Drowning is the second most common cause of death from injuries among kids under the age of 14. Drowning can happen so suddenly—sometimes in less than 2 minutes after your head goes under the water—that often there's precious little time for someone to rescue you. Many drownings and near drownings of youths occur when they accidentally fall into a swimming pool, but accidents can occur anywhere—at someone's home or even at your own house. That's why you need to know how to be safe around water.

 **Predict** | Predicting what a Web site might say is important.

343

You find lots of useful information from the *Beaches* link.

Edit   View   Favorites   Tools   Help

http://www.url.here

Beaches

Check out more stuff below!

- Swimming Pools
- Lakes and Ponds
- **Beaches**
- Water Parks

"Never underestimate the power of the ocean. It isn't like a swimming pool. The ocean is so large that it's harder to spot you if you get in trouble," Dr. Kate Cronan says. In some places swimmers may encounter strong undertows or ocean currents.

Rip currents are so strong that they can carry swimmers away from shore before they know what's going on. If you are caught in a current, swim parallel to the shore until the water stops pulling you, then swim back to shore.

You probably won't see any sharks, but jellyfish and Portuguese man-of-wars are another story. These umbrella-shaped, nearly transparent animals can grow to be as large as several feet in diameter! They are often found floating near the shore. Getting stung is no fun—it can hurt and blister your skin. If you get stung, tell an adult immediately.

More advice on Beach Safety

You decide to click on the link for more advice on beach safety.

jellyfish

A second screen appears with a list of more safety tips to keep you safe on the beach.

File   Edit   View   Favorites   Tools   Help

http:/

Beaches

Check out more stuff below!

- Swimming Pools
- Lakes and Ponds
- **Beaches**
- Water Parks

Here's some other good advice for the beach:

- Never swim alone and always swim where a lifeguard can see you.

- Wear protective footwear, especially on rocky beaches.

- Don't swim out too far.

- Never fake trouble or calls for help.

- Don't turn your back to the ocean—you may be swept into the water by waves that come without warning.

Reading Across Texts

Both this and "Learning to Swim" help you understand the power of the ocean. Compare how each selection helps you learn about safety tips to practice when swimming in large bodies of water.

Writing Across Texts Use the selections to write a list of Safety Dos and Don'ts when you are around water.

 **Sequence**   Is the sequence of steps important when caught in a rip current?

Comprehension

Skill
Generalize

Strategy
Predict

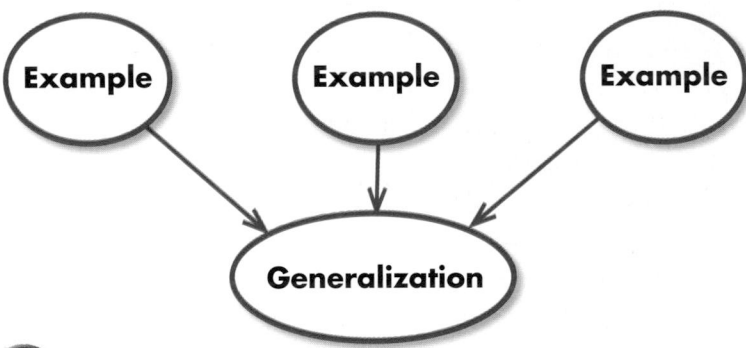

Generalize

Skill

- A generalization is a broad statement or rule that applies to many examples.

- Sometimes authors generalize about a group of people or things. Sometimes when you read, you too can generalize. You are given ideas about several things or people, and you can make a statement about all of them together.

- Valid generalizations are supported by examples, facts, or good logic. Invalid generalizations are not supported.

Example → Generalization ← Example ← Example

Strategy: Predict

Strategy

Good readers try to predict what will happen next. Generalizations can help. If you make a generalization about the way people act, you can use it to predict how someone might act.

Write

1. Read "Tall-Tale Town." Make a graphic organizer like the one above to help you make a generalization about the town.

2. Add to the story. Create and write about another example of a character acting in a way that fits your generalization.

Tall-Tale Town

Rahim was the new kid in town. One day he ventured out, looking to shoot some hoops and make some friends in the process.

"Hi," he said, as he approached a boy mowing the lawn. "Like to play basketball?"

"Sure, just yesterday I was shooting some hoops at the playground and made 551 free throws in a row," the boy said.

"That's astounding!" exclaimed Rahim.

"Yeah, but I can't play now. I have to finish mowing the lawn. Maybe later."

Rahim continued on until he came to a boy washing the family car. "Like to play basketball?" he asked.

"Love to. I scored 242 points in a game once. Would have scored more, but my coach took me out for the second half. My knee is bothering me now. Maybe some other time."

Rahim was speechless. "Like to play basketball?" he asked a third boy, a little hesitantly.

"Nope. Soccer's my game. Last week I blocked 863 shots on goal. We won the game, 1–0."

Rahim slowly wandered home.

"How'd it go, honey?" his mother inquired as he entered the back door. "Do you think you'll like it here?"

Rahim paused. "Yeah. Who wouldn't? We just moved to the greatest, smartest, most talented town in the world."

Skill Note this example of how one boy responds.

Skill What generalization might be suggested about the town?

Strategy Based on your generalization, how do you predict the boy will respond?

Strategy Was your prediction correct? Why or why not?

Words to Know

repay

fulfill

dismounted

confidently

vigorously

distressed

permission

flourish

Remember

Try the strategy. Then, if you need more help, use your glossary or a dictionary.

Vocabulary Strategy
for Prefixes

Word Structure Sometimes when you are reading, you find a word you do not know. See if the word begins with a prefix. The prefix may help you to figure out the meaning of the word. For example, usually the prefix *re-* adds the meaning "again" to a word, as in *reschedule*, or "back" as in *rewind*. Usually, the prefix *dis-* adds the meaning "to remove" or "the opposite of," as in *disrespect*.

1. Cover the prefix.

2. Look at the base word. See if you know what it means.

3. Uncover the prefix. Think about its meaning.

4. Combine the meaning of the prefix with the meaning of the base word.

5. Check the context. Does this meaning make sense in this sentence?

As you read "Kindness for Kindness," look for words that begin with prefixes. Use the prefixes to help you figure out the meaning of the words.

Kindness for Kindness

As she rode along the lane, Terry tried to think of a way to repay Miss Posy. The elderly woman had been the one to fulfill Terry's dream of owning her own horse. Miss Posy had offered Terry a job cleaning stalls and grooming horses on her dude ranch. A year later, Terry had enough money to buy Biscuit from Miss Posy. He was old but gentle and easy to ride, and Terry loved the horse to an unreasonable degree.

Arriving at the ranch, Terry dismounted and put Biscuit in a pasture to graze. Then she got to work. Terry moved confidently among the horses in the barn. As she forked clean straw vigorously into stalls, she thought of something she could do for her employer.

Last winter, Miss Posy had suffered a stroke and now spent much of her time sitting on the porch. This had distressed Terry, who knew how much Miss Posy loved being outdoors. Smiling, Terry marched to the porch and got permission for her project. Soon a beautiful big garden of flowers began to flourish next to that porch.

What could you do to help someone you love? Write about your plan. Use as many words from the Words to Know list as you can.

Juan Verdades

The Man Who Couldn't Tell a Lie

 retold by Joe Hayes
illustrated by Joseph Daniel Fiedler

Genre

Folk tales are stories with no known author that have been told by one generation to the next. As you read, think about stories you've heard or read that are like *Juan Verdades*.

Is honesty always the best policy?

One late summer day a group of wealthy rancheros was gathered on the village plaza, joking and laughing and discussing events on their ranches.

One of the men, whose name was don Ignacio, had a fine apple tree on his land. The rancher called the apple tree *el manzano real*—the royal apple tree—and was extremely proud of it. It had been planted by his great-grandfather, and there was something about the soil it grew in and the way the afternoon sun struck it that made the apple tree flourish. It gave sweeter and more flavorful fruit than any other tree in the country round about.

Every rancher for miles around knew about *el manzano real,* and each year they all hoped don Ignacio would give them a small basket of its sweet fruit. And so each of the ranchers asked don Ignacio how the fruit of the apple tree was doing. To each one don Ignacio replied, "It's doing beautifully, amigo, beautifully. My foreman takes perfect care of the tree, and every evening he reports how the fruit is ripening."

When don Ignacio said this to his friend don Arturo, the other man replied, "Do you mean to say, don Ignacio, that you don't tend your magnificent tree yourself? How can you have such faith in your employee? Maybe he's not doing all he says he is. Maybe he's not telling you the truth."

Don Ignacio wagged a finger at his friend. "*Mi capataz* has never failed me in any way," he insisted. "He has never told me a lie."

"Are you sure, *compadre?*" said don Arturo. "Are you sure that he has never lied to you?"

"Absolutely certain, *compadre*, absolutely certain. The young man doesn't know how to tell a lie. His name is Juan Valdez, but everyone calls him Juan Verdades because he is so truthful."

"I don't believe it. There never was an employee who didn't lie to his boss. I'm sure I can make him tell you a lie."

"Never," replied the proud employer.

The two friends went on arguing good-naturedly, but little by little they began to raise their voices and attract the attention of the other men on the plaza.

Finally don Arturo declared loudly, "I'll bet you whatever you want that within two weeks at the most I'll make this Juan Verdades tell you a lie."

"All right," replied don Ignacio. "It's a deal. I'll bet my ranch against yours that you can't make my foreman lie to me."

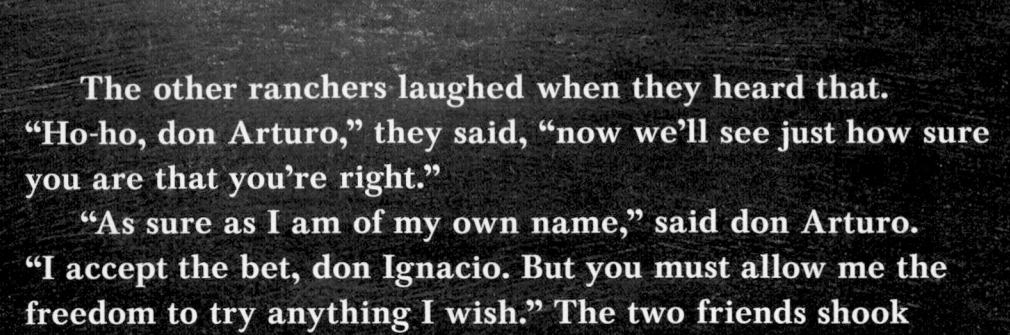

The other ranchers laughed when they heard that. "Ho-ho, don Arturo," they said, "now we'll see just how sure you are that you're right."

"As sure as I am of my own name," said don Arturo. "I accept the bet, don Ignacio. But you must allow me the freedom to try anything I wish." The two friends shook hands, and the other men in the group agreed to serve as witnesses to the bet.

The gathering broke up, and don Arturo and don Ignacio rode confidently away toward their ranches. But as don Arturo rode along thinking of what he had just done, he no longer felt so sure of himself. When he arrived home and told his wife and daughter about the bet, his wife began to cry. "What will we do when we lose our ranch?" she sobbed. And don Arturo began to think he had made a terrible mistake.

But his daughter, whose name was Araceli and who was a very bright and lively young woman, just laughed and said, "Don't worry, *Mamá.* We're not going to lose our ranch."

Araceli suggested to her father that he make up some excuse for them all to spend the next two weeks at don Ignacio's house. "If we're staying on don Ignacio's ranch," she said, "we'll surely discover a way to come out the winners."

The next day don Arturo rode to don Ignacio's ranch and told his friend, "My men are mending the walls of my house and giving them a fresh coat of whitewash. It would be more convenient for my family to be away. Could my wife and daughter and I stay at your house for a while?"

"Of course, my friend," don Ignacio answered. "Feel perfectly free."

That afternoon don Arturo and his family moved into don Ignacio's house, and the next morning Araceli rose at dawn, as she always did at home, and went to the ranch kitchen to prepare coffee. The foreman, Juan Verdades, was already there, drinking a cup of coffee he had made for himself and eating a breakfast of leftover tortillas. She smiled at him, and he greeted her politely: **"*Buenos días, señorita.*"** And then he finished his simple breakfast and went off to begin his day's work.

That night don Arturo and his daughter made up a plan. Araceli rose before dawn the next day and went to the kitchen to prepare coffee and fresh tortillas for the foreman. She smiled sweetly as she offered them to Juan. He returned her smile and thanked her very kindly. Each morning she did the same thing, and Juan Verdades began to fall in love with Araceli, which was just what the girl and her father expected.

What Araceli hadn't expected was that she began to fall in love with Juan Verdades too and looked forward to getting up early every morning just to be alone with him. She even began to wish she might end up marrying the handsome young foreman. Araceli continued to work on the plan she and her father had made—but she now had a plan of her own as well.

Of course, Juan knew that he was just a worker and Araceli was the daughter of a wealthy ranchero, so he didn't even dream of asking her to marry him. Still, he couldn't help trying to please her in every way. So one morning when they were talking, Juan said to Araceli, "You're very kind to have fresh coffee and warm food ready for me every morning and to honor me with the pleasure of your company. Ask me for whatever you want from this ranch. I'll speak to don Ignacio and see that it's given to you."

This is exactly what the girl and her father thought would happen. And she replied just as they had planned. It was the last thing Juan expected to hear.

"There's only one thing on this ranch I want," she said. "I'd like to have all the apples from *el manzano real.*"

The young man was very surprised, and very distressed as well, because he knew he couldn't fulfill her wish.

"I could never give you that," Juan said. "You know how don Ignacio treasures the fruit of that tree. He might agree to give you a basket of apples, but no more. I would have to take the fruit without permission, and then what would I say to don Ignacio? I can give you anything else from the ranch, but not what you're asking for."

With that the conversation ended, and they separated for the day. In the evening Juan reported to don Ignacio, and they exchanged the exact words they said every evening:

"Good evening, *mi capataz*," the rancher said.

"Good evening, *mi patrón*," replied the foreman.

"How goes it with my cattle and land?"

"Your cattle are healthy, your pastures are green."

"And the fruit of *el manzano real?*"

"The fruit is fat and ripening well."

The next morning Juan and Araceli met again. As they sipped their coffee together, Juan said, "I truly would like to repay you for the kindness you've shown me. There must be something on this ranch you would like. Tell me what it is. I'll see that it's given to you."

But again Araceli replied, "There's only one thing on this ranch I want: the apples from *el manzano real.*"

Each day they repeated the conversation. Araceli asked for the same thing, and Juan said he couldn't give it to her. But each day Juan was falling more hopelessly in love with Araceli. Finally, just the day before the two weeks of the bet would have ended, the foreman gave in. He said he would go pick the apples right then and bring them to the girl.

Juan hitched up a wagon and drove to the apple tree. He picked every single apple and delivered the wagonload of fruit to Araceli. She thanked him very warmly, and his spirits rose for a moment. But as he mounted his horse to leave, they sank once again. Juan rode away alone, lost in his thoughts, and Araceli hurried off to tell her father

the news and then to wait for a chance to talk to don Ignacio too.

Juan rode until he came to a place where there were several dead trees. He dismounted and walked up to one of them. Then he took off his hat and jacket and put them on the dead tree and pretended it was don Ignacio. He started talking to it to see if he could tell it a lie.

"Good evening, *mi capataz,*" he pretended he heard the tree say.

"Good evening, *mi patrón.*"

"How goes it with my cattle and land?"

"Your cattle are healthy, your pastures are green."

"And the fruit of *el manzano real?*"

"The....the crows have carried the fruit away..."

But the words were hardly out of his mouth when he heard himself say, "No, that's not true, *mi patrón*. I picked the fruit. . . ." And then he stopped himself.

He took a deep breath and started over again with, "Good evening, *mi capataz*."

And when he reached the end, he sputtered, "The . . . the wind shook the apples to the ground, and the cows came and ate them. . . . No, they didn't, *mi patrón*. I . . ."

He tried over and over, until he realized there was no way he could tell a lie. But he knew he could never come right out and say what he had done either. He had to think

of another way to tell don Ignacio. He took his hat and coat from the stump and sadly set out for the ranch.

All day long Juan worried about what he would say to don Ignacio. And all day long don Ignacio wondered what he would hear from his foreman, because as soon as Araceli had shown the apples to her father, he had run gleefully to tell don Ignacio what had happened.

"Now you'll see, *compadre*," don Arturo gloated. "You're about to hear a lie from Juan Verdades."

Don Ignacio was heartsick to think that all his apples had been picked, but he had agreed that don Arturo could try whatever he wanted. He sighed and said, "Very well, *compadre*, we'll see what happens this evening."

Don Arturo rode off to gather the other ranchers who were witnesses to the bet, leaving don Ignacio to pace nervously up and down in his house. And then, after don Ignacio received a visit from Araceli and she made a request that he couldn't deny, he paced even more nervously.

All the while, Juan went about his work, thinking of what he would say to don Ignacio. That evening the foreman went as usual to make his report to his employer, but he walked slowly and his head hung down. The other ranchers were behind the bushes listening, and Araceli and her mother were watching anxiously from a window of the house.

The conversation began as it always did:

"Good evening, *mi capataz*."

"Good evening, *mi patrón*."

"How goes it with my cattle and land?"

"Your cattle are healthy, your pastures are green."

"And the fruit of *el manzano real?*"

Juan took a deep breath and replied:

"Oh, *patrón,* something terrible happened today.
Some fool picked your apples and gave them away."

Don Ignacio pretended to be shocked and confused. "Some fool picked them?" he said. "Who would do such a thing?"

Juan turned his face aside. He couldn't look at don Ignacio. The rancher asked again, "Who would do such a thing? Do I know this person?"

Finally the foreman answered:

"The father of the fool is my father's father's son.

The fool has no sister and no brother.

His child would call my father 'grandfather.'

He's ashamed that he did what was done."

Don Ignacio paused for a moment to think about Juan's answer. And then, to Juan's surprise, don Ignacio grabbed his hand and started shaking it excitedly.

The other ranchers ran laughing from their hiding places. "Don Arturo," they all said, "you lose the bet. You must sign your ranch over to don Ignacio."

"No," said don Ignacio, still vigorously shaking Juan's hand. He glanced toward the window where Araceli was watching and went on: "Sign it over to don Juan Verdades. He has proved that he truly deserves that name, and he deserves to be the owner of his own ranch as well."

Everyone cheered and began to congratulate Juan. Don Arturo's face turned white, but he gritted his teeth and forced a smile. He shook Juan's hand and then turned to walk away from the group, his shoulders drooping and his head bowed down.

But Araceli came running from the house and put her arm through her father's. "*Papá,*" she said, "what if Juan Verdades were to marry a relative of yours? Then the ranch would stay in the family, wouldn't it?"

Everyone heard her and turned to look at the girl and her father. And then Juan spoke up confidently. "*Señorita* Araceli, I am the owner of a ranch and many cattle. Will you marry me?"

Of course she said she would, and don Arturo heaved a great sigh. "Don Juan Verdades," he said, "I'll be proud to have such an honest man for a son-in-law." He beckoned his wife to come from the house, and they both hugged Juan and Araceli.

The other ranchers hurried off to fetch their families, and a big celebration began. It lasted all through the night, with music and dancing and many toasts to Juan and Araceli. And in the morning everyone went home with a big basket of delicious apples from *el manzano real*.

Reader Response

Open for Discussion Retell the story of Juan Verdades inside your head or to a willing listener. Surely the ending is satisfying, with everyone happy—but what if Juan had failed? What then? Did Araceli have a back-up plan? Discuss with yourself or a willing listener.

1. Joe Hayes is a storyteller, so it's no wonder that a riddle appears in this story, for riddles find their way into stories everywhere. Why does the storyteller tell a riddle instead of having Juan say, "I am ashamed to admit it, but I picked those apples"?

2. Is it a generalization to say that Juan Verdades never lies? Why or why not?

3. Do you think that the rancheros will ever make another bet with don Ignacio? Why or why not?

4. Work with classmates to find sentences that use words from the Words to Know list. Write the sentences and highlight the words. Then suggest other words the author might have chosen to use and why the one the author used works best.

Test Practice

Look Back and Write Juan Verdades makes an offer that gets him into trouble. Look back at page 357 to find the offer. Write it in his own words and then write what trouble the offer brought.

Meet the Author and the Illustrator
Joe Hayes and Joseph Daniel Fiedler

Read more books by Joe Hayes and Joseph Daniel Fiedler.

Because he enjoyed listening to his dad's stories as a child, **Joe Hayes** began telling stories to his two children, then to other children. "I would go anywhere kids were gathered together—the elementary school, the public library, the YMCA, Boy Scouts and Girl Scouts—and offer to tell a story." That's how he got to be a storyteller.

Mr. Hayes has advice for young writers. "Always remember that writing is based on speaking. When you write, listen for the sound of the words. When you speak, your language has a rhythm and flow to it. If you hear a voice in your imagination saying the words as you write, your writing will have that same pleasant cadence."

Joseph Fiedler has created artwork for many newspapers and magazines around the world. Critics call his art "exquisite," and his landscapes have been called "magical." Mr. Fiedler grew up in Pittsburgh. He currently lives in New Mexico with his two cats, Iko and Obeah.

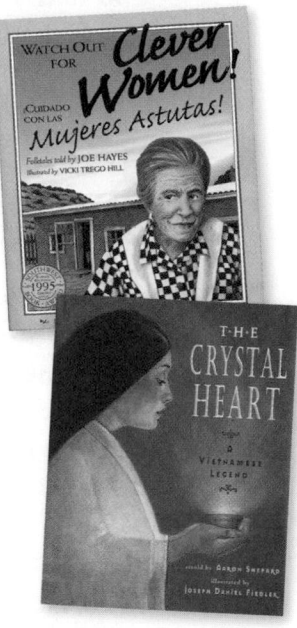

*Watch Out for Clever Women!
¡Cuidado con las mujéres
astutas!* by Joe Hayes

*The Crystal Heart: A
Vietnamese Legend*
illustrated by Joseph
Daniel Fiedler

Legend

Genre

- A legend is a story from the past, told from generation to generation until someone writes it down.

- Legends often give an explanation for a culture's history or practices.

- Unlike myths, which generally are about gods or superhuman characters, legends tend to have human characters who may or may not carry out exaggerated actions.

Link to Reading

This legend comes from Guatemala, in Central America. Find a legend from another country and share it with your class.

Song of the Chirimia

A Guatemalan legend retold by Jane Anne Volkmer

On the night of the 20th full moon of Clear Sky's kingly reign, a child was born to him. Under the moon's bright light, he stood motionless, gazing at the baby girl in his servant's arms.

"I shall name my daughter Moonlight," Clear Sky declared, "to honor the light in which I first saw her." The child was all the king had now. His beloved Queen had died at Moonlight's birth.

As Moonlight grew, Clear Sky's love for her deepened. Some days he would take her out in a boat on a nearby lake. They would watch the fishermen throw their nets into the clear blue waters. Patiently the two would wait until the men lifted the nets wriggling with fish.

Other days the two would walk through the marketplace to see the merchants' displays. Moonlight's eyes reflected the sun's

sparkle on gold necklaces. Her voice had the softness and warmth of woven cloth.

As she talked gaily to Clear Sky, she danced past the displays, breathing the fragrance of cacao beans.

But one day, the happiness ended. Moonlight sat on the palace steps, staring at the ground, not caring what could be seen at the market or how many fish were netted. She would not talk to anyone, not even her father.

She wanted to be alone.

Her father tried to bring back her laughter and chatter.

He gave her glistening jade beads from the highlands. He had his hunters bring exotic birds to her from the jungle. He called the best ballplayers in the kingdom to play in the ballcourt before her.

But Moonlight remained silent.

Clear Sky could not sleep.

He told his counselors, "My grieving will not end until I see a smile on Moonlight's face."

Clear Sky summoned governors, priests, and scribes to his chambers to ponder this problem of gloom. The learned men sat quietly for many hours, trying to think of a solution.

Finally, a scribe who recorded marriages in his village broke the silence. "Moonlight has become a young woman. It is the time of her life to marry. When she marries, her sorrow will leave."

"She shall be married!" proclaimed the king.

Clear Sky ordered all the young, unmarried men in the kingdom to come to the central plaza on the day of the 224th full moon of his rule. On this day, Moonlight could choose her husband.

Predict What kind of man might Moonlight choose?

As ordered, the suitors arrived at the palace on the day of the full moon. Many brought expensive gifts of jade, pottery, gold, and birds. Handsome men, strong men, knowledgeable men—all stood waiting. Each paraded before Moonlight in elegant clothing and spoke to her of his best qualities.

But she did not smile. She did not even listen.

As the sun lowered, the faint sounds of a song drifted through the crowd. On the path leading to the plaza, a man walked. He had no gifts. He carried no weapons. His clothes were not elegant. He was singing a joyful song. The evening breeze captured his low, sweet voice and carried it to Moonlight's ears. Smiling, she lifted her head to hear the song better.

"Tell that young man to come into my chambers," the king commanded.

The dark-haired singer was brought before the king. He stood tall and slender before Clear Sky and Moonlight.

"What is your name?" Clear Sky asked.

"I am called Black Feather," he replied.

"Black Feather, you have brought pleasure to my daughter. If she wishes, you may marry her."

Moonlight smiled at Black Feather. "Your voice is clear and your song more pure than any I have ever heard," she said. "But I still prefer to listen to the harmony of singing birds. If you can make your song and your voice become one as the birds do, I shall marry you."

"I will learn to sing like the birds," he said, "but it will take me some time. Will you grant me time to learn?"

"How much time will you need?" she asked.

"Three full moons," he answered.

"I shall listen for your return."

With love in his heart, Black Feather left the king's chambers. He hurried down the palace steps. A large cluster of ceiba trees at the plaza's edge rustled for him to come to them. A small opening between the trees led to a path. This path would take him far into the woods, where it was said that the birds never stop singing.

Black Feather disappeared down the steep and narrow path. He walked through the darkness till he could go no farther. Black Feather lay on the ground and fell asleep.

At dawn, Black Feather woke to the sound of singing birds. He listened intently. Morning, noon, and evening, Black Feather tried his best to sing as sweetly as they did.

But he could not.

Two full moons passed, and Black Feather grew weary from trying.

Alone in the woods, Black Feather thought he would never be able to return to Moonlight. Suddenly, leaves started falling around him, and the wind blew cold and moist.

Startled, Black Feather looked up. Like a large tree bent in the wind, the Great Spirit of the Woods floated above him.

Predict Will Black Feather likely find an answer? How?

"Why do you look so sad?" whispered the Great Spirit.

With much dismay, Black Feather told the spirit his story.

"I know a way for your voice and your song to join in harmony so you can sing like a bird," crackled the Great Spirit. "But you must do as I tell you. First, cut a branch from that tree."

Black Feather took his knife and cut the branch. He handed it to the Great Spirit.

Howling, the spirit flew into a treetop, setting it ablaze. The spirit roared and hissed as he transformed the branch into a long, hollow pipe with holes in one side.

The flames vanished, and the spirit drifted slowly back to Black Feather.

The Great Spirit gave the pipe to the young man saying, "What you hold in your hands is called a *chirimia*, and its song is more pleasing to the ear than that of the birds. Learn to play it well, and when the princess hears the chirimia's song, she will marry you."

Black Feather stared at the pipe.

"Take it to your lips and blow through it," the spirit commanded. "Move your fingers along the holes and listen."

Then the Great Spirit swirled into a spiral of blue-gray smoke and disappeared into the pipe.

Black Feather put his lips to the chirimia and blew. A remarkable sound filled the air, a sound so melodious that even the birds stopped their singing.

Black Feather practiced playing on the pipe all day long. The sounds became clearer and purer with every note he played.

Many days passed, and the time came for Black Feather to return. As he walked swiftly through the woods, Black Feather held tightly onto the pipe.

When he neared the small opening in the ceiba trees, he put the chirimia to his lips and began to play a song from his heart.

The melody brought the princess out of the palace to listen. Her eyes fell upon Black Feather, and she exclaimed, "Your song is lovelier than those of the birds!"

On that night, the 227th full moon of Clear Sky's reign, Moonlight and Black Feather married. Under the moon's bright light, Clear Sky stood motionless, listening to the song of the chirimia while Moonlight danced in the plaza below.

Today, if you travel to Guatemala, you may hear music sweeter than that of any bird, lilting in the wind. If you ask what it is you hear, the reply will be, "It is the song of the chirimia, the most harmonious song in the woods."

Reading Across Texts
Both Juan Verdades and Black Feather had to meet a challenge in order to marry the women they loved. Which challenge do you think was greater?

Writing Across Texts Tell why you answered this question as you did.

Generalize How do chirimias affect Moonlight?

371

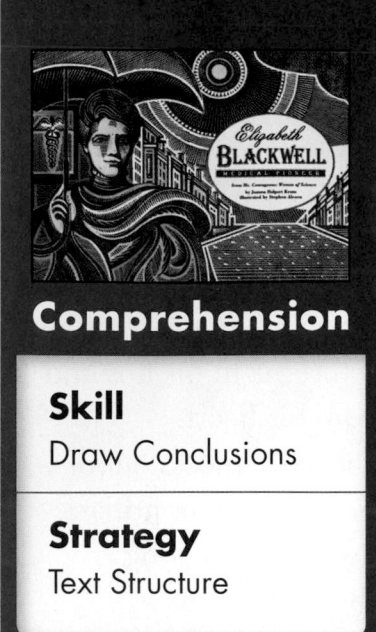

Comprehension

Skill
Draw Conclusions

Strategy
Text Structure

Draw Conclusions

- When you draw a conclusion, you form a reasonable opinion about something you have read. Drawing conclusions is also called making inferences.

- Use what you know about real life to help you draw conclusions.

- When you draw a conclusion, it should make sense. Ask, "Is my conclusion based on facts? Does what I have read support the conclusion?"

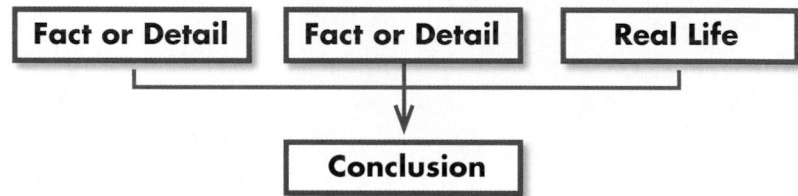

| Fact or Detail | Fact or Detail | Real Life |

Conclusion

Strategy: Text Structure

You can use the structure of an article or story to help you understand what you read. First look at the title, headings, and illustrations. Then as you read, look for patterns of ideas in the text. For example, the text may tell events in a specific order. It may compare and contrast two people or two places. Whatever the text structure is, the pattern of ideas will allow you to draw conclusions.

1. Read "How to Become a Doctor." Make a graphic organizer like the one above to help you draw a conclusion about what kind of student studies to become a doctor.

2. Make a graphic organizer like the one above to draw a conclusion about the way one becomes a doctor. Write a paragraph about the process.

How to Become a Doctor.

COLLEGE The long road to becoming a doctor begins in college. Students take many science classes and spend a lot of time in laboratories learning to use various instruments. Most students graduate after four years. Then they must pass an exam in order to go to medical school.

MEDICAL SCHOOL Medical school usually lasts for about four years. There students study the parts of the human body and how the parts work. They also study diseases.

IN THE HOSPITAL After medical school, students spend the next two to three years working with doctors in a hospital. The students observe how the doctors work and help them treat patients. During this time students must work long hours for many days in a row.

FINISHING UP The students conclude their training by working as doctors in hospitals for one or two years. This time is called residency. Experienced doctors watch the students to make sure that they do things correctly. Once their residency is completed, the students are officially doctors.

Strategy By previewing the title and headings, can you tell if the text is presenting ideas in sequence? comparing or contrasting two things? defining a problem and its solution?

Skill What conclusion can you draw about the grades most doctors received in college?

(a) Most got poor grades.

(b) Most got very good grades.

(c) Most didn't care about their grades.

Strategy The word *next* helps you follow the order of steps in becoming a doctor. What other words also help you follow the order of these steps?

Skill What conclusion can you draw about how the students might feel during the time they are working in the hospital?

Words to Know

diploma

absurd

obedient

behalf

reject

delirious

dean

candidate

hovers

Remember

Try the strategy. Then, if you need more help, use your glossary or a dictionary.

Vocabulary Strategy
for Antonyms

Context Clues When you are reading, sometimes you find a word you do not know. You can often figure out its meaning by finding a clue in the words around it. The writer may include an antonym, or a word with the opposite meaning, as a clue.

1. Reread the sentence in which the unknown word occurs.

2. Look for a word or phrase that gives a clue to its meaning.

3. Are two things being contrasted? Look for words that point to opposites, such as *unlike*, *however*, *but*, or *on the other hand*.

4. Determine the meaning of the antonym.

5. Give the unknown word the opposite meaning of the antonym. Does this meaning make sense in the sentence?

As you read "On Behalf of Women," check the context of words you don't know. See if an antonym gives you a clue to meaning.

On Behalf of Women

Today, we expect that most young women will get an education. This is the only sensible thing to do because a diploma is needed to get a good job. However, less than a hundred years ago, the idea of women needing education or jobs was thought absurd by most people. A woman should be obedient, care for the home, and raise the children. If she tried for more, she was thought willful, a bad influence.

Over that same hundred years, many brave women fought to change this attitude. On behalf of all women, they took action. To the idea that woman could not and should not have a profession, they said, "We reject your thinking. Instead, we choose to learn, to work, to be full members of our society."

Today, that old way of thinking seems delirious.

It is not rational that half of the human race be kept from achieving all it can. A woman can be the dean of a college, an astronaut, or a candidate for President. The spirit of those who spoke up hovers above all women who carry out their dreams.

Write

Write about the dreams and ambitions of a woman you know, such as a relative or a family friend. Use as many of the Words to Know as you can.

375

What qualities must a doctor have to be effective?

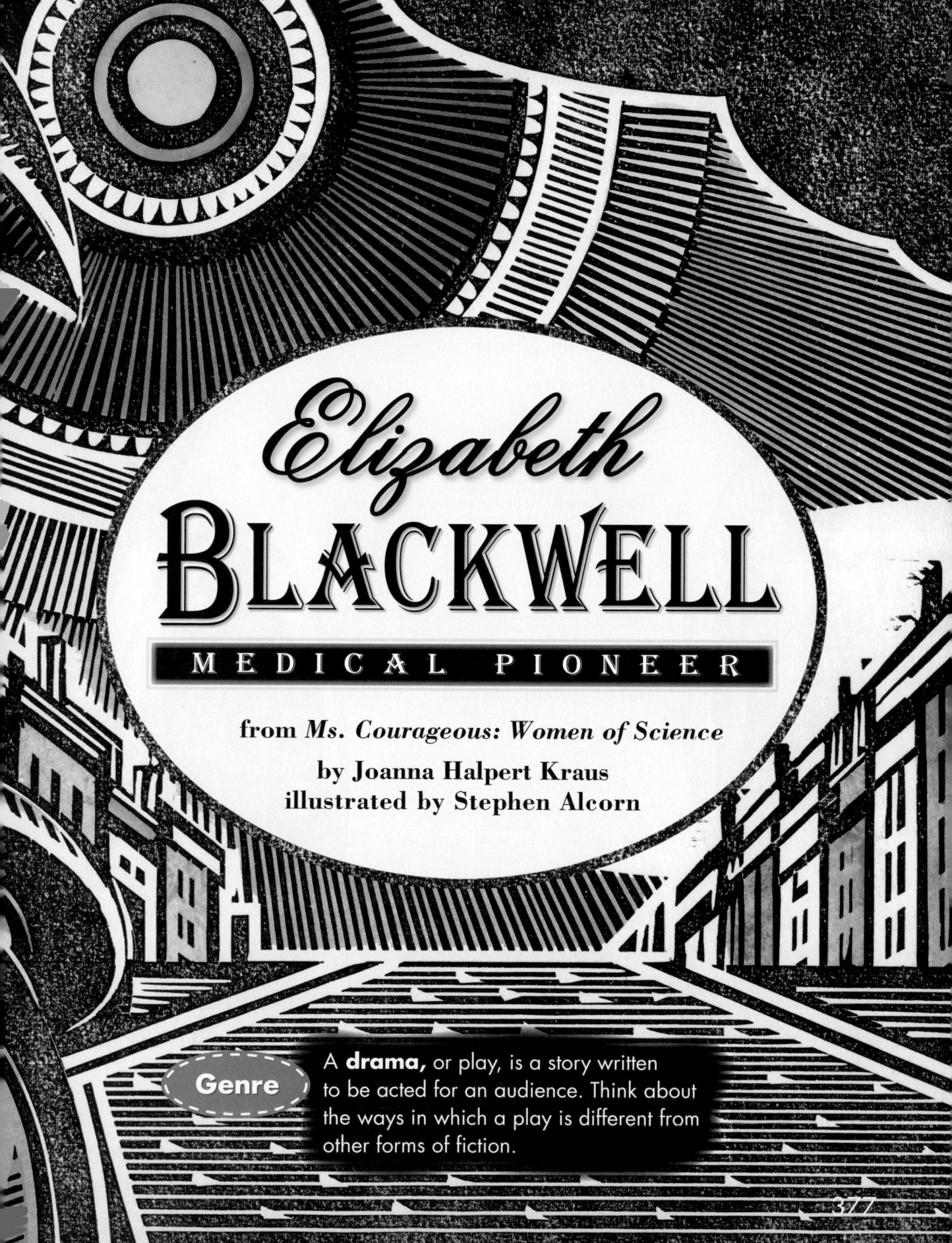

Elizabeth BLACKWELL

MEDICAL PIONEER

from *Ms. Courageous: Women of Science*

by Joanna Halpert Kraus

illustrated by Stephen Alcorn

→ CAST·OF·CHARACTERS ←

Narrators

Percussion Players or Other Musicians

Elizabeth Blackwell, a medical student

Dr. Barnes, her teacher

Dean Snyder, Dean of Admissions

James, his colleague

Dean Richards, Geneva Medical College Dean

Raymond, first Geneva colleague

Herbert, second Geneva colleague

John, Student Council President

Elmer, a student

Phillip, another student

Betsy, a young servant

Lily Barnes, Dr. Barnes's wife

Dr. Benjamin Hale, Geneva College President

Lulu, a new student nurse

Anna, Elizabeth's older sister

Dr. Claude Blot, an intern at La Maternité hospital

Anthony, a recent immigrant

Helga, Anthony's sister

Zac, a physician and Elizabeth's colleague

Sean, an Irish longshoreman

Dean Reynolds

Sean

Elizabeth

(Setting: A bare stage with varying performance levels and an easel for signs. Costume pieces and properties are available.)
(At Rise: Three NARRATORS *stand in different areas of the stage. The two* PERCUSSION PLAYERS *are on stage and remain there throughout the play.)*

(SOUND: Percussion instruments.)

NARRATOR ONE: Meet—

NARRATOR TWO: Elizabeth Blackwell.

NARRATOR THREE: Medical pioneer.

*(*PERCUSSION PLAYER *flips sign on easel to read "Philadelphia."* ELIZABETH BLACKWELL *appears, attired in a modest gown and bonnet, carrying a small traveling case. She is in her mid-20s, stubborn, determined, restless, and independent. She mimes walking in place.) (The* NARRATORS *take poses, backs to us in separate parts of the stage.)* (ELIZABETH *flings her arms wide to the world, as she sets her case down.)*

ELIZABETH: I want to be—

NARRATOR ONE *(turns):* Want to be—

NARRATOR TWO *(turns):* Want to be—

ELIZABETH: The first lady surgeon in the United States. No. I want to be the first—in the entire world!

NARRATOR ONE: The first—

NARRATOR TWO: In the world.

NARRATOR THREE *(turns):* CRAZY! (NARRATORS *confer.)*

NARRATOR ONE: Not practical.

NARRATOR TWO *(authoritatively):* A well brought up lady cannot be a doctor.

NARRATOR ONE *(reading from a large period magazine):* "A woman's sphere is in the home." *(Closes magazine decisively.)*

NARRATOR THREE *(reading from a book): The Young Lady's Book* says she must be "obedient, submissive, and humble."

(**NARRATORS** *look at one another, then back at* ELIZABETH, *glaring at her.*)

NARRATOR ONE: Shocking!

NARRATOR TWO: Shameful!

NARRATOR THREE: Sinful!

ALL NARRATORS (*pointing at* ELIZABETH): SCANDALOUS!

(NARRATORS *exit.* DR. BARNES *enters. 40s. Wise, pragmatic.*)

DR. BARNES: My dear Miss Blackwell, woman was designed to be the helpmate of man. Man must be the physician; woman the nurse.

ELIZABETH: Doctor, I've paid for three years of pre-medical study with you. I've attended your lectures, used your library, been with you to visit patients. Please! You've got to help me get admitted to medical school.

DR. BARNES: No woman has ever gone to medical school!

ELIZABETH: You told me I had the ability.

DR. BARNES: You do! But it's 1847, Miss Blackwell. There isn't a college in the country that will accept you.

ELIZABETH: Times won't change unless we make them change!

DR. BARNES (*slowly*): There is one way.

ELIZABETH: What? What?

DR. BARNES: Disguise yourself as a man, and go study in Paris.

ELIZABETH (*shocked*): How can I help other women, if I'm in disguise? There must be some school, one school, in this huge nation brave enough to accept a woman. Won't you please write a letter on my behalf?

DR. BARNES: I'll do better than that! I'll send you to a friend, who's Dean of Admissions here in Philadelphia. But don't expect miracles.

ELIZABETH: Miracles are something you make happen!

(DR. BARNES *exits.*)

(ELIZABETH *marches back to her room and takes out a writing box and begins a letter.*)

Dear Sir, I wish to apply to your medical college.

(*As she writes,* DEAN SNYDER *and* JAMES *enter a different area.* DEAN SNYDER *is 40s, hard-nosed.* JAMES *is his colleague, 30s, a "yes" person.*)

DEAN SNYDER (*waving* ELIZABETH's *letter*): If we admit a woman, our enrollment will decline. Therefore, I urge us all to reject the application, despite a fine recommendation.

JAMES (*applauding*): Hear! Hear!

DEAN SNYDER: She can hardly expect us to give her a stick with which to break our own heads! (*to* JAMES.) Do you know what will happen if women patients start going to women doctors?

JAMES: What?

DEAN SNYDER: We'll lose our jobs! This is the most absurd application I've ever had. Suddenly there are all these quacks trying to get into medical college. With water cures, electrical cures. We might as well let in all the charlatans as let in a woman!

(*They exit.* ELIZABETH *opens her letter, reading.*)

ELIZABETH: Rejection from Philadelphia. (*Throws it down. Opens another letter.* NARRATORS *have entered.*) Rejection from New York.

ALL NARRATORS: Twenty-five rejections.

ELIZABETH (*thinks aloud*): All these years I've tried to earn enough to pay for medical school. Teaching music to children who are tone deaf. Trying to pound an education into students who don't care. All these years trying to prepare for medical school, learning Greek, learning anatomy. But it doesn't matter how hard I've worked. As soon as they see my name, Elizabeth, the answer is "No!" Because I'm a female. That's the only reason.

(ELIZABETH *turns away from audience as staff of Geneva Medical College enters:* DEAN RICHARDS, *smooth administrator;* RAYMOND, *his first colleague, action-oriented;* HERBERT, *his second colleague, who follows the rules. All are men in their 30s.*)

(PERCUSSION PLAYER *flips sign to read "Geneva, New York."*)

DEAN RICHARDS: We have a very awkward situation, gentlemen. I need your advice.

RAYMOND AND HERBERT *(turn):* Y-e-e-s.

DEAN RICHARDS *(with a sheaf of papers):* A well-qualified applicant. With an excellent recommendation from Dr. Barnes.

RAYMOND: Philadelphia's best! Find a scholarship for him. Any candidate he recommends, I say we take.

DEAN RICHARDS: I'm afraid it's a graver matter than mere scholarship.

RAYMOND: More serious than money?

HERBERT: An incurable disease?

DEAN RICHARDS: You might say so. The fact is, gentlemen— *(Pauses.)* The *he* is a *she*.

HERBERT: A she!

(SOUND: Percussion.)

RAYMOND: Out of the question!

HERBERT: Impossible.

DEAN RICHARDS: I agree. Of course. But what do we write Dr. Barnes?

HERBERT: We don't want to insult him.

DEAN RICHARDS: We want to keep his goodwill. *(They pace.)*

RAYMOND: The request is highly unusual, and it concerns the students. Let them decide!

DEAN RICHARDS: Brilliant! And if any of the students object to admitting a woman, we'll reject the application.

HERBERT: The students have never agreed on anything!

DEAN RICHARDS *(smoothly):* Then we can tell Dr. Barnes it was the students' decision—not ours!

(They exit, as students enter a different area. JOHN, *Student Council President, is 18; bright, fair-minded but not above pranks.* ELMER, *17, is bored. Anything for a laugh.* PHILLIP, *17, is a reactionary.)*

JOHN *(bangs gavel):* I call this meeting of the Student Council to order.

(SOUND: Hoots, whistles, catcalls.)

ELMER: Hurry it up.

PHILLIP: All members present.

JOHN: Good! The Dean has asked the Student Council to make a momentous decision. One that could change this institution.

ELMER: Anything for a change.

JOHN: A lady has applied to Geneva Medical College.

PHILLIP: Can't be a lady if she applied here.

(SOUND: Raucous laughter.)

JOHN: The dean wants our decision this afternoon. May we have some discussion?

ELMER: Heck, just for argument's sake, I say let her come. She'd liven up the place.

PHILLIP: Liven up the place! She'd ruin our reputation!

JOHN: She could put Geneva Medical College on the map.

PHILLIP: If we let her in, she'll slow the whole class down.

ELMER *(to* PHILLIP*):* Then someone else besides you would be at the bottom!

(SOUND: Laughter.)

JOHN: It's my belief scientific education should be open to all.

PHILLIP: I agree. As long as "all" ain't women!

(SOUND: More laughter.)

ELMER: Call the vote! Call the vote!

JOHN: All those in favor?

PHILLIP: Aye!

(SOUND: Simultaneous chorus of "Ayes.")

JOHN: All those opposed?

PHILLIP: NAY!

(ELMER *rushes to* PHILLIP.)

ELMER: Toss him out the window! Throw him down the stairs!

PHILLIP *(hastily):* Aye! Aye! I vote Aye!

JOHN: Then it's unanimous! *(Grinning.)* This is more fun than Halloween!

(SOUND: "Yeas," whistles, catcalls as students exit.)

(PERCUSSION PLAYER *flips sign to read "Philadelphia".)*

(SOUND: Knock. BETSY, *an eight to ten-year-old servant, active, curious, mimes running up the stairs.)*

BETSY *(rushes into* ELIZABETH'S *room):* Miss Blackwell. Miss Blackwell. A letter for you.

ELIZABETH: Thank you.

BETSY: Ain't ya gonna open it? I ran up two flights. I never saw anyone get so many letters as you do, Miss Blackwell. More than the Doctor himself. You get more than anyone in the whole city of Philadelphia, I warrant.

ELIZABETH: But they all say the same. They all say "No."

BETSY: The Doctor and the Missus say you're to come down for tea. Hot mince pies, Miss Blackwell.

ELIZABETH: In a minute. I will in a minute.

(BETSY *exits.* LILY BARNES, *the doctor's wife, brings tea into the parlor.* LILY *is in her 30s, supportive. Unobtrusively she puts the tea out, as* ELIZABETH *opens her letter halfheartedly.* ELIZABETH *rises, more and more astonished by the letter's content. She races out of her room, delirious with joy.*)

Everybody! Listen! Everybody!

(ELIZABETH *flies into the parlor and whirls around the room.*)
I've been accepted.

LILY BARNES (*hugs* ELIZABETH): Congratulations.

DR. BARNES: I knew one of those schools would have common sense.

ELIZABETH: They've approved me. Gentlemen—(*Curtsies to an imaginary group.*) I accept.

LILY BARNES: When will you leave?

ELIZABETH: Immediately! Before they change their minds!

(DR. BARNES *brings* ELIZABETH *her travel case and exits as* ELIZABETH *crosses to a new area and* LILY BARNES *exits.*)

(*SOUND: Graduation processional march.*)

(DR. BENJAMIN HALE, *Geneva Medical College president, enters. 40s. Dignified. He wears a black velvet mortarboard to suggest academic regalia.*)

DR. HALE (*addresses audience*): No one at the college expected her to show up. And when she did no one thought she'd stay. And certainly no one ever thought she'd graduate with top honors!

(*SOUND: Applause. Processional march as* ELIZABETH *comes forward.*)

Dr. Blackwell! Congratulations! (*Hands her diploma.*)

ELIZABETH: Dr. Benjamin Hale, faculty, family, friends, ladies, and gentlemen, I will do everything in my power to bring honor to this diploma. I promise you!

(*SOUND: More wild applause. Shouts of "Hurray for Elizabeth."*
DR. BENJAMIN HALE *exits as* NARRATORS *enter and* ELIZABETH *crosses to a new area.*)

NARRATOR ONE: Elizabeth tried to keep her promise.

NARRATOR TWO: She went to Paris to fulfill her dream.

NARRATOR THREE: But no hospital would admit her.

ELIZABETH: What good is my diploma!

NARRATOR TWO: Only the maternity hospital would take her. As a —

ELIZABETH *(reading the letter, shocked):* Student nurse. A STUDENT NURSE! I have a medical degree! *(Squares her shoulders, determined.)* If that's how I have to start, then I will! *(Reflects.)* Besides, I'll learn more in three months there than in three years of reading books.

(ELIZABETH *picks up her traveling bag and marches over to don a hospital apron of heavy toweling with huge pockets.)*

(SOUND: PERCUSSION PLAYERS *beat a fast rhythm under chanted work poem.* ELIZABETH *mimes portions of the work poem.)*

NARRATOR THREE: Work.

NARRATOR ONE: Up at five.

NARRATOR TWO: Scrub the floors.

NARRATOR THREE: Dust the corners. Fill the pans.

NARRATOR ONE: Feed the patients.

NARRATOR TWO: Class at seven.

NARRATOR THREE: Follow doctors.

NARRATOR ONE: Visit wards.

NARRATOR TWO: Rushing, rushing.

NARRATOR THREE: Bolt it down.

NARRATOR ONE: A bit of bread.

NARRATOR TWO: A chunk of cheese.

NARRATOR THREE: On the run. On the run.

NARRATOR ONE: Babies born. Night and day.

NARRATOR TWO: Day and night.

NARRATOR THREE: Complications.

NARRATOR ONE: Operations.

NARRATOR TWO: Emergencies. Emergencies.

NARRATOR THREE: Middle of the night.

NARRATOR ONE: Middle of the day.

NARRATOR TWO: No sleep.

NARRATOR THREE: No time.

(ELIZABETH *collapses in a chair and falls asleep.* NARRATORS *exit.*)

(SOUND: Church bells chime three.)

(LULU *runs on and shakes* ELIZABETH. LULU *is a new student nurse. 20s. Anxious.*)

LULU: Mademoiselle! Mademoiselle Blackwell!

ELIZABETH *(groggy):* So tired. Go away, please. So tired.

LULU: The baby's worse.

ELIZABETH *(jumps up):* I'll be right there.

(ELIZABETH *runs down the hall to the ward. She picks up the swaddled baby.* LULU *hovers in the background.*)

(SOUND: Baby crying.)

ELIZABETH *(soothing):* Sh-h. Of course, it hurts. You can't see. Not with that infection in your eyes. (ELIZABETH *puts baby back in the crib.*) Sh-h. There now. Lie still. I have to use the syringe. Lie still. If only the light were better.

(SOUND: Sharp, discordant.)

ELIZABETH *(screams):* OH-H-H-H! OW-W-W-W-W-! OH-H-H-H.

(LULU *runs off.*)

(SOUND: More discordant sounds to indicate a passage of time.)

*(*DR. CLAUDE BLOT *enters a different area. Mid-20s. He is an intern at* La Maternité. *Knowledgeable.)*

*(*ELIZABETH *covers her left eye with her hand and crosses to* DR. BLOT.*)*

DR. BLOT *(very concerned):* How did it happen, Mademoiselle?

ELIZABETH: I was syringing the fluid from the baby's eye. I was very tired; the light was bad. Somehow when I leaned over the crib, some of the fluid squirted into my eye. *(Attempting to make light of it.)* You know the way a lemon squirts.

DR. BLOT *(examining):* More serious than a lemon, Mademoiselle. Why didn't you come to me as soon as it happened?

ELIZABETH: I had so much to do. I washed the eye out immediately. But this morning I couldn't open it at all.

DR. BLOT *(still examining):* The left eye is very inflamed and swollen. I pray to God it doesn't spread.

ELIZABETH: How am I going to do my work in the wards today?

DR. BLOT: You're not! Not for quite some time, Mademoiselle.

ELIZABETH *(shocked):* Not work!

DR. BLOT *(gently but firmly):* That's an order.

ELIZABETH: But I have to!

DR. BLOT: What you have to do, Mademoiselle, is get well. Unfortunately, you have the same disease as the baby you were treating.

ELIZABETH: The same? Are you sure?

DR. BLOT: It's a classic case of purulent ophthalmia. I'm sure you know the dangers already.

ELIZABETH *(slowly):* With a baby, it can mean permanent blindness. That's why I was trying so hard to save his sight.

DR. BLOT: You're a doctor, so I'll be frank. There's no guarantee—

ELIZABETH *(distraught):* Doctor, can you save my eye? Can you?

DR. BLOT: I will do everything I can. But I'm a doctor, not a magician.

(SOUND: To indicate the passage of time.)

(NARRATORS *help* ELIZABETH *remove hospital apron.* DR. BLOT *bends over* ELIZABETH *with a pincer.)*

DR. BLOT: Are you ready? I'm going to remove the film from the pupil of your eye. *(He performs the delicate procedure.)*

DR. BLOT: Sit up very slowly. You've been in bed for three weeks. (ELIZABETH *does.*) Now tell me what you can see.

ELIZABETH *(as she looks):* Pull the curtains and I will.

DR. BLOT *(stunned):* Mademoiselle . . . there are no curtains.

ELIZABETH *(grabbing and holding* DR. BLOT'*s hand):* Doctor, tell me I'll get better! Please, tell me I'll get better. A surgeon cannot be blind!

DR. BLOT: Mademoiselle, you mustn't excite yourself. Your sister's here. She's come to take you home.

ELIZABETH: Doctor, tell me the truth, please! Am I blind?

DR. BLOT *(upset):* We used the latest medical procedures. And I was there. Every day. Every night.

ELIZABETH *(quietly):* Will I see again?

DR. BLOT: You might regain the sight in your right eye. But only if you have absolute rest. That's why I've sent for your sister.

ELIZABETH: And the left eye?

DR. BLOT *(shakes his head):* I did all I could. I wish to God I could have done more. (ANNA *rushes in. 30. She is* ELIZABETH's *older sister. Protective.* DR. BLOT *exits.*)

ANNA: Elizabeth!

ELIZABETH: Anna! Anna! (ELIZABETH *starts to cry.*)

ANNA: Don't, Elizabeth. Don't.

ELIZABETH: Anna, I can't give up. For years I've planned. For years! (ANNA *holds her as* ELIZABETH *sobs silently.*)

ANNA: We can't always do what we planned. Now, you must get your strength back.

ELIZABETH: What's the point in getting well, Anna, unless I can follow my dream?

ANNA: Sh-h. Put this shawl around you. It's cold outside. (ANNA *helps* ELIZABETH *cross to a chair in a different area.*)

(SOUND: To indicate the passage of time.)

ELIZABETH *(calls):* Anna! Anna!

ANNA *(rushes in):* What is it? What's wrong, Elizabeth?

ELIZABETH: I can see the lamp. On the table. It's like through a mist. But I can see it. I can see it!

(ANNA *hugs her.*)

ANNA: I've waited six months to hear you say that! Oh, Elizabeth. Finally. Your eyes are beginning to heal! *(Producing a letter.)* A letter came this afternoon from St. Bartholomew's Hospital in London.

ELIZABETH: Read it! Don't keep me in suspense. Quick! It is yes or no? (ANNA *quickly hopes before she opens the letter to read it.*)

ANNA: It's . . . YES! For next fall. You've been accepted to study surgery. Or to study practical medicine.

ELIZABETH: SURGERY! They accepted me! Anna, cover my eyes. Quickly! One at a time. First the left.

(ANNA *covers the left eye.*)

ANNA: What do you see?

ELIZABETH: You. Better than before. You're wearing a yellow dress.

(ANNA *smiles.* ELIZABETH *looks hungrily.*) And the brass lamp. The mist is lifting. And the flowered wallpaper. And tomorrow I'll see even more. The right eye is healing. It's healing! I'm sure of it! *(Tensely.)* Now cover it. (ANNA *covers the right eye.*)

ANNA *(anxiously):* Can you see anything?

(There is a horrible pause.)

ELIZABETH: Darkness. A wall. *(With a sob.)* Anna, Anna, how do you give up a dream?

ANNA *(gently):* By dreaming another.
(ANNA *holds her distraught sister in her arms. Abruptly* ELIZABETH *holds her head up. She's made a decision.*)

ELIZABETH: Write St. Bartholomew's Hospital. I'm coming.

ANNA: Coming?

ELIZABETH: Not surgery. That door is closed. Forever. But dear sister, Anna, didn't you just say "dream another."

ANNA: But I meant—

ELIZABETH: Practical medicine! Tell them I'll study that. If I can't be a surgeon, Anna, I will be a doctor!

(ELIZABETH *crosses to a new area, as* ANNA *exits and* NARRATORS *enter.*)
(PERCUSSION PLAYER *flips sign to read "New York City."*)

(As NARRATORS *speak, two crowd members,* ANTHONY *and* HELGA, *enter.* ANTHONY, *20s, is a recent immigrant, angry.* HELGA, *also 20s and a recent immigrant, is curious.)*

NARRATOR ONE: After St. Bartholomew's, Elizabeth returned to America ready to be a doctor.

NARRATOR TWO: But it was a constant struggle.

NARRATOR THREE: No hospital wanted to hire her.

NARRATOR ONE: No landlord wanted to rent space to her.

NARRATOR TWO: Finally she opened a clinic in the immigrant slums of New York City.

NARRATOR THREE: Her medical ideas were shocking!

*(*ELIZABETH *stands on a platform addressing a crowd.)*

ELIZABETH: Fresh air, exercise, a balanced diet. Children are born to live, not die!

ANTHONY: We need a doctor who can cure the cholera! Not a preacher!

HELGA: What's fresh air got to do with tuberculosis?

ELIZABETH: Everything! Everything! If the body can't breathe, if the body isn't clean, if the body is malnourished, it cannot get well!

(SOUND: Applause and "boos.")

NARRATOR ONE: She worked around the clock seeing patients, sometimes the only figure on a darkened street hurrying through the night to save someone.

*(*ZAC *enters, crosses to clinic area.* ZAC, *20s, a physician, is* ELIZABETH's *colleague.)*

NARRATOR TWO: But one tragic night, a few months later, a patient died.

(SOUND: Angry voices, threatening mob.)

*(*PERCUSSION PLAYERS *add to the noise of the crowd. If possible, they become crowd members.)*

*(*ANTHONY *runs across stage, yelling toward the hospital area.)*

ANTHONY: Call yourself a doctor, do you? You killed her. My sister. The lady doctor killed her. And I've got a good mind to do the same to you. Murderer!

(SOUND: Approaching footsteps, voices screaming.)

(From the hospital area, ELIZABETH *and* ZAC *peer nervously out a hospital window.)*

ELIZABETH: I'd better stop that mob before they break in.

*(*ZAC *holds* ELIZABETH *back.)*

ZAC: Elizabeth, they've got pickaxes and shovels. And rocks. If you walk out there, you'll start a riot!

(SOUND: Window glass shattering.)

ELIZABETH *(shakes loose):* The riot's already started! Someone has to stop it.

*(*SEAN, *late 20s, a burly Irish longshoreman, races on and bounds up a higher platform area carrying a huge stick.)*

ZAC *(looks out):* Wait! There's a man bounding up the stairs. *(They peer out.)*

(SOUND: Crowd noises.)

SEAN: Quiet! Quiet down, all of you. One more rock, and I'll get the entire New York police force here. *(Grins.)* And five of them are my own brothers.

(SOUND: Laughter. SEAN *holds out his stick.)*

Anybody who tries to hurt the good doctors will have to get past me first! Now, listen!

(SOUND: Noise subsides.)

Dr. Blackwell saved my wife, when she nearly died of pneumonia. How many of you out here have husbands, wives, and children she's tended?

(SOUND: Crowd mumbles.)

I thought so. And did she come to your home, when you were too sick to go out?

(SOUND: Crowd mumbles in agreement. "Aye." "Yes, she did," etc.) Did you get the same care, whether you paid or not?

(SOUND: Crowd louder in agreement. "Yes." "We did." "That's true," etc.)

Some of you couldn't stand here and screech your lungs out, if she hadn't given you the strength!

(SOUND: Crowd ad-libs. "She saved my boy." "You're right," etc.)
Are you forgetting that even a doctor can't keep a patient from dying,

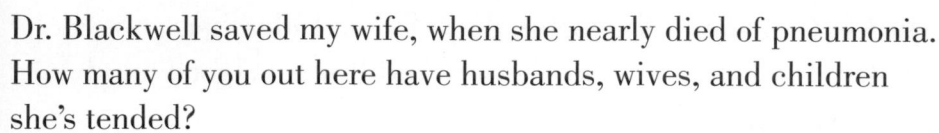

when it's the Lord's will? Sure tonight is a heartache. Sure we're all grieving. But I'll tell you this, I'd grieve more if we lost the hospital!

(SOUND: Crowd reaction.)

Do you want to know what kind of medical care the likes of us would get without her? I'll tell you. NOTHING! So, put your rocks down, and go home. We'll never have a better doctor. Don't be making her go away!

(SOUND: Mumbling crowd disperses and exits.)

ZAC: They're going! They're going.

(ELIZABETH dashes to catch SEAN.)

ELIZABETH: Wait! WAIT!

(ZAC exits, as ELIZABETH catches up with SEAN on the street.)

SEAN: Why, it's the little doctor herself. Sorry about that ruckus.

ELIZABETH: Thank you! Thank you for stopping that mob! You saved the Infirmary.

SEAN: Now don't be letting them scare you away.

ELIZABETH: It takes more than a shovel and a stone to scare a Blackwell!

SEAN *(trying to explain):* They just never saw a lady doctor before.

ELIZABETH *(firm):* They're going to see more of us! More and more. Just like me.

SEAN: Begging your pardon, Dr. Blackwell. Not like you. There's only one like you! *(Tips his cap.)* Evening, Doctor.

(SEAN exits, as NARRATORS enter.)

NARRATOR ONE: It wasn't the first time Dr. Blackwell was threatened.

NARRATOR TWO: And it wasn't the last.

ELIZABETH: Because the real sickness is prejudice! And until I conquer that, I can never stop!

ELIZABETH BLACKWELL

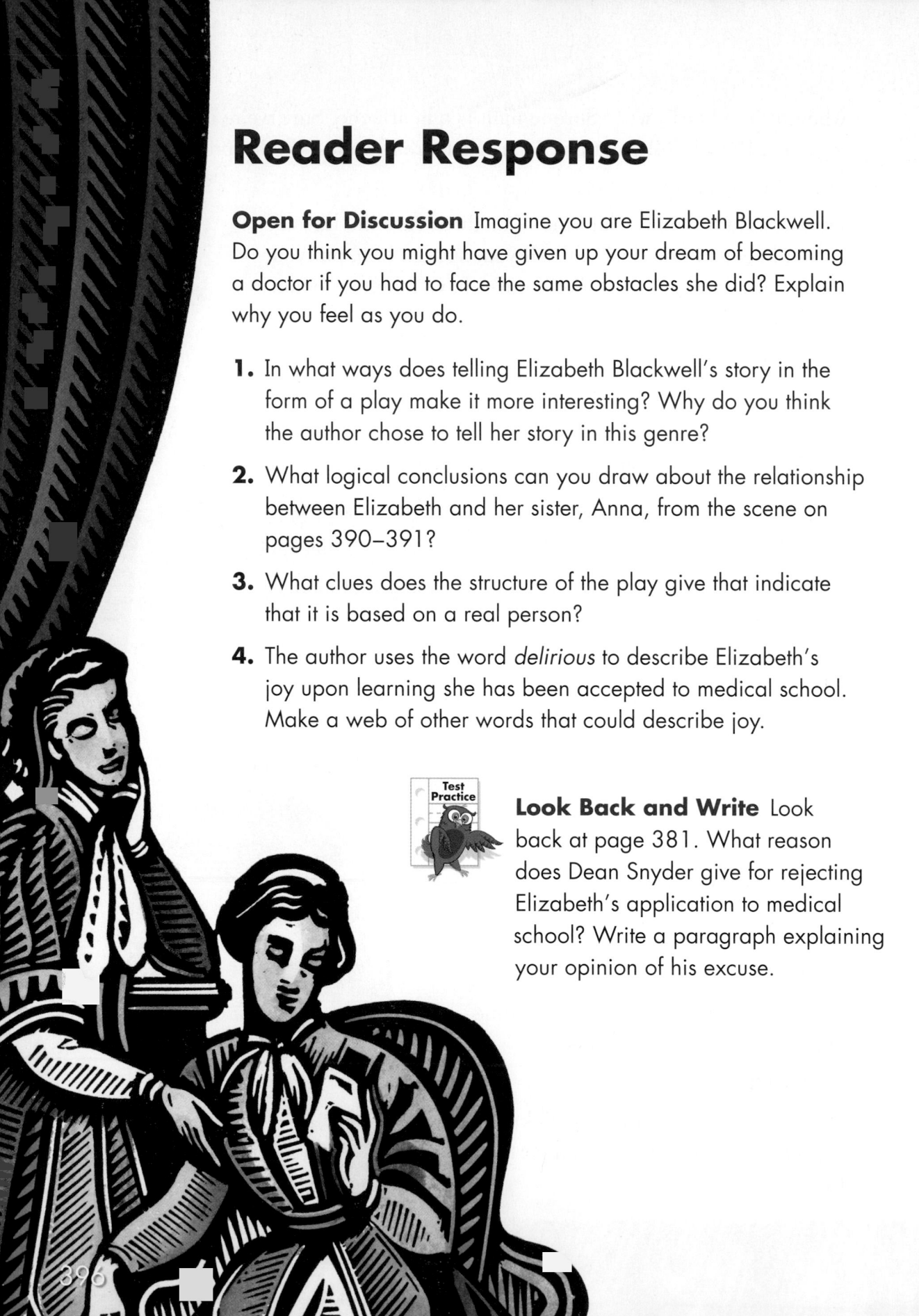

Reader Response

Open for Discussion Imagine you are Elizabeth Blackwell. Do you think you might have given up your dream of becoming a doctor if you had to face the same obstacles she did? Explain why you feel as you do.

1. In what ways does telling Elizabeth Blackwell's story in the form of a play make it more interesting? Why do you think the author chose to tell her story in this genre?

2. What logical conclusions can you draw about the relationship between Elizabeth and her sister, Anna, from the scene on pages 390–391?

3. What clues does the structure of the play give that indicate that it is based on a real person?

4. The author uses the word *delirious* to describe Elizabeth's joy upon learning she has been accepted to medical school. Make a web of other words that could describe joy.

Look Back and Write Look back at page 381. What reason does Dean Snyder give for rejecting Elizabeth's application to medical school? Write a paragraph explaining your opinion of his excuse.

Joanna Halpert Kraus

Read more books by Joanna Halpert Kraus.

Joanna Halpert Kraus was part of an acting company from an early age. "When I was thirteen," she says, "my life was changed by a marvelous director of children's theater, Margaret Dutton. We toured towns in Maine, where no live theater for young audiences had ever appeared. The children were spellbound, but no more so than we, the players. I vowed then to pass on that touch of magic."

Ms. Kraus has been true to her vow. Almost her entire career has centered around young people and the theater. "Children should have stories to grow on and should never have anything less than the best," she says. "Young people are a wonderful audience, for they listen with their hearts as well as their minds." Plays she has written include *Mean to Be Free,* about Harriet Tubman and the Underground Railroad, and *The Ice Wolf,* about an Eskimo village. In her plays, Ms. Kraus entertains and educates adults as well as children.

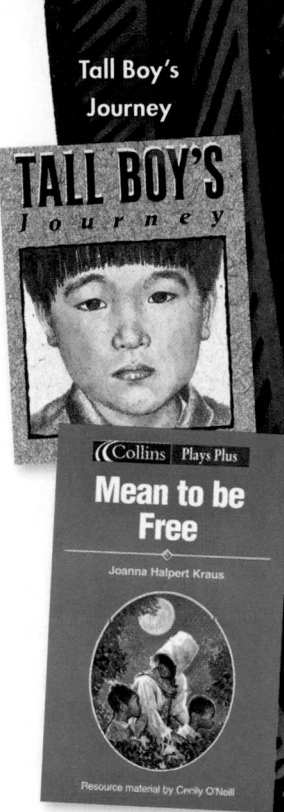

Tall Boy's Journey

Plays Plus: Mean to Be Free

Biography

Genre

- Biography is an account of a person's life, written by someone other than the subject.

- The writer must decide which events and details to include.

Text Features

- This is a very brief description of Rebecca Lee Crumpler's life and accomplishments.

- Most biographies show the subject, but no photos or drawings of Dr. Crumpler exist.

Link to Social Studies

Rebecca Lee Crumpler worked very hard to receive her education. She also published a book later in her life. Research more of her life to find out about some of the problems she had to overcome.

Rebecca Lee Crumpler

by Joan Potter and Constance Claytor

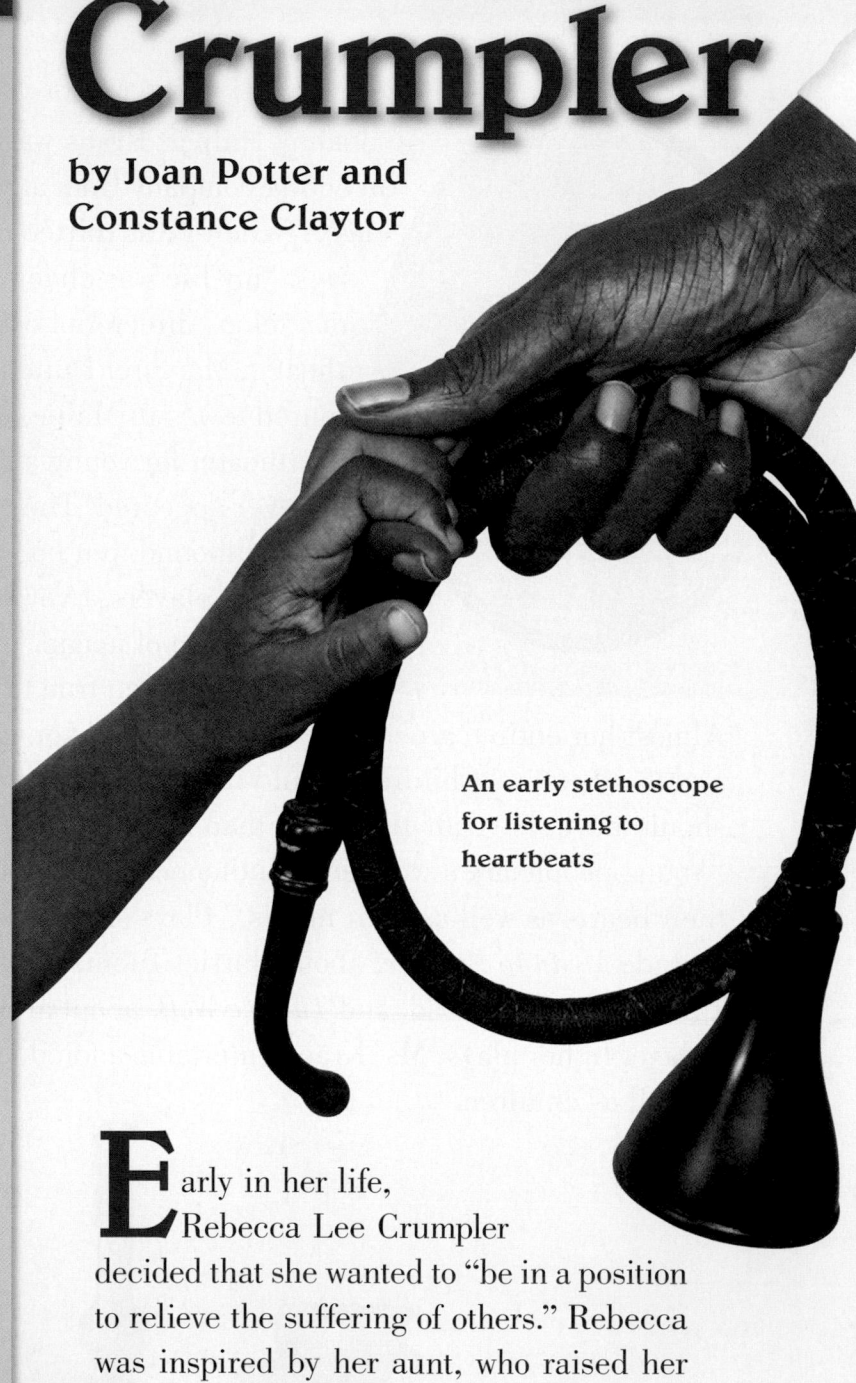

An early stethoscope for listening to heartbeats

Early in her life, Rebecca Lee Crumpler decided that she wanted to "be in a position to relieve the suffering of others." Rebecca was inspired by her aunt, who raised her

Text Structure Why is this article's structure sequential?

after she was born in 1833. Rebecca's aunt gave medical care to the people in her community, and Rebecca wanted to follow in her footsteps.

When she was nineteen, she started working as a nurse in Massachusetts. The people she worked for encouraged her to continue her medical education, and at the age of twenty-six she entered New England Medical College in Boston. She was awarded a Doctress of Medicine degree in 1864, and was the first African American woman in the United States to earn a medical degree.

When the Civil War ended, Dr. Crumpler returned to Richmond, Virginia, the city of her birth. There she provided medical care to the newly freed slaves. After years as a successful doctor in Richmond, she went back to Boston.

Dr. Crumpler treated women and children such as these.

In 1883, she published a book on a subject to which she had dedicated her life—health care for women and children. At a time when almost all doctors were men, Rebecca Lee Crumpler was an inspiration for women, and especially African American women who wanted to enter the medical profession.

Reading Across Texts

Although Dr. Blackwell and Dr. Crumpler were both "firsts" in their field, there were many differences in their lives. Name some of them.

Writing Across Texts Make a chart of differences between Dr. Blackwell and Dr. Crumpler.

Concord Hymn

by Ralph Waldo Emerson

By the rude bridge that arched the flood,
  Their flag to April's breeze unfurled,
Here once the embattled farmers stood,
  And fired the shot heard round the world.

The foe long since in silence slept;
  Alike the conqueror silent sleeps;
And Time the ruined bridge has swept
  Down the dark stream which seaward creeps.

On the green bank, by this soft stream,
  We set today a votive stone;
That memory may their deed redeem,
  When, like our sires, our sons are gone.

Spirit, that made those spirits dare
  To die, and leave their children free,
Bid Time and Nature gently spare
  The shaft we raise to them and thee.

Abe

by Alice Schertle

And so,
young Abe
     of the too-short pants
     and too-long legs,
young Abe spitting into his palms,
wrapping his bony fingers around
     the handle of an axe,
sinking the bright blade deep
     into heartwood,
young Abe splitting the rails apart

grew into Abe
     of the sad eyes
     of the face carved deep
     by sorrow,
wrapping his strong hands
     around a nation,
trying to hold the bleeding halves
together

until they healed.

Martin Luther King, Jr.

by Gwendolyn Brooks

A man went forth with gifts.

He was a prose poem.
He was a tragic grace.
He was a warm music.

He tried to heal the vivid volcanoes.
His ashes are
    reading the world.

His Dream still wishes to anoint
    the barricades of faith and of control.

His word still burns the center of the sun,
    above the thousands and the
    hundred thousands.

The word was Justice. It was spoken.

So it shall be spoken
So it shall be done.

Another Mountain

by Abiodun Oyewole

Sometimes there's a mountain
that I must climb
even after I've climbed one already
But my legs are tired now
and my arms need a rest
my mind is too weary right now
But I must climb before the storm comes
before the earth rocks
and an avalanche of clouds buries me
and smothers my soul
And so I prepare myself for another climb
Another Mountain
and I tell myself it is nothing
it is just some more dirt and stone
and every now and then I should reach
another plateau and enjoy the view
of the trees and the flowers below
And I am young enough to climb
and strong enough to make it to any top
You see the wind has warned me
about settling too long
about peace without struggle
The wind has warned me
and taught me how to fly
But my wings only work
After I've climbed a mountain

Sing a Song of Struggle

connect to
MUSIC

Many of the songs Marian Anderson sang were spirituals. In this type of song, people often describe hardships they face and how they overcome them.

Write new words set to music you know or write a completely new song. Use words that describe the obstacle faced by one of the other characters in Unit 3. Include a verse about how the character overcomes that challenge. Practice your song and share it with classmates.

She's Been Swimming in the Ocean

Sung to the tune of "I've Been Working on the Railroad"

How are the results of our efforts sometimes greater than we expect?

Lessons from Our Elders

connect to
WRITING

Interview an older person you know about a difficult challenge or obstacle that person once faced. Then write a couple of paragraphs about that experience and what lesson it teaches.

Challenges You Face

connect to
SOCIAL STUDIES

Literature often shows how people deal with conflict, either with other people in society (as in *When Marian Sang*), with nature (as in *Hatchet*), or within themselves (as in *Juan Verdades*).

With a partner, discuss different types of challenges or obstacles sixth graders might face with friends, in school, in nature, and on their own. Then make a chart to show examples of these different challenges or obstacles and ways they might respond.

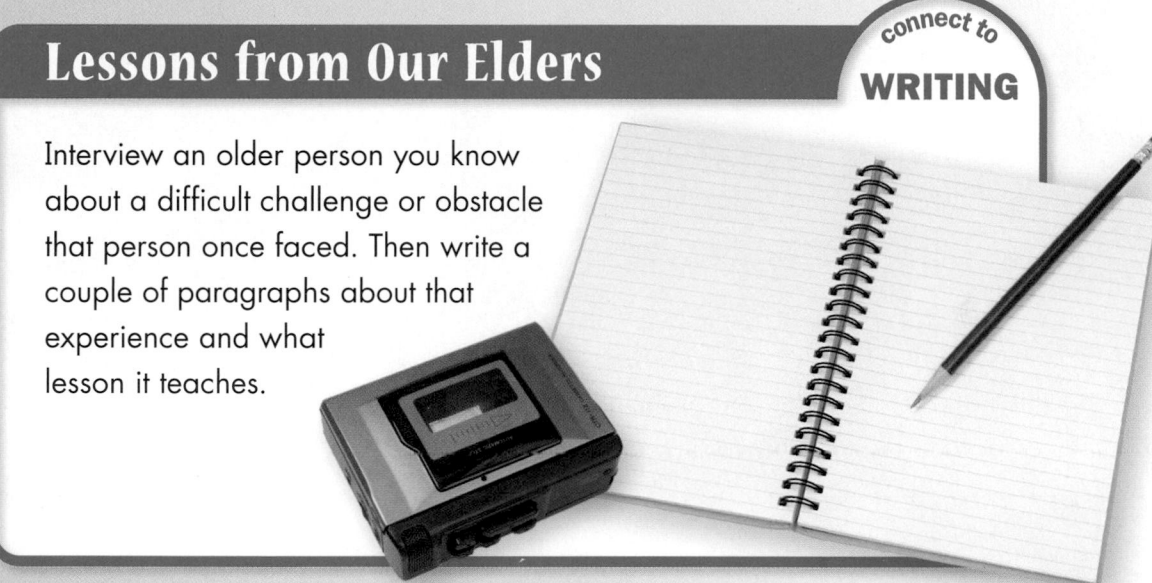

Types of Conflict or Challenge | Ways of Responding
Other People

Nature

Oneself

Read It
ONLINE
sfsuccessnet.com

Explorers, Pioneers, and Discoverers

How have those who've gone first influenced those who've gone after?

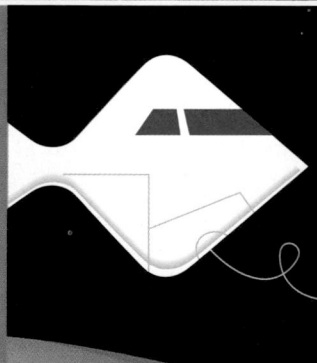

Comprehension

Skill
Cause and Effect

Strategy
Summarize

Cause and Effect

- An *effect* is something that happens. A *cause* is why something happens. To find a cause, ask yourself, "Why did this happen?" To find an effect, ask yourself, "What happened because of this?"

- Clue words such as *because, so,* and *due to* can help you spot cause-and-effect relationships.

- Sometimes there are no clue words, and a cause is not directly stated. When this is the case, think about why something happened.

Strategy: Summarize

Good readers summarize by stating the most important information or ideas in an article or story. A good summary is only a few sentences long. It does not include minor details. As you read, you can make a list or graphic organizer of causes and effects to help you summarize. Then write a summary that includes all these important ideas.

1. Read "The Arctic." Make graphic organizers like the one above to note cause-effect relationships in the article.

2. Write a summary of "The Arctic." Listing important causes and effects as you read can help you.

THE ARCTIC

Land and Water

THE ARCTIC IS located on the northernmost part of Earth. It is often considered to lie north of the "tree line," which marks where trees cannot grow because of frigid year-round temperatures. This area includes Greenland as well as parts of Alaska, Canada, Europe, and Siberia. It also includes the Arctic Ocean and, of course, the North Pole.

Ice and snow cover two-fifths of Arctic land year-round, while the rest of the land has grasses and shrubs. Ice covers more than half the Arctic Ocean all the time. This mass of jagged ice is called pack ice.

> **Strategy** Stop here and summarize. What are the most important ideas you've read so far?

Arctic Temperatures

THERE ARE LARGE temperature differences throughout the Arctic. Due to Earth's tilt, the sun's rays do not even reach the northern Arctic during the winter. Yet the coldest Arctic temperatures are not at the North Pole. That's because the North Pole is located on the Arctic Ocean pack ice. Water—even as ice—slowly takes in heat during the summer. It slowly gives it off during the winter. The most extreme temperatures, then, occur on the land in northern Canada, Alaska, and Siberia.

On the pack ice, winter air is still and dry. Most of the water is already frozen. In fact, more snow falls in New York City!

> **Skill** Clue words like *due to* help you spot cause-and-effect relationships. Why don't the sun's rays reach the northern Arctic in winter?

> **Skill** Why aren't the coldest temperatures at the North Pole?

> **Strategy** Summarize the entire article to remember its important causes and effects.

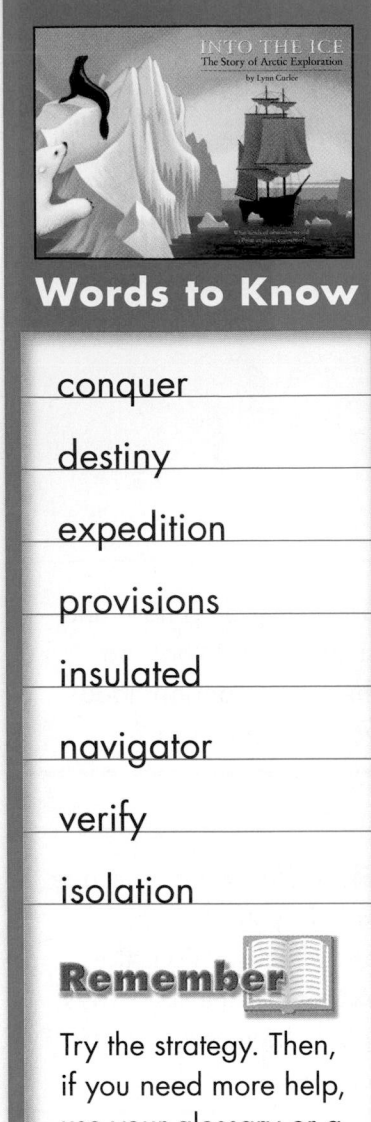

Words to Know

conquer

destiny

expedition

provisions

insulated

navigator

verify

isolation

Remember

Try the strategy. Then, if you need more help, use your glossary or a dictionary.

Vocabulary Strategy
for Unfamiliar Words

Context Clues Sometimes when you are reading, you find a word that is unfamiliar. Often the author provides clues in the text that can help you figure out the meaning of the word. Look at the context, or the words and sentences around the unknown word, for clues.

1. Reread the sentence in which the unknown word appears.

2. Look for a specific clue to the word's meaning.

3. If there isn't one, think about the overall meaning of the sentence. Does that give a clue?

4. If you need more help, read the sentences near the unknown word. They may have clues or additional information that suggests the word's meaning.

5. Determine a meaning for the word based on any clues. Try your meaning in the sentence. Does it make sense?

As you read "Exploring the Unknown," use the context to help you figure out the meanings of unfamiliar words.

Exploring the Unknown

There have always been people determined to conquer the unexplored corners of the world. Whether they have battled their way to the top of the world, the bottom of the ocean, or the silence of the moon, explorers feel it is their destiny to be the first.

They plan, organize, and outfit their expedition. To improve their odds of surviving, they take along food, clothing, transportation, and tools. They gather everything they think they will need to protect them from the cold or the heat and the extremes of nature. However, for all their provisions and planning, they still are not insulated against the dangers of the unknown.

The navigator may be able to tell them exactly where they stand. Yet he or she can never verify that the group will make it safely there and back. Think of a little knot of people standing on Mars sometime in the future. They will have reached their goal. Nonetheless, in the cold and dark of space, they must feel keenly their isolation from all other humans.

What frontier would you like to explore? Write about your expedition. Use as many of the words from the Words to Know list as possible.

Genre

Narrative nonfiction often recounts a series of events. Look for a number of related events as you read.

INTO THE ICE
The Story of Arctic Exploration

by Lynn Curlee

What kinds of obstacles would
a Polar explorer encounter?

The great pioneer in the search for the North Pole was a brilliant young Norwegian scientist named Fridtjof Nansen. Also an athlete, outdoorsman, artist, and poet, Nansen wrote of the strange atmospheric effect called the *northern lights,* "The aurora borealis shakes over the vault of heaven its veil of glittering silver—changing now to yellow, now to green, now to red. . . . It shimmers in tongues of flame . . . until the whole melts away in the moonlight . . . like the sigh of a departing spirit."

In 1888, at the age of twenty-six, Nansen organized his first expedition—a trek across Greenland on skis, a feat never before accomplished. Dropped off by ship on the uninhabited east coast, Nansen and five companions had no choice but to ski westward to civilization, carrying only the provisions required for the one-way journey.

This kind of bold yet calculated risk-taking was typical of Nansen. He carefully planned every detail, even designing his own equipment. He also knew how to improvise off the land, adopting Inuit methods such as the use of dog sledges, kayaks, and snow houses.

After the Greenland trek, Nansen became interested in the idea of *polar drift.* In 1884, in the ice near Greenland, some debris was found from the *Jeannette,* a ship crushed in the ice off Siberia in 1881. There was only one possible explanation: the ice and debris had drifted around the entire Arctic Ocean. Nansen had a breathtaking proposal: he would sail a ship directly into the ice pack off Siberia, deliberately let it be frozen in, and drift with the ice across the top of the world, penetrating the heart of the Arctic.

Nansen's small ship, the *Fram* (*Onward* in Norwegian), was specially designed with a hull that would ride up over the crushing ice and living spaces insulated with cork and felt. Fully provisioned with scientific equipment and supplies for five years, the *Fram* had workshops, a smithy, and even a windmill for electricity. On June 24, 1893, the *Fram* sailed from Norway. By September 25, Nansen and his crew of twelve were frozen fast in the polar ice pack off Siberia.

Fridtjof Nansen and the Fram

As they drifted slowly northward, the expedition settled into a routine of scientific observation. The ship was so comfortable that by the end of the second winter Nansen was restless and bored. Now only 360 miles from the North Pole, Nansen decided to strike out over the ice.

In the arctic dawn of mid-March 1895 Nansen set out with one companion, Hjalmar Johansen, three sledges of provisions, twenty-eight dogs, and two kayaks. As in Greenland, there could be no turning back—this time their home base was drifting. For three weeks they struggled northward, maneuvering the sledges over jumbled fields and immense ridges of broken ice. By early April they were still 225 miles from the Pole, and the drifting ice was carrying them south almost as quickly as they could push north. Provisions were also running low, so they reluctantly headed for the nearest land, three hundred miles to the south. As the weeks passed and the sun rose higher, the broken surface of the ice pack became slushy, then treacherous as lanes of water call *leads* opened and

closed between the ice floes. It took four months to reach land. After provisions ran out, the men survived by hunting seals in the open leads and by feeding the weak dogs to the stronger ones.

Nansen and Johansen finally found a remote island. With no hope of rescue, the two men prepared for the winter, building a tiny hut and butchering walrus and bears for a supply of meat and warm furs. They survived the winter in isolation, burning greasy blubber for heat and light and growing fat on the diet of oily meat. When the ice broke up in the spring, Nansen and Johansen set out in their kayaks. On June 13, 1896— one year and four months after leaving the *Fram*—they were picked up by an English expedition. Two months later the *Fram* and its crew broke free of the ice in the ocean east of Greenland, more than a thousand miles from their starting point. The scientific expedition was a triumphant success, and Nansen and Johansen had gone farther north than anyone had before.

The Fram *drifts in the Arctic night.*

Now the race to the North Pole was on. Another daring attempt was made the very next year—a flight to the Pole in a balloon. Salomon Andrée was a Swedish engineer with experience in aeronautics and an interest in the Arctic. He had built a large hydrogen-filled balloon with a passenger gondola designed to hold three men, four months of supplies, sledges, and a small boat.

Developed more than one hundred years earlier, balloons were still the only means of flight in the 1890s. As transportation they have serious limitations: first, they cannot be steered; and second, they are sensitive to temperature changes. Andrée tried to solve the first problem with a complicated system of sails and drag lines. He completely ignored the second problem, and the result was disastrous.

In midsummer 1897 the *Ornen* (*Eagle* in Swedish) lifted off from Spitsbergen, an island north of Norway. As they sailed northward Andrée wrote in his journal, "The rattling of the drag lines in the snow and the flapping of the sails are the only sound, except for the whining of the wind." As the balloon was alternately heated by the sun and cooled by freezing fog, the precious gas that kept them aloft leaked away. By the third day the *Ornen* was down on the ice, two hundred miles from land. In the arctic summer at the edge of the ice pack, Andrée and his two companions faced a terrifying world of slushy, grinding floes and open leads; it took them three months to struggle to the nearest island. But inexperienced and unprepared, they were unable to survive the winter. We know what happened only because thirty-three years later their frozen remains were found, along with Andrée's journal and another eerie relic—undeveloped images of the doomed expedition that were still in their camera.

PHYSICALLY THE NORTH Pole is nothing more than a theoretical point on the Earth's surface—but reaching it came to symbolize mankind's mastery of the entire planet—and a landmark human achievement. An American naval engineer desperately wanted to be the first explorer to stand on the North Pole. Robert E. Peary first entered the Arctic in 1886. For twenty years he mounted expeditions to northwest Greenland, looking for the best route north. Peary was not particularly interested in

The Ornen *comes down on the ice.*

Dog sledging on the ice pack

scientific discovery or mapping. He had one goal: the glory of being first. Over the years, Peary came to believe that it was his destiny to conquer the North Pole.

Vain and arrogant, Robert Peary ran his expeditions like a military campaign. His chief lieutenant was his personal assistant, Matthew Henson, a man of African descent. This was unusual at the turn of the century, but then, Peary was unconventional in many ways. He also took his wife on some of his early expeditions. Josephine Peary was the first white woman in the High Arctic, and she gave birth to their daughter while on expedition. Inuit came from miles around to see the newborn blond "snowbaby."

As an explorer, Peary was innovative, taking ideas from everyone and improving on them. But the Polar Inuit were the key to his success. Inuit women made his furs, and Inuit men used their own dogs to pull his sledges. They built his snowhouses on the trail and hunted for his

meat in exchange for metal
tools and other material goods.
On one occasion Peary pushed himself so relentlessly
that his feet froze. When his fur boots were removed,
several of his toes snapped off. As soon as the stumps healed, he
was back on the trail.

In 1906 Peary made a full-scale assault upon the North Pole. His plan
was to take a ship as far north as possible, winter over in Greenland
or the Canadian Islands, then strike out for the Pole in late February,
before the ice pack started breaking up. The Arctic did not cooperate,
however. When only a hundred miles out on the ice pack, the expedition
was delayed several days by a broad lead, then a blizzard kept them
camp-bound for another week. Supplies dwindled, and the disappointed
Peary had to settle for a new farthest-north record, 175 miles from
the Pole.

After another appeal to the men who financed his expeditions, Peary sailed from New York in July 1908 in the *Roosevelt,* named for Theodore Roosevelt, then President of the United States and the explorer's most enthusiastic supporter. Peary was fifty-two years old, and he knew that this was his last expedition.

But Peary was not the only explorer in the Arctic in 1908. There was also Dr. Frederick A. Cook, a veteran of both the Arctic and the Antarctic, which was just then being explored. Cook had been the physician on one of Peary's earlier expeditions. Always jealous and overbearing, Peary had refused to allow Cook to publish an article about his experiences and they had quarreled. Now the doctor was rumored to be thinking about his own attempt on the North Pole. Peary dismissed the rumors; he considered Cook an amateur, not in the same league as himself.

On March 1, 1909, Peary stood on the frozen shore of the Arctic Ocean and faced north. With him were 23 men, 19 sledges, and 133 dogs. For the next month Matt Henson led out in front, breaking trail, while Peary rode a sledge in the rear, supervising the troops. Other sledges traveled back and forth relaying tons of supplies northward, provisions for the return trip that were stored in snowhouses strung out over almost five hundred miles of floating, shifting ice. Everything had been carefully calculated, down to the sacrificing of weak dogs to feed the strong.

For the final dash to the Pole, Peary took only Henson and three Inuit. The entry in his diary for April 6, 1909, reads, "The Pole at last!!! The prize of 3 centuries, my dream & ambition for 23 years. MINE at last."

Or was it?

PEARY CAME HOME to the stunning news that Dr. Cook had already returned, claiming to have reached the North Pole on April 21, 1908, a year before Peary. In the investigations that followed, Peary accused Cook of lying, and it was demonstrated that Cook had lied once before when he claimed to have climbed Mt. McKinley in Alaska, North America's highest peak. Lacking documentation or witnesses, except for two Inuit companions who said they were never out of sight of land, Cook's claim to have reached the Pole was officially rejected.

Peary claims the North Pole.

Then, incredibly, Peary was also unable to completely verify his own claim. The careful explorer was a sloppy navigator, and from his solar observations and daily journal it was impossible to say that he had stood at the Pole. Henson and the Inuit were unable to take solar readings, so it was Peary's word against Cook's. Commander Robert E. Peary was finally given the credit and made a rear-admiral, but his great prize was tarnished, and he died an embittered man. As for Cook, he vowed until his dying day that he had reached the North Pole. In recent years, historical researchers have determined that neither man actually stepped foot on the northernmost point of the globe.

THE CLASSIC ERA of Arctic exploration ended with Peary. Attention then shifted to the Antarctic and to the South Pole, which Roald Amundsen reached in 1911. Three years later the world was at war and most exploration was postponed. When it resumed in the 1920s the world was a different place. Balloons were no longer the only means of flight, and several attempts were made to fly to the North Pole in small airplanes.

For many years Richard E. Byrd was given credit for the first successful flight, but his claim is now disputed. In 1926 Roald Amundsen flew across the entire Arctic Ocean in an Italian dirigible piloted by its designer, Umberto Nobile. The first person to stand at the North Pole, whose claim is undisputed, is Joseph Fletcher, a United States Air Force pilot who landed there in 1952. Arctic flights are great achievements, but they are achievements of technology, somehow different from crossing nearly five hundred miles of shifting ice by dog sledge and then returning. Although many people have now stood at the North Pole, no one has ever completed Peary's journey without being resupplied by plane or airlifted out.

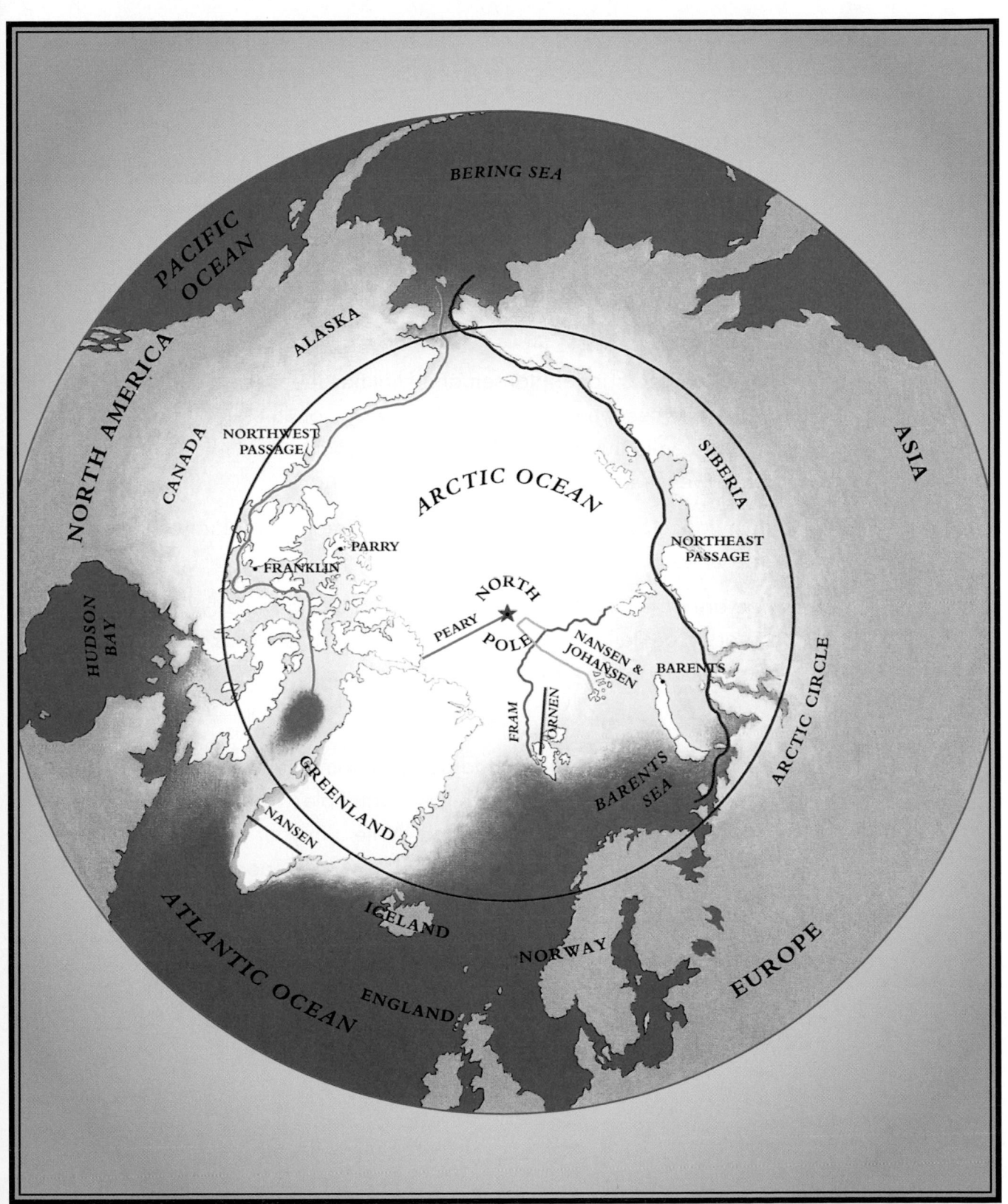

This map shows the routes of various Arctic explorers.

Reader Response

Open for Discussion Pick from this history the best incident for a scene in a movie or TV documentary. Describe why you chose it and how it would appear.

1. This author gives you a bit of information about the personalities of two of the explorers. How does he help you get to know Nansen and Peary?

2. What caused Fridtjof Nansen and Hjalmar Johansen to leave the *Fran* when they were 360 miles away from the North Pole and frozen in the polar ice? What were some of the effects of this adventure?

3. Summarize Salomon Andrée's attempt to reach the North Pole in a balloon.

4. You are an explorer who is organizing a trip to Mars. Write an ad to get fellow adventurers to join you. Use words from the Words to Know list and from the selection.

Look Back and Write Beyond personal fame, why would explorers have attempted to reach the North Pole? Look back at page 423 to find the author's answer. Write it in your own words. Then discuss in writing whether that reason still is important today.

Lynn Curlee says his book career began when he had the opportunity to illustrate a book written by another author. "With my second book I began writing myself and started the series of nonfiction informational picture books for older children which continues to this day," he says.

The illustrations in Mr. Curlee's books have an easily recognized style. He begins by creating works on large canvases using acrylic paints. These paintings are then photographed and reduced to the size needed for the book.

Many of Mr. Curlee's books are about monuments such as the five in Washington, D.C., featured in *Capital.* He says, "I have had the rare privilege and honor of making books about some of the most important and iconic monuments of our American heritage."

Mr. Curlee grew up in North Carolina. Today he lives in the village of Southold, New York, where he is the owner of a gallery.

Liberty

Capital

Polar Zones

from *Weather* from The Nature Company Discoveries Library

Expository Nonfiction

Genre

- Expository nonfiction explains ideas through facts and information presented in written and visual forms.

- There are usually photographs with captions in expository nonfiction.

Text Features

- The author of this article includes extra information outside of the main text to keep the reader's attention on what is most important.

- The author uses words such as *severe*, *fierce*, and *extreme* to convey the harshness of the winter. As you read, think about how this article would have been different without those words.

Link to Science

The polar zones are areas with extremely cold and hazardous weather. Make a list of the kinds of clothing you would need to protect against such weather.

Climates near the North and South Poles are characterized by freezing temperatures and permanent snow and ice. Polar summers are short and cold. The extreme climate is caused by lack of heat because the sun is weaker and the ice reflects much of the heat from the sun back into the atmosphere. For six months of the year, the Arctic experiences winter as the North Pole is tilted away from the sun. At the same time, Antarctica, the continent around the South Pole, enjoys a brief summer. Temperatures rise to freezing, or just above, near the coast. The pack ice drifts northward and melts in the warmer waters. Winter in the Antarctic, however, is severe. Antarctica doubles in size as the sea freezes over, and pack ice extends for hundreds of miles around the continent. Frequent blizzards and fierce winds rage across the icy surface.

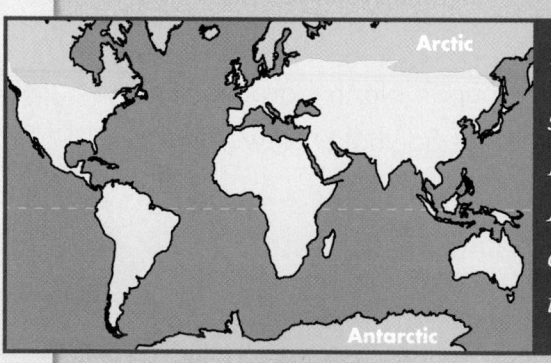

Arctic

Antarctic

The Arctic is a frozen sea surrounding the North Pole, while the Antarctic is a frozen continent around the South Pole.

COAT OF COLORS

The fur of the Arctic fox changes color during the year. In winter, it turns from smoky gray to white to camouflage the fox against the snow.

ARCTIC DWELLERS

The Inuit (Eskimos), who live in the Arctic, have adapted well to the extreme climatic conditions.

WHITE OUT

Blizzards are strong winter snowstorms. They are particularly severe in the polar zones, where they may last for weeks at a time. Snow falls on more than 150 days of the year and is swept into huge piles by the wind. Winds are equally severe and reach speeds of more than 186 miles (300 km) per hour. The average winter temperatures plummet to -76°F (-60°C). In these extreme temperatures, unprotected human skin will freeze in seconds. People need layers of warm clothing and protective shelters to survive this bitter cold.

Reading Across Texts

Referring to what you have read in *Into the Ice* and "Polar Zones," tell why you think explorers are drawn to the Arctic.

Writing Across Texts Write some reasons for which explorers are drawn to polar regions.

Cause & Effect What causes the extreme polar climate?

429

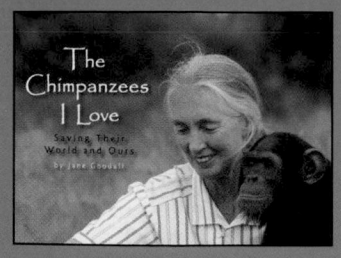

Comprehension

Skill
Author's Purpose

Strategy
Answer Questions

Author's Purpose

- Authors may write to persuade, inform, express ideas or feelings, or entertain.

- If you know the author's purpose, you can adjust the way you read. If the purpose is to entertain, you may choose to read faster. If the purpose is to inform, read more slowly.

- As you preview a selection, predict the author's purpose. After reading, ask if the author met the purpose.

> **Before Reading** Preview to decide purpose. Set reading pace.
>
> ↓
>
> **During Reading** Look for clues to purpose.
>
> ↓
>
> **After Reading** Ask if purpose was met and how.

Strategy: Answer Questions

Good readers search for important information to answer questions completely and accurately. Often it is right in the text because the author's purpose is to inform you clearly. Some questions, though, require you to combine the information in the text with what you already know.

1. Read "Jane Goodall's Career." Make a graphic organizer like the one above in order to determine the author's purpose.

2. Use your graphic organizer to write complete and accurate answers to these questions: In your opinion, did the author meet her purpose? Why or why not?

Jane Goodall's Career

JANE GOODALL is known worldwide for studying chimpanzees. As a child she became interested in how animals behaved. She left school at age 18 and eventually traveled to Africa, where in 1960 she started a camp in the Gombe Stream Game Reserve. From there she could carefully research the chimpanzees that lived in the region.

Goodall and her family lived in Gombe until 1975. Over the years Goodall discovered many surprising facts about chimpanzees. For example, she learned that chimpanzees are omnivorous. This means that they eat both plants and animals. Before her discovery most scientists believed that chimpanzees were vegetarians, or plant eaters. Goodall also discovered that chimpanzees are capable of making and using their own tools, using twigs and the like.

Goodall wrote several fascinating books about her research with chimpanzees. In 1971 she told about her first years at Gombe in the book *In the Shadow of Man*. Later, in 1986, she wrote all she had learned about chimpanzee behavior in *The Chimpanzees of Gombe*.

Skill What is the purpose of this paragraph?
(a) to persuade you that Jane Goodall was a poor scientist
(b) to express what it felt like to live in Africa
(c) to inform you about Jane Goodall's career

Strategy If you were asked, "What did Goodall learn about chimpanzees?" you could find the answer in the text. What does that tell you about the author's purpose?

Strategy What makes you think the author did or did not meet her purpose?

Skill Do you think the author met her purpose in writing this article?

431

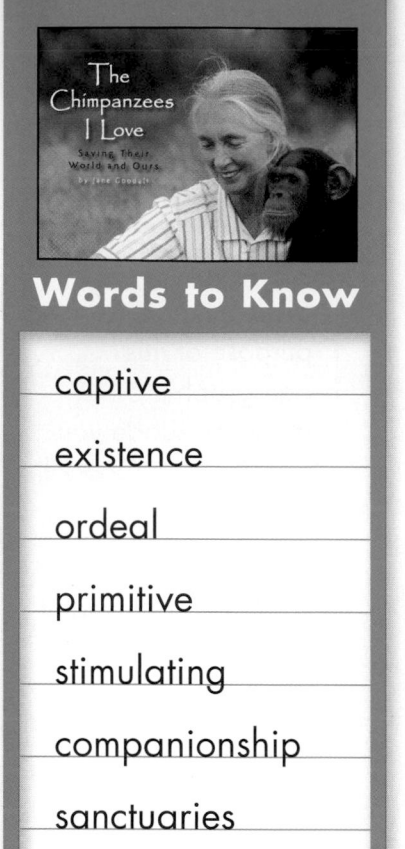

Words to Know

captive

existence

ordeal

primitive

stimulating

companionship

sanctuaries

Vocabulary Strategy
for Unfamiliar Words

Dictionary/Glossary Sometimes when you are reading, you find a word you do not know. If the sentences around the word do not give good clues to its meaning, you may need to look up the word in a dictionary or in the glossary of your book.

1. Check the back of your book to see if there is a glossary. If there is not, look in a dictionary.

2. Find the entry for the word. Words in both dictionaries and glossaries are listed in alphabetical order.

3. Read the pronunciation of the word, if one is given. You may recognize the word when you say it.

4. Read all the meanings listed in the entry.

5. Choose the meaning that makes sense in your sentence.

As you read "Zoos Then and Now," use this book's glossary or a dictionary to determine the meanings of unfamiliar words that the text does not define.

Zoos Then and Now

The first zoos existed to entertain people, who came to see strange wild animals from around the world. Hardly anyone thought about the health and happiness of these captive animals. For the most part, they were kept in small cages. Little was known about them, so no one knew what they needed for food or homes. Zoo life was nothing like their existence in the wild. Being shut in a tiny space and looking at metal and concrete all day was surely an ordeal.

Today, zoos are very different from those early, primitive places. They try hard to make life interesting and "normal" for their animals. The best zoos provide environments like those the animals would have in the wild. They offer many stimulating objects to keep the animals from getting bored. Animals are grouped in ways that make sure they have companionship. One aim is to set up family groups so babies can be born, helping endangered species increase their numbers. Zoos have become important to the survival of many animals. They are both sanctuaries and places of learning. They offer a safe place for animals to live and opportunities for people to understand them.

Write

Look at the pictures in *The Chimpanzees I Love*. Choose one to write about. Use as many words from the Words to Know list as you can.

The Chimpanzees I Love

Saving Their World and Ours

by Jane Goodall

How are chimpanzees unlike most other animals?

435

The Mind of the Chimpanzee

ANIMALS ARE much smarter than scientists used to think. I was told at school (fifty years ago) that only human beings have personalities, can think and reason, feel pain, or have emotions. Luckily, as a child, I had spent hours learning about animal behavior from my dog, Rusty—so I knew none of that was true!

The more we have learned about chimpanzees, the clearer it is that they have brains very like ours and can, in fact, do many things that we used to think only humans could do. I've described how the Gombe chimps use grass stems and twigs to fish termites from their nests. The chimps also use long smooth sticks to catch vicious biting army ants. They use crumpled leaves to soak up water from hollows in trees that they cannot reach with their lips, then suck the homemade sponge. They wipe dirt from their bodies with leaf napkins. They use stout sticks to open up holes in trees to get at birds' nests or honey and as clubs to intimidate one another or other animals. They pick up and throw rocks as missiles. In other parts of Africa, chimps have different tool-using behaviors. For instance, in west Africa and parts of central Africa, they use two stones, a hammer and an anvil, to crack open nuts. It seems that infant chimps learn these behaviors by watching the adults, and then imitating and practicing what they have seen. So the chimps have their own primitive culture.

Many scientists are finding out more about the chimpanzee mind from tests in captive situations. For example, chimps will go and find sticks to pull in food that has been placed outside the cage, beyond their reach. They can join two short sticks together to make one long tool. They have excellent memories—after eleven years' separation, a female named Washoe recognized the two humans who had brought her up. A chimp can plan what he or she is going to do. Often I've watched a chimp wake up, scratch himself

"How many times I have wished that I could look out onto the world through the eyes, with the mind, of a chimpanzee. One such minute would be worth a lifetime of research."

Chimpanzees can communicate by means of calls, gestures, postures, and facial expressions.

Ai has been learning language skills at Kyoto University since 1978. Her infant, Ayumu, will learn to stack blocks.

slowly, gaze around in different directions, then suddenly get up, walk over to a clump of grass, carefully select a stem, trim it, and then travel quite a long way to a termite mound that was out of sight when he made his tool.

Chimpanzees can be taught to do many of the things that we do, such as riding bicycles and sewing. Some love to draw or paint. Chimps can also recognize themselves in mirrors. But they cannot learn to speak words because their vocal cords are different. Two scientists, the Hayeses, brought up a little chimp named Vicky and tried to teach her to talk. After eight years she could only say four words, and only people who knew her could understand even those.

The Gardners had another idea. They got an infant chimpanzee, named her Washoe, and began teaching her American Sign Language (ASL) as used by deaf people. Then other infant chimps were taught this language. Chimps can learn 300 signs or more. They can also invent signs. The chimp Lucy, wanting a Brazil nut but not knowing its name, used two signs she knew and asked for a "rock berry." A fizzy soda became "listen drink," a duck on a pond, "water bird," and a piece of celery, "pipe food." Washoe's adopted son learned fifty-eight signs from Washoe and three other signing chimps by the time he was eight years old. He was never taught these signs by humans. Other chimps have been taught computer "languages" and can punch out quite complicated sentences. These experiments have taught us, and continue to teach us, more and more about the chimpanzee mind.

These two young chimps are good friends.

Fifi is a very good mother. Here she is with offspring Ferdinand, Faustino, and Fanni.

Chimpanzees in Captivity

UNFORTUNATELY chimpanzees, so like us in many ways, are often very badly treated in many captive situations. Chimpanzees were first brought to Europe from Africa in the middle of the seventeenth century. People were amazed by these humanlike creatures. They dressed them up and taught them tricks.

Since then we have often treated chimpanzees like slaves, shooting their mothers in Africa, shipping them around the world, caging them in zoos, training them to perform in movies and circuses and advertisements, selling them as pets, and imprisoning them in medical research laboratories. Some chimps become famous. J. Fred Muggs starred on TV's *Today* show for years and was known by millions of viewers. What they didn't know was that whenever J. Fred Muggs got too big and strong for the show, he was replaced by a younger one.

A young male called Ham was sent up into space. He was shot up in a Mercury Redstone rocket in January 1961, and because he survived the ordeal (he was terrified), it was decided that it was safe for the first human astronauts. Ham was taught his routine by receiving an electric shock every time he pressed the wrong button. Often circus chimps are taught, right at the start of their training, that instant obedience is the way to avoid a beating. The beatings are given when the trainer and chimp are on their own, so no one sees. It is the same for other animals—and for many of those used in movies and other forms of entertainment.

Infant chimpanzees are adorable and, for the first two or three years, are gentle and easy to handle. People buy them and treat them like human children. But as they grow older they become more and more difficult. They are, after all, chimpanzees, and they want to behave like chimpanzees. They resent discipline. They can—and do—bite. And by the time they are six years old they are already as strong as a human male. What will happen to them then? Zoos don't want them, for they have not been able to learn chimpanzee social behavior and they do not mix well with others of their kind. Often they end up in medical research labs.

It is because their bodies are so like ours that scientists use chimps to try to find out more about human diseases and how to cure and prevent them. Chimpanzees can be infected with almost all human diseases. Hundreds have been used (with no success) in AIDS research. The virus stays alive in their blood, but they do not show the symptoms. It is very unfair that, even though chimpanzees are being used to try to help humans, they are almost never given decent places to live.

Zoos are improving gradually, but thousands of chimpanzees around the world spend their lives in barren cement-floored cages with nothing to do.

Jou-Jou has been caged alone in a Congolese zoo. He reaches to touch me, desperate for contact.

Hundreds of them are shut up in a 5' x 5' x 7' bare, steel-barred prisons, all alone, bored, and uncomfortable. Measure out this space and imagine having to live in it your whole life. (Many closets are much bigger!)

I shall never forget the first time I looked into the eyes of an adult male chimpanzee in one of these labs. For more than ten years he had been living in his tiny prison. The sides, floor, and ceiling were made of thick steel bars. There was a car tire on the floor. His name, I read on the door, was JoJo. He lived at the end of a row of five cages, lined up along a bare wall. Opposite were five more cages. At either end of the room was a metal door. There was no window. JoJo could not touch any of his fellow prisoners—only the ends of his fingers fitted between the bars. He had been born in an African forest, and for the first couple of years he lived in a world of greens and browns, leaves and vines, butterflies and birds. Always his mother had been close to comfort him, until the day when she was shot and he was snatched from her dead or dying body. The young chimpanzee was shipped away from his forest world to the cold, bleak existence of a North American research lab. JoJo was not angry, just grateful that I had stopped by him. He groomed my fingers, where the ridges of my cuticles showed through the surgical gloves I had to wear. Then he looked into my eyes and with one gentle finger reached to touch the tear that rolled down into my mask.

JoJo and I touch through the bars of his prison cage in a research lab.

La Vieille spent years alone in a Congolese zoo. We were able to move her to our Tchimpounga sanctuary and introduce her to other chimpanzees.

"Chimpanzees are more like us than any other living beings."

In the United States, several hundred chimpanzees have been declared "surplus"—they are no longer needed for medical research. Animal welfare groups are trying to raise the money to build them sanctuaries so that they can end their lives with grass and trees, sunshine and companionship. Some lucky ones—including JoJo— have already been freed from their laboratory prisons. Many others are waiting.

Zoos are getting better, but there are still many chimps in small concrete and metal cages with no soft ground and nothing to occupy them. Good zoos keep their chimpanzees in groups and provide them with all kinds of stimulating things to do, different things each day, so that they don't get bored. Many zoos now have artificial termite mounds. Chimps use sticks or straws to poke into holes for honey or other foods. These innovations make a world of difference.

Protecting the Chimpanzees

CHIMPANZEES live in the forested areas of west and central Africa. In some places, where there is a lot of rain, these are thick tropical rain forests. In other places there are strips of dense forest along the rivers, with woodland and even open grassland in between. The chimpanzees usually cross open ground in groups, traveling without stopping until they reach the safety of the trees again. Chimpanzees can survive in quite dry areas, but there they have very big home ranges, for they must travel widely to get food. Like the other African great apes, the gorillas and bonobos, they are disappearing very fast. One hundred years ago we think there were about two million chimpanzees in Africa; now there may be no more than 150,000. They are already extinct in four of the twenty-five countries where they once lived. There are more chimpanzees in the great

Congo basin than anywhere else—but that is where they are disappearing the fastest. They are disappearing for various reasons:

1   All over Africa, their forest homes are being destroyed as human populations grow and need even more land for their crops and for their homes, and even more wood for making charcoal or for firewood.

2   In many places chimpanzees are caught in snares set for bushpigs or antelopes. Snares were once made of vines, but now hunters use wire cable. Often the chimps are strong enough to break the wire, but they cannot get the noose off. Some die; others lose a hand or a foot, after months of agony.

3   There are still dealers who are trying to smuggle chimpanzees out of Africa for the live animal trade. Mothers are shot so that hunters can steal their infants for entertainment or medical research. Many individuals die in the forest (including adult males who rush to the rescue and are shot) in order for one infant to reach its destination alive. The dealers pay the hunters only a few dollars while they themselves can sell an infant chimp for $2,000 or more.

4   The greatest threat to chimpanzees in the great Congo basin is commercial hunting for food. Local tribes, like the Pygmies, have lived in harmony with the forest and its animals for hundreds of years. Now logging companies have made roads deep into the heart of the last remaining forests. Hunters ride the trucks to the end of the road and shoot everything—chimps, gorillas, bonobos, elephants, antelopes—even quite small birds. The meat is smoked or even loaded fresh onto the trucks and taken for sale in the big towns. The trouble is that so many people living there prefer the taste of meat from wild animals, and they will pay more for it than for that from domestic animals. If this trade (known as the "bush-meat" trade) cannot be stopped, there will soon be no animals left.

There are many people and organizations trying to help protect chimpanzees and their forests, but the problems are very hard to solve. Most of the people destroying the forests are very poor. They can't afford to buy food from elsewhere, so they cut down more trees for

"Every individual has a role to play. Every individual makes a difference. And we have a choice: What sort of difference do we want to make?"

Fanni gazes down at Fax.

their farms and shoot or snare more animals for food. Because the soil needs the shelter of the trees in the tropics, the people are soon struggling to survive in a desert-like place. So they cut down more trees. And the bushmeat trade has become a very big money-making operation, with many high-up government officials involved. We shall not give up until solutions have been found.

Chimpanzee Facts

- A fully grown male chimpanzee at Gombe is about 4 feet tall and weighs up to 115 pounds. The female is about as tall, but she is lighter, seldom weighing more than 85 pounds.
- In west and central Africa the chimpanzees are a little bigger and heavier. Often they are heavier in captivity, too, at least when they are well fed and given medicine. This is not surprising, as they have much less exercise than when they live in the wild.
- Chimpanzees in the wild seldom live longer than fifty years, though some captive individuals have lived more than sixty years.
- A female chimpanzee in the wild raises two to three offspring, on average. But she may raise as many as eight or nine.

Chimpanzee Habitats

Chimpanzees are found in twenty-one African countries, from the west coast of the continent to as far east as western Uganda, Rwanda, Burundi, and Tanzania. Chimps live in the greatest concentrations in the rain forest areas along the equator. Due to the fast-paced destruction of these rain forests, as well as other pressures, chimpanzees are considered an endangered species.

The Gombe Stream Research Center is located on the eastern shore of Lake Tanganyika, in Tanzania.

CHIMPANZEE RANGE

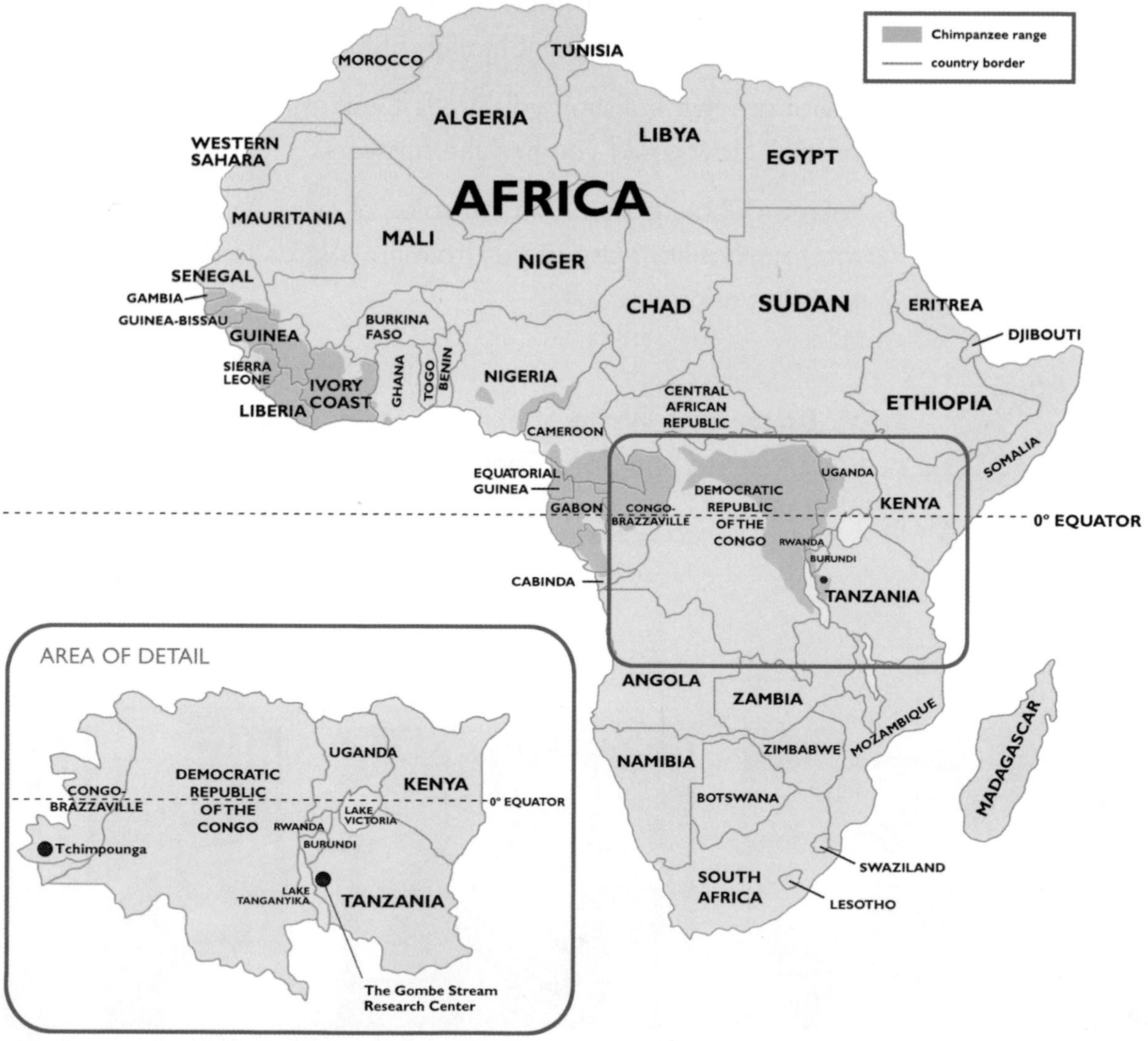

Chimpanzee range
country border

MOROCCO
TUNISIA
ALGERIA
LIBYA
EGYPT
WESTERN SAHARA
AFRICA
MAURITANIA
MALI
NIGER
SENEGAL
GAMBIA
GUINEA-BISSAU
GUINEA
BURKINA FASO
CHAD
SUDAN
ERITREA
DJIBOUTI
SIERRA LEONE
GHANA
TOGO
BENIN
NIGERIA
CENTRAL AFRICAN REPUBLIC
ETHIOPIA
IVORY COAST
LIBERIA
CAMEROON
EQUATORIAL GUINEA
UGANDA
SOMALIA
GABON
CONGO-BRAZZAVILLE
DEMOCRATIC REPUBLIC OF THE CONGO
KENYA
0° EQUATOR
RWANDA
BURUNDI
CABINDA
TANZANIA
ANGOLA
ZAMBIA
MOZAMBIQUE
MADAGASCAR
NAMIBIA
ZIMBABWE
BOTSWANA
SWAZILAND
SOUTH AFRICA
LESOTHO

AREA OF DETAIL

CONGO-BRAZZAVILLE
DEMOCRATIC REPUBLIC OF THE CONGO
UGANDA
KENYA
0° EQUATOR
RWANDA
LAKE VICTORIA
BURUNDI
Tchimpounga
LAKE TANGANYIKA
TANZANIA
The Gombe Stream Research Center

Reader Response

Open for Discussion The author tells us that some chimpanzees in captivity live in small metal cages. Based on what you've learned, what features might you combine to create a "dream living space" for a chimp?

1. Jane Goodall tells readers a great deal about chimpanzees. Which passages or details of her story did you find most interesting, and why?

2. Do you think the author's purpose in writing *The Chimpanzees I Love* was to inform, to persuade, to entertain, to express an idea or feeling, or a combination of these? Explain your answer.

3. What are two question you are left with after reading this article? How could you find the answers?

4. Take a debate position on the value of zoos. Write an argument for your position. Use words from the Words to Know list and from the selection.

Look Back and Write Look back at page 441 to review the author's meeting with JoJo. Then rewrite the passage from JoJo's point of view. Explain what he was doing, seeing, and feeling.

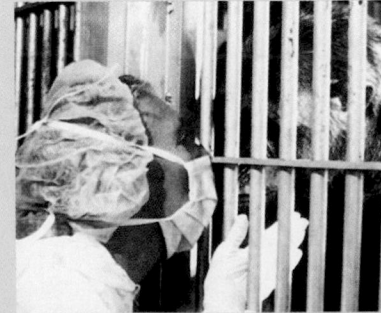

Jane Goodall

Read more books by Jane Goodall.

DR. JANE GOODALL

says it all began when she was a child and loved animals of all kinds. From the time she was ten years old, Dr. Goodall had dreamed of living in Africa and writing books about animals. In *The Chimpanzees I Love,* she wrote, "Luckily, I had a wonderful mother who encouraged my interest. . . . She was the only person who did not laugh at me. Instead she told me that if I worked hard, took advantage of opportunities, and never gave up, I would find a way. And, of course, I did!"

When she was in her twenties, Jane Goodall visited an old school friend in Kenya and arranged a meeting with the scientist Dr. Louis Leakey. He invited her to join an archaeological dig. Later he provided the opportunity for her to live in the wild and learn about chimpanzees.

Today Dr. Goodall is known throughout the world for her scientific research with the chimpanzees of Gombe National Park in Tanzania and for her efforts to preserve the environment. She encourages young people to join her "Roots and Shoots" program. She says, "Hundreds and thousands of roots and shoots—young people like you—around the globe can break through and make the world a better place for all living things."

The Chimpanzee Family Book

My Life with the Chimpanzees

Expository Nonfiction

Genre

- There are different kinds of nonfiction compositions.

- Expository nonfiction tells and explains facts and information.

- Sometimes it includes stories that are more typical of narrative nonfiction.

Text Features

- In this article, the author includes stories about the subjects to make the facts more relevant and interesting to the reader.

- The author uses quotation marks to mean many things, yet she never uses them for dialogue. As you come across words in quotation marks, think about what the author means by them.

Links to Science

The apes in this selection learned some basic symbols to communicate with their trainers. If you were training apes, what words do you think would be important to teach first? Why?

"Going Ape" over Language

by Natalie M. Rosinsky

Humans Talking with Apes?

Such conversations were once found only in fables or in science fiction like *Planet of the Apes.* But, since the 1960s, scientists have "gone ape" over other methods of interspecies communication.

Great apes physically cannot produce the consonants or some vowel sounds of human speech. So, instead of spoken language, researchers are using **American Sign Language (ASL)** and technology to teach human language to other primates.

A Chimpanzee Named Washoe

In 1966, Dr. Allen Gardner and his wife, Beatrix, began teaching ASL to a year-old female chimpanzee named Washoe. They taught Washoe by "cross-fostering" her—that is, treating her like a deaf human child. Washoe had a stimulating environment filled with toys and attentive human companions who used ASL to "discuss" daily activities. In those first years, one important topic of conversation was—of course—potty training! Dr. Roger Fouts, an early companion, and his wife, Debbi, have now spent more than 30 years with "Project Washoe." In 1992, the Fouts founded the Chimpanzee and Human Communication Institute at Central Washington University, where Washoe lives with an adoptive family of four other ASL-using chimpanzees.

Washoe is the most "talkative" member of this group, with an ASL vocabulary of 240 signs. She often "translates" spoken words she understands into ASL. Washoe signs correctly even when an object is out of sight—signaling "DOG," for example, whenever she hears canine barking. She also accurately puts together short "sentences"—signing "ROGER TICKLE WASHOE" when this is what has occurred. If she does not know the sign for an item, Washoe creatively yet logically "renames" it. She called her first candy bar a "CANDY BANANA"!

Yet emotion, not just logic, has filled some of Washoe's most memorable conversations with humans. Washoe had already had two unsuccessful pregnancies when she learned that a caregiver's baby had died. The chimpanzee looked groundward, then directly into the woman's eyes, and signed "CRY" while touching the woman's cheek just below her eye. Later that day, Washoe wouldn't let her caregiver go home without further consolation, signing "PLEASE PERSON HUG."

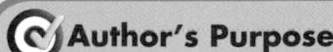 **Author's Purpose** How do the author's section heads help?

"Aping Their Betters"?

Linguist Noam Chomsky insists that human beings are the only primates neurologically capable of language. Some other scientists, including MIT's Dr. Steven Pinker, share this view. They conclude that "Project Washoe" and similar research prove only that apes can be trained, and that they will imitate the behavior of trainers just for rewards or approval. These critics maintain that investigators, along with animal rights activists, have misinterpreted the results of these research projects because they *want* to believe that apes can "talk."

But there are answers to these objections. The private signing done by chimpanzees is evidence that apes use language for more than rewards or approval. And the technology used to teach "Yerkish" to bonobos lessens the possibly questionable element of imitation in this and similar research. Furthermore, as Dr. Sue Savage-Rumbaugh notes, comprehension and visual cues between humans are themselves part of a broader definition of language. It may be unfair to define language for apes only in the narrowest sense. Lastly, current research into how apes communicate among themselves in the wild is reshaping our views of them. Geographically separated groups of bonobos have their own "dialects" of communicative gestures and sounds. And bonobos already may communicate symbolically among themselves, smashing plants and placing them at particular angles as "road signs."

Researchers are also excited by the chimpanzees' use of ASL among themselves. Washoe, her adoptive son Loulis, and other family members have been videotaped having ASL conversations on their own about games, food, and "housecleaning." Birthday parties and holiday celebrations are other "hot" topics of conversation. The chimpanzees have even been observed "talking to themselves," much as a human might mutter under her breath. When Loulis mischievously ran away with one of her favorite magazines, an annoyed Washoe signed "BAD, BAD, BAD" to herself.

It is Loulis's use of ASL, though, that may be most significant. In a planned experiment, researchers avoided signing in Loulis's presence during his first five years. Yet Loulis—like deaf human children—learned ASL by watching and imitating his adoptive mother and other family members! Chimpanzees, it seems, not only can learn human language, but also can transmit it to others.

"Bad, Bad, Bad"

A Gorilla Named Koko

Koko, a female lowland gorilla, began learning ASL in 1972, when she was one year old. Her teacher, Dr. Francine Patterson, provided her with a gorilla companion in 1976, when three-year-old Michael joined them at the official start of the Gorilla Foundation.

Koko has a working vocabulary of 1,000 signs and understands 2,000 spoken words. Michael—before his unexpected death in 2000—used 600 signs to communicate. Both gorillas, like Washoe, have shown creativity and logic in naming unknown objects. It was obvious to Koko that a face mask is an "EYE HAT," while Michael had no difficulty at all in titling his painting (yes, gorillas paint) of a bouquet of flowers "STINK GORILLA MORE"! Koko has even used ASL to "talk" herself out of trouble. When a teacher caught her eating a crayon, Koko signed "LIP" and pretended to be applying lipstick! Koko also likes to joke using ASL, calling herself an "ELEPHANT" after pointing to a long tube held out in front of her like that animal's trunk.

Koko has also used ASL to express sadness and some complex ideas. She mourned the death of her kitten, named All Ball, by repeatedly signing "SAD." When asked when gorillas die, Koko signed "TROUBLE OLD." When she was then asked what happens to gorillas after they die, Koko answered "COMFORTABLE HOLE." With Dr. Patterson as an interpreter, Koko has even participated in online, computerized "chats"!

"Trouble Old"

"Lip"

"Eye Hat"

"Sad"

Author's Purpose Why are there both funny and sad incidents here?

453

Dr. Sue Savage-Rumbaugh teaches Panibasha to speak using a complex sign language called Yerkish.

A Bonobo Named Kanzi

Kanzi, a male bonobo born in 1980, "speaks" a different human language than Washoe and Koko. He communicates in "Yerkish," a visual code invented by researchers at Georgia State University and the Yerkes Primate Research Center. "Yerkish" is a set of several hundred geometric symbols called "lexigrams," each representing a verb, noun, or adjective. These lexigrams are placed on an adapted computer keyboard, which bonobos learn to use while learning the meanings of the lexigrams. Kanzi communicates by computer! (Outdoors, Kanzi points to lexigrams on a carry-around tagboard.)

Kanzi, who also understands more than 1,000 spoken English words, first learned Yerkish by watching humans train his mother. Like a silent toddler who astonishes parents by first speaking in complete sentences, two-year-old Kanzi amazed researchers on the day he first "spoke" Yerkish by using most of the lexigrams taught to his mother. By the age of six, he had a Yerkish vocabulary of 200 lexigrams. According to Dr. Sue Savage-Rumbaugh, Kanzi and other bonobos construct logical sentences in Yerkish and even use the lexigram for "later" to discuss future activities.

Dr. Savage-Rumbaugh and an assistant teach sign language to a chimp.

Reading Across Texts

After reading *The Chimpanzees I Love* and "'Going Ape' over Language," what are some amazing things you learned about what apes can do?

Writing Across Texts Write about the most amazing thing you learned about chimps from these selections.

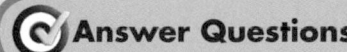 **Answer Questions** | How is Kanzi different from Koko?

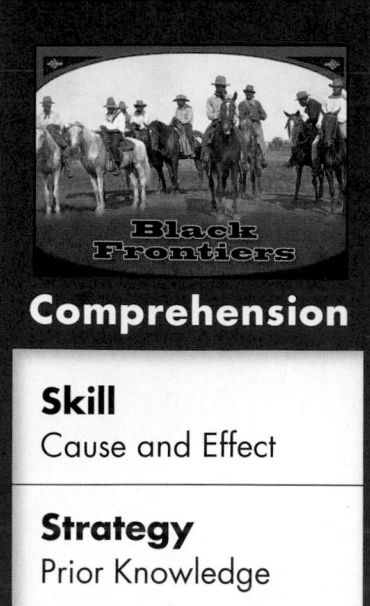

Comprehension

Skill
Cause and Effect

Strategy
Prior Knowledge

Cause and Effect

- A *cause* is why something happens. An *effect* is something that happens. Sometimes several causes lead to one effect.

- Clue words and phrases, such as *consequently*, *as a result*, and *therefore*, can help you spot cause-effect relationships. Sometimes, though, there are no clue words.

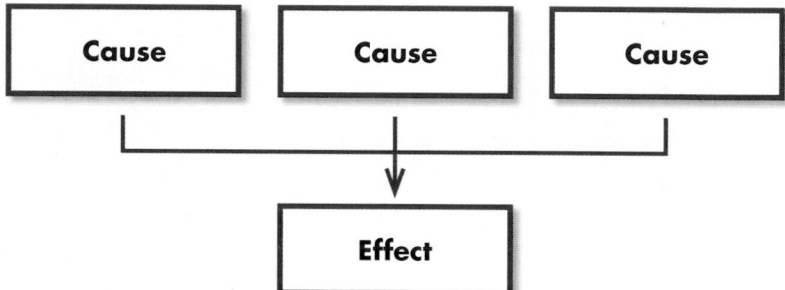

| Cause | Cause | Cause |

↓

| Effect |

Strategy: Prior Knowledge

Prior knowledge is all of what you know about a given topic. Connecting your prior knowledge to what you are reading helps you comprehend better and is especially helpful when looking for cause-effect relationships. For example, suppose you are asked to state how a heat wave might affect a town. To answer, think about what you know about hot days and how people respond to them.

1. Read "Goodbye, Jim Crow." Make a graphic organizer like the one above in order to describe an overall effect and its causes.

2. Use the graphic organizer and your prior knowledge to help you write a brief paragraph about the way many black Americans might have felt in 1964 when the Civil Rights Act was passed.

Goodbye, Jim Crow

It took many years for black people to receive full legal rights in the United States. The push for fair laws began after the Civil War ended. ●

Unfair Laws Starting in 1865, a group of laws called black codes stopped blacks from having basic rights. Citizens in the northern part of the United States disagreed with these laws. This led to the Reconstruction laws, which got rid of the black codes. But soon new laws were passed that segregated, or separated, blacks from whites in many areas of life. These were called the Jim Crow laws. ●

New Laws In 1954, the United States Supreme Court ruled that it was not fair or lawful to have separate black and white schools. This helped the civil rights movement move forward with a strong, organized push to end segregation. In 1963, leaders of the movement staged a huge march in Washington, D.C. to speak out against racial discrimination. ●

President Kennedy could not get Congress to pass equal rights laws. After President Kennedy was murdered, President Johnson got Congress to pass the Civil Rights Act in 1964, which ended legal segregation. Then, in 1965, Congress passed the Voting Rights Act. ● This led to a huge increase in the number of blacks registered to vote.

Strategy Use your prior knowledge to answer this question: Why did the civil rights movement start *after* the Civil War ended?
(a) Once the war ended, slaves were free.
(b) There wasn't interest on the part of black people until then.
(c) Before the war, discrimination was illegal.

Skill What caused the United States to pass the Reconstruction laws? Are there clue words?

Skill What was the effect of the important 1954 Supreme Court decision? Notice the pronoun *this*.

Strategy Think about what you know about voting and elections. Why was it important for black citizens to have the right to vote?

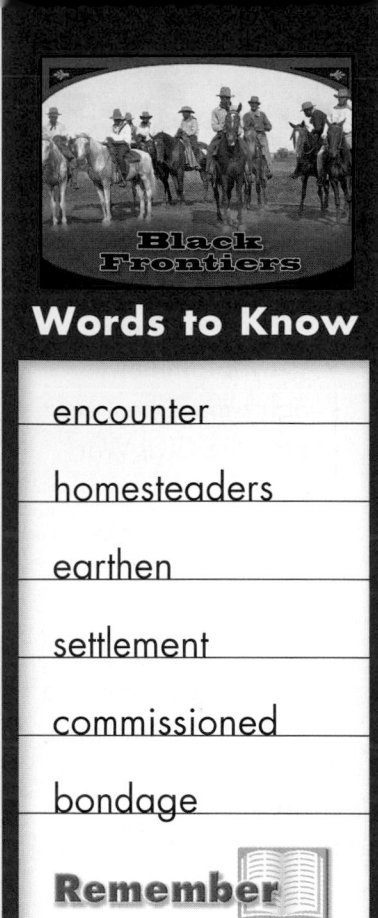

Words to Know

encounter

homesteaders

earthen

settlement

commissioned

bondage

Remember

Try the strategy. Then, if you need more help, use your glossary or a dictionary.

Vocabulary Strategy
for Unfamiliar Words

Context Clues If you find a word you do not know while reading, check the context, or the words and sentences around the unknown word. Often the author provides clues that suggest the meaning of a difficult word.

1. Reread the sentence in which the unknown word appears. Look for a specific clue to the word's meaning.

2. Think about the overall meaning of the sentence.

3. If more help is needed, read the sentences near the sentence with the unknown word. They may contain enough information about the subject to suggest the meaning of the word.

4. See if your meaning makes sense in the original sentence.

As you read "Settling the West," use the context to help you figure out the meanings of unfamiliar words.

Settling the West

Settling in the American West took bravery and staying power. Men, women, and children traveled by boat or wagon, taking all their goods along. They never knew when they might encounter Native Americans. If the settlers did meet them, would these people be friendly or angry?

Once they chose a plot of land, the pioneers faced many difficulties. Homesteaders were pioneers who bought public land cheap and set up farms or ranches. In the grasslands, they often had to build makeshift earthen homes. They built with dirt or sod because wood was so scarce.

Over time, their numbers grew. In time, a settlement, or community in the wilderness, was established.

Battles between settlers and Native Americans continued in many places, as the Native Americans saw their land disappearing. There were losses on both sides. The U.S. government saw the land as their own. They commissioned officers and sent troops to battle the Native Americans. After many years of conflict and negotiation, Native Americans were mostly forced into the bondage of living on reservations. They no longer had the freedom to live as they once had.

Write

Choose a picture from the selection and write a description of the picture. Use words from the Words to Know list.

Black Frontiers

by
Lillian Schlissel

What roles did
African Americans play
in the history of the old West?

Leaving the South

When the Civil War ended, men and women who had been slaves waited to see what freedom would bring. The land they farmed still belonged to the families who had once owned them, and because they had no money, former slaves were expected to pay back a share of their crops in exchange for seed, plows, and mules. They had to pay back a share of everything they raised for rent and food. These sharecroppers soon found they were perpetually in debt.

In 1879, a Louisiana sharecropper named John Lewis Solomon, his wife, and four children packed their belongings and started walking toward the Mississippi River. Along the riverbank they found other black families waiting for a chance to travel north. Some built rafts to carry them over the river's dangerous undertows and eddies. Others had money for passage, but riverboat captains would not let them on board. When a steamboat called the *Grand Tower* came close to shore, John Lewis Solomon called to the captain that he could pay his way. He said he had been a soldier in the Union Army. "I know my rights, and if you refuse to carry me on your boat, I will go to the United States Court and sue for damages." Solomon took a great risk, but the captain agreed to let him and his family board the steamboat.

Reaching Kansas, Solomon said, "This is free ground. Then I looked on the heavens, and I said, 'That is free and beautiful heaven.' Then I looked within my heart, and I said to myself, 'I wonder why I was never free before'."

Black families waited on the banks of the Mississippi River for a chance to go north.

Black Homesteaders

Homesteading was not easy for black or white settlers. Rocks, grass, and trees had to be cleared before crops could be planted. A farmer needed a horse, a mule, and a plow. He needed seed to plant and food for his family until the crops were ready to harvest. Most of all a pioneer needed a home.

In regions where there were trees, pioneers built log cabins. But in Kansas and Nebraska, there was only tall grass, as high as a man's shoulder. Pioneers learned that tough root systems under the grass held the dirt firmly, and sod could be cut like bricks and piled, layer upon layer, until it took the shape of a house. These homesteaders were called *sod busters,* and their homes were called *soddies.*

Sod homes could be warm and comfortable. Some were two stories high, with glass windows and chimneys. But in heavy rain, smaller sod houses leaked, and some families remembered being surprised by a snake slithering through a wall.

In North and South Dakota, where the land was rocky and winter temperatures fell to 30 degrees below zero, early pioneers burrowed into the ground and covered themselves with an earthen roof. They brought their small animals into the house in the winter, while cows and goats

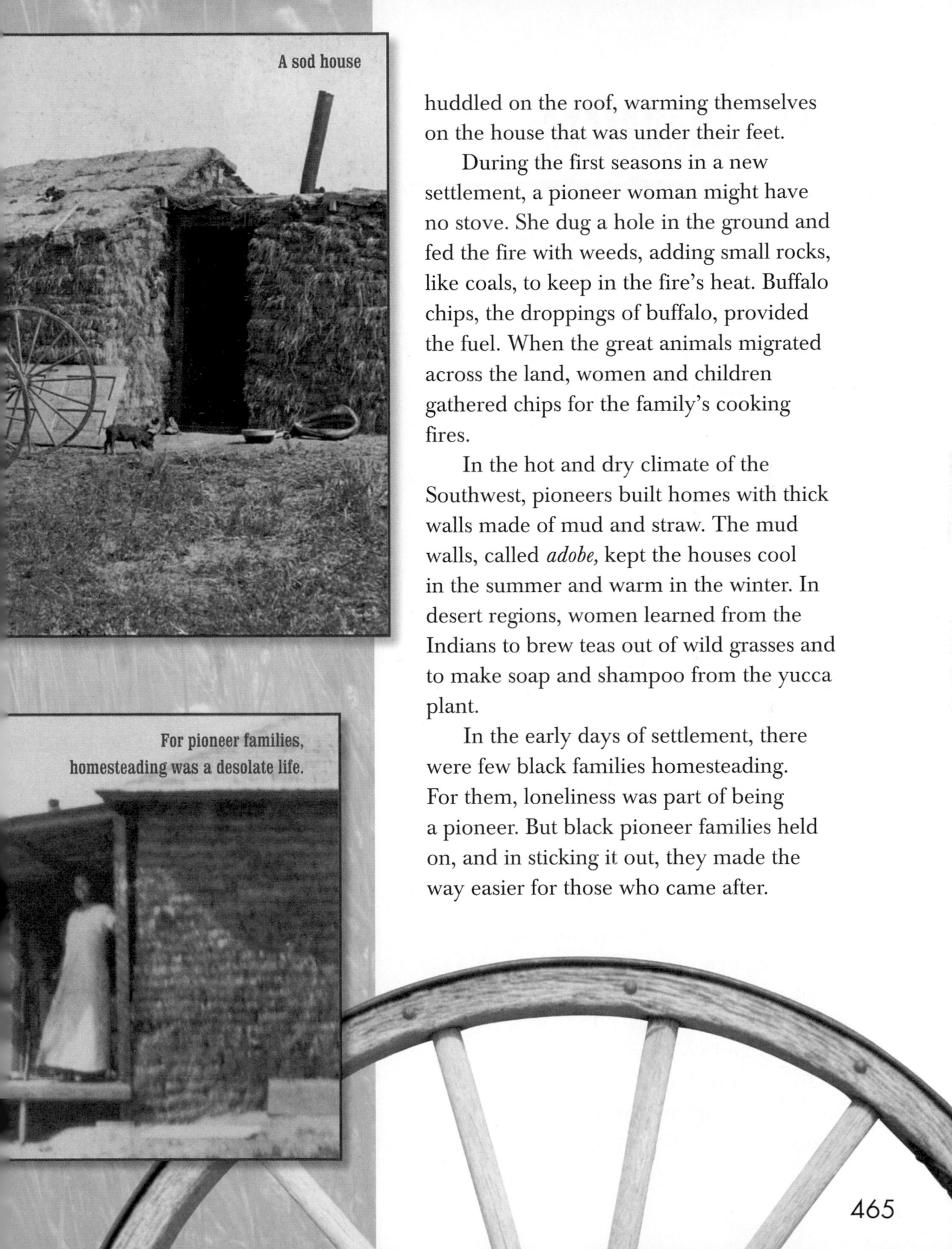

A sod house

For pioneer families, homesteading was a desolate life.

huddled on the roof, warming themselves on the house that was under their feet.

During the first seasons in a new settlement, a pioneer woman might have no stove. She dug a hole in the ground and fed the fire with weeds, adding small rocks, like coals, to keep in the fire's heat. Buffalo chips, the droppings of buffalo, provided the fuel. When the great animals migrated across the land, women and children gathered chips for the family's cooking fires.

In the hot and dry climate of the Southwest, pioneers built homes with thick walls made of mud and straw. The mud walls, called *adobe,* kept the houses cool in the summer and warm in the winter. In desert regions, women learned from the Indians to brew teas out of wild grasses and to make soap and shampoo from the yucca plant.

In the early days of settlement, there were few black families homesteading. For them, loneliness was part of being a pioneer. But black pioneer families held on, and in sticking it out, they made the way easier for those who came after.

The Exodusters

Benjamin Singleton, founder of the black community of Dunlap, Kansas

Men and women who had been slaves read in the Bible about the ancient Israelites who were brought out of bondage and delivered into freedom. Benjamin Singleton, born a slave in Tennessee, was determined that he would bring his people to free soil if it was the last thing he ever did.

After the Civil War, Singleton visited Kansas and over a period of years, he and his friends managed to buy part of a Cherokee reservation. In 1877 they advertised for homesteaders to start an all-black community there. They hoped to attract two hundred families. Fliers promised that settlers who paid one dollar "in installments of 25 cents at a time or otherwise as may be desired" could be part of the new community. By 1879 an exodus of black families out of the Old South began, and before long, there were eight hundred homesteaders in the new Kansas communities of Dunlap and Nicodemus. Benjamin Singleton said, "My people that I carried to Kansas came on our own resources. We have tried to make a people of ourselves . . ." They were known as the Exodusters.

In the early days of the town the farmers in Nicodemus owned only three horses. One man plowed with a milk cow,

Ho for Kansas!

Brethren, Friends, & Fellow Citizens:

I feel thankful to inform you that the

REAL ESTATE
AND
Homestead Association,

Will Leave Here the

15th of April, 1878,

In pursuit of Homes in the Southwestern Lands of America, at Transportation Rates, cheaper than ever was known before.

For full information inquire of

Benj. Singleton, better known as old Pap,
NO. 5 NORTH FRONT STREET.

Beware of Speculators and Adventurers, as it is a dangerous thing to fall in their hands.

Nashville, Tenn., March 18, 1878.

and others broke ground with shovels and spades. White farmers saw how hard their new neighbors worked and lent the new settlers a team of oxen and a plow. Black farmers planted their first crops and in time they prospered. By the turn of the century there were about eight thousand black homesteaders in Nicodemus and Dunlap.

Handbills encouraged black families to move to Kansas. Notice the warning at the bottom of the flier.

Schoolhouse in Dunlap, Kansas. Pupil in foreground carries a sign that reads, "God Bless Our School."

467

The Shores family in front of their sod house near Westville, Custer County, Nebraska, 1887. The Shores became famous as musicians.

Some black settlers moved farther west to Nebraska and Oklahoma where they built three new black communities–Taft, Langston, and Boley. George Washington Bush went all the way to Oregon Territory where he introduced the first mower and reaper into the area around Puget Sound.

Of all the black communities, however, Nicodemus and Dunlap remained the most famous. Each year they celebrated the Fourth of July, and they had their own special holiday, Emancipation Day. On July 31 and August 1, a square mile of land was set aside as a carnival fairground. There were boxing matches and baseball games. In

1907 the town formed one of the nation's first black baseball teams—the Nicodemus Blues. The Blues played black teams as far away as Texas, Nevada, and Louisiana. Satchel Paige, one of the greatest black pitchers in American baseball history, played ball in Nicodemus.

In 1976 Nicodemus was designated a National Historic Landmark. The town's history is being recorded and buildings restored. It marks the proud legacy of black homesteaders in America.

The Moses Speese family—neighbors of the Shores family—outside their sod house near Westville, Custer County, Nebraska

The Buffalo Soldiers

Henry Flipper, first black graduate of West Point

During the Civil War, nearly 180,000 black troops fought with the Union Army against the Confederacy, and more than 33,000 gave their lives to end slavery. After the war, General Ulysses S. Grant ordered Generals Philip Sheridan and William Tecumseh Sherman to organize regiments of black cavalry. These were designated the Ninth and Tenth Cavalry, each containing about a thousand men under the command of white commissioned officers—Colonel Edward Hatch for the Ninth and Colonel Benjamin Grierson for the Tenth. Two black regiments of infantry were organized, the Twenty-fourth and the Twenty-fifth. George Armstrong Custer refused to command black troops, but others accepted their tasks gladly.

Black troops who had been farmers, cooks, carpenters, and blacksmiths came from all parts of the country. The Army paid them thirteen dollars a month plus rations and sent them to the most desolate and dangerous frontier outposts where they served under the harshest conditions with the oldest equipment. They fought Indian tribes few soldiers wished to encounter—the Cheyenne, Comanche, Kiowa, Apache, Ute, and Sioux.

It was the Indians who gave the black troops the name Buffalo Soldiers because their hair resembled the shaggy coats of the buffalo. The buffalo was sacred to the Indians, and the men of the Ninth and Tenth Cavalry and the Twenty-fourth and Twenty-fifth Infantry accepted the name as a badge of honor, and the buffalo became a prominent part of their regimental crest.

Thirteen men of the Buffalo Soldiers won the highest military award of the nation, the Congressional Medal of Honor.

Serving under harsh conditions, these Buffalo Soldiers of the Tenth Calvary camped on Diamond Creek in New Mexico.

When all-black regiments were disbanded after World War II, almost one hundred years after they were organized, the Tenth Cavalry became the 510th Tank Battalion. But memories of frontier days were strong, and the 510th was redesignated the Tenth Cavalry in 1958 and stationed at Fort Knox, Kentucky.

A bronze statue in memory of the Ninth and Tenth Cavalry and the Twenty-fourth and Twenty-fifth Infantry was dedicated in 1992 at Fort Leavenworth, Kansas, to commemorate the courage of the Buffalo Soldiers and mark their place in American military history.

The Buffalo Soldiers helped to bring law and order to regions where ranchers fought with farmers, where Indian tribes warred with each other and with settlers, and where bandits threatened to overrun small towns. On rare occasions, settlers acknowledged their great debt to the black troops. When the Twenty-fifth was ordered to duty in the Spanish-American War, the people of Missoula, Montana, postponed Easter church services so that they could line up along the town's main street and wave goodbye to the black troops who had become their protectors and friends.

Over the years, that strange name, Buffalo Soldiers, became a prized possession of those black troops who left a legacy of courageous service in U.S. military history.

John Hanks Alexander, an African American graduate of West Point, class of 1887. He served among the respected Buffalo Soldiers during the Indian Wars.

Conclusion

It would be wrong to suggest that the frontier was without prejudice. It had its share of violence and racial injustice. As settlements grew into cities, Jim Crow segregation laws confronted black settlers. But on those lonely, dangerous, and beautiful lands we call the frontier, black pioneers built new lives. Born into slavery, African Americans had the same dreams of freedom and independence as did all other Americans. Given the chance, they proved time and again that they possessed skills, initiative, and courage.

West of the Mississippi, between 1850 and 1900, there were some ten thousand African American exodusters, homesteaders, and sod busters. There were also four thousand miners, eight thousand wranglers and rodeo riders, and some five thousand Buffalo Soldiers. According to some historians, there were some eighty thousand African Americans doing whatever else the frontier demanded. They were trappers and mountain men, hotel keepers, and scouts. They were businessmen and women, teachers, and nurses.

And they were cowboys. From the Chisholm Trail to Hollywood, the American cowboy is a hero who walks tall. It is important to remember, then, that some of America's best cowboys and rodeo riders were black, and that some of our bravest pioneers were African Americans who lived and worked on America's western frontiers.

Reader Response

Open for Discussion   They went West. What were their reasons? What roles did they fulfill? What would you put into a collage, drama, or notebook to commemorate African Americans in the western frontier?

1. To see why this author included old photographs, select one and study it for one full minute. Then cover it and report the scene as if you were there.

2. The author tells us that the Indians gave the black troops the name Buffalo Soldiers because of their hair. How did the troops respond to this name given to them?

3. How did what you already know about pioneers and the Old West help you to better understand what you read in this piece?

4. Write a journal entry that a homesteader might have written during his or her first winter in South Dakota. Use words from the Words to Know list.

Test Practice

Look Back and Write Who and where were the exodusters? Did they succeed? Review pages 466–467 before writing your answer.

Lillian Schlissel

Read more books about settling the West.

Lillian Schlissel dedicated her book *Black Frontiers: A History of African American Heroes in the Old West* to her daughter and son, Rebecca and Daniel, and to her mother, Mae Fischer. About the book, Ms. Schlissel points out, "The black presence in the West is sometimes most powerfully expressed in old photographs."

In addition to her two books for young people, Ms. Schlissel has written several adult books about the western frontier. Her *Women's Diaries of the Westward Journey* received critical praise. The book is a collection of letters and diaries written by women traveling to California and Oregon between 1849 and 1870.

Ms. Schlissel is a scholar and a lecturer. Educated at Brooklyn College, she earned a doctorate degree from Yale University. She has also worked as a consultant for a PBS television series about women of the West.

The Way West: Journal of a Pioneer Woman
by Amelia Stewart Knight

The Story of Women Who Shaped the West
by Mary Virginia Fox

Genre

- Poems are compositions arranged in lines. The lines do not have to rhyme, but many poems have lines with a clear, regular rhythm.

- Poems have the ability to make readers feel a diverse range of emotions.

- Poets use their life experiences or views as they compose their poems.

- A poet might create new words or combinations of words to reflect the mood or image.

- Notice that a poet might write short poems in a single verse or a few short verses.

Link to Writing

Write a few lines or thoughts that you have about dreams or hopes.

Poems
by Langston Hughes

The Dream Keeper

Bring me all of your dreams,

You dreamers.

Bring me all of your

Heart melodies

That I may wrap them

In a blue cloud-cloth

Away from the too-rough fingers

Of the world.

Cause/Effect What are some causes and effects in these poems?

Youth

We have tomorrow
Bright before us
Like a flame.

Yesterday
A night-gone thing,
A sun-down name.

And dawn-today
Broad arch above the
   road we came.

We march!

Dreams

Hold fast to dreams
For if dreams die
Life is a broken-winged bird
That cannot fly.

Hold fast to dreams
For when dreams go
Life is a barren field
Frozen with snow.

Reading Across Texts

What message do you think the poet Langston Hughes would have for the black settlers of communities like Nicodemus and Dunlap?

Writing Across Texts Write a message of hope for frontier settlers. Use lines from the poems if you wish.

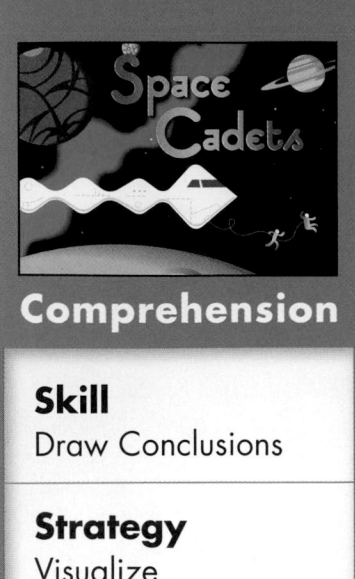

Skill
Draw Conclusions

Strategy
Visualize

Draw Conclusions

- When you draw a conclusion, you form a reasonable opinion about what you have read. Use what you know about real life to help you draw conclusions.

- Be sure that there are enough facts or information in the text to support your conclusions.

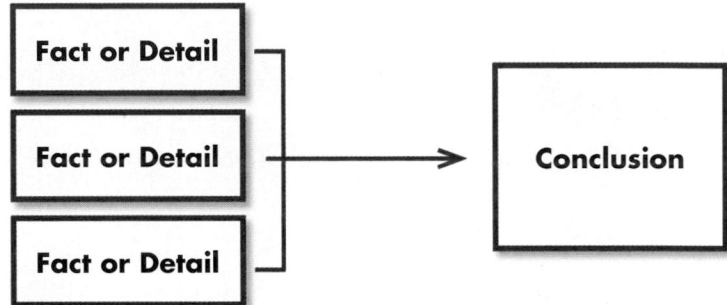

Strategy: Visualize

When you visualize, you create pictures in your mind. This strategy helps you make sense of a story. It can help you place yourself into the story, as if you were there. Visualize the details that the writer has given you. That can also help you to draw conclusions the writer has not stated.

1. Read the letter from Isabel. Make a graphic organizer like the one above to show how you would support the conclusion that technology in the time period the letter was written has advanced from what it is today.

2. Draw or write a detailed description of the place where Isabel now lives.

478

Earth Date: April 12, 2099

1221 Galaxy Way
Planet Enilorac

Greetings, Rachel,

How are you, old buddy? It has been ten Earth-weeks now since we moved to this planet. This is a different place from Earth, that's for sure. The atmosphere is greenish, and we have two suns and three moons.

The entire planet is really urban. We live on a busy flyway, with lots of aircars zipping past. So much for cruising on our air scooters like we used to, huh? Remember how much we would scooter up and down and back and forth in front of my house on Earth? It is so quiet and safe there where you are.

My new school is called Albert Einstein School. Last week the telecommunicator of this one boy—his name is Santino—started smoking and almost blew up, right in the middle of our History of the Galaxy class. He got in trouble because we are supposed to switch our telecommunicators off at school.

At recess, I sort of sit on the sidelines and watch the other kids duel with their laser swords or play dodge orb. There's no one like you here. Are you doing all right? Are you still spying on Ellen and Juanita at recess like we used to? That was awesome!

Sincerely,
Isabel

Strategy Visualize this scene. What do you see in your mind? How would it make you feel?

Skill Which conclusion can you draw about Isabel's view of her new home?
(a) She felt more comfortable on Earth.
(b) She wishes it were busier.
(c) She likes her new home better than her old home.

Skill What conclusion can you draw about how Isabel is feeling?

Strategy How would you visualize Isabel on the school playground? What details must you add to the picture that aren't in the text?

479

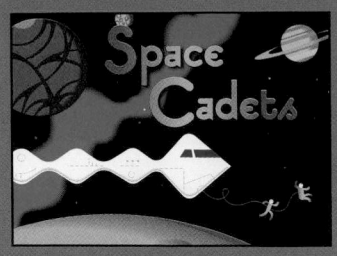

molten
aliens
hospitable
refrain
universal
ore
barge
version

Remember

Try the strategy. Then, if you need more help, use your glossary or a dictionary.

Vocabulary Strategy
for Multiple-Meaning Words

Context Clues Some words have more than one meaning. You can use the words and sentences around a multiple-meaning word to figure out which meaning the author is using.

1. Read the words and sentences around the unknown word.

2. Think about the possible meanings of the word. For example, *refrain* can mean "to keep oneself back" or "a phrase repeated over and over."

3. Decide which meaning makes sense in the sentence: Everyone sang the *refrain*.

4. Reread the sentence and replace the word with the meaning you chose.

5. Does this meaning make sense? If not, try another meaning.

As you read "The Universe According to Hollywood," use the context and your knowledge to decide which meaning a multiple-meaning word has in this article. For example, does *barge* mean "a large, flat-bottomed boat" or "to enter quickly"?

THE UNIVERSE
ACCORDING TO HOLLYWOOD

Travel to outer space is not a dream. It is part of the real world. We have had a close look at planets hot enough to turn glass to a molten pool and cold enough to put the North and South Poles to shame. So far, we have found no proof of life on other planets. However, in movies people travel to the ends of the galaxy and meet all sorts of aliens.

These beings are not always hospitable to the visiting humans. In fact, misunderstandings are always leading to trouble. It sometimes seems as though none of these beings can refrain from war and crime. It seems these ills do not belong to Earth alone. They are universal truths.

Of course, beings all over the universe also have ambition and honor. Suppose a precious ore has been discovered on Planet X. Three-eyed aliens with tentacles are just as likely as humans to be greedy. A barge loaded with valuable cargo may well be stolen by space pirates and then returned to its rightful owners by "the forces for good." In fact, the Hollywood version of life in outer space is like life at home, with special effects.

Cafe
No Pets
No Earthlings

Write

What do you imagine life would be like on a distant planet? Write a description, using as many words from the Words to Know list as you can.

? I.N.EPT

Is there any intelligent life in outer space?

A **drama** is a story written to be acted for an audience. As you read, think about how this story might appear if it were being acted out.

Genre

482

Space Cadets

by **David LaBounty**

illustrated
by **Doug Ross**

Captain
First Officer
Ensign
Tom [cadet]
Harold [cadet]
Space Cow [alien]
Og [alien]
Mog [alien]

Scene 1

TIME: *The days of warp drive and phasers set to stun.*

SETTING: *The bridge of the spaceship* Inter Nova *(I. N.) Ept. Captain's chair is center. It sits high enough above stage so that he can see over control panel, placed several feet in front of him.*

AT RISE: CAPTAIN *is sitting on the edge of his chair, staring intently at the view screen (audience). He is wearing bright blue shirt, black pants, and boots.* FIRST OFFICER *is standing behind and to the right of* CAPTAIN. *Her hands are folded behind her back. She is wearing bright red shirt, black pants, and boots. There is a curious look on her face as she examines view screen.* ENSIGN, *sitting at control panel, is wearing a bright yellow shirt, black pants, and boots. He is looking from view screen to his controls, checking to make sure they are still on course. Each crew member is wearing identical watches that serve as both timepieces and communication devices.*

Captain: Spacedate: Wednesday *(Checks watch, taps it)*—what time do you have, First Officer?

First Officer *(Consulting watch):* Nine thirty A.M., sir.

Captain *(Looking back at watch and frowning):* Is that Earth Standard Time?

First Officer: No, sir. We crossed over into Alpha Centauri Time two days ago. Did you forget to set your watch ahead an hour?

Captain *(Testily):* I didn't forget. I was just making sure the computers were operational. *(Turns his back on* FIRST OFFICER *so she won't see him adjust his watch, which she does anyway. Turning back)* Where was I? Oh, yes Spacedate:

Wednesday, 9:30 A.M. We've entered a new solar system, 73 light years from Earth. Seven planets orbit this system's star, Mensa.

First Officer: Sir.

Captain: Yes?

First Officer: I don't mean to interrupt, sir. But whom are you talking to?

Captain *(As if this were a silly question):* The ship's log, of course.

First Officer: We don't have a ship's log, sir.

Captain: Sure we do. It's the thing that records everything I say—you know, for posterity. It turns on when I say "spacedate."

First Officer *(After slowly shaking her head):* It's a novel idea, sir, but all information about our journey is typed into the computer at the end of the day by Ensign Smith and beamed back to Star Base 12, where it is saved in triplicate with one copy returning to us, one forwarded to Earth Command, and one kept in Star Base's files.

Captain: Impressive. Wait a minute. You're telling me for the past three weeks I've been talking for no reason? Out loud?

First Officer: We thought you liked to hear the sound of your voice, sir. (ENSIGN *stifles a laugh.*)

Captain: I do, but that's not the point. *(Shakes head, turns back to view screen)* I can't believe I've been talking to myself like some crazy old man sitting on a park bench feeding breadcrumbs to Neruvian pigeons. Maybe I need a vacation, or at the very least a nap. (*Looking over at* FIRST OFFICER) I'm doing it again, aren't I? (FIRST OFFICER

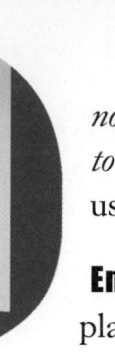

nods. CAPTAIN *clears throat, gets out of his chair and moves to stand next to* ENSIGN.) What are the scanners telling us, Ensign?

Ensign: We're detecting seven planets: four R-class planets, two L-class, and an M-class.

Captain: M-class, you say? We should probably stay away from that one. (*To* FIRST OFFICER) M. What's that stand for? Molten? Menacing?

First Officer: Actually, Sir, M-class planets are the most hospitable for carbon-based life forms. (CAPTAIN *looks confused.*) Humans. Us. (*Checking her computer*) My computers show the atmosphere to be breathable, and I am picking up signs of several types of life forms on the planet's surface.

Captain (*Nodding*): Cool.

First Officer (*Drolly*): Yes, sir. Most excellent. (*Pause*) Sir?

Captain: Yes?

First Officer: What exactly was it you were the captain of before this assignment?

Captain: I was the captain of a space barge. We mostly transported garbage from Mars to the Sun, but sometimes we would move ore from the moon to the inner planets. (*Laughs*) Funny story—(*Notices impatient look on* FIRST OFFICER'*s face and interested smile on* ENSIGN'*s*) Yes, well. We can always save that for later. (*Claps hands and returns to chair*) As we all know, our mission is to make first contact. I can't think of a better place to make first contact than with this M-Class planet. How do we land this puppy?

First Officer: We don't. As I am sure you know, the *I. N. Ept* is a starship, suitable for long, long, voyages between the stars. This puppy orbits planets, it does not land.

Captain: Then we need to assemble an away team.

First Officer *(Impressed):* Excellent idea, sir. Who will be joining you?

Captain: Me? Oh, I'm not going down there. We don't know what kind of scary, freaky creatures live on that rock. Uh uh. No way. My momma didn't raise no Voloreain space slug.

First Officer: In this case, I think it is in the best interest of your *safety*— *(Aside)* and the galaxy's—that you remain on board. So whom should we send?

Captain *(Thinking a moment):* We need a team of intelligent, fearless, somewhat pleasing-to-look-at people. Someone with the intestinal fortitude to withstand any repulsive or violent species they may encounter while on the planet below. (ENSIGN *starts to look worried and shrinks down in his chair.*) Who knows what flesh-eating, mind-warping aliens they will find down there? We need someone who isn't afraid to lose a limb—and possibly his or her life—in order to bring peace to the galaxy. *(Touches a button on the arm of his chair)* Tom, Harold, report to the bridge, on the double.

First Officer: Are you sure that's wise?

Captain: Why not? They're perfect.

First Officer: They're cadets. (TOM *and* HAROLD *come "floating" on, as if trying to walk in zero gravity.*)

Captain *(Grabbing arms of chair):* Red Alert! The gravity stabilizers must be off-line.

First Officer *(Checking computer):* Actually, sir, the stabilizers are fine. *(Jumps up and down in place)* Gravity seems to be normal.

Captain: Cancel red alert. (*Frowns at* TOM *and* HAROLD) What are you doing?

Tom: Practicing our space walking.

Captain: Why?

Harold: Section 7 paragraph 3 of the Space Cadet Training Guide states that you should always stay alert in case of a loss of gravity.

Tom (*Crashing into* HAROLD *and bouncing off wildly*): We're practicing in case of an emergency.

Captain: Not a bad idea.

First Officer: Actually, section 7 paragraph 3 of the Space Cadet Training Guide states, and I quote: "Stay away from the moss on planet Grassy T." (HAROLD *pulls small book from back pocket, thumbs to proper page, reads to himself, nods.*)

Harold: Well, I'll be. She's right. How do we practice that? (TOM *shrugs.*)

Captain: We can worry about that later. Men, I have an assignment for you. I want you to beam down to the planet below, seek out the first life forms you find, and make contact.

First Officer: Again, sir, not to question your command, but do you think it is wise to send these two—cadets—on this mission? They are not exactly trained to represent Earth Command when it comes to a first contact with unknown aliens.

Tom: I've been on several first-contact missions.

Captain and First Officer: Really?

Tom: Sure. Every time I ask a girl out on a date, it's my first contact with her—and it's usually my last, as well. (HAROLD *consolingly pats* TOM *on the shoulder.*)

First Officer (*Rolling her eyes*): I don't doubt it.

Captain: Sounds good to me. I know I don't understand women. Aren't they from Venus or someplace like that?

First Officer: We wish. However, I still believe these men are ill-prepared for a mission of this magnitude.

Captain (*Slowly nodding*): You may be right. That's why I want you to accompany them.

First Officer: Me?

Captain: You.

First Officer (*Obviously disappointed, but seeing no way out of it*): Yes, sir.

Tom and Harold (*Ad lib*): We won't let you down, sir. Absolutely not. (*Etc. They exit as if floating in zero gravity.* FIRST OFFICER *follows, shaking her head.*)

Ensign: This should be interesting.

Captain (*Getting out of his chair and moving to control panel*): Yes, it should. You think we could watch on this view screen thingy we've got here? (*Curtain*)

Scene 2

TIME: *A few minutes later.*

SETTING: *The surface of the alien planet, a strange and exotic world. May be played before curtain, if desired.*

AT RISE: *SPACE COW, MOG, and OG are standing left. FIRST OFFICER, TOM, and HAROLD enter right. HAROLD is holding a small scanner and whistling a trilling sound.*

First Officer (*To* HAROLD): What are you doing?

Harold: Scanning for life signs.

First Officer: What's with the whistling?

Harold: Sound effects.

First Officer (*Rolling her eyes*): Please refrain from making that noise.

Harold (*Disappointed*): Yes, sir.

Tom (*Consolingly*): I thought it sounded pretty cool.

Harold: Thanks. You should hear the sound I can make when I fire my phaser. (FIRST OFFICER *suddenly notices* SPACE COW *and holds up her hand.*)

First Officer: Sh-hh! Look. (TOM *and* HAROLD *look toward* SPACE COW *and take a step back.*)

Tom (*In awe*): An alien.

Harold: Do you think it's friendly?

Tom: What are we supposed to do?

Harold: Section 2 paragraph 6 of the Space Cadet Training Guide says we should approach aliens with cotton.

Tom (*Confused*): Cotton? I didn't bring any cotton. Where are we going to find some cotton?

490

First Officer (*Annoyed*): First of all, there is no section 2 paragraph 6 in the Space Cadet Training Guide. Second, the section you are probably referring to is section 6 paragraph 2, which states, and I quote, "Approach aliens with *caution*."

Tom and Harold (*Together*): Ohhhh.

Tom: That makes sense. (SPACE COW *makes a grunting noise.* TOM *takes another step back.*) What did it say?

First Officer (*Puzzled*): I do not know. Our universal translators do not seem to be functioning.

Harold (*Holding out hands to* SPACE COW *and taking a bold step forward*): Greetings, alien. We come in peace. (SPACE COW *makes a grunting noise.*)

Tom: Do you think it understands?

First Officer: It does not seem so.

Harold (*Speaking louder*): Greetings, alien! We come in peace!

First Officer (*Sarcastically*): Oh, yes. That should do it. Speaking louder will help it understand.

Tom: She's right. Maybe it doesn't have ears. Maybe it communicates with thoughts. (*Closes eyes and strains*)

First Officer: What are you doing?

Tom (*Eyes still closed, still straining*): Trying–to–send–it–a–telepathic–message. Ugh! (*Opens eyes and sways, almost falling*)

Harold (*Catching* TOM): What happened? Did it hear you? Did it try to melt your mind?

Tom: No. I'm O.K. All that hard thinking made me a little dizzy.

First Officer: I do not doubt it.

Harold (*To* FIRST OFFICER): Do you have any ideas?

First Officer: I have been observing the two creatures behind the alien.

Tom: Those creepy, crawly-looking things?

First Officer: Yes. Your scientific language needs some work, but those creepy, crawly-looking things seem to be observing us, following our movements.

Harold: Come on. They're just a couple of dogs.

First Officer: What do you mean?

Harold: Look at them. The blank looks on their faces, tongues hanging out of their mouths. They're like space dogs, or this planet's version of space dogs. Obviously the alien is taking them out for their morning walk.

Tom: Aren't they cute? (*Taking a step toward aliens with one hand outstretched*) Hey, little fella. Don't be scared. I just wanna pet you.

Harold (*Grabbing* TOM): You fool! You have no idea where that dog has been. It could have rabies, for all we know.

Tom: You're right.

First Officer (*Rubbing her forehead*): How did you two ever get into the Academy training program?

Tom: Just walked right in the front door.

First Officer: No. I mean, how did you pass the entrance exam?

Harold: I didn't have to take a test.

First Officer: Why not?

Harold: My father wrote a letter to the Dean.

First Officer: Who is your father?

Harold: Admiral Hastings.

First Officer *(In disbelief)*: Your father is Admiral Hastings?

Harold *(Surprised)*: You know him?

First Officer: He is the Commander of Star Base One.

Harold *(Impressed)*: Really? (*During this conversation,* SPACE COW *has been slowly walking toward* TOM.)

Tom: Um, you guys, the alien is coming over here. (SPACE COW *walks up to* TOM, *who is frozen with fear.* SPACE COW *reaches out a hand, touching* TOM*'s head.*) Um—what's it doing?

First Officer: It seems to be scanning you.

Harold: Or getting ready to suck out your brains! (*TOM yells and pushes* SPACE COW*'s hand away.* SPACE COW *screams.* TOM *and* HAROLD *start running around.*)

First Officer *(Speaking hurriedly into her watch)*: First Officer to Ept. Three to beam up—and make it fast. (*TOM and* HAROLD *run off;* FIRST OFFICER *follows. There is a pause.*)

Mog: Well, Og, that was strange.

Og *(Nodding)*: Yes, definitely. Where do you think they were from?

Mog: Not from around here.

Og: Why do you suppose they kept trying to talk to Bessie?

Mog: Maybe she reminded them of someone they know.

Og *(Looking up and shaking his head)*: Like I've always said, Mog. There is no intelligent life out there. (*To* SPACE COW) Come on, Bessie, let's get you back to the barn. (SPACE COW *grunts and follows* OG *and* MOG *off. Curtain*)

The End

Reader Response

Open for Discussion   Science fiction is about smart humans coping splendidly in alien space, right? Then why is *Space Cadets* so different? How does the play depart from the pattern?

1. The author did not describe the clothes and appearance of Space Cow, so an artist drew an impression. Based on Scene Two, give another description of a Space Cow.

2. How does the First Officer feel about the other members of *Inter Nova Ept*'s crew? Support your answer with information from the play's text.

3. Mog and Og are supposed to be "creepy-crawly looking" aliens. How do you picture the actors as they play these parts? What costumes and make-up do you see them wearing to make them look like the aliens?

4. Draw a picture of the alien planet described as a "strange and exotic world" in this story. Include in the picture all life forms mentioned. Add labels using words from the Words to Know list and from the selection.

Test Practice

Look Back and Write   Look at page 486. What was *Inter Nova Ept*'s mission, and did it fulfill that mission? Write your answer in the form of a message to Earth.

David LaBounty

Read more plays.

About *Space Cadets,* David LaBounty says, "Actually it's the third play in a series. In the first play, *Keystone Knights,* three bumbling knights in training try to defeat a dragon. In the second play, *Ship of Fools,* the clueless captain of a pirate ship finds himself in hot water on an island inhabited by cannibals. I wondered what it would be like if I combined the bumbling knights in the first play, the clueless captain in the second play, and threw them in space. *Space Cadets* was born."

Mr. LaBounty believes that practice is key to good writing. To young writers, he says, "Show your stories to friends and family, get their reactions, and don't be afraid of rejection. For those who want to write comedy, be able to laugh at yourself—try and get other people to laugh at your expense. Watch old television shows, variety and comedians' acts, and even cartoons." He adds, "Also read a lot of joke books. Most of the jokes in those books are old, but they may give you ideas for new ones."

Mr. LaBounty has a degree in psychology and was a teacher for several years. In addition to writing plays, he is now the editor of *The First Line,* a literary magazine.

The Most Boring Kingdom in the World
by David LaBounty from
***Plays* magazine**

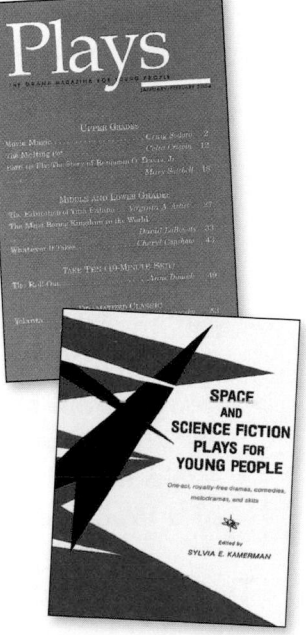

Space and Science Fiction Plays for Young People

Reading Online

Exploring Space Travel

Evaluating Sources

Genre

- You can find information fast on the Internet. Not all of it will be reliable, truthful, or dependable. You need to think carefully about it.

- You need to learn how to tell reliable from not-so-reliable Web sites. Think carefully about what you know about statements of fact and opinion when evaluating the reliability of a Web site.

Text Features

- The addresses of reliable and useful Web sites often end in .gov, .edu, or .org.

- Web sites that end in .com may also be reliable.

- Use both the source and the descriptions of the Web sites to help narrow your search.

Link to Science

Find two useful and reliable sources on any subject you are studying in science class. Tell why they are useful and reliable.

Let's say you are using the Internet for a report on space travel. You perform an Internet search. Which of these might prove useful for your report? Note both the source of the information and the *description* of the information.

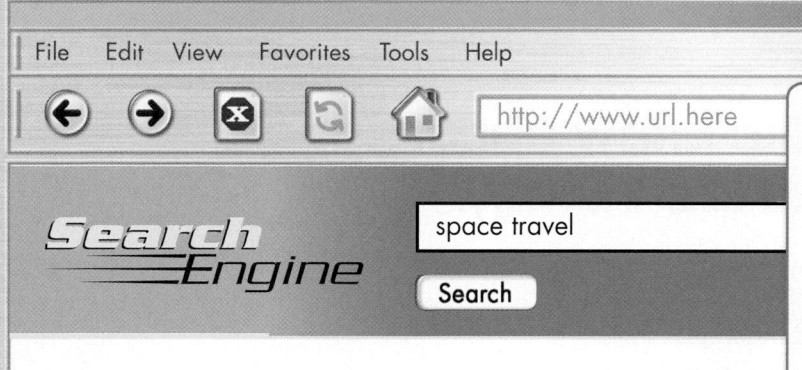

File   Edit   View   Favorites   Tools   Help

http://www.url.here

Search Engine

space travel

Search

Space Travel. Sheets and pillows that glow in the dark. You'll feel like an astronaut at bedtime!   www.website_here.com ●

This is a .com Web site. The letters *com* are short for *commercial*. A .com site often wants to sell something. It may or may not be reliable. After you read the description, you decide it is not useful.

How the U.S. Traveled Through Space to the Moon. The story of Apollo 11.   www.website_here.edu ●

This is an .edu Web site. The letters *edu* are short for *education*. An .edu site is usually a school. It is probably reliable. After you read the description, though, you decide it is not useful.

NASA Space Place: Amazing Facts. Cool stuff to know about space, Earth, and technology.   www.website_here.gov

Lisa's Journey The story of a girl who finds a time machine and travels to another galaxy.   www.website_here.com

This is a .gov Web site. The letters *gov* are short for *government*. It is probably reliable. After you read the description, you decide it is worth looking at. You click on the link NASA Space Place: Amazing Facts. This Web site is from the National Aeronautics and Space Administration. It should be very reliable.

Draw Conclusions   What conclusions might be drawn about NASA's site?

497

You look at this list of links about space and click on the <u>Launch a rocket as planet spins</u> link.

http://www.url.here

NATIONAL AERONAUTICS
AND SPACE ADMINISTRATION

Cool stuff to know about space, Earth, and technology.

Name the trees from space.

Launch a rocket as planet spins.

Solve an extraterrestrial riddle.

How do I get to space with no launch pad?

What is the "secret code" of the Voyager spacecraft?

Games

Animations

Cool Subjects

Amazing Facts

Projects

File   Edit   View   Favorites   Tools   Help

Here is what you learn about launching a rocket.

NATIONAL AERONAUTICS
AND SPACE ADMINISTRATION

Launch a "Rocket" from a Spinning "Planet"

Nothing in space stands still. Everything either orbits around something else, or moves toward or away from something else. So how do space engineers aim a spacecraft so it lands on Mars or meets up with a particular comet or asteroid?

If you don't think this is a hard problem, try this:

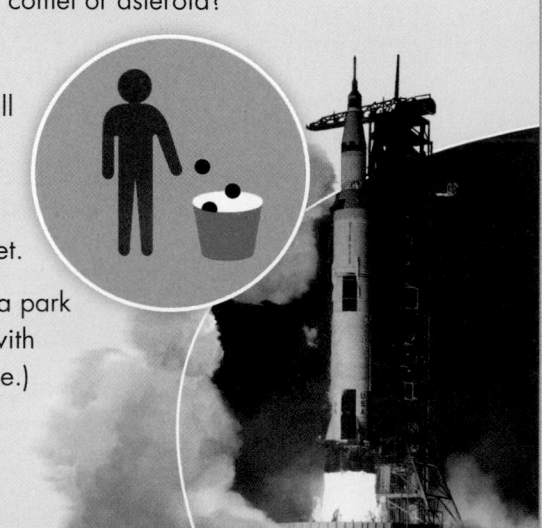

1. Gather up some tennis balls or bean bags. Or make small "paper balls" by tightly wadding up pieces of paper.

2. Put the balls in a bucket or bag.

3. Find another empty container like a bucket or wastebasket.

4. Take the balls (in their container) and the empty basket to a park or playground that has a merry-go-round. (Not the kind with horses, but the kind you push around then hop on and ride.)

498

NATIONAL AERONAUTICS AND SPACE ADMINISTRATION

5. Place the empty basket on the ground about 9 to 12 feet from the merry-go-round. Then, step up on the merry-go-round with your container of balls.

6. Without moving the merry-go-round, try tossing a few balls into the empty basket.

7. Leave the container of balls on the merry-go-round, hop off, push to get it going slowly. Then hop back on.

8. Try tossing the balls into the basket on the ground as you go around.

Adding the motion makes it a lot harder to hit your target, doesn't it? Now imagine the target is on another spinning merry-go-round on the other side of the playground. Even if your paper balls were real basketballs or baseballs, you'd have a lot of trouble.

The Earth moves around the sun counter-clockwise and the Earth spins around its own axis counter-clockwise. This motion can be used to give a boost to a rocket as it launches.

As you begin to learn more about space travel, you can take notes and extend your research into more areas by using online directories.

Reading Across Texts

Would you use either *Space Cadets* or "Launch a 'Rocket' from a 'Spinning Planet'" to write a report on space travel? What was the author's purpose in each of these?

Writing Across Texts Explain how the author's purpose affects what you learned in each selection.

 **Visualize**   Mentally picturing each of the eight steps will help you.

Inventing
the
Future

Comprehension

Skill
Author's Purpose

Strategy
Monitor and Fix-Up

Skill

Author's Purpose

- Authors may write to persuade, inform, express, or entertain. Preview the title, headings, and pictures to help predict the author's purpose. Set your reading speed.

- As you read, you may need to adjust your ideas about the author's purpose. If so, you may need to read more slowly or more quickly.

- When you finish, ask yourself, "How did the language or style help meet the purpose?"

| **Before Reading** |
| Preview to decide purpose. Set reading pace. |

↓

| **During Reading** |
| Look for clues to purpose. Adjust pace if needed. |

↓

| **After Reading** |
| Ask if purpose was met and how. |

Strategy

Strategy: Monitor and Fix-Up

Good readers make sure they understand what they are reading. If you do not understand, use a fix-up strategy. For example, as you read, you may discover the author is giving you brand-new information using difficult words. You might slow down so that you make sure you understand.

Write

1. Read "The Age of Inventions." Make a graphic organizer like the one above in order to determine the author's main purpose.

2. Make notes about what you didn't understand in "The Age of Inventions." Write about what you might do to help you better understand what you read.

The Age of Inventions

The period from the mid-1800s to the early 1900s was one of great significance in human history. Many of the machines invented during this time changed the world.

First, new ways to power machines were developed. Inventors learned to generate and use electricity, leading to the widespread use of electric lights and trains. The first gasoline-fueled engine was perfected in 1859, and these engines were soon used in many factories.

Second, transportation changed dramatically. The first motorcycles and motorcars were introduced in 1885. The first large iron ships were constructed during this time as well and soon replaced ships powered by sails. The Wright brothers piloted the first plane flight in 1903.

Third, people were able to communicate in more sophisticated ways. For example, the telephone, which was made in 1876, and the wireless telegraph, invented in 1895, let people converse across long distances. The radio was invented in 1901.

The world changed in so many ways from the mid-1800s to the early 1900s. Was it a better place because of all these inventions? Many people would say yes. However, some might disagree. Transportation and communication were speedier, but noise, pollution, and a faster pace of life also resulted.

Skill What do you predict the main purpose of the article is?

(a) to inform you which machines were invented during this time period

(b) to entertain you by joking about inventions of the 1800s

(c) to persuade you that this time was very important

Strategy Are you understanding the author's purpose and the information he is giving you? Do you need to change your reading speed?

Skill What does the purpose of this final paragraph seem to be —to inform, to entertain, or to express ideas?

Strategy What could you do here if you had trouble understanding this paragraph?

devise

transmitted

efficiency

converts

reproduce

generated

percentage

proclaimed

Remember

Try the strategy. Then, if you need more help, use your glossary or a dictionary.

Vocabulary Strategy
for Prefixes

Word Structure A prefix is a word part that is added at the beginning of a base word. The prefix changes the base word's meaning. When you come across an unknown word, check to see if it has a prefix. Knowing the meaning of the prefix may help you figure out the meaning of the word. For example, the prefix *re-* means "again"; *pro-* means "forth" or "forward"; and *trans-* means "across," "beyond," or "through."

1. Look at an unfamiliar word to see if it has a base word you know.

2. Check to see if the prefix *re-*, *pro-*, or *trans-* has been added to the base word.

3. Think about what meaning the prefix adds to the meaning of the base word.

4. Try the meaning in the sentence.

As you read "Hats Off to Inventors," look for words that have prefixes. Use the prefixes to help you figure out the meaning of the words.

ALEXANDER GRAHAM BELL, c. 1915, inventor of the telephone.

Hats Off to Inventors

We owe the comfort and convenience of our lives to inventors. These creative geniuses devise better ways to do or make something. Sometimes this means coming up with a whole new invention, such as the telephone. Thanks to this machine, sound is transmitted over great distances. At other times, inventors have just improved the efficiency of a machine that already exists. The radial tire, for example, meant that cars would get better gas mileage. Even simple inventions can make a big difference. For example, the sticky note converts paper into a message that can be placed right where you want it. The inventor is a practical dreamer. He or she wants to make a product that is easy to reproduce and useful, so the public will buy it.

Inventors have been around for thousands of years, but in the last 150 years they have generated by far the greatest percentage of new gadgets ever invented. In many ways, their work has made life better for us all. Don't you think a special Inventors Day should be proclaimed?

THOMAS EDISON

Write

Choose an invention you think is important. Write about how it has changed people's lives. Use as many words from the Words to Know list as you can.

Inventing the Future

A Photobiography of Thomas Alva Edison

by Marfé Ferguson Delano

Genre

A **biography** is the story of a real person's life written by another person. Before you read, think about what you may already know about Thomas Edison.

Why are Thomas Edison's inventions so important to us today?

Pictured here during his "tramp telegrapher" days, Edison preferred to work night jobs, which he said gave him "more leisure to experiment."

In 1868, Thomas Edison took a job in the Western Union telegraph office in Boston. He found the city an exciting place. Not only did it have a large telegraphic community, it was filled with inventors. One of them was Alexander Graham Bell, who in 1876 would invent the telephone. Edison worked nights as a press operator and spent his days exploring the shops where telegraphs and other electrical devices were designed and made. Inspired by all the activity he found, Edison soon quit his job to focus full time on bringing out inventions. He met with people who had money to invest and persuaded them to provide the funds he needed to develop his ideas and have his inventions made. He specialized in telegraphic devices, but he also worked on other inventions.

When he was 22 years old, Edison received his first patent. It was for an electric vote recorder. A patent is an official document issued by the government that gives a person or company the sole right to make or sell an invention. Edison hoped the device would be used by state legislatures, but lawmakers were not interested in buying it. The experience taught him a valuable lesson: Never again would he invent something that people didn't want to buy.

In 1869, Edison moved to New York City. Many telegraph companies, including Western Union, had their headquarters in the city, which brimmed with business opportunities for an ambitious young inventor. Edison worked for a while for the Laws Gold Indicator Company, where he repaired and improved the company's stock printers. Also called stock tickers because of the noise they made, stock printers were a kind of telegraph that sent minute-by-minute reports of the changing price of gold to stockbrokers' offices.

"Anything that won't sell, I don't want to invent. Its sale is proof of utility, and utility is success."

That fall, Edison started a business called Pope, Edison and Company with a fellow inventor named Franklin Pope. They advertised themselves as electrical engineers who could "devise electrical instruments and solve problems to order." The company offered a variety of services having to do with telegraph technology and was also committed to bringing out new devices—Edison's specialty. He patented a number of telegraphic improvements that were eagerly bought by the telegraph industry. Finally he was inventing what people wanted and were willing to pay for.

By the age of 23, Edison had earned a reputation as one of the best electrical inventors in the country, which helped him attract more financial backers. In 1870, his partnership with Pope broke up, and Edison opened his very own manufacturing company and laboratory in Newark, New Jersey.

Edison hired more than 50 employees to make and sell his stock printers and other equipment and to assist with his many experiments. Among the skilled machinists and clockmakers he hired were Charles Batchelor and John Kruesi. A British-born machinist and draftsman, Batchelor soon became Edison's right-hand man as well as his friend. They worked closely together for nearly 25 years. Kruesi, born in Switzerland and trained as a clockmaker, worked with Edison for 20-some years.

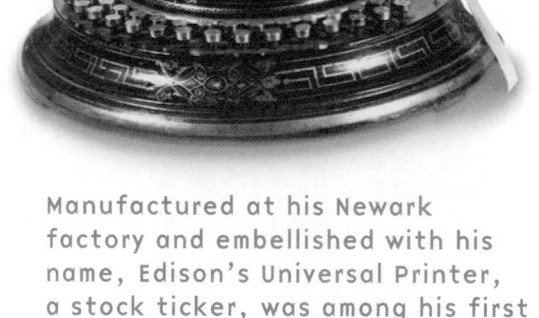

Manufactured at his Newark factory and embellished with his name, Edison's Universal Printer, a stock ticker, was among his first commercially successful inventions.

In the fall of 1871, 24-year-old Edison started his own news service, the News Reporting Telegraph Company. Among the company's employees was a pretty 16-year-old clerk named Mary Stilwell, a Newark girl whose father worked in a sawmill. Edison set his sights on Mary, and after a brief courtship, they married on Christmas Day, 1871. When the couple's first child was born, a daughter named Marion, Edison

Mary Stilwell (top) married Edison on Christmas Day, 1871. The couple had three children: Marion (middle), Thomas Alva, Jr., (bottom right), and William (bottom left).

nicknamed her "Dot," after the telegraph signal. Their second child, Thomas Alva, Jr., was dubbed "Dash," of course. The Edisons' third child was named—and called—William.

Soon after their marriage, Mary discovered that she played second fiddle to her husband's true love—inventing. He often spent several days straight at the lab, working through the nights and catching naps on a workbench or desktop when exhaustion overwhelmed him. Whenever Edison was involved with a project, he became totally wrapped up in it. And since he almost always had dozens of inventions going at once, he had little time for anything else.

In Newark, Edison first developed the method of team inventing that would characterize the rest of his career. Whenever a new idea for an invention inspired him, he sketched it out in a notebook and then shared the drawing with Batchelor and Kruesi or other trusted assistants. Their job was to take the sketch and see that it was made into a working model. Lab workers then experimented with the model to see how the invention worked—or did not work, which was often the case. Edison was not discouraged when things went wrong. He and his workers would just keep trying until they found out what did work.

Edison's workers tended to be very loyal to "the old man," as they called their young boss. They admired and respected him for the way he worked alongside them, plunging into the dirtiest jobs with enthusiasm and putting in longer hours than anyone else. Moreover, Edison could be generous. He often gave assistants who worked closely with him on an invention a percentage of the profits it made.

"Negative results are just what I want. They're just as valuable to me as positive results. I can never find the thing that does a job the best until I find the ones that don't do."

Although Edison's Newark laboratory focused mainly on devices that improved the speed and efficiency of the telegraph, other electrical inventions were also under development. One of these was the electric pen, which could create multiple copies of a handwritten document. Business owners, from lawyers to mapmakers, immediately saw the value of the device, and it sold well. Although Edison manufactured and sold many of his inventions, he also sold the patents for many others. This gave the buyer the exclusive right to make and sell a device. Despite the income this generated, Edison was usually short of cash. That's because he tended to spend most of what he earned from one invention on the next.

In 1876, Edison sold his Newark business. He moved his family and about 20 of his best workers—including Batchelor and Kruesi—

The electric pen was among the inventions Edison developed and manufactured at his Newark facility. An advertisement for the device claimed that it could produce "5,000 copies from a single writing."

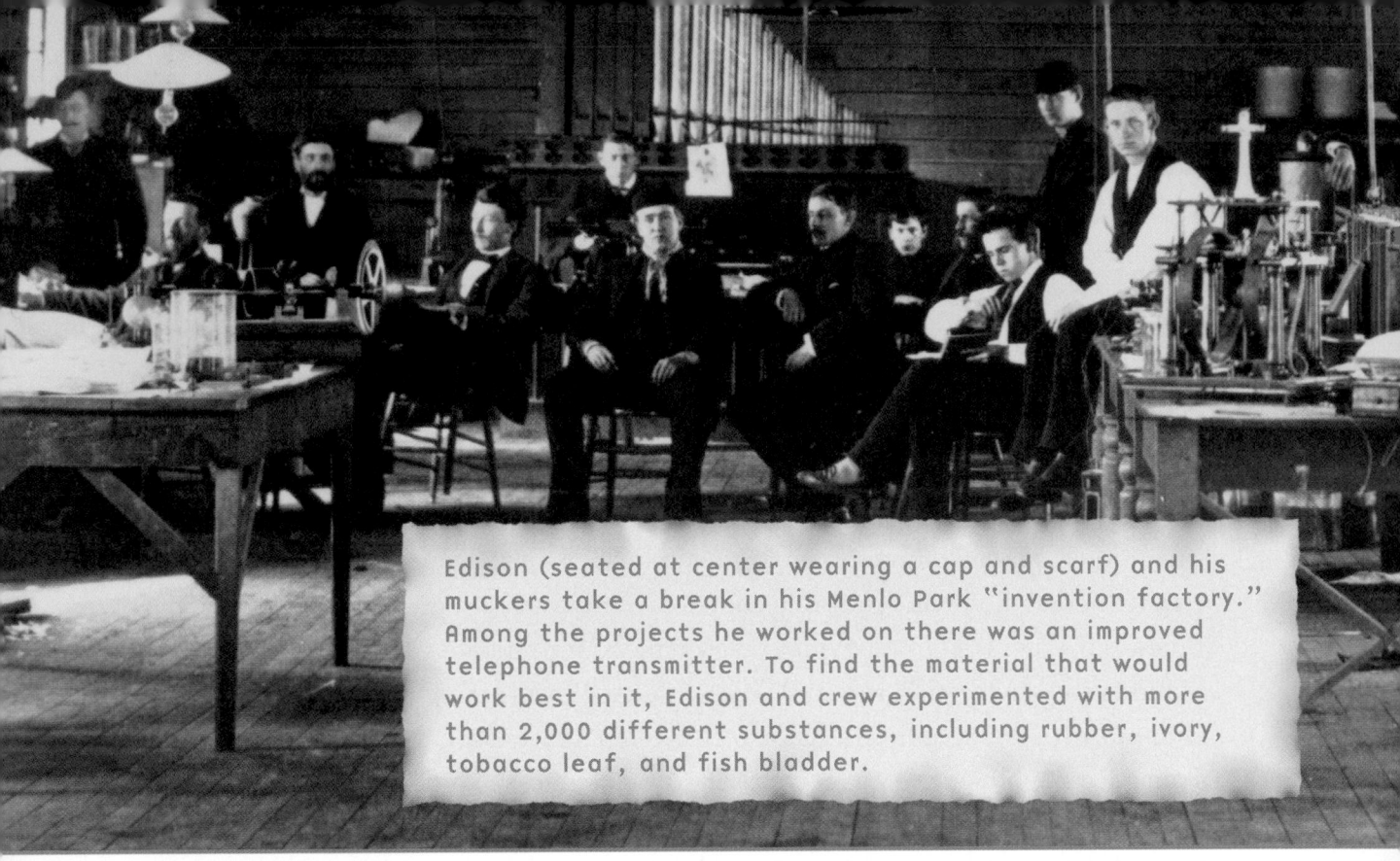

Edison (seated at center wearing a cap and scarf) and his muckers take a break in his Menlo Park "invention factory." Among the projects he worked on there was an improved telephone transmitter. To find the material that would work best in it, Edison and crew experimented with more than 2,000 different substances, including rubber, ivory, tobacco leaf, and fish bladder.

to a small farming village in New Jersey called Menlo Park, located about 20 miles from New York City. There he had a two-story laboratory built to his design. Unlike most other labs of the time, which combined inventing with manufacturing, Edison's new laboratory was devoted exclusively to researching and developing his ideas. It contained well-equipped chemistry and electrical labs and a machine shop for making models of his inventions. Edison often referred to the place as his "invention factory." He bragged that it would turn out "a minor invention every ten days and a big thing every six months or so."

Edison and his "muckers," as he fondly called his crew of fellow experimenters, lived up to the boast. Known as the "Chief Mucker," Edison patented 75 different inventions in the first two years at Menlo Park. Among them was an improved version of Alexander Graham Bell's telephone.

"Genius is 1 percent inspiration and 99 percent perspiration."

The biggest problem with Bell's telephone was that the sound it transmitted, or sent, was weak. A caller had to shout into it in order to be heard on the other end of the line. Edison felt sure he could not only find a way to make the telephone sound louder and clearer, he also could make it send messages over longer distances. Eager to gain the advantage in the budding telephone industry, Western Union hired him to do just that.

Edison knew that improving the transmitter—the device that converts the sound of a speaker's voice into electrical signals—was the key to better quality sound. The challenge was to find the material that would work best in it.

In 1877, less than a year after Bell's invention of the telephone, Edison discovered that tiny pieces of carbon encased in a small container, or button, gave the best results. Called the carbon button transmitter, the invention not only produced excellent sound, but greatly increased the range of the telephone. A version of it is still used in most telephones today.

Paying customers listen through earphones to a recording in a "phonograph parlor" in Salina, Kansas, in the 1890s. Edison manufactured phonographs with a special coin-in-slot device for use in saloons and other places of entertainment.

"*I had the faculty of sleeping in a chair anytime for a few minutes at a time.*"

A taker of catnaps since his days as a young telegrapher, Edison wasn't picky about where he nodded off. Here he snoozes atop a lab table in his West Orange laboratory in 1911.

While he was working on the telephone, another sound-related idea occurred to Edison. If the human voice could travel over wires, he reasoned, then there should be a way to record the sound so that it could be listened to later. In November 1877, Edison gave a sketch of an invention he called the phonograph to John Kruesi and asked him to build it. A few days later, Kruesi had a model ready for testing. A simple machine, it consisted of a hand-cranked cylinder covered in tinfoil, a mouthpiece with a metal disk called a diaphragm, and a needle.

With his muckers gathered around him, Edison turned the handle of the machine while he shouted a nursery rhyme into the mouthpiece. As the sound waves of his voice vibrated the diaphragm, the attached needle scratched grooves in the foil. When he finished reciting, he rewound the cylinder, put the needle into the tracks it had made, and cranked the handle again. To everyone's surprise, the machine worked the very first time! Out of the phonograph came Edison's voice, faint but clear: "Mary had a little lamb, its fleece was white as snow, and everywhere that Mary went, the lamb was sure to go." The excited experimenters stayed up all night recording themselves with the invention, which was the ancestor of modern CD players.

The next morning Edison took his brand-new "baby" to New York City and dazzled the editors of *Scientific American* magazine with a demonstration. Word of the amazing invention spread rapidly, and Edison became a celebrity overnight. The phonograph's ability to reproduce human speech seemed like a miracle. Newspaper headlines proclaimed him the "Inventor of the Age" and the "Wizard of Menlo Park."

Edison, who enjoyed the attention the phonograph attracted, envisioned a variety of commercial uses for the device, including toys and dictation machines. He soon set it aside, however, to concentrate on the greatest challenge of his career—the development of an electric lighting system that could be used in homes and businesses.

Electric lighting was not a new idea. Brightly burning lamps called arc lights (which glowed when a current of electricity jumped between two carbon rods) had already replaced gas street lamps in some large cities by the 1870s. But they were not suitable for home use. Not only

> *"This [the phonograph] is my baby and I expect it to grow up to be a big feller and support me in my old age."*

In 1878, Edison demonstrated his phonograph at the National Academy of Sciences in Washington, D.C. While there, he posed with his invention for this photograph taken by famed Civil War photographer Mathew Brady.

Over the years, Edison produced a variety of phonographs for home use. The records he made to play on them were delivered to homes and could also be bought in stores.

was their glare too intense for indoors, they were also smelly. So people still used candles, oil lamps, or gas lamps to light their homes after dark.

Aware that other inventors were racing toward the same goal as he, Edison vowed to get there first. To gain the financial support he needed, he took a gamble. In September 1878, he announced to reporters that he was very close to developing a practical incandescent lamp, or light bulb. Not only that, he said he expected to have a safe, affordable electric lighting system ready to go in just six weeks. He was exaggerating his progress greatly, but so strong was his reputation at the time that few questioned his claim. Confident of Edison's genius, several rich investors established the Edison Electric Light Company to cover his expenses. Edison's gamble paid off. It was time for the real work to begin.

The groundwork for the incandescent light bulb had been laid many years earlier by an English chemist named Sir Humphry Davy. In 1802, Davy discovered that by passing an electric current through strips of metal, he could make them hot enough to glow brightly, or incandesce, for a few seconds before they burned up.

The Menlo Park lab hummed with round-the-clock activity as Edison and his muckers—including several newly hired electrical experts—tackled the problem of the light bulb. Edison set some of his associates the task of finding a way to get all the air out of the glass bulb, so that the material giving off the light, called the filament, would not burn up too quickly. Other workers tested more than 1,600 materials—including horsehair, coconut fibers, fish line, spider webs, and even the hair from John Kruesi's beard—to find the best filament.

Finally his persistence was rewarded. In the fall of 1879, Edison and his muckers tested a piece of cotton sewing thread. First they carbonized it by baking it until it charred and turned into carbon. Then they inserted the carbonized thread into the glass bulb, forced out the air with a special vacuum pump, and sealed the glass. When connected to an

The front page of *The Daily Graphic* from July 9, 1879, (top) pictures Edison in sorcerer's garb, a reference to his nickname, the "Wizard of Menlo Park." The cartoon below it illustrates the fear electrical wiring inspired in some people in the 1880s.

This portrait of Edison associate Charles Batchelor is the first photograph ever taken by electric light. Edison sketched hundreds of different designs and tested more than 1,600 different materials in his quest to invent a practical, long-burning light bulb.

The inventor mixes chemicals in his West Orange laboratory.

electric current, the bulb glowed steadily for more than 13 hours! Within a few weeks, the lab had produced an improved bulb that burned many hours longer.

In late December 1879, Edison invited the public to Menlo Park to see his marvelous new invention. As visitors got off the train in the evening, they were astounded by the brightly shining electric street lamps lighting their way. Even more impressive was the laboratory, which one newspaper article described as "brilliantly illuminated with twenty-five lamps."

Over the next two years, Edison and his crew worked feverishly to invent the many other devices besides the light bulb that were needed to get a full lighting system up and running. At the top of the list was an efficient generator, or dynamo, to produce the electricity from the generators, which would be housed in central power stations, to streets and buildings. Sockets, switches, safety fuses, and lamp fixtures also had to be designed. Ever practical, Edison didn't forget to devise a meter to measure the amount of electricity that customers used, so they could be charged accordingly. His lighting would be cheap, yes, but not free!

This lab sketch from 1879 expresses the jubilation felt by Edison and his Menlo Park muckers at finally producing a long-burning light bulb.

By 1882, Edison had set up the world's first commercially successful electric power station, on Pearl Street in New York City. He and his family had moved to the city sometime earlier, so that he could personally supervise the installation of his lighting system. On September 4 of that year, he was finally ready to deliver what he had promised four years earlier. Standing in the office of millionaire businessman J. P. Morgan—one of his investors—Edison flicked a switch and current from the Pearl Street station lit the office lamps.

By nightfall, some two dozen buildings in the city's financial district glowed with Edison's electric lights. As crowds gathered in the streets to

Edison's earliest movies were filmed in West Orange. They were viewed through a peephole machine called a kinetoscope (above).

marvel at the latest magic from the Wizard of Menlo Park, his fame soared even higher.

Edison devoted the next few years to improving his electrical system and spreading it around the country and the world. He set up numerous companies to handle the manufacturing and installation of his products and made millions of dollars.

In 1887, Edison built the laboratory of his dreams. Located about a mile from Glenmont, it was the largest, best-equipped research facility in the world. Ten times bigger than Menlo Park, the main lab was three stories high and 250 feet long. Housed in separate buildings were a physics lab, a chemistry lab, and a metallurgical lab. In his new laboratory, Edison continued to improve his lighting system.

Edison's West Orange lab also contributed to the birth of the motion picture industry. Around 1889, Edison and a team of muckers led by William K. L. Dickson started work on "an instrument which does for the Eye what the phonograph does for the Ear."

In a few years, they had invented a movie camera, called a kinetograph, and a peep-hole machine, called a kinetoscope, for watching the movies. To make films for the kinetoscopes, Edison opened the world's first motion picture studio in West Orange in 1893. Only 20 to 30 seconds long, these early movies featured a variety of subjects, from acrobats to boxers to ballet dancers.

Edison also returned to his "baby," the phonograph, in West Orange. While Edison had been working on electric lights, inventors Chichester Bell (a cousin of Alexander Graham Bell) and Charles Tainter had created

TIME LINE OF EDISON'S INVENTIONS

1869—Electric vote recorder	1875—Electric pen 1875—Quadruplex telegraph	1877—Tinfoil phonograph 1877—Carbon-button telephone transmitter	1879—First practical light bulb

As part of the 1929 Jubilee, Edison (seated) reenacts the lighting of his famous bulb 50 years earlier. Looking on are Henry Ford (standing, left) and former Edison employee Francis Jehl.

their own, improved version of the machine, which used wax cylinders rather than tinfoil for recording. Spurred by the competition, Edison developed an even better wax-cylinder phonograph. Although he originally envisioned the device as a business machine for taking dictation, people were eager to purchase it for home entertainment. Edison was happy to satisfy them. Not only did he produce a variety of phonographs for home use over the next 40 years, he also made prerecorded cylinders, or records, of popular tunes to play on them. In the process, he helped to create what we now call the recording industry.

Edison phonograph from 1911

1888—'Perfected' phonograph	1893—System for making and showing motion pictures	1909—Storage battery

Reader Response

Open for Discussion Suppose that you are a talk show host. Thomas Alva Edison is to be your next guest. You want your audience to learn more about him than a list of his inventions. What are some questions you will ask him?

1. The biographer organizes this article by time. She lists a date followed by Edison's accomplishments during that time, then moves on to another date and another set of accomplishments. How would this way of organizing help you if you were studying to remember the information? How well does it encourage you to find out more about this subject?

2. The author's purpose for writing *Inventing the Future* was to inform you about Thomas Alva Edison's inventions. What is another purpose the author had for writing this piece? Why do you think this?

3. Some of Edison's inventions were improvements of other people's inventions. Create a T-Chart. Write *telephone* on the top left and *light bulb* on the top right. Under each head, record the ways in which Thomas Edison improved upon each of these inventions.

4. What might Thomas Edison tell prospective investors to get them to offer money for his work on the phonograph? Use words from the selection and the Words to Know list in your answer.

Test Practice

Look Back and Write Look back at page 508 to review the steps involved in team inventing. Then write the steps in your own words, placing them in order and numbering them. In one sentence, tell how these steps might help future inventors.

Meet the Author

Marfé Ferguson Delano

Read other books by Marfé Ferguson Delano.

Marfé Ferguson Delano is an award-winning author. Her book *Inventing the Future: A Photobiography of Thomas Alva Edison* was named a 2003 Notable Book for Children by the American Library Association. She teamed up with Nancy Aulenbach, an elementary schoolteacher, and Hazel Barton, a microbiologist and award-winning mapper of caves, to write *Exploring Caves: Journeys into the Earth*. This book was named an Outstanding Science Trade Book for Students K–12 by the National Science Teachers Association in 2002.

Ms. Delano has written many books for the National Geographic Society about nature subjects including these three books in the Animal Safari series: *Kangaroos, Tree Frogs,* and *Sea Otters.* She is a graduate of Duke University and now lives in Virginia with her husband and three children.

Exploring Caves: Journeys into the Earth
by Nancy Holler Aulenbach, Hazel A. Barton, and Marfé Ferguson Delano

Wildflowers (National Geographic: My First Pocket Guide)

Social Studies in Reading

Biography

Genre

- Biography is nonfiction centered on someone's life but written by another person.

- Biographies are usually organized according to time—the sequence in which events happened in the person's life.

Text Features

- The author uses section headings to separate topics within Garrett Morgan's life to help the reader more easily organize the concepts.

- The author writes about Garrett Morgan doing things. This shows that Garrett Morgan controlled his life and behavior rather than passively letting the things happen. As you read, look for words that show Garrett Morgan taking active control.

Link to Social Studies

Biographies describe events in the lives of important people. Write a short biography of someone important in your life.

Garrett Augustus Morgan

Garrett Augustus Morgan was an African American businessman and inventor whose curiosity and innovation led to the development of many useful and helpful products. A practical man of humble beginnings, Morgan devoted his life to creating things that made the lives of other people safer and more convenient.

Among his inventions was an early traffic signal that greatly improved safety on America's streets and roadways. Indeed, Morgan's technology was the basis for modern traffic signal systems and was an early example of what we know today as Intelligent Transportation Systems.

The Inventor's Early Life

The son of former slaves, Garrett A. Morgan was born in Paris, Kentucky, on March 4, 1877. His early childhood was spent attending school and working on the family farm with his brothers and sisters. While still a teenager, he left Kentucky and moved north to Cincinnati, Ohio in search of opportunity.

Although Morgan's formal education never took him beyond elementary school, he hired a tutor while living in Cincinnati and continued his studies in English grammar.

In 1895, Morgan moved to Cleveland, Ohio, where he went to work as a sewing machine repairman for a clothing manufacturer. News of his proficiency for fixing things and experimenting traveled fast and led to numerous job offers from various manufacturing firms in the Cleveland area.

In 1907, Morgan opened his own sewing equipment and repair shop. It was the first of several businesses he would establish. In 1909, he expanded the enterprise to include a tailoring shop that employed 32 employees. The new company turned out coats, suits, and dresses, all sewn with equipment that Morgan himself had made.

In 1920 Morgan moved into the newspaper business when he established the *Cleveland Call*. As the years went on, he became a prosperous and widely respected business-man, and he was able to purchase a home and an automobile. Indeed it was Morgan's experience while driving along the streets of Cleveland that led to the invention of the nation's first patented traffic signal.

A sewing machine from the early 1900s

 **Monitor & Fix Up** How could you keep track of all these dates?

The Garrett Morgan Traffic Signal

The first American-made automobiles were introduced to U.S. consumers shortly before the turn of the century. The Ford Motor Company was founded in 1903 and with it American consumers began to discover the adventures of the open road.

In the early years of the 20th century, it was not uncommon for bicycles, animal-powered wagons, and new gasoline-powered motor vehicles to share the same streets and roadways with pedestrians. Accidents were frequent. After

Before the invention of the traffic signal, road intersections were often chaotic and dangerous.

witnessing a collision between an automobile and a horse-drawn carriage, Morgan was convinced that something should be done to improve traffic safety.

While other inventors are reported to have experimented with and even marketed traffic signals, Garrett A. Morgan was the first to apply for and acquire a U.S. patent for such a device. The patent was granted on November 20, 1923. Morgan later had the technology patented in Great Britain and Canada as well.

The Morgan traffic signal was a T-shaped pole unit that featured three positions: Stop, Go, and an all-directional stop position. This "third position" halted traffic in all directions to allow pedestrians to cross streets more safely.

Morgan's traffic management device was used throughout North America until it was replaced by

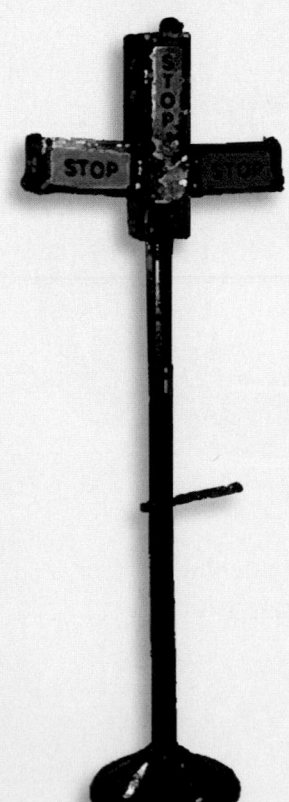

the red, yellow and green-light traffic signals currently used around the world. The inventor sold the rights to his traffic signals to the General Electric Corporation for $40,000. Shortly before his death, in 1963, Morgan was awarded a citation for his traffic signal by the United States Government.

Other Morgan Inventions

Garrett Morgan was constantly experimenting to develop new concepts. Though the traffic signal came at the height of his career and became one of his most renowned inventions, it was just one of several innovations he developed, manufactured, and sold over the years.

Morgan invented a zig-zag stitching attachment for manually operated sewing machines. He also founded a company that made personal grooming products, such as hair dying ointments and the curved-tooth pressing comb.

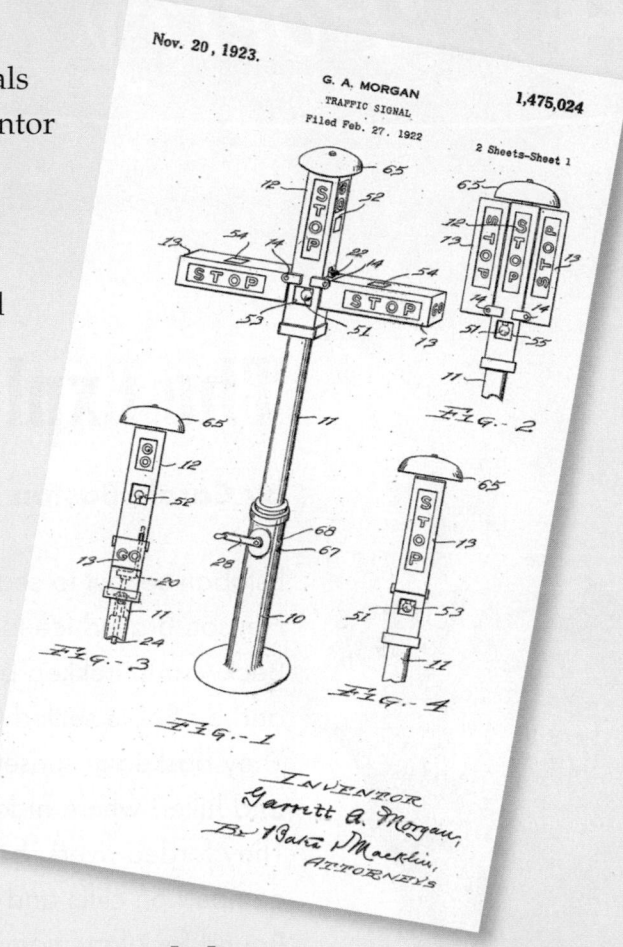

Morgan's sketch of his invention as submitted to the U.S. Patent Office

Reading Across Texts

How were the two inventors, Thomas Edison and Garrett Morgan, alike and different?

Writing Across Texts Write at least two similarities and two differences between Edison and Morgan.

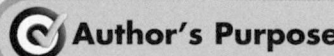 **Author's Purpose** Why did the author write this article?

The Explorers

by Carole Boston Weatherford

Estaban set out to search for gold.
Henson braved ice to find the Pole.
Beckwourth trekked beyond the bounds,
and du Sable settled Chicago town.
They basked in sunsets few had seen
and hiked where hidden springs ran clean.
They forded rivers, bathed in creeks,
camped on cliffs and climbed high peaks.
Bound for glory, compass in hand,
they boldly conquered newfound lands.
Some sailed seas and some rode west,
but one went farther than the rest.
Mae Jemison gazed at this earthly sphere,
rocketed through the space frontier.

Bronze Cowboys

by Carole Boston Weatherford

When bison roamed the wild, wild West
dark riders rode the Pony Express
over the mountains, across the plains,
past coyotes, bobcats and wagon trains.
Bronze cowboys rode in cattle drives
where deserts met the turquoise skies.
They busted broncos and bulldogged steer,
made peace with the Indians and showed no fear.
A mail carrier named Stagecoach Mary
fought off wolves on the lonesome prairie.
Nat Love was the surest shot in the land.
Bill Pickett was known as a mean cowhand.
Around the campfire, they strummed guitars,
imagined they could lasso stars.

Seeds

by Ann Turner

When the dust gets in my mouth
I remember the taste of pork
roasted over hickory wood
the night before we left
and how Gran filled a sack
with peach pits,
like dried brown hearts to carry west.
Someday I'll dig some black sweet soil,
set each seed to catch the light,
and one day I'll watch those peaches ripen.
Each bite
will be a taste of our old farm.

Science Fair Project

by Carol Diggory Shields

PURPOSE:
The purpose of my project this year
Is to make my brother disappear.

HYPOTHESIS:
The world would be a better place
If my brother vanished without a trace.

MATERIALS:
3 erasers
White-out
Disappearing ink
1 younger brother
1 kitchen sink

PROCEDURE:
Chop up the erasers.
Add the white-out and the ink.
Rub it on the brother
While he's standing in the sink.

RESULTS:
The kid was disappearing!
I had almost proved my theorem!
When all at once my mom came home
And made me re-appear him.

CONCLUSION:
Experiment a failure.
My brother is still here.
But I'm alrcady planning
For the science fair *next* year.

Wrap-Up

Interview Me

With a partner, choose one of the real people you read about in this unit. Plan questions you would ask if you could interview this person in real life. Think about how this person would answer the questions. When you are prepared, take turns as an interviewer and the person being interviewed.

- How do you like living in Africa?
- Have you worked with animals other than chimpanzees?

How have those who've gone first influenced those who've gone after?

Advertise It

connect to
SOCIAL STUDIES

Suppose you were one of the people you read about in this unit who had invented a useful gadget, started a community, or led an exploration into a new area. Write an ad that would get other people to buy your invention, live in the community, or take part in your exploration.

Great Inspiration

connect to
WRITING

Inspired by those who have gone before them, people often find and create new things.

Choose a person from the unit who inspires you. Do you want to follow in his or her footsteps or do something else? Write about the ways in which this person inspires you.

Read It
ONLINE
sfsuccessnet.com

Resources

What are resources and why are they important to us?

Plot

- A plot includes (1) a *problem* or *goal,* (2) *rising action*, as a character tries to solve the problem or meet the goal, (3) a *climax,* when the character meets the problem or goal head on, and (4) a *resolution,* or outcome.

- Sometimes a writer hints at an event that will happen later in the story. Such a hint is called foreshadowing.

- Sometimes a writer goes back in time to tell about an earlier event. The earlier event is called a flashback.

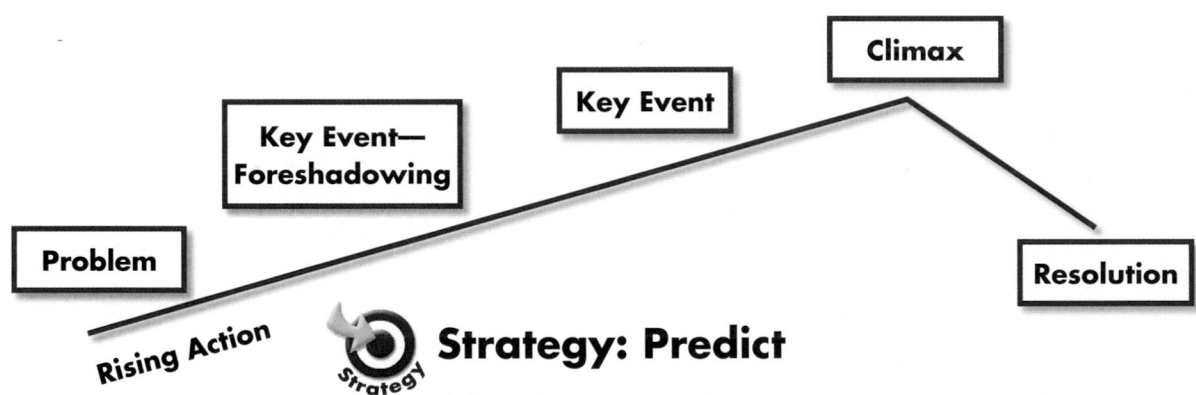

Strategy: Predict

Active readers predict. They think what might happen next in a story. Use your understanding of plot as well as what you know about the way people act to predict. For example, if one event seems to be a foreshadowing, you can use the foreshadowing to predict what will happen.

1. Read "Jarrett's Journal." Make a graphic organizer like the one above to describe the plot of the story. Decide which key event is a foreshadowing.

2. Use your graphic organizer to write a short summary of the plot of "Jarrett's Journal."

Jarrett's Journal

April 16— It's a very relaxing evening—the very opposite of today! Today I was going to host a dinner at 5 o'clock in my new apartment for my grandparents, parents, and 12-year-old brother Billy. *Was going to* is the operative phrase.

This morning I rolled over in bed and glanced at the clock. It was noon! I had neglected to set my alarm. Hastily I darted out of bed and started sweeping and scrubbing and piling stuff that was lying around into closets and drawers.

Then I dashed out to the supermarket. When I got back, I rinsed the chicken I'd just purchased, plopped it into a pan, poured a gourmet sauce over it, and stuck it in the oven.

Next I readied the potatoes and asparagus and set the table. Finally I readied myself—showering and donning a clean pair of jeans. Five o'clock—the security buzzer rang.

With my family peering over my shoulder, I opened the oven and *voilà!* a pink, flabby, raw chicken. I had neglected to turn the oven on.

"Nice going," my brother said with a smirk. "*Now* what are we going to eat?" he whined.

It's a good thing there's an outstanding pizza parlor just down the block.

Skill What was the narrator's goal in this story?

Strategy Based on the first paragraph, do you predict the narrator met his goal? Why or why not?

Strategy What do you predict will happen next?

Skill Why is this the climax? How was this event foreshadowed?

Words to Know

presence

decline

unaccompanied

former

accustomed

Remember

Try the strategy. Then, if you need more help, use your glossary or a dictionary.

Vocabulary Strategy
for Antonyms

Context Clues Antonyms are words that mean the opposite of one another. A writer may include an antonym near a difficult word to give you a clue to the word's meaning.

1. Reread the words and sentences around the unknown word. Are two things being contrasted? Look for words and phrases that point to opposites, such as *unlike, not, however, but,* and *on the other hand.*

2. If there is an antonym, think about a word that means the opposite and substitute it for the unknown word.

3. Does this meaning make sense in the sentence?

4. If not, look up the unknown word in the dictionary.

As you read "An Invitation to a Wedding," look for antonyms that may give you clues to the vocabulary words' meanings.

An Invitation to a Wedding

The invitation began "Mr. and Mrs. Harold Smith request the honor of your presence . . ." I thought to myself, "Oh, no! Not another wedding!" And I began thinking of ways to excuse my absence from this celebration.

I didn't always feel this way. I enjoyed the joyous occasion and the party that followed as much as the next person. But as I grew older, my enthusiasm for weddings went into a decline. The more friends and cousins married, the more people asked me, "Isn't it time you were getting married?" If I attended a wedding unaccompanied, people shot me sympathetic glances. ("Poor thing," they thought. "All alone again.") If I escorted a friend to the wedding, we were at once claimed by the hordes of matchmakers who seem to live for weddings. ("Have you set a date yet?")

One day I'll meet the right person. Then I'll be ready to take my turn in front of the well-wishers. My former distaste for weddings will dissolve as I relish my own future wedding. By then, my family will have become so accustomed to my single state that it will be hard for them to get used to the idea that I'm getting married.

Write

Write a description of a wedding you have attended or watched on TV. Use as many words from the Words to Know list as you can.

The View from Saturday

by E. L. Konigsburg
illustrated by Janan Cain

Can a little creativity save a
wedding from disaster?

541

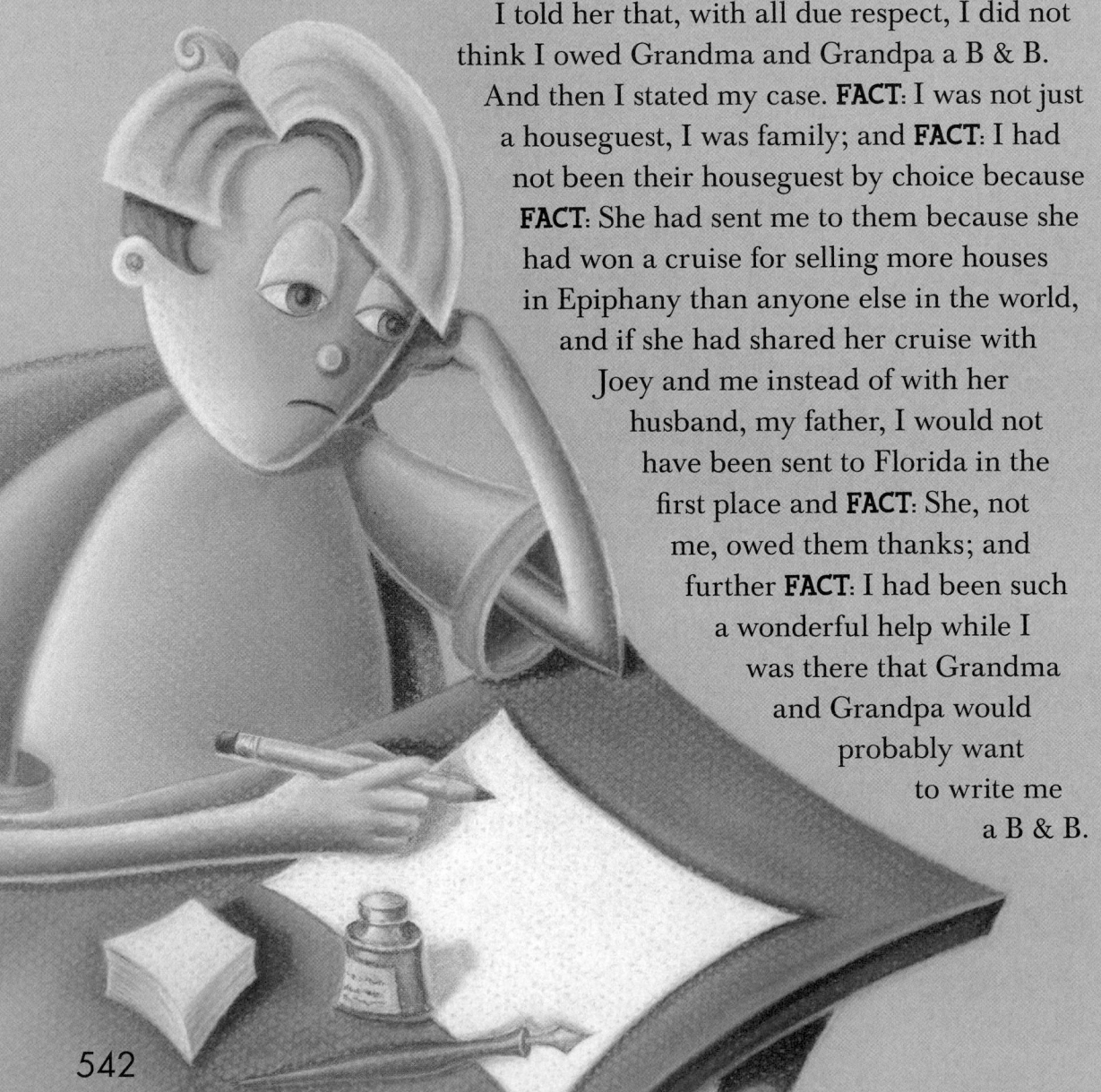

My mother insisted that I write a B & B letter to my grandparents. I told her that I could not write a B & B letter, and she asked me why, and I told her that I did not know what a B & B letter was. She explained—not too patiently—that a B & B letter is a *bread and butter letter* you write to people to thank them for having you as their houseguest. I told her that I was taught never to use the word you are defining in its definition and that she ought to think of a substitute word for *letter* if she is defining it. Mother then made a remark about how Western Civilization was in a decline because people of my generation knew how to nitpick but not how to write a B & B letter.

I told her that, with all due respect, I did not think I owed Grandma and Grandpa a B & B. And then I stated my case. **FACT**: I was not just a houseguest, I was family; and **FACT**: I had not been their houseguest by choice because **FACT**: She had sent me to them because she had won a cruise for selling more houses in Epiphany than anyone else in the world, and if she had shared her cruise with Joey and me instead of with her husband, my father, I would not have been sent to Florida in the first place and **FACT**: She, not me, owed them thanks; and further **FACT**: I had been such a wonderful help while I was there that Grandma and Grandpa would probably want to write me a B & B.

My brother Joey had been sent to my other set of grandparents, who live in a normal suburb in Connecticut. "Is Joey writing a B & B to Grandma and Grandpa Eberle?"

"Even as we speak," Mother replied.

"Well, maybe he has something to be thankful for," I said.

Mother drew in her breath as if she were about to say something else about what children of my generation were doing to Western Civilization, but instead, she said, "Write," and closed my bedroom door behind her. I opened the door and called out to her, "Can I use my computer?"

She said, "I know you can use the computer, Noah, but you *may* not." I was about to make a remark about who was nitpicking now, but Mother gave me such a negative look that I knew any thoughts I had had better be about bread and butter and not nitpicking.

I gazed at my closed bedroom door and then out the window. Door. Window. Door. Window. There was no escape.

I took a box of notepaper out of my desk drawer. The notes were bigger than postage stamps, but not by much. I took out a ballpoint pen and started pressing it against a piece of scrap paper, making dents in the paper but not making a mark. Ballpoint pens sometimes take a while to get started. When I was down in Florida, Tillie Nachman had said, "The ballpoint pen has been the biggest single factor in the decline of Western Civilization. It makes the written word cheap, fast, and totally without character." My mother and Tillie should get together. Between them, they have come up with the two major reasons why Western Civilization is about to collapse.

Not because I was trying to save Western Civilization but because I wanted to actually get my B & B letter written, I put the ballpoint pen back into the drawer and took out my calligraphy pen, the one that uses wet ink. I didn't fill it. I would fill it when I was ready to write. I also took out a sharpened pencil and a pad of Post-it notes to jot down any ideas that might come to mind.

I wrote *red wagon.* The red wagon had definitely been a gift—even though, under the circumstances, I didn't bring it back to Epiphany with me. I thought a while longer and wrote *tuxedo T-shirt.* It, too, had been a gift, but I didn't have that either. I wrote *calligraphy pen and bottle of ink.* A wet ink pen and a bottle of ink had been given to me, but the ones I took out of my desk drawer were ones I had bought myself. The calligraphy pen made me remember about the Post-it notes I had bought to correct the problem that had developed with the ink. Even though I had bought the Post-it notes myself, I added *Post-it notes* to my list. I peeled off the Post-it note containing my list and stuck it on the wall in front on my desk, and then, as my mother had commanded, I thought again.

red wagon
tuxedo T-shirt
calligraphy pen
and bottle of ink
Post-it notes

Century Village where my Gershom grandparents live is not like any place I had ever been to. It is in Florida, but it is not exactly Disney World or Sea World or other regular destinations. It is like a theme park for old people. Almost everyone who lives there is retired from useful life. Grandma Sadie and Grandpa Nate fit in nicely.

It all started when Margaret Draper and Izzy Diamondstein decided to get married, and the citizens of Century Village called a meeting in the clubhouse to organize the wedding.

In their former lives, Grandma Sadie and Grandpa Nate had owned a small bakery right here in Epiphany, New York, so Grandma volunteered to do the wedding cake, and Grandpa Nate, whose chief hobby had always been violin playing, promised to arrange for the music.

Mr. Cantor, a retired postman from Pennsylvania, who was devoted to growing orchids, said that he would have enough blossoms for the corsages. And Mrs. Kerchmer said that she would lend her African violets for the centerpieces.

Tillie Nachman volunteered to do the invitations, and Rabbi Friedman, who was a rabbi in his former life, said he would perform the ceremony even though Margaret Draper was not Jewish and Izzy Diamondstein was. This was a late second marriage, and there wouldn't be any concern about what religion they should choose for their children since all their children were already grown up and chosen. Grandpa Nate later explained to me that unlike the average citizen of Century Village, rabbis don't have former lives. They are what they were; once a rabbi, always a rabbi.

Many citizens of Century Village were widows who had once been great family cooks, so they formed a committee to plan the wedding dinner. Everyone agreed to share the cost, and they made up a menu and a master shopping list.

After that first meeting, Grandpa Nate and I took Tillie Nachman, a former New York City person who had never learned to drive, to the stationery store so that she could buy the invitations. While she shopped for the invitations, Grandpa and I went to Wal-Mart to pick up Grandma's prescription, and that is when we saw the red wagon special. Grandpa bought it for me, and it's a good thing he did. It came in handy until Allen came along.

I checked my list. *Post-it notes.* I had bought them when we ran out of invitations. Of course, we didn't run out of invitations until Tillie's cat got its paws into the ink.

Tillie was filling in the *who-what-when-and-where* on the invitations when I noticed that she had the prettiest handwriting

I had ever seen. "Calligraphy," she said. "It means beautiful writing," and she asked me if I would like to learn how to write like her. I said yes. She said she would give me lessons if I would help her address the envelopes. So Grandpa drove us to an art supply store where she bought me a calligraphy pen and a bottle of ink. It was while Tillie was trying out various pen points (called *nibs*) that she made the remark about the ballpoint pen being the biggest single factor in the decline of Western Civilization.

After choosing a nib Tillie said, "I hope in the future, Noah, that you will use a ballpoint pen only when you have to press hard to make multiple carbons."

I couldn't promise that. There were times in school when a person had to do things fast, cheap, and without character.

Tillie said, "There are pens that come with ink in a cartridge, Noah, but I will have nothing to do with them." So when we were back at her condo, Tillie taught me how to fill a pen, or, as she said, "How to *properly* fill a pen."

One: Turn the filling plunger counterclockwise as far as it will go. Two: Dip the nib completely into the ink. Three: Turn the filling plunger clockwise until it stops. Four: Hold the nib above the ink bottle and turn the plunger counterclockwise again until three drops of ink fall back into the bottle. Five: Turn the plunger clockwise to stop the drops. Six: Wipe the excess ink completely from pen and nib.

When I told Tillie that six steps seemed a lot to have to do before you begin, she said, "You must think of those six steps not as preparation for the beginning but as the beginning itself."

I practiced my calligraphy. I practiced all twenty-six letters of the alphabet, including *X,* which was not part of any of the who-what-when-and-wheres or any of the addresses but is a very good letter to practice because **FACT**: It is not easy.

When Tillie decided that I was good enough to help with the invitations, I sat on the floor of her living room and used her coffee table as my desk. She sat at the kitchen table. **FACT**: Many of the domiciles in Century Village do not have family rooms with desks.

Your Presence but no presents.

There was a lot of writing to do because at the bottom of each and every one of those invitations, we wrote: Your presence but no presents. Tillie said that practically all the invitations that went out from Century Village said that. "Besides," she said, "I think that making the wedding is enough of a present."

I was doing a wonderful job until Thomas Stearns, called T.S., Tillie's cat, pounced into my lap, and I jumped up and spilled the ink, and the cat walked through the spilled ink and onto a couple of the invitations I was addressing. A few—five altogether—now had cat's paws.

Tillie was pretty upset because she had not bought extras because she said, "I don't make mistakes." In her former life Tillie had been a bookkeeper. I heard her say, "I can add up a column of figures with the best of them." I didn't know if she meant the best of the computers or the best of the bookkeepers, and I didn't ask because I was afraid I already knew.

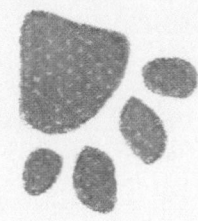

I told Tillie not to worry. I told her that I would think of something. And I did. That's when I bought the Post-it notes. I put a Post-it into each of the invitations that had a cat's paw mark. On the Post-it I wrote (in faultless calligraphy): Bring this specially marked invitation to the wedding and receive a surprise gift. When Tillie asked me

margarine

what the surprise would be, I told her not to worry, that I would think of something. And I did. But **FACT**: It wasn't easy.

On the day the groceries were to be purchased, the citizens of Century Village formed their version of the Home Shopping Network. They met in the clubhouse again. Everyone sat in rows, holding coupons they'd clipped since printing began. They asked me to be master of ceremonies.

I sat at a table in front of the clubhouse room and called out items from the master grocery list. It was a lot like a game of Go Fish. I said, "I need one Crisco, four margarines, *pareve*, and let's have all your paper towels." Everyone searched through their fistfuls of coupons and gave me the ones that were needed. Tillie circled the items we had coupons for.

Then we checked the newspaper for supermarket specials and made out lists for each of the stores, depending on which one had the best buy in a particular item. I wrote the Gershom list in calligraphy. It didn't slow things down too much, and the citizens of Century Village are accustomed to waiting.

Later that day, everyone returned to the clubhouse with the groceries and the store receipts. Tillie added, divided, and straightened out who owed and who was owed, and no one bothered to check because everyone knew that Tillie Nachman did not make mistakes. Then we had to check the grocery list

Crisco

against the menu and who was cooking what. I helped distribute the groceries to the proper households, using the new red wagon.

FACT: I did a wonderful job.

On the day of the wedding I was in great demand to take things over to the clubhouse in my wagon. The African violets alone took three trips, and the briskets took two. Next, Mr. Cantor and I delivered the orchid corsages to the bride and her maid of honor. In the real world, I had never met anyone who spent as much time with flowers as Mr. Cantor. Mrs. Draper's maid of honor was to be her daughter, Mrs. Potter. Mrs. Draper used to live in my hometown, which is Epiphany, New York, and her daughter, Mrs. Potter, still does. Mrs. Potter bought a new dress and flew down for the wedding, but we didn't fly down together. I had come weeks before—my first trip as an unaccompanied minor.

Mr. Cantor and I took flowers over to the groom and his best man to put in their buttonholes. Allen, who was Izzy Diamondstein's son, was to be best man. They both live in Florida and have the same last name.

Allen Diamondstein still lived in the real world because even though he was Izzy's child and even though he was full-grown, he was too young to live in Century Village. **FACT**: Allen Diamondstein was the most nervous human being I have ever seen in my entire life. **FACT**: His wife had left him. She had moved to Epiphany and taken a job with my father, who is the best dentist in town (**FACT**).

Allen Diamondstein kept saying, "Isn't it ironic? My father is getting married just as I am getting divorced." This was not the greatest conversation starter in the world. No one knew what to say after he said it. Some cleared their throats and said nothing. Others cleared their throats and changed the subject.

I must have heard him say it a dozen times, and I never knew what to say either. At first I wondered if that was because I didn't know the meaning of *ironic*. So I looked it up.

The meaning that best fits (and does not use the same word in its definition) is "the contrast between what you expect to happen and what really happens." But after I looked it up, I couldn't figure out what was ironic about Allen Diamondstein's getting divorced and

549

Izzy Diamondstein's getting married. The way Allen Diamondstein acted, I can tell you that divorce would be the only possible thing you could expect from marriage to him. And the way Izzy acted around Margaret, marriage would not only be expected, it would be necessary. *Sha! a shanda far die kinder.* They were embarrassing to watch, but not so embarrassing that I didn't.

Wedding cakes are not baked as much as they are built. In the real world, people don't build wedding cakes. They order in. If you are going to build it yourself, it is not done in a day. It takes three. On the first day, Grandma Sadie baked the layers. On the second, she constructed the cake, using cardboard bases and straws for supports, and made the basic icing to cover the layers. On the third day, she made the designer icing for the rosebuds and put the little bride and groom on top. **FACT**: The cake was beautiful.

Fortunately, Grandpa Nate took its picture right after she finished it, so Grandma Sadie can remember how it looked for a little while. Allen Diamondstein would tell you that the red wagon was the problem, but I would say that it's ironic that he should say so. It definitely wasn't. He was. How else were we supposed to deliver the cake to the clubhouse? It was too tall to fit in the trunk of the car, and since on an average day the outside temperature in Century

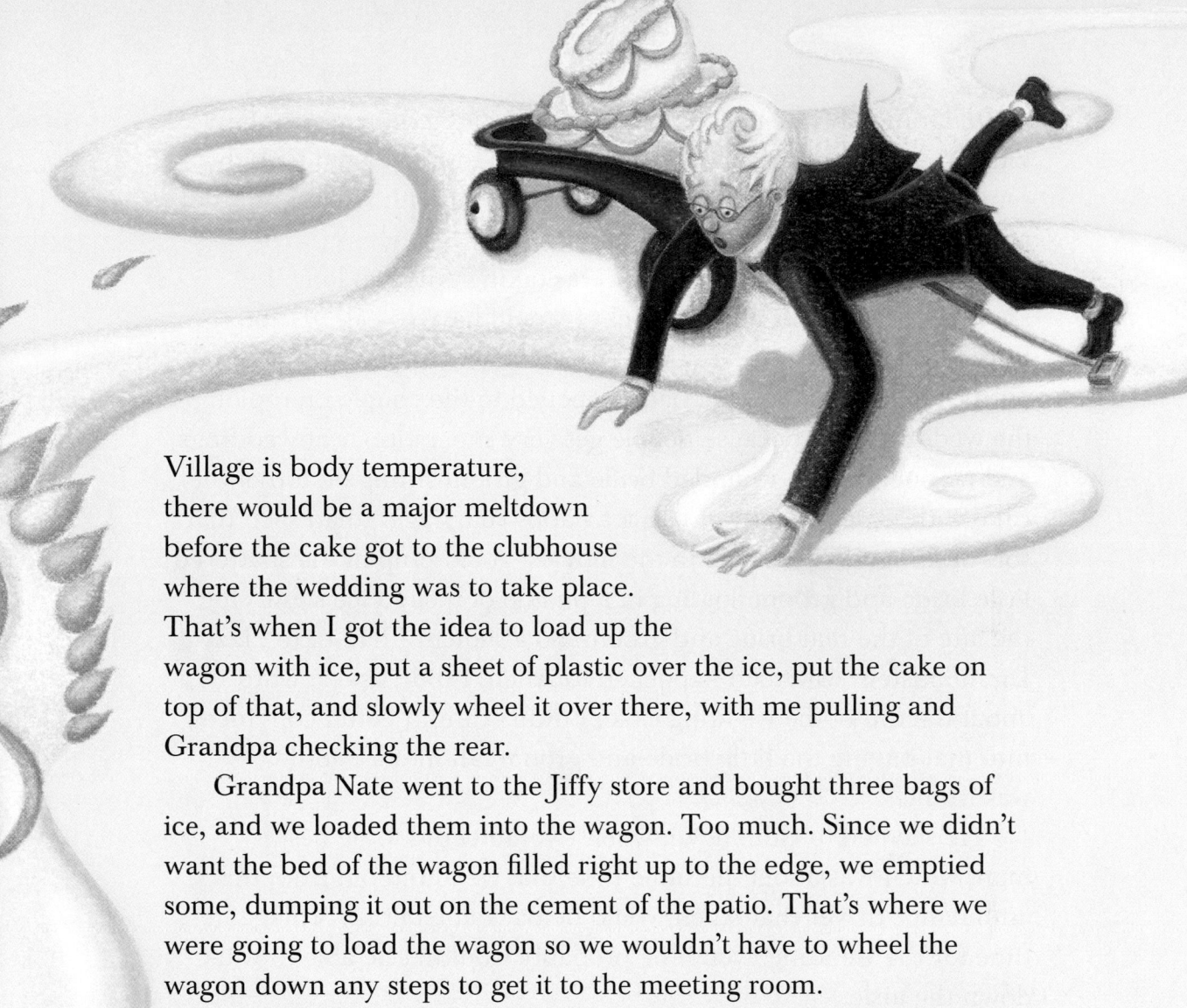

Village is body temperature,
there would be a major meltdown
before the cake got to the clubhouse
where the wedding was to take place.
That's when I got the idea to load up the
wagon with ice, put a sheet of plastic over the ice, put the cake on
top of that, and slowly wheel it over there, with me pulling and
Grandpa checking the rear.

Grandpa Nate went to the Jiffy store and bought three bags of
ice, and we loaded them into the wagon. Too much. Since we didn't
want the bed of the wagon filled right up to the edge, we emptied
some, dumping it out on the cement of the patio. That's where we
were going to load the wagon so we wouldn't have to wheel the
wagon down any steps to get it to the meeting room.

Just after we loaded the cake onto the wagon, Allen Diamondstein
came over to Grandma's. He said his father wanted him to pick up a
prayer book, but I think his father sent him because he was making
the groom nervous.

No one answered when he rang the front doorbell because we
were all in the back loading the cake into the red wagon, so he
walked around back to the patio. Unfortunately, he didn't see the
wagon handle, so he tripped on it, slid on the wet concrete, fell in the
puddle of melted ice, and, unfortunately, toppled the wedding cake.

The little top layer was totally smashed; it fell in the same puddle
as Allen, and the little bride and groom were seriously maimed.

So was Allen's ankle. Which fact I detected when he grabbed
his foot and started to moan while still sitting in the puddle on the

patio. Grandpa Nate called 911. Grandma Sadie returned to the kitchen to whip up a repair batch of icing. Grandpa Nate took the remains of the cake to the clubhouse, and I sat with Allen until the ambulance came. He was not good company.

The groom called to see what was taking Allen so long. I answered the phone, and I thought I would have to call 911 for him, too. "Don't panic," I said. "I'll be your best man."

I did not tell Izzy what had happened to the couple on top of the wedding cake because people get very superstitious at weddings, and no one wants a wounded bride and groom sitting on top of the cake with which they are to start a happy marriage. I had seen that sort of thing often enough in the movies: A close-up of the shattered little bride and groom floating in a puddle of melted ice signifying the fate of the real bride and groom. So although I had to tell Izzy Diamondstein what had happened to Allen, I didn't say a word about the top of the wedding cake. I didn't think I could convince him that having the little bride and groom fall into a puddle was ironic.

He seemed to calm down when I volunteered to be best man, which was about the same time that we found out from the ambulance driver that Allen would be back at Century Village in time for the wedding even if he probably wouldn't be able to walk down the aisle.

As soon as the ambulance took Allen away, I ran over to Mr. Cantor's place and asked him to please, please find another orchid for the top of the cake although it would be better if he could find two since the second layer was now the top layer and was bigger. Mr. Cantor found two beautiful sprays of orchids, which Grandma Sadie artistically arranged around the new top layer.

Since I had promised to be best man, not having a tux was a problem. I couldn't fit in Allen's, not that I would have wanted to if I could. That's when Grandpa Nate called Bella Dubinsky.

In her former life, Bella had been an artist. She painted the pictures that went into the pattern books for people who sew their own clothes. In the real world I had never met anyone who sewed

her own clothes, but in Century Village, I had met three. Bella had a supply of fabric paints, and within two hours, we had painted a T-shirt that looked like a tuxedo and a red bow tie. I say *we* because I helped color in the lines she drew. It's not easy filling in the lines on T-shirt material; it scrunches up under the weight of the brush, leaving skip marks. You have to go over it again and again. Fortunately, the paints dry fast, and by four o'clock, it was ready to wear.

Repaired, the wedding cake looked beautiful. If Allen had not told, no one would have guessed that those orchids didn't belong on top. But Allen told. He told everyone. He also apologized for my being best man. I didn't think that I was someone he had to apologize for. I had helped a lot, and I looked totally presentable in my tuxedo T-shirt, which was a real work of art.

FACT: Being best man is not hard. You walk down the aisle with the maid of honor. Who, in this case, was a matron of honor because she is married. I admit that having the son of the groom, Allen, as the best man would have been a better match, size-wise, for the daughter of the bride even though one is married and the other divorced, but the essential fact is that I did a very good job.

I stood beside the groom. Mrs. Potter stood beside the bride, and the four of us stood in front of the rabbi, and all five of us stood under a bridal canopy, which I know is called a *chupah* and which I think is spelled the way I spelled it. I didn't yawn, sneeze, or scratch any visible thing. I held the wedding ring until the rabbi nodded, and I handed it over.

Whatisit?

I did an excellent job of being best man even though when I was under the chupah, I was under a lot of pressure trying to think of surprises for the cat's-paw invitations. The idea came to me at the very moment Izzy smashed the glass and everyone yelled *mazel tov*. Even before Izzy stopped kissing the bride, I knew what I could do. (**FACT**: It was a very long and thorough kiss.)

It wouldn't be easy. It would mean giving up things I loved, but I had to do it.

When everyone except Allen was dancing the *hora*, I slipped out of the clubhouse and ran back to Grandma Sadie's. I took off my tuxedo T-shirt, folded it nicely, and put it in my red wagon. I found the package of Post-it notes, my calligraphy pen, and bottle of ink and after making sure that the ink was tightly closed, I put those in the wagon, too. When I returned to the wedding party, the dance was over, and everyone was sitting around looking exhausted. My moment had arrived.

I tapped a glass with a spoon as I had seen grown-ups do, and I said, "Ladies and gentlemen, will those lucky few who have the specially marked invitations, please come forward. It is time to choose your surprise gift." I saw them pick up their cat's-paw invitations and walk over to the band where I was standing beside my red wagon. "First," I said, "we have one hand-painted T-shirt, which is an original work of art done by Mrs. Bella Dubinsky. In addition, we have a calligraphy pen, almost new, and a bottle of ink, almost full. These are the perfect instruments for beautiful handwriting. We have one packet of Post-it notes, complete except for five." I swallowed hard and added, "And we have one red wagon."

Tillie Nachman, who could count precisely, said, "But that's only four gifts, and there were five cat's-paw invitations."

"Oh yes," I said, "the fifth gift is the best gift of all."

Everyone asked at once, *Whatisit? Whatisit? Whatisit?*

I sucked in my breath until my lungs felt like twin dirigibles inside my ribs. "The best gift of all is . . . the very best . . . the very best gift of all is . . . to give up your gift."

A thick silence fell over the room. Then Tillie Nachman started clapping. Soon the others joined in, and I noticed Grandma Sadie and Grandpa Nate looking proud.

At first everyone who held a cat's-paw invitation wanted to be the one to give up his gift, but I did not want that. If they didn't take my presents, I would feel as if they didn't matter. Mr. Cantor stepped forward and took the Post-it notes. He said he could use them for labeling his plants. He said that he was donating an orchid plant as the fifth gift. Then Tillie promised calligraphy lessons to the person who took the pen and ink, and Bella promised fabric painting lessons to the person who took the tuxedo T-shirt. In that way each of my gifts kept on giving.

Four cat's-paw gifts were now taken.

Only the red wagon remained. Guess who had the fifth cat's-paw invitation?

Allen, the son of.

Allen said he didn't want the little red wagon. He said that he had no use for a wagon in the real world where he was an accountant.

When Izzy, the groom, rose from the table to make a toast, he lifted his glass of wine and said, "Margy and I want to thank all our friends in Century Village. We don't know if we can ever thank you enough for giving our life together this wonderful start. As you know, Margy and I have pooled our resources and bought a little condo on the ocean. Not exactly *on* the ocean. It is, after all, a high-rise. We will miss the community life here, but we don't want to miss our friends. We'll visit. We want you to visit us. Our welcome mat is out. Always. We leave many memories behind. And we are also leaving this little red wagon. Every time you use it, please think of this happy occasion."

Izzy started to sit down, but halfway he got up again and added, "Consider it a gift to everyone from the best man." He never said which best man he meant, but I'm pretty sure he meant me.

Now back in the real world, I sat at my desk and crossed every single item off the list. I didn't have the wagon, the Post-it notes, the T-shirt that Bella Dubinsky had designed, or the pen and ink that Tillie Nachman had bought me. I did have a new pad of Post-it notes and a new calligraphy pen—both of which I had bought with my own money when I got back to Epiphany.

I never had to write a B & B letter when we stayed at Disney World or Sea World. Of course, Century Village is not exactly Disney World or Sea World either. Century Village is not like any other place in Western Civilization. It is not like any other place in the entire world.

I picked up my pen and filled it *properly,* the six-step process that Tillie had taught me. She had said, "You must think of those six steps not as preparation for the beginning but as the beginning itself." I knew then that I had started my B & B. I let my pen drink up a whole plunger full of ink and then holding the pen over the bottle, I squeezed three drops back into the bottle.

And I thought—a B & B letter is giving just a few drops back to the bottle. I put away the tiny notepad and took out a full sheet of calligraphy paper and began,

Dear Grandma Sadie and Grandpa Nate,
Thank you for a vacation that was out of this world...

Reader Response

Open for Discussion   It sounds ironic, but Noah may enjoy writing that B & B letter despite his protests. Help him along; tell him what you think he should write.

1. A one-liner gets a laugh when you're reading a story. Example: "This was not the greatest conversation starter in the world" (p. 549). Find two more one-liners. If you can, practice reading them aloud for a laugh.

2. Near the beginning of the story, Noah writes "red wagon" on a Post-it note. What is the wagon used for and why is it an important part of the story?

3. What do you think Noah included in his letter? How do you predict his grandparents will react to the letter he has written? How do you predict his mother will react?

4. The phrase "decline of Western Civilization" is used by adults in the story to describe something they feel is ruining the world as we know it. Find places in which it is used. Do you agree with the assessment of the world?

Test Practice

Look Back and Write   What was written at the bottom of every wedding invitation (page 547)? Explain what it means.

...decline of Western Civilization...

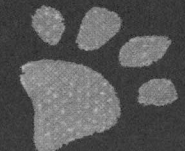

E. L. Konigsburg

Read more books by E. L. Konigsburg.

E. L. Konigsburg says, "Readers let me know they like books that have more to them than meets the eye. Had they not let me know that, I never would have written *The View from Saturday*."

She goes on to explain that she had started writing about a bed and breakfast inn—also called a B and B—when she stopped to take a walk along the beach. She says, "When I write a book, I more or less start a movie in my head, and there I was doing a rerun of what I had written." During that rerun, she remembered she already had a story in her files about Noah, whose mother insisted he write a bread-and-butter letter. Noah's story reminded her of another story, and that story reminded her of one about an Academic Bowl team. The links grew into a novel about four young people and their teacher coach.

The View from Saturday won the Newbery Medal in 1997. It was the second time one of her books received the top honor.

From the Mixed-up Files of Mrs. Basil E. Frankweiler

Altogether, One at a Time

Social Studies
in Reading

Expository Nonfiction

Genre

- **Expository nonfiction explains the *who, what, where, when, why,* and *how* about an idea or subject.**

- **Expository nonfiction can tell about a series of events that lead to an idea or invention.**

Text Features

- **A paragraph introduces and summarizes what the paragraphs will describe.**

- **The boldfaced heads are like titles telling the readers what they will learn about next.**

Link to Social Studies

Choose an item and investigate its origin. Use the library or Internet to research your choice. Share what you learn with the class.

Who THOUGHT of That?

by Bonnie Kepplinger

Noah uses a ballpoint pen and Post-It™ Notes—both popular items in modern life. You may be surprised to learn how these and other everyday items came about.

Post-It Notes

In 1970, a man named Spencer Silver was working in the 3M research laboratory. He hoped to develop a strong adhesive, but ended up with a weak one. It stuck to things but could easily be pulled off. Four years later, another 3M scientist named Arthur Fry was marking his places in a hymnal while singing in the church choir. However, the bits of paper kept falling out of the book. He had saved some of Silver's weak glue and used it to fasten his markers. This was the birth of Post-It Notes, today one of the most widely used office products available.

 **Predict** | What can you predict about this article?

The Amazing Spring

What can walk, although it's not alive? You're right if you guessed a Slinky®! This toy was accidentally invented by Richard James, a Philadelphia engineer, during World War II (1939-1945). James was experimenting with coil springs for the U.S. Navy. One day a spring fell from a shelf and appeared to "walk" across a pile of books. He and his wife came up with the name Slinky®, and made 400 of these gadgets to sell as toys. Slinkies were an instant hit, selling out in 90 minutes at a New York department store during the Christmas holidays.

The Ballpoint Pen

More than 100 years ago, people were trying to invent a fountain pen that did not have to be refilled with ink. By the mid-1940s, ballpoint pens were being sold—for over $12 each! But these pens leaked, smudged, and clogged. Although the price dropped, the pens stopped selling. In 1949, a chemist named Fran Seech sold his ideas for a new ink formula to Patrick J. Frawley, Jr., who began selling the first pen with a retractable ballpoint tip. This non-smear pen, named the "Papermate," was soon selling in the millions. Another ballpoint pen, patented by Ladislas and Georg Biro, was introduced by Marcel Bich as the "Ballpoint Bic." It is a best-seller today.

Reading Across Texts
Two of the inventions in "Who Thought of That?" were used by Noah in *The View from Saturday*. Which one did Tillie Nachman say was responsible for the decline of western civilization?

Writing Across Texts Tell why you think Tillie Nachman said what she did about this invention.

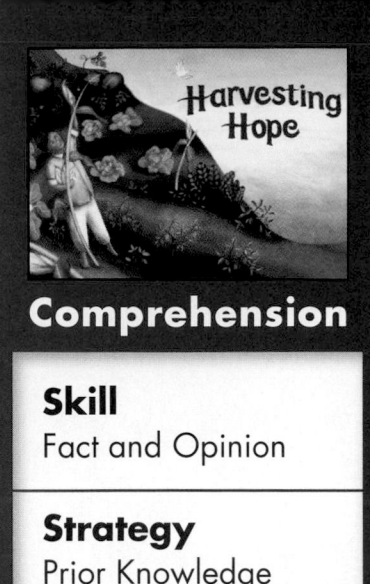

Fact and Opinion

- Statements of opinion are someone's beliefs or way of thinking about something. The statement *Cars are the best way to travel* is a statement of opinion.

- Statements of fact can be proved true or false. Statements of opinion cannot be proved but can be shown to be valid or faulty. Valid statements of opinion are supported by facts or experts. Faulty statements are not supported by facts.

Statement of Opinion	Support	Valid or Faulty
Statement	Sentence from reference book	Valid
Statement	Opinion or incorrect fact	Faulty

Strategy: Prior Knowledge

Prior knowledge refers to everything you know about a certain topic from what you have read or seen and your own personal experiences. Good readers critically examine statements of opinion by activating their prior knowledge. To determine if a statement of opinion is valid or faulty, think about what you already know about the subject. Is your knowledge based on facts or information from reliable sources?

1. Read "The Best Job in the World." Make a graphic organizer like the one above in order to identify valid and faulty statements of opinion in the article.

2. Use your graphic organizer to help you explain whether or not you think the author supported her argument that movers have the best job in the world.

The Best Job
IN THE WORLD

Movers transport people's belongings from one location to another. Movers have the best job in the world because they are healthy, get to help people every day, and get to see many interesting places.

Movers use their muscles when they work. I think exercising your muscles makes you strong. Movers are the strongest workers in the world because they use their muscles more than any other job.

Movers have the best job because each day they get to help other people and that makes movers happy. I think movers are happy because Dr. David Kell recently did a study showing that helpful people tend to be happier. Everyone enjoys helping others. Think of how nice it would be to do so all day, every day.

Finally, movers always get to see new and interesting places. Office workers who sit at their desks each day can't say that. Movers get to see mansions, unique apartments, and other types of living places. That is always fun to do.

In conclusion, movers have the best job in the world because they exercise, help others, and get to see new places every day. Now, don't you want to be a mover?

Strategy To decide if this statement of opinion is valid or faulty, tap your prior knowledge about exercise. Based on what you know, do you think the statement is valid or faulty? Why?

Skill How can you tell that this statement of opinion is faulty?
- **(a)** It is based only on another opinion.
- **(b)** It was stated by an expert.
- **(c)** It is based on incorrect facts.

Skill Is the author's statement of opinion well supported or poorly supported?

Strategy Based on your prior knowledge, do those statements of fact seem reasonable? Do they need to be proved?

563

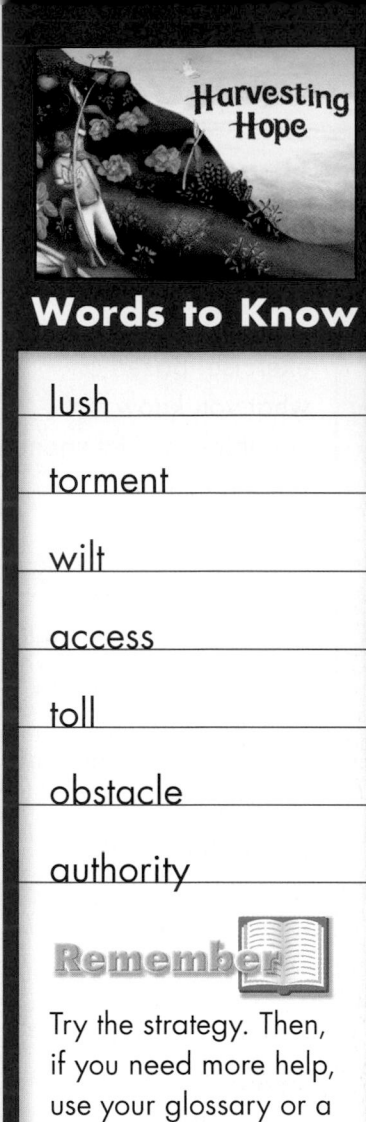

Words to Know

lush

torment

wilt

access

toll

obstacle

authority

Remember

Try the strategy. Then, if you need more help, use your glossary or a dictionary.

Vocabulary Strategy
for Homonyms

Context Clues When you are reading, you may come to a word whose meaning you know, but that meaning doesn't make sense in the sentence. The word may be a homonym. Homonyms are two or more words that are spelled the same but have different meanings because they developed from different words. For example, *lean* could mean either "thin" or "to rest against something for support." You can use the context—the words and sentences around the word—to figure out which meaning is being used.

1. Reread the sentence in which the homonym appears.

2. Look for clues to the homonym's meaning.

3. If you need more help, read the sentences around the sentence with the homonym. Look for clues or additional information that suggests the homonym's meaning.

4. Try the meaning in the sentence. Does it make sense?

As you read "Migrant Work Is No Picnic," look for homonyms. Use the context to determine the meanings of the homonyms.

Migrant Work Is No Picnic

We tend to think of farm work as being healthy. You get fresh air and sunshine and use your muscles. You can lean against your hoe and look at the lush green crops growing in straight rows. It sounds like a satisfactory life, doesn't it?

On the contrary, for migrant workers field work means long hours, poor pay, and torment for the body and mind. With bare hands and bent backs, these workers labor from sunup to sundown in the hot sun. Even a plant will wilt under the sun's punishing rays without enough water. Sometimes the workers are not provided with water. They may not even have access to bathrooms. And as for fresh air, workers instead often breathe the fumes of insecticides.

All this hard labor takes a toll on workers' health. Yet they often fail to get proper health care. When your pay is scarcely enough to buy food for your family, a doctor's bills become an obstacle that can't be overcome. Getting people the authority to fight for the rights of migrant workers has been an important issue for decades.

Choose one of the illustrations in the next selection, *Harvesting Hope.* Write a description of it using as many words from the Words to Know list as you can.

Genre

A **biography** is the story of a real person's life that has been written by another person. As you read, notice the clues that tell you this is a story about a real person.

Harvesting Hope

THE STORY OF CESAR CHAVEZ

by Kathleen Krull
illustrated by Yuyi Morales

How can one person change
the lives of many?

Until Cesar Chavez was ten, every summer night was like a fiesta. Relatives swarmed onto the ranch for barbecues with watermelon, lemonade, and fresh corn. Cesar and his brothers, sisters, and cousins settled down to sleep outside, under netting to keep mosquitoes out. But who could sleep—with uncles and aunts singing, spinning ghost stories, and telling magical tales of life back in Mexico?

Cesar thought the whole world belonged to his family. The eighty acres of their ranch were an island in the shimmering Arizona desert, and the starry skies were all their own.

Many years earlier, Cesar's grandfather had built their spacious adobe house to last forever, with walls eighteen inches thick. A vegetable garden, cows, and chickens supplied all the food they could want. With hundreds of cousins on farms nearby, there was always someone to play with. Cesar's best friend was his brother Richard; they never spent a day apart.

Cesar was so happy at home that he was a little afraid when school started. On his first day, he grabbed the seat next to his older sister, Rita. The teacher moved him to another seat—and Cesar flew out the door and ran home. It took three days of coaxing for him to return to school and take his place with the other first graders.

Cesar was stubborn, but he was not a fighter. His mother cautioned her children against fighting, urging them to use their minds and mouths to work out conflicts.

Then, in 1937, the summer Cesar was ten, the trees around the ranch began to wilt. The sun baked the farm soil rock hard. A drought was choking the life out of Arizona. Without water for the crops, the Chavez family couldn't make money to pay its bills.

There came a day when Cesar's mother couldn't stop crying. In a daze, Cesar watched his father strap their possessions onto the roof of their old car. After a long struggle, the family no longer owned the ranch. They had no choice but to join the hundreds of thousands of people fleeing to the green valleys of California to look for work.

Cesar's old life had vanished. Now he and his family were migrants—working on other people's farms, crisscrossing California, picking whatever fruits and vegetables were in season.

When the Chavez family arrived at the first of their new homes in California, they found a battered old shed. Its doors were missing and garbage covered the dirt floor. Cold, damp air seeped into their bedding and clothes. They shared water and outdoor toilets with a dozen other families, and overcrowding made everything filthy. The neighbors were constantly fighting, and the noise upset Cesar. He had no place to play games with Richard. Meals were sometimes made of dandelion greens gathered along the road.

Cesar swallowed his bitter homesickness and worked alongside his family. He was small and not very strong, but still a fierce worker. Nearly every crop caused torment. Yanking out beets broke the skin between his thumb and index finger. Grapevines sprayed with bug-killing chemicals made his eyes sting and his lungs wheeze. Lettuce had to be the worst. Thinning lettuce all day with a short-handled hoe would make hot spasms shoot through his back. Farm chores on someone else's farm instead of on his own felt like a form of slavery.

The Chavez family talked constantly of saving enough money to buy back their ranch. But by each sundown, the whole family had earned as little as thirty cents for the day's work. As the years blurred together, they spoke of the ranch less and less.

The towns weren't much better than the fields. WHITE TRADE ONLY signs were displayed in many stores and restaurants. None of the thirty-five schools Cesar attended over the years seemed like a safe place, either. Once, after Cesar broke the rule about speaking English at all times, a teacher hung a sign on him that read, I AM A CLOWN. I SPEAK SPANISH. He came to hate school because of the conflicts, though he liked to learn. Even he considered his eighth-grade graduation a miracle. After eighth grade he dropped out to work in the fields full-time.

His lack of schooling embarrassed Cesar for the rest of his life, but as a teenager he just wanted to put food on his family's table. As he worked, it disturbed him that landowners treated their workers more like farm tools than human beings. They provided no clean drinking water, rest periods, or access to bathrooms. Anyone who complained was fired, beaten up, or sometimes even murdered.

So, like other migrant workers, Cesar was afraid and suspicious whenever outsiders showed up to try to help. How could they know

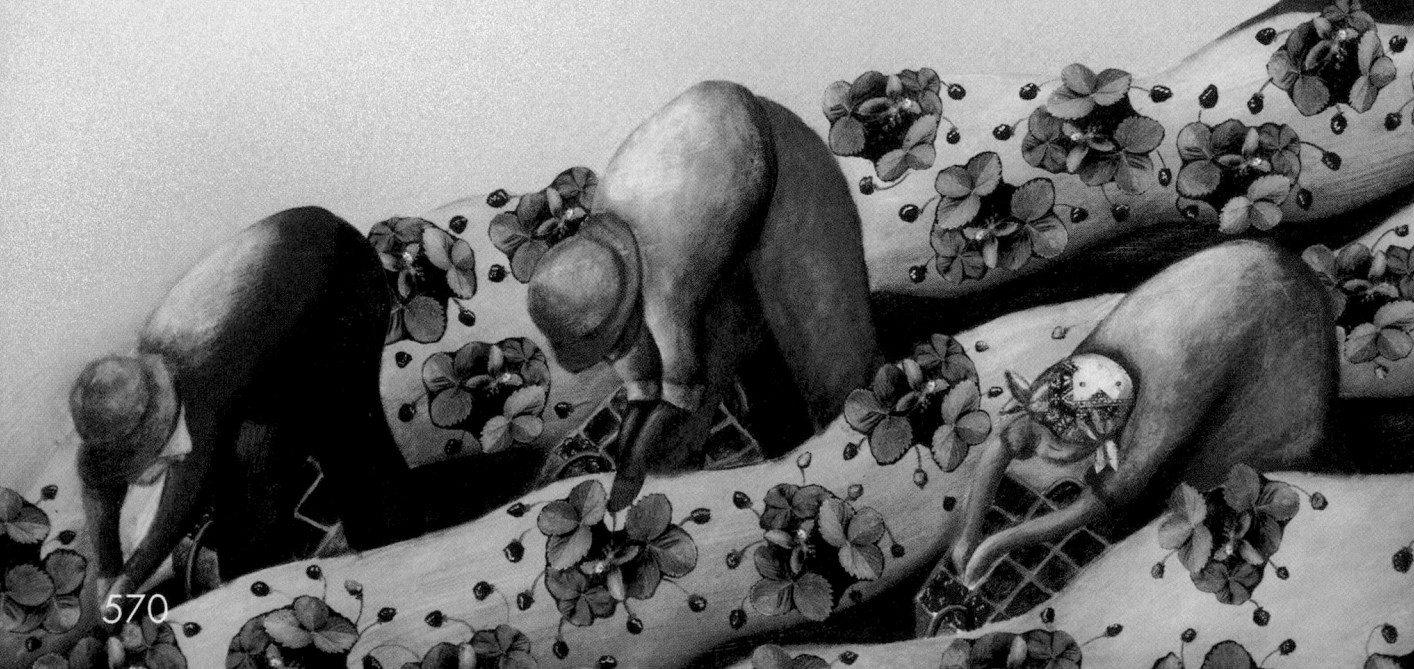

about feeling so powerless? Who could battle such odds?

Yet Cesar had never forgotten his old life in Arizona and the jolt he'd felt when it was turned upside down. Farmwork did not have to be this miserable.

Reluctantly, he started paying attention to the outsiders. He began to think that maybe there was hope. And in his early twenties, he decided to dedicate the rest of his life to fighting for change.

Again he crisscrossed California, this time to talk people into joining his fight. At first, out of every hundred workers he talked to, perhaps one would agree with him. One by one—this was how he started.

At the first meeting Cesar organized, a dozen women gathered. He sat quietly in a corner. After twenty minutes, everyone started

wondering when the organizer would show up. Cesar thought he might die of embarrassment.

"Well, I'm the organizer," he said—and forced himself to keep talking, hoping to inspire respect with his new suit and the mustache he was trying to grow. The women listened politely, and he was sure they did so out of pity.

But despite his shyness, Cesar showed a knack for solving problems. People trusted him. With workers he was endlessly patient and compassionate. With landowners he was stubborn, demanding, and single-minded. He was learning to be a fighter.

In a fight for justice, he told everyone, truth was a better weapon than violence. "Nonviolence," he said, "takes more guts." It meant using imagination to find ways to overcome powerlessness.

More and more people listened.

One night, 150 people poured into an old abandoned theater in Fresno. At this first meeting of the National Farm Workers Association, Cesar unveiled its flag—a bold black eagle, the sacred bird of the Aztec Indians.

La Causa—The Cause—was born.

It was time to rebel, and the place was Delano. Here, in the heart of the lush San Joaquin Valley, brilliant green vineyards reached toward every horizon. Poorly paid workers hunched over grapevines for most of each year. Then, in 1965, the vineyard owners cut their pay even further.

Cesar chose to fight just one of the forty landowners, hopeful that others would get the message. As plump grapes drooped, thousands of workers walked off that company's field in a strike, or *huelga*.

Grapes, when ripe, do not last long.

The company fought back with everything from punches to bullets. Cesar refused to respond with violence. Violence would only hurt *La Causa*.

Instead, he organized a march—a march of more than three hundred miles. He and his supporters would walk from Delano to the state capitol in Sacramento to ask for the government's help.

Cesar and sixty-seven others started out one morning. Their first obstacle was the Delano police force, thirty of whose members locked arms to prevent the group from crossing the street. After three hours of arguing—in public—the chief of police backed down. Joyous marchers headed north under the sizzling sun. Their rallying cry was *Sí Se Puede*, or "Yes, It Can Be Done."

The first night, they reached Ducor. The marchers slept outside the tiny cabin of the only person who would welcome them.

Single file they continued, covering an average of fifteen miles a day. They inched their way through the San Joaquin Valley, while the unharvested grapes in Delano turned white with mold. Cesar developed painful blisters right away. He and many others had blood seeping out of their shoes.

The word spread. Along the way, farmworkers offered food and drink as the marchers passed by. When the sun set, marchers lit candles and kept going.

Shelter was no longer a problem. Supporters began welcoming them each night with feasts. Every night was a rally. "Our pilgrimage is the match," one speaker shouted, "that will light our cause for all farmworkers to see what is happening here."

Another cried, "We seek our basic, God-given rights as human beings . . . ¡*Viva La Causa!*"

Eager supporters would keep the marchers up half the night talking about change. Every morning, the line of marchers swelled, Cesar always in the lead.

On the ninth day, hundreds marched through Fresno.

The long, peaceful march was a shock to people unaware of how California farmworkers had to live. Now students, public officials, religious leaders, and citizens from everywhere offered help. For the grape company, the publicity was becoming unbearable.

And on the vines, the grapes continued to rot.

In Modesto, on the fifteenth day, an exhilarated crowd celebrated Cesar's thirty-eighth birthday. Two days later, five thousand people met the marchers in Stockton with flowers, guitars, and accordions.

That evening, Cesar received a message that he was sure was a prank. But in case it was true, he left the march and had someone drive him all through the night to a mansion in wealthy Beverly Hills. Officials from the grape company were waiting for him. They were ready to recognize the authority of the National Farm Workers Association, promising a contract with a pay raise and better conditions.

Cesar rushed back to join the march.

On Easter Sunday, when the marchers arrived in Sacramento, the parade was ten-thousand-people strong.

From the steps of the state capitol building, the joyous announcement was made to the public: Cesar Chavez had just signed the first contract for farmworkers in American history.

The parade erupted into a giant fiesta. Crowds swarmed the steps, some people cheering, many weeping. Prancing horses carried men in mariachi outfits. Everyone sang and waved flowers or flags. They made a place of honor for the fifty-seven marchers who had walked the entire journey.

Speaker after speaker, addressing the audience in Spanish and in English, took the microphone. "You cannot close your eyes and your ears to us any longer," cried one. "You cannot pretend that we do not exist."

The crowd celebrated until the sky was full of stars.

The march had taken its toll. Cesar's leg was swollen, and he was running a high fever. Gently he reminded everyone that the battle was not over: "It is well to remember there must be courage but also that in victory there must be humility."

Much more work lay ahead, but the victory was stunning. Some of the wealthiest people in the country had been forced to recognize some of the poorest as human beings. Cesar Chavez had won this fight—without violence—and he would never be powerless again.

Reader Response

Open for Discussion Think about Cesar Chavez's early life, before the march to Sacramento. What resources outside himself and inside himself helped him become a leader?

1. Biographies tell not only a person's life but also conditions that surrounded that life. What do this author and illustrator tell you about conditions in the lives of migrant workers?

2. On page 573, the author writes, "Poorly paid workers hunched over grapevines for most of the year." Is this a statement of fact or a statement of opinion? Give support for your answer.

3. The strike by the National Farm Workers Association brought better working conditions and pay for farm workers. In what other ways have people fought to improve their working or living conditions? Are they still fighting now? How do you know?

4. Cesar Chavez overcame many obstacles in his pursuit of fairness for farm workers. Make a web with the word *obstacle* in the center. Add words and phrases from the Words to Know list and from the selection that describe some of these obstacles.

Test Practice

Look Back and Write The march grew from sixty-eight people to a parade of ten thousand. Look back at pages 574–576 and write a list of those who learned of the march and gave their support.

Kathleen Krull and Yuyi Morales

Read more books by Kathleen Krull and Yuyi Morales.

Kathleen Krull says, "When I was fifteen, I was fired from my part-time job at the library. The reason? Reading too much—while I was supposed to be working." Today she is a full-time writer of books for young people and lives in San Diego with her husband.

"As a child," she says, "I thought books were the most important thing in the world, and that perception is actually more intense now. I'm grateful, for so many reasons, to be able to work in a vital and exhilarating field: preserving literacy. One of its benefits is that I can't be fired. Especially for reading too much."

The Boy on Fairfield Street: How Ted Geisel Grew Up to Become Dr. Seuss
by Kathleen Krull

Yuyi Morales is an artist, writer, puppet maker, and Brazilian folk dancer. She lives in California with her husband, son, and cat.

Ms. Morales says, "I was born in the city of flowers, Xalapa, Mexico. When I was a child, I spent most of the time thinking about extraterrestrials and waiting for them to come in their UFOs to take me away. I practiced to be an acrobat too—and broke many things at home. Then I grew up and became an artist and a writer. Oh, well."

Just a Minute: A Trickster Tale and Counting Book
written and illustrated by Yuyi Morales

Poetry

Genre

- A poem is a composition arranged in lines. Some poems have lines that rhyme, while others do not.

- Poetry often expresses the poet's serious, deep thoughts on a subject.

- Poetry often makes readers think about a new or un-expected way of looking at human experiences.

Link to Writing

Find some other poems written by Alma Flor Ada or Leobardo V. Cortéz. Choose a poem and write a paragraph about how it makes you feel.

Fieldworkers

by Leobardo V. Cortéz

Early,
when the sun comes out,
lumps move throughout the field like
clockwork every sunrise,
until the moon comes.

Their bronze hands
wave
like
rifles in a war.

Fighting
for survival
a new tomorrow
for our children. . . .

The white vests
our innocence
purity
and wealth. . . .

Come child, leave your life
    upon the land.
I am
the slave of my children.

I am
their owner as well.
Yes!

I am
the *campesino*
in the fields. . . .

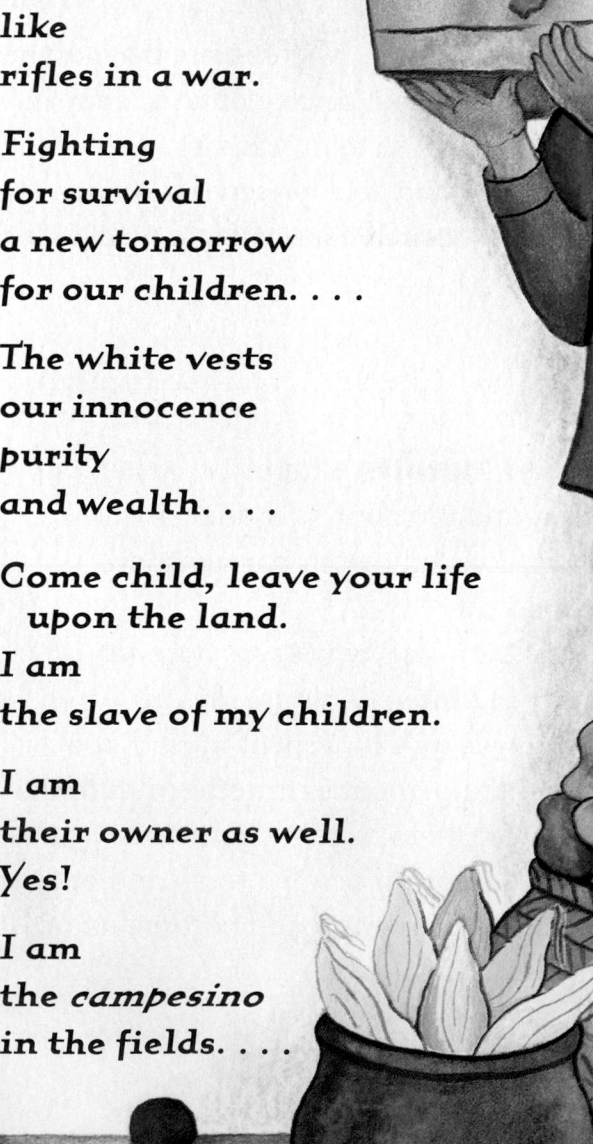

Farmworkers

by Alma Flor Ada

Farmworkers is the name we give
to the people who work the land,
who harvest the fields,
united beneath one sky.

Thank you, farmworker,
for the fruits your hands have
    brought me.
I will grow stronger and kinder
as I eat what you have grown.

Reading Across Texts

Which poem reflects the life and struggles of Cesar Chavez and his family? Whose voice do we hear in the other poem?

Writing Across Texts Write what you think Chavez would say about the poem that reflects his life and struggles.

Prior Knowledge What must you recall to understand these poems?

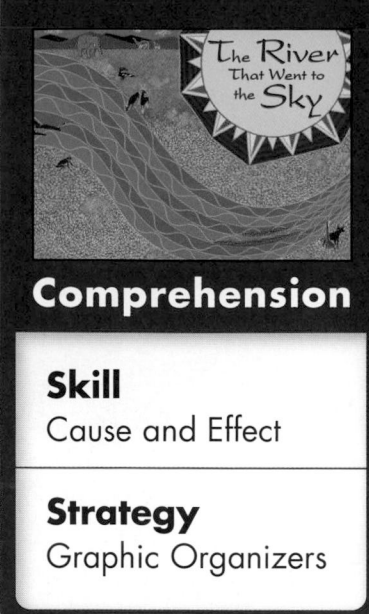

Comprehension

Skill
Cause and Effect

Strategy
Graphic Organizers

Cause and Effect

- An *effect* is something that happens. A *cause* is why something happens. Clue words such as *since, thus, as a result, therefore,* and *consequently* point to cause-effect relationships.

- When a cause is not directly stated, you must think about why something happened.

- You can use graphic organizers to show cause-effect relationships.

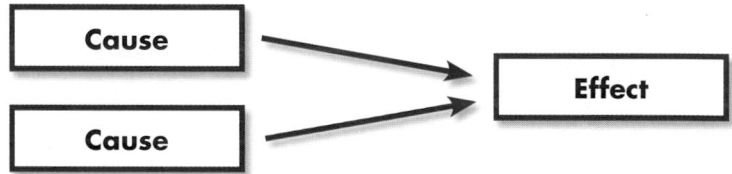

Strategy: Graphic Organizers

Making and filling in a graphic organizer can help you connect ideas described in the text. For example, completing a cause-effect chart like the one above can help you see cause-effect relationships. With some articles, it may be possible to fill in the organizer while reading. With others, you may need to read the entire article before completing the organizer.

1. Read "The Theory of Plate Tectonics." Make a graphic organizer like the one above to show cause-effect relationships described in the article.

2. How did making and filling in graphic organizers help you better understand the information in this article? Write down your explanation.

The Theory of Plate Tectonics

Why do earthquakes occur? What causes volcanoes? How do mountain ranges form? Scientists have been studying these questions for years. They can be answered by the theory of plate tectonics.

Strategy Before reading, make a cause-effect T-chart. Under the side you label *Effect*, write *Volcano, Mountains, Earthquakes*. Fill in the causes as you read the article.

The Theory The surface of the Earth is made up of large plates, which are huge chunks of the Earth's crust. Continents and oceans rest on these plates. The plates slowly glide along the surface of the Earth. Depending on the way in which the plates meet, they can cause earthquakes, volcanoes, or mountain ranges.

Volcanoes Some plates are thicker than others. When two plates meet, the thinner one is pushed underneath the thicker one. This thinner plate goes beneath the Earth's crust, which is very hot, and melts. Melted rock is called magma. The magma then rises to the surface of the Earth to form a volcano.

Skill What causes the thinner plate to melt?
(a) It turns into magma.
(b) It slides over the thicker plate.
(c) It goes underneath the Earth's surface.

Mountain Ranges Plates can carry both oceans and continents. When two plates carrying continents meet, neither one can go beneath the other. So they collide, forcing the Earth's crust to crumple and buckle. Thus, mountain ranges are formed.

Skill What causes mountain ranges to form? Look for clue words.

Earthquakes Sometimes two plates pass each other going in opposite directions, like cars driving on opposite sides of a street. But they rub against each other and often get stuck. When they break free and move again, the movement causes an earthquake.

Strategy Look at the cause-effect graphic organizer that you completed. Can you draw any comparisons between volcanoes and mountain ranges?

The River That Went to the Sky

Words to Know

densest

ventured

expanse

eaves

moisture

Remember

Try the strategy. Then, if you need more help, use your glossary or a dictionary.

Vocabulary Strategy
for Synonyms

Context Clues Synonyms are two or more words that mean almost the same thing. An author may use a synonym near a difficult word to help you understand the word's meaning.

1. Read the words and sentences around the word you don't know.

2. Look for clues that indicate the unknown word has a synonym. A synonym is often preceded by the word *or* or *like* and may be set off by commas.

3. If there is a synonym, try using it in place of the unknown word. This will help you understand the meaning.

4. If this does not help you understand the word, read on or look the word up in a dictionary.

As you read "Tropical Rain Forest," look for synonyms to help you figure out the meanings of unknown words.

Tropical Rain Forest

The tropical rain forest is a green super-city. We think of cities as being crowded places, but the rain forests have the densest, or most crowded, populations of living things. A city may grow to hold many millions of people, but the world's rain forests contain nearly half the world's species, or kinds, of plants as well as a huge variety of animals.

Those who have ventured into the rain forest know that its vast expanse, or area, includes towering trees and miles of long vines. Under the eaves of these giants, many kinds of ferns, mosses, flowers, and shrubs grow. Because it gets so much moisture (from as little as 80 inches to as much as 250 inches of rainfall each year) and warmth, a tropical rain forest is always lush and green.

Of course, animals of all kinds love it there—fish, frogs, birds, snakes, and monkeys, to name a few. Insects, however, are the most plentiful animal in the rain forest. Scientists have counted some 40 different species of ants in a single tree of the South American rain forest.

Write

Imagine an animal living in a tropical rain forest. Write a paragraph describing a typical day in its life. Use as many words from the Words to Know list as you can.

585

Genre

A **myth** is a story told by word of mouth that explains something about nature. As you read, look for clues which show that this story is a myth.

The River
That Went to the Sky

A Story from Malawi

retold by Kasiya Makaka Phiri
illustrated by Stéphan Daigle

**How did Africa's Sahara
desert come to be?**

Once there was a River. It ran from one side of the great continent to the other, and it was so wide it looked like a lake, and the land around it was rich. All the animals that lived there had plenty of everything. Grass to graze, fruit to eat, nuts to crack, roots to chew, bark to nibble, and leaves to eat. The animals ambled all day long, eating a little, stopping, gazing into the distance, eating a little more, and going on slowly, for there was no hurry. The great vast River meandered across the land avoiding all the mountains, choosing only the plains and the valleys but always spreading wide, wide across the land. It rolled gently from one side of the vast continent and went to sleep and glided on the night tide to the other side. Backward and forward. It felt good and made happy noises on the banks, like the sound of calabashes filling with water, one gulp at a time.

On the banks grew the low grasses that like to trail their roots in cool river water. With them grew the papyrus and bulrushes. Behind them grew those grasses that like to smell the water every day and hear the happy sounds of the River. Water trees stood knee-deep in the water, looking toward the grasses of the low plains that gave way to ankle-high grass, then knee-high grass, all the way to the towering elephant grass. Then came the tall trees of the woods, beyond which were the high plains and foothills of great mountains. The high plains were covered in shorter grasses where the swift wind blew, keeping everything down except in the sheltered folds of the rolling ridges. In these hidden valleys were groves of rare trees and flowers and many other plants.

So everything was all right, until one day the River, gliding sleepily, looked up and saw the stars in the night sky.

"What is that?" said the River in a sleepy voice.

Hyena, who happened to be nearby taking a sip of water, looked up and said, "What's what, where?"

"Up there with the many eyes," said the sleepy River.

"That is the night sky," Hyena said and went on his way.

"Oh, how I wish I could go to the sky," said the River, sighing as it fell asleep.

The grass with the roots in the water heard this and whispered: "The River wants to go to the sky."

The whisper went on, to the papyrus, to the reeds, to the short plain grass, and to the knee-high grass.

"The River wants to go to the sky!"

"The River . . ."

" . . . wants to . . ."

" . . . go to . . ."

" . . . the sky. . . ."

The whisper went very fast until it was at the edge of the woods that are hedged by bushes guarding the foothills of the great mountains and the high plains.

"The River wants to go to the sky," said a bush, and the trees whispered from trunk to branch to leaf to leaf to leaf like a gentle stir in an invisible breeze all the way to the wind-swept high plains where the grass lay low below the swift wind.

The wind was quick at picking up whispers from the lower plains, so it snapped the whisper up and dragged it over the high plains up to the mountains and over the peaks, where nothing grew because it was too cold. Away into the sky the wind carried the whisper.

"*Shoosh-whoosh, whoosh-whoosh,* the River wants to go to the sky."

The night sky heard it, the stars heard it, and early the following day before dawn, just as it was eating its breakfast ready to start the day, the Sun heard it.

589

"Very well, I'll visit the River today," said the Sun.

The River woke up very early, and soon after, the Sun came to visit.

"I hear you want to go to the sky, meandering River?" said the Sun.

"Yes! Oh, to walk the blue and see the twinkling eyes," the River sighed.

"Very well," said the Sun. "I can help you up but you'll have to find your way down."

"Down! It looks so beautiful up there, I won't want to find my way down."

Gazelle, who happened to be taking a drink just then, sprang up and ran to Elephant and said, "The Sun is going to take the great River up to the sky, and she says she'll never come back here again!"

Elephant thought for a while then raised her trunk and blew a message into the air. The wind, who was always quick at picking up messages, snapped it up, and everywhere it blew, the animals and the plants heard it.

The trees were the first to react. They gathered together into the densest forest ever and talked over the matter for days and days. The gathering of trees and creepers became a jungle, but the grasses, thinking it was too dark under the eaves of those huge trees, wandered out onto the plains, and they were so happy they rocked in the wind singing in their throaty voices. They spread as far as the eye could see. Some small thorn trees and bushes came out and dotted the grassy plains, and this became the savanna.

When the animals gathered they too talked for days and days.

"This is a serious matter," said Elephant.

"It is time to migrate to faraway places," said Rhino. Saying so, he put down his head and followed his nose South. South, South, always South. That started the exodus, and animals wandered in all directions. Great Gorilla and Brainy Chimpanzee, feeling that they did not want to go too far, simply went into the jungle. Tree Pangolin, Leopard, Gabon Viper, and Royal Antelope did the same.

Elephant led a whole delegation South following the rhinoceros. Buffalo, Lion, Giraffe, Gazelle, Hyena, Zebra, Cheetah, and many others wandered South and roamed the grasslands. But rock-climbing Barbary Sheep, Camel, Addax, Sand Cat, Desert Hedgehog, Fennec Fox, Jerboa, Sand Grouse, and many others remained exactly where they were.

Meanwhile, the Sun had gathered all its strength. It sent its hottest rays to heat the River, and slowly, oh so slowly you could not see what was happening, the River started to lift in particles too tiny for the eye to see. Up, up, up they went until they were so high that it felt cold. Then the tiny particles of the River huddled together and formed white fluffy clouds of all sizes. They were so happy to be floating in the air, and they waited in excitement for the spectacle of the night sky when they would walk among the many winking stars.

Sure enough, in the evening, the night sky prepared to lay out the best winking stars for the visiting clouds to walk among, and as it got darker the stars winked and twinkled and sparkled.

"Oh, isn't this wonderful!" said a cloud. "Simply stupendous!"

Whoosh! A gust of wind came in.

"You're sitting on my bit of sky ledge," the wind said.

"Oh, I beg your pardon," said the cloud, and she moved over to one side.

Whoosh! Gusts of wind came over and over again, here and everywhere. They claimed parts of the sky where the clouds were. Sometimes they came while the clouds were trying to get some sleep, and they would shake them awake and push them over.

Now, pushing and shoving is about the only thing that the gentle River would not stand. And all the clouds remembered the peaceful days of being water down on Earth. They remembered the gentle flow in one direction and the gliding back on the tide, and a small cloud said, "I want to go home."

Yes. They all wanted to go home. But how? The wind, so quick at picking up conversations, snapped up the news of the clouds trying to go home, and it gathered all its sisters, cousins, and brothers.

WWHHOOOSSSHH!!

They carried the clouds high and made them feel colder, and as the clouds huddled together they grew heavy and began to fall as rain. Down below, the Sun was still burning out any manner of moisture that remained in the river bed.

But it rained. It rained all day long and all night long. It rained everywhere but never in the old river bed. It rained in Abyssinia and formed the Blue Nile. It rained and rained and formed the While Nile and Lake Victoria and Lake Tanganyika and Lake Malawi and Lake Chad, Lake Turkana, and many small lakes besides. It rained and rained and formed the Shire River. It rained and formed the Zambezi. It rained some more and the Limpopo, the Orange, the Niger, the Luangwa, and many, many other rivers were born. It rained heavily and lightly, day and night, and if you put your hands over your ears and moved them on and off, you could hear something like a song but not quite a song. Something like words but not quite like words:

"I am the River, the River that went to the sky for a walk. I am the River, the River that went to the sky for a walk."

It rained and rained everywhere but never in the place where the River once lived. If any of the drops ventured anywhere near that place, the Sun bore down on them and sent them back into the sky. And it is true. If you go to the great continent of Africa today you will see the vast expanse of sand where the meandering River lived. Sand everywhere, even in places where grass had been plenty. To this day the wildebeest have not stopped running away from the Sun, following their noses to wetter places where the grass would be as it used to be once upon a time, a long time ago, on the great continent of Africa.

Reader Response

Open for Discussion   This story needs a powerful storyteller or story reader. Choose a scene and demonstrate how effective a telling or reading can be.

1. The description of African topography is real. Read about the river and its surroundings (page 588). Draw a diagram to fit this label: a setting showing where the story begins.

2. On page 589, the River first whispers, "Oh, how I wish I could go to the sky." How does the whisper finally reach the Sun?

3. Create a cause-effect graphic organizer that shows how the disappearance of the River affects the plants and animals of the Sahara.

4. What part of the land would you describe with the word *densest*? Find other words that the author uses to describe its land and animals.

Look Back and Write   A turning point in the story is that the River wanted to go home. Why? Look on page 593 and write your answer.

Read more tales from Africa.

Kasiya Makaka Phiri is a poet, playwright, and storyteller. He says that "The River That Went to the Sky" was inspired by many experiences—"the Limpopo River, a flight over the Sahara, the migration of wildlife on the plains of East Africa, and the great spectacle of the transition from the dry to the wet season."

Mr. Phiri tells new stories and retells old ones. He tries out his stories on his three daughters, and later he tells them in front of an audience.

Born in Zimbabwe and educated in Malawi, Kasiya Makaka Phiri now lives in Wisconsin. About collecting and publishing African stories, he says it is "a great support for the evolution of our African culture in these days of rockets, lasers, and bombs."

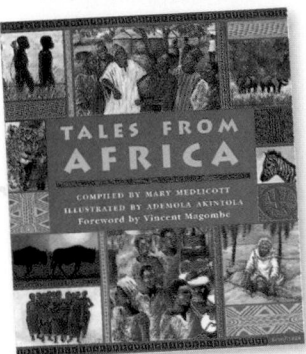

Tales from Africa
compiled by Mary Medlicott

The Lion's Whiskers and Other Ethiopian Tales
by Brent Ashabranner and Russell Davis

Folk Literature

Tall Tale

Genre

- A tall tale is a greatly exaggerated account of real, imaginary, or impossible acts of humor or heroism.

- While some tall tales are based on the life or undertakings of a real person, many involve totally fictitious people.

- Tall tales often center on the culture of the nineteenth century pioneer Americans and their hardships.

Link to Reading

Find other tall tales in the library or on the Internet. Report to your class on other characters and their superhuman feats.

Pecos Bill and the Cyclone

from AMERICAN TALL TALES by Mary Pope Osborne

Once Bill settled down with the gang, his true genius revealed itself. With his gang's help, he put together the biggest ranch in the Southwest. He used New Mexico as a corral and Arizona as a pasture. He invented tarantulas and scorpions as practical jokes. He also invented roping. Some say his rope was exactly as long as the equator; others argue it was two feet shorter.

Things were going fine for Bill until Texas began to suffer the worst drought in its history. It was so dry that all the rivers turned as powdery as biscuit flour. The parched grass was catching fire everywhere. For a while Bill and his gang managed to lasso water from the Rio Grande. When that river dried up, they lassoed water from the Gulf of Mexico.

No matter what he did, though, Bill couldn't get enough water to stay ahead of the drought. All his horses and cows were starting to dry up and blow away like balls of tumbleweed. It was horrible.

Just when the end seemed near, the sky turned to a deep shade of purple. From the distant mountains came a terrible roar. The cattle began to stampede, and a huge black funnel of a cyclone appeared, heading straight for Bill's ranch.

The rest of the gang shouted, "Help!" and ran.

But Pecos Bill wasn't scared in the least. "Yahoo!" he hollered, and he swung his lariat and lassoed that cyclone around its neck.

Bill held on tight as he got sucked up into the middle of the swirling cloud. He grabbed the cyclone by the ears and pulled himself onto her back. Then he let out a whoop and headed that twister across Texas.

The mighty cyclone bucked, arched, and screamed like a wild bronco. But Pecos Bill just held on with his legs and used his strong hands to wring the rain out of her wind. He wrung out rain that flooded Texas, New Mexico, and Arizona, until finally he slid off the shriveled-up funnel and fell into California. The earth sank about two hundred feet below sea level in the spot where Bill landed, creating the area known today as Death Valley.

"There. That little waterin' should hold things for a while," he said, brushing himself off.

After his cyclone ride, no horse was too wild for Pecos Bill.

Reading Across Texts

Both the myth "The River That Went to the Sky" and this tall tale tell about land and water formations that actually exist. What are they?

Writing Across Texts Make a chart that lists the formations you read about in the myth and in this tall tale.

Cause & Effect Can you tell what ended the drought?

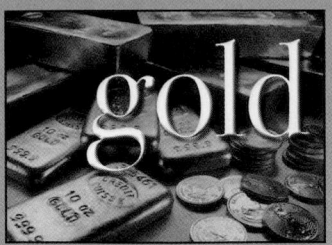

Comprehension

Skill
Main Idea
and Details

Strategy
Text Structure

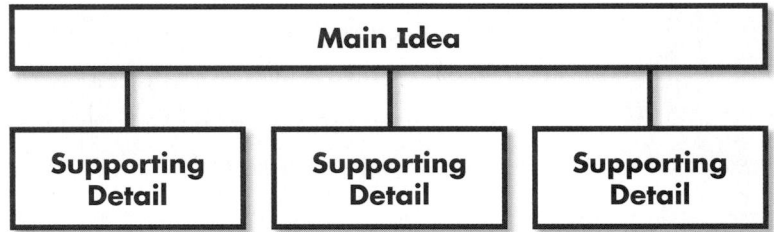

Main Idea
and Details

- The topic is what a paragraph is about and can usually be stated in a word or two.

- To find the main idea of the paragraph, think about all of the important information the paragraph gives about the topic.

- Supporting details tell more about the topic. They are less important pieces of information that support the main idea.

Main Idea

Supporting Detail	Supporting Detail	Supporting Detail

Strategy: Text Structure

Each piece of writing has a structure, or way of being organized. Sometimes the piece may describe events in a sequence, as in a fairy tale. Or a piece may use a cause-effect pattern for explaining ideas, as is sometimes found in a nonfiction article. Good readers use the text structure to help them understand the main idea of the article. As you read, look for patterns that show the text structure.

Write

1. Read "Metals." Make a graphic organizer like the one above giving the main idea of each section.

2. Use your graphic organizer to write a summary of "Metals."

METALS

WHAT ARE METALS? Some substances, such as gold, iron, aluminum, and silver, are called metals. Almost all metals are in solid form and look shiny. They are good conductors, meaning that it is easy for heat or electricity to flow through them. Metals are also malleable and ductile, which means they can be shaped and made flat.

ARE THERE MANY METALS? There are many different metals on Earth. In fact, three-fourths of all of the chemical substances humans know about are metals. Many, such as iron, are found in the Earth's crust.

WHAT TYPES OF METALS ARE THERE? Metals are grouped in three categories based on their characteristics. There are alkali metals, alkaline-earth metals, and transition metals. Alkali metals, such as sodium, dissolve in water. The molecules in these metals often join with other elements to form new substances. Alkaline-earth metals also dissolve in water, and the new substances they form are often found in nature. Calcium, which is found in your bones, is an alkaline-earth metal. Transition metals are the largest group of metals. Most metals that are used in everyday life, such as copper and iron, are transition metals. These metals are hard, strong, and shiny.

Strategy In a question/answer format, the basic answer to each question is the main idea of that section. What is the main idea of this paragraph?

Skill The topic of this paragraph is the quantity of metals. What is the main idea of the paragraph—what is it basically saying about that?

Strategy The structure of this paragraph is compare-contrast because each metal's unique characteristics are explained.

Skill What is the main idea of this paragraph? What are some important details?

Words to Know

characteristic

corrode

extract

exploit

hoard

engulfed

Remember

Try the strategy. Then, if you need more help, use your glossary or a dictionary.

Vocabulary Strategy
for Unfamiliar Words

Context Clues If you find a word you do not know while reading, check the context, or the words and sentences around the unknown word. Often an author provides clues that can help you figure out the meaning of a word.

1. Reread the sentence in which the unknown word appears. Look for specific clues to the word's meaning.

2. Think about the overall meaning of the sentence.

3. If you need more help, reread other sentences near the sentence with the unknown word. They may contain enough information about the subject to suggest the word's meaning.

4. Try your meaning in the original sentence. Does it make sense?

As you read "All That Glitters," use the context to help you figure out the meanings of unfamiliar words.

All That Glitters

Gold and silver are the metals most often used for making jewelry. Both have a **characteristic** shine. Because they reflect light, people have long been drawn to both metals. However, you may know that silver will **corrode**. This means that its atoms mix with oxygen. Eventually, a coat of tarnish appears on the surface. The process actually eats away the outer layer of silver. Gold does not corrode.

Both metals must be mined. That is, it is necessary to **extract** them from the Earth. This can only be done where they are found in a concentrated form. If the metal is not found in pure chunks, it must somehow be pulled out of the ore in which it is found.

Many people are drawn to places where large pockets of ore are discovered. Gold and silver miners hope to **exploit**, or profit by, the rich veins of metal. For centuries, people have wanted to **hoard** piles of the stuff. A stockpile of gold and silver tells the world, "I am powerful and rich!" Normally kind people can be **engulfed** by greed and selfishness at the thought of getting all that gold and silver!

Write

Look closely at a piece of jewelry and then write a description of it. Use as many words from the Words to Know list as you can.

Why is gold so precious?

Genre

Expository nonfiction explains the nature of an object or idea. As you read, look for explanations of the nature and uses of gold.

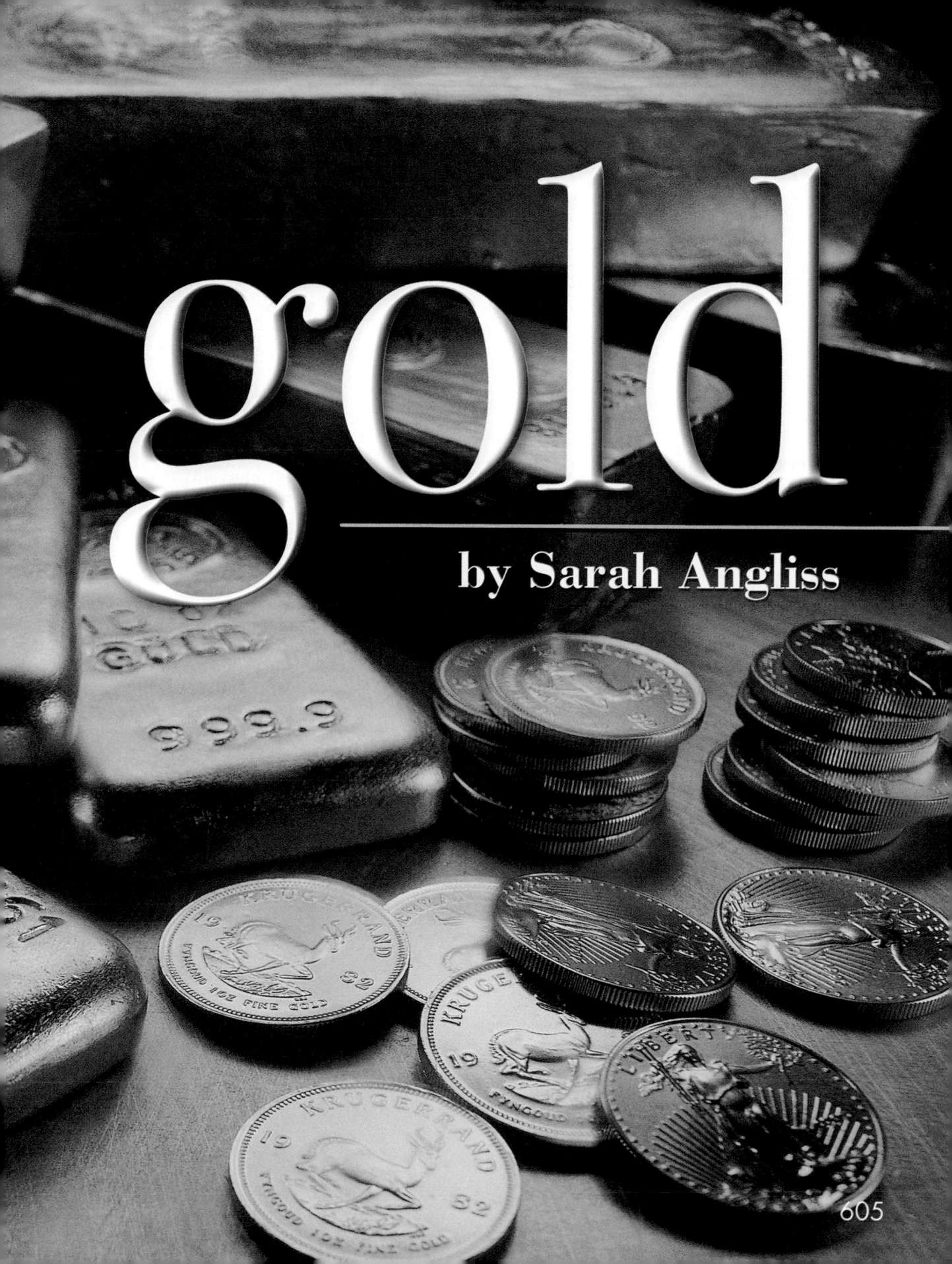

gold

by Sarah Angliss

What Is Gold?

Glistening bright yellow, gold is a heavy metal that is treasured in every country of the world.

Almost all metals have a characteristic luster (shininess)—that is, they reflect light in a mirrorlike way. Gold is special because its luster never fades. That is because gold does not react with air, water, or any ordinary chemical. In other words, it doesn't corrode. Roman coins, masks from Ancient Egypt, decorated books from Persia, and other golden treasures from the ancient world shine as brilliantly now as they did the day they were made.

Gold excites people all over the world. The gold jewelry that people own is often among their most valued possessions.

Melting Pots

At room temperature, gold is solid. Gold melts at 1,943°F (1,062°C). It is often heated to this temperature so that it can be poured into molds.

Gold is 19.3 times denser than water and three times denser than iron. Density means the mass of a substance that fills a given volume. It is usually measured in grams per cubic meter. So, one cubic meter of pure gold is 19.3 times heavier than one cubic meter of water. Imagine this: if you could just manage to lift a pail of water, you would need 19 friends to help you lift that pail if it were filled with gold instead.

Despite its great density, pure gold is soft enough to cut with a knife. This makes gold the perfect metal for intricate jewelry, artwork, and many industrial components.

This gold has been heated until it has melted and is now being poured so that it can be shaped into bars.

Nuggets of gold like this are usually found in veins of the mineral quartz. Often, the gold is combined with another precious metal—silver.

Many prospectors have been misled by this very believable "look-alike" for gold. This is not a gold nugget but a sample of a mineral rich in iron rather than gold, commonly referred to as "fool's gold."

Where Gold Is Found

Gold is extremely rare, which is one of the many reasons why we value it so highly. The proportion of Earth's crust that is made of gold is only five billionths.

As gold reacts with very few other chemicals, gold prospectors (people who search for gold) usually find it in its pure form. Occasionally, they come across gold that has combined with the metals bismuth, tellurium, or selenium.

Prospectors usually extract tiny crystals of gold, just a few millimeters in size. If they are very lucky, they may come across larger lumps of gold, known as nuggets. Gold is most often found in veins of a mineral called quartz. Sometimes it is discovered in loose chunks that pepper sand or gravel. These chunks are called placer deposits. They form when gold breaks free from rocks that have eroded (worn away). Running water, wind, or rain can erode rocks like this over millions of years.

The leading areas for goldmining include South Africa, Russia, the United States, Canada, Australia, Brazil, and China. The single most productive area is the Transvaal Province of South Africa, a country that now produces over a quarter of the world's annual gold production of 3,300 tons (3,000 tonnes).

Wealth Beneath the Waves

The oceans, which cover about three-quarters of Earth's surface, contain a much higher proportion of gold than the land. On average, one cubic foot (0.09 m3) of ocean is between 1,000 and 50,000 times more likely to contain gold than one cubic foot of Earth's crust.

Rich Oceans but Poor Returns

Some 80 years ago, when people thought that there was more gold in seawater than there really is, German scientist Fritz Haber (1868–1934) was asked to find a way to extract the oceans' gold. His government wanted gold to pay the debts it had built up by the end of World War I (1914–1918).

Did You Know?

A RIVETING STORY

The design of jeans may well have been perfected during the American gold rush. At that time, people needed hard-wearing trousers with pockets that could safely store nuggets of gold. People made their trousers of rugged denim and put metal rivets around the pockets to ensure that their seams would not break.

This astronaut's tether is his lifeline. It contains strands of gold that are guaranteed never to corrode. That means the tether should not snap and cause the astronaut to drift off into space.

In fact, the proportion of gold in seawater is a mere 10 parts per trillion, so Haber succeeded only in showing that it would cost more to extract the gold than the gold would be worth.

Searching for Gold

As traces of gold have been found and used by many ancient civilizations, it is impossible to say who first discovered this metal. But historic treasures and records that survive to this day show that many early peoples had a passion for gold. Cities have been founded and expeditions and wars started by people scrabbling for more of this precious metal.

Early gold prospectors, such as those in Persia and Ancient Egypt, probably panned for gold. Using river water, they would wash sand or gravel through a sieve. Any lumps of gold would be left behind in their sieve for them to collect.

Over the centuries, people have also developed the technology to dig gold out of solid rock. In the 16th century, the Spanish invaders of South America used slave labor to mine vast amounts of gold, changing the world economy forever. The population of states like Nevada mushroomed in the 19th century as people rushed there to exploit newly discovered reserves of gold.

Gold mining is still big business, especially in South Africa. Today, gold prospectors use satellite technology and chemical rock analysis to search for new reserves. They can blast gold from rock using high-pressure water. They can even extract gold economically from low-grade ores (rocks that contain very small amounts of the metal). Gold can be dissolved from these rocks using the chemical potassium cyanide.

Precious Properties

Gold catches our eye and is attractive to many people because it shines so brilliantly. People also like it because it is so rare and precious. But gold is valued for more than its scarcity and beauty. It has several other unusual properties that make it a perfect metal for many tasks.

Most metals, such as iron and copper, corrode over time. Corrosion happens when a metal combines with another element—usually the gas oxygen in the air—to form a compound that covers the metal's surface as a dull film. Gold objects never corrode. That is why they still look new even centuries after they were made. In fact, gold does not react in any way with water, air, and most acids, or with any other common substance.

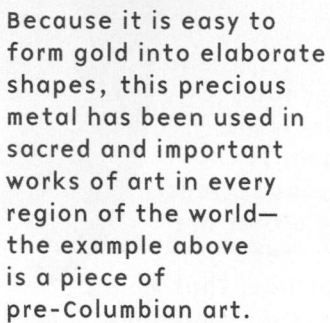

Because it is easy to form gold into elaborate shapes, this precious metal has been used in sacred and important works of art in every region of the world— the example above is a piece of pre-Columbian art.

Stamped to show its authenticity, 45 percent of the world's gold is kept under lock and key in bank vaults as bars of gold bullion.

Did You Know?

A LITTLE GOES A LONG WAY

A cube of gold the size of a plum could be beaten to form a sheet of gold leaf that could cover a tennis court, or it could be stretched to form a wire nearly 2 miles (3.2 km) long. Less than 1/250,000 in. (1/10,000 mm) thick, gold leaf can be folded and torn as easily as paper.

Bend Me, Shape Me

Pure gold is extremely malleable, which means that it is soft enough to bend or beat into many different shapes. You can beat a lump of gold with a hammer, for example, to turn it into a thin, flexible sheet of "gold leaf."

Gold is also very ductile. This means that it can be easily stretched into extremely fine wire, especially when first softened by heat.

Gold is an excellent thermal and electrical conductor—in other words, it lets heat and electricity flow through it very easily. Only silver and copper are more effective conductors of heat and electricity than gold.

Gold has these properties because of the way its atoms, the tiny particles that make it up, are arranged. Compared to most metals, gold has atoms that are bonded together very loosely. This means that they are able to slide past each other easily when only a tiny force is applied to them—for instance, when you try to bend or stretch a lump of gold.

With so many special properties, it is no wonder that gold can be put to so many different uses.

Reader Response

Open for Discussion Let's hear it for gold: its special features, its uses, its sources, where it may be found in the future. Organize a speech around those sub-topics.

1. The author writes about the fact that gold is noncorrosive. Why do you think she included this information in the article?

2. On page 609, the author states that one of the reasons gold is valuable is because it is so rare. What detail in the passage supports this idea? Is this statement supported by other details in the article?

3. What is the function of the *Did You Know?* sidebars? Why do you think the author put these pieces of information into sidebars rather than with the other text?

4. One of the characteristics of gold is that its luster never fades— it doesn't corrode. Find other phrases in the selection that you could include in a list called *Characteristics of Gold.*

Look Back and Write Why wouldn't gold prospectors be wiser to look for gold in the sea than in the hills? Read all of pages 610–611; then write a useful answer.

614

Meet the Author

Sarah Angliss

Read more books by Sarah Angliss.

Sarah Angliss is an acoustic engineer and composer who creates exhibits for institutions, including the Science Museum in London. In addition to creating new exhibits, Ms. Angliss spends her time editing video and presenting live events. She says, "When I'm not working with sound, I'm usually dreaming up new exhibits and galleries, digging out facts and stories from archives, editing video for use in theater shows, presenting live events, . . . or writing books and articles on science."

Two of Ms. Angliss's exhibits, *Booth of Truth* and *Urban Monitor,* immersed visitors in imaginary worlds through use of sound. In recent years she has toured around Great Britain with *Instant Hit Machines,* an interactive sound show.

Recently, Ms. Angliss won a Dream Time award from the National Endowment for Science, Technology, and the Arts. She is using the money to explore new ways to use sound in science centers and museums.

Cosmic Journeys: A Beginner's Guide to Space and Time Travel

Electricity and Magnets

615

Online Reference Sources

Genre

- You can find reference sources such as encyclopedias, atlases, and dictionaries on Internet Web sites.

- Some sites give you several different reference sources all in one place.

Text Features

- These electronic sources look much like printed sources, and they are usually organized the same way—often alphabetically.

- You use a computer mouse to move through an online resource instead of turning pages by hand.

Link to Science

In addition to gold, what other metals and minerals are valuable? Report your findings to the class.

The California Gold Rush

Pablo learned a lot about gold in the selection Gold. But he was also interested in the California Gold Rush and the famous "Forty-Niners." He decided to find out more by going to an online reference source run by the United States Department of State.

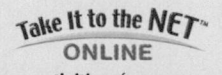
Take It to the NET™
ONLINE
more activities sfsuccessnet.com

Pablo sees that there are several reference sources on this site—biographies, fast facts, almanacs, dictionaries, encyclopedias, and sources of quotations, as well as other Web sites. He clicks on one of the encyclopedia links.

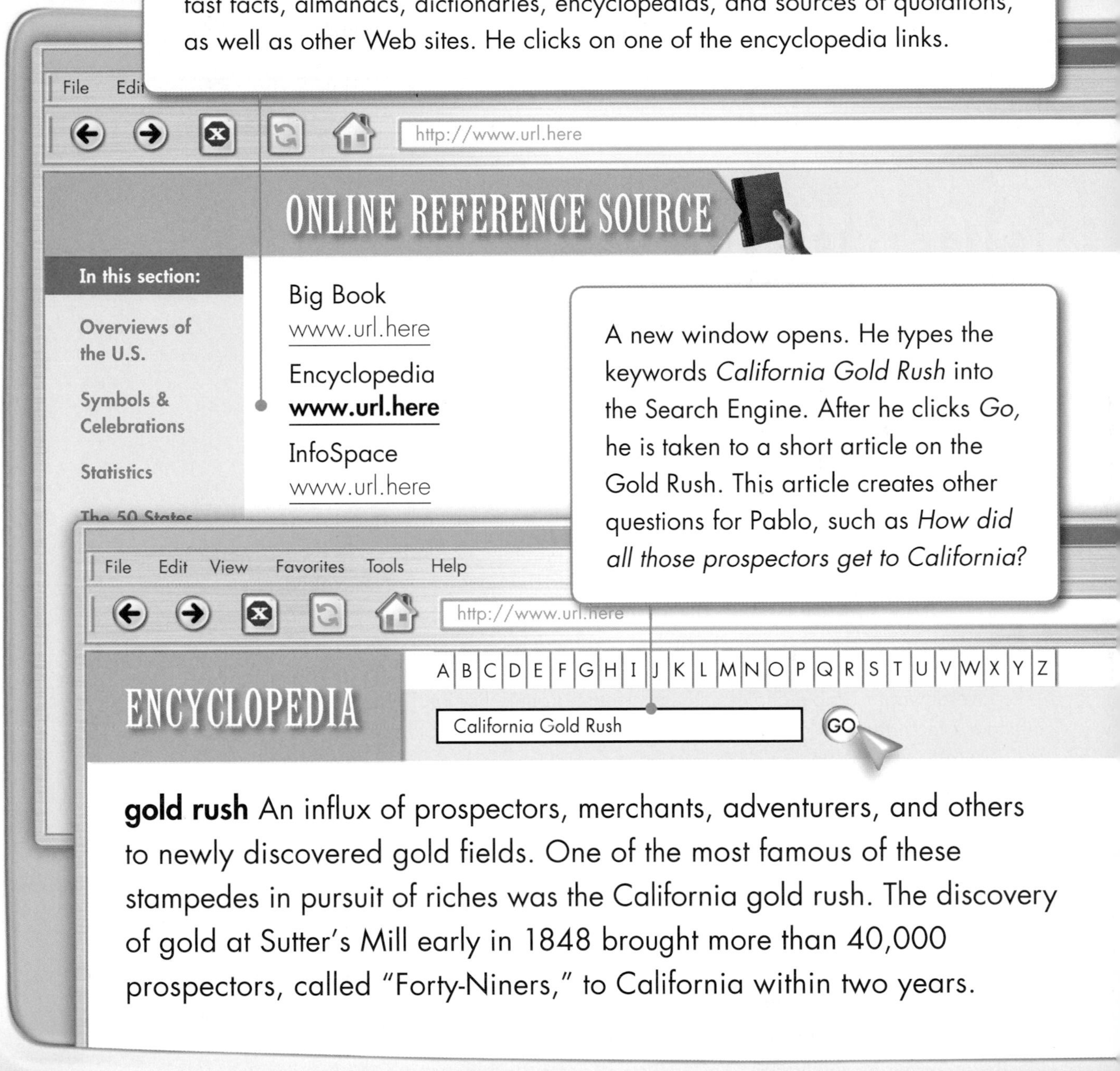

File   Edit

http://www.url.here

ONLINE REFERENCE SOURCE

In this section:

Overviews of the U.S.

Symbols & Celebrations

Statistics

The 50 States

Big Book
www.url.here

Encyclopedia
www.url.here

InfoSpace
www.url.here

A new window opens. He types the keywords *California Gold Rush* into the Search Engine. After he clicks *Go*, he is taken to a short article on the Gold Rush. This article creates other questions for Pablo, such as *How did all those prospectors get to California?*

File   Edit   View   Favorites   Tools   Help

http://www.url.here

A B C D E F G H I J K L M N O P Q R S T U V W X Y Z

ENCYCLOPEDIA

California Gold Rush   GO

gold rush An influx of prospectors, merchants, adventurers, and others to newly discovered gold fields. One of the most famous of these stampedes in pursuit of riches was the California gold rush. The discovery of gold at Sutter's Mill early in 1848 brought more than 40,000 prospectors, called "Forty-Niners," to California within two years.

Main Idea & Details   The link you click on is actually a topic.

Pablo types in *Forty-Niners* and searches again. He finds this Web site from a state university. This is what he reads:

The Gold Rush

"The reports of the gold regions are as encouraging here as they were back in Massachusetts. Just imagine yourself seeing me return with $10,000 to $100,000."

— ANONYMOUS '49ER

The Journey

Sea Route

The departing gold-seekers, called "Forty-Niners," faced an immediate problem. California was far away. There was no railroad to whisk them west; no river to float them to California. Instead, the journey would be a painful test of endurance.

There were two miserable choices. The sea route around the tip of South America often took more than six months. The sea route was favored by gold seekers from the eastern states. but on a ship, seasickness was rampant; food was often full of bugs or rancid. Water stored for months on a ship was almost impossible to drink.

For Americans who lived in the central states, there was another way west: the Oregon-California Trail. The overland road was much shorter than the sea route, but it wasn't faster. Most had no idea how severe the overland journey would be.

Oregon-California Trail

All they could think about was gold as they plodded alongside covered wagons at two miles per hour—for up to six months.

The real danger of the overland journey was the lack of water. At some points there were no water resources at all, and some people would die of thirst. A number of people in California heard of this and they came out with just about anything filled with water. They would sell the water for $1 a glass or more. The price for water could go as high as $100 per drink. Those without money were sometimes left to die. It was a lesson in supply and demand in frontier California.

The Gold Rush

On the same university Web site, Pablo comes across a link to *Fun Facts about the Gold Rush.* This is what he found:

Weird Ways West

A California-bound airline in 1849!? Don't laugh; it almost happened. Rufus Porter, founder of *Scientific American* magazine, planned to fly '49ers west on propeller-driven balloons. He advertised the expedition, and 200 brave souls signed up for the trip. But the "airline" never got off the ground.

Then there was the "wind wagon," sort of a cross between a sailboat and a wagon. A prototype was built, and for a brief moment it barreled across the plains at the advertised 15 miles-per-hour. Then it went out of control and crashed. The inventor—Frederick "Wind-wagon" Thomas—kept trying for years to make his invention work, but never succeeded.

Frederick Thomas's "wind wagon".

Others took another approach, making the trip with only a wheelbarrow. It's hard to imagine pushing a fully-loaded wheelbarrow for 2,000 miles, but several dozen attempted the trip. For a time, they could outpace everything on the Trail, but human endurance has its limits. No one is quite sure if any of them made it all the way with their wheelbarrows.

Why all the weird contraptions? Everyone was in a big hurry to get west—to strike it rich.

Reading Across Texts

What do you learn about gold's effects on people from reading these selections?

Writing Across Texts In a paragraph or two, compare what you think are the good things that gold brings to people against the bad it can cause.

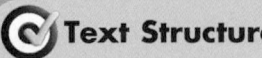 **Text Structure**   How would the text structure help you summarize this article?

Sequence

- Sequence refers to the order of events or the steps of a process.

- Dates, times, and clue words such as *first, next, then,* and *last* can help you determine the order of events.

- Sometimes a text will present events out of order. In this case, you can read on, review, or reread the text in order to learn the correct sequence of events.

First Event	Second Event	Third Event	Fourth Event

Strategy: Monitor and Fix Up

One strategy good readers use to get back on track when they are confused is to keep reading. Often your confusion will be cleared up once you read the entire section or text. Reading on allows you to learn about all of the events before placing them in their correct sequence. You can also reread and review to make sure you have the order correct.

 **Write**

1. Read "July 8, 1933." Make a graphic organizer like the one above in order to show the sequence of important events in the story.

2. Write a paragraph summarizing the actual sequence of places where the diary writer has lived.

JULY 8, 1933

We are on the move again, looking for suitable housing and wondering whence our next substantial meal will come. We just left the city and are heading off into a more rural area of the state.

A few weeks ago we found decent shelter at an abandoned motel. Father found us what we needed, and we had a few reasonable weeks there until the police evicted us. Now we are on the road once more, doing our best to get by.

It is decidedly different from the old days—our spacious house, the gorgeous, tree-lined street we lived on. Oh, I wish we could go back to that time. This "Great Depression," as it is being called, has certainly altered our lives.

When these horrible economic problems first started, we were able to retain the house, but then the bank claimed it. Father packed us in the car, and we motored off to the city to locate an apartment. That worked for a while until we couldn't pay the rent and had to leave.

Strategy Since it is difficult to determine the order of events from this first paragraph, you should read on. What words or phrases in this paragraph tell you that the event that takes place *first* in this story is not mentioned in this paragraph?

Skill What clue words tell you these events take place before the first paragraph?

Skill Is the time described in this paragraph one of the first or last items in the sequence of events? How can you tell?

Strategy Why might you need to reread or review and think about this last paragraph?

621

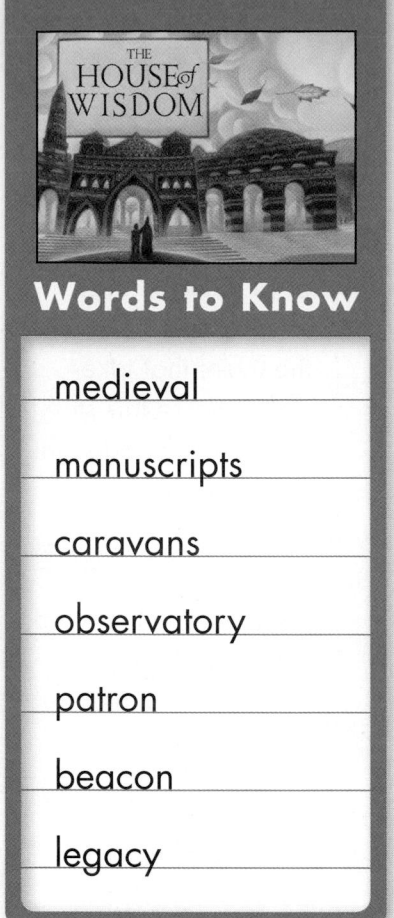

Words to Know

medieval

manuscripts

caravans

observatory

patron

beacon

legacy

Vocabulary Strategy
for Unfamiliar Words

Dictionary/Glossary Dictionaries and glossaries provide lists of words and their meanings. Glossaries appear at the back of some books and list definitions for important words in the books. Dictionaries list many more words and provide pronunciations, parts of speech, and spellings as well as definitions.

1. If you come to an unfamiliar word as you read, you can look up the word in the glossary at the back of the book or in a dictionary.

2. If you are using a dictionary, use guide words to help you locate the word. Guide words appear in dark type at the top of each page and show the first and last words on that page.

3. When you find the correct entry word (usually in boldfaced type), look at all the meanings listed. Try the one that seems most appropriate.

4. If the meaning you choose doesn't make sense, try another meaning.

As you read "Shining Cities," use the glossary in this book or a dictionary to help you find out the meanings of new words.

SHINING CITIES

In medieval times, Europe was a "dark" place. Learning and the sciences had fallen by the wayside. Only a few people, such as officials of the church, could read and write. Most people did not go to school. Monks carefully lettered religious manuscripts with beautiful illustrations, but few people could read them. These books were shut in monasteries. They were kept safe, but they were not shared.

However, at that same time, some cities in the Far East and Middle East shone brightly. Gold, spices, silk, and many other goods traveled by caravans over thousands of miles for trade. Scientists studied the sky from an observatory and discovered truths about the world. Wise rulers summoned the most learned people and collected their knowledge. They understood that by being a patron to the sciences and arts, they could improve the world. In these places, knowledge shone like a beacon to the world. Thanks to their legacy, much of the learning of past ages was not lost to the world.

Write

Look at the illustrations in *The House of Wisdom*. Choose one to write about. Imagine being a scholar in the Middle East or Far East and wanting to learn. Use as many words from the Words to Know list as you can.

THE
HOUSE of
WISDOM

by Florence Parry Heide & Judith Heide Gilliland

illustrated by Mary GrandPré

What inspires the desire for knowledge?

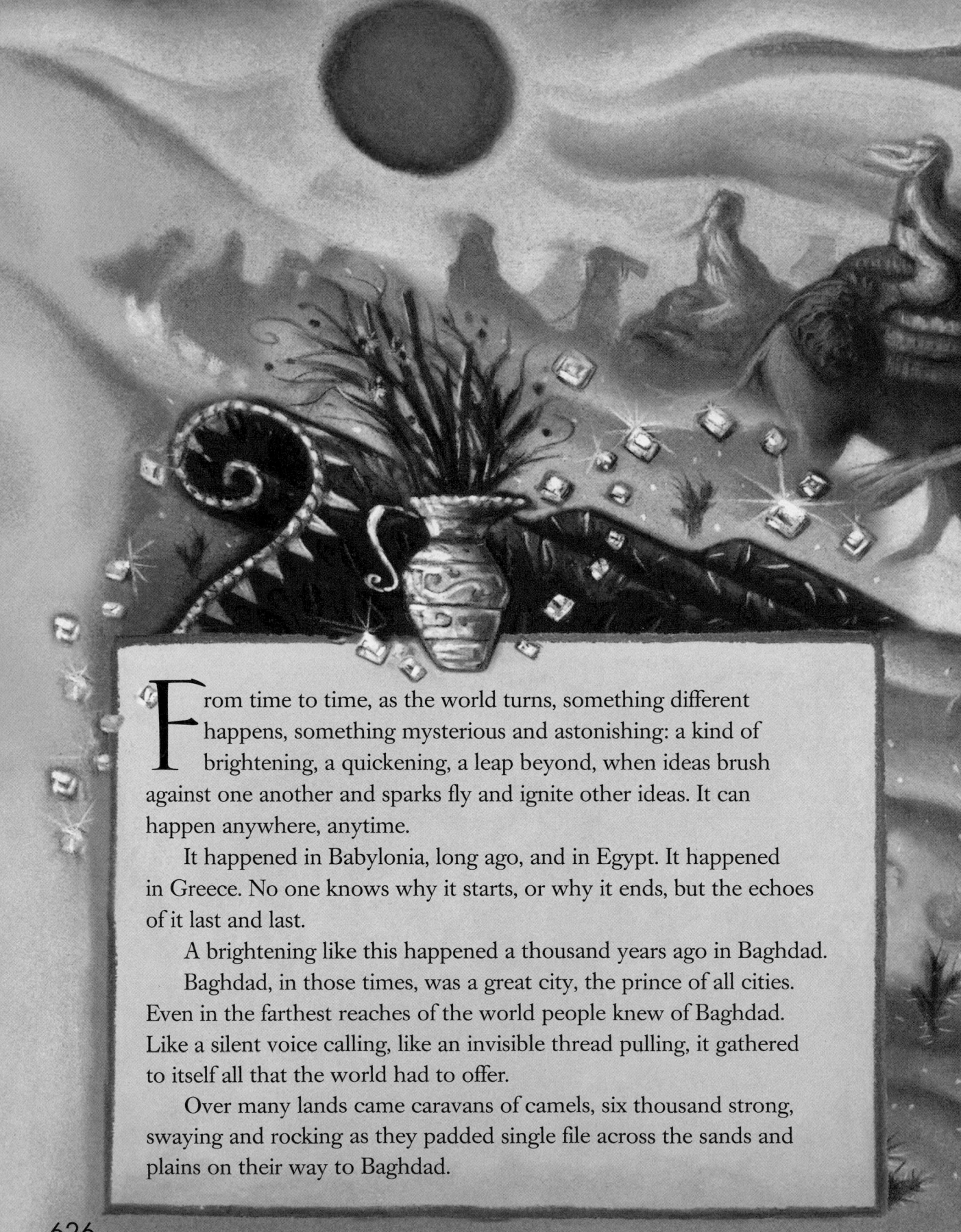

From time to time, as the world turns, something different happens, something mysterious and astonishing: a kind of brightening, a quickening, a leap beyond, when ideas brush against one another and sparks fly and ignite other ideas. It can happen anywhere, anytime.

It happened in Babylonia, long ago, and in Egypt. It happened in Greece. No one knows why it starts, or why it ends, but the echoes of it last and last.

A brightening like this happened a thousand years ago in Baghdad.

Baghdad, in those times, was a great city, the prince of all cities. Even in the farthest reaches of the world people knew of Baghdad. Like a silent voice calling, like an invisible thread pulling, it gathered to itself all that the world had to offer.

Over many lands came caravans of camels, six thousand strong, swaying and rocking as they padded single file across the sands and plains on their way to Baghdad.

They carried porcelain and silks from China, cinnamon and cardamom from India, perfumes and brocades from Persia, gold and diamonds from Africa.

And along with the silk and the gold and the spices came something else: ancient books filled with treasures of their own, filled with ideas and knowledge from other places, other times.

The caravans came. The dust rose and the sun burned, and still they came.

And across seas and up rivers and into the crowded harbor of Baghdad sailed ships, ships of all kinds, some shaped like dolphins, some like eagles, some like lions. They came carrying fragrant musk and brilliant dyes, rubies and lapis lazuli, pearls and daggers.

And with these treasures came the other riches, the books and manuscripts from far and forgotten times.

The ships came. The winds blew and the waves crashed, and still they came.

Now the ruler of Baghdad at that time was the Caliph al-Ma'mun. He enjoyed his riches and everything that his gold could buy. But of all the treasures that came to Baghdad by land and by sea, he most valued the books.

He built a great library to hold them, and he called it the House of Wisdom. But it was more than a house, it was more than a library, it was more even than a palace. It was the very center of the brightening that was Baghdad.

The House of Wisdom became like a beacon, drawing to itself a thousand scholars from all over the world. They came to read the precious books, books that had been written in languages and alphabets that only scholars could read: ancient Greek and Syriac, Persian and Sanskrit. Once the scholars had translated these books into Arabic, everyone could read them and share their ideas.

And as these ideas sparked new ideas, Baghdad shone brighter.

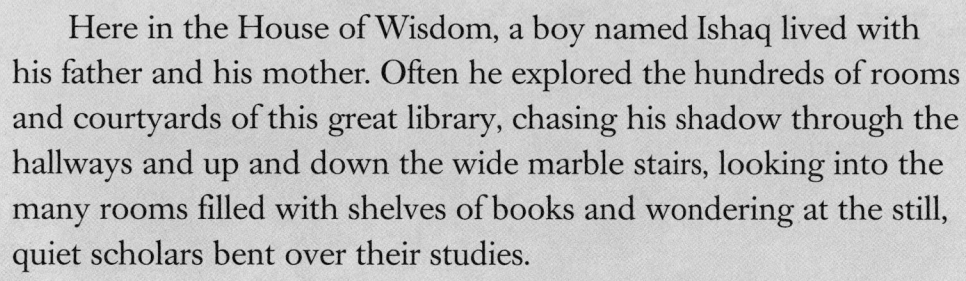

Here in the House of Wisdom, a boy named Ishaq lived with his father and his mother. Often he explored the hundreds of rooms and courtyards of this great library, chasing his shadow through the hallways and up and down the wide marble stairs, looking into the many rooms filled with shelves of books and wondering at the still, quiet scholars bent over their studies.

Ishaq's father, Hunayn, worked all day at his books. He was the best translator in all of Baghdad. The Caliph himself so prized Hunayn's translations that for each completed manuscript, the Caliph gave him its equal weight in gold. But Ishaq knew it was not the gold that was important to his father. It was something else, something that could not be weighed or touched or measured or found even in Baghdad's famous market.

The souk, Baghdad's crowded marketplace, offered almost everything imaginable. It seemed that all the world came there to buy and sell. Ishaq watched the crowds of people from faraway places with curiosity: Russian traders in fur caps, Indians in white dhotis, Turks in billowing pantaloons, Africans in brilliant orange robes. They spoke in languages he had never heard.

"They speak so strangely," Ishaq whispered one day.

"You may not understand them, but that does not mean they have nothing to say," said Hunayn.

Later that night Ishaq looked for his father and found him in his study, reading a manuscript in Greek.

"You are so often alone here, Father," he said.

Hunayn smiled and touched the book before him. "I am never alone. I am with Aristotle, who reaches out to me across time and shows us how to search for the answers. That searching is the great adventure; it is the fire in our hearts."

"But he lived a thousand years ago. People did not know much then," Ishaq said. "They were not like us."

"They were not so different," said Hunayn. "And the ones who come after us will not be so different either. We are like leaves of the same tree, separated by many autumns."

When Ishaq left his father's study, he climbed the stairs around and around and up and up to his favorite room. There the scholars studied the stars and measured the earth. Aristotle would have looked at these same stars a thousand years ago. And someday someone in the future would look at them and wonder too. *Maybe it is only time that separates us,* he thought. There was so much to know.

"I want to be a man of learning," he decided. "Like my father. Like Aristotle."

And so, many mornings Ishaq sat with his books, reading the ancient Greek words one at a time, then writing them in Arabic, slowly. How different it was when he threw the javelin, when he raced his horse, or when he hunted the wild boar with the cheetah. Then the time flew! But studying was long, difficult, slow work.

He thought of his father's joy when a special manuscript had come to him through time and distance, by camel and by ship. How could ancient words mean so much? Yes, he wanted to be a scholar, but he also wanted to travel, to explore the world.

"I wish I could lead one of the Caliph's expeditions in search of books," he told his father.

"One day you will; seeing the world is part of becoming a learned man. But first you must study, you must prepare yourself, you must make room in your head and in your heart for all you will see."

So Ishaq studied, he read, he translated. He became a good student, even a scholar. He learned about astronomy and mathematics, about geography and medicine. He studied the writings of ancient Greek thinkers such as Galen and Plato and Hippocrates.

But still he did not feel the fire.

And then one day the Caliph chose Ishaq to lead an expedition to search for books. Now he could explore! At last he would see the world.

His father went with him to the great caravansary, where the drivers and their camels had gathered in preparation for the long journey. He embraced Ishaq. "On your travels you will learn much— from the storyteller in rags, from the birds, from the stars. It will all become part of you."

Ishaq rode by camel and horse through desert and plain, along well-traveled roads and desolate trails. He sailed from river to sea and from port to port.

He listened to the trumpeting of elephants beside the Ganges and talked with learned scholars in fragrant gardens in Persia.

He hunted the crocodile along the Nile and wrapped himself against fierce sandstorms in the Sahara.

To Cordova and Samarkand, to India and China he traveled, visiting distant cities and hidden cloisters. And everywhere he went he met holy men and merchants, adventurers and explorers. They brought him books, for they knew he paid handsomely for them in the name of the Caliph.

Everything he saw and heard and felt was new and strange, but for the rising of the sun each day and the canopy of stars at night.

In Athens he walked the streets that Aristotle had once walked. He thought of Aristotle surrounded by students. For a moment he imagined he was one of them, and felt a quickening in his mind. Maybe the ideas they shared, the excitement they felt, could reach across time.

He traveled even to the west, to the dark, ruined land of the barbarians. Here the people were superstitious. In this land scarcely anyone could read or write. But hidden away in hills and forests and caves there lived quiet, robed monks who spent their days copying old books, saving what little wisdom and learning they could in those dark times.

Ishaq thought of the thousand scholars bent over their books in the House of Wisdom, their lanterns shining deep into the night. He longed for home.

But he continued his journey, everywhere gathering more books. There were so many books and manuscripts that Ishaq could not know them all, armfuls and basketfuls of books of all kinds, pages of books, pieces of books, old and forgotten books.

For three years he traveled the world.

At last it was time to return home to Baghdad. He wondered if he was now ready to live the life of a scholar.

As his ship finally entered the harbor of Baghdad one summer night, Ishaq looked to the House of Wisdom on the hillside.

It seemed to him that the lights of the scholars' lanterns were like new stars that had come close to Earth, and that the glow of those lanterns might reach to the darkness of the land he had seen.

Ishaq saw his father and mother waiting on the dock, and he hurried to meet them. They embraced for a long time.

Hunayn looked into Ishaq's eyes. "You have grown in many ways, my son."

"I have learned many things, Father. But come and see what I have brought you," Ishaq said proudly. "Manuscripts from Damascus and Alexandria, from Aleppo and Constantinople and Tripoli. Hundreds and hundreds, Father, thousands and thousands!"

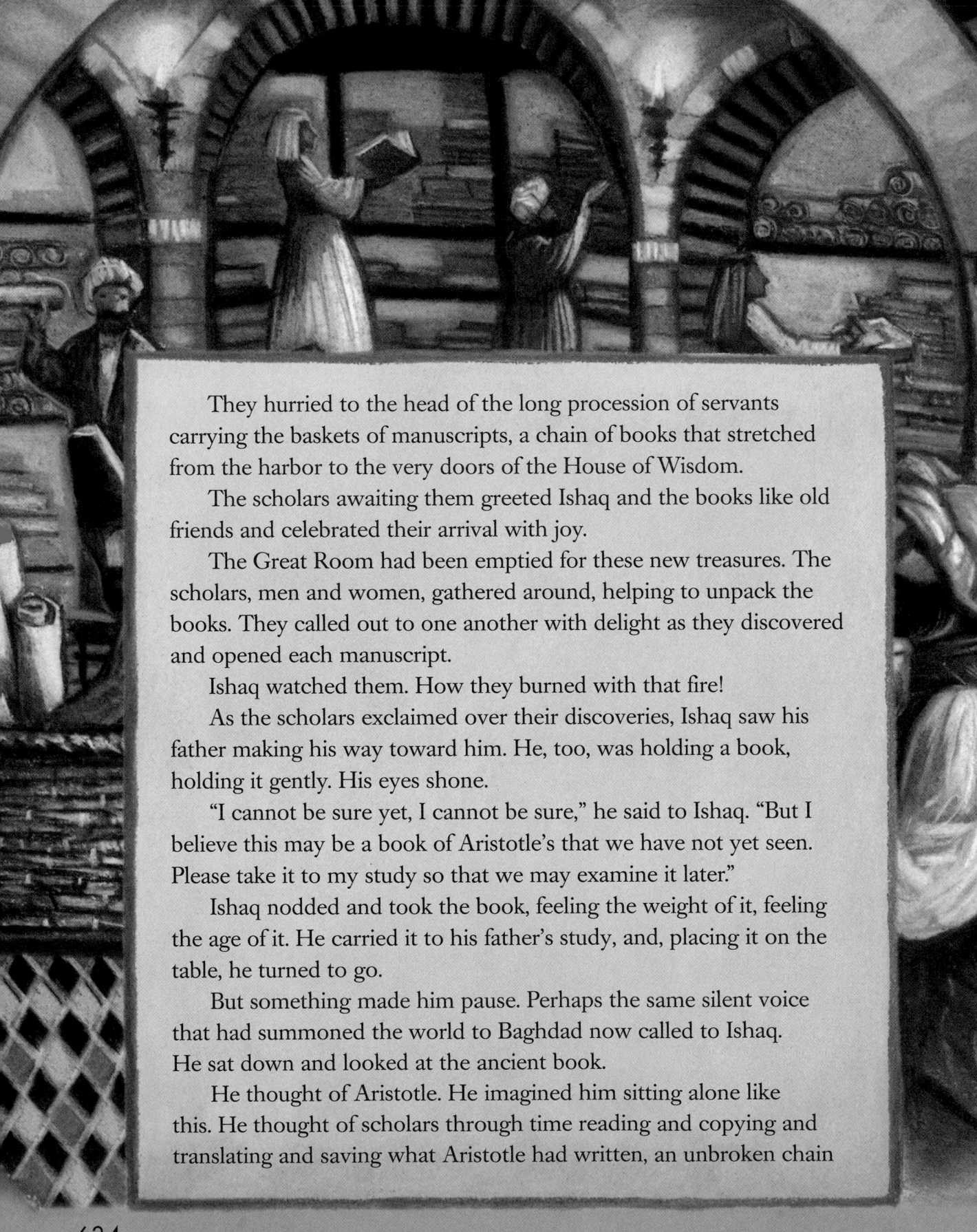

They hurried to the head of the long procession of servants carrying the baskets of manuscripts, a chain of books that stretched from the harbor to the very doors of the House of Wisdom.

The scholars awaiting them greeted Ishaq and the books like old friends and celebrated their arrival with joy.

The Great Room had been emptied for these new treasures. The scholars, men and women, gathered around, helping to unpack the books. They called out to one another with delight as they discovered and opened each manuscript.

Ishaq watched them. How they burned with that fire!

As the scholars exclaimed over their discoveries, Ishaq saw his father making his way toward him. He, too, was holding a book, holding it gently. His eyes shone.

"I cannot be sure yet, I cannot be sure," he said to Ishaq. "But I believe this may be a book of Aristotle's that we have not yet seen. Please take it to my study so that we may examine it later."

Ishaq nodded and took the book, feeling the weight of it, feeling the age of it. He carried it to his father's study, and, placing it on the table, he turned to go.

But something made him pause. Perhaps the same silent voice that had summoned the world to Baghdad now called to Ishaq. He sat down and looked at the ancient book.

He thought of Aristotle. He imagined him sitting alone like this. He thought of scholars through time reading and copying and translating and saving what Aristotle had written, an unbroken chain

leading all the way to Baghdad, all the way to Ishaq, a thousand years later.

And then, lighting the lantern, he began to read.

As Ishaq read, he felt that Aristotle was in the room with him, was at his side, was speaking to him. He felt he was lighting a candle for him, a flame to guide him.

He did not notice that the moon had set, or that his father had looked in on him, had smiled and quietly closed the door.

When Ishaq looked up, he saw that it was morning. As he looked out the window at the trees in the courtyard and then at the book before him, he finally understood what his father had meant

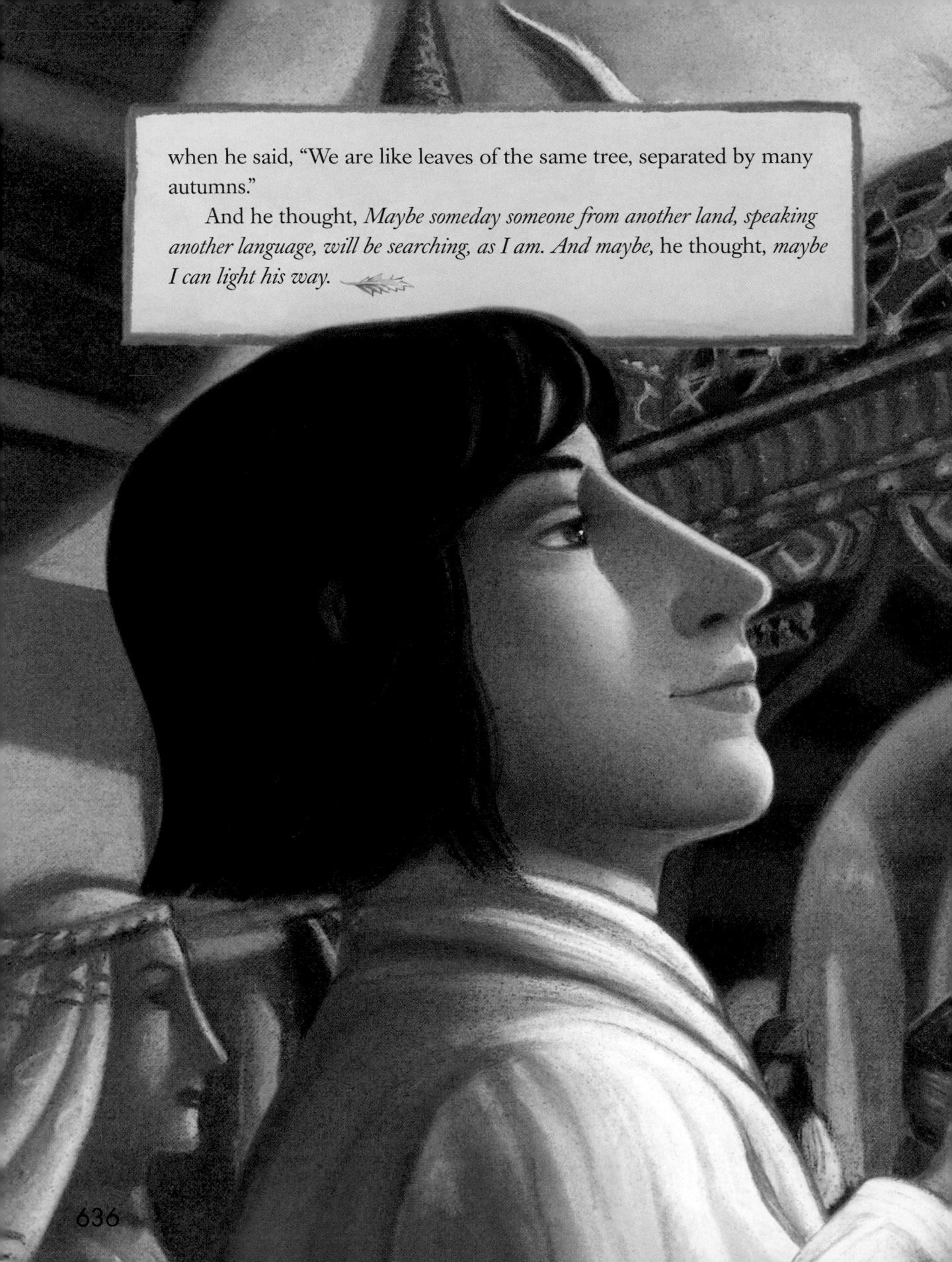

when he said, "We are like leaves of the same tree, separated by many autumns."

And he thought, *Maybe someday someone from another land, speaking another language, will be searching, as I am. And maybe,* he thought, *maybe I can light his way.*

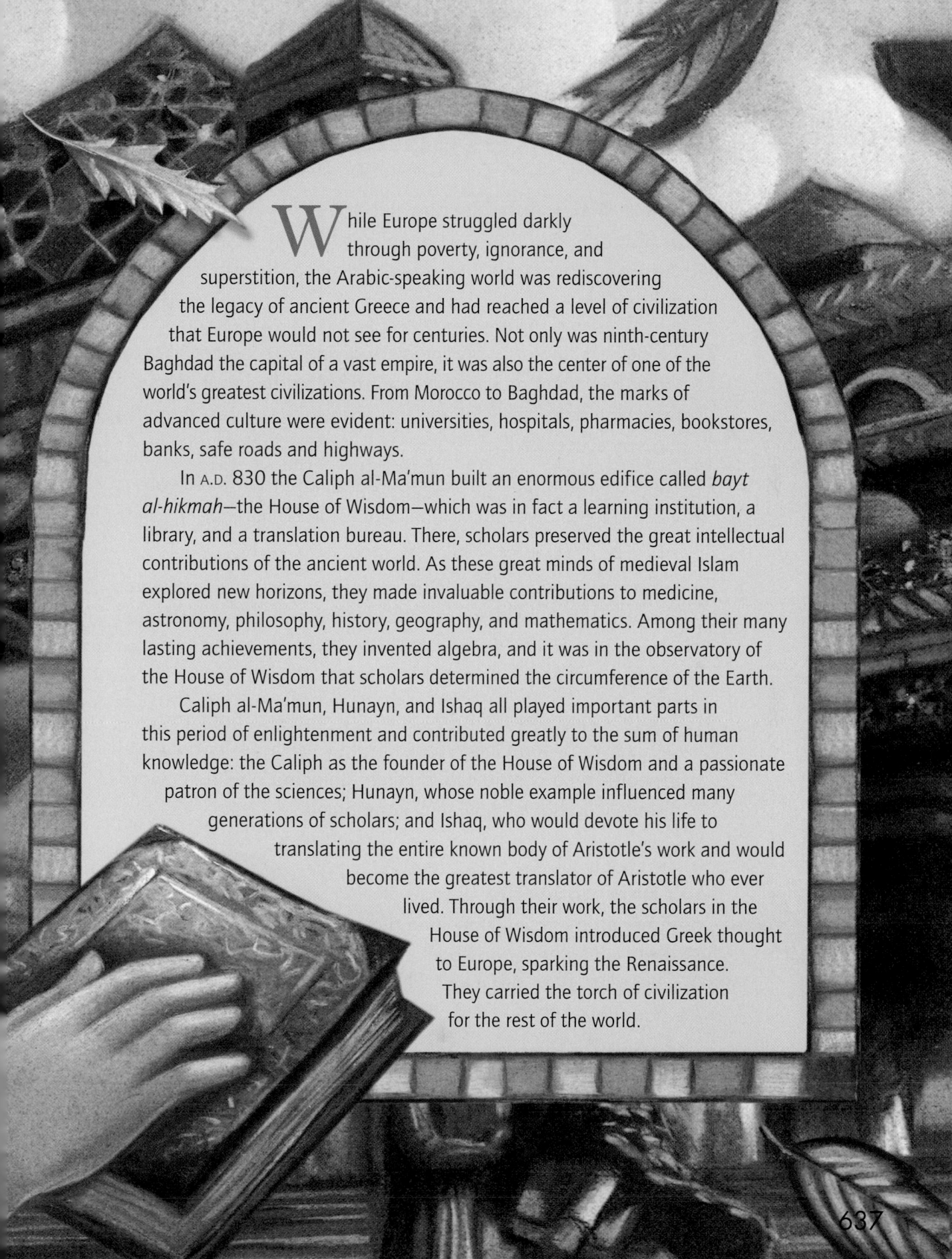

While Europe struggled darkly through poverty, ignorance, and superstition, the Arabic-speaking world was rediscovering the legacy of ancient Greece and had reached a level of civilization that Europe would not see for centuries. Not only was ninth-century Baghdad the capital of a vast empire, it was also the center of one of the world's greatest civilizations. From Morocco to Baghdad, the marks of advanced culture were evident: universities, hospitals, pharmacies, bookstores, banks, safe roads and highways.

In A.D. 830 the Caliph al-Ma'mun built an enormous edifice called *bayt al-hikmah*—the House of Wisdom—which was in fact a learning institution, a library, and a translation bureau. There, scholars preserved the great intellectual contributions of the ancient world. As these great minds of medieval Islam explored new horizons, they made invaluable contributions to medicine, astronomy, philosophy, history, geography, and mathematics. Among their many lasting achievements, they invented algebra, and it was in the observatory of the House of Wisdom that scholars determined the circumference of the Earth.

Caliph al-Ma'mun, Hunayn, and Ishaq all played important parts in this period of enlightenment and contributed greatly to the sum of human knowledge: the Caliph as the founder of the House of Wisdom and a passionate patron of the sciences; Hunayn, whose noble example influenced many generations of scholars; and Ishaq, who would devote his life to translating the entire known body of Aristotle's work and would become the greatest translator of Aristotle who ever lived. Through their work, the scholars in the House of Wisdom introduced Greek thought to Europe, sparking the Renaissance. They carried the torch of civilization for the rest of the world.

Reader Response

Open for Discussion   Reading this true tale, you reach halfway across history to find Ishaq, who reaches halfway across history to find Aristotle. Why is this trip through time important to the scholars of Baghdad? to you?

1. The authors and artist are intent on giving you setting: time and place. Examine one layout (words and illustration), then look away and describe what you saw. Have the authors, the artist, and you succeeded?

2. Using a world map, the story, and a dictionary to help you with modern names for ancient places, trace the journey Ishaq may have taken from Baghdad.

3. Reread pages 634–636. What did Ishaq's father mean when he said, "We are like leaves of the same tree, separated by many autumns"? How does understanding this quote help you understand the meaning of the story?

4. The story talks about the "brightening" that was Baghdad. Choose words from the Words to Know list that tell about events or people who contributed to this brightening. Write the words in sentences that tell how they contributed.

Look Back and Write   Ishaq's life was changed by travel. How long did he travel—and when? Look back at pages 632–633, and then write your answer.

WISDOM

Read another book by the authors and the illustrator.

Florence Parry Heide (pronounced "high-dee") got a late start as an author. She began writing books only after all five of her children had started school. She says, "It is magical that something I might think of can be put into words, stories, ideas, and that those words end up in the heads of readers I will never meet."

Florence Parry Heide's daughter, **Judith Heide Gilliland**, lived for five years in the Middle East. Mother and daughter teamed up to write *The House of Wisdom* and two other award-winning books set in that region.

Sami and the Time of the Troubles
by Florence Parry Heide and Judith Heide Gilliland

Mary GrandPré's art has received numerous awards, and her illustrations for the Harry Potter books were featured on the cover of *TIME* magazine.

When asked in an interview if she had advice for young illustrators, she replied, "I would just say keep working hard and don't give up. Illustration, like any form of art, is up for criticism, but it has to come from the heart or it's not good. If you're not enjoying what you're doing, keep trying new things because your best work will come from work you enjoy."

Batwings and the Curtain of Night
illustrated by Mary GrandPré

Folk
Literature

Folk Tale

Genre

- A folk tale is a story from a particular culture handed down for generations until someone writes it down.

- The same folk tale may have different versions because different storytellers have changed or added their own details.

Link to Writing

Continue the story. Write what you think the greedy magician might do next. How does Aladdin escape?

Around the time that libraries were being established in the Middle East, other literature was being preserved orally by storytellers. These tales, now called the Arabian Nights, *began to be collected and written down in the ninth century. Here is a portion of one of the best-known of these stories.*

Aladdin

retold by Bonnie Vaughan

Once there lived a magician who longed to possess all the treasures of the world. One night he lit a magic potion and chanted a spell. Through the smoke, he saw a vision of a mountain and a dark cave sealed by a stone slab with a gleaming copper ring on top. Only a boy named Aladdin, living in China, could open the stone and obtain the unimaginable riches inside. The magician traveled to China, where he found the boy among silks and fragrant spices in a market. Posing as Aladdin's long-lost uncle, he grabbed the boy and took him to the mountain. There he chanted another spell, causing a loud clap of thunder. The earth trembled and a huge hole tore into the mountain. Above the hole was a stone slab and a copper ring.

Sequence In folk literature, events are told in their correct order.

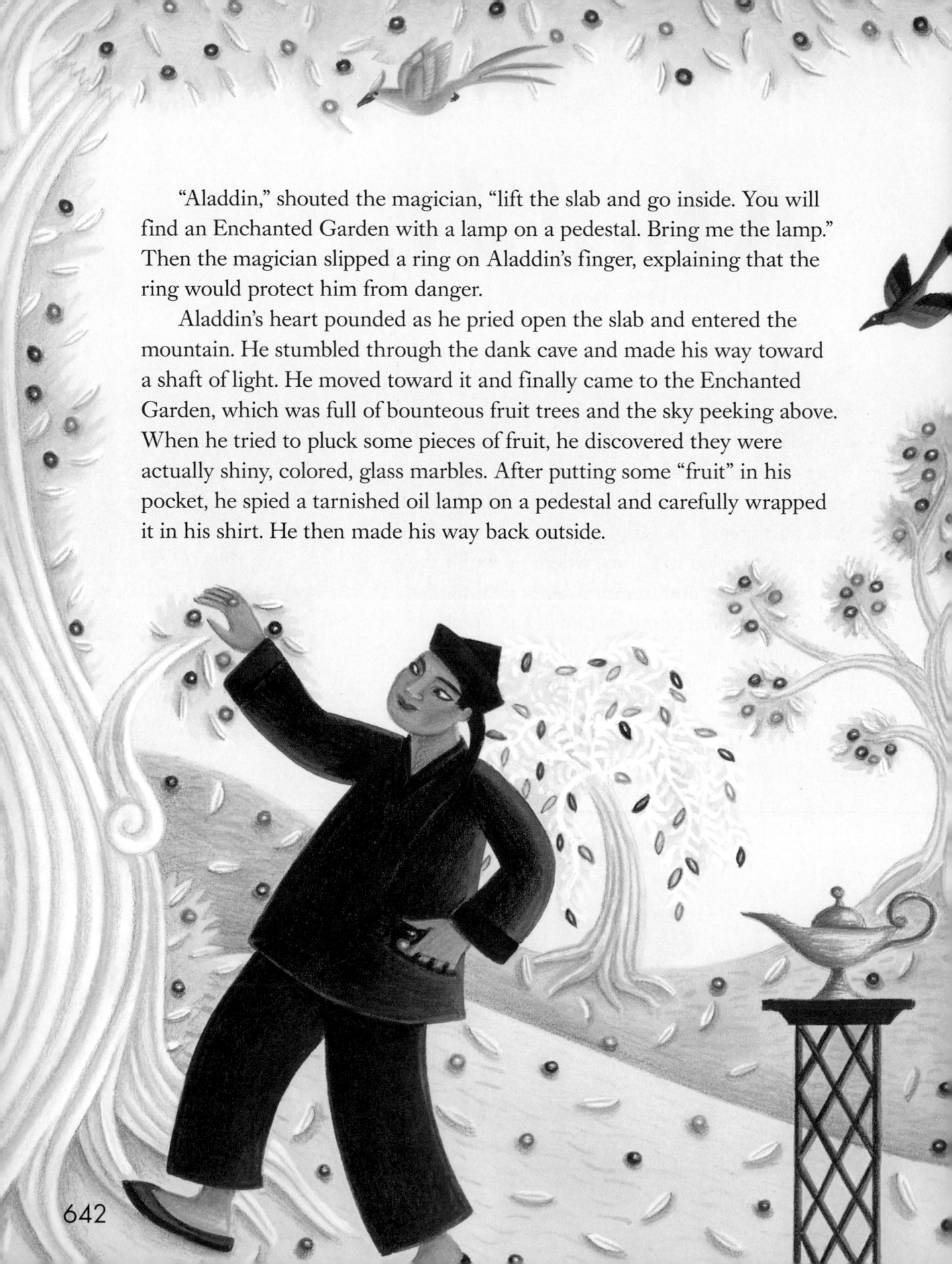

"Aladdin," shouted the magician, "lift the slab and go inside. You will find an Enchanted Garden with a lamp on a pedestal. Bring me the lamp." Then the magician slipped a ring on Aladdin's finger, explaining that the ring would protect him from danger.

Aladdin's heart pounded as he pried open the slab and entered the mountain. He stumbled through the dank cave and made his way toward a shaft of light. He moved toward it and finally came to the Enchanted Garden, which was full of bounteous fruit trees and the sky peeking above. When he tried to pluck some pieces of fruit, he discovered they were actually shiny, colored, glass marbles. After putting some "fruit" in his pocket, he spied a tarnished oil lamp on a pedestal and carefully wrapped it in his shirt. He then made his way back outside.

The magician awaited him and tried to snatch the lamp from Aladdin as he approached the opening of the cave. As the two scuffled over the lamp, Aladdin stumbled and fell back into the cave. The stone slab slammed shut, and the enraged magician was left without the lamp or access to the cave. Meanwhile Aladdin realized that he was trapped in the cave. He cried and wrung his hands together, rubbing the magician's ring by mistake. Immediately, a huge and terrifying genie billowed out saying, "I am the slave of the ring. Master, I will give you whatever you wish." Aladdin wished he were back home, and he suddenly found himself whirling through space. Soon he was in his kitchen telling his mother about his strange adventure.

Aladdin's poor mother had no money to buy food for her hungry son. "Go sell this dirty lamp," she said. When she began to polish it, another genie—this one more formidable than the last—appeared in a puff of smoke. "I am the genie of the lamp. What is your wish?" he thundered. Aladdin wished for food, and immediately a silver tray appeared, full of roast meats, ripe fruits, and luscious pastries. After this feast, Aladdin showed the glass "fruits" from the Enchanted Garden to his mother. She gasped as she held each one to the light, exclaiming, "These are rubies, emeralds, and sapphires, not marbles." Aladdin and his mother never lived in poverty again.

But in a faraway land, the greedy magician still lived, resenting Aladdin's good fortune and determined to get revenge. Aladdin had not yet seen the last of the magician or his fiendish deeds.

Reading Across Texts

Compare and contrast the "treasures" that Ishaq and Aladdin had.

Writing Across Texts Tell which boy you think had the most lasting treasure and why.

Monitor & Fix Up How can you get on track if you get confused reading fiction?

FOR THE EARTH DAY CONTEST

by Bobbi Katz

Someday there may be no "away"
to throw stuff anymore,
so we better all start thinking
and we better know the score.
We better ask some questions
about the things we choose:
Do we want a certain something
to use
   and use
      and use?
When it's broken, small, or empty,
will that be that something's end?

Can we fix it?
   Can we fill it?
      Can we give it to a friend?
Can we make that something something else
   or will that something be
      just a use-it-one-time-toss-it-out,
        a trash-it—1-2-3?
The garbage trucks
   roll
      down
        the streets
when it is garbage day.
But where will they be rolling to
when there is no "away"?

PODS POP AND GRIN

by James Berry

Strong strong sun, in that look
you have, lands ripen
fruits, trees, people.

Lands love the flame of your gaze.
Lands hide some warmth
of sun-eye for darkness.

All for you pods pop and grin.
Bananas hurry up and grow.
Coconut becomes water and oil.

Palm trees try to fly to you
but just dance everywhere.
Silk leaves of bamboo rustle wild.

And when the rain finished falling
winds shake diamonds from branches
that again feel your eye.

Strong strong sun, in you
lands keep ripening
fruits, trees, people.

Birds go on tuning up
and don't care at all—
more blood berries are coming.

Your look strokes up all
summertime. We hear streams running.
You come back every day.

maggie and milly and molly and may…

by e.e. cummings

maggie and milly and molly and may
went down to the beach (to play one day)

and maggie discovered a shell that sang
so sweetly she couldn't remember her troubles, and

milly befriended a stranded star
whose rays five languid fingers were;

and molly was chased by a horrible thing
which raced sideways while blowing bubbles: and

may came home with a smooth round stone
as small as a world and as large as alone.

For whatever we lose (like a you or a me)
it's always ourselves we find in the sea

Maple Talk

by Lilian Moore

Plant us.
Let our roots go
deeply down.
We'll hold the soil
when rain tugs
at the earth.

Plant us.
You will better know
how seasons come
and go.

Watch for
our leaves unfurling
in spring green,

our leafy roofs of summer
over pools of shade,

our sunset red and gold
igniting autumn's blaze.

When cold winds
leave us bare
we'll show you treetop nests
where songbirds hid
their young.

And when
in early spring
the sweet sap flows again,
have syrup for your pancakes!

Plant us.

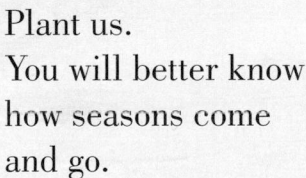

Special Person Celebration

connect to
**SOCIAL
STUDIES**

Choose a person in your community whom you consider to be a community treasure. How could you let others know what makes this person so valuable? Plan a community event that would celebrate the special skills, talents, or knowledge that makes this person a unique resource.

Person	Why Valuable	How to Celebrate

What are resources and why are they important to us?

connect to
SOCIAL STUDIES

The Gift That Keeps On Giving

Sit in a circle with a group of classmates. Talk about how the prizes that Noah handed out at the wedding in *The View from Saturday* led other guests to offer a prize in return.

Then one person in the circle will name a resource that he or she could give another person in the circle. (It should not be something you buy. It may be something you cannot see or touch.)

Have the next person think of a resource that he or she could give another person in the group. Continue around the circle until everyone has shared an idea.

> I would help Alex study for the math test.

connect to
WRITING

Preserving a Resource

Write a newspaper editorial. Persuade readers about the importance of one of the characters or natural resources in a selection from this unit. Explain why and how the work of this person or this natural resource must be preserved.

Rivers are one of our most important natural resources. They provide drinking water for animals and people and irrigation for plants. When River went to the sky, the animals

649

Exploring Cultures

In what ways does one culture affect another?

Skill
Author's Purpose

Strategy
Ask Questions

Skill

Author's Purpose

- Authors have different reasons for writing. They may write to persuade, inform, entertain, or express thoughts and feelings. They may have more than one purpose for writing.

- You can draw conclusions from what the author writes to help you determine the purpose or purposes for writing.

- You can adjust the way you read based on the author's purpose. If the purpose is to entertain, you may want to read faster. If the purpose is to inform, you may want to read more slowly.

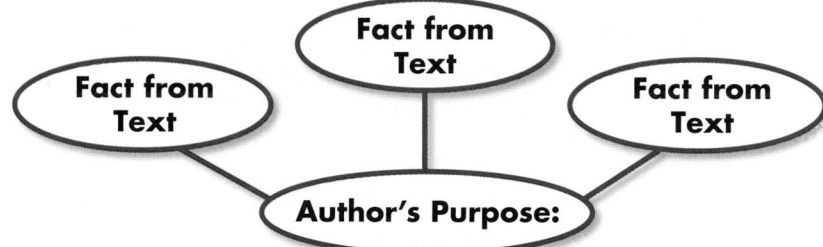

Strategy

Strategy: Ask Questions

Active readers ask frequent questions before, during, and after reading. Questioning helps readers predict what an article will be about and what the author's purpose is for writing the article. Asking questions during and after reading can help you decide if the author succeeded in meeting his or her purpose.

Write

1. Read "Gina's Adventures in Italy." Make a graphic organizer like the one above in order to determine the author's purpose.

2. Write a paragraph telling what you think was the author's purpose(s) and why you think this.

Gina's Adventures in Italy

My sister Gina has always been unique. She repeatedly showed this during the summer we spent in Italy.

In Florence, Gina was admiring a row of scooters parked on the sidewalk. In typical Gina fashion, she accidentally bumped into one, and they all fell like a row of dominoes. Later I suggested we go see Michelangelo's famous sculpture, *David.* "David who? Do we know this fellow?" Gina asked. Like always, I gave up trying to explain and just took her there. She loved it.

Our next stop was Rome. I had always wanted to see the Fountain of Trevi, the gorgeous old fountain that many tourists wade in on hot days. Gina had obviously heard about this because as we walked toward the fountain, I saw her donning a bathing cap and swim goggles. "What are you doing?" I asked.

"I read that you can go in. I'm having a swim!" she said. I watched as she galloped to the fountain and jumped in. Other tourists watched the strange scene with amazement. "Man, I wish I had my flippers!" Gina said as she came up for air.

Strategy Based on the title and art, what questions can you ask in order to predict what this piece will be about or set a purpose for reading it?

Skill How do you know the purpose of this paragraph is to entertain you by describing some silly situations, rather than to inform you about scooters in Florence or the works of Michaelangelo?

Skill Which details in this paragraph tell you that its purpose is to entertain you?

Strategy What questions can you ask to help you determine the author's purpose for writing this story?

DON QUIXOTE AND THE WINDMILLS

Words to Know

quests

misfortune

renewed

renowned

squire

lance

resound

Remember

Try the strategy. Then, if you need more help, use your glossary or a dictionary.

Vocabulary Strategy
for Prefixes

Word Structure Sometimes when you are reading, you come across a word you do not know. One way to figure out the meaning of a word is to understand the meanings of its parts. A prefix is a syllable added at the beginning of a base word that changes its meaning. The prefix *re-* means "again" or "back," as in *retell* and *recall*. The prefix *mis-* means "bad" or "wrong," as in *misspell*.

1. Identify the prefix in the unknown word.

2. Cover the prefix and look at the base word. Think about its meaning.

3. Uncover the prefix and identify its meaning.

4. Add the prefix's meaning to the meaning of the base word.

5. Check the context. Does this meaning make sense in this sentence?

As you read "Knights of Old," look for words that have prefixes. Use the prefixes to help you figure out the meanings of the words.

KNIGHTS OF OLD

Medieval knights were actually soldiers, not just the brave heroes of adventure stories. Stories tell us that knights went on quests. A knight might fight an evil beast or save a fair lady whom misfortune had placed in danger. In spite of great hardship, he always renewed his devotion and carried on. One of the most renowned of these legendary knights was Lancelot.

Real knights did go through a ceremony in which they promised to use their weapons for noble causes and high ideals. A boy who was to become a knight first served as a squire. At 15 or 16 he became the personal servant of a knight. He trained hard and rode with his master into battle. Knights wore heavy armor and used a lance as well as a sword to fight.

Knights sometimes fought in tournaments, which at first were much like battles. The air would resound with the clanging of swords. Over time, the contest changed. Pairs of knights would square off and try to unseat each other using blunt lances. Today, fights similar to these are sometimes re-created for educational and entertainment purposes.

Write

Imagine that you are watching two knights battle. Describe the scene. Use as many words from the Words to Know list as you can.

Can Don Quixote
save the countryside
from the enemy?

Don Quixote and the Windmills

retold and adapted by Eric A. Kimmel

illustrations by Leonard Everett Fisher

658

Are you one who loves old stories? Does your heart beat faster when you hear tales of knights in armor? of castles and dragons? of ogres, sorcerers, and damsels in distress? Beware! Those tales can drive you mad. It happened to a certain Spanish gentleman who lived four centuries ago in the province of La Mancha.

Señor Quexada was his name. He was a tall, lean figure and wore a woeful expression on his face, as if his heart held some secret sorrow.

Indeed, it did. Señor Quexada longed to live in days gone by, when gallant knights battled for the honor of ladies fair. Books of their adventures filled his library. *Amadis of Gaul, The Mirror of Chivalry,* and *The Exploits of Esplandián* were but a few of the volumes that tumbled from his shelves.

Señor Quexada buried himself in these books. He read all day and far into the night, until his mind snapped. "Señor Quexada is no more," he announced to his astonished household. "I am the renowned knight and champion Don Quixote de la Mancha."

In the attic he found a rusty suit of armor, his grandfather's sword, a round leather shield, and an antique lance. His helmet was a foot soldier's steel cap that lacked a visor. Don Quixote made one out of paperboard and tied it on with ribbons. It would serve until he won himself a proper helmet on the field of battle.

A knight must have a noble steed. Don Quixote owned a nag as tall and bony as himself. He named the horse Rocinante, which means "Nag No More."

A knight must also have a squire, a faithful companion to share his quests. Don Quixote invited Sancho Panza, a short, fat farmer from the neighborhood, to accompany him. "Come with me, Sancho," Don Quixote said. "Within a week I will conquer an island and make you king of it."

"That will be no bad thing," Sancho replied. "If I were king of an island, my wife would be queen, and all my children princes and princesses." So Sancho agreed to come along. Although he was not as crackbrained as Don Quixote, he certainly saw no harm in seeing a bit of the world.

Finally, a knight must have a fair lady to whom he has pledged his loyalty and his life. "A knight without a lady is like a tree without leaves or fruit, a body without a soul," Don Quixote explained to Sancho. After considering all the damsels in the district, he chose a pretty farm girl— Aldonza Lorenzo—from the village of Toboso.

Don Quixote rechristened his lady as he had rechristened his horse. He called her "Dulcinea," meaning "Sweetness." The very word breathed music and enchantment.

"Dulcinea of Toboso . . . Dulcinea . . . Dulcinea . . ." The knight's heart overflowed with devotion as he whispered the sacred name.

662

One moonless night, while everyone in town lay asleep, Don Quixote and Sancho set forth. By dawn they were miles away. Don Quixote rode ahead, scanning the plain for ogres and sorcerers. Sancho followed on his little donkey, munching his breakfast of bread and cheese.

Don Quixote halted. "Fortune has favored our quest, good Sancho. Can you see what lies yonder? There stand the monstrous giants who have plagued this countryside long enough. I intend to strike them down and claim their wealth as our just reward."

Sancho squinted into the distance. "Giants, Master? What are you talking about? I see no giants."

"There they are. Straight ahead. Can't you see them? They have four arms, each one more than six miles long."

"Oh, Master, you are mistaken. Those aren't giants. They're windmills. What you call arms are really sails to catch the wind. The wind turns the sails and makes the millstones go round and round."

"It is plain you know nothing at all," Don Quixote replied. "I say those are giants, whether or not you recognize them as such. I intend to slay them. If you are frightened, you may hide yourself away and say your prayers while I challenge them to mortal combat."

Having said this, Don Quixote lowered his visor and put his spurs to Rocinante. He galloped across the plain to do battle with the windmills.

"Take to your heels, cowardly giants! Know that it is I, the noble Don Quixote, Knight of La Mancha, who am attacking you!"

"Master! They are only windmills!" Sancho called after him.

The wind picked up. The sails billowed. The great arms of the windmills began to turn.

Don Quixote laughed with scorn. "Do you think to frighten me? Though you have more arms than the giant Briareus, I will still make

an end of you!" He lifted his eyes toward heaven. "Beautiful damsel, Dulcinea of Toboso, in your honor do I claim the victory. If I am to die, let it be with your sweet name upon my lips."

Shouting defiance, he charged at the nearest windmill.

His lance pierced the canvas sail and became tangled in the ropes. Attempting to pull free, Don Quixote became caught as well. The windmill's rumbling arm dragged him out of the saddle, carrying him higher and higher.

Don Quixote drew his sword. "Release me, Giant, before you feel the sharp sting of my blade!" He slashed at the ropes. The windmill's arm swept past its zenith. It began hurtling toward the ground at an ever-increasing speed.

Sancho trotted up on his donkey. "Master, I will save you!" He grasped Don Quixote's ankle when the knight swept by. The faithful squire found himself pulled off his donkey and carried aloft with his master.

"Do not fear, good Sancho. I feel the giant weakening. I will soon make an end of this villain." Don Quixote hacked at the ropes with renewed vigor.

Sancho saw the cords begin to fray. "Master! Spare the poor giant a few moments of life. At least until he brings us closer to the ground."

"Giant, in the name of my lady, Dulcinea of Toboso, I command you to yield or die."

Don Quixote made one last thrust. The ropes parted. The sail blew away. Don Quixote, with Sancho clinging to his ankle, plunged straight down. Together they would have perished, knight and squire, dashed to a hundred pieces, had the sail of the following arm not caught them and sent them rolling across the plain.

They tumbled to a stop at Rocinante's feet. Sancho felt himself all over for broken bones. "Ay, Master!" he groaned. "Why didn't you listen to me? I tried to warn you. Could you not see that they were only windmills? Whatever possessed you to attack them?"

Don Quixote dusted off his battered armor. He tied the crushed visor back onto his helmet. "Be silent, Sancho. Your words reveal your ignorance. You know nothing about these matters. It is true that the giants now have the appearance of windmills. This is because they were bewitched by my enemy, the wizard Frestón. At the last moment, he transformed the giants into windmills to deprive me of the glorious victory that was rightfully mine.

Never fear, Sancho. We will meet him again. All the power of his magic arts will not save him when he feels the edge of my mighty sword."

"I hope so," said Sancho as he pushed Don Quixote back onto Rocinante. "Another tumble like this and we will all go home in pieces."

Don Quixote took the reins in hand. "Never fear, faithful Sancho. The road to victory is often paved with misfortune. A true knight never complains. Follow me, and I promise we will dip our arms up to the elbow in what common people call 'adventures.' Our names and the stories of our matchless deeds will resound through the ages."

"Ay, Master! When I hear you say those words, I can almost believe they are true. Perhaps I really will have my island someday."

"Of course you will, Sancho. Why would you ever doubt it?"

Sancho mounted his donkey and went trotting after Rocinante, vowing to follow Don Quixote wherever fortune's winds might carry him.

667

Reader Response

Open for Discussion Call Don Quixote's battle a case of mistaken identity. What caused it? Why are people still reading about it and talking about it after 400 years?

1. Reread the first paragraph. Examine illustrations of Don Quixote attacking windmills sideways and upside down. How can you tell that the author and illustrator had fun with their jobs?

2. Why did the author retell this classic story? What was he trying to accomplish? Was he successful?

3. Did the story give you all the information you wanted about Don Quixote? Did it leave unanswered questions? What might you ask the author about the story of Don Quixote if you could?

4. *Lance* and *squire* are words that were used more in medieval times than they are today. Make a web with *Medieval Words* in the center. Add these two words from the Words to Know list along with others in the story that might fit.

Test Practice

Look Back and Write Finally, Quixote realizes that the windmills are windmills. Still he believes in his mortal combat with giants. Read the bottom of page 664 and pages 666–667 for his explanation. Then summarize his case.

Read more books by Eric A. Kimmel and Leonard Everett Fisher.

Eric A. Kimmel travels throughout the world visiting schools to tell stories and talk about his books. His first love is sharing stories from different countries and cultures. He says, "I don't have any set routine for writing other than I think about the story a lot before I actually sit down at my desk. Most of the work is done before I write the first word. The real work of creating a story comes in the thinking. The rest is just a matter of revision."

Mr. Kimmel's interests range from bluegrass music to horses. He lives with his wife in Portland, Oregon.

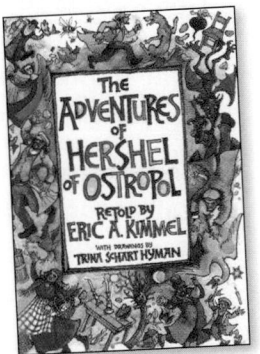

The Adventures of Hershel of Ostropol retold by Eric A. Kimmel

Leonard Everett Fisher was just two years old when he added his own touches to a painting his father had left on an easel. Although he ruined the painting, he was given his own small studio in a hall closet, complete with worktable, crayons, paper, and pencils. Today he is a painter, illustrator, educator, and author of more than two hundred books. His illustrations have won many awards. He lives with his wife in Westport, Connecticut.

William Tell illustrated by Leonard Everett Fisher

Textbook

Genre

- Textbooks are used in classrooms to teach facts, provide information, and offer explanations in a particular subject area.

- The information has been well researched for accuracy.

- The facts and details found in textbooks may help students excel on tests.

Text Features

- In textbooks, heads and subheads help to organize information.

- Pictures and captions add more information.

Link to Social Studies

Research the life of a monarch, lord, knight, or serf, and report to the class on what you learn.

Feudalism

from *Scott Foresman Social Studies: The World*

During the Middle Ages, Europe had few strong central governments. People formed their own system to meet their need for protection and justice. **Feudalism** was a political, social, and economic system that began in the 800s. It provided the needed protection for people.

Feudalism resembled a social structure. At the top was the **monarch**, a king or queen who was the supreme ruler. The next level included lords who pledged their loyalty to the monarch and military support in the event of a war or conflict. In return, the monarch granted the lord an estate.

The lord owned the land. He also received a large percentage of the crops produced on the land and received all the income from the crops. He collected taxes, maintained order, enforced laws, and protected the serfs. **Serfs** were the people who lived on the land and farmed it.

serf

lord

Author's Purpose The purpose is to inform. How should you read this?

Many lords had **knights**, or warriors trained and prepared to fight on horseback. Knights were supposed to have deep faith, be ready to die for the church, give to all, and stand against injustice.

Feudalism Declines

Serfs, who are sometimes called peasants, formed the base of the society in the Middle Ages. Unlike kings, lords, and knights, who were bound to be faithful to one another, serfs had no such loyalty to anyone. Serfs were not slaves, yet could not become knights. They could not be bought or sold separate from the land. Even so, serfs were tied to the land they worked and could not leave it without the lord's permission.

As time passed, some lords had many faithful knights, therefore building up much military power. These lords became independent of the monarch, who originally granted the land to them. The lords substituted payment in money for actual military support. By the 1400s, feudalism had begun to decline.

monarch

lords

knights

serfs or peasants

In feudalism, peasants made up 90 percent of the population. Monarchs, lords, and the church had all the power and wealth.

castle or manor house

church

knight

Reading Across Texts

You read about knights in the article "Feudalism." If Señor Quexada, or Don Quixote, were really a knight, do you think he would have been a good one?

Writing Across Texts Write your answer about Don Quixote.

Comprehension

Skill
Graphic Sources

Strategy
Graphic Organizers

Graphic Sources

- Graphic aids include maps, charts, diagrams, and other illustrations.

- While reading, study the information in the graphics and ask: What does this information tell me about this topic? How does this graphic connect to what I'm reading in the text?

Greek Clothing		
Clothing type	**Indoor**	**Outdoor**
Regular clothing	chiton	chiton
Heavier clothing		himation (cloak)
On feet	shoeless	sandals
On head	hatless	veil or hat

Strategy: Graphic Organizers

Creating a graphic organizer while reading allows you to organize and summarize key information from the text. Sometimes the text you are reading will include a graphic aid. You can complete a graphic organizer to connect the information in the aid to the text.

1. Read "Greece: Land and Climate." Make a web to organize the information as you read.

2. Write a brief paragraph suggesting the types of clothing visitors should bring when traveling in Greece in the summer, and why.

GREECE: Land and Climate

Greece is a country in Europe. It is made up of a mainland and more than 2,000 islands that have a total area of 50,949 square miles. While Greece is known as a rocky place with many mountains, it does have level ground, as the pie chart illustrates.

The Land Because Greece touches the Mediterranean, Ionian, and Aegean Seas, it has a great deal of coastline. In fact, there is only one small area in all of Greece that is farther than 50 miles from the coast.

There are several mountain ranges that run across the country, forming many narrow valleys. Some of the tallest mountains in Greece are Mt. Smolikas (8,652 feet), Mt. Orvilos (7,287 feet), Mt. Olympus (9,570 feet), and Mt. Parnassus (8,061 feet).

The Climate Greece has a comfortable climate. Warm, southern winds blow on Greece during the winter months. The average January temperature in Thessaloniki, in the north, is 43°F, while Athens, farther south, averages 50°F and Iraklion, even farther south, averages 54°F. In summer, it is dry and hot all over Greece. The normal July temperature is 80°F.

THE LAND OF GREECE

☐ = mountains
■ = lowlands

Strategy The title gives a clue to the main arms on your web.

Skill Which of these does this pie chart tell you about the land of Greece? Compare the colors to the key.

a) It has more lowlands than mountains.

b) Most of its land is mountainous.

c) Greeks like the mountains.

Skill Does the information in the pie chart relate to the information presented in this paragraph of the text? Why or why not?

Strategy Make a chart or table that would organize the information in this paragraph.

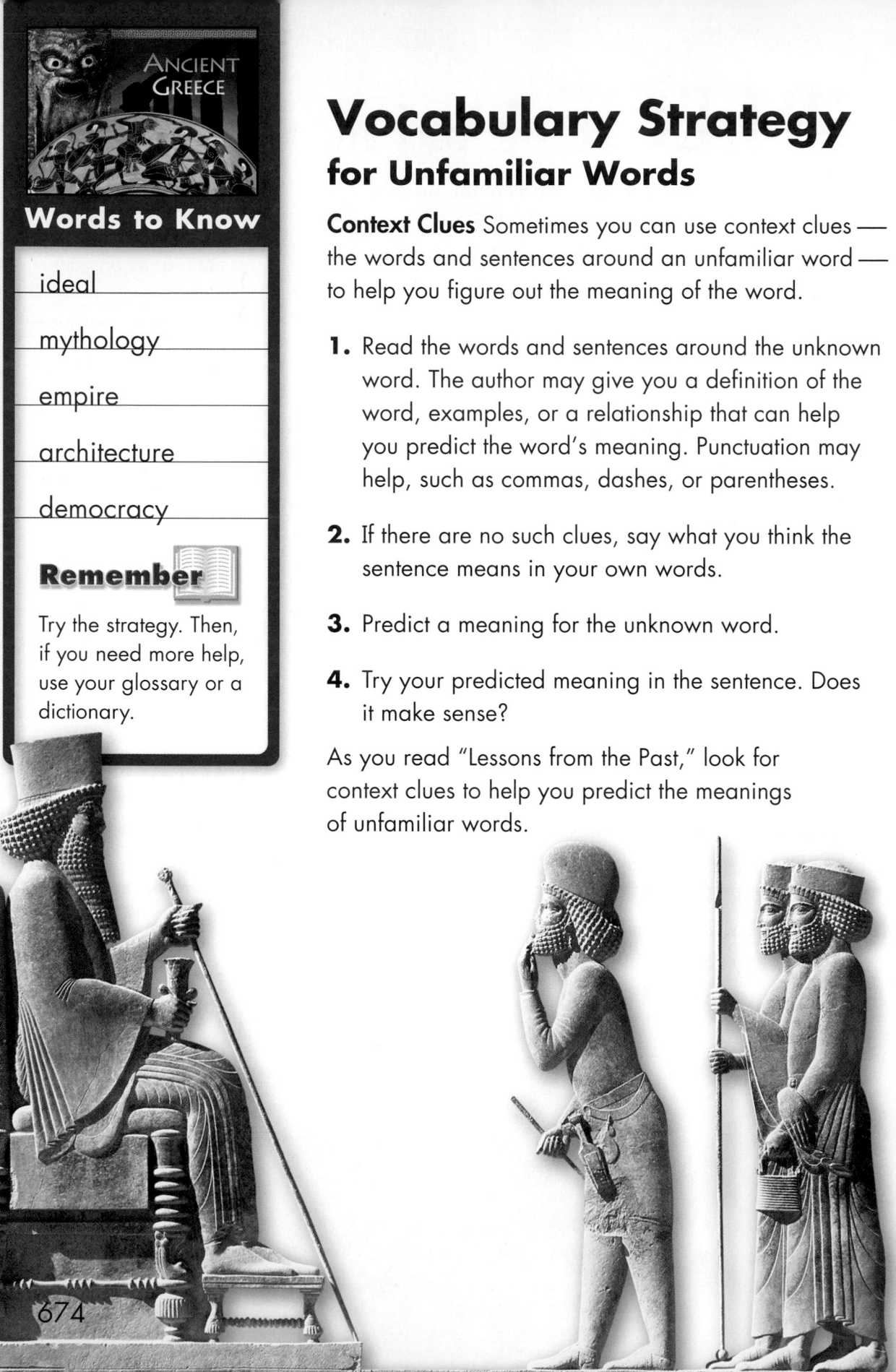

Words to Know

ideal

mythology

empire

architecture

democracy

Remember

Try the strategy. Then, if you need more help, use your glossary or a dictionary.

Vocabulary Strategy
for Unfamiliar Words

Context Clues Sometimes you can use context clues — the words and sentences around an unfamiliar word — to help you figure out the meaning of the word.

1. Read the words and sentences around the unknown word. The author may give you a definition of the word, examples, or a relationship that can help you predict the word's meaning. Punctuation may help, such as commas, dashes, or parentheses.

2. If there are no such clues, say what you think the sentence means in your own words.

3. Predict a meaning for the unknown word.

4. Try your predicted meaning in the sentence. Does it make sense?

As you read "Lessons from the Past," look for context clues to help you predict the meanings of unfamiliar words.

Lessons *from the* Past

Human beings have always asked themselves: "How should we live? What way of life is best?" We can study the past to try to answer these questions. By asking still more questions ("What kind of government has been best? When have people been happiest?"), we can learn from the past. We can try to comprehend what would make up the ideal, or perfect, way of life.

Ancient civilizations have sent us messages. Their literature and history communicate how they lived and felt. Every civilization has its mythology— a body of stories that explain the workings of the world and religion. These tales, filled with struggle, show us what ancestors believed to be the meaning of life. However, they contain little of happiness or contentment.

The empire was a common type of government in many past civilizations. The strong rule of a single person might lead to astounding art, architecture, and invention. But most subjects were not free to enjoy these boons. Over thousands of years, humans have moved away from government with a single all-powerful ruler toward democracy. We have come to believe that each person should be free and have a voice in how the community is governed.

In which past era would you most like to have lived? Write a journal entry telling about this era and why you admire it. Use words from the Words to Know list.

*How did the
ancient Greeks influence
the modern world?*

Genre

Expository nonfiction explains the nature of something. Look for facts about the nature of ancient Greece as you read.

ANCIENT GREECE

by Kim Covert

CHAPTER 1
THE ANCIENT OLYMPICS

Twenty runners get into position on the starting line. A trumpeter sounds the start of the race. Sand flies up as the runners race down the 210-yard (192-meter) track. The crowd cheers as the runners cross the finish line. The judges place a wreath of olive leaves on the winner's head.

Later, horse-drawn chariots line up on an oval track. At the sound of the trumpet, each driver urges his horses forward. In the first turn, a driver cuts in front of another chariot. The two chariots run into each other and tip over. The horses and drivers crash to the ground. Several more chariots fall in the pileup. Many horses and drivers are hurt. The drivers who missed the wreck bolt to the finish line. The owner of the winning chariot receives a wreath of olive leaves.

Footraces and chariot races were part of the Olympic games of ancient Greece. Wrestling, boxing, and the pentathlon were other events. The pentathlon included javelin, discus, long jump, running, and wrestling.

The first recorded Olympics were held in 776 B.C. The games took place in Olympia, a town in western Greece. They honored the Greek god Zeus. In Greek mythology, Zeus was the ruler of all the Olympian gods.

For 1,000 years, the Olympic games were held every four years. Before each Olympics, the Greeks stopped all warfare. No wars could be fought just before, during, or just after the

CHARIOT RACE This is a scene on a vase from the 500s B.C. It shows a chariot race, one of the ancient Olympic events.

games. Wars were stopped so athletes and people coming to watch could travel to and from the games safely.

The modern Olympics are one of many traditions developed in Greece. Ancient Greece is often called the cradle of Western civilization. It was the birthplace of many modern ideas. Greek ideas are found in today's governments, art, architecture, and literature. They are also seen in science, drama, and athletics.

CHAPTER 2
EARLY GREEKS

The Minoans

The first civilization in Greece formed on the island of Crete. The Minoans lived from 2200 B.C. to 1450 B.C. They built a huge port on Crete and a large fleet of ships. Their ships allowed them to trade with people in other areas.

The Minoans also built palaces. They covered the palace walls with paintings. The paintings show peaceful, happy people. The Minoans built their largest palace at Knossos. The palace honored King Minos. In Greek mythology, Minos was a son of Zeus.

RUINS OF A MINOAN PALACE at Knossos can be seen today. Sir Arthur Evans discovered the ruins in the early 1900s.

The Mycenaeans

By about 1600 B.C., the Mycenaeans had settled in cities on the Greek mainland. A king ruled each city. Mycenaeans built huge walls around their palaces. Paintings, gold, and jewels decorated their palaces.

The Mycenaeans were great warriors. Around 1450 B.C., the Mycenaeans invaded Crete. They conquered the Minoans, who disappeared from history at this time.

According to legend, around 1220 B.C. the Mycenaeans conquered Troy. This city was on the northwestern coast of Asia Minor. Today this area includes the country of Turkey. Stories about the Trojan War have lasted to the present day.

Few Mycenaeans remained in Crete or Greece by 1200 B.C. Their palaces on the mainland were destroyed. Historians believe they were invaded by another civilization. Soon after, the Dorians took over Crete. They came from northern Greece.

The Trojan War

According to legend, the Mycenaeans attacked the city of Troy to rescue Helen. She was the wife of King Menelaus of Sparta. A Trojan prince had kidnapped her.

The tall walls around Troy kept the Greeks out for 10 years. Finally, the Greeks built a huge hollow wooden horse. They gave it to the Trojans as a gift. The Trojans dragged the horse into Troy. They did not know that Greek warriors were hiding inside. That night, the warriors climbed out and opened the city's gates. The Greek army then defeated the Trojans.

Around 750 B.C., two long poems about the Trojan War were written. *The Iliad* describes the long struggle between Greek and Trojan soldiers. *The Odyssey* tells the story of the hero Odysseus.

TROJAN HORSE

He suffers many difficulties while trying to get home after the Trojan War. Historians disagree about who wrote the poems. Many people believe the Greek poet Homer wrote them.

The Dark Age

Historians know little about Greece from 1100 B.C. to 800 B.C. During this time, Greece was a land of small farming villages. These villages had little contact with one another. Historians call this period the Dark Age.

Around 800 B.C., the Greeks appeared in history again. They built new colonies in parts of Europe and Africa. They traded with western Asia and learned to make iron objects. With iron, the Greeks could more easily make tools for farming and other tasks.

The Phoenicians lived across the Mediterranean Sea. The Greeks traded with the Phoenicians and learned their alphabet and system of writing. They also learned about Phoenician art and shipbuilding. This progress helped end the Dark Age.

CHAPTER 3
THE RISE OF GREECE

By the end of the Dark Age, the Greeks had built many villages. Many villages centered around a high hilltop, called an acropolis. The farms and villages surrounding each acropolis joined to form a city-state. Each city-state ruled itself and had its own customs. By 700 B.C., hundreds of independent city-states had formed. The two most powerful city-states were Athens and Sparta.

ANCIENT GREECE
500 B.C.—336 B.C.

Athens and Sparta

Athens was a city-state located slightly inland from the Aegean Sea. Athens built a port city called Piraeus. This port allowed Athens to launch its powerful navy and trade ships. Long walls joined Athens and Piraeus.

Athenians welcomed new ideas and customs. Athenians believed that a city-state should serve all of its citizens. They created a new type of government called a democracy. Each free male citizen in Athens could vote on laws and choose leaders. Women and slaves could not vote. An assembly made governmental decisions.

Sparta was located 150 miles (241 kilometers) from Athens. Mountains around Sparta protected the city-state. Spartans were different from Athenians. Spartans wanted no contact with outsiders. They were against change.

Sparta's government was also different from Athens's government. Two kings and a council of elders ruled Sparta. Only rich people served on the council.

Each Greek city-state formed an army. In Athens, men between ages 17 and 59 were required to serve in the military.

Sparta's society was based on the military. Every adult male was a full-time soldier. Soldiers were not allowed to work at other jobs.

PIRAEUS Ships sailed from Athens's port Piraeus. Long walls connected Pireaus to Athens.

PERSIAN GUARDS c. 5th century B.C.

The Persian Wars

Persia was a large empire east of Greece. The Persians' territory covered much of Asia and the Middle East. King Darius I of Persia wanted to rule Greece. In 490 B.C., Darius's army landed at the village of Marathon, northwest of Athens. An army of 10,000 Athenians marched to Marathon to face 60,000 Persians. Athens defeated them in a surprise victory.

Ten years later, Darius's son Xerxes returned to Greece. He brought an army of 200,000 men. Athens and Sparta led a united army of all Greek city-states. After fighting for a year, the Greeks defeated Persia. Their victory in 479 B.C. kept the Persians from taking over Europe.

The Golden Age of Athens

After the Persian Wars, Athens entered its Golden Age. During this period, Athens reached its peak of power. The Greeks enjoyed great achievements in art, science, and government during this time.

Pericles was the leader of Athens from 461 to 429 B.C. He supported democracy. He also started a system of payment for government service. The earlier system did not pay government workers. Only rich people could afford to serve in the government. The new system of payment allowed anyone to earn a living by working at a government job.

Pericles planned to make Athens a model for other cities. He helped build a strong navy. Athens became wealthy through trade with other lands. Athens was also a model for art and culture. The government supported the work of architects, artists, and writers.

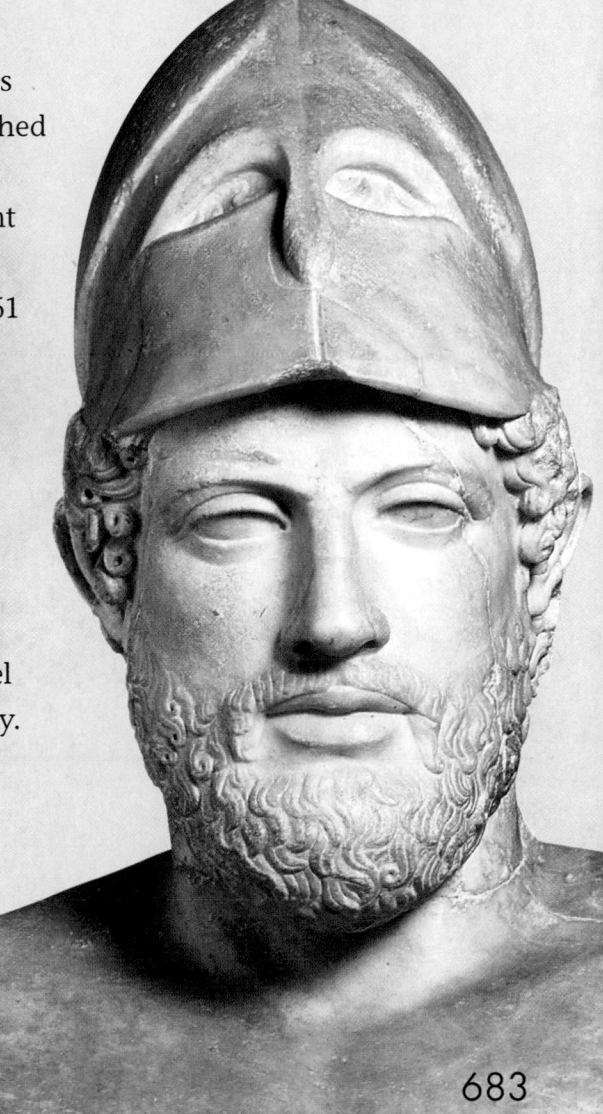

This sculpture of Pericles shows him wearing a helmet because he was a general.

CHAPTER 4
FALL FROM POWER

Coin featuring
Alexander the Great

After the Greeks beat Persia, many Greek city-states joined together. They agreed to protect each other. This alliance was known as the Delian League. Delian League members contributed ships or money to the league. They kept the money in the Delian League treasury.

People in Athens began taking the league's money. Athens's government made decisions for the league. Athens used the money to build temples and new colonies. Athens built a large and powerful empire throughout the Mediterranean.

The Peloponnesian War

For many years, Sparta and Athens were rivals. The two city-states did not trust each other. Athens wanted to spread democracy, freedom, and self-rule.

Sparta was afraid that Athens's power would reach too far. Other Greek city-states also were unhappy with Athens. They were upset that Athens was taking money from the Delian League.

In 431 B.C., Sparta declared war on Athens. For 27 years, Athens and Sparta and their allies fought in the Peloponnesian War. Athens finally surrendered in 404 B.C.

Alexander the Great

In 359 B.C., Philip II became the king of Macedonia. Philip wanted to rule the Persian Empire. He asked the Greeks to help him defeat Persia. In return, he would let them govern themselves. In 336 B.C., before Philip could organize an attack on Persia, he was killed. His son, Alexander, became king at age 20. A strong military leader, he became known as Alexander the Great.

ALEXANDER THE GREAT This statue was created between the first and second centuries B.C.

In 334 B.C., Alexander led an army of Macedonians and Greeks. They attacked Persia. In three years, he defeated the Persian king.

Alexander's army later conquered Egypt, western Persia, and western India. He also conquered the countries now known as Afghanistan and Pakistan. Alexander founded many military colonies in the lands he conquered. These settlements helped provide supplies to his armies.

After his death in 323 B.C., Alexander's generals fought to control his empire. They divided Greece into three kingdoms.

The Hellenistic Age

The Greek language was spoken in Alexander's colonies. The colonists copied Greek architecture, law, and art. They studied Greek science and philosophy. The most famous city Alexander founded was Alexandria, Egypt. It became the world's most important center of trade and learning.

After Alexander's death, the power of the Greek city-states faded. But the rulers of Greek kingdoms promoted Greek culture. Elements of Greek culture spread from southern present-day France to what is now northern Afghanistan. This period is known as the Hellenistic Age.

The Roman Empire

Around 275 B.C., the Romans defeated the Hellenistic King Pyrrhus in Italy. Rome gradually took over other kingdoms. It conquered Sicily in 241 B.C. and Spain in 201 B.C. Rome began conquering other areas. By 31 B.C., Rome defeated the last Greek kingdom. It was the end of the Hellenistic Age.

THIS STATUE OF THE GODDESS ATHENA is an example of art from the Hellenistic Age.

GREEK INFLUENCE Part of Roman Emperor Hadrian's villa uses Greek columns.

After conquering the Greeks, the Roman Empire grew. The Romans adopted the best ideas of the people they conquered. The Romans used Greek styles in literature and architecture. They modeled many public buildings after Greek temples. The Romans based their government on some of Greece's democratic ideas.

Rome fell in the A.D. 400s. The Visigoths, a tribe from Germany in northern Europe, defeated the last Roman emperor. Rome's influence faded.

Europeans once again took interest in Greek culture in the A.D. 1400s and 1500s. This period was known as the Renaissance. Classical ideas of ancient Greece influenced artists, writers, and architects. For 300 years after the Renaissance, Europe developed colonies around the world. The Europeans spread these classical ideas to the colonies. Greek culture continued to thrive.

CHAPTER 5
LASTING ACHIEVEMENTS

The ancient Greeks made lasting contributions to art, architecture, science, and medicine. They also developed drama, literature, and philosophy. Their ideas still influence the modern world.

Architecture and Art

Greek water jug from 530 B.C. showing women filling vases at a fountain.

The Greeks built many structures that still stand today. Temples are the most famous of their buildings. Most of the temples have a similar design. The buildings are rectangular with columns holding up the sloping roof. Modern architects base many of their designs on Greek styles.

The most famous example of Greek architecture is the Parthenon. Completed in 432 B.C., this temple honored the goddess Athena. She was the goddess of war and wisdom.

The Greeks created their own forms of sculpture, pottery, and painting. They were the first to sculpt human statues in a natural style. Greek statues usually showed perfect bodies. Earlier statues had looked stiff and unnatural. Athenians made the most valued pottery of the ancient Western world. They painted their pots with pictures of gods, heroes, and ordinary people. Greek artists decorated buildings with beautiful paintings called frescoes. These wall paintings on plaster showed scenes from Greek myths.

Sculptures of women support the roof on this porch of the Erechtheum, a temple on the Acropolis in Athens.

Science and Medicine

Ancient Greeks were among the first to use logic to explain the world around them. They wanted to discover the reasons why things worked.

Anaxagoras was an early Greek astronomer. He learned that the moon did not make its own light. Instead, Anaxagoras believed that the moon's light was a reflection from the sun.

Archimedes was an inventor and mathematician. He discovered the principle of a lever. Archimedes created a complicated set of levers and pulleys. He used them to lift a large ship from water to land by himself.

Hippocrates was a Greek doctor. He is often called the father of medicine. He developed the Hippocratic oath, a promise to heal the sick. Today, many medical students take this oath when they become doctors.

ARCHIMEDES

PARTHENON
the most famous example
of Greek architecture

Menander with theatrical masks

Drama and Literature

The ancient Greeks created drama. The earliest Greek plays were religious ceremonies. A chorus sang and acted out stories about the gods. Later, dramas told legends of Greek heroes. Many plays were about gods. Other plays told about the Persian Wars.

The Greeks were the Western world's first writers of history. Around 450 B.C., Herodotus explored the Mediterranean region. He wrote long reports of wars, geography, customs, and legends. Herodotus is often called the father of history.

Aesop is one of the most famous Greek writers. Historians believe Aesop was a Greek slave who had been freed. In the 500s B.C., Aesop wrote hundreds of fables. These short stories about animals taught a lesson. Aesop's fables include "The Tortoise and the Hare" and "The Fox and the Grapes." Many of Aesop's fables are still told today.

Philosophy

Early Greek philosophers studied life, death, and other mysteries of the natural world. Socrates was the most famous philosopher from Athens. He was one of the first to study ethics. He taught students by asking questions, rather than giving them answers. This teaching method is now known as the Socratic method.

Plato was a student of Socrates. In his book *The Republic*, Plato describes his ideas for an ideal government. He also founded a school called the Academy.

Plato's most famous student was Aristotle. Aristotle became a great philosopher and scientist. He developed a scientific system to help understand the world. The ideas of Socrates, Plato, and Aristotle are still discussed today.

Plato and Aristotle, from exterior of belltower of Santa Maria del Flore in Florence

Daily Life in Ancient Greece

Most people in ancient Greece were farmers. Their farms were usually small and run by one family. Often, slaves helped them.

Men and women lived in separate parts of the house. The women had a special room. There, they played with their children, spun thread, and sewed. The men often held parties in the men's area. Slaves brought them food and drink. At the center of each home was an outdoor courtyard. There, children played games.

Each day people filled the market-place, or *agora*. People came to shop, meet friends, and do business. Farmers brought their goods to market on donkeys. Pottery, cloth, and jewelry were also sold there.

When they became adults, children brought their toys to the temple. Girls did this before they married. Boys did this around age 14. The children offered their toys to the Greek gods Apollo and Artemis. The children then took part in a ceremony that welcomed them to adult life.

SOCRATES

CHAPTER 6

GREEK INFLUENCE TODAY

Greece has influenced many modern governments. Democracy is now a common form of government. Ancient Greeks developed political speeches, debates, and voting. Trial by jury is another system created by the Greeks. A jury is a group of people who listens to and decides a court case.

The ancient Greeks believed in the rights of the male citizen. Aristotle wrote that the pursuit of happiness was important. When the 13 Colonies in North America separated from Great Britain, the colonists created the Declaration of Independence. This document borrowed Aristotle's idea. It states that people have the right to life, liberty, and the pursuit of happiness.

Often, government buildings also have Greek influence. Court buildings, capitols, and presidential homes have all used Greek architecture.

Every day, people take part in activities invented by the ancient Greeks. They read novels, attend plays, or exercise in a public gym. Athletes wrestle, box, and compete in track and field events. Philosophers explore the meaning of life. Scientists search for logical answers to problems. Ideas from ancient Greece continue to influence modern life.

Greek architecture influenced the U. S. Supreme Court building in Washington, D. C.

EQUAL JUSTICE UNDER LAW

Reader Response

Open for Discussion We can see influences from the ancient Greek culture all around us. Which of these influences do you think was the most important and lasting?

1. Much of this article tells about the different ages and conquests of ancient Greece or Greek leaders. But Chapter 5 discusses the arts. Why do you think the author thought it was important to include this information?

2. How do the photos, drawings, and map add to the depth of your understanding of the text?

3. Create a simple outline to organize the information in Chapter 2, using the section heads from the text as the headings in your outline. Under each heading, list at least two details discussed in the text.

4. Write a short speech about the main accomplishments of the ancient Greeks. Use words from the Words to Know list in your writing.

Look Back and Write What does the term *the Golden Age of Athens* mean? When was the Golden Age of Athens? Look back at page 683 and write a summary of this particular time period in Greek history.

Kim Covert has written many nonfiction books, but *Ancient Greece* is her favorite. She did extensive research for the book. "When writing about events that occurred thousands of years ago, it's especially important to use accurate sources. I based my research on books written by historians and archaeologists who specialize in ancient Greece."

Ms. Covert has traveled to many places around the world, including China, Russia, Europe, Australia, and New Zealand. She visited Greece several years ago and saw the Acropolis and the Parthenon. "Greece is one of the countries I'd most like to visit again," she says.

As a child, Ms. Covert lived in many different places. "My father was a pilot in the Air Force, and our family moved frequently when I was growing up. We lived in Japan, England, Germany, and many states in the U.S. I continued to travel as an adult and taught third and first grade at international schools in Japan and Hong Kong. Today, I live in Minnesota with my two teenaged children. After a lifetime of moving around, I've been content to stay in one place for the past ten years."

Ancient Greece
by Peter Hicks

Ancient Greek Children
by Richard Tames

Newspaper Article

Genre

- Newspaper articles provide current, accurate information on recent events. They should include few or no opinions.

- Newspaper articles include a date and often have descriptive and interesting headlines.

Text Features

- This newspaper article contains details about the *who, what, when, where, why,* and *how* of the 2004 Olympic Games.

- The reporter gives facts in a well-written, interesting style.

Link to Social Studies

Choose another of the modern Olympics to research. Compare and contrast its opening ceremony with the one in Athens in 2004. Share what you learn with your class.

Journal-Star Olympic Bureau
by Darleen Ramos

OPENING CEREMONY IN ATHENS:

Fire and Water

AUGUST 14, 2004

ATHENS—After 108 years, the Olympic Games have finally returned to Greece. Greece is the birthplace of the Olympics. It is also the country that hosted the first modern Games in 1896. As is the custom, an opening ceremony marks the start of the Games. This opening ceremony not only reminded the audience that the Games began in Greece, but it also paid respect to the tradition of the Olympics.

The ceremonies began with a theatrical performance. On a giant video screen, a drummer standing on a field in Olympia, where the games originated, began a drumbeat. Then, drummers filled the aisles in the Olympic Stadium, gathering energy from the crowd. They marched down to the infield, the Stadium's field of play. The pounding sounded like a heartbeat, an ancient call that joined the past to the present.

 Graphic Organizers What graphic could help you keep track of events in this text?

evening to represent the sea, an element of nature that the Greeks have long treasured. Like Neptune rising from the sea, the Olympic Rings burst through the water, flames licking the night air. The five connected circles symbolize the union of what are called the five continents—Africa, Asia, the Americas, Europe, and Australia.

Dancers, musicians, and actors all participated in bringing the ceremony to life. It began with a boy sailing across the man-made sea in what looked like a paper boat, waving a Greek flag. Next, a centaur—the mythological half man, half horse—waded through the water. He tossed a spear of light across the water toward a marble carving. The spear was meant to give the illusion that the centaur was throwing a comet.

The huge marble carving was in the form of a face. The form broke open three times. Each time it cracked open, the figure underneath represented another stage of Greek sculpture. As the pieces of the sculpture fell, a cube rose from the water with a man perched on top.

This segment of the performance ended with Eros, the ancient Greek god of love, floating above two people dancing in the sea.

As Eros floated above the water, the audience was treated to a parade of performers who were painted white and gray to look like statues. The procession of characters included Greek gods and Trojans on horses. The performers represented 4,000 years of Greek history, from the first civilization of the Minoans who lived on Crete to the present day.

For the production's finale, the performers entered the water and an olive tree rose from it. The olive tree is a symbol of life to the Greeks. In the ancient Games, winners were awarded an olive wreath that they wore upon their heads. In the 2004 Olympics, winners will also wear the traditional wreath.

The Athletes Parade

After the theatrical portion of the ceremonies, it was time for the parade of nations to enter the stadium. Traditionally, Greece leads the parade, as it is the birthplace of the ancient and modern Olympics. But it is also tradition that the host country enters last. To solve the problem, the Greek weightlifter, Pyrros Dimas, led the athletes into the field with his country's flag. Then, he joined his teammates who marched in last.

Over ten thousand athletes poured into the stadium.

Marching in the order of the Greek alphabet, 202 nations entered the stadium. Many of the athletes wore their country's national colors or traditional costumes. Two hours later, Greece finally entered the stadium. Members of the Olympic Organizing Committee made speeches and welcomed the athletes as "Olympians where it all began."

This centaur (half man, half horse) is an artistic example of ancient Greek mythology.

Once the Olympic flag was paraded around the stadium, the crowd waited for the torchbearer to enter. It was an historic moment. This opening ceremony marked the first time that the Olympic flame was carried around the world before returning to its birthplace in Greece. It was carried on all five Olympic continents. After five separate torchbearers carried the flame around the stadium, Greek Olympic windsurfing champion, Nickolaos Kaklamanakis, lit the Olympic cauldron.

From the water that filled the stadium and the sailor who lit the cauldron to the burning flames of the Olympic rings and torch, the ceremony truly reflected all that is Greek.

Reading Across Texts

What struck you as the most remarkable differences between the ancient and modern Olympic Games? Use your prior knowledge and what you read in *Ancient Greece* and this newspaper account.

Writing Across Texts Which Olympic Games would you have preferred to attend—an ancient or modern one? Tell why.

Graphic Sources How do the photos help you understand the text?

Comprehension

Skill
Compare
and Contrast

Strategy
Visualize

Compare and Contrast

- When you compare, you tell how two or more things are alike. When you contrast, you tell how two or more things are different.

- Clue words, such as *like*, *similarly*, and *both* can show comparison. Clue words such as *unlike*, *on the other hand*, and *however* can indicate contrast.

Place A
characteristic
characteristic

Both
characteristic
characteristic

Place B
characteristic
characteristic

Strategy: Visualize

To *visualize* means to create mental pictures of what you read. This helps you better understand a story and place yourself into it. Visualizing can help you compare and contrast. For example, if you are comparing and contrasting two different places, carefully read the descriptions of each place and picture them in your mind. Then think about how they are alike and different.

1. Read "My Fifth-Grade Teachers." Make a graphic organizer like the one above to compare and contrast Mrs. Wallen and Mrs. Casa.

2. How did visualizing help you compare and contrast the two teachers? Give your answer in writing.

My Fifth-Grade Teachers

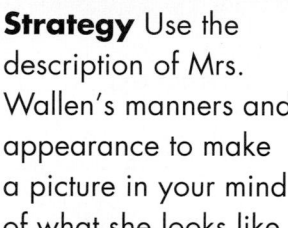

When I was in fifth grade, our school combined two classes together in one extra-large classroom. We were co-taught by two teachers, Mrs. Wallen and Mrs. Casa.

Mrs. Wallen was very strict. She had clear procedures for everything from how you stood in line to how you raised your hand. She tended to be serious and curt. But she expected a lot from us, and made sure we learned everything we were supposed to learn. Mrs. Wallen's appearance was flawless. Her blonde hair was always perfectly done. Her clothes were always carefully pressed, and her posture was always perfect. ● She was like a well-dressed statue. ●

Mrs. Casa, on the other hand, was a lot softer. She had a wonderful sense of humor and enjoyed a little playful banter during lessons. However, if we ever got out of control or lost our focus, she would very strongly bring us back to attention. She was inconsistent at enforcing the rules but always insisted that we worked hard, paid attention, and learned. Well-dressed and pretty, she was a welcome sight each morning. ●

Despite their differences, Mrs. Casa and Mrs. Wallen worked well together. They were both great teachers, and I learned a lot that year. ●

Strategy Use the description of Mrs. Wallen's manners and appearance to make a picture in your mind of what she looks like.

Skill When the author uses the phrase *like a statue* to describe Mrs. Wallen, in what way are a statue and Mrs. Wallen alike?
(a) They both have perfect posture.
(b) They both are made of stone.
(c) They both have many rules to follow.

Strategy How do you picture Mrs. Casa in your mind?

Skill In what ways are the two teachers similar? Look back at the descriptions of each. Do you see any clue words that might help you compare?

promoted

progress

revolting

relish

disgraced

unison

retreat

Remember

Try the strategy. Then, if you need more help, use your glossary or a dictionary.

Vocabulary Strategy
for Multiple-Meaning Words

Context Clues Some words have more than one meaning. Use words and sentences near a multiple-meaning word to figure out which meaning the author is using.

1. Read the sentences near the word in question.

2. Think about the different meanings the word can have. For example, *drum* can be a musical instrument, a metal container, or the act of tapping.

3. Decide which meaning makes sense in the sentence: He began to *drum* his fingers on the desk.

4. Reread the sentence, replacing the word with the meaning you chose.

5. If this meaning seems right, read on. If not, try another meaning.

As you read "A Party for Mom," use the context and your knowledge to decide which meaning a multiple-meaning word has in the article. For example, does *relish* mean "a liking for something" or "a food eaten with others to add flavor"?

A Party for Mom

When Mom was promoted at work, our family had a party to celebrate. We were all proud of her progress in the company. She had been employed at Merritt Controls for only three years, and she had been made a manager.

I hoped Dad wasn't planning to serve any revolting foods, such as avocado or broccoli, at the party. Of all the foods I dislike, those are my least favorite. To my relief, my parents put me in charge of the chips, dip, and relish trays. My orders were to be sure that there were plenty of eye-popping green, red, and yellow or orange colors on those trays. The pickles were green. I added green food coloring to pep them up! The cherries were red, and cheese curls added an orange-yellow color. When I saw my parents' shock, I knew I had disgraced myself.

"That's not what we meant!" they sputtered in unison. They wanted carrots, peppers, and cherry tomatoes. Then the doorbell rang. It was too late to change the trays. I beat a retreat to my room then and there. Later, I found out that because the trays were so interesting and different, they turned out to be a big hit with all the guests.

Write

Describe a family party or special event that you have enjoyed. Use words from the Words to Know list.

The All★American
Slurp

by Lensey Namioka

illustrated by Stephane Jorisch

Is it impolite to slurp your food?

The first time our family was invited out to dinner in America, we disgraced ourselves while eating celery. We had emigrated to this country from China, and during our early days here we had a hard time with American table manners.

In China we never ate celery raw, or any other kind of vegetable raw. We always had to disinfect the vegetables in boiling water first. When we were presented with our first relish tray, the raw celery caught us unprepared.

We had been invited to dinner by our neighbors, the Gleasons. After arriving at the house, we shook hands with our hosts and packed ourselves into a sofa. As our family of four sat stiffly in a row, my younger brother and I stole glances at our parents for a clue as to what to do next.

Mrs. Gleason offered the relish tray to Mother. The tray looked pretty, with its tiny red radishes, curly sticks of carrots, and long, slender stalks of pale green celery. "Do try some of the celery, Mrs. Lin," she said. "It's from a local farmer, and it's sweet."

Mother picked up one of the green stalks, and Father followed suit. Then I picked up a stalk, and my brother did too. So there we sat, each with a stalk of celery in our right hand.

Mrs. Gleason kept smiling. "Would you like to try some of the dip, Mrs. Lin? It's my own recipe: sour cream and onion flakes, with a dash of Tabasco sauce."

Most Chinese don't care for dairy products, and in those days I wasn't even ready to drink fresh milk. Sour cream sounded perfectly revolting. Our family shook our heads in unison.

Mrs. Gleason went off with the relish tray to the other guests, and we carefully watched to see what they did. Everyone seemed to eat the raw vegetables quite happily.

Mother took a bite of her celery. *Crunch*. "It's not bad!" she whispered.

Father took a bite of his celery. *Crunch*. "Yes, it *is* good," he said, looking surprised.

I took a bite, and then my brother. *Crunch, crunch*. It was more than good; it was delicious. Raw celery has a slight sparkle, a zingy taste that you don't get in cooked celery. When Mrs. Gleason came around with the relish tray, we each took another stalk of celery, except my brother. He took two.

There was only one problem: long strings ran through the length of the stalk, and they got caught in my teeth. When I help my mother in the kitchen, I always pull the strings out before slicing celery.

I pulled the strings out of my stalk. *Z-z-zip, z-z-zip*. My brother followed suit. *Z-z-zip, z-z-zip*. To my left, my parents were taking care of their own stalks. *Z-z-zip, z-z-zip, z-z-zip*.

Suddenly I realized that there was dead silence except for our zipping. Looking up, I saw that the eyes of everyone in the room were on our family. Mr. and Mrs. Gleason, their daughter Meg, who was my friend, and their neighbors, the Badels—they were all staring at us as we busily pulled the strings of our celery.

That wasn't the end of it. Mrs. Gleason announced that dinner was served and invited us to the dining table. It was lavishly covered with platters of food, but we couldn't see any chairs around the table. So we helpfully carried over some dining chairs and sat down. All the other guests just stood there.

Mrs. Gleason bent down and whispered to us, "This is a buffet dinner. You help yourselves to some food and eat it in the living room."

Our family beat a retreat back to the sofa as if chased by enemy soldiers. For the rest of the evening, too mortified to go back to the dining table, I nursed a bit of potato salad on my plate.

Next day, Meg and I got on the school bus together. I wasn't sure how she would feel about me after the spectacle our family made at the party. But she was just the same as usual, and the only reference she made to the party was, "Hope you and your folks got enough to eat last night. You certainly didn't take very much. Mom never tries to figure out how much food to prepare. She just puts everything on the table and hopes for the best."

I began to relax. The Gleason's dinner party wasn't so different from a Chinese meal after all. My mother also puts everything on the table and hopes for the best.

Meg was the first friend I had made after we came to America. I eventually got acquainted with a few other kids in school, but Meg was still the only real friend I had.

My brother didn't have any problems making friends. He spent all his time with some boys who were teaching him baseball, and in no time he could speak English much faster than I could—not better, but faster.

I worried more about making mistakes, and I spoke carefully, making sure I could say everything right before opening my mouth. At least I had a better accent than my parents, who never really got rid of their Chinese accent, even years later. My parents had both studied English in school before coming to America, but what they had studied was mostly written English, not spoken.

Father's approach to English was a scientific one. Since Chinese verbs have no tense, he was fascinated by the way English verbs changed form according to whether they were in the present, past imperfect, perfect, pluperfect, future, or future perfect tense. He was always making diagrams of verbs and their inflections, and he looked for opportunities to show off his mastery of the pluperfect and future perfect tenses, his two favorites. "I shall have finished my project by Monday," he would say smugly.

Mother's approach was to memorize lists of polite phrases that would cover all possible social situations. She was constantly muttering things like "I'm fine, thank you. And you?" Once she accidentally stepped on someone's foot, and hurriedly blurted, "Oh, that's quite all right!" Embarrassed by her slip, she resolved to do better next time. So when someone stepped on *her* foot, she cried, "You're welcome!"

In our own different ways, we made progress in learning English. But I had another worry, and that was my appearance. My brother didn't have to worry, since Mother bought him blue jeans for school, and he dressed like all the other boys. But she insisted that girls had to wear skirts. By the time she saw that Meg and the other girls were wearing jeans, it was too late. My school clothes were bought already, and we didn't have money left to buy new outfits for me. We had too many other things to buy first, like furniture, pots, and pans.

The first time I visited Meg's house, she took me upstairs to her room, and I wound up trying on her clothes. We were pretty much the same size, since Meg was shorter and thinner than average. Maybe that's how we became friends in the first place. Wearing Meg's jeans and T-shirt, I looked at myself in the mirror. I could almost pass for an American—from the back, anyway. At least the kids in school wouldn't stop and stare at me in the hallways, which was what they did when they saw me in my white blouse and navy blue skirt that went a couple of inches below the knees.

When Meg came to my house, I invited her to try on my Chinese dresses, the ones with a high collar and slits up the sides. Meg's eyes were bright as she looked at herself in the mirror. She struck several sultry poses, and we nearly fell over laughing.

The dinner party at the Gleasons' didn't stop my growing friendship with Meg. Things were getting better for me in other ways too. Mother finally bought me some jeans at the end of the month, when Father got his paycheck. She wasn't in any hurry about buying them at first, until I worked on her. This is what I did. Since we didn't have a car in those days, I often ran down to the neighborhood store to pick up things for her. The groceries cost less at a big supermarket, but the closest one was many blocks away. One day, when she ran out of flour, I offered to borrow a bike from our neighbor's son and buy a ten-pound bag of flour at the big supermarket. I mounted the boy's bike and waved to Mother. "I'll be back in five minutes!"

Before I started pedaling, I heard her voice behind me. "You can't go out in public like that! People can see all the way up to your thighs!"

"I'm sorry," I said innocently. "I thought you were in a hurry to get the flour." For dinner we were going to have pot-stickers (fried Chinese dumplings), and we needed a lot of flour.

"Couldn't you borrow a girl's bicycle?" complained Mother. "That way your skirt won't be pushed up."

"There aren't too many of those around," I said. "Almost all the

girls wear jeans while riding a bike, so they don't see any point buying a girl's bike."

We didn't eat pot-stickers that evening, and Mother was thoughtful. Next day we took the bus downtown and she bought me a pair of jeans. In the same week, my brother made the baseball team of his junior high school, Father started taking driving lessons, and Mother discovered rummage sales. We soon got all the furniture we needed, plus a dart board and a 1,000-piece jigsaw puzzle (fourteen hours later, we discovered that it was a 999-piece jigsaw puzzle). There was hope that the Lins might become a normal American family after all.

Then came our dinner at the Lakeview restaurant.

The Lakeview was an expensive restaurant, one of those places where a headwaiter dressed in tails conducted you to your seat, and the only light came from candles and flaming desserts. In one corner of the room a lady harpist played tinkling melodies.

Father wanted to celebrate, because he had just been promoted. He worked for an electronics company, and after his English started improving, his superiors decided to appoint him to a position more suited to his training. The promotion not only brought a higher salary but was also a tremendous boost to his pride.

Up to then we had eaten only in Chinese restaurants. Although my brother and I were becoming fond of hamburgers, my parents didn't care much for western food, other than chow mein.

But this was a special occasion, and Father asked his coworkers to recommend a really elegant restaurant. So there we were at the Lakeview, stumbling after the headwaiter in the murky dining room.

At our table we were handed our menus, and they were so big that to read mine I almost had to stand up again. But why bother? It was mostly in French, anyway.

Father, being an engineer, was always systematic. He took out a pocket French dictionary. "They told me that most of the items would be in French, so I came prepared." He even had a pocket flashlight, the size of a marking pen. While Mother held the flashlight over the menu, he looked up the items that were in French.

"Pâté en croûte," he muttered. "Let's see . . . *pâté* is paste . . . *croûte* is crust . . . hmm . . . a paste in crust."

The waiter stood looking patient. I squirmed and died at least fifty times.

At long last Father gave up. "Why don't we just order four complete dinners at random?" he suggested.

"Isn't that risky?" asked Mother. "The French eat some rather peculiar things, I've heard."

"A Chinese can eat anything a Frenchman can eat," Father declared.

The soup arrived in a plate. How do you get soup up from a plate? I glanced at the other diners, but the ones at the nearby tables were not on their soup course, while the more distant ones were invisible in the darkness.

Fortunately my parents had studied books on western etiquette before they came to America. "Tilt your plate," whispered my mother. "It's easier to spoon the soup up that way."

She was right. Tilting the plate did the trick. But the etiquette book didn't say anything about what you did after the soup reached your lips. As any respectable Chinese knows, the correct way to eat your soup is to slurp. This helps to cool the liquid and prevent you from burning your lips. It also shows your appreciation.

We showed our appreciation. *Shloop*, went my father. *Shloop*, went my mother. *Shloop, shloop*, went my brother, who was the hungriest.

The lady harpist stopped playing to take a rest. And in the silence, our family's consumption of soup suddenly seemed unnaturally loud. You know how it sounds on a rocky beach when the tide goes out and the water drains from all those little pools? They go *shloop, shloop, shloop.* That was the Lin family, eating soup.

At the next table a waiter was pouring water. When a large *shloop* reached him, he froze. The pitcher continued to pour, and water flooded the tabletop and into the lap of a customer. Even the customer didn't notice anything at first, being also hypnotized by the *shloop, shloop, shloop.*

It was too much. "I need to go to the toilet," I mumbled, jumping

to my feet. A waiter, sensing my urgency, quickly directed me to the ladies' room.

I splashed cold water on my burning face, and as I dried myself with a paper towel, I stared into the mirror. In this perfumed ladies' room, with its pink-and-silver wallpaper and marbled sinks, I looked completely out of place. What was I doing here? What was our family doing in the Lakeview restaurant? in America?

The door to the ladies' room opened. A woman came in and glanced curiously at me. I retreated into one of the toilet cubicles and latched the door.

Time passed—maybe half an hour, maybe an hour. Then I heard the door open again, and my mother's voice. "Are you in there? You're not sick, are you?"

There was real concern in her voice. A girl can't leave her family just because they slurp their soup. Besides, the toilet cubicle had a few drawbacks as a permanent residence. "I'm all right," I said, undoing the latch.

Mother didn't tell me how the rest of the dinner went, and I didn't want to know. In the weeks following, I managed to push the whole thing into the back of my mind, where it jumped out at me only a few times a day. Even now, I turn hot all over when I think of the Lakeview restaurant.

But by the time we had been in this country for three months, our family was definitely making progress toward becoming Americanized. I remember my parents' first PTA meeting. Father wore a neat suit and tie, and Mother put on her first pair of high heels. She stumbled only once. They met my homeroom teacher and beamed as she told them that I would make honor roll soon at the rate I was going. Of course Chinese etiquette forced Father to say that I was a very stupid girl and Mother to protest that the teacher was showing favoritism toward me. But I could tell they were both very proud.

The day came when my parents announced that they wanted to give a dinner party. We had invited Chinese friends to eat with us before, but this dinner was going to be different. In addition to a Chinese American family, we were going to invite the Gleasons.

"Gee, I can hardly wait to have dinner at your house," Meg said to me. "I just *love* Chinese food."

That was a relief. Mother was a good cook, but I wasn't sure if people who ate sour cream would also eat chicken gizzards stewed in soy sauce.

Mother decided not to take a chance with chicken gizzards. Since we had western guests, she set the table with large dinner plates, which we never used in Chinese meals. In fact we didn't use individual plates at all, but picked up food from the platters in the middle of the table and brought it directly to our rice bowls. Following the practice of Chinese-American restaurants, Mother also placed large serving spoons on the platters.

The dinner started well. Mrs. Gleason exclaimed at the beautifully arranged dishes of food: the colorful candied fruit in the sweet-and-sour pork dish, the noodle-thin shreds of chicken meat stir-fried with tiny peas, and the glistening pink prawns in a ginger sauce.

At first I was too busy enjoying my food to notice how the guests were doing. But soon I remembered my duties. Sometimes guests were too polite to help themselves, and you had to serve them with more food.

I glanced at Meg, to see if she needed more food, and my eyes nearly popped out at the sight of her plate. It was piled with food: the sweet-and-sour meat pushed right against the chicken shreds, and the chicken sauce ran into the prawns. She had been taking food from a second dish before she finished eating her helping from the first!

Horrified, I turned to look at Mrs. Gleason. She was dumping rice out of her bowl and putting it on her dinner plate. Then she ladled prawns and gravy on top of the rice and mixed everything together, the way you mix sand, gravel, and cement to make concrete.

I couldn't bear to look any longer, and I turned to Mr. Gleason. He was chasing a pea around his plate. Several times he got it to the edge, but when he tried to pick it up with his chopsticks, it rolled back toward the center of the plate again. Finally, he put down his chopsticks and picked up the pea with his fingers. He really did! A grown man!

All of us, our family and the Chinese guests, stopped eating to watch the activities of the Gleasons. I wanted to giggle. Then I caught my mother's eyes on me. She frowned and shook her head slightly, and I understood the message: the Gleasons were not used to Chinese ways, and they were just coping the best they could.

For some reason I thought of celery strings.

When the main courses were finished, Mother brought out a platter of fruit. "I hope you weren't expecting a sweet dessert," she said. "Since the Chinese don't eat dessert, I didn't think to prepare any."

"Oh, I couldn't possibly eat dessert!" cried Mrs. Gleason. "I'm simply stuffed!"

Meg had different ideas. When the table was cleared, she announced that she and I were going for a walk. "I don't know about you, but I feel like dessert," she told me when we were outside. "Come on, there's a Dairy Queen down the street. I could use a big chocolate milkshake!"

Although I didn't really want anything more to eat, I insisted on paying for the milkshakes. After all, I was still hostess.

Meg got her large chocolate milkshake, and I had a small one. Even so, she was finishing hers while I was only half done. Toward the end she pulled hard on her straws and went *shloop, shloop*.

"Do you always slurp when you eat a milkshake?" I asked, before I could stop myself.

Meg grinned. "Sure. All Americans slurp."

717

Reader Response

Open for Discussion When two cultures meet, there are bound to be differences. How did the Lin family cope with those differences? How would you?

1. When you are faced with embarrassing situations, humor helps. Find examples to show how the Lin daughter applied humor.

2. Compare the dinner at the Gleasons' house with the dinner at the Lins'. What were the similarities and differences between the two situations?

3. Read again the scene with the Lin family *schlooping* their soup in the Lakeview restaurant. What and whom do you see in the scene? What other details do you picture in your mind?

4. Make a chart with the following heads: *Word/Story Meaning/ Other Meaning.* In the first column, write the multiple-meaning words from the Words to Know list. In the second column write the meaning of each word as it is used in the story. In the third column, write another meaning for each word. Use a dictionary if you need help.

Test Practice

Look Back and Write What is the all-American slurp? How does it make an appropriate ending to this account of the Lin family? Write your response.

Read more books by Lensey Namioka.

Lensey Namioka says, "I wrote 'The All-American Slurp' when a Chinese relative visited us in America and he vigorously slurped his soup. After I had lived in America for so many years, my attitude had changed on table manners, so that I found his slurping startling. I wrote the story to illustrate the differences in manners."

Born in China, Lensey Namioka moved to the United States when she was nine years old. She remembers what it was like to be a little girl in China and what it was like to move to a new country. The celery story comes from another family experience. She says, "When we were invited by an American family to dinner, we all started pulling the strings from our celery, to the great amusement of our hosts."

Ms. Namioka also writes about Japanese history and the samurai. She became interested in Japan after visiting there with her husband, who is Japanese.

Although she studied mathematics in school, Lensey Namioka chose to become a writer. In all, she has written twenty-two books, of which many have won awards. "My advice to young writers," she says, "is to have a thick skin and not be discouraged when you get criticized or rejected." She lives in Seattle, Washington, and speaks frequently at schools and bookstores.

Half and Half

The Coming of the Bear

719

Expository Nonfiction

Genre

- Expository nonfiction conveys information and facts.

- Expository nonfiction pieces can examine everyday, useful things found in the real world.

Text Features

- The title and the short opening paragraph provide the reader with a quick summary of the information in the article.

- Notes in the margin give additional interesting facts.

Link to Social Studies

The end of the article states, "We can only guess what tomorrow's utensils will look like!" Work with a partner and invent a new utensil. Share your creation with the class.

THE EVOLUTION OF
Eating Utensils

BY LINDA WASHINGTON

Think about the eating utensils you use every day. Have you ever wondered how they came about? Utensils have a long history.

The Knife

The knife is one of the oldest eating utensils. The first knives were made from flint, a gray stone discovered during—you guessed it—the Stone Age. A knife was handy not only for protection, but also for spearing food. And, unlike a sharp stick, which could also be used for spearing, a flint knife did not break so easily.

Over time, knives became thinner and sharper as metals like bronze and iron were discovered. In early centuries, rich Egyptians, Greeks, and Romans ate with knives to avoid getting their fingers dirty. In their own way, knives became a symbol of wealth.

Prehistoric knives of flint

During the Middle Ages knives became more common among all people. Using two knives—one to cut with and one to carry food to the mouth—was a sign of good manners. But, as you might guess, using a sharp knife to eat with was dangerous.

Table knives like the ones you see in your family's silverware drawer or the school cafeteria, came about in 1669. King Louis XIV wanted to put a stop to violence in France. He declared that all knives must have a rounded edge. Used for cutting food rather than piercing it, these safer, rounded-end knives became increasingly more common on dinner tables.

King Louis XIV declared all table knives must have a rounded end to put a stop to violence.

Chopsticks

Chopsticks, which originated in China, have been around for more than 5,000 years. The earliest chopsticks might have been twigs used to take hot food from a pot. These sticks kept the fingers from being burned. Chinese chop-sticks were usually made from ivory, jade, or wood.

In Japan, most chopsticks were made from either wood or bamboo. And instead of two separate sticks like you see today, chopsticks were attached at one end the way tweezers are today. During the tenth century, however, the sticks were separated.

The chopsticks we use today often have a square end, to fit the hand better, as well as a rounded tip.

Chopsticks are called kuai-zi in Mandarin Chinese.

Compare & Contrast In some articles, comparisons are easy to make.

The Fork

The first forks had only two tines. Greeks and Romans used a long-handled fork in the first century, but not to eat with. At that time, forks were used for carving and serving meat only. In sixth century, smaller forks became more common in the Middle East. In Germany, during the eighteenth century, the fork gained more tines—rather than two, there were now four. But this four-tined fork didn't make its way to the United States until the nineteenth century.

When Catherine de Médicis of Italy married King Henry II in 1533, she brought the fork to France. Yet in France, as well as Italy, forks were not popular at first. Many people thought they were weird.

A man named Thomas Coryate claimed that he brought the fork to England. He stated in his writings that while traveling in Italy and France in 1608, he saw people using forks and decided to use one too. But back in England his friends made fun of him. They called him *ferciferus*, which meant "pitchfork handler." To this he replied, "Wait and see; one day you will each have a fork. Mark my words!" And he was right. Years later, the fork caught on among the rich, and eventually most everyone else.

Origins of Eating Utensils

prehistoric times	c. 3000 B.C.	first century A.D.	sixth century A.D.	18th century A.D.	19th century A.D.
crude knives developed	chopsticks first used	modern spoon developed	fork first used as eating utensil	four-tined fork created	spork created

The Spoon

Some form of the spoon has been around since prehistoric times. Both the Greek and Latin words for *spoon* are derived from *cochlea*, meaning "a spiral-shaped snail shell." The earliest spoons were probably sticks with seashells attached to them. Later spoons were made from wood, ivory, metals, and other materials—even bone!

We have the Romans to thank for the spoon we use today. During the first century, the Romans developed two types of spoons. One had an oval bowl and a long, thin handle. The other had a round bowl. Modern spoons were modeled from these designs.

During the Middle Ages, most people used spoons made of wood, pewter, or tin. Only rich people had fancy silver spoons. That's probably why the phrase *born with a silver spoon in his mouth* means "born into a wealthy family."

The Spork

The spork is a combination fork and spoon. It has a spoon shape and short tines on the end. You've probably used a plastic one at a fast-food restaurant. The spork has been around since the 1800s when they were made from silver or stainless steel. Large stainless steel or silver sporks are still used as serving utensils.

We can only guess what tomorrow's utensils will look like!

Reading Across Texts

What historical information about the eating utensils of their cultures might the Lins and the Gleasons of "The All-American Slurp" exchange?

Writing Across Texts Write your favorite bit of historical trivia about eating utensils.

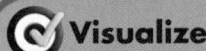 **Visualize** Why is visualizing important when comparing utensils?

Comprehension

Skill
Draw Conclusions

Strategy
Answer Questions

Draw Conclusions

- When you draw a conclusion, you form a reasonable opinion about something you have read.

- Evaluate whether your conclusions are valid. Ask yourself: Do the facts and details in the text support my conclusion? Is my conclusion valid, based on logical thinking and common sense?

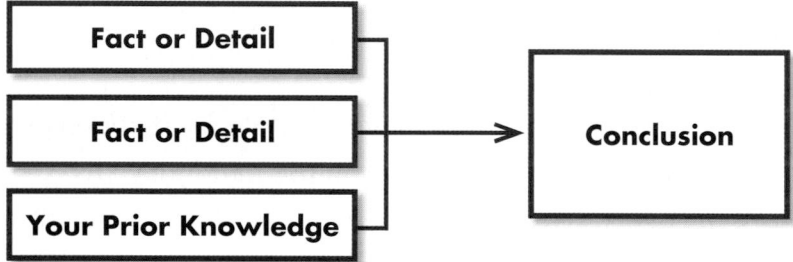

Strategy: Answer Questions

Good readers show their understanding of what they read by giving accurate and complete answers to questions. When the question asks you to draw a conclusion, sometimes the information needed to do so is stated right in the text. But some questions may require you to combine the information in the text with what you already know.

1. Read "The Conquistadores." Make a graphic organizer like the one above in order to draw a conclusion about the character traits of these people.

2. Evaluate your conclusion by answering these questions: What facts and details support your conclusion? Is your conclusion based on common sense and logical thinking? Explain.

The Conquistadores

During the 1500s, Spaniards sailed to the Americas and began to explore the land there. In time, some of them began to conquer and take control over parts of the Americas. These Spaniards were called *conquistadores,* which is the Spanish word for *conquerors.* These men were arguably most interested in fighting and searching for gold.

Francisco Pizarro is known for conquering the Inca people of South America. In 1531, Pizarro set sail for Peru, the center of the mighty Inca empire. He had with him 180 men and nearly forty horses. The Incas had a much larger army, but they were fighting among themselves. Pizarro and his men made a surprise attack against the Incas and captured their leader. Later, this leader was killed by Pizarro's men, even after he gave the Spaniards a room full of gold and silver.

Sebastián de Belalcázar was another well-known conquistador. He traveled to the Americas in 1519 and conquered Nicaragua in 1524. In 1531, he went to Peru with Pizarro. Later, Belalcázar conquered Ecuador and part of Colombia.

History demonstrates that most of the conquistadores were better at fighting than governing. Because of this, other Spanish leaders eventually took their places.

Strategy Good answers are accurate and complete. Answer this question: What are conquistadores?

Skill Which of the following conclusions about Pizarro is valid?

(a) He was generous.

(b) He was clever.

(c) He was afraid.

Think about his actions.

Strategy Why were Pizarro and his men able to defeat the Incas? Where is the information?

Skill Draw a conclusion in order to answer the following question: What do you think the conquistadores were like as rulers?

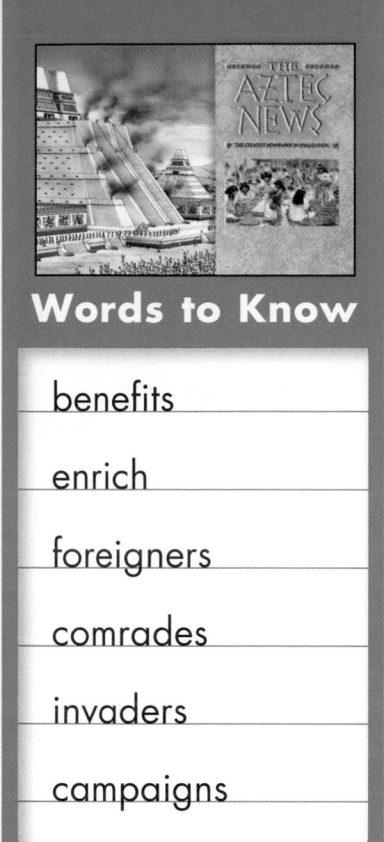

Words to Know

benefits

enrich

foreigners

comrades

invaders

campaigns

Vocabulary Strategy
for Multiple-Meaning Words

Dictionary/Glossary Some words have more than one meaning. If the words and sentences around a multiple-meaning word do not give clues to which meaning the author is using, refer to a dictionary or glossary.

1. Think about the different meanings a word can have. For example, a *bug* can be a crawling insect, a disease germ, or a small hidden microphone.

2. Find the entry word in the dictionary. Read the definitions. Think about the way the word is used in the text.

3. Decide which meaning makes sense in the sentence: The *bug* recorded the thieves' conversation.

4. Reread the sentence, replacing the word with the meaning you think fits best.

5. If this meaning seems right, read on. If not, try another meaning.

As you read "The End of the Aztecs," use a dictionary or glossary to decide which meaning a multiple-meaning word has in the article.

The End of the Aztecs

During the 1500s, through exploration, Europe had learned of the Americas. They called this place across the ocean to the west the "New World." European people had long dreamed of finding a better route to the East with its wealth of spices, silk, jewels, and gold. A good, quick route to the East would give the discoverer many trade benefits. Instead, adventurers sailed west and found the lands and native peoples of the Americas.

Natives such as the Aztecs of Mexico had a rich kingdom with much gold. These people had vast knowledge, including ways that would help to enrich the soil to provide good crops; they had built a huge city on a lake. The Aztecs were truly ingenious people. The Spanish, who sought riches, organized armies and ships and set sail. What must the proud Aztec people have thought of these white-skinned foreigners? It is likely that the Aztec leader believed the Spanish leader was a god. The Aztecs offered valuable gifts and welcomed the Spanish. The Spanish, however, did not want to be comrades to the Aztecs. They came as invaders, not friends. Their campaigns against the Aztecs were bloody but successful. In just two years, the Aztecs had been conquered and enslaved.

Write

Write a summary of a battle or war that you have studied or read about. Use words from the Words to Know list.

In what ways were the Aztecs
like we are today?

728

THE AZTEC NEWS

 THE GREATEST NEWSPAPER IN CIVILIZATION

by PHILIP STEELE

Genre

Informational text is text that is based on factual information. Though not a real newspaper, look for details that demonstrate that *The Aztec News* is based on real information about Aztec history and culture.

729

SUCCESS IS OURS!

Illustrated by ANGUS McBRIDE

OUR VICTORY over the Mixtec city of Coixtlahuaca in 1458 marked the start of our triumphant rise to power under Montezuma I. A reporter from *The Aztec News* witnessed the final battle and sent back this report.

I AM STANDING in the center of Coixtlahuaca. All around me, the streets are filled with dead and dying Mixtecs.

The sky is thick with smoke as the Mixtec temple goes up in flames. This fire is a triumphant sign to the world that victory is ours.

Ahead of me, I can see our army's finest warriors, the Eagles and the Jaguars, rounding up captives to be sent back to our city for sacrifice.

Today's events bring to a close one of the largest campaigns we Aztecs have ever waged. There were more than 200,000 warriors in the army that left Tenochtitlán, along with 100,000 porters to carry their supplies.

I am told that the Mixtecs shook with fear as they saw row after row of our warriors marching toward them. No matter how hard the Mixtecs fought, they had no hope of defeating us.

This glorious victory will be remembered for years to come. Not only will the sacrifice of so many captives delight our gods, but the people of Coixtlahuaca must now pay a high price if they wish to be left in peace.

The Mixtecs are known throughout the land for the wealth of their traders and the fine skills of their craftworkers. The tribute payments they must send to Montezuma will fill his treasury with riches. ▣

CLASH OF STRENGTH: The Mixtecs are forced back by our Jaguar and Eagle warriors.

COUNTDOWN TO CONFLICT

Illustrated by IAN THOMPSON

March 1519

Stories begin to reach Tenochtitlán from the east coast, telling of tall wooden towers floating on the sea. Reports say there are 11 of these strange ships.

April 1519

Over 600 pale-skinned foreigners leave the ships and set up camp at Veracruz. Our spies learn that the men call themselves Spaniards. This news is taken to Montezuma II. He sends splendid gifts of gold to the Spanish leader, Hernán Cortés.

August 1519

The Spaniards burn their ships — do they plan never to leave our land? Riding on the great deer they call horses, they set off toward Tenochtitlán.

September 1519

Cortés persuades our enemies, the Tlaxcalan people, to join him as he marches through their land.

November 8, 1519

Cortés reaches Lake Texcoco, where he is greeted by Montezuma. The Spaniards and the Tlaxcalans are invited to stay in one of the palaces in our city.

November 24, 1519

Cortés tries to control Tenochtitlán by taking Montezuma hostage.

May 1520

At a religious festival, the Spaniards murder a number of our nobles. Fighting breaks out and the foreigners retreat to their palace.

June 1520

Montezuma tells us we must make peace with the Spaniards. These are not the words of a brave ruler.

Our nobles turn their backs on Montezuma and choose Cuitlahuac, his brother, as ruler.

Montezuma begs us to make peace, but we will listen to this traitor no longer. Instead, we pelt him with stones. He falls, the Spaniards carry him back to their palace, and he is never seen alive again. ◼

SPANIARDS FLEE CITY

Illustrated by GINO D'ACHILLE

THIS GLORIOUS DAY, June 30, 1520, is one that our people will remember forever. At long last the Spanish cowards have been chased from our city—Tenochtitlán is free!

TODAY, the murderous invaders lie dead in the thousands, many of them still clinging greedily to their stolen gold.

Last night the Spanish leader made a foolish mistake. Having realized that he could not easily defeat us, Cortés decided to lead his army out of our city. And knowing that we Aztecs rarely fight at night, he waited until it was dark to escape. The gods seemed to be on his side. There was no moon, and the night was pitch-black.

The Spaniards and their Tlaxcalan allies crept through the city toward the lake, hoping to sneak across the eastern causeway to the mainland.

But they had barely reached the edge of the city when they were seen by some women fetching water from the lake.

These brave women swiftly gave the alarm, and the whole city arose to give chase.

TRAPPED AT THE GAP

As the enemy fled, our warriors took to their canoes. They planned to trap the Spaniards and Tlaxcalans at the first of the four gaps in the causeway and to attack them from the water.

Our warriors thought the enemy wouldn't be able to cross the gaps—as usual, the wooden bridges that span them had been removed to prevent anyone from entering our city at night.

But knowing this, the Spaniards had built their own bridge. Only when they came to the second gap in the causeway did they realize their mistake. The Spaniards had only one bridge, and the last of their army was still using it to cross the first gap!

By this time our warriors had reached the causeway in their canoes.

CAUSEWAY CHAOS: The enemy die in the thousands as they attempt to flee the city.

And now they let loose a deadly hail of stones, spears, and arrows. Some of the enemy were killed outright. Others were wounded and fell into the lake.

Many of the Spaniards drowned, weighed by their heavy armor. In a desperate bid to escape, others clambered over the bodies of their dead comrades. And in this way a number of them managed to reach the mainland.

When day dawned and the bodies were counted, it became clear that as few as a third of the Spaniards and Tlaxcalans had gotten away.

Cortés must now be weeping like a cloud in the rainy season. Surely he will never dare to return to Tenochtitlán.

THE PRICE OF POWER

Illustrated by LUIGI GALANTE

HAVE YOU EVER wondered what life would be like as a noble? If so, remember that life at the top isn't everything it's cracked up to be.

OF COURSE, there are many benefits to being a noble. For starters, they're seriously rich! Apart from anything else, whenever tribute payments are sent to our great ruler by conquered peoples, every noble is given a share of the goods.

And, as we all know, nobles can have two-story houses and live right in the city center.

NOBLE: Fine clothes, but is it all fun and games?

Then, there's the fact that noblemen are able to marry as many women as they want to. And they and their families are allowed to wear top-quality clothing, like long cotton or feather capes, and jewelry made from gold and precious stones.

Commoners, on the other hand, can't wear any jewelry other than clay-bead or shell necklaces and earrings. And may the gods help them if they're ever seen in anything not made out of maguey-cactus cloth!

TWO SIDES TO EVERY STORY

But there's a downside to everything, of course.

For example, if a noble is found guilty of a crime, he'll be punished far more harshly than a commoner. A commoner caught for a particular crime might be forced into slavery, but a noble might lose his life for the same offense.

Then there are your children to think of. As a noble, you'll probably send them to a calmecac school so they'll get a better choice of job when they grow up. If they study hard, they may even become a judge, a general, or a priest. But as calmecac students aren't ever allowed to visit their homes, you'll never get to see them.

COMMONER:
A simple life, but a happy one?

As a commoner, you will probably prefer your children to go to a local telpochcalli school. They may have to sleep there, but at least they'll be free to come home to eat with you every day.

The simple truth of the matter is you're better off the way you are. So count your blessings—and just be glad that you're an Aztec! ⏎

PUBLIC NOTICES

RUNAWAY SLAVES

Anyone caught touching a runaway slave will be forced into slavery. Only their owners may try to catch them. All slaves who escape win their freedom.

KNOW YOUR PLACE!

An increasing number of commoners have been seen wearing cotton clothes. This is a luxury allowed only to nobles. Commoners are reminded that they are forbidden to wear any clothing not woven from the fiber of the maguey cactus.

OFFENDERS WILL BE TAKEN INTO SLAVERY.

TENOCHTITLÁN, A GUIDE

Illustrated by CHIRIS FORSEY

HEART OF THE CITY: The Great Temple stands at the center of Tenochtitlán—use it as a landmark and you'll never get lost.

OUR BEAUTIFUL CITY attracts visitors from all over the empire, but finding your way around can be tricky. So let *The Aztec News* help you to make the most of your stay in Tenochtitlán.

YOUR FIRST sight of our glorious island city will take your breath away—if, that is, you have any left after the long climb over the mountains that surround Lake Texcoco!

As you come down into the valley, you'll see Tenochtitlán glimmering in the distance ahead of you, like a golden jewel set in jade green water. It may not look so big from where you are now, but you'll soon discover that it's vast. Covering nearly 6 square miles, our city is home to more than 250,000 people.

GETTING AROUND

Once you reach the lake's edge, you have a choice. You can either paddle across the water in a dugout canoe, or you can enter the city by one of three long causeways, all of them wide enough for eight people to walk along side by side.

Once in Tenochtitlán, you can also choose to travel by canoe or walk, as the city is crisscrossed by a network of canals and streets.

But be warned, the canals can be very smelly. You might find yourself traveling next to a canoe taking sewage from the city's public toilets to enrich the soil of the chinampas—the farms at the edge of our island.

But don't let this stop you from taking a trip around the chinampas. Paddle out there some fine evening, then drift through the peaceful tunnels of leaves—it's a truly unforgettable experience!

SIGHTSEEING

Towering above the city skyline is our famous Great Temple with its twin shrines. One shrine is to Huitzilopochtli, the awesome god of the sun, war, and our nation. The other is to Tlaloc, our mighty god of rain.

Sadly, only nobles are allowed inside the Great Square where the temple stands. But even if you aren't permitted to enter the square, you'll be able to glimpse the shrines over the high stone wall that surrounds it.

Around the outside of the square are the three royal palaces and the houses of the nobles.

But to discover how ordinary people live, head out of the city center to the busy streets that lie beyond. Here you'll find whitewashed cottages noisy with turkeys, dogs, and children.

EATING OUT

Our city is well known for its mouthwatering tortilla pancakes—buy one from a street vender.

Fresh from mountain springs, water is carried into the city by aqueducts.

SOUVENIRS

Whatever you're looking for, from the simple to the exotic, the place to go is Tlatelolco Market. To find it, just head north from the Great Square. Most traders will accept a variety of goods in exchange for their wares, but you might find it easier to take along some cocoa beans or pieces of copper instead.

FESTIVALS

If you can, go to one of our religious festivals while you're in the city—there's at least one every month. The costumes, dancing, and music at these spectacular events will make your visit to Tenochtitlán one you'll always remember! ▣

UNDER COVER

Illustrated by LUIGI GALANTE

OUR TRAVELING merchants, the pochtecas, are often envied for their great wealth. But the trade reporter of *The Aztec News* believes that their riches are well earned in view of the dangers they face.

I REMEMBER the very first time I saw the pochtecas. I was 5 years old. It was a hot night and I couldn't sleep, so I wandered out onto the road.

There, in the moonlight, I saw a long line of porters shuffling by, straining beneath their loads. And leading them were shadowy figures dressed in capes.

"Who are those men?" I asked my mother.

"They're pochtecas," she said, smiling. "They are the merchants who bring in marvelous things for us to buy at the market.

"They carry so much wealth with them that they travel under the cover of darkness for fear of robbers. And they store their goods in secret warehouses in the city."

My mother went on to talk of the far-off lands the pochtecas visited and of the many treasures they brought back—golden jewelry, feather capes, tortoiseshell cups, spices, cocoa beans. . . .

Of course, it wasn't surprising that I hadn't yet come across these merchants. They keep to themselves. They live in a separate part of the city and have their own temples and laws. They even have their own god— Yacatecuhtli.

But when I was a young warrior marching across the empire with the army, I often saw these merchants trading in faraway cities. And I began to realize that it's the pochtecas who help to make our city so rich. Since then, I've wondered if they do more than just buy and sell. . . .

I SPY A TRADER

I've heard people say that the pochtecas spy for our ruler in the lands they visit. We can't know this for certain, of course, but they do have the perfect cover—they speak many languages, and they do their best to blend in with other tribes.

BY THE LIGHT OF THE MOON: Three pochtecas and their porters quietly leave the city.

There's no question that many pochtecas are even richer than nobles. But then, traveling beyond the borders of the empire can be dangerous—let alone spying! Personally, I admire their courage, and I have ever since that magical night when I was a little boy.

LOOKING FOR ADVENTURE?

Could you carry a 60-pound load for more than 20 miles a day? Then you could be a _tlamene_, a porter on our next trading expedition.

You'll get regular food rations and a chance to travel.

Apply to the Pochteca Committee, Tlatelolco.

THROWING THE PERFECT PARTY

Illustrated by ANGUS McBRIDE

WHETHER YOU'RE celebrating a birthday or doing your best to impress your friends, organizing a party can be hard work—unless, that is, you do it *The Aztec News* way.

THE GUEST LIST

Choose your guests with care. Nobles: You will want to invite men in positions of power who can help you or your family. Commoners: Ask as many people as you can afford, to show how generous your are.

THE PLACE TO PARTY

Make sure the seating areas for men and women are clearly separated. If you don't have enough space inside

LET'S PARTY! Noble men and women gather for a feast.

your house, a courtyard will work just as well. Decorate the area with fresh flowers, incense burners, and torches for when it gets dark.

THE MENU

Bear in mind that if your guests don't like the food you give them, they can invite themselves back again the following day for another party. So really make an effort with the menu!

If you can afford it, serve specialties like hot turkey potpies with chili and tomato sauce or lobster with avocado. And it wouldn't be much of a party without plenty of frothy hot chocolate, would it?

ENTERTAINMENT

It goes without saying that no party is complete without music and dancing. So, if you can afford to, hire some entertainers. Otherwise, invite along a few friends who are good singers or dancers.

DRESS TO IMPRESS

Everything is ready, and your guests will soon be arriving. But have you thought about what to wear? It's vital that you look your best in honor of the occasion.

Men: You'll want to wear your most brilliantly patterned cape and loincloth. If you're a noble, take the chance to show off your finest headdress and armbands and your best nose- and lip-plugs.

And ladies: Make sure that your most colorful skirt and overblouse are fresh and clean.

If you're a commoner, it's worth thinking about making a new outfit—maguey cloth does look best when it's new.

Noblewomen should add some amber or jade earrings and perhaps a gold necklace. Precious metals and stones are forbidden to commoners, of course. Instead, wear your finest clay-bead or shell necklace.

AND FINALLY. . .

Don't forget that as the host of the party you will be expected to give each one of your guests a suitable present at the end of the evening. ▣

 **About A.D. 1100**

The Aztecs leave their homeland in the north of Mexico to travel south in search of a new home.

 **About 1195**

The Aztecs arrive in the Valley of Mexico.

 **1325**

The city of Tenochtitlán is founded on an island in Lake Texcoco.

The first Great Temple is built by the Aztecs in thanks to their gods.

The Aztecs have to pay tribute to the ruler of Atzcapotzalco, the most powerful city on the lake.

 **1375**

Acamapichtli, the first-known ruler of the Aztecs, comes to the throne.

 **1428**

The Aztecs join forces with the nearby cities of Texcoco and Tlacopan, forming what is known as the Triple Alliance.

Together they conquer the city of Atzcapotzalco and dominate the Valley of Mexico.

 **1440**

Montezuma I comes to the throne. Under his leadership the Aztec empire expands.

 **1486**

Ahuizotl becomes ruler. During his reign the empire continues to grow.

 **1502**

Montezuma II becomes ruler. The Aztec empire is now at its height.

 **1519**

A fleet of Spanish ships lands on the east coast of Mexico. The Spaniards set up camp at Veracruz.

Led by Hernán Cortés, the Spanish army heads toward Tenochtitlán. It is joined by warriors of the Tlaxcalan people.

Montezuma invites the Spaniards and their allies to stay in one of the royal palaces in Tenochtitlán. Once there, they take Montezuma prisoner.

 **1520**

Cuitlahuac, Montezuma's brother, is elected ruler. Montezuma dies, and the Spaniards flee the city.

Smallpox breaks out. Thousands die, including Cuitlahuac. Cuauhtémoc becomes the new ruler.

 **1521**

The Spaniards and their Tlaxcalan allies return and surround Tenochtitlán. On August 13, after a siege lasting 93 days, the Aztecs surrender and their city is destroyed. More than 240,000 Aztecs die during the siege.

 **1522**

Tenochtitlán is rebuilt and named Mexico City. It is declared the capital of the Spanish colony of New Spain.

Ahuizotl	*ah-wi-zotl*	**Tlaloc**	*tla-lok*
chinampa	*chee-nam-pa*	**tlamene**	*tla-may-nay*
Coixtlahuaca	*ko-eesh-tla-hwah-kah*	**Tlatelolco**	*tla-tay-lo-ko*
Huitzilopochtli	*hwee-tsee-lo-potch-tlee*	**Tlaxcalan**	*tlahsh-kah-lan*
maguey	*mah-gway*	**tortilla**	*tor-tee-ya*
Mixtec	*meesh-tek*		
Montezuma	*mon-tay-zu-ma*		
pochteca	*potch-tay-kah*		
telpochcalli	*tel-potch-kah-yee*		
Tenochtitlán	*teh-nosh-teet-lan*		
Texcoco	*tesh-ko-ko*		

Some of the names used in this book are modern ones, such as America or Mexico. The Aztecs would have used different names.

MAP OF THE
AZTEC EMPIRE

NORTH AMERICA

SOUTH AMERICA

HUAXTEC PEOPLE

CHICHIMEC PEOPLE

THE VALLEY OF MEXICO

Tlacopan

Texcoco

Tenochtitlán

TLAXCALAN PEOPLE

Gulf of Mexico

Veracruz

TEOTITLÁN PEOPLE

Coixtlahuaca

YOPITZINGO PEOPLE

MIXTEC PEOPLE

MAYAN PEOPLE

Pacific Ocean

THE VALLEY OF MEXICO

Lake Zumpango

Lake Xaltocan

Lake Texcoco

Tenochtitlán

Lake Chalco

Lake Xochimilco

N
W E
S

Extent of the Aztec Empire at A.D. 1521

Reader Response

Open for Discussion   Suppose that over 400 years from now some eager author writes a mock newspaper about your culture today. How would the news stories resemble *The Aztec News?* How would they be different?

1. *The Aztec News* combines information and imagination. Find statements that impart information. Then find statements that seem to spring from the author's imagination.

2. Though we know they're not real, the advertisements in *The Aztec News* give us information about the culture of the Aztecs. What conclusion could you draw about the pochtecas from the ad at the bottom of page 739?

3. Does having this information about the Aztecs in the format of a newspaper make it seem more ancient or more modern? Explain your answer.

4. There were pluses and minuses to being noblemen and commoners in Aztec society. Make a chart. List some of each. Use words from the Words to Know list and the selection.

Look Back and Write   In 1520, the Spaniards are driven from the city. What happens a year later? Find the fateful outcome hidden on page 742. Write about it in your own words.

744

Read more books by Philip Steele.

Philip Steele learned about the world of publishing during the years he worked as an editor. "I still find the most exciting part of my work begins with the planning and visualization of a title, sitting around the table with designers, artists, and editors."

After working as an editor in England, Mr. Steele moved to Wales to do freelance writing. He says, "The move was a stimulating one. I learned to speak the Welsh language, made new friends, and relaxed in some of the most beautiful scenery in the British Isles." Today he lives in Wales with his wife and his daughter, Elin Rhiannon.

Mr. Steele likes to travel and does so whenever he can. He has backpacked across the Middle East, India, the former Soviet Union, and China. He has also spent time in the United States, Canada, Mexico, and Africa. He says these experiences have given him background material for his children's books about countries, peoples, and natural history.

Mr. Steele has published more than sixty books in Britain. Yet he says that he would still like to write a historical novel for younger readers, "if I can ever find the time!"

Castles

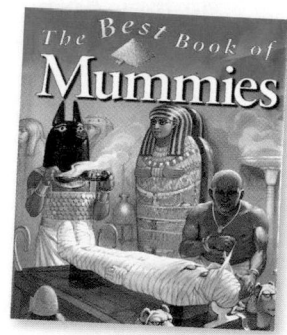

The Best Book of Mummies

Reading Online

Online Directories

Genre

- Internet Web sites called online directories list links to many Web sites about a given topic.

- You can use an online directory instead of a search engine to learn about a topic.

Text Features

- Directories list topics as links on their home page. You may click on any topic link.

- You may instead choose to type in keywords and click on the search button.

- Your next stop is a list of links to Web sites that are all about your topic.

Link to Social Studies

The Mayans used a calendar very different from the one we use. Research the Mayan calendar or the history of various calendars and present your findings to the class.

The Mayans

The Mayans, Aztecs, and Incas were the largest civilizations in the lands now considered part of *Latin America*. The oldest of these three great civilizations, the Mayans, built their empire in what is now southern Mexico and Central America.

Since you have just read about the Aztecs, you might be curious about the Mayans as well. You could use your Web browser to help you find an Internet online directory. Here are some of the topics you will likely find listed there.

Take It to the NET
ONLINE
more activities sfsuccessnet.com

746

The closest general topic is Ancient Civilizations, so you click on this link. It takes you to a page of specific categories about this general topic.

ONLINE DIRECTORY

Today's Pictures	Health & Wellness	Ancient Civilizations
Earth Science	Kids' Health	World War II
Weather	History	

File   Edit   View   Favorites   Tools   Help

http://www.url.here

Ancient Civilizations

1. Aztecs— A description of the history, religion, economy, society, and writings of the culture that dominated Mexico in the fifteenth and sixteenth centuries.

2. Ancient Egypt— Explore over 5000 years of Egyptian civilization through artifacts, articles, maps, and models.

3. Mayan Life— The Maya originated in Yucatán in Mexico. They developed astronomy, calendar systems, and their own writing method. They built elaborate pyramids and observatories, all without metal tools.

4. Mesopotamia— Mesopotamia is often referred to as the "cradle of civilization," because it was the first known civilization in the world. It was located between the Tigris and Euphrates Rivers in parts of what are now Turkey and Iraq.

You decide to click on Mayan life.

 **Draw Conclusions**   Draw at least one conclusion about the Mayan people.

Here is the result of the Mayan Life link.

File   Edit   View   Favorites   Tools   Help

http://www.url.here

PEOPLE   PLACES   BELIEFS   GLOSSARY   GAMES   CLIPART   MAYAN

The Ancient Maya

They built their cities in the rain forest. They also played games that went on for days and are famous for their knowledge of the stars. They chewed "gum," pierced their bodies, and raised bees without stingers so they could harvest honey without getting stung. Like the Egyptians, they built pyramids. Click on the links above to help you learn more about the Maya.

Edit   View   Favorites   Tools   Help

http://www.url.here

> When you click on Places, you would find this information.

PEOPLE   PLACES   BELIEFS   GLOSSARY   GAMES   CLIPART   MAYAN

Mayan Places

Chichén Itzá—The Snake and the Sun

This temple looks like a pyramid and is called **El Castillo.** It's 75 feet tall. On the first day of spring and the first day of fall, the sun casts shadows on the steps that look like a snake wiggling down the pyramid. To the Maya, this was a lucky symbol. It meant that it was time to plant corn or prepare for the harvest.

Merida: Temple of the Seven Dolls

Dzibilchaltun means "the place where there's writing on the stones." This city is close to Merida on the north coast of Yucatán. Some parts of Dzibilchaltun are more than 2,500 years old. By far the most impressive structure is the Temple of the Seven Dolls. A small but fascinating museum on site displays the seven dolls which were found inside the temple.

If you clicked on <u>People</u>, you would find this information.

PEOPLE   PLACES   BELIEFS   GLOSSARY   GAMES   CLIPART   **MAYAN**

Mayan Customs

The Maya had a sense of beauty that was quite different from ours. They shaped the skulls of their newborn children by tying boards to the forehead. They admired a forehead that sloped back.

Jade earrings and jewelry box. ▲

The Maya had tattoos and pierced their bodies. The Maya wore many different forms of jewelry. The most common was jade. Jade was worn in beads, earrings, and ear spools. It was also one of the materials that the Maya traded. The Maya also wore gold.

The Maya would put body paint on themselves for special occasions. They filed their teeth to make them pointed and put jade in the spaces. Men wore an **ex,** which is a loincloth. Women wore loose sacklike dresses. The clothes of the priests and nobles were made with finer materials and had many shells and beads on them. For ceremonies, they wore wonderful headdresses.

Reading Across Texts

Look for similarities among the Aztecs, Mayans, and people of today. What things are the same?

Writing Across Texts Write at least two paragraphs to a friend in which you tell about how the people today are different from the Maya and Aztecs.

⊙ Answer Questions   Look in several places to answer the questions above.

Comprehension

Skill
Generalize

Strategy
Ask Questions

 # Generalize

- A generalization is a broad statement or rule that applies to many examples. Authors sometimes make generalizations about a group of things or people to get a message across.

- A generalization is often signaled by clue words such as *most, all, always,* or *never.*

- A generalization can be either valid or faulty. Valid generalizations are supported by examples, facts, or sound logic. Invalid generalizations are not supported.

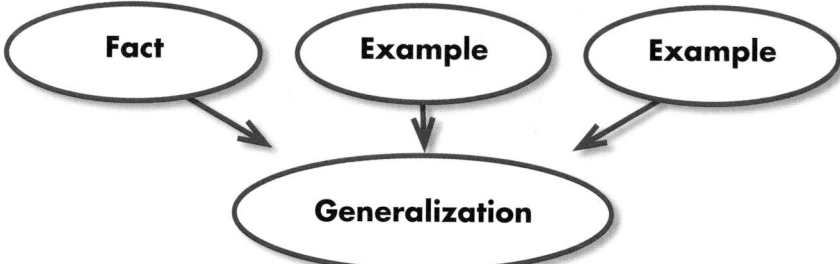

Fact **Example** **Example**

Generalization

 ## Strategy: Ask Questions

Good readers ask themselves questions before, during, and after they read. Before you read, look over the article and ask: *What will this be about?* While you're reading, ask yourself what the author is trying to say. Look for any generalizations the author is making. After you read, ask yourself whether those generalizations were valid or faulty.

 **Write**

1. Read "Traveling Men" and make a graphic organizer like the one above to make a generalization.

2. Write a paragraph making a generalization about A. Philip Randolph and supporting it.

Traveling Men

After the Civil War, two important events happened at about the same time. Slaves were freed, and the first intercontinental railroad was finished.

With the new, longer train trips, passengers needed a comfortable place to sleep on the train. Chicago businessman George Pullman claimed that his new sleeping cars had luxury and service at affordable prices. Pullman hired former slaves, who did an excellent job working as porters on these luxury sleeping cars.

It was work the former slaves were glad to get. It gave them a steady job and respect in the neighborhood. They were known as "traveling men."

However, their jobs were far from fair. Hours were long, pay was quite low, and there was no job security. Porters could be fired for no reason. As time progressed, younger porters, who had not been born into slavery, began to see that they deserved much better treatment. However, the Pullman company refused to make changes.

Because of the refusal, the porters formed a union in 1925 called the Brotherhood of Sleeping Car Porters, led by A. Philip Randolph. It took twelve long years of struggle, but the union finally won better pay and working conditions.

And it was this courage and perserverance that, in part, helped the modern Civil Rights movement gain momentum.

Skill The Emancipation Proclamation was signed in 1863. The Civil War ended in 1865. The railroad was completed in 1869. You might use these examples to generalize that this was a time of great change in the United States.

Strategy What questions could you ask to find out whether the generalization about the quality of the porters' work is valid or faulty?

Strategy Write down a question you have about the Pullman porters' job. See if it will be answered as you read.

Skill Would it be a *valid* generalization to say that *all* porters wanted to join a union and fight for better treatment and wages? Explain your thinking.

751

Words to Know

rural
urban
burden
sufficient
maintenance
leisure
conformed

Remember

Try the strategy. Then, if you need more help, use your glossary or a dictionary.

Vocabulary Strategy
for Synonyms

Context Clues When you find a word you do not know, look at words near the unknown word. Often the author will provide clues to help you figure out the meaning of the word. One kind of clue that might help you determine a word's meaning is a synonym, a word that has the same or almost the same meaning as another word.

1. Read the words and sentences near the unknown word. The author may give you a synonym of the word that can help you predict the word's meaning. Authors sometimes use synonyms in their writing to help define other, more difficult words.

2. Look for a synonym to the unknown word. Substitute the synonym in place of the word. Does this meaning make sense in the sentence?

3. If not, read on. The larger context may make the meaning clear.

As you read "Country Versus City," look for synonym clues to help you understand the meanings of unfamiliar words.

Country Versus City

The twentieth century was a time of great change in America. In this time, America began the change from a more rural country to one that had larger and larger urban populations. In the early 1900s, most American people lived on small farms in the country. But in large cities, industry was growing. However, world wars placed a burden—or hardship—on supplies of everything. The nation began to build more factories, and production of goods was stepped up. People were needed to work in the factories, so many people who had worked in smaller rural areas moved to urban centers where the jobs were.

Some of these migrants had troubles. For example, a large influx of workers could mean there was not sufficient, or enough, housing. Families crowded into small apartments. They were not responsible for the maintenance, or upkeep, of the apartments. Even so, the owner might not make needed repairs. Life in the city meant changes in lifestyle. For example, what people did with their leisure, or free, time changed. Cities offered more action but less spacc.

As the century wore on and America became richer and more productive, urban populations became more sophisticated. Their interests conformed to, or matched up with, the opportunities they had come to know—better libraries, theaters, and other social and educational resources.

Look through the pictures in the selection and pick one to write about. Use as many words from the Words to Know list as you can.

Where Opportunity Awaits

by James R. Grossman
paintings by Jacob Lawrence

Genre

Expository nonfiction tells the nature of a true event. In addition to what you will read, notice the visual information that helps to inform you about the Great Migration.

Why did so many African Americans migrate from the South to the North in the early 1900s?

Painting by Jacob Lawrence. The Migration of the Negro, Panel 1, 1940-1941.

THE THOMAS FAMILY ARRIVED IN CHICAGO IN THE SPRING of 1917. Like thousands of other black southerners moving north, they first had to find a home.

For a week, they pounded the pavements of the city's South Side. Mr. and Mrs. Thomas, their 19-year-old daughter, and 17-year-old son eventually crowded into a five-room apartment — it was cramped but probably larger than the farmhouse they had left behind in Alabama.

Their second task was to find work. The men went to the stockyards, and the women earned money doing laundry.

African Americans hoped for better jobs as well as better education when they left to go to Northern cities.

Optimistic about the future, the teenagers spent their evenings at night school, hoping to improve on the grade-school education they had earned in a rural southern schoolhouse. In their free time, the family explored the leisure activities available on Chicago's South Side, carrying picnics into the park and venturing into theaters and ice cream parlors.

THE THOMASES WERE PART OF THE FIRST GREAT MIGRATION—the collective journeys of a half-million black southerners to northern cities between 1916 and 1919. By 1918, migration chains that linked South to North enabled thousands of southerners to choose destinations where they had friends or relatives to offer a welcoming hand. A native of Abbeville, South Carolina, for example, could move to Philadelphia without worrying about where she might sleep the first night in town. From Hattiesburg, Mississippi, a newcomer could easily find the Hattiesburg Barber Shop in Chicago and be directed to the appropriate boarding house. In most cases, these patterns conformed largely to patterns established by railroad routes. North and South Carolinians went to New York, Philadelphia, and other eastern seaboard cities. Pittsburgh's African American newcomers were likely to hail from Alabama, Georgia, or Kentucky. From Mississippi, Louisiana, Tennessee, and parts of Georgia and Alabama, people headed for Chicago. Because of the influence of *The Chicago Defender* newspaper and the long tentacles of the Illinois Central Railroad, Chicago was an especially popular destination.

"To Let" signs such as this one in Pittsburgh, Pennsylvania, were often difficult to find as the numbers of migrants increased.

The "chains" allowed prospective migrants to make arrangements before leaving home. "Let me know what day you expect to leave and over what road, and if I don't meet you I will have someone there to

Painting by Jacob Lawrence.
Tombstones, 1942.

meet you and look after you until I see you," one woman wrote from Chicago to a member of her former church in Mississippi. These kinds of community and family contacts had tied southern cities to their hinterlands for decades; they now extended north. A thin strand even stretched west from Texas and Oklahoma to the West Coast.

Because these migrants arrived during a wartime housing shortage, most encountered difficulty finding a place to live. Usually, a black northerner in 1920 was likely to have at least several white neighbors within a few blocks. But by 1930, that likelihood had diminished considerably, with African Americans segregated into ghettoes.

GHETTOES, HOWEVER, WERE NOT NECESSARILY SLUMS. PROPERTY values have not always declined as neighborhoods shift from "white" to "black." During the Great Migration and throughout much of the 1900s, the process was complicated. As southerners—most of them poor and unaccustomed to urban life—moved into the least expensive and oldest neighborhoods, established residents tended to seek better housing in less crowded districts. But housing discrimination meant that black neighborhoods could expand only slowly, and only at their edges.

Black northerners generally paid more than whites would pay for similar living space. At the same time, black workers earned less than their white counterparts. Hence, African Americans spent a very high percentage of their income on shelter. In some cases, this left homeowners without sufficient funds to maintain their houses adequately. In New York City's Harlem, rents generally commanded nearly half of the earnings of

African American residents. Naturally, this placed a considerable burden on family resources. In addition, because there was a constant need for housing, landlords collected rents more diligently than they maintained their buildings.

Tenants who demanded proper maintenance (and many did) could usually be replaced with newcomers who knew little about what to expect or who took what they could get because they had few choices. Gradually, the turnover of residents and the deterioration of buildings due to overcrowding and shoddy construction methods took its toll on the surrounding block. As a result, the neighborhood declined.

DURING WORLD WAR I AND AT TIMES DURING THE 1920s, black newcomers found places to work in northern cities much more easily than they found places to live. In fact, the first Great Migration was stimulated by the opening of thousands of new railroad jobs.

By 1917, African Americans were also working in heavy industry across the Northeast and Midwest. Most of the jobs in steel mills, auto plants, packinghouses, and rubber factories could be learned quickly. It was far more difficult for many migrants from the South to adapt to a different approach to time. They were not, however, the only ones who faced this difficulty. Rural workers around the world had faced the same difficulty when introduced to industrial employment.

In the rural South, just as in other agricultural societies, the calendar and the weather determined the work pace. One planter described cotton cultivation as "a

The first Great Migration was stimulated by the opening of thousands of railroad jobs.

The Migration of the Negro #17 comments on the sharecropping system that left many African Americans in poverty.

series of spurts rather than a daily grind." In those areas where southern workers did not have to sustain a regular pace — railroad-tie layers, dock hands, construction gangs, for example — a work song set the rhythm. These songs were flexible. A song leader, who set the tempo, could change the pace.

By the 1910s, most workers in northern factories were punching time clocks. Arrive 10 minutes late, and your pay was docked one hour. On the "disassembly lines" of the packinghouses, conveyer belts moved animal carcasses from worker to worker, each of whom would make a single cut. Tardiness or absence could disrupt the whole process. Once a line began moving, a newcomer had no control over the pace of work.

Women sorting peanuts in Chicago factory in 1928.

WHAT DID NOT REQUIRE adjustment, however, was hard work. "I will & can do eny kind of worke," declared one man just before heading north from his Florida home. Men with farm experience were accustomed to a workday that began at dawn and ended at sundown. Black women, responsible in both rural and urban settings for household labor as well as for producing income, began their work earlier and ended later. "I came here to Philadelphia because people said it was better," recalled Ella Lee of her early years in Philadelphia, "so much better living in the North than it was in the South. But so far as I am concerned you have got to work like a dog to have anything anywhere you go."

Home Chores, painted in 1945.

The difference for most migrants—the reason why most not only stayed but also encouraged their friends and relatives to join them— was that the hard work produced rewards during the war years and in the 1920s. In interviews and in letters back home, migrants spoke enthusiastically of sending their children to school, voting, sitting where they pleased on streetcars, and countless other accomplishments. Although black women in the North were pushed out of industry and into domestic employment after World War I, even domestic service paid better in the North than in the South. Black men retained their industrial footholds, putting more cash in their pay envelopes and looking forward to the possibility of promotion down the road.

Reader Response

Open for Discussion   Suppose your family, living in the South, is trying to decide whether to join the Great Migration. Make two lists: one labeled *Advantages,* the other labeled *Disadvantages.* What do you decide?

1. True to his title, the author presents advantages of the Great Migration. What about the disadvantages? Find examples. Then decide whether this author presents a balanced view.

2. Make two generalizations about the experiences of those who moved north during the Great Migration. Support your generalizations with information from the text.

3. The Jacob Lawrence paintings shown in this article represent the struggles of African Americans during this time period. Are Jacob Lawrence's feelings clear in his art? What questions would you ask him about his works of art if you could?

4. Write an ad designed to encourage African Americans living in the South in the 1900s to move north. State the advantages. Use words from the Words to Know list and from the selection.

Test Practice

Look Back and Write   What were migration chains (pages 757–758)? Write an explanation and give an example.

Meet the Author and the Illustrator
James R. Grossman and Jacob Lawrence

Read more books about the Great Migration and Jacob Lawrence.

James R. Grossman has researched and written books about the African Americans who journeyed from the South to the North in the first half of the twentieth century. He believes that we can learn "the meaning and boundaries of American citizenship and opportunity" from the Great Migration.

The Great Migration: An American Story
paintings by Jacob Lawrence

Story Painter: The Life of Jacob Lawrence
by John Duggleby

Jacob Lawrence once wrote, "The Great Migration is part of my life. I grew up knowing about people on the move from the time I could understand what words meant." Mr. Lawrence did a series of paintings on the Great Migration. "I started the Migration series in 1940, when I was twenty-two years old, and finished it one year later," he explained. "I can still remember all the panels spread out in my studio on tables made from boards and sawhorses. My wife, Gwen, helped me to prepare the surfaces. I painted the panels all at once, color by color, so they share the same palette."

Before his death in 2000, Mr. Lawrence created more than 1,200 works of art. His paintings are known for their bold images and vivid colors.

Social Studies in Reading

Expository Nonfiction

Genre

- Expository nonfiction contains facts and information that may be written using a text structure of sequence.

- In expository nonfiction, photographs and captions help to give information.

Text Features

- The photographs provide visual information about the immigrants and their relocation.

- This article has captions with the pictures. You can look at the pictures and read the captions first or study them after you have read the article.

Link to Social Studies

Ask family members, neighbors, or friends if they know someone who was an immigrant. Find out where the person immigrated from, and find the country on a map. Share the names and locations with your class.

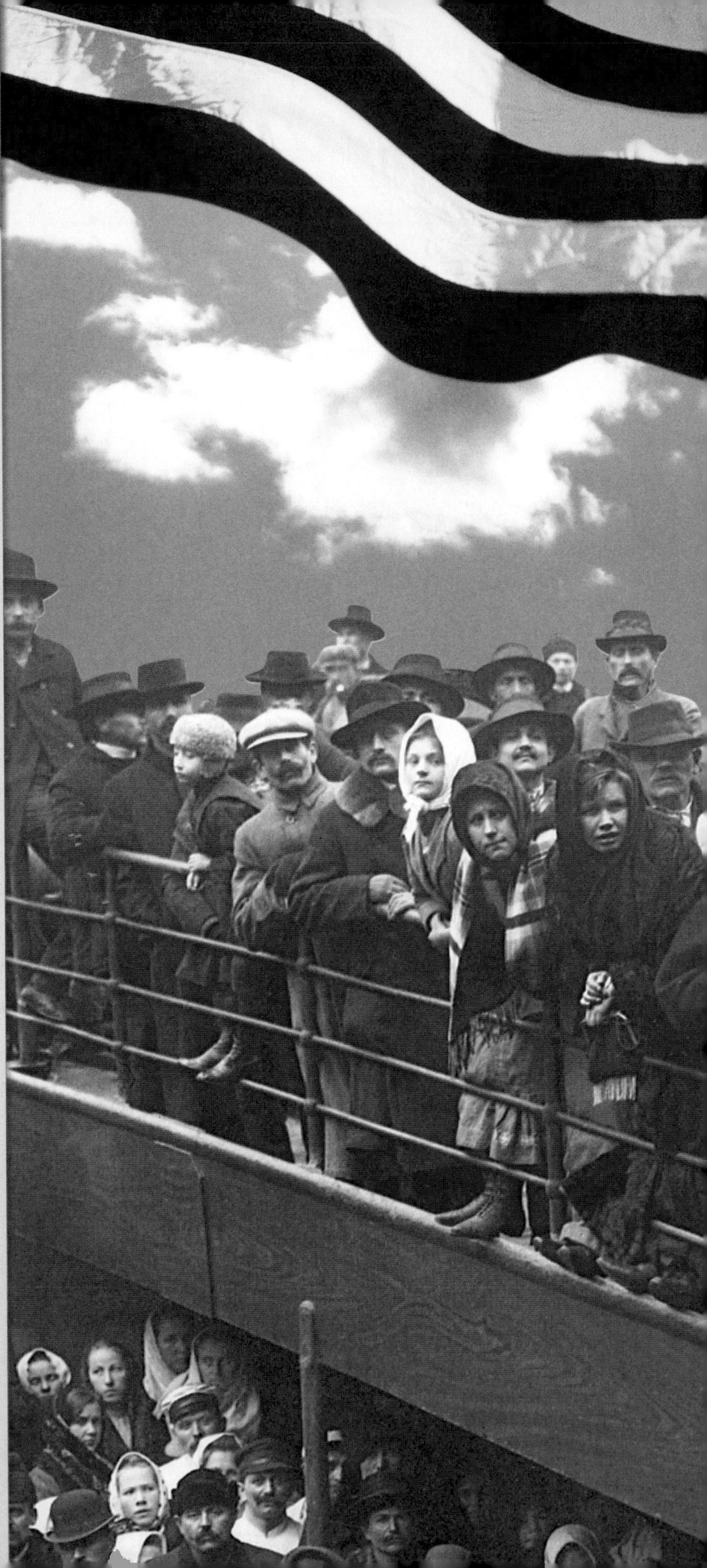

Coming Over

by Russell Freedman

BETWEEN 1880 AND 1920, TWENTY-three million immigrants arrived in the United States. They came mainly from impoverished towns and villages in southern and eastern Europe. The one thing they had in common was a fervent belief that in America, life would be better.

Most of these immigrants were poor, and many immigrant families arrived penniless. Often the father came first, found work, and sent for his family later.

Immigrants usually crossed the Atlantic as steerage passengers. Reached by steep, slippery stairways, the steerage lay deep down in the hold of the ship. It was occupied by passengers paying the lowest fare.

Generalize The author makes generalizations based on historical facts.

An Italian woman and her children arrive at Ellis Island, 1905.

Men, women, and children were packed into dark, foul-smelling compartments. They slept in narrow bunks stacked three high. They had no showers, no lounges, and no dining rooms. Food served from huge kettles was dished into dinner pails provided by the steamship company. Because steerage conditions were crowded and uncomfortable, passengers spent as much time as possible up on deck.

THE GREAT MAJORITY OF IMMIGRANTS landed in New York City, at America's busiest port. Edward Corsi, who later became United States Commissioner of Immigration, was a ten-year-old Italian immigrant when he sailed into New York Harbor in 1907. He wrote, "My first impressions of the New World will always remain etched in my memory, particularly that hazy October morning when I first saw Ellis Island. The steamer *Florida,* fourteen days out of Naples, filled to capacity with sixteen hundred natives of Italy, had weathered one of the worst storms in our captain's memory; and glad we were, both children and grown-ups, to leave the open sea and come at last through the Narrows into the Bay.

"My mother, my stepfather, my brother Giuseppe, and my two sisters, Liberta and Helvetia, . . . looked with wonder on this miraculous land of our dreams.

". . . Passengers all about us were crowding against the rail. Jabbered conversation, sharp cries, laughs and

New arrivals wait in long lines in the Great Inspection Hall at Ellis Island.

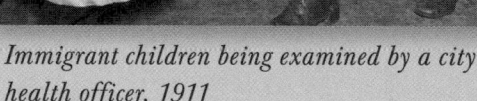
Immigrant children being examined by a city health officer, 1911

cheers—a steadily rising din filled the air. Mothers and fathers lifted up babies so that they too could see, off to the left, the Statue of Liberty. . . ."

BUT THE JOURNEY WAS NOT YET OVER. Before they could be admitted to the United States, immigrants had to pass through Ellis Island, which became the nation's chief immigrant-processing center in 1892. There they would be questioned and examined. Those who could not pass all the exams would be detained; some would be sent back to Europe. And so their arrival in America was filled with great anxiety. Among the immigrants Ellis Island was known as Heartbreak Island.

When their ship docked at a Hudson River pier, the immigrants had numbered identity tags pinned to their clothing. Then they were herded onto special ferryboats that carried them to Ellis Island. Officials hurried them along, shouting, "Quick! Run! Hurry!" in half a dozen languages.

Filing into an enormous inspection hall, the immigrants formed long lines separated by iron railings that made the hall look like a great maze.

First the immigrants were examined by two doctors of the United States Health Service. One doctor looked for physical and mental abnormalities. When a case aroused suspicion, the immigrant received a chalk mark on the right shoulder for further inspection: *L* for lameness, *H* for heart, *X* for mental defects, and so on.

Ask Questions | What questions of yours might the text answer as you keep reading?

767

Lower New York City and Ellis Island, 1936

The second doctor watched for contagious and infectious diseases. He looked especially for infections of the scalp and at the eyelids for symptoms of trachoma, a blinding disease. Since trachoma caused more than half of all medical detentions, this doctor was greatly feared. He stood directly in the immigrant's path. With a swift movement, he would grab the immigrant's eyelid, pull it up, and peer beneath it. If all was well, the immigrant was passed on.

Those who failed to get past both doctors had to undergo a more thorough medical exam. The others moved on to the registration clerk, who questioned them with the aid of an interpreter: What is your name? Your nationality? Your occupation? Can you read and write? Have you ever been in prison? How much money do you have with you? Where are you going?

Some immigrants were so flustered that they could not answer. They were allowed to sit and rest and try again. About one immigrant out of every five or six was detained for additional examinations or questioning.

Most immigrants made it through Ellis Island in about one day. Carrying all their worldly possessions, they waited on the dock for the ferry that would take them to Manhattan, a mile away. Some of them still faced long journeys overland before they reached their final destinations. Others would head directly for the teeming immigrant neighborhoods of New York City. But no matter where they went, they all hoped to find the same thing: a better life for themselves and their children.

Reading Across Texts

Migrants from the South and immigrants from Europe both faced challenges in their moves. What were some of the challenges?

Writing Across Texts Make lists of the challenges faced by each group.

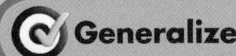 **Generalize** What generalizations can you make about the immigrants?

Borders

by Arnold Adoff

Great Grandma Ida came from a small village
in Poland
    on the Russian border
    to America,
    on a ship that sailed
    for weeks,
    on the rough Atlantic
        Ocean:

to make a new place for her self;
to work in a factory; to find her father;
to find a man
    from a German town on the Polish
        border

to marry; to have and raise a daughter
    who would find and marry
    a man from a Russian town
        on the Polish
        border.

And in 1935 they would have a baby boy
        in a New York City hospital
Who is daddy now to
        me.

My Bird Day

by Janet S. Wong

When my grandfather says *birthday*
in his Chinese accent,
it sounds like "bird day,"
which is closer to truth—
for us, anyway.

At my birthday parties
we never have
paper streamers,
piñatas in trees,
balloons taped up
on the wall.
We decorate with platters
of peking duck,
soy sauce chicken and squab
in lettuce cups.
Food is all
that matters.

Other Chinese families
might do things
differently,
but my grandfather,
whose name is Duck,
thinks it's good
luck to make
a bird day
special.

Happy Bird day!

The Colors Live

by Mary O'Neill

The Colors live
Between black and white
In a land that we
Know best by sight.
But knowing best
Isn't everything,
For colors dance
And colors sing,
And colors laugh
And colors cry—
Turn off the light
And colors die,
And they make you feel
Every feeling there is
From the grumpiest grump
To the fizziest fizz.
And you and you and I
Know well
Each has a taste
And each has a smell
And each has a wonderful
Story to tell. . . .

The New Colossus

by Emma Lazarus

Not like the brazen giant of Greek fame,
With conquering limbs astride from land to land;
Here at our sea-washed sunset gates shall stand
A mighty woman with a torch, whose flame
Is the imprisoned lightning, and her name
Mother of Exiles. From her beacon-hand
Glows world-wide welcome; her mild eyes command
The air-bridged harbor that twin-cities frame.
"Keep, ancient lands, your storied pomp!" cries she
With silent lips. "Give me your tired, your poor,
Your huddled masses yearning to breathe free,
The wretched refuse of your teeming shore.
Send these, the homeless, tempest-tossed to me—
I lift my lamp beside the golden door!"

Where I'm From

connect to
SOCIAL
STUDIES

Talk with members of your family about where your ancestors lived before migrating to the area where you live today. Try to go back a few generations.

Then make a map of the United States and other parts of the world your family members came from. Trace the route family members may have taken and add labels to show the approximate dates.

In what ways does one culture affect another?

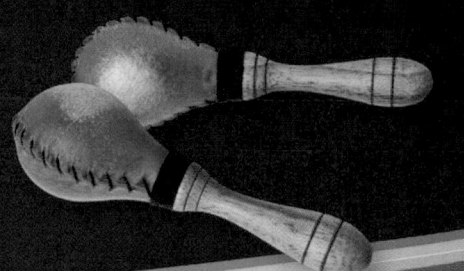

A New Way of Looking

connect to
ART

In his mind, Don Quixote transformed objects around him into something different, seeing windmills as giants, for instance. Suppose that Don Quixote were in your neighborhood today. What vehicles, animals, buildings, or other landmarks might he see and interpret as something else?

Draw a part of your community as Don Quixote might see it. Then show your illustration to classmates. Describe the part of the community you drew and explain how history might shape Don Quixote's way of looking at it.

From One Culture to Another

connect to
WRITING

You read about many cross-cultural influences in Unit 6. Research one of the contributions from a culture you read about in this unit. Write a booklet about it. You might include sections such as facts about the culture, how a certain object was made, and similar objects in use today. Add an illustration for each page. Make a cover for your booklet.

Everything You Ever Wanted to Know About Chopsticks

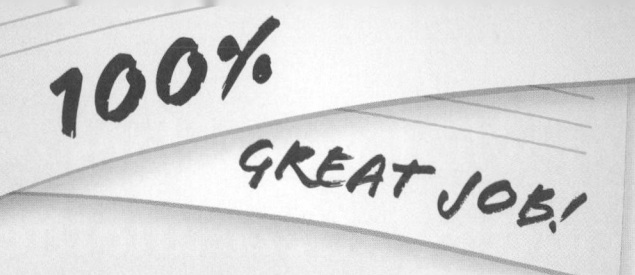

Answering Questions Well

Different Kinds of Questions

As a student, you must answer many questions.

- Your teacher asks you questions.
- Your textbooks contain questions.
- Practice books and workbooks contain questions.
- The tests you must take are full of questions.

Some tests have one kind of question. Other tests have more than one kind of question.

You might find multiple-choice or fill-in-the-blank questions. You might be asked to write your answers. If you write, your answers might have to be short or long.

To help you answer questions and take tests, read the pages that follow. You will learn strategies to help you read questions and find the answers. You can also use these strategies when you take tests. Some pages ask you to try to find the answers yourself. Write your answers on a separate sheet of paper.

Remember, you can develop the skills you need to do well.

A Lifelong Skill

The skills you are learning will help you do well on tests while you are in school. They will also help you after you finish school.

Throughout your life, you will have to answer questions that come from many sources. You may need to answer questions on a job. You will need to understand what you are being asked and answer the best you can.

Tips for Tests
Study for a test, but don't worry ahead of time. Get a good night's rest. Eat a good breakfast. Then, believe in yourself. Help yourself take a test by knowing you can do it. You have studied. You have learned test-taking skills. You are prepared!

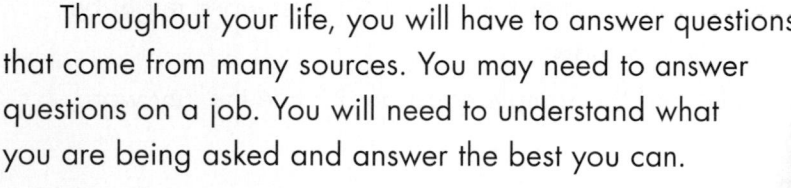

Understand the Question

Key Words

Before you can answer a question in a book or on a test, you must understand it. One way is to find key words. These tips will help you.

Read the question slowly. Ask yourself, "Whom or what is this question about?" The words that tell whom or what the question is about are **key words**.

Look for other key words in the question. Often the first word of the question is another key word. The first word might be *who, what, where, when,* or *how.*

Read the sentence and the sample question. Notice the key word.

> **Tip** Look for **key words** in the question. The question often uses words that are clues to the answer.

The asteroid Eros was discovered in 1898.

1 *When* was the asteroid Eros discovered?

Turn the question into a statement. Use the key words in a sentence that begins "I need to find out. . . ." After you read a question that begins with *when,* you might think to yourself, "I need to find out *when.* . . ."

You might think, "I need to find out *when* the asteroid Eros was discovered." Then look back at the text. The answer must be "in 1898."

Here is a sample text.

The National Weather Service uses computers to track storms across the United States. The computers use information provided by satellites orbiting the Earth to form pictures of storms.

Here is a sample question about the text. See how one student makes sure she understands the question.

Test Question

1 What does the National Weather Service use to track storms?

I've read the question. What is it about? Well, it's talking about the National Weather Service and what it uses to track storms. **National Weather Service** and **track storms** must be key words.

Okay, I'm going to read the question again. There's the key word **what**, and there's the key word **use**. I need to find out what the National Weather Service uses to track storms.
    The answer must be "computers."

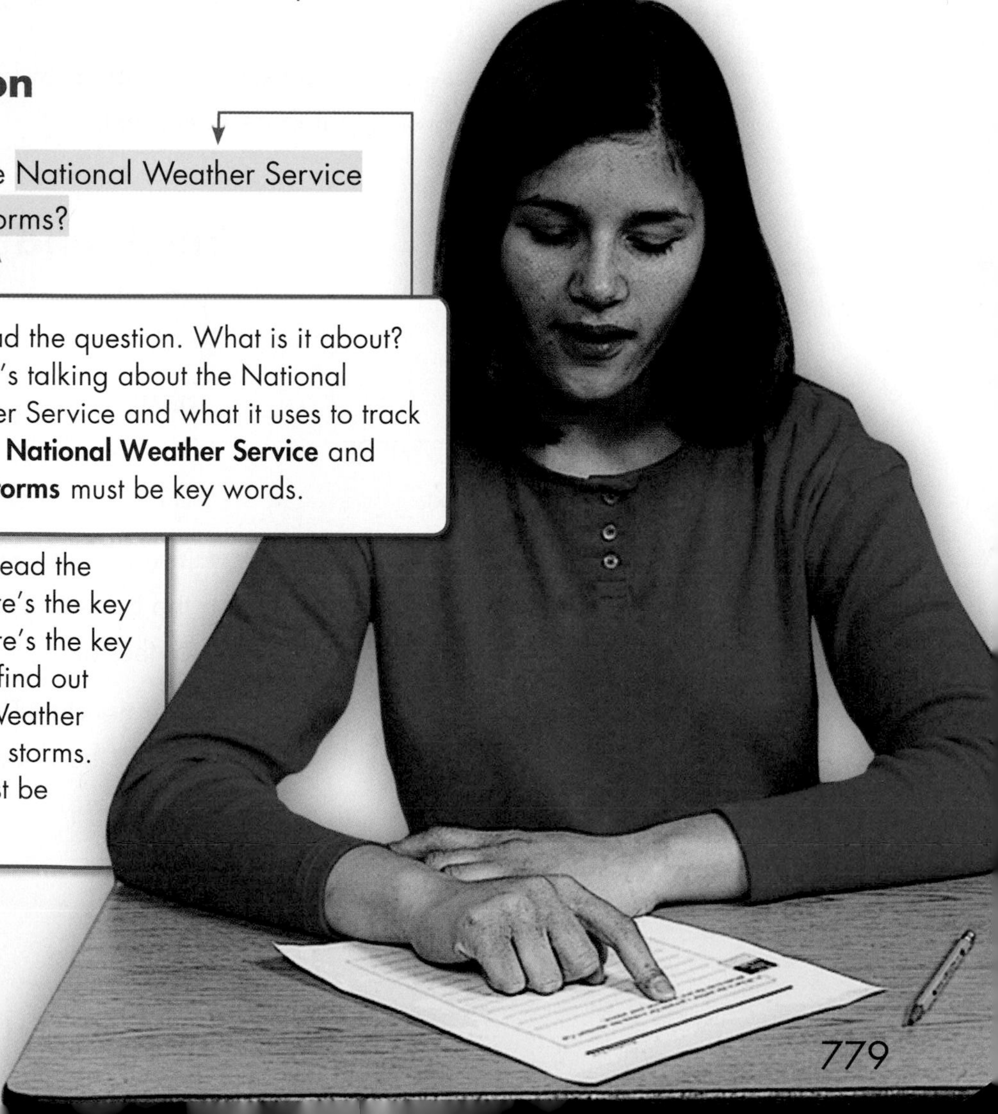

Here are strategies that will help you when you answer questions anytime. Think about each one. Which have you tried before? Which are new to you?

In the Book

Sometimes the answer to a question is **in the book.** You can find these answers right there in the text.

Right There

- The answer is RIGHT THERE in one spot in the text.

- The answer is usually easy to find.

- You can put your finger on the answer.

Think and Search

- The answer IS in the text, but NOT in one spot.

- You need to SEARCH for the answer in different parts of the text.

- You need to THINK how to put the information together.

In My Head

Sometimes the answers to questions are **in your head.**
The answers are NOT right there in the text.

Author and Me

- The answer is NOT written in the text.

- The AUTHOR gives you clues about the answer.

- You also must use what YOU already know.

- You put all this together to find the best answer.

On My Own

- The answer is NOT in the text at all.

- You must think about what you already know.

- You need to use your background knowledge to find the answer.

I Can Find the Answer

Right There

When you answer questions, sometimes you can find the answer RIGHT THERE in the text. You can find the answer in one sentence.

Read this selection and the test question. Notice that the answer to the question is RIGHT THERE in the text. You can find the answer in one sentence and put your finger on it. The answer is highlighted for you.

The answer is **right there.**

Though technology is slowly changing the lives of the different people living in Arctic lands, life in the Arctic is a challenge. The Arctic peoples make warm clothing from the skins of seals, bears, and deer. The Lapps keep herds of deer for meat, while the Inuits and Aleuts concentrate on fishing. In the cold, harsh weather, the Arctic peoples have **learned** to work together within the group **for survival**. For example, the task of gathering food is divided among the members of the group.

1 What have Arctic peoples **learned for survival?**

(A) to work together within the group

(B) to divide the task of gathering food

(C) to wear animal skins

(D) to eat fish and meat

When you read a question, decide what the key words are. Then look for key words in the text. The key words in this question and in the text are marked for you in bold type. Find the answer near the key words in the text.

Try It!

Now you decide the correct answers. Read this selection and the questions. Look for key words in the questions and in the text. Find the answers RIGHT THERE in the text. Then choose the correct answer in the test.

During colonial times there was no uniform system of money. From 1652 to 1686, Massachusetts made the first coins in the colonies. Soon other colonies made coins too. Most of the coins used in colonial times, however, were from other countries. After the United States became independent, the government decided it needed its own currency. In 1792, Congress passed a law to make the dollar the basic unit of American currency. At the same time, the first mint was opened in Philadelphia.

 Tip Read carefully. Look for key words in the question and in the text.

 Tip Remember: Sometimes you can find the answer to a test question *right there* in the text. The answer is near the key words in the text.

1 Where did most of the coins used in colonial times come from?

- (A) Massachusetts
- (B) the U.S. government
- (C) the Philadelphia mint
- (D) other countries

2 When did the government decide there was a need for its own currency?

- (F) when Massachusetts stopped issuing coins
- (G) when Congress passed a law against using money from other countries
- (H) when the United States became independent
- (J) when the first mint opened in Philadelphia

I Can Find the Answer

In the Book

 ## Think and Search

Sometimes the answer to a question is in the text, but it is not in just one sentence. You may need to SEARCH for the answer in two or more places in the text. Then you need to THINK how to put the information together for your answer.

Most of the time the selections you read will contain the answer in different places in the text. Sometimes a selection has a chart. To answer the question, you may need to look at both the selection and the chart.

Read this selection and study the chart. Then read the question. The key words are marked for you in bold type. Put together the information from the selection and the chart. The answer is highlighted for you.

Beaufort Wind Scale

Beaufort Number	Description of Wind	Miles per Hour
0	Calm	less than 1
1	Light Air	1–3
2	Light Breeze	4–7
3	Gentle Breeze	8–12
4	Moderate Breeze	13–18
5	Fresh Breeze	19–24
6	Strong Breeze	25–31
7	Moderate Gale	32–38
8	Fresh Gale	39–46
9	Strong Gale	47–54
10	Whole Gale	55–63
11	Storm	64–73
12–17	Hurricane	74 and above

The Beaufort wind scale is a series of numbers used to indicate wind speeds. For example, when the Beaufort number is 0, the effect on land is calm. Smoke rises vertically. The wind speed is less than 1 mile per hour. When the **Beaufort number** is **5**, the **wind speed** is higher and **small trees sway.**

1 Based on the **Beaufort number,** what is the **wind speed** in miles per hour when **small trees sway?**

(A) less than 1
(B) 19–24
(C) 32–38
(D) 64–72

Notice that the key words are **Beaufort number**, **5**, **wind speed**, and **small trees sway**. To get the answer, look in *both* the text and the chart. *Think* about the text and the chart. Then *search* for information and put it together to find the correct answer.

Try It!

Now you decide the correct answers. Read this selection and these test questions. Remember that you may have to SEARCH in more than one place to find the answers. Then THINK about how the information fits together.

Tip Key words can help you. These clues may be words with similar meanings, words used in measurements, or numbers.

Tip Remember that sometimes you need to **think** and **search** to put together information from two or more places.

For many years, surveyors disagreed on the exact height of Mount Everest. In the mid-1800s, a British team estimated the height to be 29,002 feet (8,840 meters). In 1954 an Indian government survey set the present official height at 29,028 feet (8,848 meters). Many people have tried to make the hard climb to the top of Mount Everest. On May 29, 1953, Sir Edmund Hillary of New Zealand and Tenzing Norgay, a Nepalese Sherpa man, became the first people to reach the top of Mount Everest.

1 Compared to an earlier height estimate, how much higher officially is Mount Everest?

(A) 8 feet
(B) 48 feet
(C) 8,848 meters
(D) 26 feet

2 How high did Sir Edmund Hillary believe Mount Everest was when he reached its top?

(F) 29,002 feet
(G) 8,848 meters
(H) 29,028 feet
(J) nearly 6 miles above sea level

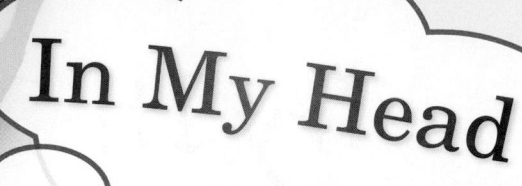

I Can Find the Answer — In My Head

Author and Me

Sometimes your reading does not give you every part of the answer to a question. You have to find the answer by putting together what the author tells you and what you already know. YOU and the AUTHOR work together.

Read the text and the question. Notice how the author gives you some of the information you need to answer the question. A sample answer is written for you.

Once there was a boy, Gawain, who did nothing but read books. His brothers told him to go out and make money. Gawain went out. He saw a house with a sign that read "Help Wanted." A scientist came to the door. He asked Gawain one question: Could he read? Gawain said that he could. The scientist said, "Too bad. I am looking for someone who cannot read. I need someone to dust my book collection." Gawain was determined to get the job. He said to himself: "I need to find a wig, a fake beard, and another coat."

1 What do you predict Gawain will do next?

To predict an outcome, look for clues in the text. Use what the **author** tells you and what **you** already know about how people might act in such a situation.

> Gawain will find a way to disguise himself. Then he will go back to the scientist and apply for the job again. This time he will say that he cannot read.

Try It!

Now you decide the best answers. Read the text and the questions. Think about what the AUTHOR tells you and what YOU know.

 Tip Read carefully. Think about what the author tells you.

 Tip Sometimes *you* and the *author* work together. Remember: information from the **author +** information from **me** = the best answer.

    Peter stood on the beach, straining to catch sight of his sister's rainbow-colored sail on the ocean. The sea threw a salty-tasting, bitter spray at him. The wind seemed to howl and moan, "Go back!" Peter pulled his fuzzy hat over his ears to shut out the chilling noise. He could smell the wild scent of the approaching storm. Then, in the far distance, he saw the colorful sail of his sister's boat appear above the horizon like a warm sunrise.

1 Which word best describes how Peter feels before he sees the boat?

(A) worried

(B) pleased

(C) angry

(D) impatient

2 Why do you think the author ended the scene with the words "like a warm sunrise"? Write your answer on a separate sheet of paper.

I Can Find the Answer In My Head

On My Own

Sometimes the answer to a question is *not* in the text. You have to think about it and about what you already know. For this kind of question, you can answer ON YOUR OWN.

Sometimes a test will ask you to write about a topic. Your answer should give details that tell what you know about the topic.

Read this selection and test directions. Then read how one student wrote an answer.

> The key words are highlighted. They tell the *topic* to write about.

The cell phone is one of the best communication devices ever invented. First of all, much business is conducted over the phone. Appointments are set up through phone calls. The cell phone lets business people stay in touch no matter where they are. If a person needs help, it is easy to dial the doctor, fire department, or police. The cell phone helps family members communicate.

Directions: Write about a device that you think is especially useful. Give details about why the device is useful.

Tip Remember to think about the topic before you write so you can give clear details about your own ideas.

> The computer has changed the world. Every business seems to have a computer system. Business people aren't the only ones to use a computer for keeping records. Every home seems to need a computer too. My dad keeps accounts on our computer. He uses it to figure his income tax. Besides, the computer is fun. I use it for playing video games, burning CDs, and sending e-mails to my friends.

Notice that the student did not find the answer in the text. The student had to use personal ideas and experiences to write the answer.

Try It!

Read the text below. Notice that you do not need the text to write an answer. The text helps you start thinking about a writing topic. Remember that sometimes you need to write an answer ON YOUR OWN.

Students should be allowed to use the school gym and the gym equipment after school on certain days. The gym and the equipment are paid for, so the only cost would be to pay someone to supervise. Students could use the gym and the equipment to improve their physical education skills. Open gym time would help students who have no place else to go.

Directions: Think about your school or your community. What improvement would you make if you could? Tell what you think should be done, and why. Choose either your school or your community to write about. Write your answer on a separate sheet of paper.

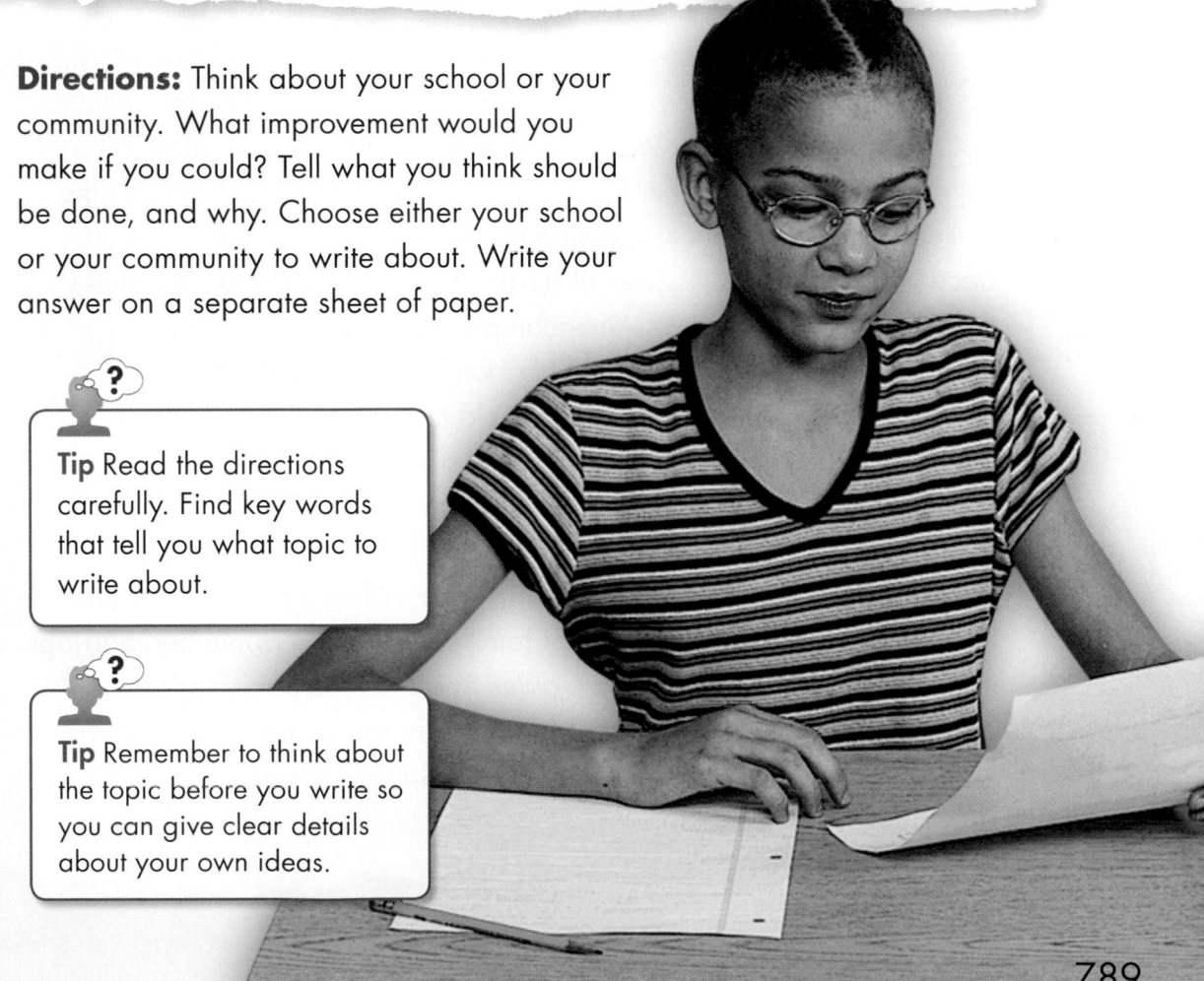

Tip Read the directions carefully. Find key words that tell you what topic to write about.

Tip Remember to think about the topic before you write so you can give clear details about your own ideas.

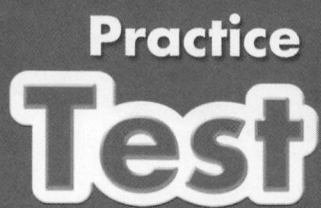

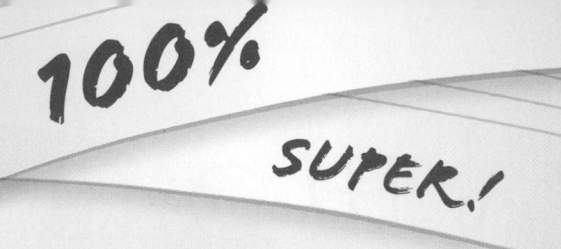

Directions: You might find a selection like this one on a real test. Read the selection. Then answer the questions that follow.

Laura Ingalls Wilder was born in Pepin, Wisconsin, in 1867. As a child, she traveled with her family throughout the Middle West and the Dakotas. Her experiences growing up on the American frontier later became the basis for a series of books. These wonderful stories evoke the spirit and difficulties of American pioneer life.

The first book in the series, *Little House in the Big Woods*, was published in 1932. Laura is six years old in this first story. One part of the book beautifully re-creates a special day when she receives a doll as a present. It also tells about many of the dangers and hardships Laura's family faced, such as floods, droughts, and attacks by wild animals.

In 1885 Laura Ingalls married Almanzo Wilder of New York. She later united the Ingalls and Wilder families by writing about her marriage in a book called *These Happy Golden Years*. It was published in 1943.

Laura Ingalls Wilder's books have been popular for more than 60 years. They contain many warmhearted, inspiring stories that everyone should read and enjoy.

Write the correct letter of each answer. **Use a separate sheet of paper.**

1 How old was Laura in the first book in the series?

(A) five
(B) six
(C) ten
(D) thirty-two

2 Where was Laura Ingalls Wilder born?

(F) Southwestern United States
(G) New York
(H) Dakotas
(J) Wisconsin

3 When was the first *Little House* book published?

(A) 1885
(B) 1910
(C) 1932
(D) 1943

4 About how many years later than the first *Little House* book was *These Happy Golden Years* published?

(F) about 10
(G) about 32
(H) 43
(J) 60

5 What is the author's opinion of Laura Ingalls Wilder's books?

(A) The author dislikes the books.
(B) The author expresses no opinion.
(C) The author likes the books very much.
(D) The author thinks only children should read the books.

6 How long have Laura Ingalls Wilder's books been popular?

(F) more than 43 years
(G) more than 50 years
(H) more than 60 years
(J) more than 90 years

7 Which of the following did Laura Ingalls Wilder *not* write about?

(A) pioneer life
(B) city adventures
(C) family ties
(D) American pioneer spirit

8 Write about a book you read. Tell why you liked it, or why you disliked it. Include details about the book in your answer.

Glossary

How to Use This Glossary

This glossary can help you understand and pronounce some of the words in this book. The entries in this glossary are in alphabetical order. There are guide words at the top of each page to show you the first and last words on the page. A pronunciation key is at the bottom of every other page. Remember, if you can't find the word you are looking for, ask for help or check a dictionary.

The entry word is in dark type. It shows how the word is spelled and how the word is divided into syllables.

> *The pronunciation is in parentheses. It also shows which syllables are stressed.*
>
> > *Part-of-speech labels show the function or functions of an entry word and any listed form of that word.*

con·quer (kong′kər), *V.* to overcome; get the better of: *conquer a bad habit.* ❑ *V.* **con·quered, con·quer·ing, con·querers.**

> *Sometimes, irregular and other special forms will be shown to help you use the word correctly.*

The definition and example sentence show you what the word means and how it is used.

Aa

ab·surd (ab sėrd′), *ADJ.* plainly not true or sensible; foolish; ridiculous: *The idea that the number 13 brings bad luck is absurd.*

a·bun·dant (ə bun′dənt), *ADJ.* more than enough; very plentiful: *an abundant supply of food.*

ac·cess (ak′ses), **1.** *N.* right to approach, enter, or use; a dmittance: *All students have access to the library during the afternoon.* **2.** *V.* to make information available by putting into or retrieving from a computer memory: *access a list of names.* ❑ *V.* **ac·cessed, ac·ces·sing.**

ac·cus·tomed (ə kus′təmd), **1.** *ADJ.* usual; customary: *By Monday I was well again and was back in my accustomed seat in class.* **2.** *ADJ.* accustomed to; used to; in the habit of: *I am accustomed to getting up early.*

a·drift (ə drift′), *ADJ.* floating without being guided; drifting: *During the storm, our boat was adrift on the lake.*

ag·gres·ive (ə gres′iv), *ADJ.* taking the first step in an attack or a quarrel; ready to attack others: *a warlike and aggressive nation.*

al·ien (ā′lyən), **1.** *N.* person who is not a citizen of the country in which he or she lives. **2.** *N.* an imaginary creature from outer space. ❑ *N. PL.* **al·iens.**

ap·par·ent·ly (ə par′ənt lē), *ADV.* seemingly; with the appearance of.

ap·pli·ca·tion (ap′lə kā′shən), *N.* a request for something, such as employment, an award, a loan, etc.: *I filled out an application for a job at the supermarket.*

aliens

ar·chi·tec·ture (är′kə tek′chər), *N.* style or special manner of building: *Greek architecture made much use of columns.*

ar·ti·fact (är′tə fakt), *N.* anything made by human skill or work, especially a tool or weapon. ❑ *N. PL.* **ar·ti·facts.** (*Artifact* comes from two Latin words, *artem* meaning "art" and *factum* meaning "made.")

as·tron·o·mer (ə stron′ə mər), *N.* an expert in astronomy, the science that deals with the sun, moon, planets, stars, etc. ❑ *N. PL.* **as·tron·o·mers.** (*Astronomer* comes from the Greek root *astr* meaning "star.")

at·tire (ə tīr′), *V.* to clothe or dress; array: *The king was attired in a robe trimmed with ermine.* ❑ *V.* **at·tired, at·tir·ing.**

au·thor·i·ty (ə thôr′ə tē), *N.* power to enforce obedience; right to command or act: *Parents have authority over their children.*

Bb

barge (bärj), *N.* **1.** a large, strongly built vehicle or flat-bottomed boat for carrying freight: *a grain barge.* **2.** *N.* a large boat used for excursions, pageants, and special occasions.

ba·sin (bā′sn), *N.* all the land drained by a river and the streams that flow into it: *The Mississippi basin extends from the Appalachians to the Rockies.*

bea·con (bē′kən), *N.* fire or light used as a signal to guide or warn.

be·half (bi haf′), *N.* side, interest, or favor: *I acted on her behalf.*

ben·e·fit (ben′ə fit), **1.** *N.* anything which is for the good of someone or something; advantage: *Good roads are of great benefit to travelers.* **2.** *V.* to do good to; be good for: *Rest will benefit a sick person.* ❑ *V.* **ben·e·fits, ben·e·fit·ed, ben·e·fit·ing.**

bi·o·di·ver·si·ty (bī′ō di vėr′sə tē), *N.* a wide variety of different species living together in one place.

birth·right (bėrth′rīt′), *N.* right or privilege that someone is entitled to by birth.

bond·age (bon′dij), *N.* condition of being held against your will under the control or influence of some person or thing; lack of freedom; slavery.

bug (bug), **1.** *N.* a crawling insect with a pointed beak for piercing and sucking. **2.** *N.* a disease germ. **3.** *N.* a very small microphone hidden in a room and used to overhear conversations.

bur·den (bėrd′n), *N.* something carried; load of things, care, work, duty, or sorrow: *Everyone in my family shares the burden of housework.*

Cc

ca·coph·o·ny (kə kof′ə nē), *N.* series of harsh, clashing sounds; discord.

cal·a·bash (kal′ə bash), *N.* gourd or gourdlike fruit whose dried shell is used to make bottles, bowls, drums, pipes, etc. ❑ *N. PL.* **cal·a·bash·es.**

cam·paign (kam pān′), **1.** *N.* in a war, a series of related military operations which are aimed at some special purpose: *In order to capture the enemy's most important city, the general planned one of the largest campaigns of the war.* **2.** *N.* series of connected activities to do or get something: *Our town had a campaign to raise money for a new hospital.* ❑ *N. PL.* **cam·paigns.**

a in hat	ō in open	sh in she
ā in age	ȯ in all	th in thin
â in care	ô in order	ᴛʜ in then
ä in far	oi in oil	zh in measure
e in let	ou in out	ə = a in about
ē in equal	u in cup	ə = e in taken
ėr in term	u̇ in put	ə = i in pencil
i in it	ü in rule	ə = o in lemon
ī in ice	ch in child	ə = u in circus
o in hot	ng in long	

can·di·date (kan′də dāt), *N.* person who seeks, or is suggested by others for some office, honor, or acceptance: *There is only one candidate for president of the club.*

cap·tive (kap′tiv), *ADJ.* kept in confinement: *captive animals.*

car·a·van (kar′ə van), *N.* group of merchants, pilgrims, etc., traveling together for safety through difficult or dangerous country. ❑ *N. PL.* **car·a·vans.**

car·bon di·ox·ide (kär′bən dī ok′sīd), *N.* a colorless, odorless gas, present in the atmosphere and formed when any fuel containing carbon is burned. The air that is breathed out of an animal's lungs contains carbon dioxide. Plants absorb it from the air and use it to make plant tissue. Carbon dioxide is a greenhouse gas.

car·da·mom (kär′ də məm), *N.* a spicy seed used as seasoning and in medicine.

chap·ar·ral (shap′ə ral′), *N.* dense, often thorny thicket of low bushes.

char·ac·ter·is·tic (kar′ik tə ris′tik), *ADJ.* distinguishing one person or thing from others; special: *Bananas have their own characteristic smell.*

char·i·ty (char′ə tē), *N.* fund or organization for helping the sick, the poor, the helpless, or the environment: *She gives money regularly to the Red Cross and to other charities.* ❑ *N. PL.* **char·i·ties.**

clois·ter (kloi′stər), *N.* place of religious retirement; convent or monastery. ❑ *N. PL.* **clois·ters**

col·lapse (kə laps′), *V.* to fold or push together: *The card table would collapse so that it could be stored easily.* ❑ *V.* **col·lapsed, col·laps·ing.**

col·lide (kə līd′), *V.* to hit or strike violently together; crash: *Two ships collided in the harbor and sank.* ❑ *V.* **col·lid·ed, col·lid·ing.**

com·bus·tion (kəm bus′chən), *N.* act or process of burning. Many houses are heated by the rapid combustion of coal, oil, or gas.

com·mis·sioned (kə mish′ənd), *ADJ.* holding the rank of second lieutenant or above in the U.S. Army, Air Force, or Marine Corps, or of ensign or above in the U.S. Navy.

com·pact (kom′pakt), *ADJ.* firmly packed together; closely joined: *Cabbage leaves are shaped into a compact head.*

com·pan·ion·ship (kəm pan′yən ship), *N.* friendly feeling among companions; fellowship.

com·pas·sion·ate (kəm pash′ə nit), *ADJ.* wishing to help those who suffer; sympathetic; pitying.

com·rade (kom′rad), **1.** *N.* a close companion and friend. **2.** *N.* fellow worker; partner. ❑ *N. PL.* **com·rades.**

con·fi·dent·ly (kon′fə dənt lē), *ADV.* certainly; surely; with firm belief.

con·form (kən fôrm′), *V.* to agree; be the same as. ❑ *V.* **con·formed, con·form·ing.**

con·quer (kong′kər), *V.* to overcome; get the better of: *conquer a bad habit.* ❑ *V.* **con·quered, con·quer·ing.**

con·sump·tion (kən sump′shən), *N.* act or process of using up; use: *We took along some food for consumption on our trip.*

con·ven·tion·al (kən ven′shə nəl), *ADJ.* of the usual type or design; commonly used or seen: *conventional furniture.*

con·vert (kən vėrt′), *V.* to turn to another for a particular use or purpose; change: *The generators at the dam convert water power into electricity.* ❑ *V.* **con·verts, con·vert·ed, con·vert·ing.**

co·or·di·nate (kō ôrd′n āt), *V.* to work or cause to work together in the proper way; fit together: *I have difficulty trying to coordinate the movements of my arms and legs in ballet class.* ❑ *V.* **co·or·di·nat·ed, co·or·di·nat·ing.**

cor·ri·dor (kôr′ə dər), *N.* a long hallway; passage in a large building into which rooms open: *There are many corridors leading from the school's front entrance to the numerous classrooms.* ❑ *N. PL.* **cor·ri·dors.**

cor·rode (kə rōd′), *V.* to wear or eat away gradually: *Acid caused the pipes to corrode.* ❑ *V.* **cor·rod·ed, cor·rod·ing.**

cor·sage (kôr säzh′), *N.* a small bouquet of flowers to be worn on the shoulder of a woman's clothes or on her wrist. ❑ *N.* **cor·sages**

cos·mic (koz′mik), *ADJ.* having to do with the whole universe: *Cosmic forces produce galaxies.*

coun·sel·or (koun′sə lər), *N.* person who gives advice; adviser.

cus·tom·ar·y (kus′tə mer′ē), *ADJ.* according to custom; usual: *Ten o'clock is her customary bedtime.*

Dd

dean (dēn), *N.* head of a division or school in a college or university: *the dean of the law school.*

de·cline (di klīn′), *N.* process of losing power, strength, wealth, beauty, etc.; growing worse: *Lack of money led to a decline in the condition of the school.*

de·cree (di krē′), *N.* something ordered by authority; official decision; law: *The new state holiday was one of three new decrees by the governor.* ❑ *N. PL.* **de·crees.**

de·lir·i·ous (di lir′ē əs), *ADJ.* wildly excited: *The students were delirious with joy when their team won the tournament.*

de·moc·ra·cy (di mok′rə sē), *N.* government that is run by the people who live under it. In a democracy, the people rule either directly through meetings that all may attend, such as the town meetings in New England, or indirectly through the election of representatives to attend to the business of government.

dense (dens), *ADJ.* closely packed together; thick: *In the densest fog it is difficult to see your hand held out in front of your face.* ❑ *ADJ.* **dens·er, dens·est.**

de·prive (di prīv′), *V.* to keep from having or doing: *Crash diets can deprive the dieter of proper nutrition.* ❑ *V.* **de·prived, de·priv·ing.**

des·o·late (des′ə lit), *ADJ.* not lived in; deserted: *a desolate house.*

desolate

a	in hat	ō	in open	sh	in she
ā	in age	ȯ	in all	th	in thin
â	in care	ô	in order	ᴛʜ	in then
ä	in far	oi	in oil	zh	in measure
e	in let	ou	in out	ə	= a in about
ē	in equal	u	in cup	ə	= e in taken
ėr	in term	u̇	in put	ə	= i in pencil
i	in it	ü	in rule	ə	= o in lemon
ī	in ice	ch	in child	ə	= u in circus
o	in hot	ng	in long		

des·ti·na·tion (des′tə nā′shən), *N.* place to which someone or something is going or is being sent.

des·ti·ny (des′tə nē), *N.* what becomes of someone or something; your fate or fortune: *It was young Washington's destiny to become the first president of the United States.*

de·tect (di tekt′), *V.* to find out; discover; catch: *Can you detect any odor in the room?* ❑ *V.* **de·tec·ted, de·tec·ting.**

de·vise (di vīz′), *V.* to think out; plan or contrive; invent: *She needed to devise a way of raising boards up to her tree house.* ❑ *V.* **de·vised, dev·is·ing.**

dic·ta·tion (dik tā′shən), *N.* words said or read aloud to another person who writes them down or to a machine that records them: *The secretary took the dictation in shorthand and typed it out later.*

dil·i·gent·ly (dil′ə jənt lē), *ADV.* carefully; steadily.

din·gy (din′jē), *ADJ.* lacking brightness or freshness; dirty-looking; dull: *Dingy curtains covered the windows of the dusty room.*

di·plo·ma (də plō′mə), *N.* a written or printed paper given by a school, college, or university, which states that someone has completed a certain course of study or has graduated after a certain amount of work.

dis·grace (dis grās′), *V.* to cause loss of honor or respect; to bring shame upon: *The embezzler disgraced her family.* ❑ *V.* **dis·graced, dis·grac·ing.**

dis·mount (dis mount′), *V.* to get off something, such as a horse or bicycle: *The riders dismounted and led their horses across the stream.* ❑ *V.* **dis·mount·ed, dis·mount·ing.**

dis·tress (dis tres′), *V.* to cause great pain or sorrow to; to make unhappy: *Her tears distressed me.* ❑ *V.* **dis·tressed, dis·tress·ing.**

doc·u·men·ta·tion (dok′yə men tā′shən), *N.* proof or support of a claim or opinion by documentary evidence: *Your essay provides good and proper documentation.*

dom·i·nate (dom′ə nāt), *V.* to control or rule by strength or power: *She has the authority needed to dominate the meeting.* ❑ *V.* **dom·i·nat·ed, dom·i·nat·ing.**

dra·mat·ic (drə mat′ik), *ADJ.* like a drama; of or about plays: *a dramatic actor.*

du·bi·ous·ly (dü′bē əs lē), *ADV.* doubtfully; uncertainly.

Ee

earth·en (ėr′thən), *ADJ.* made of ground, soil, or earth.

an earthen house

eave (ēv), *N.* the projecting lower level. ❑ *N. PL.* **eaves.**

ed·i·fice (ed′ə fis), *N.* a building, especially a large one.

ef·fi·cien·cy (ə fish′ən sē), *N.* ability to produce the effect wanted without waste of time, energy, etc.: *The skilled carpenter worked with great efficiency.*

e·lude (i lüd′), *V.* to avoid or escape by cleverness or quickness; slip away from: *The fox could always elude the hunting dogs.* ❑ *V.* **e·lud·ed, e·lud·ing.**

em·pha·size (em′fə sīz), *V.* to stress; call attention to: *The number of car accidents emphasized the need for careful driving.* ❑ *V.* **em·pha·sized, em·pha·siz·ing.**

em·pire (em′pīr), *N.* group of countries or states under one ruler or government: *The Roman Empire consisted of many separate territories and different peoples.*

en·coun·ter (en koun′tər), *v.* to meet as an enemy; meet in a fight or battle: *He knew he would encounter the enemy in direct combat.* ❑ *V.* **en·coun·tered, en·coun·ter·ing.**

en·gulf (en gulf′), *V.* to swallow up; overwhelm: *A wave engulfed the small boat.* ❑ *V.* **en·gulfed, en·gulf·ing.**

en·rage (en rāj′), *V.* to make very angry; make furious: *The dog was enraged by the teasing.* ❑ *V.* **en·raged, en·rag·ing.**

en·rich (en rich′), *V.* to make rich or richer: *Some companies add vitamins or minerals to enrich their food products.* ❑ *V.* **en·riched, en·rich·ing.**

en·roll·ment (en rōl′mənt), *N.* number who are members, who are registered: *The school has an enrollment of 200 students.*

en·thu·si·as·ti·cal·ly (en thü′zē as′tik lē), *ADV.* with great and eager interest: *The audience applauded enthusiastically.*

e·qua·tor (i kwā′tər), *N.* an imaginary circle around the middle of the earth, halfway between the North Pole and the South Pole. The equator divides the earth into the Northern Hemisphere and the Southern Hemisphere.

e·ro·sion (i rō′zhən), *N.* the process of gradually eating or wearing away by rain, glaciers, running water, waves, or wind: *Trees help prevent the erosion of soil.*

e·ter·ni·ty (i tėr′nə tē), *N.* the endless time period after death.

eth·ics (cth′iks), *N. SING.* the study of standards of right and wrong; the part of philosophy dealing with moral conduct, duty, and judgment.

et·i·quette (et′ə ket), *N.* the customary rules for behavior in polite society: *Etiquette requires that we eat peas with a fork, not a knife.*

e·vap·o·rate (i vap′ə rāt′), *V.* to change from a liquid into a gas: *Boiling water evaporates rapidly.* ❑ *V.* **e·vap·o·rates, e·vap·o·rat·ed, e·vap·o·rat·ing.**

ex·as·pe·ra·tion (eg zas′pə rā′shən), *N.* extreme annoyance; irritation; anger.

ex·ca·va·tion (ek′skə vā′shən), *N.* the act of or process of uncovering by digging: *The excavation revealed an ancient, buried city.*

ex·clu·sive (ek sklü′siv), *ADJ.* not divided or shared with others; single; sole: *exclusive rights to sell a product.*

a	in hat	ō	in open	sh	in she
ā	in age	ȯ	in all	th	in thin
â	in care	ô	in order	ᴛʜ	in then
ä	in far	oi	in oil	zh	in measure
e	in let	ou	in out	ə	= a in about
ē	in equal	u	in cup	ə	= e in taken
ėr	in term	u̇	in put	ə	= i in pencil
i	in it	ü	in rule	ə	= o in lemon
ī	in ice	ch	in child	ə	= u in circus
o	in hot	ng	in long		

ex·ist·ence (eg zis′təns), *N.* condition of being: *Dinosaurs disappeared from existence millions of years ago.*

ex·o·dus (ek′sə dəs), *N.* act of going out; departure: *Every June, there is an exodus of students from the college.*

ex·panse (ek spans′), *N.* open or unbroken stretch; wide, spreading surface: *The Pacific Ocean is a vast expanse of water.*

ex·pe·di·tion (ek′spə dish′ən), *N.* journey for some special purpose, such as exploration, scientific study, or military purposes.

ex·ploit (ek sploit′), *V.* to make use of: *The men wanted to exploit the mine for its minerals.* ❏ *V.* **ex·ploit·ed, ex·ploit·ing.**

ex·port (ek spôrt′), *V.* to send goods out of one country for sale and use in another: *The United States has exported corn for many years.* ❏ *V.* **ex·port·ed, ex·port·ing.**

ex·tract (ek strakt′), *V.* to pull out or draw out, usually with some effort: *extract iron from the earth.* ❏ *V.* **ex·tract·ed, ex·tract·ing.**

Ff

fes·tive (fes′tiv), *ADJ.* of or suitable for a feast, festival, or holiday; merry: *A birthday is a festive occasion.*

fix·ture (fiks′chər), *N.* thing put in place to stay: *a bathroom fixture, light fixtures.* ❏ *N. PL.* **fix·tures.**

flam·ma·ble (flam′ə bəl), *ADJ.* easily set on fire; inflammable: *Paper is flammable.*

flim·sy (flim′zē), *ADJ.* easily torn or broken; not strongly made: *I accidentally tore the flimsy paper.*

flour·ish (flėr′ish), *V.* to grow or develop well; thrive: *His radishes flourish with the right conditions.* ❏ *V.* **flour·ished, flour·ish·ing.**

fo·reign·er (fôr′ə nər), *N.* person from another country; alien. ❏ *N. PL.* **fo·reign·ers.**

for·mal (fôr′məl), **1.** *ADJ.* according to set customs or rules: *The ambassador paid a formal call on the prime minister.* **2.** *ADJ.* done with or having authority; official: *A written contract is a formal agreement to do something.*

for·mer (fôr′mər), *ADJ.* earlier; past: *In former times, cooking was done in fireplaces instead of stoves.*

for·ti·tude (fôr′tə tüd), *N.* courage in facing pain, danger, or trouble; firmness of spirit.

frag·ile (fraj′əl), *ADJ.* easily broken, damaged, or destroyed; delicate; frail: *Be careful; that thin glass is fragile.*

fran·tic (fran′tik), *ADJ.* very much excited; wild with rage, fear, pain, or grief: *The trapped animal made frantic efforts to escape.*

fres·co (fres′kō), *N.* picture or design created by painting with water colors on clean, fresh plaster. ❏ *N. PL.* **fres·coes.**

fresco

frus·tra·tion (fru strā′shən), *N.* a feeling of anger and helplessness, caused by bad luck, failure, or defeat.

ful·fill (fúl fil′), *V.* to perform or do a duty, command, etc.: *She felt she was able to fulfill all the teacher's requests.* ❑ *V.* **ful·filled, ful·fill·ing.**

Gg

gal·ax·y (gal′ək sē), *N.* group of billions of stars forming one system. Earth and the sun are in the Milky Way galaxy. Many galaxies outside our own can be seen with a telescope. (*Galaxy* comes from the Greek word *galaktos* meaning "milk.")

gen·e·rate (jen′ə rāt′), *V.* to cause to be; bring into being; produce: *The politician generated a great deal of enthusiasm among voters.* ❑ *V.* **gen·e·rat·ed, gen·e·rat·ing.**

ge·ol·o·gist (jē ol′ə jist), *N.* scientist who studies the composition of the earth or of other solid heavenly bodies, the processes that have formed them, and their history. ❑ *N. PL.* **ge·ol·o·gists.**

gloat (glōt), *V.* to think about or gaze at with great satisfaction: *She gloated over her success.* ❑ *V.* **gloat·ed, gloat·ing.**

grope (grōp), *V.* to feel about with the hands: *He was groping in the dark for a flashlight after the lights went out.* ❑ *V.* **groped, grop·ing.**

Hh

has·sle (has′əl), *N.* bother; trouble: *the hassle of fixing a broken bicycle.*

hatch·et (hach′it), *N.* a small ax with a short handle, for use with one hand.

heart·sick (härt sik′), *ADJ.* sick at heart; very depressed; very unhappy.

hoard (hôrd), *N.* what is saved and stored away; things stored: *They have a hoard of candy.*

home·stead·er (hōm′sted′ər), n. a person who owns and lives on land granted by the U.S. government. ❑ *N. PL.* **home·stead·ers.**

hos·pi·ta·ble (ho spit′ə bəl), *ADJ.* friendly; receptive.

hov·er (hov′ər), *V.* to stay in or near one place; wait nearby: *My mother tells me not to hover by the kitchen door before dinner.* ❑ *V.* **hov·ers, hov·ered, hov·er·ing.**

hu·mil·i·ty (hyü mil′ə tē), *N.* humbleness of mind; lack of pride; meekness.

Ii

i·de·al (ī dē′əl), *ADJ.* just as you would wish; perfect: *A warm, sunny day is ideal for a picnic.*

i·den·ti·ty (ī den′tə tē), *N.* who or what you are: *The writer concealed her identity by signing her stories with a pen name.*

ig·nite (ig nīt′), *V.* to set on fire: *A spark from a campfire can ignite dry grass.* ❑ *V.* **ig·nit·ed, ig·nit·ing.**

a in hat	ō in open	sh in she
ā in age	ȯ in all	th in thin
â in care	ô in order	ŦH in then
ä in far	oi in oil	zh in measure
e in let	ou in out	ə = a in about
ē in equal	u in cup	ə = e in taken
ėr in term	ú in put	ə = i in pencil
i in it	ü in rule	ə = o in lemon
ī in ice	ch in child	ə = u in circus
o in hot	ng in long	

im·bed (im bed′), *V.* to enclose in a surrounding mass; fasten or fix firmly: *Precious stones are often found imbedded in rock.* ❑ *V.* **im·bed·ded, im·bed·ding.**

im·mor·tal (i môr′tl), *ADJ.* living forever; never dying; everlasting: *Most religions teach that the soul is immortal.* (*Immortal* comes from the Latin word *mort* meaning "death.")

im·po·lite (im′pə līt′), *ADJ.* not polite; having or showing bad manners; rude; discourteous.

im·print (im print′), *V.* to fix firmly in the mind: *His boyhood home was imprinted in his memory.* ❑ *V.* **im·print·ed, im·print·ing.**

in·ci·dent (in′sə dənt), *N.* something that happens; event: *an exciting incident.* (*Incident* comes from the Latin word *incidentem* meaning "happening, befalling.")

in·dus·tri·al (in dus′trē əl), *ADJ.* engaged in or connected with business, trade, or manufacture: *industrial worker, industrial development.*

in·fin·i·ty (in fin′ə tē), *N.* condition of having no limits; endlessness: *the infinity of space.*

in·laid (in lād′), *ADJ.* set in the surface as a decoration or design.

in·su·late (in′sə lāt), *V.* to keep something from losing electricity, heat, or sound by lining or surrounding it with a material that does not conduct the kind of energy involved: *Telephone wires are often insulated by a covering of rubber.* ❑ *V.* **in·su·lat·ed, in·su·lat·ing.**

in·vad·er (in vād′ər), *N.* person who enters with force or as an enemy: *The invaders conquered the country.* ❑ *N. PL.* **in·vad·ers.**

i·so·la·tion (ī′sə lā shən), *N.* the state of being separated from others, of being alone.

Ll

lance (lans), *N.* a long, wooden spear with a sharp iron or steel head: *The knight carried a lance as he rode into battle.*

leg·a·cy (leg′ə sē), *N.* something handed down from an ancestor or predecessor; heritage.

lei·sure (lē′zher *or* lezh′ər), *ADJ.* free; not busy: *leisure hours.*

lunge (lunj), *V.* to move suddenly forward; thrust: *The dog is always lunging at strangers.* ❑ *V.* **lunged, lung·ing.**

lush (lush), *ADJ.* having thick growth; covered with growing things: *The hillside was lush with spring flowers.*

lush

Mm

main·te·nance (mān′tə nəns), *N.* act or process of keeping in good repair.

mal·nour·ished (mal nėr′isht), *ADJ.* improperly nourished: *The stray cat looked malnourished.*

man·u·script (man′yə skript), *N.* a handwritten or keyboarded book or article. Manuscripts are sent to publishers to be made into printed books, magazine articles, and the like. ❑ *N. PL.* **man·u·scripts.**

ma·ter·i·al·ize (mə tir′ē ə līz), *V.* to appear or cause to appear suddenly in material or bodily form: *A woman would materialize from the smoke of the magician's fire.* ❑ *V.* **ma·ter·i·al·ized, mat·ter·i·al·iz·ing.**

me·an·der (mē an′dər), *V.* to follow a winding course: *The hikers meandered through the woods.* ❑ *V.* **me·an·dered, me·an·der·ing.**

me·di·e·val (mē dē′vəl or med ē′vəl), *ADJ.* of or belonging to the Middle Ages (the years from about A.D. 500 to about 1450).

men·ac·ing (men′is ing), *ADJ.* threatening: *The dog had a menacing growl.*

mi·gra·tion (mī grā′shən), **1.** *N.* the act of going from one region to another with the change in the seasons. **2.** *N.* the act of moving from one place to settle in another.

mis·for·tune (mis fôr′chən), *N.* bad luck: *She had the misfortune to break her arm.*

mois·ture (mois′chər), *N.* slight wetness; water or other liquid suspended in very small drops in the air or spread on a surface. Dew is moisture that collects at night on the grass.

mol·ten (mōlt′n), *ADJ.* made liquid by heat; melted: *molten steel.*

mo·men·tous (mō men′təs), *ADJ.* very important: *Choosing between peace and war is a momentous decision.*

mon·grel (mong′grəl), *N.* animal or plant of mixed breed, especially a dog.

my·thol·o·gy (mi thol′ə jē), *N.* a group of legends or stories about a particular country or person: *Greek mythology.*

Nn

nav·i·ga·tor (nav′ə gā′tər), *N.* person in charge of finding the position and course of a ship, aircraft, or expedition.

ne·go·ti·ate (ni gō′shē āt), *V.* to talk over and arrange terms; confer; consult: *The two countries came together to negotiate for peace.* ❑ *V.* **ne·go·ti·at·ed, ne·go·ti·at·ing.**

no·ble·man (nō′bəl mən), *N.* man of noble rank, title, or birth. ❑ *N. PL.* **no·ble·men.**

non·vi·o·lence (non vi′ə ləns), *N.* belief in the use of peaceful methods to achieve any goal; opposition to any form of violence.

nub (nub), *N.* lump or small piece.

Oo

o·be·di·ent (ō bē′dē ənt), *ADJ.* doing what you are told; willing to obey: *The obedient dog came at its owner's whistle.*

ob·serv·a·to·ry (əb zėr′və tôr′ē), *N.* building equipped with telescopes and other devices for watching and studying astronomical objects.

ob·sta·cle (ob′stə kəl), *N.* something that prevents or stops progress; hindrance: *The fallen tree was an obstacle to traffic.*

a in hat	ō in open	sh in she
ā in age	ȯ in all	th in thin
â in care	ô in order	ŦH in then
ä in far	oi in oil	zh in measure
e in let	ou in out	ə = a in about
ē in equal	u in cup	ə = e in taken
ėr in term	ů in put	ə = i in pencil
i in it	ü in rule	ə = o in lemon
ī in ice	ch in child	ə = u in circus
o in hot	ng in long	

op·er·a (op′ər ə), *N.* a play in which music is an essential and prominent part, featuring arias, choruses, etc., with orchestral accompaniment.

op·ti·mis·tic (op′tə mis′tik), *ADJ.* hoping for the best: *I am optimistic about the chance of continued good weather.*

or·deal (ôr dēl′), *N.* a severe test or experience: *I dreaded the ordeal of going to the dentist.*

ore (ôr), *N.* rock containing enough of a metal or metals to make mining profitable. After it is mined, ore must be treated to extract the metal.

out·burst (out′bėrst′), *N.* act of bursting forth. ❏ *N. PL.* **out·bursts.**

Pp

pack·ing·house (pak′ing hous′), *N.* place where foods are prepared and packed to be sold.

pains·tak·ing (pānz′tā′king), *ADJ.* very careful; particular; diligent: *a painstaking painter.*

pa·le·on·tol·o·gist (pā′lē on tol′ə jist), *N.* a scientist who studies the forms of life existing in prehistoric time, as represented by fossil animals and plants. ❏ *N. PL.* **pa·le·on·tol·o·gists.**

pa·py·rus (pə pī′rəs), *N.* a tall water plant from which the ancient Egyptians, Greeks, and Romans made a material upon which to write.

par·ti·cle (pär′tə kəl), *N.* a very little bit: *I got a particle of dust in my eye.* ❏ *N. PL.* **par·ti·cles.** (*Particle* comes from the Latin word *partem* meaning "part.")

pa·trol·man (pə trōl′ mən), *N.* a policeman or policewoman who keeps watch over a particular area in order to protect life and property.

pa·tron (pā′trən), *N.* person who gives approval and support to some person, art, cause, or undertaking: *A well-known patron of art, she has helped several young painters.*

per·cent·age (pər sen′tij), *N.* allowance, commission, discount, etc., figured by percent.

per·mis·sion (pər mish′ən), *N.* consent; leave: *My sister gave me permission to use her camera.*

per·sist (pər sist′), *V.* to keep on; refuse to stop or be changed: *Though we've asked her not to, she persisted in reading at the table.* ❏ *V.* **per·sist·ed, per·sist·ing.**

per·sist·ence (pər sis′təns), *N.* act of refusing to stop or be changed: *Her persistence in practicing led to her making the team.*

phys·i·cal (fiz′ə kəl), *ADJ.* of or for the body: *physical exercise, physical strength, physical work.*

plea (plē), *N.* request or appeal; an asking: *The firefighters heard many pleas for help.* ❏ *N. PL.* **pleas.**

poi·son·ous (poi′zn əs), *ADJ.* containing dangerous substance; very harmful to life and health: *The rattlesnake's bite is poisonous.*

poul·tice (pōl′tis), *N.* a soft, moist mass of mustard, herbs, etc., applied to the body to reduce pain or swelling.

prej·u·dice (prej′ə dis), *N.* unreasonable dislike of an idea, group of people, etc.

pres·ence (prez′ns), *N.* condition of being present in a place: *I just learned of her presence in the city.*

prey (prā), *N. SING.* or *PL.* animal or animals hunted and killed for food by another animal: *Mice and birds are the prey of cats.*

prim·i·tive (prim′ə tiv), *ADJ.* very simple, such as people had early in history: *A primitive way of making fire is by rubbing two sticks together.*

priv·i·leged (priv′ə lijd), *ADJ.* having some special rights, advantage, or favor: *The nobility of Europe was a privileged class.*

pro·claim (prə klām′), *V.* to make known publicly and officially; declare publicly: *The congresswoman proclaimed that she would run for reelection.* ❑ *V.* **pro·claimed, pro·claim·ing.**

pro·gress (prog′res), *N.* an advance or growth; development; improvement: *the progress of science, showing rapid progress in your studies.*

pro·mote (prə mōt′), **1.** *V.* to raise in rank, condition, or importance: *Pupils who pass the test will be promoted to the next higher grade.* **2.** *V.* to further the sale of something by advertising. ❑ *V.* **pro·mot·ed, pro·mot·ing.**

pro·vi·sions (prə vizh′əns), *N. PL.* a supply of food and drinks: *After a long winter, the settlers were low on provisions.*

Qq

quest (kwest), *N.* expedition by knights in search of something: *There are many stories about the quests of King Arthur's knights.* ❑ *N. PL.* **quests.**

quill (kwil), *N.* a stiff, sharp hair or spine like the pointed end of a feather. A porcupine has quills on its back.

quills

Rr

rab·bi (rab′ī), *N.* teacher of the Jewish law and religion; leader of a Jewish congregation.

re·cede (ri sēd′), *V.* to go backward; move backward; withdraw: *When the tide receded, we dug for clams.* ❑ *V.* **re·ced·ed, re·ced·ing.**

re·cit·al (ri sī′ tl), *N.* a musical entertainment, given usually by a single performer. ❑ *N. PL.* **re·cit·als**

re·cy·cle (rē sī′kəl), *V.* to process or treat something so that it can be used again. ❑ *V.* **re·cy·cled, re·cy·cling.**

re·frain[1] (ri frān′) *V.* to keep yourself from doing something: *refrain from wrongdoing.* ❑ *V.* **re·frained, re·frain·ing.**

re·frain[2] (ri frān′) *N.* phrase or verse repeated regularly in a song or poem. In "The Star-Spangled Banner," the refrain is "O'er the land of the free and the home of the brave."

reg·is·ter (rej′ə stər), *V.* to have some effect, to make an impression. ❑ *V.* **reg·is·tered, reg·is·ter·ing.**

reign (rān), *V.* to rule: *The king and queen reigned over the kingdom.* ❑ *V.* **reigned, reign·ing.**

a in hat	ō in open	sh in she
ā in age	ȯ in all	th in thin
â in care	ô in order	ᴛʜ in then
ä in far	oi in oil	zh in measure
e in let	ou in out	ə = a in about
ē in equal	u in cup	ə = e in taken
ėr in term	u̇ in put	ə = i in pencil
i in it	ü in rule	ə = o in lemon
ī in ice	ch in child	ə = u in circus
o in hot	ng in long	

re·ject (ri jekt′), *V*. to refuse to take; turn down: *The army will reject any applicants under the age of eighteen.* ❑ *V*. **re·ject·ed, re·ject·ing.**

rel·ish (rel′ish), **1.** *N*. a pleasant taste; good flavor: *Hunger gives relish to simple food.* **2.** *N*. a side dish to add flavor to food. Olives and pickles are relishes.

re·new (ri nü′), *V*. make like new; restore: *The rain renewed the greenness of the fields.* ❑ *V*. **re·newed, re·new·ing.**

re·nowned (ri nound′), *ADJ*. famous: *a renowned scientist.*

re·pay (ri pā′), *V*. to do something in return for something received: *No thanks can repay such kindness.* ❑ *V*. **re·paid, re·pay·ing.**

re·pro·duce (rē′prə düs′), *V*. to make a copy of: *to reproduce a photograph.* ❑ *V*. **re·pro·duced, re·pro·duc·ing.**

re·pul·sive (ri pul′siv), *ADJ*. causing strong dislike or aversion: *the repulsive smell of a skunk.*

re·sound (ri zound′), *V*. be much talked about: *They knew that the fame of the first flight across the Atlantic would resound all over the world.* ❑ *V*. **re·sound·ed, re·sound·ing.**

re·treat (ri trēt′), **1.** *N*. act of moving back or withdrawing: *The army's retreat was orderly.* **2.** *N*. a retirement or period of retirement by a group of people for religious exercises, meditation, etc.: *The monks conducted a retreat.*

re·volt·ing (ri vōl′ting), *ADJ*. disgusting; repulsive: *a revolting odor.*

riv·et (riv′it), *N*. a metal bolt with a head at one end, the other end being hammered into a head after insertion: *The rugged blue jeans had a rivet on each corner of the pockets.*

romp (romp), *V*. to play in a rough, boisterous way; rush and tumble. ❑ *V*. **romped, romp·ing.**

row·dy (rou′dē), *ADJ*. rough; disorderly; quarrelsome: *The gym was full of rowdy kids.*

rur·al (rùr′əl), *ADJ*. in the country; belonging to the country; like that of the country: *a rural school, rural roads.*

rural

Ss

sanc·tu·ar·y (sangk′chü er′ē), *N*. place of refuge or protection: *Wildlife sanctuaries help ensure animals' safety.* ❑ *N. PL*. **sanc·tu·ar·ies.**

se·cre·tive (si krē′tiv), *ADJ*. having the habit of secrecy; not frank and open.

seg·re·gate (seg′rə gāt), *V*. to separate people of different races by having separate schools, restaurants, etc. ❑ *V*. **seg·re·gat·ed, seg·re·gat·ing.**

set·tle·ment (set′l mənt), *N*. group of buildings and the people living in them: *The prairie settlement was a day's ride from the next town.*

share·crop·per (shâr′krop′ər), *N*. person who farms land for the owner in return for part of the crops. ❑ *N. PL*. **share·crop·pers.**

sling (sling), *V.* to throw; cast; hurl; fling: *I slung the bag of oats into the truck.* ❑ *V.* **slung, sling·ing.**

slug·gish (slug′ish), *ADJ.* slow-moving; not active; lacking energy or vigor: *When I stay up too late, I am often sluggish the next day.*

smol·der (smōl′dər), *V.* to burn and smoke without flame: *The campfire smoldered for hours after the blaze died down.* ❑ *V.* **smol·dered, smol·der·ing.**

smug·gle (smug′əl), *V.* to bring something into or take something out of a country secretly and unlawfully, especially without payment of legal duties. ❑ *V.* **smug·gled, smug·gling.**

sol·vent (sol′vənt), *N.* substance, usually a liquid, that can dissolve other substances: *Water is a solvent of sugar and salt.* ❑ *N. PL.* **sol·vents.**

spa·cious (spā′shəs), *ADJ.* containing much space; with plenty of room; vast: *The rooms were bright and spacious.*

spec·i·men (spes′ə mən), *N.* one of a group or class taken to show what the others are like; sample: *He collects specimens of all kinds of rocks and minerals. The two statues were fine specimens of Greek sculpture.* ❑ *N. PL.* **spec·i·mens.**

speck·led (spek′əld), *ADJ.* marked with many small spots: *A speckled bird flew out of the bush.*

squawl (skwȯl), *v.* to cry; bawl. ❑ *V.* **squawl·ed, squawl·ing.**

squire (skwīr), *N.* attendant.

stif·fen (stif′ən), *V.* to make or become rigid, fixed: *Her muscles stiffened in the cold wind.* ❑ *V.* **stif·fened, stif·fen·ing.**

stim·u·lat·ing (stim′yə lāt ing), *ADJ.* lively; engaging. *The stimulating conversation made the party interesting.*

stun (stun), *V.* to daze; bewilder; shock; overwhelm: *She was stunned by the news of her friend's injury.* ❑ *V.* **stunned, stun·ning.**

sub·scribe (səb skrib′), *V.* to give your consent or approval; agree: *She does not subscribe to my opinion.* ❑ *V.* **sub·scribed, sub·scrib·ing.** (**Subscribe** comes from two Latin words, *sub* meaning "under" and *scribe* meaning "to write.")

suf·fi·cient (sə fish′ənt), *ADJ.* as much as is needed; enough: sufficient proof.

su·per·sti·tious (sü′pər stish′əs), *ADJ.* having belief or practice based on ignorant fear or mistaken reverence.

sur·plus (sėr′pləs or sėr′plus), *N.* amount over and above what is needed; extra quantity left over; excess: *The bank keeps a large surplus of money in reserve.*

sur·vive (sər vīv′), *V.* to continue to exist; remain; to continue to live: *No one thought the old, bent tree would survive being hit by lightning.* ❑ *V.* **sur·vived, sur·viv·ing.**

Tt

tech·nol·o·gy (tek nol′ə jē), *N.* the use of scientific knowledge to control physical objects and forces: *overcome problems by technology.*

tol·e·rate (tol′ə rāt′), *V.* to allow or permit: *Gum chewing in the classroom was not tolerated.* ❑ *V.* **tol·e·rat·ed, tol·e·rat·ing.**

a	in hat	ō	in open	sh	in she
ā	in age	ȯ	in all	th	in thin
â	in care	ô	in order	ᴛʜ	in then
ä	in far	oi	in oil	zh	in measure
e	in let	ou	in out	ə	= a in about
ē	in equal	u	in cup	ə	= e in taken
ėr	in term	u̇	in put	ə	= i in pencil
i	in it	ü	in rule	ə	= o in lemon
ī	in ice	ch	in child	ə	= u in circus
o	in hot	ng	in long		

toll[1] (tōl), *V.* to sound with single strokes which are slowly and regularly repeated. **2.** *N.* something paid, lost, suffered, etc.: *Accidents take a heavy toll of human lives.* ❑ *V.* **tolled, tol·ling.**

toll[2] (tōl), *N.* tax or fee paid from some right or privilege. We pay a toll when we use the bridge.

tor·ment (tôr′ment), *N.* a cause of very great pain: *A bad burn can be a torment.*

tour·ism (tŭr′iz′əm), *N.* the business of serving people who are traveling for pleasure.

tou·sle (tou′zəl), *V.* to put into disorder; make untidy; muss: *tousled hair.* ❑ *V.* **tou·sled, tou·sling.**

trades·man (trādz′mən), *N.* storekeeper; shopkeeper.

trans·mit (tran smit′ or tranz mit′), *V.* to send out signals by means of electromagnetic waves or by wire: *Some station is transmitting every hour of the day.* ❑ *V.* **trans·mit·ted, trans·mit·ting.**

trav·erse (trav′ərs), *V.* to pass across, over, or through: *Explorers traversed the desert by truck.* ❑ *V.* **tra·versed, tra·vers·ing.**

treach·er·ous (trech′ər əs), *ADJ.* having a false appearance of strength, security, etc.; not reliable; deceiving: *Thin ice is treacherous.*

tread (tred), **1.** *V.* to set a foot down; walk; step: *Don't tread on the flower beds.* **2.** *V.* tread water; to keep the body straight in the water with the head above the surface by moving the arms and legs. ❑ *V.* **trod, tread·ed, tread·ing.**

trop·ics (trop′iks), *N. PL.* the regions between the equator and imaginary circles 23.45 degrees north and south of the equator. The hottest part of the Earth is in the tropics.

tropics

tu·i·tion (tü ish′ən), *N.* money paid for instruction: *a $300 increase in college tuition.*

tur·bu·lent (tèr′byə lənt), *ADJ.* stormy; tempestuous: *turbulent weather.*

Uu

un·ac·com·pa·nied (un′ə kum′pə nēd), *ADJ.* not accompanied; alone.

un·can·ny (un kan′ē), *ADJ.* strange and mysterious; weird: *The trees took uncanny shapes in the mist.*

un·con·ven·tion·al (un′kən ven′shə nəl), *ADJ.* not bound by or conforming to convention, rule, or precedent; free from conventionality.

u·ni·son (yü′nə sən), *N.* agreement: *The marchers' feet moved in unison. We spoke in unison.*

u·ni·ver·sal (yü′nə vėr′səl), **1.** *ADJ.* of or belonging to all; concerning all: *Food is a universal need.* **2.** *ADJ.* existing everywhere: *The law of gravity is universal.*

un·la·dy·like (un lā′dē lik′), *ADJ.* impolite; not like a lady; not well-bred.

ur·ban (ėr′bən), *ADJ.* typical of cities: *urban life.*

urban

Vv

ven·ture (ven′chər), *V.* to dare to come or go: *We ventured out on the thin ice and fell through.* ❑ *V.* **ven·tured, ven·tur·ing.**

ver·i·fy (ver′ə fi), *V.* to prove to be true; confirm: *The witness's account of the accident would verify the driver's report.* ❑ *V.* **ver·i·fied, ver·i·fy·ing.**

ver·sion (vėr′zhən), **1.** *N.* one particular statement, account, or description: *Each of the three boys gave his own version of the quarrel.* **2.** *N.* a special form or variant of something: *I liked the movie version better than the book.*

vig·or·ous·ly (vig′ər əs lē), *ADV.* strongly; actively; energetically.

vis·ta (vis′tə), *N.* opening or passage through or from which you see a wide view.

vol·can·ic (vol kan′ik), *ADJ.* of or caused by a volcano; about volcanoes: *a volcanic eruption.*

Ww

waft (wäft), **1.** *V.* to carry over water or through air: *A breeze wafted the aroma of fresh bread to me.* ❑ *V.* **waft·ed, waft·ing. 2.** *N.* a breath or puff of air, wind, scent, etc.: *A waft of fresh air came through the window.*

wane (wān), *V.* to go through the moon's regular reduction in the amount of its visible portion. The moon wanes when the side facing the Earth moves gradually out of the sun's light. ❑ *V.* **waned, wan·ing.**

wel·fare (wel′fâr′), *N.* health, happiness, and prosperity; condition of being or doing well: *My uncle asked about the welfare of everyone in our family.*

wilt (wilt), *V.* to become limp and bend down; wither: *Flowers wilt when they don't get enough water.* ❑ *V.* **wilt·ed, wilt·ing.**

Zz

ze·nith (zē′nith), *N.* the highest point: *the zenith of a ferris wheel.*

a	in hat	ō	in open	sh	in she
ā	in age	ȯ	in all	th	in thin
â	in care	ô	in order	₮H	in then
ä	in far	oi	in oil	zh	in measure
e	in let	ou	in out	ə	= a in about
ē	in equal	u	in cup	ə	= e in taken
ėr	in term	u̇	in put	ə	= i in pencil
i	in it	ü	in rule	ə	= o in lemon
ī	in ice	ch	in child	ə	= u in circus
o	in hot	ng	in long		

English/Spanish
Selection Vocabulary List

Unit 1
Old Yeller

English	Spanish
lunging	embestir
nub	trozo (completamente agotado)
romping	retozando
rowdy	alborotado
slung	arrojé
speckled	moteada

Mother Fletcher's Gift

English	Spanish
apparently	aparentemente
fixtures	accesorios
flimsy	frágil
incident	incidente
subscribe	suscribir
survive	sobrevives

Viva New Jersey

English	Spanish
corridors	pasillos
destination	destino
groping	agarrando a tientas
menacing	amenazador
mongrel	perro callejero
persisted	persistió
pleas	súplicas

Saving the Rain Forests

English	Spanish
basin	cuenca
charities	organizaciones benéficas
equator	ecuador
erosion	erosión
evaporates	evapora
exported	exportados
industrial	industrial
recycled	reciclada
tropics	trópico

When Crowbar Came

English	Spanish
aggressive	agresiva
detect	detectar
dubiously	dudosamente
frustration	frustración
imprinted	dejar huella
materialize	aparecer
migration	migración
secretive	reservados
tolerated	tolerado

Unit 2

The Universe

English	Spanish
astronomers	astrónomos
collapse	colapsa
collide	chocan
compact	compacto
galaxy	galaxia
particles	partículas

Dinosaur Ghosts: The Mystery of *Coelophysis*

English	Spanish
fragile	frágiles
poisonous	venenosos
prey	presa
sluggish	especímenes
specimens	soñolientos
treacherous	peligroso
volcanic	volcánica

A Week in the 1800s

English	Spanish
counselor	consejera
identity	identidad
physical	físico
surplus	excedente
technology	tecnología

Goodbye to the Moon

English	Spanish
combustion	combustión
dingy	deslucidos
negotiate	negociar
traversed	atravesaba
waft	aroma
waning	menguando

Egypt

English	Spanish
abundant	abundantes
artifacts	artefactos
decrees	decretos
eternity	eternidad
immortal	inmortales
receded	retrocedían
reigned	reinaron

Unit 3
Hatchet

English	Spanish
hatchet	hacha
ignite	encender
painstaking	esmerado
quill	púa
registered	se registraran
smoldered	humearon
stiffened	(se) entumeció

When Marian Sang

English	Spanish
application	(una) solicitud
dramatic	dramático
enraged	enfurecidos
formal	formal
momentous	de suma importancia
opera	ópera
prejudice	los prejuicios
privileged	privilegiado
recital	recital

Learning to Swim

English	Spanish
customary	habitual
emphasized	enfatizaba
frantic	frenéticos
stunned	estupefactos
treaded	se mantenían a flote

Juan Verdades: The Man Who Couldn't Tell a Lie

English	Spanish
confidently	con seguridad
dismounted	desmontó
distressed	angustiado
flourish	crecer con vigor
fulfill	satisfacer
permission	permiso
repay	reembolsar
vigorously	vigorosamente

Elizabeth Blackwell: Medical Pioneer

English	Spanish
absurd	absurda
behalf	a favor de (de recomendación)
candidate	candidato
dean	decano
delirious	loca (de alegría)
diploma	diploma
hovers	ronda
obedient	obediente
reject	rechazar

Unit 4
Into the Ice

English	Spanish
conquer	conquistar
destiny	destino
expedition	expedición
insulated	aislados
isolation	aislamiento
navigator	navegador
provisions	provisiones
verify	verificar

The Chimpanzees I Love

English	Spanish
captive	cautivos
companionship	compañía
existence	existencia
ordeal	difícil experiencia
primitive	primitiva
sanctuaries	santuarios
stimulating	estimulantes

Black Frontiers

English	Spanish
bondage	esclavitud
commissioned	comisionados
earthen	de tierra
encounter	enfrentar
homesteaders	nuevos colonos
settlement	asentamiento

Space Cadets

English	Spanish
aliens	extraterrestres
barge	barcaza
hospitable	hospitalarios
molten	fundido
ore	mineral
refrain	absténgase
universal	universales
version	versión

Inventing the Future: A Photobiography of Thomas Alva Edison

English	Spanish
converts	convierte
devise	concebir
efficiency	eficiencia
generated	generaba
percentage	porcentaje
proclaimed	proclamaron
reproduce	reproducir
transmitted	transmitía

Unit 5

The View from Saturday

English	Spanish
accustomed	acostumbrados
decline	deterioro
former	anterior
presence	presencia
unaccompanied	solo

Harvesting Hope: The Story of Cesar Chavez

English	Spanish
access	acceso
authority	autoridad
lush	exuberante
obstacle	obstáculo
toll	(había hecho) estragos
torment	tormentos
wilt	marchitarse

The River That Went to the Sky: A Story from Malawi

English	Spanish
densest	más tupido
eaves	aleros (techo de árboles)
expanse	extensión
moisture	humedad
ventured	aventuraban

Gold

English	Spanish
characteristic	característico
corrode	se corroen
engulfed	sumida
exploit	explotar
extract	extraen
hoard	botín

The House of Wisdom

English	Spanish
beacon	faro
caravans	caravanas
legacy	legado
manuscripts	manuscritos
medieval	medieval
observatory	observatorio
patron	patrón

Unit 6

Don Quixote and the Windmills

English	Spanish
lance	lanza
misfortune	desventura
quests	hazañas
renewed	renovado
renowned	célebre
resound	resonarán
squire	escudero

Ancient Greece

English	Spanish
architecture	arquitectura
democracy	democracia
empire	imperio
ideal	ideal
mythology	mitología

The All-American Slurp

English	Spanish
disgraced	deshonramos
progress	progreso
promoted	promovido
relish	aperitivos
retreat	retirada
revolting	repugnante
unison	(al) unísono

The Aztec News

English	Spanish
benefits	beneficios
campaigns	campañas
comrades	camaradas
enrich	enriquecer
foreigners	extranjeros
invaders	invasores

Where Opportunity Awaits

English	Spanish
burden	carga
conformed	conformaban
leisure	de ocio
maintenance	mantenimiento
rural	rural
sufficient	suficientes
urban	urbanos

Acknowledgments

Text

22: From *Old Yeller* by Fred Gipson. Copyright © 1956 by Fred Gipson. Reprinted by permission of HarperCollins Publishers, Inc.; **38:** "A Dog's Life" by Iain Zaczek. Reprinted by permission of Carus Publishing Company from *Muse* magazine, November/December 2002, Vol. 6, No. 9, introduction © 2002 by Iain Zaczek; **46:** "Mother Fletcher's Gift" (originally titled "A Christmas Story") from *145th Street: Short Stories* by Walter Dean Myers, copyright © 2000 by Walter Dean Myers. Used by permission of Random House Children's Books, a division of Random House, Inc.; **64:** "The Harlem Renaissance" from *Cobblestone* Magazine, Volume 12, Number 2, February, 1991. Copyright © 1991, Cobblestone Publishing, 30 Grove Street, Suite C, Peterborough, NH 03458. All Rights Reserved. Reprinted by permission of Carus Publishing Company; **70:** "Viva New Jersey" by Gloria Gonzalez, copyright © 1993 by Gloria Gonzalez, from *Join In, Multiethnic Short Stories* by Donald R. Gallo, ed. Used by permission of Dell Publishing, a division of Random House, Inc.; **92:** *Saving the Rain Forests* by Sally Morgan, Franklin Watts, 1999; **108:** "Not a Drop to Drink" from *Kids Discover*, April 2003; **116:** "When Crowbar Came," from A *Tarantula in My Purse and 172 Other Wild Pets* by Jean Craighead George. © 1996 by JULIE PRODUCTIONS, INC. Used by permission of HarperCollins Publishers; **134:** "They've Got Personality" by Aline Alexander Newman from *National Geographic World* magazine, April 2002. Used by permission of National Geographic Society; **138:** "Those Winter Sundays" from *Angle of Ascent: New and Collected Poems* by Robert Hayden, Liveright Publishing Corporation, 1962; **139:** "Grandma" from *Relatively Speaking: Poems About Family* by Ralph Fletcher. Published by Orchard Books, a Division of Scholastic Inc. Copyright © 1998 by Scholastic Inc. Reprinted by permission of Scholastic Inc.; **140:** "Song to Mothers" from *A Tribute to Mothers* by Pat Mora, Lee & Low Books, 2001; **141:** "Louisa Jones Sings a Praise to Caesar" by Emanuel di Pasquale. Copyright © 1990 by Emanuel di Pasquale. Reprinted by permission of the author; **150:** From *The Universe* by Seymour Simon. Text copyright © 1998 by Seymour Simon. Used by permission of HarperCollins Publishers; **164:** "So Long Sol!" by Seth Shostak from *Odyssey's* April 2001 issue: "The Fate of the UNIVERSE," © 2001, Cobblestone Publishing, 30 Grove Street, Suite C, Petersborough, NH 03458. All Rights Reserved. Reprinted by permission of Carus Publishing Company; **172:** From *Dinosaur Ghosts: The Mystery of Coelophysis* by J. Lynett Gillette, Dial Books for Young Readers, 1997; **190:** "Dino Hunting" by Kristin Baird Rattini from *National Geographic World* Magazine, December 2000. Used by permission of National Geographic Society; **198:** "A Week in the 1800's" from *Ultimate Field Trip 4* by Susan E. Goodman, photographs by Michael J. Doolittle. Reprinted with the permission of Atheneum Books for Young Readers, an imprint of Simon & Schuster Children's Publishing Division. Text copyright © 2000 Susan E. Goodman. Photographs copyright © 2000 Michael J. Doolittle; **224:** "Goodbye to the Moon" from *Crisis on Conshelf Ten* by Monica Hughes, Atheneum Books for Young Readers, 1977; **240:** "Zoo" by Edward D. Hoch. *Fantastic Universe*, 1958; reprinted by permission of the Sternig & Byrne Literary Agency; **248:** "Land of the Pharaohs" from *Egypt: Enchantment of the World* by Ann Henrichs. Copyright © 1997 by Ann Heinrichs. Used by permission of Children's Press/Franklin Watts a Scholastic Library Publishing Company, Inc. a division of Scholastic Inc.; **264:** "The Rosetta Stone" from The British Museum Website at www.ancientegypt.co.uk; **266:** "Fossils" from *Something New Begins* by Lilian Moore, Atheneum Publishers, Inc., 1982; **267:** "Tradition" from *Under the Sunday Tree* by Eloise Greenfield, Harper & Row, 1988; **268:** "Arrival" from *It's About Time: Poems* by Florence Parry Heide, Judith Heide Gilliland & Roxanne Heide Pierce. Text copyright © 1999 by Florence Parry Heide, Judith Heide Gilliland & Roxanne Heide Pierce. Reprinted by permission of Clarion Books/Houghton Mifflin Company. All rights reserved; **268:** "The Time Machine" from *It's About Time: Poems* by Florence Parry Heide, Judith Heide Gilliland & Roxanne Heide Pierce. Text copyright © 1999 by Florence Parry Heide, Judith Heide Gilliland & Roxanne Heide Pierce. Reprinted by permission of Clarion Books/Houghton Mifflin Company. All rights reserved; **269:** "Suit of Armor" by Beverly McLoughland, as appeared in *Cricket* Magazine, September 1994. Used by permission of the author; **278:** *Hatchet* by Gary Paulsen. Text copyright © 1987 by Gary Paulsen. Reprinted with the permission of Simon & Schuster Books for Young Readers, an imprint of Simon & Schuster Children's Publishing Division; **302:** From *When Marian Sang* by Pam Muñoz Ryan, illustrations by Brian Selznick. Text copyright © 2002 by Pam Muñoz Ryan, illustrations copyright © 2002 by Brian Selznick. Published by Scholastic Press/Scholastic Inc. Reprinted by permission; **326:** "Learning to Swim," from *When I Was Your Age* by Kyoko Mori. Copyright © 1999 by Kyoko Mori. Published by Candlewick Press. Used by permission of the author; **342:** From "Staying Safe in the Water," www.KidsHealth.org. This information was provided by KidsHealth, one of the largest resources online for medically reviewed health information written for parents, kids, and teens. For more articles like this one, visit www.KidsHealth.org or www.TeensHealth.org. © 1995-2004. The Nemours Foundation. Reprinted by permission; **350:** From *Juan Verdades: The Man Who Couldn't Tell a Lie* by Joe Hayes, illustrated by Joseph Daniel Fiedler. Text copyright © 2001 by Joe Hayes, illustration copyright © 2001 by Joseph Daniel Fiedler. Published by Orchard Books/Scholastic Inc. Reprinted by permission; **366:** *Song of the Chirimia* by Jane Anne Volkmer. Copyright 1990 by Jane Anne Volkmer. Reprinted by permission of Carolrhoda Books, Inc., a division of Lerner Publishing Group. All rights reserved; **376:** From *Ms. Courageous: Women of Science* by Joanna Halpert Kraus. Copyright © 1997 Joanna Halpert Kraus. Used by permission of New Plays Incorporated, P. O. Box 5074, Charlottesville, VA 22905; **398:** "Rebecca Lee Crumpler," from *African Americans Who Were First* by Joan Potter and Constance Clayton, copyright © 1997 by Joan Potter and Constance Clayton, text. Used by permission of Cobblehill Books, an affiliate of Dutton Children's Books, A Division of Penguin Young Readers Group, A Member of Penguin Group (USA) Inc., 345 Hudson Street, New York, NY 10014. All rights reserved; **401:** "Abe" by Alice Schertle. Used by permission of the author, who controls all rights; **402:** "Martin Luther King, Jr." by Gwendolyn Brooks. Reprinted by Consent of Brooks Permissions; **403:** "Another Mountain" from *Rooted In The Soil* by Abiodum Oyewole, 1983; **412:** From *Into the Ice: The Story of Arctic Exploration* by Lynn Curlee. Copyright © 1998 by Lynn Curlee. Reprinted by permission of Houghton Mifflin Company. All rights reserved; **428:** "Polar Zones" text by Sally Morgan from *Discoveries: Weather*. © 1996 Weldon Owen Pty Ltd. Reprinted by permission; **434:** From *The Chimpanzees I Love* by Jane Goodall. Text copyright © 2001 by Jane Goodall, map copyright © 2001 by Byron Preiss Visual Publications, Inc. Reprinted by permission of Scholastic, Inc.; **450:** "Going Ape Over Language," by Natalie M. Rosinsky from *Odyssey's* October 2001 issue: "Passionate About Primates," © 2001, Cobblestone Publishing, 30 Grove Street, Suite C, Petersborough, NH 03458. All Rights Reserved. Reprinted by permission of Carus Publishing Company; **460:** From *Black Frontiers* by Lillian Schlissel. Copyright © 1995 Lillian Schlissel. Reprinted with the permission of Simon & Schuster Books for Young Readers, an imprint of Simon & Schuster Children's Publishing Division; **476:** "The Dream Keeper," from *The Collected Poems of Langston Hughes* by Langston Hughes, copyright © 1994 by The Estate of Langston Hughes. Used by permission of Alfred A. Knopf, a division of Random House, Inc.; **477:** "Youth," from *The Collected Poems of Langston Hughes* by Langston Hughes, copyright © 1994 by The Estate of Langston Hughes. Used by permission of Alfred A. Knopf, a division of Random House, Inc.; **477:** "Dreams," from *The Collected Poems of Langston Hughes* by Langston Hughes, copyright ©

1994 by The Estate of Langston Hughes. Used by permission of Alfred A. Knopf, a division of Random House, Inc.; **482:** "Space Cadets" by David LaBounty from *Plays, The Drama Magazine for Young People*, April 2002. Reproduced with the permission of Sterling Partner, Inc./Plays, The Drama Magazine for Young People, P. O. Box 600160, Newton, MA 02460; **504:** From *Inventing the Future: A Photobiography* of Thomas Alva Edison by Marfe Ferguson Delano. Copyright © 2002 National Geographic Society. Reprinted by permission; **528:** "The Explorers" from *Remember the Bridge* by Carole Boston Weatherford, Philomel Books, 2002; **529:** "Bronze Cowboys" from *Remember the Bridge* by Carole Boston Weatherford, Philomel Books, 2002; **530:** "Seeds" from *Mississippi Mud: Three Prairie Journals* by Ann Turner, HarperCollins, 1997; **531:** "Science Fair Project" from *Almost Late to School* by Carol Diggory Shields, illustrations by Paul Meisel, Dutton Children's Books, 2003; **540:** From *The View from Saturday* by E. L. Konigsburg. Copyright © 1996 by E. L. Konigsburg. Reprinted with the permission of Atheneum Books for Young Readers, an imprint of Simon & Schuster Children's Publishing Divison; **566:** From *Harvesting Hope: The Story of Cesar Chavez* by Kathleen Krull, illustrated by Yuyi Morales. Text copyright © 2003 by Kathleen Krull. Illustrations copyright © 2003 by Yuyi Morales. Reprinted by permission of Harcourt, Inc.; **580:** "Fieldworkers" by Leobardo V. Cortèz from *Voices From the Fields* by S. Beth Atkin. Copyright © 1993 by S. Beth Atkin. Reprinted by permission of Little, Brown and Company, (Inc.); **581:** "Farmworkers" from *Gathering the Sun by* Alma Flor Ada, Lothrop, Lee & Shepard Books, 1997; **586:** "The River That Went to the Sky" by Kasiya Makaka Phiri. Reprinted by permission of Ursula A. Barnett acting as agent for the author; **598:** "Pecos Bill" from *American Tall Tales* by Mary Pope Osborne, Borzoi Book, Alfred A. Knopf, Inc., 1991; **604:** From *Gold* by Sarah Angliss. © 2000 Marshall Cavendish Corporation. Reprinted with permission of Marshall Cavandish Corporation; **617:** "Gold Rush" from the *Columbia Encyclopedia, 6th ed.* from www.encyclopedia.com; **618–619:** From "California Gold Rush" from The Idaho State University website at www.isu.edu/~trinmich; **624:** From *The House of Wisdom* by Florence Parry Heide and Judith Heide Gilliland, Illustrated by Mary GrandPré, 1999; **644:** "For the Earth Day Essay Contest" by Jeanette Neff, from *We the People* by Bobbi Katz, Greenwillow Books, 1998, 2000; **645:** "Pods Pop and Grin" from *When I Dance* by James Berry, Harcourt Brace Jovanich, Publishers, 1991; **646:** "maggie and milly and molly and may..." from *Complete Poems, 1913-1962* by E. E. Cummings, Liveright Publishing Corporation; **647:** "Maple Talk" from *Poems Have Roots* by Lilian Moore. Copyright © 1997 by Lilian Moore. Reprinted with the permission of Atheneum Books for Young Readers, an imprint of Simon & Schuster Children's Publishing Division. All rights reserved; **656:** *Don Quixote and the Windmills* by Eric Kimmel, Shearwater Books, 2004; **670:** "Feudalism" from Scott Foresman Social Studies: *The World* - Grade 6. Copyright © 2003 Pearson Education, Inc. Reprinted by permission of Pearson Education, Inc.; **676:** From *Ancient Greece* by Kim Covert. © 2004 by Capstone Press. Reprinted by permission of Coughlan Publishing; **702:** "The All-American Slurp," by Lensey Namioka, copyright © 1987, from *Visions*, edited by Donald R. Gallo. Reprinted by permission of Lensey Namioka. All rights are reserved by the Author; **728:** *The Aztec News*. Text Copyright © 1997 by Philip Steele. Illustrations copyright © 1997 by Walker Books Ltd. Reproduced by permission of the publisher, Candlewick Press, Inc., Cambridge, MA, on behalf of Walker Books Ltd, London; **746:** From www.mayankids.com; **754:** "Where Opportunity Awaits" (originally titled "The Promise of the Cities"), pp. 111-119 from *A Chance to Make Good* by James R. Grossman, copyright © 1997. Used by permission of Oxford University Press, Inc.; **764:** "Coming Over" adapted from *Immigrant Kids* by Russell Freedman, copyright © 1980 by Russell Freedman. Used by permission of Dutton Children's Books, A Division of Penguin Young Readers Group, A Member of Penguin Group (USA) Inc., 345 Hudson Street, New York, NY 10014. All rights reserved; **770:** "Borders" from *All the Colors of the Race* by Arnold Adoff, Lothrop, Lee & Shepard Books, 1982; **771:** "My Bird Day" from *Good Luck Gold and other Poems* by Janet S. Wong. Copyright © 1994 by Janet S. Wong. Reprinted with the permission of Margaret K. McElderry Books, an imprint of Simon & Schuster Children's Publishing Division. All rights reserved; **772:** "The Colors Live," from *Hailstones and Halibut Bones* by Mary O'Neill and Leonard Weisgard, III, copyright © 1961 by Mary LeDuc O'Neill. Used by permission of Random House Children's Books, a division of Random House, Inc.

Illustrations

Photographs

Glossary

The contents of this glossary have been adapted from *Thorndike Barnhart Intermediate Dictionary* and *Thorndike Barnhart Advanced Dictionary*. Copyright © 1997, Pearson Education, Inc.